THE BEST PLAYS OF 1993–1994

THE OTIS GUERNSEY BURNS MANTLE THEATER YEARBOOK

THE BEST PLAYS OF 1993–1994

EDITED BY OTIS L. GUERNSEY JR.
AND JEFFREY SWEET

Illustrated with photographs and with drawings by HIRSCHFELD

LIMELIGHT EDITIONS

ISBN: 0-87910-183-0

ISSN: 1071-6971

Printed in the United States of America

EDITOR'S NOTE

THE Best Plays of 1993-94 is the 75th volume in continuous annual publication of this theater yearbook series started by Burns Mantle with *The Best Plays of 1919-20*. In observance of our diamond anniversary, we glance backward down the three-quarter-century path trodden indelibly into history by the momentous achievements of our theater's creative and interpretive artists. Taking the long view, we notice first that the major esthetic development over those years was the sophistication of the musical book from a mere convenience on which to hang song numbers to a dramatization of the highest order in which, for example, this season's best musical, James Lapine's and Stephen Sondheim's *Passion*, studies a searingly memorable character in a deep emotional crisis, but without a single identified musical number in its prizewinning score.

Accordingly, we invited Peter Stone, author of 14 musical books including *1776* and president of the Dramatists Guild, to trace this development for our record. With his special flair and insight, he has obliged us and our readers in detail in our 75th anniversary edition's leading article.

A more diffuse characteristic of the three-quarter century has been the playwright's effort to break open the mold of form and exercise as much imagination in structure and language as in content, often with such brilliant results as this season's *Three Tall Women* by Edward Albee or *All in the Timing* by David Ives. This trend has shown up as a number of individual impulses by individual authors, rather than as a steady movement, but its examples are easily recognized within our list of the 750 Best Plays, ten a year cited by the succession of six *Best Plays* critics. In special recognition of our 75th anniversary, we've listed the golden 750 in groups of ten in this volume, season by season. And to each seasonal group we've added a footnote mentioning those shows which were passed over in Best Play selection but went on to glory in popular esteem or major award citations, so as to remember each year in full perspective. And we've updated our list of playwrights most often cited for Best Plays (Maxwell Anderson is still the champ, but Neil Simon is gaining rapidly).

After celebrating the past, *The Best Plays of 1993-94* plunges deep into its comprehensive coverage of our theater's immediate present in New York and cross-country, beginning with Jeffrey Sweet's incomparably detailed review of the new plays, musicals and revivals produced this year on and off Broadway. And Sweet is doubly represented in this volume, as his play *American Enterprise* is specially cited and synopsized as a 1993-94 Best Play. Mel Gussow reviews the bests of off off Broadway, and Camille Dee has compiled her listing of the year's productions OOB which, like our Broadway and off-Broadway listings of complete casts and credits, takes in all

OOB's major features. Jeffrey A. Finn has traced the important Broadway and off-Broadway cast replacements for the record, together with the casts of touring Broadway shows (whose grosses, added to those of the current Broadway productions, rose above the $1 billion mark this year).

Rue E. Canvin has recorded the important publication of new and classical playscripts and our necrology of theater folk whose names take us by sad surprise with every passing year and cause us to reflect that in this volume, most of those listed were not even born when the first *Best Plays* yearbook was published. Sheridan Sellers has provided an extensive cast-and-credits report of major productions of new plays in cross-country theater, among which the American Theater Critics Association committee chaired by Michael Grossberg has cited three standouts to be celebrated in our regional theater section. And keeping close attention to the clarity and accuracy of the entire package were and are, as usual, the editor's persevering wife and our indefatigable colleague, Jonathan Dodd.

Editorial contributors who helped make *The Best Plays of 1993-94* possible include William Schelble (Tony Awards), Sally Dixon Wiener (a Best Play synopsis), Thomas T. Foose (historical advisories), Michael Kuchwara (New York Drama Critics Circle voting), Henry Hewes (former *Best Plays* editor, providing the Hall of Fame listing), Ralph Newman of the Drama Book Shop and—indispensably—the dozens of patient and cooperative members of the producers' press offices who supply most of the information in these pages.

Like the present editors and staff of the *Best Plays* yearbooks, Al Hirschfeld is still going strong, illuminating the New York theater with his drawings. The Hirschfeld visions of the 1993-94 season are featured prominently in the contemporary section of this volume, and a few of his drawings from the past are a stylish asset of our 75-year backward glance. The "look" of the theater is enhanced by them and by the photographs of stage action in New York and across the country made available to us by the production offices and including the work of Chris Bennion, Barbara Bordnick, Marc Bryan-Brown, David Cooper, Donald Cooper, Paula Court, Leon Daniels, T. Charles Erickson, Gerry Goodstein, Ken Howard, Sherman Howe Jr., Suzanne Karp Krebs, Brigitte Lacombe, Joan Marcus, Inge Morath/Magnum Photos, Stuart Morris, Timothy Raab, Roya, Terry Shapiro, Lee Snider/Photo Images, David Swanson, Martha Swope Associates (Martha Swope, Carol Rosegg, William Gibson) and Sandy Underwood.

As the three-quarter-century roster of the 750 Best Plays flamboyantly illustrates, our theater is primarily the creation of the playwright, composer and book and lyric writer, and so is this yearbook series. It's the scripts themselves which the six *Best Plays* editors have contemplated in making their 750 selections, and it's the scripts themselves that are primarily celebrated here with scenes illustrating the style and construction of each work. What we cannot illustrate—but cordially and devotedly celebrate—is the entire body of that iceberg of creativity, on the tip of which each theater season shows itself at its best. It is this mass of effort and talent represented in the not-quites and even in the not-at-alls out of which our wonderful theater arises, as *The Man Who Had All the Luck* evolves into *Death of a Salesman*, or *Battle of Angels* into *A Streetcar Named Desire*. We don't have space to synopsize every promising new script that appears on our stages, but we can record the arrival of and offer our thanks for each and every one of them, together with our appreciation for their authors' devotion to the form. At any level, it is the dramatist's original commitment and essential contribution to the still-living theater which has been the progenitor and brightly shining highlight of the 75 *Best Plays* yearbooks.

OTIS L. GUERNSEY Jr.
Editor

September 1, 1994

CONTENTS

Drawings by HIRSCHFELD

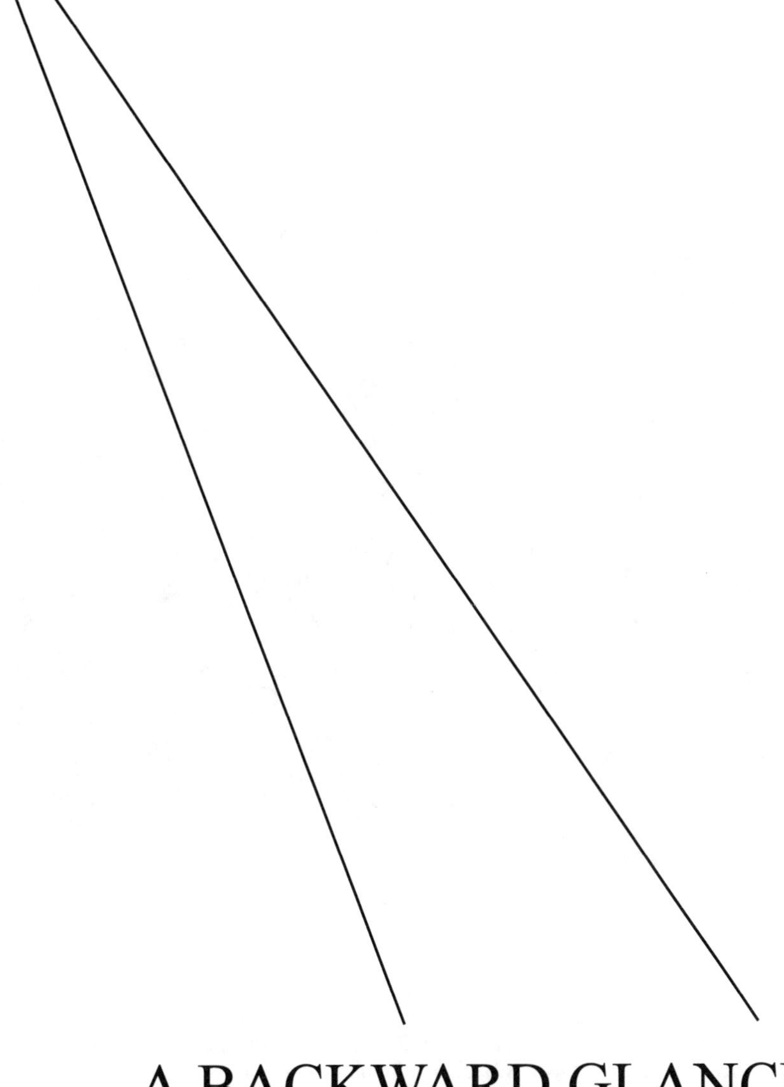

A BACKWARD GLANCE AT 75 YEARS ON AND OFF BROADWAY

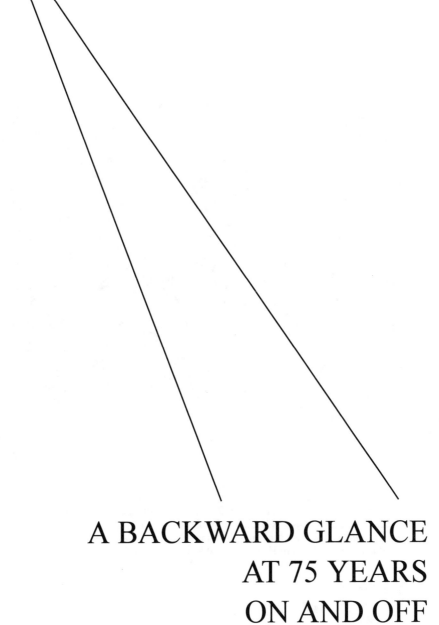

1776—Al Hirschfeld's drawing of the original 1969 production of the Peter Stone-Sherman Edwards musical about the Declaration of Independence *(above)* featured *(seated)* Howard Da Silva as Benjamin Franklin and William Daniels as John Adams, with *(standing)* Paul Hecht as John Dickinson, Clifford David as Edward Rutledge, Ronald Holgate as Richard Henry Lee and Ken Howard as Thomas Jefferson

THE MUSICAL BOOK: ONWARD AND UPWARD FROM *SHOW BOAT*

By Peter Stone

Author of 14 musical books and president of The Dramatists Guild

LET'S get one thing settled right off the bat: we "librettists" don't much care for the term "libretto." Operas and the recent British spectacles in which the entire text is sung have "libretti." Musicals, with spoken words and scenes, have "books." Now we can proceed.

It is fair to say that the musical book, as it is now recognized, is almost entirely the creation of one man—Oscar Hammerstein II. This is not to downgrade John O'Hara's effort in *Pal Joey,* or the abridged version of the Gershwins' opera *Porgy and Bess,* both of which presaged the new form.

And though it is generally accepted that the appearance, in 1943, of Rodgers and Hammerstein's *Oklahoma!* began what is now called the era of the modern musical, one cannot dismiss Hammerstein's book for *Show Boat,* which preceded his work with Richard Rodgers. That classic 1927 show contained nearly all of the properties now present in today's book musicals. (Only the apparently happy ending of Act I differs from the current practice of inducing, through plot or character complications, the audience's return for Act II.)

Prior to the Hammerstein era, the American and English musicals of the 1920s and 1930s were collections of songs tied together by a lighthearted (and -headed) plot, its premise seldom deeper or more complicated than an impending birthday party to be celebrated at a country house in Connecticut. The spoken words, relying on farcical incidents and punchlines to render them as painless as possible, were entirely devoted to setting up the songs, no matter how convoluted and improbable the context became. After all, a good song was a good song, and worth any improbability to gain its inclusion in the show.

But *Oklahoma!* and *Show Boat,* adapted from serious literary works, contained songs that were actually devoted to setting up the story. With these works the form had graduated from musical comedy to musical theater, to the glories that were *Guys and Dolls, West Side Story, Gypsy, My Fair Lady* and *A Chorus Line.* This development turned out to be welcomed by American theatergoers after the social realism of the 1930s, an extension of 19th century middle and northern European naturalism.

These movements had all but eliminated the classic theatrical conventions—poetry, soliloquies, asides and the like—in favor of fourth-wall reality with its dialogue and settings indistinguishable from life outside on the street.

By the beginning of the second World War, audiences had enough reality on the front pages of their newspapers; they yearned, whether they knew it or not, for theatricality. It was Aristotle, after all, who had catalogued the six vital properties of theater. He had listed not only plot, character and theme (all present in naturalism), but also poetry, dance and spectacle. And it was Hammerstein's new kind of musicals which were to return to us these last three important elements: poetry (in the form of lyrics), choreography and lavish, impressionistic settings, as well as the rest of the nearly forgotten stage conventions. (Can it be a coincidence that arguably the finest single piece of our musical theater is actually called "Soliloquy"?)

That Hammerstein was also a lyricist—a combination not that common in the history of the form—made his complex job simpler to perform. It not only helped the lead-ins to the songs appear more seamless, but enabled him to reconceive the very form of those songs as well. For example: the romantic ballad, surely the bread-and-butter of any score, became more than slightly endangered as a first act utility when, as more realistic stories containing more fully-drawn characters emerged, the romance between the boy and girl couldn't possibly have developed sufficiently in the first act to warrant the emotion dished out in a ballad. To remedy this (a musical can always use a first act ballad), Hammerstein created what I have termed the *conditional* ballad. It made its first appearance in *Show Boat* with "Only Make Believe" (we can't be in love yet, so let's just make believe), reappeared in *Oklahoma!* with "People Will Say We're in Love" (we're not, of course, but you can't stop folks from talking), continued on in *Carousel* with "If I Loved You" (we only just met, but already I can imagine what it might be like once we get to know each other better), and still again in *South Pacific* with "Some Enchanted Evening" (I will meet a stranger and when I do . . .), etc., etc., etc. (to quote the King of Siam).

But more and more, through the late 1940s and early 1950s, the score was becoming subordinate to the book, with most of the back-sliding coming from the surviving practitioners of the old ways. In *Annie Get Your Gun,* Irving Berlin, the composer-lyricist of literally dozens of shows in the 1920s and 1930s, met the challenge of serving the book and its three-dimensional characters head-on. "I Can Do Anything Better Than You" is a perfectly motivated development of the headstrong leading woman and man, each of whom have too much ego to yield a single thing to the other. But another song, "I'm an Indian, Too," is a shamefully old-fashioned remnant from earlier times when a piece of pure entertainment was dragged in by the heels, plot and characters be damned. Coincidentally, *Annie Get Your Gun* was produced by the very same Rodgers & Hammerstein who, as creators, would never have countenanced such a relapse.

And, throughout that period, composers and lyricists still clung to the commercial possibilities of their songs being performed outside the show, on records and the radio, which forced the book to make room for the notorious (to book writers) "reprise of the ballad," usually somewhere in Act II. This practice could drive some authors mad: George S. Kaufman, on becoming rankled during rehearsals of *Silk Stockings,* finally confronted Cole Porter and was told that the audience *enjoyed* the ballads and wanted to hear them again; Kaufman thereupon demanded (without success) that some of his first act jokes should also be reprised.

But with the coming of rock and roll, book writers gained some relief. Whereas *South Pacific* had opened on Broadway with at least five of its songs already on the hit parade—it was said that audiences hummed the tunes *entering* the theater—by the early 1960s one could no longer hear show tunes on the radio, nor were they any longer popular on records or tape. In fact, in the best-seller charts of the past 20 years, it would be difficult to find five songs from all of the Broadway shows *combined.*

This development not only did much to restrain rampant reprising, it also freed the ballads themselves from the sort of generalized lyrics that facilitated outside-the-show performance. Now lyricists could devote all of their time and enterprise to serving, not Sinatra and Streisand, but the specific needs of the book.

What exactly is a musical book? And how does it differ from a play? I had asked myself those same two questions when I was offered my first opportunity to write a Broadway musical. It was in February of 1961, and, though considering myself a playwright, I had never even contemplated writing a musical, though I was an enthusiastic fan of the form. The show was *Kean,* to be based on the play by Jean-Paul Sartre (out of Alexandre Dumas *fils*) that had been a huge success in Paris in the early 1950s, that dealt with the life and career (and the confusion between the two) of Edmund Kean, one of England's greatest actors, and to star America's foremost actor-singer on the musical stage, Alfred Drake. It was irresistible.

But how to do it? Fortunately, I had as a friend Frank Loesser who was not only a composer-lyricist of towering talent *(Guys and Dolls, Where's Charley? How to Succeed in Business Without Really Trying* and *The Most Happy Fella),* but the possessor of uncommon and arcane knowledge of what makes musicals tick, plus the articulation to pass it along. I went to Frank with all my questions and, as always, he answered them:

1. What's the difference between a musical book and a straight play? More than anything else—more than the jokes and dialogue, more than the characters and individual scenes—the book is the *construction* of the show, the blueprint used by all of the other creative and interpretive members of the collaboration, containing the order and balance of the scenes, and, even more important, the *concept* and overall style of the show, what Frank called the "level." He said that if all of the members of the collaboration did not agree on this level, the show could not possibly succeed. (This was brought home to me on my fifth show when the composer, lyricist and director, each of whom was experienced and successful in his own field, all had different ideas of the show's level, due either to my failure to communicate the one I intended or their unwillingness to accept it. The show was profitable, owing to the drawing power of its star, but ended up satisfying no one.)

2. I then asked Frank how to determine where in a scene the songs were supposed

to go. His answer was clear and concise: when a character can no longer express himself in normal language and must resort to interjections—oh! gosh! gee! wow!—that's when it would be permissible to change from speech to song. And that's why, he said, so many wonderful theater songs actually begin with interjections (the word "Oh!" being by far the most popular—"Oh, What a Beautiful Morning," "Oh, Kay," "Oh, Sweet and Lovely Lady, Be Good," "Oh, How I Hate to Get Up in the Morning"—Lorenz Hart used "Oh" to begin 22 songs, Cole Porter 51 and Ira Gershwin a stunning 63).

3. What's a "lead-in" and how do you write one? Frank explained that the lead-in—which he called the "gozinta" ("goes into")—is not only the set-up for a song, but also the bridge which facilitates the change from prose into poetry. Toward that end the book writer must subtly alter his prose, utilizing a more lyrical phraseology. This is one of the ways to make the individual voices of the collaboration seem one.

4. I then asked Frank how the collaboration should work—should the book be

GUYS AND DOLLS—Here are the Damon Runyon types in the original 1950 staging of the Frank Loesser-Jo Swerling-Abe Burrows musical, according to Hirschfeld: Sam Levene as Nathan Detroit *(center)* surrounded by Douglas Deane (Rusty Charlie), Tom Pedi (Harry the Horse), Stubby Kaye (Nicely-Nicely Johnson), Johnny Silver (Benny Southstreet), Robert Alda (Sky Masterson), B.S. Pully (Big Jule), Vivian Blaine (Miss Adelaide), Pat Rooney Sr. (Arvide Abernathy) and Isabel Bigley (Sarah Brown)

written first? Or the score? But he said neither. In order to create with one voice, and to avoid duplication and/or misunderstandings, and to prevent the rancor of one author's work being appropriated by the others, and for many other reasons, the book and score should, whenever possible, be written *simultaneously;* i.e., planned out together, scene by scene, song by song, neither creator getting ahead of the others.

5. Finally, Frank returned to the differences between a musical book and a play and elaborated on what he felt was the most important: because the score, though using up a full hour of stage time, rarely advances the plot or characters by more than a few minutes, the book writer is allowed only one hour to tell two hours of story. This requires the development of a discipline, one that utilizes a kind of shorthand as well as the intervention of new and different methods of telling the story.

Toward this end, I have found that, with the proliferation of television and its ubiquitous accessory, the remote clicker, audiences have become not only more sophisticated in their need for linear plot development and its attendant exposition (having viewed literally thousands of hours of TV comedy and melodrama), but also, as a result, are more impatient with the erstwhile methods of transmitting these dramatic elements. This induces them to go "surfing" with their clickers, grazing through the complete menu of TV fare, stopping only when their interest has been snared, then continuing on again until they return to their starting point, seemingly able to retain the basics of several stories simultaneously.

This development offers a very rich vein for musical books to quarry. For example: in *The Will Rogers Follies,* I have Will, on first meeting his future wife, discover that they both have six single sisters (fact). He turns to the audience, remarking on the coincidence, then adds that he'll "skip the next part as it didn't add up to much and get right to the good part." Without skipping a beat, he turns back to the girl and expresses his love. Thus, breaking through the fourth wall to confide in the audience is one way of condensing the art of story-telling by taking advantage of the newer methods of doing so.

Similarly, in *Grand Hotel,* I caused two (and, at one moment, as many as five) scenes to play concurrently, held together in some instances by connecting phrases, in others by similarities in emotion or circumstance, much the way a motion picture is intercut.

Other new approaches include the dislocation of time or space or both—that is, the use of other film techniques such as the flash-back or -forward. I firmly believe it is imperative that the style and form of the musical book should continue to advance and broaden to meet the ever-changing interests and capacities of the audience.

But the rules have always been for breaking. What one generation believes to be iron-clad is re-evaluated by the next. When I wrote *1776,* the notion that a book scene could continue for more than four or five minutes was practically unheard of. But in order to establish the two dozen or so members of the Continental Congress, to explain the major political differences between the various colonies and to set out the parliamentary maneuvers their seriously divided representatives used to promote their individual interests, a long, sustained dialogue scene was written. But by the time it reached the stage it was over 30 minutes long, uninterrupted by either singing, dancing or even underscoring. The creative coalition, concerned with this colossal abnormality, explored every possible way of breaking it up with some musical element; but any attempt to do so accomplished nothing except to weaken the scene. Finally the bullet was bitten and the scene was allowed to remain as it was.

Further, at the end of the show, the final 15 minutes were also without any musical accompaniment whatsoever. In all, at least two-thirds of the musical was pure dialogue, surely a still-standing record. And yet, neither critics nor audience members ever remarked that anything aberrant had taken place. The lesson was clear: what works works.

The last thing Frank gave me was a warning. The rewards for writing musical books would have to come from the satisfaction of doing it well and/or having a hit show. As for the other rewards, well, they could, at times, seem rather meager. Having your musical forever known as the composer and lyricist's show—Bock and

Harnick's *Fiddler on the Roof,* Jerry Herman's *Hello, Dolly!,* Kander and Ebb's *Cabaret* or Stephen Sondheim's *Company*—had to be a painful pill for book writers Joseph Stein, Michael Stewart, Joe Masteroff or George Furth to swallow. But, Frank added, that doesn't prevent the critics from blaming the book if the show doesn't work; most critics, unversed in music and dance, are only comfortable dealing with the words. (The only safe solution to this problem is to do away with the book altogether—i.e. *Dancin', Ain't Misbehavin', Sophisticated Ladies,* and *Cats*—thereby eliminating any possibility of having the book attacked.)

Finally Frank remarked (though, as a composer, without much sympathy) on the financial rewards—one third of the royalty to book writers for what they contend is half of the show, surely a hangover from those days when the book was merely filler between the songs. And *no* share in the future life of the songs, even though the book writer might have come up with the idea for the show, had his scenes and dialogue musicalized, and suggested the subject matter and often the title for one of the individual numbers.

But, Frank concluded, were I to get him drunk he'd have to admit that the success of a modern book musical is due mostly to the book. A show, he admitted, could succeed with a so-so score if the book were strong. But one with a weak book is doomed, even with the strongest score in the world. "That's what Hammerstein has wrought, even if you'll never hear it from a sober composer." How can you not love a man like that?

Frank Loesser's advice was invaluable, but so, too, was experience gained in the field. The routine of pre-production, as the collaboration expands to include a producer, director, choreographer, set/costume/lighting/sound designers, then, through auditions, the actors, followed by the rehearsals, can teach more about the craft and practice of writing a musical book than a full curriculum of drama school courses.

But the most educational experience by far is to accompany a show on its out-of-town pre-Broadway tryout. It is during this period that musical books are *really* created—shaped, reordered, rewritten. Though often (if not always) a trying, grisly and thoroughly horrific experience filled with frenzy, frustration and unpleasant surprises (Larry Gelbart, a fine author of musical books, once characterized this experience by saying, "If Hitler's alive I hope he's out of town with a musical"), it is the final, postgraduate course of study in musical theater.

It is not until this step that the authors can actually *see and hear* the show they've written, complete with orchestra, sets, costumes, lighting and, most important, *audiences*—customers who have paid money to see your work. They never lie. (Another thing Frank told me was never listen to individual members of an audience, they are almost always wrong; but collectively they are always right: "If they don't laugh, if they don't applaud, if they cough or nod off or, yes, *walk out*—it's *your* fault, pal, not theirs. Don't argue with them, fix it.")

That today's producers find the taking of a show out of town expendable in the face of rising costs is a great pity; to open cold in New York City, even after weeks of previews, is no replacement for the freedom, informality and vacuum of an out-of-town booking. An author who, were he out of town, would dismantle an entire act in order to restructure it, thus leaving it in temporary disarray, will think twice or three times before displaying such chaotic work-in-progress to a New York preview audience, filled as it invariably is with friends, rivals, reporters, producers, agents and other theater professionals. As a result, this more complicated, drastic sort of fixing, often necessary, is routine work in Boston or Washington, but hardly ever attempted in New York City.

Producers who dispense with out-of-town tryouts because they've become too expensive should check the record, comparing the fortunes of those shows that travelled with those that opened cold in New York. Then, when they discover the truth, they should bite the bullet and call it a necessary production cost, like the scenery. That costs a bundle, too, but they'd never dream of doing without it.

So now, at this writing, 32 years and 14 musical books later, I am a confirmed and inveterate book writer. It is a form that I find theatrically vital and personally satisfying. It offers a method for expressing certain themes and subjects in ways that are not possible, considering the climate and stringencies of today's commercial theater. At their best, musical books speak directly to, and enrich the lives of, American audiences in ways that theater was originally intended to do—by satisfying the entire range of our dramatic appetites.

There is, sadly, a great lack of dedicated musical book authors at the present writing. Either playwrights don't want (or don't understand) the sort of collaboration required, or they don't see the rewards, or they don't comprehend, or feel comfortable with, the medium itself. But more and more serious straight-play authors are beginning to consider the form, and a few notable dramatists have already tried it with notable success. Until their ranks grow and prosper, we may be condemned to several more seasons when the musical revivals outnumber the original shows. For until a new generation of musical books are written, the next golden age of musical theater cannot begin.

○
○
○

1919-20 TO 1993-94: THE 750 BEST PLAYS OF THE THREE-QUARTER CENTURY AS SELECTED IN OUR 75 VOLUMES

○
○
○

WE CELEBRATE our 75th year of continuous *Best Plays* yearbook publication with this special season-by-season listing of the 750 Best Plays, ten in each year, selected by six critic-editors over three-quarters of a century. Unlike our usual alphabetical listing (which appeared in the 1992-93 edition and will reappear in future volumes), this one follows the New York theater's meandering flow from 1919 to 1994, revealing its tributaries and reminding us of how sweet its sparkling waters always tasted.

These 750 Best Plays were selected season after season by founder Burns Mantle (28 volumes 1920-1947) and his successors John Chapman (5 volumes 1948-1952), Louis Kronenberger (9 volumes 1953-1961), Henry Hewes (3 volumes that enlarged the yearbook's scope and paved the way for today's comprehensive off-off-Broadway-wide and nationwide coverage, 1962-1964), the undersigned (21 volumes 1965-1985) and our associate editor Jeffrey Sweet (9 volumes 1986-1994). Ours were individual, not committee, selections, according to standards which may have varied in detail from critic to critic but always focussed on the quality of the script itself, with as little attention as humanly possible given to size of production or intensity of performance. It is the playscript and its writer(s) that this *Best Plays* series has applauded as the stage's primary creative force.

And to allow that our judgements, though conscientiously made and strongly felt, are nevertheless in some degree debatable (no other individual ever agrees with all ten choices in any one year), we add an italic footnote to each season noting any shows which did not make the Best Plays list but won either a major award or the popular support to run about a year or longer. We remember all our selections with pride but report them here in the context of each season's whole achievement.

Who were the New York theater's sustaining artists who fulfilled its promise again and again over three-quarters of a century? A list of dramatists who were cited 4 or more times as author, adapter or composer of a Best Play gives us most of the answer, as follows:

AUTHOR	NO. OF CITATIONS	AUTHOR	NO. OF CITATIONS
Maxwell Anderson	19	David Mamet	5
George S. Kaufman	18	Clifford Odets	5
Neil Simon	15	Paul Osborn	5
Eugene O'Neill	12	John Osborne	5
Moss Hart	11	Elmer Rice	5
Philip Barry	10	Peter Shaffer	5
S.N. Behrman	9	George Abbott	4
Lillian Hellman	9	Jerry Bock	4
Robert E. Sherwood	9	Jerome Chodorov	4
Tennessee Williams	9	Russell Crouse	4
Terrence McNally	8	Rose Franken	4
Stephen Sondheim	8	Christopher Fry	4
Jean Anouilh	7	Paul Green	4
Arthur Miller	7	Sheldon Harnick	4
John van Druten	7	Lucienne Hill	4
Edward Albee	6	William Inge	4
Marc Connelly	6	George Kelly	4
Rachel Crothers	6	Arthur L. Kopit	4
Athol Fugard	6	Howard Lindsay	4
Sidney Howard	6	Harold Pinter	4
Sidney Kingsley	6	Tom Stoppard	4
Joseph Fields	5	Hugh Wheeler	4
Brian Friel	5	Thornton Wilder	4
Jean Giraudox	5	August Wilson	4
A.R. Gurney	5	Lanford Wilson	4
James Lapine	5		

Ours was the theater of Maxwell Anderson, George S. Kaufman, Eugene O'Neill—and Neil Simon with 15 citations including a 1994 Best Play, still writing at the top of his form. And Simon accomplished *twice* in contemporary circumstances what few others managed once: two Best Plays running on Broadway, not only in the same season but at the same time *(Barefoot in the Park* and *The Odd Couple* in the 1965 season and *Last of the Red Hot Lovers* and *The Gingerbread Lady* in 1971)—and in both years there were *other* Simon hits long-running beside them. Alan Ayckbourn came up with a triple in 1976 with *Table Manners, Living Together* and *Round and Round the Garden,* but it was a trilogy classified as a single Best Play, *The Norman Conquests.* Other occasional and not necessarily simultaneous doubles were achieved by Sidney Howard *(The Late Christopher Bean* and *Alien Corn* in 1933), Kaufman *(Stage Door* and *You Can't Take It With You* in 1937), Philip Barry *(Here Come the Clowns* and *The Philadelphia Story* in 1939), Moss Hart *(George Washington Slept Here* and *Lady in the Dark* in 1941), O'Neill *(Long Day's Journey Into Night* and *A Moon for the Misbegotten* in 1957), John Osborne *(Look Back in Anger* and *The Entertainer* in 1958) and Preston Jones *(The Last Meeting of the Knights of the White Magnolia* and *The Oldest Living Graduate* in 1977).

Woman playwrights? Lillian Hellman, who always hated to be so identified and called herself "a playwright who happens to be a woman," was the runaway leader with 9 Best Play citations. Backing her up were Rachel Crothers with 6 citations and Rose Franken and Lucienne Hill with 4 each. Jean Anouilh (7) and Athol Fugard (6 and still counting) make up the vanguard of foreign authorship, with Brian Friel, Jean Giraudoux and Peter Shaffer close to them with 5 citations apiece and Christopher Fry, Harold Pinter and Tom Stoppard with 4.

The scarcity of musical authors on the multi-Best-Plays list points directly to the subject of Peter Stone's article leading this 75-year reminiscence: the gradual but steady sophistication of the musical theater libretto in the last half of this century. It has always been said that with a good musical you come out humming the tunes. In the modern musical you also come out humming the characters, which now are as memorable as the score, as Stone's article suggests.

The first acknowledgement by *Best Plays* editors that a "musical comedy" book might deserve a Best Play citation was Mantle's selection of the Gershwins' *Of Thee I Sing* in the 1932 season. The second was *Lady in the Dark* in 1941 and the third *Oklahoma!* in 1943. Today it's a rare season without at least one musical on the Best Plays list.

In the absence of full recognition of musical authorship acquired by the late 1960s, Richard Rodgers and Oscar Hammerstein II were cited only twice (for *Oklahoma!* and *Allegro).* They are conspicuously absent from the multiple list, along with Alan Jay Lerner, Frederick Loewe, Leonard Bernstein and Frank Loesser, each of whom was also cited only twice (and in the Dark Ages, Cole Porter wasn't even cited for *Kiss Me, Kate,* passed over with *South Pacific* in the same season).

Among contemporaries on whom the final word hasn't nearly been spoken, Stephen Sondheim has a Secretariat lead over all other composer-lyricists with 8 handsomely deserved citations as of 1994, and his collaborator James Lapine leads librettists with 5. The only other composer on the multiple list so far is Jerry Bock with 4 plus one special citation, and librettists Sheldon Harnick and Hugh Wheeler have 4 citations apiece. Active contemporaries like John Kander and Fred Ebb, Charles Strouse, Lee Adams, Jerry Herman and Peter Stone have already been cited more than once and will probably repeat again and again before the end of the century.

The extremely popular Broadway play (and musical in recent years) usually found itself on the Best Plays list—not *because* of its popularity. Broadway's longest-running musical *(A Chorus Line,* 6,137 performances), second-longest and continuing *(Cats,* 4,862+) and longest-running play *(Life With Father,* 3,224) made the list, but not the second-longest-running play *(Tobacco Road,* 3,182), nor—before musicals took their rightful place—*Grease* (3,388), *The Sound of Music* (1,443), *The King and I* (1,245) or *Carousel* (890). Off Broadway, the all-time longest-running New York production of record, *The Fantasticks* (14,103+ and still counting) wasn't named a Best Play, probably because it opened at the very end of the first season (1959-60) that editor Kronenberger included in his coverage a formal listing of off-Broadway productions compiled by future editor Hewes—and Kronenberger cited off-Broadway's *The Connection* (722) as one of that season's Best Plays. Off Broadway's second-longest and ongoing *Nunsense* (3,513+) was also passed over. But beginning with Hewes's editorship in 1962-63, through that of the present editors and continuing, all productions, musical or straight, on or off Broadway, have been considered on a level playing field. We have cited enthusiastically the likes of *You're a Good Man Charlie Brown* (1,597), *Your Own Thing* (933), *Driving Miss Daisy* (1,195) and *The Hot 1 Baltimore* (1,166).

On the other side of the coin, the fragmentation of the New York theater audience into segments of special interest during the last few decades has influenced the citation of scripts of unusually high quality which for any number of reasons, some of them economic, had very short first runs but have almost always made a place for themselves in world theater. For the first 50 years of *Best Plays* volumes, there were only 7 cited shows which ran fewer than 20 performances, the shortest runs being those of *A Very Special Baby* (5) and *The Egg* (8). During the past 25 years there have been at least a dozen, the shortest being Jean-Claude van Itallie's intensely striking *The Serpent* (3) and including Edward Albee's *The Lady From Dubuque* (12), Terrence McNally's *It's Only a Play* (17) and Donald Margulies's *The Loman Family Picnic* (16).

Vintage seasons? Consider 1935-36: *Winterset, Dead End, Pride and Prejudice, First Lady, Boy Meets Girl, Victoria Regina, Ethan Frome, Call It a Day, End of Summer, Idiot's Delight.* Or 1946-47 for its list of Best Play authors: Eugene O'Neill, Maxwell Anderson, George Kelly, Lillian Hellman, Moss Hart, Ruth Gordon, Arthur Miller, Norman Krasna, John Patrick and the musical team of Alan Jay Lerner and Frederick Loewe. Or 1959-60, a vintage season not for its Best Play selections but for its popular off-Broadway attractions: *The Fantasticks, The Connection, The Balcony* (672 performances), *Krapp's Last Tape* and *The Zoo Story* (582), *Little Mary Sunshine* (1,143) and *Leave It to Jane* in revival (928).

Night of nights? On October 10, 1921, *two* Best Plays opened on Broadway, and there were *three* other Broadway openings that same evening. Sixty-eight years later—on February 16, 1989—there were two on the same night, one on Broadway and one off.

In our profound admiration for each and every one of the golden 750 Best Plays of the three-quarter century, we now march them past in single file, troop after seasonal troop, each title in **bold face type** followed by its number of first-run performances (in parentheses, with an asterisk * if it was still running on June 1, 1994), followed by its author(s) and opening date. In many cases when a show originated off and then moved to Broadway, we combine the totals of the two runs in this special 75-year report (though we list them separately elsewhere), and the date given is the original opening date in the smaller theater. And when a script has won the Pulitzer, Critics (for best American or foreign play or musical, or the unqualified "best regardless of category" instituted in 1962-63 with *Who's Afraid of Virginia Woolf?)* or best-play or best-musical Tony Award, we report that with the entry in this listing. Reminder: Anyone looking for a particular title of a Best Play here can determine its year by looking it up in the alphabetical listing in last year's or other *Best Plays* volumes.

Our window opens on this grand parade on September 13, 1919 with Guy Bolton's and George Middleton's *Adam and Eva.* Step in anywhere your memory suggests and join that enchanting, never-to-be-forgotten theatrical past in your imagination.

OTIS L. GUERNSEY Jr.
Editor

1919–1920

Adam and Eva (312)
By Guy Bolton and George Middleton. September 13, 1919.
The Jest (197)
By Sem Benelli; adapted by Edward Sheldon. (Opened April 19, 1919, suspended June 14, 1919.) Reopened September 19, 1919.
Clarence (306)
By Booth Tarkington. September 20, 1919.
Déclassée (257)
By Zoe Akins. October 6, 1919.
Wedding Bells (168)
By Salisbury Field. November 12, 1919.
Abraham Lincoln (193)
By John Drinkwater. December 15, 1919.
The Famous Mrs. Fair (344)
By James Forbes. December 22, 1919.
Mamma's Affair (98)
By Rachel Barton Butler. January 29, 1920.
Beyond the Horizon (160)
By Eugene O'Neill. February 2, 1920. Pulitzer Prize.
Jane Clegg (158)
By St. John Ervine. February 23, 1920.

Irene (670), The Gold Diggers (720).

1920–1921

Enter Madame (350)
By Gilda Varesi and Dolly Byrne. August 16, 1920.
The Bad Man (350)
By Porter Emerson Browne. August 30, 1920.
The First Year (760)
By Frank Craven. October 20, 1920.
The Skin Game (176)
By John Galsworthy. October 20, 1920.
The Emperor Jones (204)
By Eugene O'Neill. November 1, 1920.
Mary Rose (127)
By James M. Barrie. December 22, 1920.
Deburau (189)
By Sacha Guitry; adapted by Harley Granville Barker. December 23, 1920.
The Green Goddess (440)
By William Archer. January 18, 1921.

Nice People (247)
By Rachel Crothers. March 2, 1921.
Liliom (300)
By Ferenc Molnar; adapted by Benjamin Glazer. April 20, 1921.

The Bat (867), Miss Lulu Bett (200; Pulitzer Prize), Ladies' Night (360), Sally (570), Shuffle Along (504).

1921–1922

Dulcy (246)
By George S. Kaufman and Marc Connelly. August 13, 1921.
Six Cylinder Love (430)
By William Anthony McGuire. August 25, 1921.
The Hero (80)
By Gilbert Emery. September 5, 1921.
The Circle (175)
By W. Somerset Maugham. September 12, 1921.
Ambush (98)
By Arthur Richman. October 10, 1921.
A Bill of Divorcement (173)
By Clemence Dane. October 10, 1921.
Anna Christie (177)
By Eugene O'Neill. November 2, 1921. Pulitzer Prize.
The Dover Road (324)
By A.A. Milne. December 23, 1921.
He Who Gets Slapped (308)
By Leonid Andreyev; adapted by Gregory Zilboorg. January 9, 1922.
The Nest (152)
By Paul Geraldy; adapted by Grace George. January 28, 1922.

Abie's Irish Rose (2, 327), Blossom Time (576), Kiki (600), Chauve-Souris (520).

1922–1923

The Old Soak (423)
By Don Marquis. August 22, 1922.
Loyalties (220)
By John Galsworthy. September 27, 1922.
R.U.R. (184)
By Karel Capek. October 9, 1922.
The Fool (373)
By Channing Pollock. October 23, 1922.
Rain (648)
By John Colton and Clemence Randolph; based on the story by W. Somerset Maugham. November 7, 1922.

Merton of the Movies (381)

By George S. Kaufman and Marc Connelly; based on Harry Leon Wilson's novel. November 13, 1922.

Why Not? (120)

By Jesse Lynch Williams. December 25, 1992.

Mary the 3rd (162)

By Rachel Crothers. February 5, 1923.

Icebound (171)

By Owen Davis. February 10, 1923. Pulitzer Prize.

You and I (178)

By Philip Barry. February 19, 1923.

The Gingham Girl (422), Seventh Heaven (704).

1923–1924

Sun-Up (356)

By Lula Vollmer. May 25, 1923. (Entry appears in 1922-23 *Best Plays* volume, but was named a Best Play of 1923-24.)

The Changelings (128)

By Lee Wilson Dodd. September 17, 1923.

Chicken Feed (144)

By Guy Bolton. September 24, 1923.

Tarnish (248)

By Gilbert Emery. October 1, 1923.

The Swan (255)

By Ferenc Molnar; translated by Melville Baker. October 23, 1923.

Hell-Bent fer Heaven (122)

By Hatcher Hughes. January 4, 1924. Pulitzer Prize.

Outward Bound (144)

By Sutton Vane. January 7, 1924.

The Goose Hangs High (183)

By Lewis Beach. January 29, 1924.

The Show-Off (571)

By George Kelly. February 5, 1994.

Beggar on Horseback (224)

By George S. Kaufman and Marc Connelly. February 12, 1924.

Little Jessie James (453), White Cargo (686).

1924–1925

Dancing Mothers (312)

By Edgar Selwyn and Edmund Goulding. August 11, 1924.

What Price Glory? (433)

By Maxwell Anderson and Laurence Stallings. September 3, 1924.

Minick (141)
By George S. Kaufman and Edna Ferber. September 24, 1924.
The Firebrand (269)
By Edwin Justus Mayer. October 15, 1924.
Desire Under the Elms (208)
By Eugene O'Neill. November 11, 1924.
They Knew What They Wanted (414)
By Sidney Howard. November 24, 1924. Pulitzer Prize.
The Youngest (104)
By Philip Barry. December 22, 1924.
Mrs. Partridge Presents (144)
By Mary Kennedy and Ruth Hawthorne. January 5, 1925.
The Fall Guy (176)
By James Gleason and George Abbott. March 10, 1925.
Wild Birds (44)
By Dan Totheroh. April 9, 1925.

Is Zat So? (618), The Student Prince (608), Rose Marie (557).

1925–1926

The Green Hat (231)
By Michael Arlen. September 15, 1925.
The Butter and Egg Man (243)
By George S. Kaufman. September 23, 1925.
Craig's Wife (360)
By George Kelly. October 12, 1925. Pulitzer Prize.
The Enemy (203)
By Channing Pollock. October 20, 1925.
Young Woodley (260)
By John van Druten. November 2, 1925.
The Last of Mrs. Cheyney (385)
By Frederick Lonsdale. November 9, 1925.
The Dybbuk (120)
By S. Ansky; adapted by Henry G. Alsberg. December 15, 1925.
The Great God Brown (271)
By Eugene O'Neill. January 23, 1926.
The Wisdom Tooth (160)
By Marc Connelly. February 15, 1926.
Bride of the Lamb (109)
By William Hurlbut. March 30, 1926.

The Cradle Snatchers (478), Earl Carroll's Vanities (440), George White's Scandals (424), The Girl Friend (409), Lulu Belle (461), Sunny (517), The Vagabond King (511).

1926–1927

Broadway (603)
By Philip Dunning and George Abbott. September 16, 1926.
Daisy Mayme (112)
By George Kelly. October 25, 1926.
The Play's the Thing (326)
By Ferenc Molnar; adapted by P.G. Wodehouse. November 3, 1926.
The Constant Wife (295)
By W. Somerset Maugham. November 29, 1926.
The Silver Cord (112)
By Sidney Howard. December 20, 1926.
Chicago (172)
By Maurine Dallas Watkins. December 30, 1926.
In Abraham's Bosom (116)
By Paul Green. December 30, 1926. Pulitzer Prize.
The Cradle Song (57)
By Gregorio and Maria Martinez Sierra; translated by John Garrett Underhill. January 24, 1927.
Saturday's Children (310)
By Maxwell Anderson. January 26, 1927.
The Road to Rome (392)
By Robert E. Sherwood. January 31, 1927.

The Desert Song (471), The Ladder (789), Rio Rita (494), The Squall (444).

1927–1928

Burlesque (372)
By George Manker Watters and Arthur Hopkins. September 1, 1927.
Porgy (367)
By Dorothy and DuBose Heyward. October 10, 1927.
Escape (173)
By John Galsworthy. October 26, 1927.
Coquette (366)
By George Abbott and Ann Preston Bridgers. November 8, 1927.
The Racket (119)
By Bartlett Cormack. November 22, 1927.
The Plough and the Stars (32)
By Sean O'Casey. November 28, 1927.
Behold the Bridegroom (88)
By George Kelly. December 26, 1927.
Paris Bound (234)
By Philip Barry. December 27, 1927.

The Royal Family (345)
By George S. Kaufman and Edna Ferber. December 28, 1927.
Strange Interlude (426)
By Eugene O'Neill. January 30, 1928. Pulitzer Prize.

Blackbirds of 1928 (518), A Connecticut Yankee (418), Good News (551), Show Boat (572), Skidding (472), The Trial of Mary Dugan (437).

1928–1929

The Front Page (276)
By Ben Hecht and Charles MacArthur. August 14, 1928.
Machinal (91)
By Sophie Treadwell. September 7, 1928.
Little Accident (303)
By Floyd Dell and Thomas Mitchell. October 9, 1928.
Holiday (229)
By Philip Barry. November 26, 1928.
Wings Over Europe (90)
By Robert Nichols and Maurice Browne. December 10, 1928.
The Kingdom of God (92)
By Gregorio Martinez Sierra; adapted by Helen and Harley Granville Barker. December 20, 1928.
Street Scene (601)
By Elmer Rice. January 10, 1929. Pulitzer Prize.
Gypsy (64)
By Maxwell Anderson. January 14, 1929.
Let Us Be Gay (353)
By Rachel Crothers. February 19, 1929.
Journey's End (485)
By R.C. Sherriff. March 22, 1929.

Bird in Hand (500), Follow Thru (403), Hold Everything (413), The New Moon (509).

1929–1930

Strictly Dishonorable (577)
By Preston Sturges. September 18, 1929.
The Criminal Code (173)
By Martin Flavin. October 2, 1929.
June Moon (273)
By Ring W. Lardner and George S. Kaufman. October 9, 1929.
Berkeley Square (229)
By John L. Balderston. November 4, 1929.

Michael and Mary (246)
By A.A. Milne. December 13, 1929.
Death Takes a Holiday (180)
By Alberto Casella; adapted by Walter Ferris. December 26, 1929.
The First Mrs. Fraser (352)
By St. John Ervine. December 28, 1929.
Rebound (114)
By Donald Ogden Stewart. February 3, 1930.
The Last Mile (289)
By John Wexley. February 13, 1930.
The Green Pastures (640)
By Marc Connelly; based on Roark Bradford's *Ol Man Adam and His Chillun.* February 26, 1930. Pulitzer Prize.

1930–1931

Once in a Lifetime (406)
By Moss Hart and George S. Kaufman. September 24, 1930.
Elizabeth the Queen (147)
By Maxwell Anderson. November 3, 1930.
Grand Hotel (459)
By Vicki Baum; adapted by W.A. Drake. November 13, 1930.
Alison's House (41)
By Susan Glaspell. December 1, 1930. Pulitzer Prize.
Overture (41)
By William Bolitho. December 5, 1930.
Five-Star Final (175)
By Louis Weitzenkorn. December 30, 1930.
Tomorrow and Tomorrow (206)
By Philip Barry. January 13, 1931.
Green Grow the Lilacs (64)
By Lynn Riggs. January 26, 1931.
The Barretts of Wimpole Street (370)
By Rudolph Besier. February 9, 1931.
As Husbands Go (148)
By Rachel Crothers. March 5, 1931.

1931–1932

The House of Connelly (91)
By Paul Green. September 28, 1931.
The Left Bank (242)
By Elmer Rice. October 5, 1931.

Mourning Becomes Electra (150)
By Eugene O'Neill. October 26, 1931.

Cynara (210)
By H.M. Harwood and R.F. Gore-Browne. November 2, 1931.

Brief Moment (129)
By S.N. Behrman. November 9, 1931.

Reunion in Vienna (264)
By Robert E. Sherwood. November 16, 1931.

Of Thee I Sing (441)
Musical with book by George S. Kaufman and Morrie Ryskind; music by George Gershwin; lyrics by Ira Gershwin. December 26, 1931. Pulitzer Prize.

The Devil Passes (96)
By Benn W. Levy. January 4, 1932.

The Animal Kingdom (183)
By Philip Barry. January 12, 1932.

Another Language (344)
By Rose Franken. April 25, 1932.

1932–1933

When Ladies Meet (191)
By Rachel Crothers. October 6, 1932.

Dinner at Eight (232)
By George S. Kaufman and Edna Ferber. October 22, 1932.

The Late Christopher Bean (224)
By René Fauchois; adapted by Sidney Howard. October 31, 1932.

Biography (267)
By S.N. Behrman. December 12, 1932.

Pigeons and People (70)
By George M. Cohan. January 16, 1933.

We, the People (49)
By Elmer Rice. January 21, 1933.

Design for Living (135)
By Noel Coward. January 24, 1933.

One Sunday Afternoon (322)
By James Hagan. February 15, 1933.

Alien Corn (98)
By Sidney Howard. February 20, 1933.

Both Your Houses (72)
By Maxwell Anderson. March 6, 1933. Pulitzer Prize.

1933–1934

Men in White (351)
By Sidney Kingsley. September 26, 1933. Pulitzer Prize.

Ah, Wilderness! (289)
By Eugene O'Neill. October 2, 1933.
The Green Bay Tree (166)
By Mordaunt Shairp. October 20, 1933.
Her Master's Voice (224)
By Clare Kummer. October 23, 1933.
Mary of Scotland (248)
By Maxwell Anderson. November 27, 1933.
Wednesday's Child (56)
By Leopold Atlas. January 16, 1934.
No More Ladies (162)
By A.E. Thomas. January 23, 1934.
The Shining Hour (121)
By Keith Winter. February 13, 1934.
They Shall Not Die (62)
By John Wexley. February 21, 1934.
Dodsworth (315)
By Sidney Howard; based on the novel by Sinclair Lewis. February 24, 1934.

Tobacco Road (3,182), Sailor, Beware! (500), As Thousands Cheer (400).

1934–1935

The Distaff Side (177)
By John van Druten. September 25, 1934.
Merrily We Roll Along (155)
By George S. Kaufman and Moss Hart. September 29, 1934.
Lost Horizons (56)
By Harry Segall; revised by John Hayden. October 15, 1934.
The Farmer Takes a Wife (104)
By Frank B. Elser and Marc Connelly; based on the novel *Rome Haul* by Walter Edmonds. October 30, 1934.
The Children's Hour (691)
By Lillian Hellman. November 20, 1934.
Valley Forge (58)
By Maxwell Anderson. December 10, 1934.
Accent on Youth (229)
By Samson Raphaelson. December 25, 1934.
The Old Maid (305)
By Zoe Akins; based on the novel by Edith Wharton. January 7, 1935. Pulitzer Prize.
The Petrified Forest (197)
By Robert E. Sherwood. January 7, 1935.

Awake and Sing (209)
By Clifford Odets. February 19, 1935.

Anything Goes (420), Personal Appearance (501), Three Men on a Horse (835).

1935–1936

Winterset (195)
By Maxwell Anderson. September 25, 1935. Critics Award (American play).

Dead End (687)
By Sidney Kingsley. October 28, 1935.

Pride and Prejudice (219)
By Helen Jerome; based on the novel by Jane Austen. November 5, 1935.

First Lady (246)
By Katherine Dayton and George S. Kaufman. November 26, 1935.

Boy Meets Girl (669)
By Bella and Samuel Spewack. November 27, 1935.

Victoria Regina (517)
By Laurence Housman. December 26, 1935.

Ethan Frome (120)
By Owen and Donald Davis; based on the novel by Edith Wharton. January 21, 1936.

Call It a Day (194)
By Dodie Smith. January 28, 1936.

End of Summer (153)
By S.N. Behrman. February 17, 1936.

Idiot's Delight (300)
By Robert E. Sherwood. March 24, 1936. Pulitzer Prize.

1936–1937

St. Helena (63)
By R.C. Sherriff and Jeanne de Casalis. October 6, 1936.

Daughters of Atreus (13)
By Robert Turney. October 14, 1936.

Tovarich (356)
By Jacques Deval; translated by Robert E. Sherwood. October 15, 1936.

Stage Door (169)
By George S. Kaufman and Edna Ferber. October 22, 1936.

Johnny Johnson (68)
By Paul Green; incidental music by Kurt Weill; lyrics by Paul Green. November 19, 1936.

You Can't Take It With You (837)
By Moss Hart and George S. Kaufman. December 14, 1936. Pulitzer Prize.

The Women (657)
By Clare Boothe. December 26, 1936.

High Tor (171)
By Maxwell Anderson. January 9, 1937. Critics Award (American play).
Yes, My Darling Daughter (405)
By Mark Reed. February 9, 1937.
Excursion (116)
By Victor Wolfson. April 9, 1937.

Brother Rat (577), Room Service (500).

1937–1938

The Star-Wagon (223)
By Maxwell Anderson. September 29, 1937.
Susan and God (288)
By Rachel Crothers. October 7, 1937.
Amphitryon 38 (153)
By Jean Giraudoux; adapted by S.N. Behrman. November 1, 1937.
Golden Boy (250)
By Clifford Odets. November 4, 1937.
Of Mice and Men (207)
By John Steinbeck. November 23, 1937. Critics Award (American play).
Shadow and Substance (274)
By Paul Vincent Carroll. January 26, 1938. Critics Award (foreign play).
On Borrowed Time (321)
By Paul Osborn; based on a novel by Lawrence Edward Watkin. February 3, 1938.
Our Town (336)
By Thornton Wilder. February 4, 1938. Pulitzer Prize.
Prologue to Glory (70)
By E.P. Conkle. March 17, 1938.
What a Life (538)
By Clifford Goldsmith. April 13, 1938.

Bachelor Born (400), Pins and Needles (1,108).

1938–1939

Kiss the Boys Good-bye (286)
By Clare Boothe. September 28, 1938.
Abe Lincoln in Illinois (472)
By Robert E. Sherwood. October 15, 1938. Pulitzer Prize.
Rocket to the Moon (131)
By Clifford Odets. November 24, 1938.
Here Come the Clowns (88)
By Philip Barry. December 7, 1938.

The White Steed (136)
By Paul Vincent Carroll. January 10, 1939. Critics Award (foreign play).

The American Way (164)
By George S. Kaufman and Moss Hart. January 21, 1939.

The Little Foxes (410)
By Lillian Hellman. February 15, 1939.

The Philadelphia Story (417)
By Philip Barry. March 28, 1939.

No Time for Comedy (185)
By S.N. Behrman. April 17, 1939.

Family Portrait (111)
By Lenore Coffee and William Joyce Cowen. May 8, 1939.

Hellzapoppin (1, 404).

1939–1940

Skylark (256)
By Samson Raphaelson. October 11, 1939.

The Man Who Came to Dinner (739)
By Moss Hart and George S. Kaufman. October 16, 1939.

The Time of Your Life (185)
By William Saroyan. October 25, 1939. Pulitzer Prize and Critics Award (American play).

Margin for Error (264)
By Clare Boothe. November 3, 1939.

Life With Father (3,224)
By Howard Lindsay and Russel Crouse; based on the book by Clarence Day. November 8, 1939. Broadway's longest-running play.

The World We Make (80)
By Sidney Kingsley; based on the novel *The Outward Room* by Millen Brand. November 20, 1939.

Key Largo (105)
By Maxwell Anderson. November 27, 1939.

Morning's at Seven (44)
By Paul Osborn. November 30, 1939.

The Male Animal (243)
By James Thurber and Elliott Nugent. January 9, 1940.

There Shall Be No Night (181)
By Robert E. Sherwood. April 29, 1940. 1940–41 Pulitzer Prize.

Du Barry Was a Lady (408), Louisiana Purchase (444), Separate Rooms (613).

1940–1941

George Washington Slept Here (173)
By George S. Kaufman and Moss Hart. October 18, 1940.

The Corn Is Green (477)
By Emlyn Williams. November 26, 1940. Critics Award (foreign play).
My Sister Eileen (864)
By Joseph Fields and Jerome Chodorov; based on Ruth McKenney's stories. December 26, 1940.
Flight to the West (136)
By Elmer Rice. December 30, 1940.
Arsenic and Old Lace (1,444)
By Joseph Kesselring. January 10, 1941.
Mr. and Mrs. North (163)
By Owen Davis; based on Frances and Richard Lockridge's stories. January 12, 1941.
Lady in the Dark (162)
Musical with book by Moss Hart; music by Kurt Weill; lyrics by Ira Gershwin. January 23, 1941.
Claudia (722)
By Rose Franken. February 12, 1941.
Native Son (114)
By Paul Green and Richard Wright; based on Richard Wright's novel. March 24, 1941.
Watch on the Rhine (378)
By Lillian Hellman. April 1, 1941. Critics Award (American play).

Panama Hattie (501).

1941–1942

Candle in the Wind (95)
By Maxwell Anderson. October 22, 1941.
Blithe Spirit (657)
By Noel Coward. November 5, 1941. Critics Award (foreign play).
Junior Miss (710)
By Jerome Chodorov and Joseph Fields. November 18, 1941.
Hope for a Harvest (38)
By Sophie Treadwell. November 26, 1941.
Angel Street (1,295)
By Patrick Hamilton. December 5, 1941.
Letters to Lucerne (23)
By Fritz Rotter and Allen Vincent. December 23, 1941.
In Time to Come (40)
By Howard Koch and John Huston. December 28, 1941.
Jason (125)
By Samson Raphaelson. January 21, 1942.

The Moon Is Down (71)
By John Steinbeck. April 7, 1942.
Uncle Harry (430)
By Thomas Job. May 20, 1942.

By Jupiter (427), Let's Face It (547), Sons o' Fun (742).

1942–1943

The Eve of St. Mark (307)
By Maxwell Anderson. October 7, 1942.
Thc Damask Cheek (93)
By John van Druten and Lloyd Morris. October 22, 1942.
The Skin of Our Teeth (359)
By Thornton Wilder. November 18, 1942. Pulitzer Prize.
Winter Soldiers (25)
By Daniel Lewis James. November 29, 1942.
The Doughgirls (671)
By Joseph Fields. December 30, 1942.
The Patriots (173)
By Sidney Kingsley. January 29, 1943. Critics Award (American play).
Harriet (377)
By Florence Ryerson and Colin Clements. March 3, 1943.
Kiss and Tell (956)
By F. Hugh Herbert. March 17, 1943.
Oklahoma! (2,212)
Musical with book and lyrics by Oscar Hammerstein II; music by Richard Rodgers; based on the play *Green Grow the Lilacs* by Lynn Riggs. March 31, 1943.
Tomorrow the World (500)
By James Gow and Arnaud d'Usseau. April 14, 1943.

Janie (642), Rosalinda (521), Something for the Boys (422), Star and Garter (609), Stars on Ice (830), Three's a Family (497), Ziegfeld Follies (553).

1943–1944

Outrageous Fortune (77)
By Rose Franken. November 3, 1943.
The Innocent Voyage (40)
By Paul Osborn; based on the novel *A High Wind in Jamaica* by Richard Hughes. November 15, 1943.
Winged Victory (212)
By Moss Hart; music by David Rose. November 20, 1943.

The Voice of the Turtle (1,557)
By John van Druten. December 8, 1943.
Over 21 (221)
By Ruth Gordon. January 3, 1944.
Storm Operation (23)
By Maxwell Anderson. January 11, 1944.
Decision (160)
By Edward Chodorov. February 2, 1944.
Jacobowsky and the Colonel (417)
By S.N. Behrman; based on Franz Werfel's play. March 14, 1944. Critics Award (foreign play).
The Searching Wind (318)
By Lillian Hellman. April 12, 1944.
Pick-up Girl (198)
By Elsa Shelley. May 3, 1944.

Carmen Jones (503), Mexican Hayride (481), One Touch of Venus (567), The Two Mrs. Carrolls (585), Follow the Girls (882).

1944–1945

Anna Lucasta (957)
By Philip Yordan. August 30, 1944.
Soldier's Wife (253)
By Rose Franken. October 4, 1944.
I Remember Mama (714)
By John van Druten; based on the book *Mama's Bank Account* by Kathryn Forbes. October 19, 1944.
Harvey (1,775)
By Mary Chase. November 1, 1944. Pulitzer Prize.
The Late George Apley (385)
By John P. Marquand and George S. Kaufman; based on John P. Marquand's novel. November 23, 1944.
A Bell for Adano (304)
By Paul Osborn; based on John Hersey's novel. December 6, 1944.
Dear Ruth (683)
By Norman Krasna. December 13, 1944.
The Hasty Heart (207)
By John Patrick. January 3, 1945.
Foolish Notion (104)
By Philip Barry. March 3, 1945.
The Glass Menagerie (561)
By Tennessee Williams. March 31, 1945. Critics Award (American play).

Bloomer Girl (654), Hats Off to Ice (889), On the Town (463), Ten Little Indians

(426), Up in Central Park (504), Song of Norway (860), Carousel (890; 1945–46 Critics Award for best musical).

1945–1946

Deep Are the Roots (477)
By Arnaud d'Usseau and James Gow. September 26, 1945.
The Rugged Path (81)
By Robert E. Sherwood. November 10, 1945.
State of the Union (765)
By Howard Lindsay and Russel Crouse. November 14, 1965. Pulitzer Prize.
Dream Girl (348)
By Elmer Rice. December 14, 1945.
Home of the Brave (69)
By Arthur Laurents. December 27, 1945.
The Magnificent Yankee (160)
By Emmet Lavery. January 22, 1946.
O Mistress Mine (452)
By Terence Rattigan. January 23, 1946.
Born Yesterday (1,642)
By Garson Kanin. February 4, 1946.
Lute Song (385)
Musical with book by Sidney Howard and Will Irwin; music by Raymond Scott; lyrics by Bernard Hanighen; based on the Chinese classic *Pi-Pa-Ki.* February 6, 1946.
Antigone (64)
By Jean Anouilh; adapted by Lewis Galantière. February 18, 1946.

Show Boat (418; revival), The Red Mill (531; revival), Call Me Mister (734), Annie Get Your Gun (1,147).

1946–1947

The Iceman Cometh (136)
By Eugene O'Neill. October 9, 1946.
Joan of Lorraine (199)
By Maxwell Anderson. November 18, 1946.
The Fatal Weakness (119)
By George Kelly. November 19, 1946.
Another Part of the Forest (182)
By Lillian Hellman. November 20, 1946.
Christopher Blake (114)
By Moss Hart. November 30, 1946.
Years Ago (206)
By Ruth Gordon. December 3, 1946.

A golden moment in American playwriting passed by in the late 1940s, in masterworks by Tennessee Williams and Arthur Miller. *At right,* the Hirschfeld interpretation, in 1947, of Jessica Tandy and Marlon Brando creating the roles of Blanche DuBois and Stanley Kowalski under Elia Kazan's direction in Williams's *A Streetcar Named Desire.* For Hirschfeld's interpretation of the Miller play, turn the page.

All My Sons (328)

By Arthur Miller. January 29, 1947. Critics Award (American play).

John Loves Mary (423)

By Norman Krasna. February 4, 1947.

The Story of Mary Surratt (11)

By John Patrick. February 8, 1947.

Brigadoon (581)

Musical with book and lyrics by Alan Jay Lerner; music by Frederick Loewe. March 13, 1947. Critics Award (musical).

No Exit (31; Critics Award for best foreign play), Burlesque (439; revival), Happy Birthday (564), Icetime of 1948 (422), Finian's Rainbow (725).

1947–1948

The Heiress (410)
By Ruth and Augustus Goetz; suggested by the novel *Washington Square* by Henry James. September 29, 1947.

Command Decision (408)
By William Wister Haines. October 1, 1947.

Allegro (315)
Musical with book and lyrics by Oscar Hammerstein II; music by Richard Rodgers. October 10, 1947.

An Inspector Calls (95)
By J.B. Priestley. October 21, 1947.

The Winslow Boy (215)
By Terence Rattigan. October 29, 1947. Critics Award (foreign play).

Eastward in Eden (15)
By Dorothy Gardner. November 18, 1947.

A Streetcar Named Desire (855)
By Tennessee Williams. December 3, 1947. Pulitzer Prize. Critics Award (American play).

Skipper Next to God (93)
By Jan de Hartog. January 4, 1948.

Mister Roberts (1,157)
By Thomas Heggen and Joshua Logan; based on Thomas Heggen's novel. February 18, 1948. Tony Award.

Me and Molly (156)
By Gertrude Berg. February 26, 1948.

Make Mine Manhattan (429), High Button Shoes (727).

1948–1949

Edward, My Son (260)
By Robert Morley and Noel Langley. September 30, 1948.

Life With Mother (265)
By Howard Lindsay and Russel Crouse; based on Clarence Day's book. October 20, 1948.

Goodbye, My Fancy (446)
By Fay Kanin. November 17, 1948.

Light Up the Sky (216)
By Moss Hart. November 18, 1948.

The Silver Whistle (219)
By Robert E. McEnroe. November 24, 1948.

Anne of the Thousand Days (286)
By Maxwell Anderson. December 8, 1948.

The Madwoman of Chaillot (368)

Lee J. Cobb as Willy Loman with Mildred Dunnock as his wife Linda in Arthur Miller's *Death of a Salesman* under Elia Kazan's direction in 1948

By Jean Giraudoux; adapted by Maurice Valency. December 27, 1948. Critics Award (foreign play).

Death of a Salesman (742)

By Arthur Miller. February 10, 1949. Pulitzer Prize. Critics Award (American play). Tony Award.

Two Blind Mice (157)

By Samuel Spewack. March 2, 1949.

Detective Story (581)

By Sidney Kingsley. March 23, 1949.

South Pacific (1, 925; Critics Award for best musical; Pulitzer Prize and 1949–50 Tony Award), As the Girls Go (420), Howdy, Mr. Ice (406 for 1949 version; 430 for 1950 version), Lend an Ear (460), Where's Charley? (792), Kiss Me, Kate (1, 070; Tony Award).

1949–1950

Lost in the Stars (273)
Musical with book and lyrics by Maxwell Anderson; music by Kurt Weill; based on the novel *Cry, the Beloved Country* by Alan Paton. October 30, 1949.

I Know My Love (246)
By S.N. Behrman; adapted from *Auprès de Ma Blonde* by Marcel Achard. November 2, 1949.

Clutterbuck (218)
By Benn W. Levy. December 3, 1949.

The Member of the Wedding (501)
By Carson McCullers; adapted from her novel. January 5, 1950. Critics Award (American play).

The Enchanted (45)
By Maurice Valency; adapted from the play *Intermezzo* by Jean Giraudoux. January 18, 1950.

The Cocktail Party (409)
By T.S. Eliot. January 21, 1950. Critics Award (foreign play). Tony Award.

The Happy Time (614)
By Samuel Taylor; based on Robert Fontaine's book. January 24, 1950.

The Innocents (141)
By William Archibald; based on *The Turn of the Screw* by Henry James. February 1, 1950.

Come Back, Little Sheba (191)
By William Inge. February 15, 1950.

The Wisteria Trees (165)
By Joshua Logan; based on *The Cherry Orchard* by Anton Chekhov. March 29, 1950.

The Consul (269; Critics Award for best musical), Gentlemen Prefer Blonds (740).

1950–1951

Affairs of State (610)
By Louis Verneuil. September 25, 1950.

Season in the Sun (367)
By Wolcott Gibbs. September 28, 1950.

The Country Girl (235)
By Clifford Odets. November 10, 1950.

Bell, Book and Candle (233)
By John van Druten. November 14, 1950.

Guys and Dolls (1,200)
Musical with book by Jo Swerling and Abe Burrows; music and lyrics by Frank Loesser; based on a story and characters by Damon Runyon. November 24, 1950. Critics Award (musical). Tony Award.

Second Threshold (126)
By Philip Barry; revisions by Robert E. Sherwood. January 2, 1951.

Darkness at Noon (186)
By Sidney Kingsley; based on Arthur Koestler's novel. January 13, 1951. Critics Award (American play).

The Rose Tattoo (306)
By Tennessee Williams. February 3, 1951. Tony Award.

Billy Budd (105)
By Louis O. Coxe and Robert Chapman; based on Herman Melville's novel. February 10, 1951.

The Autumn Garden (101)
By Lillian Hellman. March 7, 1951.

The Lady's Not for Burning (151; Critics Award for best foreign play), Call Me Madam (644), The Moon Is Blue (924), Stalag 17 (472), The King and I (1,246; 1951–52 Tony Award).

1951–1952

Remains To Be Seen (199)
By Howard Lindsay and Russel Crouse. October 3, 1951.

The Fourposter (632)
By Jan de Hartog. October 24, 1951. Tony Award.

Barefoot in Athens (30)
By Maxwell Anderson. October 31, 1951.

Gigi (219)
By Anita Loos; based on Colette's novel. November 24, 1951.

I Am a Camera (214)
By John van Druten; based on Christopher Isherwood's Berlin stories. November 28, 1951. Critics Award (American play).

Point of No Return (364)
By Paul Osborn; based on J.P. Marquand's novel. December 13, 1951.

The Shrike (161)
By Joseph Kramm. January 15, 1952. Pulitzer Prize.

Jane (100)
By S.N. Behrman; suggested by W. Somerset Maugham's story. February 1, 1952.

Venus Observed (86)
By Christopher Fry. February 13, 1952. Critics Award (foreign play).

Mrs. McThing (350)
By Mary Chase. February 20, 1952.

Pal Joey (540; revival; Critics Award for best musical), Don Juan in Hell (105; special Critics citation).

1952–1953

The Time of the Cuckoo (263)
By Arthur Laurents. October 15, 1952.
Bernardine (157)
By Mary Chase. October 16, 1952.
Dial "M" for Murder (552)
By Frederick Knott. October 29, 1952.
The Climate of Eden (20)
By Moss Hart; based on the novel *Shadows Move Among Them* by Edgar Mittleholzer. November 13, 1952.
The Love of Four Colonels (141)
By Peter Ustinov. January 15, 1953. Critics Award (foreign play).
The Crucible (197)
By Arthur Miller. January 22, 1953. Tony Award.
The Emperor's Clothes (16)
By George Tabori. February 9, 1953.
Picnic (477)
By William Inge. February 19, 1953. Pulitzer Prize. Critics Award (American play).
Wonderful Town (559)
Musical with book by Joseph Fields and Jerome Chodorov; based on their play *My Sister Eileen* and Ruth McKenney's stories; music by Leonard Bernstein; lyrics by Betty Comden and Adolph Green. February 25, 1953. Critics Award (musical). Tony Award.
My 3 Angels (344)
By Samuel and Bella Spewack; based on the play *La Cuisine des Anges* by Albert Husson. March 11, 1953.

Wish You Were Here (598), The Fifth Season (654), Can-Can (892), The Seven Year Itch (1, 141).

1953–1954

Take a Giant Step (76)
By Louis Peterson. September 24, 1953.
Tea and Sympathy (712)
By Robert Anderson. September 30, 1953.
The Teahouse of the August Moon (1,027)
By John Patrick; based on Vern Sneider's novel. October 15, 1953. Pulitzer Prize. Critics Award (American play). Tony Award.
In the Summer House (55)
By Jane Bowles. December 29, 1953.
The Caine Mutiny Court Martial (415)
By Herman Wouk; based on his novel. January 20, 1954.

The Immoralist (96)
By Ruth and Augustus Goetz; based on Andre Gide's novel. February 8, 1954.
The Girl on the Via Flaminia (111)
By Alfred Hayes; based on his novel. February 9, 1954.
The Confidential Clerk (117)
By T.S. Eliot. February 11, 1954.
The Magic and the Loss (27)
By Julian Funt. April 9, 1954.
The Golden Apple (125)
Musical with book and lyrics by John Latouche; music by Jerome Moross. April 20, 1954. Critics Award (musical).

Ondine (157; Critics Award for best foreign play); Kismet (583; Tony Award), The Solid Gold Cadillac (526), Anniversary Waltz (615), Comedy in Music (849), The Pajama Game (1, 063; 1954–55 Tony Award).

1954–1955

The Boy Friend (485)
Musical with book, music and lyrics by Sandy Wilson. September 30, 1954.
The Living Room (22)
By Graham Greene. November 17, 1954.
Bad Seed (332)
By Maxwell Anderson; adapted from William March's novel. Dec. 8, 1954.
Witness for the Prosecution (645)
By Agatha Christie. December 16, 1954. Critics Award (foreign play).
The Flowering Peach (135)
By Clifford Odets. December 28, 1954.
The Desperate Hours (212)
By Joseph Hayes; based on his novel. February 10, 1955. Tony Award.
The Dark Is Light Enough (69)
By Christopher Fry. February 23, 1955.
Bus Stop (478)
By William Inge. March 2, 1955.
Cat on a Hot Tin Roof (694)
By Tennessee Williams. March 24, 1955. Pulitzer Prize. Critics Award (American play).
Inherit the Wind (806)
By Jerome Lawrence and Robert E. Lee. April 21, 1955.

The Saint of Bleeker Street (92; Critics Award for best musical), Plain and Fancy (461), Silk Stockings (478), Fanny (888), Damn Yankees (1, 019; 1955–56 Tony Award).

1955–1956

A View From the Bridge (149)
By Arthur Miller. September 29, 1955.

Tiger at the Gates (217)
By Jean Giraudoux; translated from his *La Guerre de Troi n'Aura Pas Lieu* by Christopher Fry. October 3, 1955. Critics Award (foreign play).

The Diary of Anne Frank (717)
By Frances Goodrich and Albert Hackett; based on Anne Frank's *The Diary of a Young Girl.* October 5, 1955. Pulitzer Prize. Critics Award (American play). Tony Award.

No Time for Sergeants (796)
By Ira Levin; adaped from Mac Hyman's novel. October 20, 1955.

The Chalk Garden (182)
By Enid Bagnold. October 26, 1955.

The Lark (229)
By Jean Anouilh; adapted by Lillian Hellman. November 17, 1955.

The Matchmaker (486)
By Thornton Wilder; based on Johann Nestroy's *Einen Jux Will Er Sich Machen.* December 5, 1955.

The Ponder Heart (149)
By Joseph Fields and Jerome Chodorov; adapted from Eudora Welty's story. February 16, 1956.

My Fair Lady (2,717)
Musical with book and lyrics by Alan Jay Lerner; music by Frederick Loewe; based on George Bernard Shaw's play *Pygmalion.* March 15, 1956. Critics Award (musical). 1956-57 Tony Award.

Waiting for Godot (59)
By Samuel Beckett. April 19, 1956.

Middle of the Night (477), Will Success Spoil Rock Hunter? (444), The Most Happy Fella (676; 1956-57 Critics Award for best musical), The Threepenny Opera (2,611), The Iceman Cometh (565; revival).

1956–1957

Separate Tables (332)
By Terence Rattigan. October 25, 1956.

Long Day's Journey Into Night (390)
By Eugene O'Neill. November 7, 1956. Pulitzer Prize. Critics Award (American play). Tony Award.

A Very Special Baby (5)
By Robert Alan Aurthur. November 14, 1956.

Candide (73)
Musical with book by Lillian Hellman; music by Leonard Bernstein; lyrics by Richard Wilbur, John Latouche and Dorothy Parker; based on Voltaire's satire. December 1, 1956.

A Clearing in the Woods (36)
By Arthur Laurents. January 10, 1957.

The Waltz of the Toreadors (132)
By Jean Anouilh; translated by Lucienne Hill. January 17, 1957. Critics Award (foreign play).

The Potting Shed (143)
By Graham Greene. January 29, 1957.

Visit to a Small Planet (388)
By Gore Vidal. February 7, 1957.

Orpheus Descending (68)
By Tennessee Williams. March 21, 1957.

A Moon for the Misbegotten (68)
By Eugene O'Neill. May 2, 1957.

Happy Hunting (412), The Tunnel of Love (417), New Girl in Town (431), Auntie Mame (639), L'il Abner (693), Bells Are Ringing (924).

1957–1958

Look Back in Anger (407)
By John Osborne. October 1, 1957. Critics Award (foreign play).

Under Milk Wood (39)
By Dylan Thomas. October 15, 1957.

Time Remembered (248)
By Jean Anouilh; adapted from his *Leocadia* by Patricia Moyes. November 12, 1957.

The Rope Dancers (189)
By Morton Wishengrad. November 20, 1957.

Look Homeward, Angel (564)
By Ketti Frings; based on Thomas Wolfe's novel. November 28, 1957. Pulitzer Prize. Critics Award (American play).

The Dark at the Top of the Stairs (468)
By William Inge. December 5, 1957.

Summer of the 17th Doll (29)
By Ray Lawler. January 22, 1958.

Sunrise at Campobello (556)
By Dore Schary. January 30, 1958. Tony Award.

The Entertainer (97)
By John Osborne. February 12, 1958.

The Visit (189)
By Friedrich Duerrenmatt; adapted by Maurice Valency. May 5, 1958. 1958-59 Critics Award (foreign play).

The Music Man (1,375; Critics Award for best musical; Tony Award), Jamaica

(555), West Side Story (732), Two for the Seesaw (750), The Boy Friend (763; revival), The Crucible (571; revival).

1958–1959

A Touch of the Poet (284)
By Eugene O'Neill. October 2, 1958.

The Pleasure of His Company (474)
By Samuel Taylor and Cornelia Otis Skinner. October 22, 1958.

Epitaph for George Dillon (23)
By John Osborne and Anthony Creighton. November 4, 1958.

The Disenchanted (189)
By Budd Schulberg and Harvey Breit; based on Budd Schulberg's novel. December 3, 1958.

The Cold Wind and the Warm (120)
By S.N. Behrman. December 8, 1958.

J.B. (364)
By Archibald MacLeish. December 11, 1958. Pulitzer Prize. Tony Award.

Requiem for a Nun (43)
By Ruth Ford and William Faulkner; adapted from William Faulkner's novel. January 30, 1959.

Sweet Bird of Youth (375)
By Tennessee Williams, March 10, 1959.

A Raisin in the Sun (530)
By Lorraine Hansberry. March 11, 1959. Critics Award (American play).

Kataki (20)
By Shimon Wincelberg. April 9, 1959.

La Plume de Ma Tante (835; Critics Award for best musical), The World of Suzie Wong (508), The Marriage-Go-Round (431), Redhead (452; Tony Award), Flower Drum Song (600), Destry Rides Again (472), A Majority of One (556), Once Upon a Mattress (460), Gypsy (702).

1959–1960

The Tenth Man (623)
By Paddy Chayefsky. November 5, 1959.

Fiorello! (795)
Musical with book by Jerome Weidman and George Abbott; music by Jerry Bock; lyrics by Sheldon Harnick. November 23, 1959. Pulitzer Prize. Critics Award (musical). Tony Award.

Five Finger Exercise (337)
By Peter Shaffer. December 2, 1959. Critics Award (foreign play).

The Andersonville Trial (179)
By Saul Levitt. December 29, 1959.

The Deadly Game (39)
By James Yaffe; based on Friedrich Duerrenmatt's novel. February 2, 1960.

Caligula (38)
By Albert Camus; adapted by Justin O'Brien. February 16, 1960.

Toys in the Attic (556)
By Lillian Hellman. February 25, 1960. Critics Award (American play).

A Thurber Carnival (127)
By James Thurber. February 26, 1960.

The Best Man (520)
By Gore Vidal. March 31, 1960.

Duel of Angels (51)
By Jean Giraudoux; adapted from his *Pour Lucrèce* by Christopher Fry. April 19, 1960.

Take Me Along (448), The Miracle Worker (700; Tony Award), Bye Bye Birdie (607; 1960-61 Tony Award), The Sound of Music (1,443; Tony Award), The Fantasticks (14,103; longest run on record in the American theater), The Balcony (672), Krapp's Last Tape and The Zoo Story (582), Little Mary Sunshine (1, 143), Leave It to Jane (928; revival), The Connection (722; special off-Broadway citation).*

1960-1961

The Hostage (127)
By Brendan Behan. September 20, 1960.

A Taste of Honey (376)
By Shelagh Delaney. October 4, 1960. Critics Award (foreign play).

Becket (193)
By Jean Anouilh; translated by Lucienne Hill. October 5, 1960. Tony Award.

Period of Adjustment (132)
By Tennessee Williams. November 10, 1960.

All the Way Home (333)
By Tad Mosel; based on the novel *A Death in the Family* by James Agee. November 30, 1960. Pulitzer Prize. Critics Award (American play).

Rhinoceros (240)
By Eugene Ionesco; translated by Derek Prouse. January 9, 1961.

Mary, Mary (1,572)
By Jean Kerr. March 8, 1961.

The Devil's Advocate (116)
By Dore Schary; based on Morris L. West's novel. March 9, 1961.

Big Fish, Little Fish (101)
By Hugh Wheeler. March 15, 1961.

A Far Country (271)
By Henry Denker. April 4, 1961.

Carnival (719; Critics Award for best musical), Irma La Douce (524), Do Re Mi

(400), The Unsinkable Molly Brown (532), Come Blow Your Horn (677), Camelot (873), The Blacks (1, 408).

1961–1962

The Caretaker (165)
By Harold Pinter. October 4, 1961.

How to Succeed in Business Without Really Trying (1,417)
Musical with book by Abe Burrows, Jack Weinstock and Willie Gilbert; music and lyrics by Frank Loesser; based on Shepherd Mead's novel. October 14, 1961. Pulitzer Prize. Critics Award (musical). Tony Award.

The Complaisant Lover (101)
By Graham Greene. November 1, 1961.

Gideon (236)
By Paddy Chayefsky. November 9, 1961.

A Man for All Seasons (637)
By Robert Bolt. November 22, 1961. Critics Award (foreign play). Tony Award.

Stone and Star (also called **Shadow of Heroes**) (20)
By Robert Ardrey. December 5, 1961.

The Night of the Iguana (316)
By Tennessee Williams. December 28, 1961. Critics Award (American play).

The Egg (8)
By Felicien Marceau; adapted by Robert Schlitt. January 8, 1962.

Oh Dad, Poor Dad, Mamma's Hung You in the Closet and I'm Feelin' So Sad (454)
By Arthur L. Kopit. February 26, 1962.

A Thousand Clowns (428)
By Herb Gardner. April 5, 1962.

Take Her, She's Mine (404), Milk and Honey (543), Brecht on Brecht (424), The Hostage (545; revival), No Strings (580), A Funny Thing Happened on the Way to the Forum (964; 1962-63 Tony Award).

1962–1963

Stop the World—I Want to Get Off (555)
Musical with book, music and lyrics by Leslie Bricusse and Anthony Newley. October 3, 1962.

Who's Afraid of Virginia Woolf? (664)
By Edward Albee. October 13, 1962. Critics Award. Tony Award.

Tchin-Tchin (222)
By Sidney Michaels; based on François Billetdoux's play. October 25, 1962.

P.S. 193 (48)
By David Rayfiel. October 30, 1962.

The Collection (578)
By Harold Pinter. November 26, 1962.
The Milk Train Doesn't Stop Here Anymore (69)
By Tennessee Williams. January 16, 1963.
Andorra (9)
By Max Frisch; adapted by George Tabori. February 9, 1963.
Mother Courage and Her Children (52)
By Bertolt Brecht; adapted by Eric Bentley. March 28, 1963.
Rattle of a Simple Man (94)
By Charles Dyer. April 17, 1963.
She Loves Me (301)
Musical with book by Joe Masteroff; music by Jerry Bock; lyrics by Sheldon Harnick; based on the play *Parfumerie* by Miklos Laszlo. April 23, 1963.

Beyond the Fringe (667; special Critics citation), Never Too Late (1, 007), Oliver! (774), Enter Laughing (419), Six Characters in Search of an Author (529; revival), The Boys from Syracuse (500; revival), Dime a Dozen (728).

1963–1964

The Rehearsal (110)
By Jean Anouilh; adapted by Pamela Hansford Johnson and Kitty Black. September 23, 1963.
Luther (211)
By John Osborne. September 25, 1963. Critics Award. Tony Award.
Chips With Everything (149)
By Arnold Wesker. October 1, 1963.
Barefoot in the Park (1,530)
By Neil Simon. October 23, 1963.
Next Time I'll Sing to You (23)
By James Saunders. November 27, 1963.
Hello, Dolly! (2,844)
Musical with book by Michael Stewart; music and lyrics by Jerry Herman; based on the play *The Matchmaker* by Thornton Wilder. January 16, 1964. Critics Award (musical). Tony Award.
Dylan (153)
By Sidney Michaels. January 18, 1964.
After the Fall (208)
By Arthur Miller. January 23, 1964.
The Passion of Josef D. (15)
By Paddy Chayefsky. February 11, 1964.
The Deputy (109)
By Rolf Hochhuth; adapted by Jerome Rothenberg. February 26, 1964.

The Trojan Women (600; revival; special Critics citation), Any Wednesday (982), What Makes Sammy Run? (540), Funny Girl (1, 348), The Knack (685).

1964–1965

The Subject Was Roses (832)
By Frank D. Gilroy. May 25, 1964. (Entry appears in 1963-64 *Best Plays* volume but was chosen a Best Play of 1964-65). Pulitzer Prize. Critics Award. Tony Award.

Fiddler on the Roof (3,242)
Musical with book by Joseph Stein; music by Jerry Bock; lyrics by Sheldon Harnick; based on Sholom Aleichem's stories. September 22, 1964. Critics Award (musical). Tony Award.

The Physicists (55)
By Friedrich Duerrenmatt; adapted by James Kirkup. October 13, 1964.

Luv (901)
By Murray Schisgal. November 11, 1964.

Poor Bitos (17)
By Jean Anouilh; translated by Lucienne Hill. November 14, 1964.

Slow Dance on the Killing Ground (88)
By William Hanley. November 30, 1964.

Incident at Vichy (99)
By Arthur Miller. December 3, 1964.

The Toilet (151)
By LeRoi Jones (a.k.a. Amiri Baraka). December 16, 1964.

Tiny Alice (167)
By Edward Albee. December 29, 1964.

The Odd Couple (964)
By Neil Simon. March 10, 1965.

Golden Boy (568), The Owl and the Pussycat (427), Half a Sixpence (511), A View From the Bridge (780; revival).

1965–1966

Generation (299)
By William Goodhart. October 6, 1965.

The Royal Hunt of the Sun (261)
By Peter Shaffer. October 26, 1965.

Hogan's Goat (607)
By William Alfred. November 11, 1965.

Man of La Mancha (2,328)
Musical with book by Dale Wasserman; music by Mitch Leigh; lyrics by Joe Darion; suggested by the life and works of Miguel de Cervantes y Saavedra. November 22, 1965. Critics Award (musical). Tony Award.

Inadmissible Evidence (166)
By John Osborne. November 30, 1965.

Cactus Flower (1,234)
By Abe Burrows; based on a play by Pierre Barillet and Jean-Pierre Gredy. December 8, 1965.

The Persecution and Assassination of Marat as Performed by the Inmates of the Asylum of Charenton Under the Direction of the Marquis de Sade (144)
By Peter Weiss; English version by Geoffrey Skelton; verse adaptation by Adrian Mitchell. December 27, 1965. Critics Award. Tony Award.

Philadelphia, Here I Come! (326)
By Brian Friel. February 16, 1966.

The Lion in Winter (92)
By James Goldman. March 3, 1966.

"It's a Bird It's a Plane It's Superman" (129)
Musical with book by David Newman and Robert Benton; music by Charles Strouse; lyrics by Lee Adams; based on the comic strip "Superman." March 29, 1966.

The Impossible Years (670), Sweet Charity (608), Mame (1, 508), Happy Ending and Day of Absence (504), The Pocket Watch (725), The Mad Show (871).

1966–1967

A Delicate Balance (132)
By Edward Albee. September 22, 1966. Pulitzer Prize.

The Killing of Sister George (205)
By Frank Marcus. October 5, 1966.

The Apple Tree (463)
Musical with book and lyrics by Sheldon Harnick; music by Jerry Bock; additional book material by Jerome Coopersmith; based on stories by Mark Twain, Frank R. Stockton and Jules Feiffer. October 18, 1966.

America Hurrah (634)
By Jean-Claude van Itallie. November 6, 1966.

Cabaret (1,165)
Musical with book by Joe Masteroff; music by John Kander; lyrics by Fred Ebb; based on the play *I Am a Camera* by John van Druten and stories by Christopher Isherwood. November 20, 1966. Critics Award (musical). Tony Award.

The Homecoming (324)
By Harold Pinter. January 5, 1967. Critics Award. Tony Award.

Black Comedy (337)
By Peter Shaffer. February 12, 1967.

You're a Good Man Charlie Brown (1,597)
Musical with book, music and lyrics by Clark Gesner; based on the comic strip "Peanuts" by Charles M. Schulz. March 7, 1967.

Hamp (101)
By John Wilson; based on an episode from a novel by J.L. Hodson. March 9, 1967.

You Know I Can't Hear You When the Water's Running (755)
By Robert Anderson. March 13, 1967.

Don't Drink the Water (598), I Do! I Do! (560); Hallelujah, Baby! (293; 1967-68 Tony Award).

1967–1968

After the Rain (64)
By John Bowen. October 9, 1967.

Scuba Duba (692)
By Bruce Jay Friedman. October 10, 1967.

Rosencrantz and Guildenstern Are Dead (420)
By Tom Stoppard. October 16, 1967. Critics Award. Tony Award.

Staircase (61)
By Charles Dyer. January 10, 1968.

Your Own Thing (933)
Musical with book by Donald Driver; music and lyrics by Hal Hester and Danny Apolinar; suggested by William Shakespeare's *Twelfth Night.* Opened January 13, 1968. Critics Award (musical).

I Never Sang for My Father (124)
By Robert Anderson. January 25, 1968.

A Day in the Death of Joe Egg (154)
By Peter Nichols. February 1, 1968.

The Price (429)
By Arthur Miller. February 7, 1968.

Plaza Suite (1,097)
By Neil Simon. February 14, 1968.

The Boys in the Band (1,000)
By Mart Crowley. April 15, 1968.

George M! (427), Hair (1, 750), Curley McDimple (931).

1968–1969

Lovers (148)
By Brian Friel. July 25, 1968.

The Man in the Glass Booth (268)
By Robert Shaw. September 26, 1968.

The Great White Hope (556)
By Howard Sackler. October 3, 1968. Pulitzer Prize. Critics Award. Tony Award.

Forty Carats (780)
By Jay Allen; adapted from a play by Pierre Barillet and Jean-Pierre Gredy. December 26, 1968.

Hadrian VII (359)
By Peter Luke; based on *Hadrian the Seventh* and other works by Fr. Rolfe (Baron Corvo). January 8, 1969.

Celebration (109)
Musical with book and lyrics by Tom Jones; music by Harvey Schmidt. January 22, 1969.

Adaptation/Next (707)
Two one-act plays: *Adaptation* by Elaine May and *Next* by Terrence McNally. February 10, 1969.

In the Matter of J. Robert Oppenheimer (64)
By Heinar Kipphardt; translated by Ruth Speirs. March 6, 1969.

1776 (1,217)
Musical with book by Peter Stone; music and lyrics by Sherman Edwards. March 16, 1969. Critics Award (musical). Tony Award.

No Place To Be Somebody (250)
By Charles Gordone. May 4, 1969. 1969-70 Pulitzer Prize.

Promises, Promises (1, 281), Play It Again, Sam (453), Dames at Sea (575).

1969–1970

Indians (96)
By Arthur L. Kopit. October 13, 1969.

Butterflies Are Free (1,128)
By Leonard Gershe. October 21, 1969.

Last of the Red Hot Lovers (706)
By Neil Simon. December 28, 1969.

Child's Play (342)
By Robert Marasco. February 17, 1970.

The White House Murder Case (119)
By Jules Feiffer. February 18, 1970.

Applause (896)
Musical with book by Betty Comden and Adolph Green; music by Charles Strouse; lyrics by Lee Adams; based on the film *All About Eve* and the original story by Mary Orr. March 30, 1970. Tony Award.

The Effect of Gamma Rays on Man-in-the-Moon Marigolds (819)
By Paul Zindel. April 7, 1970. 1970-71 Pulitzer Prize. Critics Award (American play).

Company (705)
Musical with book by George Furth; music and lyrics by Stephen Sondheim. April 26, 1970. Critics Award (musical). 1970-71 Tony Award.

What the Butler Saw (224)
By Joe Orton. May 4, 1970.
The Serpent: A Ceremony (3)
Created by The Open Theater Ensemble; words and structure by Jean-Claude van Itallie. May 29, 1970.

Borstal Boy (143; Critics Award; Tony Award), Oh! Calcutta! (704), Purlie (688), The Last Sweet Days of Isaac (485).

1970-1971

Boesman and Lena (205)
By Athol Fugard. June 22, 1970.
Steambath (128)
By Bruce Jay Friedman. June 30, 1970.
Conduct Unbecoming (144)
By Barry England. October 12, 1970.
Sleuth (1,222)
By Anthony Shaffer. November 12, 1970. Tony Award.
Home (110)
By David Storey. November 17, 1970. Critics Award.
The Gingerbread Lady (193)
By Neil Simon. December 13, 1970.
The Trial of the Catonsville Nine (159)
By Daniel Berrigan; New York text prepared by Saul Levitt. February 7, 1971.
The House of Blue Leaves (337)
By John Guare. February 10, 1971. Critics Award (American play).
The Philanthropist (72)
By Christopher Hampton. March 15, 1971.
Follies (521)
Musical with book by James Goldman; music and lyrics by Stephen Sondheim. April 4, 1971. Critics Award (musical).

The Rothschilds (507), The Me Nobody Knows (586), No, No, Nanette (861; revival), Lenny (455), The Dirtiest Show in Town (509), Touch (422), One Flew Over the Cuckoo's Nest (1,025; revival), The Proposition (1,109), Godspell (2,124), Oh! Calcutta! (610; transfer).

1971–1972

Where Has Tommy Flowers Gone? (78)
By Terrence McNally. October 7, 1971.
Ain't Supposed to Die a Natural Death (325)
Musical with book, music and lyrics by Melvin Van Peebles. October 20, 1971.
Sticks and Bones (366)
By David Rabe. November 7, 1971. Critics Award (special citation). Tony Award.

The Prisoner of Second Avenue (780)
By Neil Simon. November 11, 1971.
Old Times (119)
By Harold Pinter. November 16, 1971. Critics Award (special citation).
The Screens (28)
By Jean Genet; translated by Minos Volanakis. November 30, 1971. Critics Award (foreign play).
Vivat! Vivat Regina! (116)
By Robert Bolt. January 20, 1972.
Moonchildren (16)
By Michael Weller. February 21, 1972.
Small Craft Warnings (192)
By Tennessee Williams. April 2, 1972.
That Championship Season (844)
By Jason Miller. Opened May 2, 1972. 1972-73 Pulitzer Prize. Critics Award. 1972-73 Tony Award.

Two Gentlemen of Verona (627; Critics Award for best musical; Tony Award), Jesus Christ Superstar (720), Grease (3, 388), Sugar (505), Don't Bother Me, I Can't Cope (1, 065), The Real Inspector Hound and After Magritte (465).

1972–1973

6 Rms Riv Vu (247)
By Bob Randall. October 17, 1972.
Butley (135)
By Simon Gray. October 31, 1972.
Green Julia (147)
By Paul Ableman. November 16, 1972.
The Creation of the World and Other Business (20)
By Arthur Miller. November 30, 1972.
The River Niger (400)
By Joseph A. Walker. December 5, 1972. 1973-74 Tony Award.
The Sunshine Boys (538)
By Neil Simon. December 20, 1972.
Finishing Touches (164)
By Jean Kerr. February 8, 1973.
A Little Night Music (600)
Musical with book by Hugh Wheeler; music and lyrics by Stephen Sondheim; suggested by Ingmar Bergman's film *Smiles of a Summer Night.* February 25, 1973. Critics Award (musical). Tony Award.
The Changing Room (192)
By David Storey. March 6, 1973. Critics Award.

The Hot l Baltimore (1,166)
By Lanford Wilson. March 22, 1973. Critics Award (American play).

Pippin (1,944), Irene (604; revival), El Grande de Coca-Cola (1, 114), What's a Nice Country Like You Doing in a State Like This? (543).

1973–1974

The Contractor (72)
By David Storey. October 17, 1973. Critics Award.
The Good Doctor (208)
By Neil Simon; adapted from Anton Chekhov stories. November 27, 1973.
Creeps (15)
By David E. Freeman. December 4, 1973.
When You Comin' Back, Red Ryder? (302)
By Mark Medoff. December 6, 1973.
Find Your Way Home (135)
By John Hopkins. Opened January 2, 1974.
Bad Habits (273)
By Terrence McNally. February 4, 1974.
Noel Coward in Two Keys (140)
By Noel Coward; program of two plays: *Come Into the Garden Maud* and *A Song at Twilight.* February 28, 1974.
Short Eyes (156)
By Miguel Piñero. February 28, 1974. Critics Award (American play).
The Sea Horse (128)
By Edward J. Moore (a.k.a. James Irwin). April 15, 1974.
Jumpers (48)
By Tom Stoppard. Opened April 22, 1974.

Candide (740; Critics Award for best musical), Raisin (847; Tony Award), Good Evening (438), The Magic Show (1, 920), Let My People Come (1, 327).

1974–1975

The National Health (53)
By Peter Nichols. October 10, 1974.
The Wager (104)
By Mark Medoff. October 21, 1974.
Equus (1,209)
By Peter Shaffer. October 24, 1974. Critics Award. Tony Award.
The Island (52)
By Athol Fugard, John Kani and Winston Ntshona. November 24, 1974.
All Over Town (233)
By Murray Schisgal. December 29, 1974.

The Ritz (400)
By Terrence McNally. January 20, 1975.

Seascape (65)
By Edward Albee. January 26, 1975. Pulitzer Prize.

Same Time, Next Year (1,453)
By Bernard Slade. March 13, 1975.

A Chorus Line (6,238)
Musical conceived by Michael Bennett; book by James Kirkwood and Nicholas Dante; music by Marvin Hamlisch; lyrics by Edward Kleban. April 15, 1975 for 101 off-Broadway performances, followed July 25, 1975 by the longest Broadway run on record, 6,137 performances. 1975-76 Pulitzer Prize. Critics Award (musical). 1975-76 Tony Award.

The Taking of Miss Janie (42)
By Ed Bullins. May 4, 1975. Critics Award (American play).

The Wiz (1, 672; Tony Award), Absurd Person Singular (592), Sherlock Holmes (471; revival), Shenandoah (1, 050).

1975–1976

Chicago (898)
Musical with book by Fred Ebb and Bob Fosse; music by John Kander; lyrics by Fred Ebb; based on the play by Maurine Dallas Watkins. June 3, 1975.

Jesse and the Bandit Queen (155)
By David Freeman. October 17, 1975.

Travesties (155)
By Tom Stoppard. October 30, 1975. Critics Award. Tony Award.

The Norman Conquests (228)
By Alan Ayckbourn; repertory of three plays: *Table Manners, Living Together* and *Round and Round the Garden.* December 7, 1975.

Pacific Overtures (193)
Musical with book by John Weidman; music and lyrics by Stephen Sondheim; additional material by Hugh Wheeler. January 11, 1976. Critics Award (musical).

Knock Knock (193)
By Jules Feiffer. January 18, 1976.

Streamers (478)
By David Rabe. April 21, 1976. Critics Award (American play).

Serenading Louie (33)
By Lanford Wilson. May 2, 1976.

Rebel Women (40)
By Thomas Babe. May 6, 1976.

The Runner Stumbles (191)
By Milan Stitt. May 18, 1976

Threepenny Opera (307; special Best Play citation as revival), Me and Bessie (453), Bubbling Brown Sugar (766), Boy Meets Boy (463), Tuscaloosa's Calling Me . . . But I'm Not Going (429), Vanities (1,785), For Colored Girls Who Have Considered Suicide/When the Rainbow Is Enuf (862).

1976–1977

California Suite (445)
By Neil Simon. June 10, 1976.
The Last Meeting of the Knights of the White Magnolia (22)
By Preston Jones. September 22, 1976.
The Oldest Living Graduate (20)
By Preston Jones. September 23, 1976.
Comedians (145)
By Trevor Griffiths. November 28, 1976.
Sly Fox (495)
By Larry Gelbart; based on *Volpone* by Ben Jonson. December 14, 1976.
Ashes (167)
By David Rudkin. January 25, 1977.
Otherwise Engaged (309)
By Simon Gray. February 2, 1977. Critics Award.
American Buffalo (135)
By David Mamet. February 16, 1977. Critics Award (American play).
The Shadow Box (315)
By Michael Cristofer. March 31, 1977. Pulitzer Prize. Tony Award.
Annie (2,377)
Musical with book by Thomas Meehan; music by Charles Strouse; lyrics by Martin Charnin; based on Harold Gray's comic strip "Little Orphan Annie." April 21, 1977. Critics Award (musical). Tony Award.

Godspell (527; transfer), Oh! Calcutta! (5,959; Broadway's longest-run revival), Your Arms Too Short to Box With God (429), Mummenschanz (1, 326), I Love My Wife (872), The King and I (696; revival), Gemini (1, 851), Beatlemania (920), The Club (674).

1977–1978

The Gin Game (517)
By D.L. Coburn. October 6, 1977. Pulitzer Prize.
A Life in the Theater (288)
By David Mamet. October 20, 1977.
Chapter Two (857)
By Neil Simon. December 4, 1977.
A Prayer for My Daughter (127)
By Thomas Babe. December 27, 1977.

Deathtrap (1,793)
By Ira Levin. February 26, 1978.
Family Business (438)
By Dick Goldberg. April 12, 1978.
The Best Little Whorehouse in Texas (1,703)
Musical with book by Larry L. King and Peter Masterson; music and lyrics by Carol Hall. April 17, 1978.
The 5th of July (159)
By Lanford Wilson. April 27, 1978.
Da (450)
By Hugh Leonard. May 1, 1978. Critics Award. Tony Award.
Tribute (212)
By Bernard Slade. June 1, 1978.

Ain't Misbehavin' (1, 604; Critics Award for best musical; Tony Award), Dracula (925; revival), On the Twentieth Century (453), Dancin' (1, 774), The Passion of Dracula (714), I'm Getting My Act Together and Taking It on the Road (1, 165).

1978–1979

Wings (128)
By Arthur L. Kopit. June 21, 1978.
On Golden Pond (156)
By Ernest Thompson. September 13, 1978.
First Monday in October (79)
By Jerome Lawrence and Robert E. Lee. October 3, 1978.
Getting Out (259)
By Marsha Norman. October 19, 1978.
Nevis Mountain Dew (61)
By Steve Carter. December 7, 1978.
Gimme Shelter (17)
By Barrie Keeffe. December 10, 1978.
The Elephant Man (989)
By Bernard Pomerance. January 14, 1979. Critics Award. Tony Award.
Sweeney Todd, the Demon Barber of Fleet Street (557)
Musical with book by Hugh Wheeler; music and lyrics by Stephen Sondheim; based on a version of *Sweeney Todd* by Christopher Bond. March 1, 1979. Critics Award (musical). Tony Award.
Bedroom Farce (278)
By Alan Ayckbourn. March 29, 1979.
Whose Life Is It Anyway? (223)
By Brian Clark. April 17, 1979.

Buried Child (152; Pulitzer Prize), Eubie! (439), They're Playing Our Song (1, 082).

1979–1980

Loose Ends (284)
By Michael Weller. June 6, 1979.

Bent (240)
By Martin Sherman. December 2, 1979.

Home (361)
By Samm-Art Williams. December 14, 1979.

Betrayal (170)
By Harold Printer. January 5, 1980. Critics Award (foreign play).

Table Settings (264)
By James Lapine. January 14, 1980.

The Lady From Dubuque (12)
By Edward Albee. January 31, 1980.

Talley's Folly (277)
By Lanford Wilson. February 20, 1980. Pulitzer Prize. Critics Award.

Children of a Lesser God (887)
By Mark Medoff. March 30, 1980. Tony Award.

I Ought To Be in Pictures (324)
By Neil Simon. April 3, 1980.

Nuts (96)
By Tom Topor. April 28, 1980.

Sugar Babies (1, 208; special Best Play citation), Evita (1, 567; Critics Award for best musical; Tony Award), Morning's at Seven (564; revival), Barnum (854), A Day in Hollywood/A Night in the Ukraine (588), Peter Pan (551; revival), Scrambled Feet (831), One Mo' Time (1, 372); special Critics citation to Peter Brook's Le Centre International de Créations Théâtrales.

1980–1981

42nd Street (3,486)
Musical with book by Michael Stewart and Mark Bramble; music and lyrics by Harry Warren and Al Dubin; other lyrics by Johnny Mercer and Mort Dixon. August 25, 1980. Tony Award.

A Life (72)
By Hugh Leonard. November 2, 1980.

Lunch Hour (262)
By Jean Kerr. November 12, 1980.

A Lesson From Aloes (96)
By Athol Fugard. November 17, 1980. Critics Award.

Zooman and the Sign (33)
By Charles Fuller. December 7, 1980.

Crimes of the Heart (570)
By Beth Henley. December 9, 1980 (off off Broadway) and November 4, 1981. Pulitzer Prize. Critics Award (American play).

Amadeus (1,181)
By Peter Shaffer. December 17, 1980. Tony Award.

Translations (48)
By Brian Friel. April 7, 1981.

The Floating Light Bulb (65)
By Woody Allen. April 27, 1981.

Cloud 9 (971)
By Caryl Churchill. May 18, 1981.

Lena Horne; The Lady and Her Music (333; special Critics citation), The Pirates of Penzance (772; revival; special Critics citation), Fifth of July (511; return engagement; a.k.a. The 5th of July), Sophisticated Ladies (767), Woman of the Year (770).

1981–1982

The Dance and the Railroad (181)
By David Henry Hwang. July 16, 1981.

The Life & Adventures of Nicholas Nickleby, Part I (49) and **Part II** (49)
By David Edgar; adapted from Charles Dickens. October 4, 1981. Critics Award. Tony Award.

The Dresser (200)
By Ronald Harwood. November 9, 1981.

Mass Appeal (214)
By Bill C. Davis. November 12, 1981.

A Soldier's Play (468)
By Charles Fuller. November 20, 1981. Pulitzer Prize. Critics Award (American play).

Torch Song Triology (1,339)
By Harvey Fierstein. January 15, 1982. 1982–83 Tony Award.

The Dining Room (583)
By A.R. Gurney. February 24, 1982.

Agnes of God (599)
By John Pielmeier. March 30, 1982.

Master Harold . . . and the Boys (344)
By Athol Fugard. May 4, 1982.

Nine (739)
Musical with book by Arthur L. Kopit; music and lyrics by Maury Yeston; adapted from the Italian by Mario Fratti. May 9, 1982. Tony Award.

Dreamgirls (1, 522), Joseph and the Amazing Technicolor Dreamcoat (747; revival), Pump Boys and Dinettes (573), Sister Mary Ignatius Explains It All for You and The Actor's Nightmare (947).

1982–1983

Cats (4,862*)

Musical based on *Old Possum's Book of Practical Cats* by T.S. Eliot; music by Andrew Lloyd Webber; additional lyrics by Trevor Nunn and Richard Stilgoe. October 7, 1982. Tony Award.

Good (125)

Play with music by C.P. Taylor. October 13, 1982.

Angels Fall (129)

By Lanford Wilson. October 17, 1982.

Plenty (137)

By David Hare. October 21, 1982. Critics Award (foreign play).

Foxfire (213)

Play with songs by Susan Cooper and Hume Cronyn; music by Jonathan Holtzman; based on materials from the *Foxfire* books. November 11, 1982.

Extremities (325)

By William Mastrosimone. December 22, 1982.

Quartermaine's Terms (375)

By Simon Gray. February 24, 1983.

K2 (85)

By Patrick Meyers. March 30, 1983.

'night, Mother (434)

By Marsha Norman. March 31, 1983. Pulitzer Prize.

My One and Only (767)

Musical with book by Peter Stone and Timothy S. Mayer; music by George Gershwin from *Funny Face* and other shows; lyrics by Ira Gershwin. May 1, 1983.

Brighton Beach Memoirs (1, 530; Critics Award), Little Shop of Horrors (2, 209; Critics Award for best musical), Young Playwrights Festival (24; special Critics citation), Forbidden Broadway 1982 (2, 332), On Your Toes (505; revival), True West (762), Greater Tuna (501).

1983–1984

Fool for Love (1,000)

By Sam Shepard. May 26, 1983.

Ohio Impromptu, Catastrophe, What Where (350) and **Enough, Footfalls, Rockaby** (78)

Two programs of one-act plays by Samuel Beckett. June 15, 1983 and February 16, 1984. Special Critics citation (for the body of Beckett's work).

La Cage aux Folles (1,761)

Musical with book by Harvey Fierstein; music and lyrics by Jerry Herman; based on the play by Jean Poiret. August 21, 1983. Tony Award.

Painting Churches (206)
By Tina Howe. November 22, 1983.
And a Nightingale Sang . . . (177)
By C.P. Taylor. November 27, 1983.
Noises Off (553)
By Michael Frayn. December 11, 1983.
The Real Thing (566)
By Tom Stoppard. January 5, 1984. Critics Award. Tony Award.
Glengarry Glen Ross (378)
By David Mamet. March 25, 1984. Pulitzer Prize. Critics Award (American play).
The Miss Firecracker Contest (131)
By Beth Henley. May 1, 1984.
Sunday in the Park With George (604)
Musical with book by James Lapine; music and lyrics by Stephen Sondheim. May 2, 1984. 1984–85 Pulitzer Prize. Critics Award (musical).

The Tap Dance Kid (669), Isn't It Romantic (733; revised version); La Tragédie de Carmen (187; special Best Plays citation).

1984–1985

Split Second (147)
By Dennis McIntyre. June 7, 1984.
Hurlyburly (388)
By David Rabe. June 21, 1984.
Ma Rainey's Black Bottom (275)
By August Wilson. October 11, 1984. Critics Award.
The Foreigner (686)
By Larry Shue. November 1, 1984.
Tracers (186)
Conceived by John DiFusco; written by Vincent Caristi, Richard Chaves, John DiFusco, Eric E. Emerson, Rick Gallavan, Merlin Marston and Harry Stephens with Sheldon Lettich. January 21, 1985.
Pack of Lies (120)
By Hugh Whitemore. February 11, 1985.
As Is (333)
By William M. Hoffman. March 10, 1985.
Biloxi Blues (524)
By Neil Simon. March 28, 1965. Tony Award.
Doubles (277)
By David Wiltse. May 8, 1985.
The Marriage of Bette and Boo (86)
By Christopher Durang. May 16, 1985.

Big River (1,005; Tony Award), Penn & Teller (666).

1985–1986

I'm Not Rappaport (1,071)
By Herb Gardner. June 6, 1985. Tony Award.

Season's Greetings (20)
By Alan Ayckbourn. July 11, 1985.

The Mystery of Edwin Drood (632)
Musical with book, music and lyrics by Rupert Holmes; suggested by the unfinished novel of Charles Dickens. August 4, 1985. Tony Award.

Aunt Dan and Lemon (191)
By Wallace Shawn. October 1, 1985.

Benefactors (217)
By Michael Frayn. December 22, 1985. Critics Award (foreign play).

It's Only a Play (17)
By Terrence McNally. January 12, 1986.

Drinking in America (94)
By Eric Bogosian. January 19, 1986.

Execution of Justice (12)
By Emily Mann. March 13, 1986.

Largo Desolato (40)
By Vaclav Havel; translated by Marie Winn. March 25, 1986.

The Perfect Party (238)
By A.R. Gurney. April 2, 1986.

Goblin Market (89; special Best Play citation), A Lie of the Mind (186; Critics Award), The Search for Signs of Intelligent Life in the Universe (398; special Critics citation), Vampire Lesbians of Sodom and Sleeping Beauty or Coma (2,024), Nunsense (3,513), Beehive (600).*

1986–1987

Born in the R.S.A. (8)
By Barney Simon in collaboration with the cast. October 1, 1986.

Broadway Bound (756)
By Neil Simon. December 4, 1986.

The Widow Claire (150)
By Horton Foote. December 17, 1986.

Wild Honey (28)
By Michael Frayn; adapted from an untitled play by Anton Chekhov. December 18, 1986.

Kvetch (31)
By Steven Berkoff. February 18, 1987.

Les Misérables (2,949*)
Musical with book by Alain Boublil and Claude-Michel Schönberg; music by Claude-Michel Schönberg; lyrics by Herbert Kretzmer; original French text by Alain Boublil and Jean-Marc Natel; additional material by James Fenton; based on the novel by Victor Hugo. March 12, 1987. Critics Award (musical). Tony Award.

Fences (526)
By August Wilson. March 26, 1987. Pulitzer Prize. Critics Award. Tony Award.

Driving Miss Daisy (1,195)
By Alfred Uhry. April 15, 1987. 1987–88 Pulitzer Prize.

Les Liaisons Dangereuses (148)
By Christopher Hampton; from the novel by Choderlos de Laclos. April 30, 1987. Critics Award (foreign play).

Three Postcards (22)
Musical with book by Craig Lucas; music and lyrics by Craig Carnelia. May 14, 1987.

Starlight Express (761).

1987–1988

Steel Magnolias (1,126)
By Robert Harling. June 19, 1987.

The Mahabharata (25)
By Jean-Claude Carrière; adapted into English by Peter Brook. October 13, 1987.

Into the Woods (765)
Musical with book by James Lapine; music and lyrics by Stephen Sondheim. November 5, 1987. Critics Award (musical).

Real Estate (55)
By Louise Page. December 1, 1987.

A Walk in the Woods (136)
By Lee Blessing. February 28, 1988.

Wenceslas Square (55)
By Larry Shue. March 2, 1988.

M. Butterfly (777)
By David Henry Hwang. March 20, 1988. Tony Award.

Joe Turner's Come and Gone (105)
By August Wilson. March 27, 1988. Critics Award.

The Road to Mecca (172)
By Athol Fugard. April 12, 1988. Critics Award (foreign play).

Speed-the-Plow (278)
By David Mamet. May 3, 1988.

The Phantom of the Opera (2, 650; special Best Play citation; Tony Award), Burn This (437), Anything Goes (804; revival), Sarafina! (597), Frankie and Johnny in the Clair de Lune (533), Perfect Crime (2, 908*), Tony 'n' Tina's Wedding (2, 062*), A Shayna Maidel (501), Oil City Symphony (626), Tamara (1, 036).*

1988–1989

Road (62)
By Jim Cartwright. July 28, 1988.

The Cocktail Hour (351)
By A.R. Gurney. October 20, 1988.

Eastern Standard (138)
By Richard Greenberg. October 27, 1988.

Emerald City (17)
By David Williamson. November 30, 1988.

The Heidi Chronicles (702)
By Wendy Wasserstein. December 11, 1988. Pulitzer Prize. Critics Award. Tony Award.

Other People's Money (990)
By Jerry Sterner. February 16, 1989.

Shirley Valentine (324)
By Willy Russell. February 16, 1989.

Gus and Al (25)
By Albert Innaurato. February 27, 1989.

Lend Me a Tenor (481)
By Ken Ludwig. March 2, 1989.

Aristocrats (186)
By Brian Friel. April 25, 1989. Critics Award (foreign play).

Jerome Robbins' Broadway (634; special Best Play citation; Tony Award), Largely New York (35; special Critics citation), Rumors (531), Black and Blue (824), Forbidden Broadway 1988 (534).

1989–1990

The Loman Family Picnic (16)
By Donald Margulies. June 20, 1989.

Love Letters (160)
By A.R. Gurney. Opened August 22, 1989.

Grand Hotel (1,077)
Musical with book by Luther Davis; songs by Robert Wright and George Forrest; additional music and lyrics by Maury Yeston; based on Vicki Baum's play. November 12, 1989.

City of Angels (878)
Musical with book by Larry Gelbart; music by Cy Coleman; lyrics by David Zippel. December 11, 1989. Critics Award (musical). Tony Award.

My Children! My Africa! (28)
By Athol Fugard. December 18, 1989.
Sex, Drugs, Rock & Roll (103)
By Eric Bogosian. February 8, 1990.
Prelude to a Kiss (473)
By Craig Lucas. March 14, 1990.
The Grapes of Wrath (188)
By Frank Galati; adapted from the novel by John Steinbeck. March 22, 1990. Tony Award.
The Piano Lesson (329)
By August Wilson. April 16, 1990. Pulitzer Prize. Critics Award.
Once on This Island (493)
Musical with book and lyrics by Lynn Ahrens; music by Stephen Flaherty; based on Rosa Guy's novel *My Love, My Love.* May 6, 1990.

Privates on Parade (64; Critics Award for best foreign play), A Few Good Men (497), Gypsy (582; revival), Forbidden Broadway 1990 (576), Forever Plaid (1, 794).*

1990–1991

Six Degrees of Separation (640)
By John Guare. June 14, 1990. Critics Award.
Falsettoland (215)
Musical with book by William Finn and James Lapine; music and lyrics by William Finn. June 28, 1990.
The Sum of Us (335)
By David Stevens. October 16, 1990.
Shadowlands (169)
By William Nicholson. November 11, 1990.
The American Plan (37)
By Richard Greenberg. December 16, 1990.
Lost in Yonkers (780)
By Neil Simon. February 21, 1991. Pulitzer Prize. Tony Award.
The Substance of Fire (120)
By Jon Robin Baitz. March 17, 1991.
Miss Saigon (1,310*)
Musical with book by Alain Boublil and Claude-Michel Schönberg; music by Claude-Michel Schönberg; lyrics by Richard Maltby Jr. and Alain Boublil, adapted from the original French lyrics by Alain Boublil; additional material by Richard Maltby Jr. April 11, 1991.
Our Country's Good (48)
By Timberlake Wertenbaker. April 29, 1991. Critics Award (foreign play).
The Good Times Are Killing Me (207)
By Lynda Barry. May 21, 1991.

La Bête (25; special Best Play citation), The Will Rogers Follies (983; Critics Award for best musical; Tony Award), A Room of One's Own (98; special Critics citation), The Secret Garden (706), Song of Singapore (459).

1991–1992

Lips Together, Teeth Apart (406)
By Terrence McNally. June 25, 1991.

Dancing at Lughnasa (421)
By Brian Friel. October 24, 1991. Critics Award. Tony Award.

Mad Forest (54)
By Caryl Churchill. December 4, 1991.

Marvin's Room (214)
By Scott McPherson. December 5, 1991.

Sight Unseen (263)
By Donald Margulies. January 20, 1992.

Crazy for You (952*)
Musical co-conceived by Ken Ludwig and Mike Okrent; book by Ken Ludwig; music by George Gershwin; lyrics by Ira Gershwin; inspired by material (in the musical *Girl Crazy)* by Guy Bolton and John McGowan. Opened February 19, 1992. Tony Award.

Conversations With My Father (402)
By Herb Gardner. March 29, 1992.

Two Trains Running (160)
By August Wilson. April 13, 1992. Critics Award (American play).

Fires in the Mirror (109)
By Anna Deavere Smith. May 12, 1992.

The Extra Man (39)
By Richard Greenberg. May 19, 1992.

Guys and Dolls (888; revival), Jelly's Last Jam (569), Falsettos (487; revival), Beau Jest (1, 069*), Tubes (1, 044*).*

1992–1993

Red Diaper Baby (59) and **Spic-O-Rama** (86)
Red Diaper Baby by Josh Kornbluth. June 12, 1992. *Spic-O-Rama* by John Leguizamo. October 27, 1992. Cited as best monologues.

The Destiny of Me (175)
By Larry Kramer. October 20, 1992.

The Sisters Rosensweig (650*)
By Wendy Wasserstein. October 22, 1992.

Oleanna (513)
By David Mamet. October 25, 1992.

Joined at the Head (41)
By Catherine Butterfield. November 15, 1992.

Jeffrey (365)
By Paul Rudnick. March 6, 1993.

Wings (47)
Musical with book and lyrics by Arthur Perlman; music by Jeffrey Lunden; based on the play by Arthur L. Kopit. March 9, 1993.

Kiss of the Spider Woman (450*)
Musical with book by Terrence McNally; music by John Kander; lyrics by Fred Ebb; based on the novel by Manuel Puig. May 3, 1993. Critics Award (musical). Tony Award.

Angels in America, Part I: Millennium Approaches (260*)
By Tony Kushner. May 4, 1993. Pulitzer Prize. Critics Award. Tony Award.

Later Life (126)
By A.R. Gurney. May 23, 1993.

The Who's Tommy (461; special Best Play citation), Someone Who'll Watch Over Me (232; Critics Award for best foreign play), Blood Brothers (456*).*

1993–1994

A Perfect Ganesh (124)
By Terrence McNally. June 27, 1993.

The Madness of George III (17)
By Alan Bennett. September 28, 1993.

The Kentucky Cycle (34)
By Robert Schenkkan. November 14, 1993. 1991–92 Pulitzer Prize.

Laughter on the 23rd Floor (218*)
By Neil Simon. November 22, 1993.

Angels in America, Part II: Perestroika (117*)
By Tony Kushner. November 23, 1993. Tony Award.

All in the Timing (117*)
By David Ives. February 17, 1994.

Twilight: Los Angeles, 1992 (63*)
By Anna Deavere Smith. March 23, 1994. Special Critics citation.

Three Tall Women (65*)
By Edward Albee. April 5, 1994. Pulitzer Prize. Critics Award.

Passion (26*)
Musical with book by James Lapine; music and lyrics by Stephen Sondheim; based on the film *Passione D'Amore.* May 9, 1994. Tony Award.

SubUrbia (10*)
By Eric Bogosian. May 22, 1994.

American Enterprise (15; special Best Play citation), She Loves Me (269; revival), Four Dogs and a Bone (240*), Carousel (74*; revival).*

THE SEASON ON AND OFF BROADWAY

Women of the 1993-94 New York Theater Year

Above, Marian Seldes, Myra Carter and Jordan Baker in Edward Albee's *Three Tall Women; at right,* Donna Murphy in a scene from the Stephen Sondheim-James Lapine musical *Passion*

BROADWAY AND OFF BROADWAY

By Jeffrey Sweet

NO committee meets before each theater season to decide on a central theme, yet certain seasons seem to organize themselves around an implicit concern. This year, an unusual number of new works addressed the past, as if to ask the question, "How did we get here?"

Robert Schenkkan's Best Play *The Kentucky Cycle* traces the history of a corner of that state though nine acts dealing with three families; labor activist Mother Jones and Civil War terrorist Quantrill mingle with the fictional characters. Tony Kushner's Best Play *Angels in America, Part II: Perestroika,* the continuation of his Best Play *Angels in America, Part I: Millennium Approaches,* focuses on the gay experience in the Reagan-Bush years; again historical figures—lawyer Roy Cohn and Ethel Rosenberg—interact with characters of the playwright's creation. And an historical figure occupies the title and center stage of the largest new British drama, Alan Bennett's Best Play *The Madness of George III,* a revisionist portrait of the monarch against whom the American Revolution was fought.

Sometimes it was possible to trace a thread of history from play to play. Austin Pendleton's *Booth* at York Theater Company described the deterioration of 19th century matinee idol Junius Booth, father of Edwin and John Wilkes. The revival of Robert Sherwood's *Abe Lincoln in Illinois* portrayed the early days of the President whose life would tragically intersect with that of John Wilkes. Suzan-Lori Parks's *The America Play* introduced a black man who, for a fee, would impersonate Abraham Lincoln while tourists recreated the assassination. And my own off-Broadway effort, *American Enterprise,* dealt with 19th century Chicago industrialist George Pullman whose fortunes flourished partially because of the circumstances of Lincoln's final return to Illinois.

Historical backgrounds figure in still other works introduced this year. Frank Gilroy's *Any Given Day* takes place in the Bronx before America's entry into World War II. Arthur Miller's *Broken Glass* is set in 1938 as American Jews watched the events in Europe with increasing concern, while Diane Samuels charts the effect of the same events on a British household in *Kindertransport.* Both Neil Simon's Best Play *Laughter on the 23rd Floor* and Timothy Mason's *The Fiery Furnace* are set during the McCarthy era when Roy Cohn first became notorious. Written by Joan Rivers, Erin Sanders and Lonny Price, the biographical *Sally Marr . . . and Her Es-*

The 1993-94 Season on Broadway

PLAYS (8)

Mixed Emotions
The Twilight of the Golds
THE KENTUCKY CYCLE
Any Given Day
LAUGHTER ON THE 23RD FLOOR
PERESTROIKA
Broken Glass
Sally Marr . . . and Her Escorts

MUSICALS (5)

Cyrano: The Musical
The Red Shoes
Beauty and the Beast
PASSION
The Best Little Whorehouse Goes Public

FOREIGN PLAYS IN ENGLISH (2)

Wonderful Tennessee
The Rise and Fall of Little Voice

REVUE (1)

A Grand Night for Singing

ONE-ACTOR PERFORMANCES (2)

Jackie Mason: Politically Incorrect
TWILIGHT: LOS ANGELES, 1992 (transfer)

REVIVALS (20)

Roundabout:
- *She Loves Me*
- White Liars & Black Comedy
- No Man's Land
- Picnic

Camelot
Lincoln Center:
- In the Summer House
- Abe Lincoln in Illinois
- *Carousel*

N.Y. City Opera:
- The Student Prince
- The Mikado
- Cinderella

Nat'l Actors Theater:
- Timon of Athens
- The Government Inspector
- The Flowering Peach

Joseph and the Amazing Technicolor Dreamcoat
My Fair Lady
Damn Yankees
Medea
An Inspector Calls
Grease

SPECIALTIES (4)

Radio City Music Hall:
- Jesus Was His Name
- Christmas Spectacular
- Easter Show

A Little More Magic

Categorized above are all the shows listed in the Plays Produced on Broadway section of this volume.
Plays listed in CAPITAL LETTERS have been designated Best Plays of 1993-94.
Plays listed in *italics* were still running June 1, 1994.

corts tells how the comedy of Lenny Bruce's mother and that of her famous son reflected and challenged postwar social and sexual values.

A significant number of the season's few new musicals were also set in the past. Stephen Sondheim and James Lapine's Best Play *Passion* takes place in 19th century Italy. *Beauty and the Beast* is set in a story book version of France. *Cyrano: The Musical* is adapted from the classic Rostand romance of the French swordsman and poet. *Annie Warbucks,* the sequel to *Annie,* is a fairy tale of the Depression, including a cameo of President Franklin D. Roosevelt. Roosevelt's wife Eleanor is one of the subjects of *First Lady Suite,* a group musical portrait of the wives of past presidents. And *First Lady* composer-lyricist Michael John LaChiusa jumps back and forth between nine decades in *Hello Again,* his musical adaptation of *La Ronde.*

Audiences had the opportunity to see several Pulitzer Prize-winning plays, although not always in full production. This year's Pulitzer winner was Edward Albee's Best Play *Three Tall Women.* Last year's winner, *Millennium Approaches*, continued, playing in repertory with *Perestroika.* The previous year's winner, *The Kentucky Cycle,* had an all-too-brief run on Broadway. As mentioned before, Robert Sherwood's *Abe Lincoln in Illinois* was revived at Lincoln Center, and William Inge's *Picnic* was presented by the Roundabout. In addition, there were concert stagings of two Pulitzer Prize-winning musicals, *Fiorello!* and *Sunday in the Park With George.* (A Pulitzer near-miss was also revived—*The Flowering Peach* was recommended for the 1955 Pulitzer by the jury, but the final judges chose to give it to Tennessee Williams's *Cat on a Hot Tin Roof.* I doubt many today would quarrel with the choice.)

Several directors had multiple credits this season. Scott Ellis mounted two productions for the Roundabout, *She Loves Me* (which moved to a commercial run) and the aforementioned *Picnic.* Gerald Gutierrez staged two very different revivals, *Abe Lincoln* and *White Liars & Black Comedy.* Michael Langham directed two of the National Actors Theater's offerings, *Timon of Athens* and *The Government Inspector.* John Tillinger began the season with Terrence McNally's Best Play *A Perfect Ganesh* and ended it with Miller's *Broken Glass.* Nicholas Hytner remounted two of his triumphs from the Royal National Theater, *The Madness of George III* and the revival of Rodgers and Hammerstein's *Carousel.* George C. Wolfe directed two Best Plays, the New York productions of *Perestroika* and Anna Deavere Smith's *Twilight: Los Angeles, 1992,* both of which, incidentally, began their lives under other directional hands at the Mark Taper Forum.

The Mark Taper was well represented in New York this season. In addition to *Perestroika* and *Twilight,* the production of *The Kentucky Cycle* that arrived in New York and Sybille Pearson's underestimated *Unfinished Stories* (a 1993 winner of an American Theater Critics Association citation which had an off-off-Broadway run at the New York Theater Workshop) also arrived here via that Los Angeles theater. Other domestic theaters that exported plays to our neighborhood include Chicago's Lookingglass Theater *(The Arabian Nights),* Woodstock, N.Y.'s now-defunct River Arts *(Three Tall Women),* Actors Theater of Louisville *(Escape From Paradise),* New Haven's Long Wharf *(Broken Glass, Come Down Burning* and *Booth),* New

CAROUSEL—Michael Hayden and Sally Murphy in a scene from the best-musical-revival Tony winner, also a triumph of design with scenery and costumes by Bob Crowley and lighting by Paul Pyant

Brunswick's George Street Playhouse *(Greetings!),* Princeton's McCarter Theater *(Those the River Keeps),* East Hampton's John Drew Theater *(The Fiery Furnace),* Seattle's Intiman Theater (the original production of *The Kentucky Cycle*), the Arena Stage and Dallas Theater Center (both of which workshopped *The America Play*), the Pasadena Playhouse *(The Twilight of the Golds),* Burlington, Vt.'s Atlantic Theater Company *(The Lights),* Sag Harbor's Bay Street Theater Festival *(Desdemona—A Play About a Handkerchief),* the New York State Theater Institute (a remounting of *American Enterprise,* a work premiered by Chicago's Organic Theater) and the Pittsburgh Public Theater (*Edith Stein* at Jewish Repertory Theater).

As usual, the season hosted a number of plays and/or productions originating in foreign venues, mostly from the United Kingdom. British imports included three from the Royal National Theater, *An Inspector Calls, The Madness of George III* and *Carousel.* The Royal Court originated *The Treatment* and *Three Birds Alighting on a Field,* and the Soho Theater originated *Kindertransport.* Other visitors from overseas included *Wonderful Tennessee* (from the Abbey Theater), *Playland* (the Market Theater of Johnnesburg), and *Cyrano: The Musical* (which began in Holland).

Several actresses did work that introduced them to the New York audience as major talents. Myra Carter made a tremendous impact as the elderly, dying grande dame of *Three Tall Women,* a young actress named Alanna Ubach negotiated difficult transformations with extraordinary skill in *Kindertransport,* Audra Ann McDonald brightened every moment she was onstage in *Carousel,* and Marin Mazzie impressed (both in clothes and out) as Clara in *Passion.* Other, more established talents surprised by venturing into new territory. Donna Murphy had already won high praise for her comic performance in *Song of Singapore;* not many were prepared for the power she unleashed as Fosca in the decidedly uncomic *Passion.* Few are surprised by Joan Rivers's way with a joke; in *Sally Marr . . . and Her Escorts* she established her credentials as a serious dramatic actress. And then there were the pleasures of watching major actresses fulfill our expectations of excellence—among them, Diana Rigg in *Medea,* Amy Irving in *Broken Glass,* Zoe Caldwell and Frances Sternhagen in *A Perfect Ganesh,* Marian Seldes in *Three Tall Women* and Nancy Marchand in *Black Comedy.*

Several established male stars reaffirmed their reputations with major performances, too. Sam Waterston offered the evolution of Lincoln in Sherwood's play; Brian Bedford managed to embrace both extremes of Shakespeare's Timon; Ron Rifkin struggled movingly with his Jewish identity in *Broken Glass;* Ron Leibman completed the appalling trajectory he began with last season's Tony Award-winning performance as Roy Cohn in *Angels in America;* Stacy Keach was the flawed patriarch of several generations of *The Kentucky Cycle;* Frank Langella raged with a fine 19th century flair as *Booth;* Nigel Hawthorne gave a bravura performance as Alan Bennett's tortured George III, and Christopher Plummer was compellingly seedy in *No Man's Land.* Among the actors showing unexpected facets of their talent were two alumni of Wendy Wasserstein's *The Heidi Chronicles*—Peter Friedman inverting his usual dynamism to play the beleaguered father in *The Loman Family Picnic* and Boyd Gaines revealing a previously unseen flair for musical comedy in *She Loves Me.*

British productions featured some of the season's most notable achievements in design. Bob Crowley was responsible for both the sets and the costumes of *Carousel.* Set designer Peter J. Davidson collaborated with lighting designers Wayne Dowdeswell and Rui Rita in literally bringing down a substantial chunk of the house in *Medea.* Set designer Ian MacNeil provided more spectacular house-rattling in *An Inspector Calls,* augmented by striking lighting by Rick Fisher. British set designer Stewart Laing triumphed in the extraordinary task of redefining Central Park's Delacorte Theater space for *All's Well That Ends Well.*

All of these opportunities began with scripts written by dramatists, which returns us to the prime mission of this annual—to honor new work with citations for Best Plays. To quote Otis L. Guernsey Jr. in past volumes, "The choice is made without any regard whatsoever to the play's type—musical, comedy or drama—or origin on or off Broadway, or popularity at the box office or lack of same.

"We don't take scripts of bygone eras into consideration for Best Play citation in this one, whatever their technical status as American or New York 'premieres' which didn't have a previous production of record. We draw the line between adaptations and revivals, the former eligible for Best Play selection but the latter not, on a case-by-case basis. If a script influences the character of a season, or by some function of consensus wins the Critics, Pulitzer or Tony Awards, we take into account its future historical as well as present esthetic importance. This is the only special consideration we give, and we don't always tilt in its direction, as the record shows."

Our choices for the Best Plays of 1993–94 are listed in the final season-by-season grouping of the 750 Best Plays in the previous section of this volume, in the order in which they opened on or off Broadway, with an asterisk * applied to the performance numbers of those which were still running on June 1, 1994.

BROKEN GLASS—David Dukes and Ron Rifkin in Arthur Miller's play

New Plays

Increasingly, the contemporary American stage is home to the theater of anecdote—the small-scale stories of a handful of characters often told in fewer than 90 minutes. Two Broadway offerings bucked this trend by painting large canvases: Robert Schenkkan's *The Kentucky Cycle* and Tony Kushner's *Angels in America,* the second part of which, *Perestroika,* completed the journey begun last season by the celebrated *Millennium Approaches.*

At the end of *Millennium Approaches,* an angel crashes through the ceiling of AIDS sufferer Prior Walter, telling him that "the great work" awaits and that he, Prior, is to be its prophet. In *Perestroika,* it turns out that there really *is* no great work for Prior to do. Kushner's portrait of Heaven features a group of dispirited angels who can think of nothing better than to counsel the acceptance of stasis. And yes, I am a little disappointed. After waiting months to find out what Prior's message to the world would be, the announcement of cosmic ineffectualness is a bit of a letdown.

But that is the extent of my disappointment in *Perestroika.* The rest of the play

The 1993-94 Season Off Broadway

PLAYS (28)

Sheila's Day
Manhattan Theater Club:
  A PERFECT GANESH
  Four Dogs and a Bone
  Day Standing on
    Its Head
  The Arabian Nights
A Better Life
Asylum
Young Playwrights Festival
Circle Repertory:
  The Fiery Furnace
  Desdemona—A Play About
    a Handkerchief
  A Body of Water
Playwrights Horizons:
  Sophistry
  An Imaginary Life
  Moe's Lucky Seven
All That Glitters
Trophies
Papp Public Theater:
  The Swan
  East Texas Hot Links
  The America Play
Lincoln Center:
  The Lights
  SUBURBIA
A Quarrel of Sparrows
Greetings!
Those the River Keeps
ALL IN THE TIMING
AMERICAN ENTERPRISE
THREE TALL WOMEN
Hide Your Love Away

SPECIALTIES (4)

In Persons
Ricky Jay & His 52
  Assistants
Stomp
Airport Music

MUSICALS (11)

Prime Time Prophet
Whoop-Dee-Doo!
Annie Warbucks
Johnny Pye and
  the Foolkiller
First Lady Suite
Hello Again
Smiling Through
Avenue X
Fallen Angel
Bring in the Morning
Hysterical Blindness

REVUE (1)

Forbidden Broadway 1994

ONE-ACTOR
PERFORMANCES (13)

Piaf . . . Remembered
Blown Sideways Through
  Life
Family Secrets
Fire in the Rain
Out Is In
Papp Public Theater:
  Irene's Worth's
    Portrait of Edith
    Wharton
  TWILIGHT: LOS ANGELES,
    1992
  All for You
  Big Momma 'N'Em
Pounding Nails in the
  Floor With My Forehead
Escape From Paradise
Mort Sahl's America
Moonshot and Cosmos

REVIVALS (5)

Shakespeare Marathon:
  Measure for Measure
  All's Well That Ends Well
  Richard II
The Winter's Tale
The Loman Family Picnic

FOREIGN PLAYS
IN ENGLISH (6)

Playland
Brooklyn Academy:
  THE MADNESS OF
    GEORGE III
  Sacrifice of Mmbatho
The Treatment
Three Birds Alighting
  on a Field
Kindertransport

Categorized above are all the shows listed in the Plays Produced Off Broadway section of this volume.
Plays listed in CAPITAL LETTERS have been designated Best Plays of 1993–94.
Plays listed in *italics* were still running June 1, 1994.

continues the chronicle of the group of characters introduced in the first part as they cope with AIDS and the Reagan-Bush years. There are some significant shifts of emphasis in *Perestroika.* To a large degree, this part concerns the contrast between the ways in which Prior Walter and Roy Cohn face the disease they have in common. Prior gains in moral stature; Cohn continues his descent into the heart of evil. The second half also promotes supporting characters from the first half to larger roles, particularly Hannah Pitt, a Morman woman who transcends religious dogma to form an odd bond with drag queen Prior, and Belize, the gay black hospital attendant who, despite his loathing for patient Cohn, is the agent for a final gesture of compassion toward him.

A nit-picker could challenge individual moments and choices in *Perestroika,* but there is little doubt that Kushner's two-part play is a major achievement. It manages to be simultaneosly a rigorous exploration of the contradictory impulses in the national character and a gripping personal drama. An added pleasure is the large number of flat-out funny passages, proving once more that the richest humor springs out of the most serious concerns. George C. Wolfe again brought the best out of his cast. Because of the increased prominence of their roles in this episode, Kathleen Chalfant as Hannah and Jeffrey Wright as Belize made particuarly strong impressions. This is not to slight the continued excellence of the work of Stephen Spinella as Prior, Joe Mantello as his lost love Louis, and Ron Leibman as Cohn in completing the voyages they began so impressively last season. Kushner has been quoted as saying he may return to these characters in a few years to see how intervening events have registered on their lives (much as John Updike returned to Harry "Rabbit" Angstrom once a decade as a way of reading the national temperature). I know I'm not alone in looking forward to meeting them again.

Robert Schenkkan won what I believe to be a richly-deserved 1992 Pulitzer Prize for *The Kentucky Cycle.* By following the fortunes of three intertwined families over more than 200 years, Schenkkan reflects the tortured history of rural Kentucky. As the years pass, the murders, betrayals and corruption that hold center stage in a series of vividly told episodes are echoed in the larger destruction of the land on which the drama is being enacted. There is a bump or two along the way; the third play in the cycle, *The Homecoming,* jams together a dizzying series of melodramatic twists and reversals. But this is a minor quibble, in view of what Schenkkan achieves here. At the same time he pursues his serious purpose of exploring dark corners of American history, he also serves up something for which our theater hungers—virtuoso storytelling. Even as we in the audience watch tragedy being played out in generation after generation and feel the pain and the waste, we share the thrill of watching a river of narrative flow through more than six hours of theater.

Schenkkan was well-served by the production of director Warner Shook and a large ensemble of actors led by Stacy Keach, each of whom undertook a variety of roles. One of the considerable rewards of *The Kentucky Cycle* was to compare and contrast the various parts an actor undertook over the course of the play, each actor's journey being a theatrical drama in itself. Paradoxically, though Schenkkan's play was largely a chronicle of villainy, the play itself registers as a heroic undertaking.

The Kentucky Cycle didn't flourish commercially in New York, but that is more a criticism of New York than the play. Few seasons host a new work so large, ambitious and accomplished. The fact that the 1993-94 season hosted *two* such works—Schenkkan's and Kushner's—marks it as a particularly distinctive one.

Shakespeare often dealt with how the personal qualities and conditions of kings shape history. Alan Bennett explores this theme in *The Madness of George III,* a look at the monarch who sat on England's throne during the American Revolution. In Bennett's play, George is an amiable, well-liked and well-intentioned man who has the unfortunate luck of being laid low by a disease that appears to his contemporaries to be an attack of madness. Suddenly it becomes apparent that there are people more powerful than the king in England—the king's doctors, whose dubious treatments inflict pain and humiliation on their monarch. Part of Bennett's subject is the contrast between a leader's public and private faces. After viewing George sympathetically for much of the evening, and mentally booing those who plot his illness as an excuse to topple him, it comes as a shock to learn that the "villains" seek power partially to end the slave trade. Bennett's writing has always been characterized by brilliantly articulate characters, and in Nigel Hawthorne he had an actor who could both do justice to the language and uninhibitedly play the king's agonies.

Suzan-Lori Parks's *The America Play* introduces a black man who divides his time between digging the Hole of History and impersonating Abraham Lincoln in a theme park where, for a small fee, patrons may re-enact John Wilkes Booth's shooting of the President. In his review for the New York *Times,* David Richards wrote that the play is about confronting the lack of representation of the black experience in accounts of American history. Richards wrote persuasively, but I have to report that none of this occurred to either me or my guest.

Two other black writers made significant contributions to this season. Kia Corthron's *Come Down Burning* is a look at the politics of abortion against the background of poor black rural life. If the plotting relies a little too much on coincidence (the central character has to deal with the unwanted pregnancies of two of her circle within a matter of days), the integrity and vitality of the writing are unmistakable and make me eager to see more of her work. Eugene Lee's *East Texas Hot Links* deals with issues of racism and betrayal in a black cafe in 1955 Texas. Though the shift from a leisurely August Wilson-style interplay of voices to bloody violence reminiscent of Sam Peckinpah seems dictated less by the play's internal logic than by the author's desire to end with a bang, Lee definitely has a gift for language, atmosphere and characterization that marks him, too, as someone to watch.

Elizabeth Egloff's fantasy, *The Swan,* concerns a Nebraska woman who is startled when a swan she attempts to nurse back to health is transformed into a naked man who behaves, well, swanishly. Frances McDormand and Peter Stormare performed gracefully in the leads, but this fable struck me as attenuated whimsy. It has been well received in a series of regional productions, so I will cheerfully concede that this may be a case of my not being the right audience for this piece.

Othello has inspired a number of ancillary works—Verdi's opera, a ballet called *The Moor's Pavanne,* a modern movie retelling set against the British jazz world called *All Night Long* (featuring Patrick McGoohan as an Iago-like drummer), and a rock musical called *Catch My Soul* (made into a little-seen movie directed by the same Patrick McGoohan). Add to this list Paula Vogel's *Desdemona—A Play About a Handkerchief,* which was based on the conceit that, though Othello was wrong in supposing his wife to be unfaithful to him with Cassio, she was getting it on with almost everyone else in pants. I suppose this was intended to be a meditation on the sexual archetypes created by the culture of a male-dominated society and how they blind one to individual character, but I appreciated it most for the opportunity it gave three extraordinary actresses—Cherry Jones as Bianca, Fran Brill as Emilia and J. Smith-Cameron as Desdemona—to romp under Gloria Muzio's playful direction.

The entire cast romped in *The Arabian Nights,* a story theater presentation adapted and directed by Mary Zimmerman. Here again is the story of Scheherazade. Married to a king who takes his vengeance on womanhood by marrying, bedding and killing a bride on a daily basis, she nightly gets a stay of execution by telling him tales and stopping at a point when his desire to know what happens next outweighs his homicidal habit. The tales—by turn haunting, silly, bawdy and magical—become a kind of moral education for her murderous spouse. By the evening's end, he has been transformed into a loving and compassionate husband and ruler, thereby demonstrating, in Bruno Bettelheim's phrase, "the uses of enchantment." Scheherazade and her husband are the only familiar figures in this adaptation, as Zimmerman chose to dramatize the less familiar tales in the canon—no Aladdin or Ali Baba here. And out they pour, story after story. Toward the end of the evening, Zimmerman has her cast split up into different corners, each group enacting a different tale. At this point, it is impossible to follow any single thread, but the image of several tales in counterpoint makes for a dazzling display of narrative fireworks. The cast, made up of actors from Chicago (where this piece originated) came to feel like friends, with Denis O'Hare particularly impressing with his versatility.

All in the Timing is the blanket title of David Ives's evening of six short plays, all of them displaying a beguiling sense of theatrical playfulness. In *Sure Thing,* a newly-met couple constantly backtrack to revise their conversation in a hilarious patchwork of verbal options, each new take punctuated by a bell. *Words, Words, Words* concerns three monkeys named Swift, Kafka and Milton let loose in a room with typewriters. In *The Universal Language,* a teacher attempts to introduce a winsome student to a language the logic of which is constantly shifting. *Philip Glass Buys a Loaf of Bread* is a spoof on Glass and the staging affectations of his collaborator Robert Wilson. *Variations on the Death of Trotsky* resembles a vaudeville sketch, with the exiled Soviet leader playing the entire piece with an axe stuck in his head. And my favorite, *The Philadelphia,* equates states of mind with cities, the title one not being among the more desirable. Robert Stanton, who appeared in five of the six pieces, made a marvelous comic Everyman (or, playing, Swift, Everymonkey), particularly in his partnerships with Nancy Opel and Wendy Lawless. Their timing, under the direction of Jason McConnell Buzas, made *All in the Timing* whiz along with a sublime breathlessness.

Mixed Emotions by Richard Baer reunited Katherine Helmond and Harold Gould (who starred opposite each other in the original production of John Guare's *The House of Blue Leaves*), but the script gave them little to do but enact a sad dance of sitcom seduction. More ambitious but no more successful, *Day Standing on its Head* offers a confused portrait of a middle-aged Japanese-American professor haunted by what he did and did not do in the movement in the 1960s. The author, Philip Kan Gotanda, wrote a little gem of a play called *The Wash* some seasons back, so there is reason to hope for better work from him in the future. In *An Imaginary Life,* Peter Parnell returns again to his frequent theme of the writer's struggle, here setting up a game with the audience as to which scenes are real and which are the leading character's fictionalized extrapolations from his life. Individual scenes score, but the trick of constantly undercutting the audience's expectations is repeated to the point where it frustrates rather than delights.

Jonathan Marc Sherman, who made such an impressive debut with the one-act *Women and Wallace* while still a teenager, made his full-length debut with *Sophistry,* introducing a group of students coping with sexual politics among themselves and watching while one of their gay professors wrestles with a charge of sexual harassment. Moment by moment, the writing is lively, the interplay between the students (one of whom was played by Sherman himself) limned with vitality and wit, but the play is structurally confused. Sherman doesn't seem to know what story he wants to tell. The first act focuses on the impact the charge against the professor (well acted by Austin Pendleton) has on his students. In the second act, Sherman frustrates the expectation that the resolution of the professor's story will get full dramatic treatment. Instead, his story is relegated to a few sketchy scenes; there is little sense of his fate having much to do with the actions of his former students.

Eric Bogosian makes a more successful pass at portraying contemporary American youth with his Best Play *SubUrbia.* The script bears more than a passing resemblance to David Rabe's Best Play *Hurlyburly.* Both view a world in which casual drugs and sex distract from the terror of empty futures, and both are framed by the conflict between two friends' moral views. Bogosian's Jeff, like Rabe's Eddie, has moral impulses that are struggling to find expression in an atmosphere in which to profess sincere belief in any kind of value system is to invite mockery. And Bogosian's Tim, like Rabe's Mickey, takes revenge on the world by using his almost ferocious intelligence in the pursuit of what he knows to be rotten goals.

The friend with whom I saw the play loathed it, particularly the characters' habit of constantly striking in-your-face attitudes. But I think part of Bogosian's point is that "attitude" is what is put on in the absence of a thought-through system of belief. This pursuit of attitude at the expense of substance also pollutes the popular culture. None of the would-be art that three of the characters make—a profanity-laden collection of cliches of an aspiring feminist performance artist, the empty posing of a

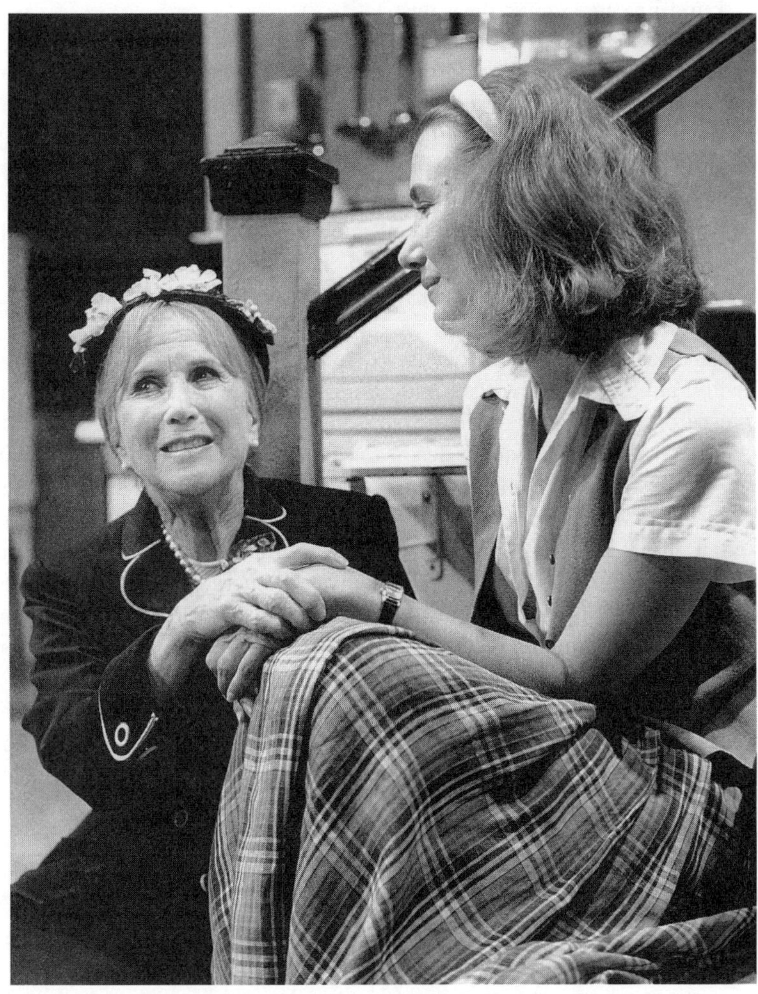

THE FIERY FURNACE—Julie Harris and Ashley Gardner in a scene from the play by Timothy Mason

bubble-headed rock singer and the random videotapings of a sweetly stupid pothead—does much but exhibit the characters' confusion. Robert Falls did a strong job shaping the action, though it was wearing to have yet another play begin with eardrum-splitting rock music to bully attention. Beginning with this sort of cacophony blasting through opening moments of darkness has become one of the most hackneyed devices of the contemporary theater.

Speaking of *Hurlyburly,* its author David Rabe returned to the Promenade Theater (where that play premiered ten years ago) with *Those the River Keeps.* Set in Los Angeles, *River* focuses on Phil, a struggling actor, in a tense relationship with his young wife. Before taking up acting, Phil was a hood who occasionally did severe and sometimes fatal damage to those who crossed his bosses. One of his partners from the old days, Sal, shows up and attempts to recruit him to join in executing a local contract. When Phil turns him down, Sal rails against Phil for turning against his own nature. Sal is determined to spring Phil from what he sees as a self-imposed exile from the authentic life, even if springing him means murdering Phil's wife Susie. When Phil sees Sal is serious about the proposed murder, he turns violently against his old friend, damn near killing him. This attack registers as an indication that, as bitter and screwed up as Phil is, at this point he still has sufficient moral equipment to fight for what he loves.

For me, the potential power of *River* is undercut by the knowledge that in *Hurlyburly* an older Phil appears as a divorced, borderline psychotic who writes an incoherent final note before committing suicide by driving his car off a cliff. Knowing Phil's future shortcircuits Rabe's evident desire for us to view him at the end of *River* as someone who has gained wisdom from his experience. Apart from that, the script has other problems—chief among them that it is an hour longer than it needs to be to get its point across. This is a shame. Were the rambling and repetition and digressions trimmed, I think a very interesting play would emerge. There might have been more chance of that happening had David Rabe not also directed the off-Broadway production. There are few playwright-directors who can bring themselves to make all the cuts necessary.

David Rabe was not the only author of a Best Play from the past to run into difficulties this season. Being authors of proven accomplishment, however, even their stumblings couldn't help being of considerable interest. Timberlake Wertenbaker, a veteran of the Royal Court Theater and author of the Best Play *Our Country's Good,* weighed in with her take on the 1980s with *Three Birds Alighting on a Field,* a satiric view of the London art world. Though individual passages aspire to Shavian wit, overall the play suffers from being facile. The art critics, dealers, speculators and artists who populate the play are drawn as such boobs and poseurs that it is hard to give them much credibility or invest much concern in their dilemmas. In a 1992 Best Play set against the art scene, *Sight Unseen,* Donald Margulies made sure that we in the audience never saw any of his painter's work so that our perception of his abilities wouldn't distract us from the issues being raised. In production, Wertenbaker and her director Max Stafford-Clark made the mistake of having the artist representing incorruptible talent explicate a painting that was in full view of the audience. That the painting looked unpersuasive couldn't help undermining the regard we held for the character. The best reason for the evening was the quietly impressive performance of Harriet Walter as a British woman who doesn't know much about art but comes to know what she likes.

Another Royal Court and Best Plays veteran, Jim Cartwright, made his Broadway debut with *The Rise and Fall of Little Voice,* a play which stumbled here after achieving a substantial success in London. This echoes the history of his Best Play, *Road,* which was a triumph in England and was given short shrift in New York. *Little Voice* is not in the same class as *Road,* though it is a further exploration of one of *Road*'s themes: the degree to which popular culture can present an escape for those who find the reality of contemporary working class life too painful. Little Voice is an English girl who rarely leaves her house in a depressed town in northern England. In fact, she barely leaves her room, which is not surprising given the brassy, belligerent, alcoholic and promiscuous mother with whom she shares the house. Hiding in her room, the girl spends hours listening to her precious records of the great female singers. One day, a seedy agent who is her mother's current bedmate overhears her singing in the voices of Judy Garland, Billy Holliday, Shirley Bassey and others. Apparently she has so absorbed these women's spirits that she can summon them up, given the proper circumstances. Smelling potential income, the agent manipulates the girl into performing at a club where she becomes something of a local sensation, though the performances threaten to kill her.

Hynden Walch made an effective Little Voice, barely audible as the terrified girl, dynamic as the spirits of her beloved entertainers took her over. Rondi Reed laid it on a bit thick as the grotesque mother, and John Christopher Jones turned in another of his perfectly calibrated cameos as a bizarre MC named Mr. Boo. The New York press was fairly unanimous in its lack of enthusiasm for the play; but, despite its heavy-handedness, it stirred most of the audience around me to cheers.

Playland, written by multiple-Best-Play author Athol Fugard, represents his attempt to dramatize the choices facing blacks and whites in today's changing South Africa. A white ex-soldier and a black night watchman—both with blood on their hands from racial wars of the past—meet in the seedy amusement park where the watchman works. During the course of the play, they clash, confess and come to terms in a gesture of new hope. While it is heartening that Fugard sees this hope in South Africa, unfortunately the play itself came across as a labored and predictable construction, despite the earnest work by Kevin Spacey and Frankie R. Faison as the pair.

With this season's *Wonderful Tennessee,* Brian Friel, author of the extraordinary Best Play *Dancing at Lughnasa,* seemed to lose his sense of how to keep the audience engaged. A group of friends spend the night on a rural Irish dock waiting for a boat to take them to visit an island holding out the promise of spiritual rejuvenation. Since there's no serious chance that the boat will show, we know we're in for an evening of reminiscence, rumination and revelation, offset by the odd song. Much of the language is lovely, but nothing seems to be riding on anything happening on the stage. Actions without consequence tend not to make compelling drama, even when offered up by a cast of world class actors including the great Donal McCann and John P. Kavanagh.

Frank Gilroy, best known for the Best Play *The Subject Was Roses,* employs younger versions of the characters in that play as supporting figures in his *Any Given Day,* a group portrait of a Bronx family in the early 1940s and how its dynamics doom a marriage. Sada Thompson starred as Mrs. Benti, the family's stern matriarch, but the most interesting writing was for the character of good-natured Gus Brower, who, in the course of the action, watches his future crumble. Andrew Robinson was wrenchingly effective in this role, and the cast was uniformly strong. An "old fashioned" family drama, this play deserved a longer run than it received.

There were several other examinations of families under strain. John J. Wooten's *Trophies,* which found favor with a number of other critics, was a familiar tale about a son returning home to do battle with a father over a retarded brother. *Greetings!,* too, involved a son on a visit home dealing with a retarded brother and coping with parents, but in Tom Dudzick's sweetly imaginative tale the brother suddenly is enlisted by a heavenly spirit to serve as a mouthpiece for a message of faith. While not a ground-breaking work, this is the sort of piece which should make audiences happy as an alternative to *A Christmas Carol* in theaters around the country.

Still more family conflict was dramatized in *The Twilight of the Golds,* which represented actor Jonathan Tolins's playwriting debut. The development of a test which can determine before birth whether the baby will be genetically inclined to homosexuality brings the Gold family to crisis. David, the gay son of the family, poses the question of whether his pregnant sister and her husband would abort the baby if the test were to indicate the baby would turn out "like" him. The fact that David's job is involved with opera production gives him the excuse to draw parallels between this contemporary domestic story and the battles in Wagner's Ring Cycle. The parallels come off as strained, and much of the script is marred by mechanical jokes, but Tolins deserved more credit than he got for writing moving passages for Phyllis, the Gold matriarch, beautifully played by Judith Scarpone. Like *Little Voice,* this is a play which stirred the audience around me despite the general critical drubbing it received.

I thought Marlane Meyer's *Moe's Lucky Seven* also deserved better than it got. A play about a group of colorful characters in a bar, Meyer signals her intention that this be viewed as a modern retelling of the story of the Garden of Eden. While I was unable to follow her allegorical connection, and the presence of two characters commenting on the action from the side seemed a coy device, the script crackled with deft turns of phrase and wry aphorisms. Deirdre O'Connell and Barry Sherman tackled their roles as stand-ins for Eve and the Snake with marvelous gusto.

Arthur Miller (who himself once took a crack at the Garden of Eden story with the Best Play *The Creation of the World and Other Business)* celebrated the 50th anniversary of his first production on Broadway (*The Man Who Had All the Luck* in 1944) with a new one, *Broken Glass,* a play set 56 years ago in the Brooklyn in which he grew up. The tale is framed as a medical detective story. Dr. Harry Hyman, a handsome general practitioner, is drawn into trying to find the source of the paralysis that has attacked the legs of Sylvia Gellburg, wife of Phillip Gellburg, the token Jew employed by a bank. Early in the play, Hyman expresses his opinion that people don't get sick one by one but in relationship with their intimates. And indeed, as the play progresses, it becomes apparent that Sylvia's paralysis is related to a connection she's made between Phillip's self-hatred as a Jew and the news stories of the persecution of the Jews in Germany.

In this effort, Miller returns to the theme that has been central to much of his work—the relationship of the family to the larger world. If people get sick in relationship with their intimates, families get sick within the context of the societies in which they live. Here Miller is trying to relate Sylvia Gellburg's paralysis to the moral paralysis of a world which watched as the Holocaust was beginning and could not rouse itself to make an effective response.

I wish I could say that I believe that Miller has fulfilled the potential of his ambitious subject. The chief problem is that after years of seeing plays, movies and TV programs (many of them written by dramatists undoubtedly influenced by Miller), the audience is way ahead of the playwright. Consequently, the revelations of the roots of Sylvia's paralysis lack the desired dramatic punch. The play also suffers from being constructed mostly as a series of scenes between two people, much of it in the form of the doctor questioning the Gellburgs separately. This lack of variety becomes a little deadening. Given that the subtext of the play is a triangle between the Gellburgs and the doctor, the absence of a substantial three-way scene between them seems a serious dramatic oversight.

As is usual with productions guided by director John Tillinger, the play was beautifully cast. Ron Rifkin has played men in conflict with their Jewishness before, most memorably in Jon Robin Baitz's Best Play *The Substance of Fire,* and he gave Gellburg a haunting mixture of arrogance and terror. Amy Irving matched him with the subtlety of her work as Sylvia. David Dukes did as well as possible with Hyman, a character whose primary functions are to cue exposition and moralize. More vivid, in secondary roles, were Lauren Klein, Frances Conroy and George N. Martin.

Diane Samuels's *Kindertransport* also traces the effect of Hitler's Germany on personal lives, though here the subject is the after-effect of history. For the first act, we follow the stories of both Eva, one of nearly 10,000 German-Jewish children sent for their protection to England in 1938, and Evelyn, an edgy middle-aged English woman in the 1980s in constant conflict with her daughter Faith. As the play proceeds, we realize that Evelyn is the grown Eva and that Samuels is concerned with the details of the growing-up.

We watch as ten-year-old Eva finds a home with a genial English woman named Lil, how she gradually loses her accent, and how, as an 18-year-old, she rejects the mother who has miraculously survived the Holocaust, preferring to continue living with Lil and to maintain her adopted identity as an Englishwoman. And we see the consequences of this denial in Evelyn's relationship with Faith, who is only just learning her mother's true story and consequently something of the cornerstone of her own identity.

Samuels has not written quite as good a play as her powerful premise deserves. The script feels as if it were constructed from an outline, and the device of having one male actor embody the various faces of evil and stupidity in the world comes across as simplistic. Nevertheless, *Kindertransport* has considerable emotional impact. Its production was the occasion of one of the season's most remarkable performances—that of Alanna Ubach as Eva. Over the course of the evening, this young American actress was utterly convincing in her evolution from a ten-year-old German-Jewish girl to an 18-year-old English woman, her accent and body language subtly mutating in a dazzling display of the actor's art.

Jenna Zark, too, engages issues of Jewish identity in her *A Body of Water,* a pair of related one-acts. In the first, a non-believing young woman finds that bathing in the mikvah (which some Orthodox women do seven days after their periods) offers her the respite she needs to cope with a difficult life with a jealous husband. In the second, a rabbi's wife compares her unwanted childlessness to the situation of a woman in her husband's congregation considering a forbidden abortion. The evening acts as a kind of theatrical meditation on the ways in which being Jewish can offer women comfort in one situation and afflict them in another. Jodi Thelan was particularly strong as the embittered rabbi's wife. This production represented Zark's New York debut. Though there were uneven patches in the writing, with this bill she establishes a dramatic voice that is unlikely to be confused with anyone else's.

Timothy Mason's *The Fiery Furnace* shifted tone at its intermission. The first act consisted of three well-observed, understated scenes focussing on the women of an upstate Wisconsin family in the 1950's. In the second act, this was replaced with melodrama, complete with a hissable villain and the threat of gunplay. It was as if Mason didn't know how to bring his story to a close without bringing in an element of physical jeopardy. Even though I was disappointed by the shift in the second act, Mason and the cast (under the precise and assured direction of Norman Rene) had made me care so much about the characters that I watched with heart in mouth. As one would expect, Julie Harris gave a subtly modulated performance as the beleaguered matriarch, and the entire cast was first rate, with special honors due to Susan Batten, who was heartbreaking in her transformation from a spirited young woman to a traumatized housewife.

Senator Joseph McCarthy's spirit haunted the background of *The Fiery Furnace.* The red-baiting terror he represented is also a presence in the Best Play *Laughter on the 23rd Floor,* Neil Simon's fictionalized portrait of his days working with the likes of Mel Brooks, Lucille Kallen and Larry Gelbart writing comedy sketches for Sid Caesar in the early days of television. Not that Simon chooses to make much of the politics, except to suggest that the explosion of mostly Jewish humor might be partially fueled by reaction to the paranoia of the times.

A musical version of the film *My Favorite Year* attempted a similar portrait of Caesar and his entourage last season. One of the reasons that show failed was the lack of a credible alter ego for Caesar. *Laughter* is more successful. This is partially due to Simon's skill as a writer in drawing the role of Max Prince, and, in production, to the casting in it of Nathan Lane, one of the most exuberant comic actors in New York. It doesn't hurt that Simon surrounds Prince with entertaining companions and that these were played by such veteran character actors as Lewis J. Stadlen, John Slattery, Ron Orbach, Randy Graff and Mark Linn-Baker. (Linn-Baker, incidentally, has made something of a specialty of this milieu, having played the juvenile lead in the original film of *My Favorite Year*, a part reportedly based on Brooks.) I

KINDERTRANSPORT—Alanna Ubach (in one of the season's best performances in a primary role), Jane Kaczmarek and Dana Ivey in Diane Samuels's play

wish that Simon had let a little more plot in the door; still, an evening offering this much opportunity to laugh is its own excuse.

Sally Marr . . . and Her Escorts invokes two other important figures in American Jewish comedy—Sally Marr and her ground-breaking son, Lenny Bruce. Co-authored by Joan Rivers, Erin Sanders and director Lonny Price, the device of having Sally deliver the overwhelming majority of the lines to mostly unspeaking actors representing a variety of supporting roles is labored. Also, if part of the point of the evening is to focus on Sally's accomplishments and influence rather than those of her famous son's, it seems odd to skimp on the story of how she spent the decades after Bruce's death. But the evening was more than justified as a display of Joan Rivers's considerable and underestimated gifts as an actress. The well-lacquered public persona of stand-up comedy gave way to moments of great sensitivity. By the end of the evening, I hungered to see her sink her teeth into *Mother Courage*.

Frank Langella had a triumph playing the troubled parent of another famous performer in Austin Pendleton's play *Booth*. In both plays, parents encourage the early efforts of children who ultimately eclipse them. Pendleton's play is constructed in a manner reminiscent of 19th century melodrama, with major developments telescoped into a handful of key scenes; Langella played the matinee idol at the end of his rope with great panache.

In John Patrick Shanley's *Four Dogs and a Bone*, a film is in the process of being shot on location in New York, and two of the actresses are doing all they can to try to persuade the idealistic writer (is there any other kind?) to revise his screen play to their advantage, such persuasions including the offer of sexual favors. Meanwhile, the film's producer tries to cope simultaneously with the infighting and a mysterious bleeding sore on his anus. Under the direction of the author, the scabrous dialogue was delivered with shameless aplomb by an expert cast (Polly Draper and Mary-Louise Parker as the actresses, Loren Dean as the writer and Tony Roberts as the producer), but I thought it was pretty familiar stuff. There have been so many black comic attacks on the venality of the movie business (*Speed-the-Plow*, *The Road to Nirvana*, *S.O.B.*, *Barton Fink* and so forth and so on) that at this point I think the only truly revolutionary depiction would be to say something nice about it. (It is possible. Francois Truffaut managed it in his lovely film *Day for Night*.) A lot of people found more to admire in this play than I did; it moved from its initial production at the Manhattan Theater Club to an extended commercial run.

More villainous show biz types are featured in Martin Crimp's *The Treatment*. The title refers not only to the film treatment a pair of shadowy producers want to derive from the trauma of an abused wife, but also to the treatment the city in general metes out to her. One of the most vivid scenes depicts her being sped through New York streets in a cab driven by a man she gradually realizes is blind, his indifference to the damage he's causing meant to be equivalent to the city's indifference to the damage it routinely inflicts upon its inhabitants. The play seems to mistake nastiness for integrity. The same week Crimp's play opened at the Public Theater, Howard Korder's bleak view of city life, *The Lights*, opened at Lincoln Center. Again, the bulk of the play is made up of familiar nightmare images of urban callousness. Unexpectedly, somewhere in the second act Korder produces a thought-provoking passage in which a character speaks of the chaos of the city as the result of millions of conscious decisions.

One of most admirable aspects of the most admirable Terrence McNally is his adventurousness, his determination to chart new ground for himself. His Best Play *A Perfect Ganesh* is a double portrait of two Connecticut matrons who journey to India together in the hopes that something about that mysterious land will help them cope with the trials of their lives. There is the expected comedy of Western values colliding with Eastern ways (the East being represented by Fisher Stevens, playing a variety of parts, and Dominic Cuskern, playing the benevolent god Ganesha who seems to watch over the ladies). There are also many moving passages as the overwhelming sights of misery and splendor trigger private associations on the part of the tourists.

If ultimately the play doesn't quite seem to arrive at a resonant conclusion, the journey more than justifies itself, especially when enacted by Frances Sternhagen and Zoe Caldwell as the alternately bedazzled and horrified twosome.

Edward Albee also provided a welcome showcase for actresses in his Best Play *Three Tall Women*. In the first act, a young woman identified in the program as C is visiting an elderly woman, A, on some legal business. A is alternately teased and guarded by her hired companion, B, a woman is her 50s with a biting wit. At the end of the first act, A suffers a stroke. In a startling shift, the second act introduces the actresses who played separate parts in the first act as A at three stages of her life. While a dummy representing the comatose A rests upstage, the three explore the contrasting perspectives of youth, middle and old age, dissecting the ignorance and insight specific to each.

This is a play not of plot but nuance, Albee being most interested in how time and experience change our voices and the way we view the options available to us. He seems to be least interested in the young woman, who comes across as callow and selfish, but he has provided the actresses playing A and B with rich verbal arias. Happily, in the New York production the actresses entrusted with these plum roles were Myra Carter and Marian Seldes, both of whom, under Lawrence Sacharow's precisely modulated direction, gave virtuoso performances. The play gained added resonance when it was revealed that the model for A was Albee's stepmother, with whom he had a turbulent relationship due to her unwillingness to accept his sexuality.

Aside from the rewards of the play itself, there was the additional satisfaction of seeing Albee, who has weathered years of critical disfavor, being greeted with a hero's welcome capped by his third Pulitzer Prize. (For those who wanted to be reminded how uncompromising a writer he remains, the Signature Theater staged a season of his less accessible work, which was received more equivocally by many of the same critics who embraced *Three Tall Women*.) In a society that has a habit of too easily discarding last season's geniuses, it was refreshing to see one of the bright lights of the theater's past stake a firm claim on the present.

Here's where we list the *Best Plays* choices for the outstanding straight play achievements of 1993-94 in New York, on and off Broadway. In the acting categories, clear distinction among "starring," "featured" or "supporting" players can't be made on the basis of official billing, which is as much a matter of contracts as of esthetics. Here in these volumes we divide acting into "primary" or "secondary" roles, a primary role being one which might some day cause a star to inspire a revival in order to appear in that character. All others, be they vivid as Mercutio, are classed as secondary. Furthermore, our list of individual standouts makes room for more than a single choice when appropriate. We believe that no useful purpose is served by forcing ourselves into an arbitrary selection of a single best when we come upon multiple examples of equal distinction.

PLAYS

BEST PLAY: *Angels in America, Part II: Perestroika* by Tony Kushner; *The Kentucky Cycle* by Robert Schenkkan

BEST REVIVAL: *All's Well That Ends Well* by William Shakespeare

BEST ACTOR IN A PRIMARY ROLE: Sam Waterston as Abraham Lincoln in *Abe Lincoln in Illinois*

BEST ACTRESS IN A PRIMARY ROLE: Myra Carter as A in *Three Tall Women*; Diana Rigg as Medea in *Medea*; Alanna Ubach as Eva in *Kindertransport*

BEST ACTOR IN A SECONDARY ROLE: Joe Mantello as Louis Ironson and Jeffrey Wright as Belize in *Perestroika*; Andrew Robinson as Gus Brower in *Any Given Day*

BEST ACTRESS IN A SECONDARY ROLE: Susan Batten as Charity in *The Fiery Furnace*; Kathleen Chalfant as Hannah Pitt in *Perestroika*

BEST DIRECTOR: George C. Wolfe for *Perestroika*; Richard Jones for *All's Well That Ends Well*

BEST SCENERY: Peter J. Davison for *Medea*; Stewart Laing for *All's Well That Ends Well*; Ian MacNeil for *An Inspector Calls*

BEST COSTUMES: Jane Greenwood for *Abe Lincoln in Illinois*; Stewart Laing for *All's Well That Ends Well*

BEST LIGHTING: Rick Fisher for *An Inspector Calls*; Mimi Jordan Sherin for *All's Well That Ends Well*; Robin Wagner for *Perestroika*

SPECIAL CITATION: Jonathan Dove for incidental music for *All's Well That Ends Well* and *Medea*

CYRANO: THE MUSICAL—Adam Pelty as Valvert and Bill Van Dijk in the title role of the musical based on Rostand's *Cyrano de Bergerac*

Musicals and Special Entertainments

I fully expect that the hundreds of thousands of people who will pay top dollar to visit the Palace Theater for the stage version of *Beauty and the Beast* (officially titled *Disney's Beauty and the Beast*) will feel that they got their money's worth. Certainly the audience around me, among whom were hundreds of children, seemed to enjoy themselves thoroughly. The show has some strong elements. The songs that composer Alan Menken collaborated on with the late lyricist Howard Ashman for the cartoon feature continue to beguile. Some of the effects, particularly the magical midair transformation of the Beast into a prince, take the breath away. And any show featuring singing by Terrence Mann, Susan Egan and Beth Fowler is going to offer pleasure.

But whereas much of the exhilaration of the 90-minute movie was the result of the swiftness of the transitions and the kind of staging possible only with the plasticity of animated performers, the stage version seems to lumber along, ultimately clocking in at two and a half hours. New material has been added, chiefly new songs by Menken written with former Andrew Lloyd Webber librettist Tim Rice. Rice's lyrics mostly articulate points that are already understood by the audience before the songs begin. Rice also seems to have stimulated Menken to write ersatz Lloyd Webber; "If I Can't Love Her" wouldn't sound out of place in any of a number of Sir Andrew's scores. If Menken is going to continue collaborating with Rice, I hope that he will more strongly reaffirm his own voice as a composer.

Several seasons ago, the Palace hosted another beauty-and-the-beast tale, a musical version of Rostand's *Cyrano de Bergerac*. That effort foundered despite a brilliant performance by Christopher Plummer in the title role. This season saw a new attempt, *Cyrano: The Musical*; but, despite energy and charm, Bill Van Dijk couldn't convey the title character's genius and pain. Ad Van Dijk's music is lush in the Europop-opera tradition, but it seems to have no strong musical character of its own. The most striking aspects of this production were its elaborate sets, lights and costumes (credited to Paul Gallis, Reinier Tweebeeke and Yan Tax respectively) and Timothy Nolen as Cyrano's nemesis, De Guiche.

The roster of talent connected with the musical version of *The Red Shoes* was impressive. Composer Jule Styne has written several of the theater's most dynamic scores, book writer and co-lyricist Marsha Norman has a Pulitzer Prize to her credit and director Stanley Donen helmed many of the great M-G-M film musicals. Unfortunately, none of these gifted people, nor their producer Martin Starger, seemed to be able to present a compelling reason to make the popular movie about the ballet world into a piece for the stage. (Marsha Norman and the project's original director, Susan H. Schulman, have gone public with their dissatisfaction over their dealings with Starger on the show, so who is responsible for which creative decisions is unclear.) In any case, the show was a virtual compilation of mistakes in judgment.

The story introduces a ballet impressario named Lermontov who is determined to dictate not only what appears on his stage but how the performers he presents are to live offstage. Virtually all of the other major characters in the piece come into conflict with Lermontov's compulsion to control them. Given that one of the functions of song in a musical is to establish and make vivid thematic ideas, the absence of a number for Lermontov articulating the rules against which the others will struggle was puzzling. With the evening's central dramatic contest insufficiently defined at the outset, there was little hope that the principal story of his tragic battle with the young ballerina Victoria Page would carry much dramatic weight. There was the further problem that, though Margaret Illmann danced the role of Victoria beautifully and acted it creditably, she didn't have a strong enough voice for the writers to trust her with the necessary songs to bring this character to full musical life.

A Grand Night for Singing began as a night club salute to Rodgers and Hammerstein. Director Walter Bobbie, in collaboration with Pamela Sousa, guided an ingratiating cast of five through a program which reminded contemporary audiences yet again why the two dominated the musical theater of their era as thoroughly as Sondheim does his. *Smiling Through* also drew on pre-existent songs in telling the story of a British music hall performer's experiences during World War II. Written by Ivan Menchell as a vehicle for his talented mother Vicki Stuart, the show ran afoul of the New York press but would probably please audiences elsewhere. Another small-scale venture, *Howard Crabtree's Whoop-Dee-Doo!*, was a cheerfully nonsensical revue on gay themes. The material was mostly forgettable, but the evening was an almost constant delight because of the parade of frequently hilarious costumes by Crabtree, who also performed, produced and wrote some of the material. I can't remember the last time costumes were reason enough to recommend a show, but such was the case here.

The *raison d'être* of *Avenue X* is the doo-wop singing that flourishes on street corners of working class neighborhoods. In John Jiler's book, the singing can serve either to define gaps or offer the promise of bridging them. The time is 1963, and the characters in the show are blacks and Italians uneasily sharing a Brooklyn neighborhood. When one Italian boy decides he wants to sing doo-wop with a recently-arrived black boy, the people around them begin to draw lines. The show asks the question why people who can sing in harmony can't live in harmony. The book is earnest, melodramatic and heavy-handed. The songs by Jiler and Ray Leslee, however, are frequently a delight. One scene, in which black and white singers set up a musical duel with their different styles of vocalizing and ultimately join together in a number, represents the show at its very best. Unfortunately, by definition a score based on one kind of musical arrangement will tend towards monotony. As stirring as many of the individual numbers are, a whole evening of doo-wop is overkill. The cast at Playwrights Horizons was chosen for its considerable singing abilities. The standout was Colette Howley as Barbara, a brassy young Italian girl in revolt who sang a bitter anthem against her narrowing options.

Bring in the Morning also deals with young people coping with urban living. Created by some of the same hands behind the similarly-structured musical *The Me Nobody Knows*, and derived in part from poetry written by inner city kids, *Bring in the Morning* featured a talented cast delivering impassioned accounts of the nearly nonstop cycle of songs, but the characters lacked sufficient specificity to engage. At any rate, that was my reaction. Most of the audience around me seemed to be genuinely thrilled with the piece.

A musical entertainment without a melody, a story or, until the very end, spoken dialogue, *Stomp* introduces a group of working class British young people in an industrial setting who turn every tool and gadget at hand into the occasion for noise-making and dancing. I couldn't help thinking what a kick Susan Stroman would get out of this evening, given how much of her choreography in *Crazy for You* is based on the manipulation of objects. She surely would appreciate the ingenuity of numbers built on shuffling sounds of brooms, the clicking and flaring of Zippo lighters and the pounding of hubcaps. There is a wistful undercurrent to the frequently comic proceedings; though there is no plot, the show seems to be about how a group consigned to the tediousness of an industrial shop manages to turn limitations into opportunities. None of the "instruments" they play, after all, was built for music; they

STOMP—Theseus Gerard and Fiona Wilkes with their rhythm instruments in the specialty show from England

have been transformed by the performers' imagination. Conceived and directed by Luke Cresswell and Steve McNicholas, *Stomp* was immediately welcomed, except by those living next door to the theater, who were less than cheerful about the schedule of eight performances a week of din.

The premise of *The Best Little Whorehouse Goes Public* had potential. The story is loosely based on a true situation. A legal Nevada brothel was seized by the IRS because of tax arrears, and the government found itself in the position of having to manage this place if it were going to have any hope of getting the money owed. Brecht would have had a field day with a story like this. But Larry L. King, Carol

Hall, Peter Masterson, Tommy Tune and Jeff Calhoun weren't aiming for a Brechtian look at the hypocrisy which results when money and public protestations of morality collide. All the collaborators on this show have in mind is clean, naughty fun—to toss out a few bad words, parade some scantily clad ladies, wink and say, "Just kidding." The ending is supposed to be a happy one—the women in the house manage to take control of the brothel, so they're working for themselves. Apparently this is intended as a feminist statement. At any rate, the end of the show has the leading lady—the brothel's former madam—newly elected as President of the United States and singing something about America with a film montage of proud-looking American women projected on a screen behind her. Somehow Dee Hoty managed the feat of giving the appearance of being in a better show, occasionally finding refuge from the general mindlessness of the proceedings in one of composer-lyricist Carol Hall's beguiling country ballads.

The Best Little Whorehouse Goes Public is a sequel to the successful *The Best Little Whorehouse in Texas*. *Annie Warbucks* is the sequel to the successful *Annie*. It would be facile to say that one shouldn't create sequels to musicals, but I can't think of one that has passed muster. *Annie Warbucks* certainly didn't. After years of development aimed toward a Broadway production, it finally opened off Broadway. Many of the elements present in the original returned—Annie, Sandy, Daddy Warbucks and Roosevelt, not to mention the bulk of the creative team—but the result was a discouragingly mechanical concoction that only came to life when Ann Reinking began to dance.

Some years back, William Finn brought Mrs. Roosevelt to a Public Theater stage as a musical character in *Romance in Hard Times*. Apparently, the Public feels it has a mission to make Eleanor sing, for she returned as a character in Michael John LaChiusa's *First Lady Suite*, flying around in Amelia Earhart's airplane. Other episodes of the show present Jacqueline Kennedy on her way to Dallas, Mamie Eisenhower musing on Ike's infidelity, and Bess Truman bullying her daughter Margaret. While it was a treat to watch performers of the caliber of Maureen Moore and Alice Playten sink their teeth into substantial roles, the evening seemed to be a queasy marriage of *National Enquirer* gossip and art song.

LaChiusa had considerably more success with *Hello Again*, his full-length, one act adaptation of Schnitzler's *La Ronde*. I can't say I understood the dramatic reason for setting every scene in a different decade of the 20th century, but it did give him the opportunity to season his score with a satirical smorgasbord of popular music influences. Elegantly staged by Graciela Daniele and orchestrated for a small ensemble by Michael Starobin, for many *Hello Again* announced the arrival of a talent who had learned some of the right lessons from Stephen Sondheim.

Which brings us to Sondheim: He returned this season with his newest collaboration with writer-director James Lapine, *Passion*. For my money, it is dramatically the most successful piece he's offered since *Sweeney Todd*. Like Sweeney, the central motif is obsession. Sweeney will go to any lengths for his revenge, and the sickly and unattractive Fosca knows no limits in her pursuit of Giorgio, the handsome, sensitive and unwilling object of her affections.

Passion is as uncompromising and relentless as its odd heroine. Sondheim and Lapine have so built their show that there is no opportunity for the audience to have the release of applauding individual numbers or getting a respite from the milieu via an intermission. In this respect, the audience's relationship to the material is similar to that of Giorgio to Fosca. And, similar to Giorgio, we ultimately succumb. By the evening's end, I felt as if I had spent nearly two hours in a hothouse surrounded by orchids, my senses intoxicated by the beauty, but feeling more than a little claustrophobic.

I have minor bones to pick. The nude sex scene between Giorgio and his married lover Clara that begins the piece acts against the interests of the material. A musical by its very nature invites an audience to enter a metaphoric world; nudity onstage is startling precisely because it is so literal. I was not thinking of Giorgio and Clara as they sang their rapturous duet; libidinous Philistine that I am, I was appreciating Marin Mazzie's beautiful body and speculating on where Jere Shea's microphone was hidden. Perhaps others in the audience have purer souls than I, but I suspect that many will be able to first appreciate the music and lyrics Sondheim has written for this scene when the recording is issued and there are fewer distractions.

Also, though I was swept along by the momentum of the story, I still can't tell you why Giorgio succumbs to Fosca. The explanation that she represents the Life Force is fine as a thematic statement, but in concrete human terms I don't understand what moves Giorgio from pity to passion. Without understanding that, it's hard to view Fosca as something appreciably different than a contemporary stalker. I ended up buying the transition because I wanted to, because that was necessary for the show to work for me.

Here's where we list the *Best Plays* choices for the musical and special-attraction bests of 1993-94.

MUSICALS AND SPECIAL ATTRACTIONS

BEST MUSICAL: *Passion*

BEST REVIVAL: *Carousel*; *She Loves Me*

BEST BOOK: James Lapine for *Passion*

BEST MUSIC: Stephen Sondheim for *Passion*

BEST LYRICS: Stephen Sondheim for *Passion*

BEST ACTOR IN A PRIMARY ROLE: Boyd Gaines as Georg in *She Loves Me*; Jere Shea as Giorgio in *Passion*

BEST ACTRESS IN A PRIMARY ROLE: Donna Murphy as Fosca in *Passion*

BEST ACTOR IN A SECONDARY ROLE: Paxton Whitehead as Col. Pickering in *My Fair Lady*

BEST ACTRESS IN A SECONDARY ROLE: Sally Mayes as Ilona in *She Loves Me*; Audra Ann McDonald as Carrie Pipperidge in *Carousel*

BEST DIRECTOR: Nicholas Hytner for *Carousel*; James Lapine for *Passion*
BEST CHOREOGRAPHY: Kenneth MacMillan and Jane Elliott for *Carousel*
BEST SCENERY: Bob Crowley for *Carousel*
BEST LIGHTING: Paul Pyant for *Carousel*
BEST COSTUMES: Howard Crabtree for *Whoop-Dee-Doo!*; Bob Crowley for *Carousel*
SPECIAL CITATION: *Stomp*

AMONG SOLO PERFORMANCES OFF BROADWAY—*Above, left to right,* Mort Sahl in *Mort Sahl's America,* Sherry Glaser in *Family Secrets* and Eric Bogosian in *Pounding Nails in the Floor With My Forehead; below,* Claudia Shear in *Blown Sideways Through Life*

Solo Performances

Somebody has done Jackie Mason a disservice in encouraging him to believe that he has the credentials to be a social commentator. As a comic with a talent for alternately invoking and tweaking ethnic stereotypes and exploring the ethos of middle-class Jews, he has few peers. But in *Politically Incorrect*, his primary focus was on politics and would-be sociological exploration. In a field calling for the stiletto-like pricks of a satirist, Mason applied a hacksaw. He couldn't help being funny some of the time, but a good deal of humor was curdled by mean-spiritedness. At one point he asked, "Does anyone here still believe this is a democracy?" A woman in the audience shouted back, "Yes!" and for the rest of the evening he made frequent jabs at her, calling her a "sick *yente*." A true satirist is not a bully.

Mort Sahl's America featured another vintage comedian observing the current political scene. Sahl at his best is a genuine satirist. He was at his best spinning new material from fresh events. Otherwise, much of what he did was familiar from other outings and, as was true of his engagement on Broadway a few years back, it was marred by relentless name-dropping, as if he were saying, "I mock these people, but I'm part of their gang." It's hard to view from the outside when you're so pleased to be on the inside. One day, I hope Sahl will create a theatrical framework for his years of old material, perhaps in the form of an explanation of how we got to Clinton from Eisenhower. With the exception of Jules Feiffer (who collected his running account of these years in a book called *Jules Feiffer's America*), there is no American satirist as well qualified to offer such a perspective of postwar American life.

In a case of fashioning theatrical lemonade out of lemons, Claudia Shear took the many trials of her life floating from job to job to job while trying to support herself as a not-very-much-in-demand actress and made of them *Blown Sideways Through Life*. Having been a supporting character in so many demeaning circumstances (including answering phones for a callgirl service), her transformation to center stage celebrity is its own happy ending, one she celebrates at the end of each performance with a dance of sheer delight as the audience cheers. Along the way, her piece offers oblique views of life in this city from perspectives theatergoers don't usually experience.

Spalding Gray's Anatomy brought Gray back to the Lincoln Center stage in another autobiographical tale. Told that he has a deteriorating eye condition, Gray dashed from one alternative treatment to another in the hope of cure. Gray managed the neat trick of simultaneously sketching Dickensian impressions of the various quacks and faith-healers lying in wait for the desperate and mocking his own hope that his notorious skepticism will be proven wrong. Ultimately, he found little could be done for the eye, but made another journey that provided rich material for his storytelling. Another case of lemonade from lemons.

As a longtime Eric Bogosian fan, I have to confess disappointment with *Pounding Nails in the Floor With My Forehead*, his latest solo outing. In previous pieces, he has dazzled audiences with his portraits of various strains of American males—the violent, the self-deluded, the over-hearty, the lost and the bewildered. While still capable of offering up a gem—his cameo of a man in a self-help group apologizing for being male is up to the best of his work—for the first time his material carries as a subtext the appreciation of his own celebrity, and for my taste this compromises his reporter's eye. Also for the first time, I sensed him calculating the shock value of his material, being aware of how this or that outrageous image might rile up his audience. I prefer the Bogosian who is content to act as the medium for his characters rather than to directly confront his audience. This is a case in which I am very much in the minority; the show got mostly rave reviews and played an extremely successful run off Broadway.

Lanford Wilson, who has contributed so many fine plays in his long career, this season was represented at Circle Rep by *Moonshot and Cosmos*, a double bill of solo pieces, one dealing with a man's reaction to his lover's death from AIDS and the other with a woman's revenge for having been abused by her stepfather as a child. Neither piece met the standard of Wilson at his considerable best, but Judith Ivey had a great time playing the increasingly inebriated author introducing her skeletons to an unsuspecting high school journalist. Regina Taylor, best known for her impressive work as the star of TV's *I'll Fly Away*, appeared at Circle Rep in her own solo play, *Escape From Paradise*, a family portrait that alternated between being vivid and incoherent. In other venues, Irene Worth presented her *Portrait of Edith Wharton*, Juliette Koka honored Edith Piaf in song in *Piaf. . . Remembered*, Holly Near sang of her own life and career in *Fire in the Rain* and Kate Clinton celebrated the gay and lesbian community in *Out Is In*.

Sherry Glaser, in collaboration with her co-author, director and husband, Greg Howells, was responsible for a solo effort called *Family Secrets*, a group portrait of a Jewish family she says is drawn from her own background. In the first two sections, in which she played the parents of the family, Glaser's material and her performance were clear-sighted, funny and compassionate. Her performance as their two daughters and a philosophical grandmother continued on a high level, though the inventiveness of the material flagged in these sections.

Reportedly, the Pulitzer jury decided that Anna Deavere Smith's *Twilight: Los Angeles, 1992* was not eligible for the drama prize because the text is not original with Smith but was derived from interviews she did with witnesses and participants in the riots touched off by the Rodney King case. In my opinion, playwriting is not primarily a matter of creating language, it is creating the opportunity for a dramatic event. Smith made a fine play where there wasn't one before. I would have voted in favor of *Twilight*'s eligibility.

The play she made juxtaposes the voices of dozens of Angelenos and a handful of observers in the attempt to suggest the variety of vectors that contributed to the resultant of the riots. All told, about four dozen people of both sexes and a variety of ages and ethnicities are heard from. Smith the dramatist set a daunting task for Smith the performer. It is to her credit as an actress that she is able to make distinctive as many of the voices as she does; but, as accomplished as she is, some of the 40-odd voices can't help blending together. I also would have wished for a simpler production. The projection of relevant tapes and photos augmented the evening, but the parade of different furniture sliding on and off stage seemed at odds with the celebration of the transformational powers of acting which is part of the kick of the piece, a Best Play of this season.

Nevertheless, the work is an impressive one, even more complex than *Fires in the*

Mirror, the exploration of the Crown Heights controversy which brought her to fame. Through skillful editing and arrangement, the various perspectives illuminate each other. I was particularly struck by the passage in which white riot victim Reginald Denny spoke of planning a room in his house to honor the spirit of peace, which slid into a section in which black Paul Parker, who defends those responsible for the attack on Denny, talks about building a room dedicated to defiance.

AN INSPECTOR CALLS—Jan Owen, Christopher Marquette and Ian MacNeil's volatile scenery in the J.B. Priestley revival at the Royale

Revivals

Several classic and semi-classic musicals returned to Broadway this season. All of these shows were period pieces when they were originally produced, with the exception of *Damn Yankees*, and for this year's revival of that show the book was revised to emphasize its distance from today. With a nod towards *Faust*, the plot concerns a middle-aged baseball fan who makes a deal with the Devil to become a young player named Joe Hardy and save his beloved Washington Senators from disgrace at the hands of the hated New York team. Featuring jazzy sets by Douglas W. Schmidt which looked as though they originated as covers of old issues of *The New Yorker*, the production benefitted from snappy staging by Old Globe artistic director Jack O'Brien, with choreographer Rob Marshall tipping his hat to original choreographer Bob Fosse while bringing his own light touch to the numbers.

O'Brien consulted with *Yankees'* original co-librettist and director, 106-year-old George Abbott, in fiddling with the script. Some of the revisions, including some gentle satiric digs at the 1950s culture from which the story emerged, gave the show new sparkle. But other revisions gutted much of the impact of the star role of Lola, the temptress assigned by the devilish Applegate to corrupt the ballplayer. In the original version, Lola's dilemma is that she falls for Joe and, for love of him (and an unrequited love at that), becomes the ballplayer's ally against Applegate, working to redeem his soul. In the second act, when all seems lost for Joe, he and Lola spend the evening together, culminating in a musical commiseration, "Two Lost Souls."

I won't go into the details of how O'Brien has altered the second act, but in this version, Joe and Lola hardly seem to know each other, so her moral dilemma hardly registers. In addition, presumably to beef up Applegate's part, O'Brien has recast the "Two Lost Souls" number as an ill-motivated duet for Lola and her employer. Some reviewers commented that this production's Lola, Bebe Neuwirth, was technically proficient but chilly in comparison to the original's legendary Gwen Verdon. I think that if she'd had the same material to play, she would have been better received. Even so, Neuwirth was more than welcome as dancer and comedienne. Victor Garber was a charming devil in a cheerfully sleazy Bill Murray mold, Jarrod Emick was a rock solid Joe, and Linda Stephens (brilliant in last season's musical version of *Wings*) gave the potentially tiresome role of Joe's middle-aged wife some real feeling.

Choreographer Rob Marshall's talents were also on display in the revival of *She Loves Me*, which played an engagement at the Roundabout before moving to a commercial run on Broadway. There was minimal fiddling with the original material here, and a good thing, too, because Joe Masteroff's script, based on Miklos Laszlo's play *Parfumerie* (also the source of the classic film *The Shop Around the Corner* is among the best constructed books of the traditional musical theater, and the melodic and witty score is a showcase of composer Jerry Bock and lyricist Sheldon Harnick's extraordinary ability to write for character. Yes, under the direction of Scott Ellis, there were some new elements to the show—Marshall's dances for the patrons at a romantic cafe and the Christmas customers at the perfume shop were showstopping additions to a show that before had not attempted to stop. But this was less a re-imagining of *She Loves Me* than a realization of its considerable strengths. The tale of a young man and woman who battle at the shop where they both work (but, unbeknownst to them, are simultaneously loving correspondents under pseudonyms) continues to enchant. The running time of this small-scale gem was nearly three hours, but it seemed shorter than many of the 90-minute one-acts presented this season.

Always an ingratiating dramatic performer, Boyd Gaines as Georg proved to have a pleasing singing voice as well, partnered with Judy Kuhn's beautifully sung Amalia. Fans of Sally Mayes were delighted to see her finally have a role worthy of her talents, playing the rueful and, uh, more experienced Ilona. Howard McGillin slinked with bravado as the supplier of some of that experience. And Lee Wilkof somehow managed to make cowardice endearing as the anxiety-ridden salesman Sipos. Much was made of the pleasures the modestly-scaled *She Loves Me* supplied, in contrast to many of the spectacle-obsessed behemoths of recent seasons. Having no need for gimmicks like fireballs and helicopters, the Masteroff-Bock-Harnick collaboration stands firmly on the foundation of musical theater writing craft at its most assured.

Pygmalion does not have to be played as a love story. Shaw himself denied that it was, and there have been some very strong revivals in recent years that have been oblivious to the tale's romantic possibilities. (Certainly a few seasons back it was impossible to believe that Peter O'Toole and Amanda Plummer were likely to find themselves contemplating a life together.) On the other hand, Lerner and Loewe's musical version, *My Fair Lady*, most definitely *is* a love story. The chief problem with Howard Davies's staging of this year's revival of the musical is that it seemed to be a production of *My Fair Lady* by people who would rather be doing *Pygmalion*. To say that there was no sexual chemistry between Richard Chamberlain's Henry Higgins and Melissa Errico's Eliza Doolittle is to put it mildly. Add to this the sets (which, according to a curious credit in the program, were "based on original designs by Ralph Koltai"); they seemed intent on dismantling the Cecil Beaton imagery from the original production and the film, but did it so thoroughly as to render Higgins's study a virtual torture chamber.

The strength of much of the material shone through nevertheless. If Miss Errico wasn't able to pull off Eliza's intellectual transformation with much conviction, her strong voice and infectious enthusiasm made for a lovely "I Could Have Danced All Night." Julian Holloway (son of Stanley) was an energetic Doolittle, doing particularly well by "With a Little Bit of Luck" (reportedly staged with an uncredited assist from Tommy Tune). Best of all was Paxton Whitehead's perfect Col. Pickering. Whitehead was Chamberlain's standby for Higgins. More than once I thought of how much I would like to see Whitehead play Higgins—in *Pygmalion*. (Another revival of a Lerner and Loewe show, *Camelot*, featuring Robert Goulet in the role of Arthur, played a brief run to sour reviews.)

I've always viewed *Grease* as an anti-*Pygmalion*, the story of a smart and sensitive 1950s high school girl compelled by social pressures to jettison her integrity and stoop to the level of those around her in order to achieve popularity. *Grease* asks the audience to celebrate the moment when she casts aside her values and becomes a tramp to be accepted by the boy she loves. But, of course, I'm taking the show too seriously. Not having thought much of the piece to begin with, I can't pretend to be as disturbed as many of the other critics by the vulgarity of the Tommy Tune-supervised revival directed and choreographed by Jeff Calhoun, though the day-glo design of John Arnone's set seemed confusing and anachronistic for a show set in the 1950s. Most of the audience around me seemed to be having a swell time, as had the audience around me when I saw the original New York production. (*Joseph and the Amazing Technicolor Dreamcoat*, an early Andrew Lloyd Webber-Tim Rice collaboration also drawing heavily on spoofs of 1950s rock 'n' roll, made a return visit, too, proving to be more popular with audiences than with critics.)

The most widely-celebrated revival of a musical this season was the Nicholas Hytner production of Rodgers and Hammerstein's *Carousel*, which originated at London's Royal National Theater. Rodgers made no secret that this was his favorite of his works, and it's easy to understand why. The courtship scene between Billy Bigelow and Julie Jordan is as exquisitely written a passage as any in American musical theater, and the rest of the score displays the composer at the height of his melodic powers. The script, however, is problematic—nothing can disguise the fact that the show's hero is a whiny bully and that, after the initial scene in which she shows so much spunk, the leading lady becomes passive to the point of invisibility. In an earlier time, with a star as charismatic as John Raitt in the lead, the audience might enter into a kind of complicity to not take Billy's flaws too seriously, but the show today plays to an audience that doesn't accept wife-beating as something that can be viewed as the regrettable but understandable action of a troubled soul.

Not that Hytner in any way attempted to downplay the troubling aspects of the Billy-Julie relationship. To the contrary. Michael Hayden's Billy was bad news from word one—moody, selfish, overbearing, immature and casually insulting. Just when one was ready to write him off, "If I Loved You" revealed the sensitivity the character is afraid to show. Sally Murphy managed to play with quiet conviction the saintly Julie's obsession with this unappealing young man. Still, it was hard to hope for the couple's reconciliation. The problem, as I say, is in the writing. But the writing also gave Audra Ann McDonald glorious opportunities as the spunky Carrie Pipperidge, and she made the most of them, singing beautifully and displaying the gifts of a born comedienne. She had a fine foil in Eddie Korbich's Mr. Snow.

Hytner's accomplishment was shared with set and costume designer Bob Crowley and lighting designer Paul Pyant. Influenced by Grandma Moses, Edward Hopper and Andrew Wyeth, they applied the film-influenced stage technique of the 1990s to a work from the 1940s. They announced their artistic intentions with a tour de force opening, placing onstage the social background that librettist Hammerstein and director Rouben Mamoulian only implied in the original. Instead of starting in the amusement park where Billy is a barker on the carousel (as specified in Hammerstein's script), Hytner and Crowley introduced us to Julie and her girlfriends working in the mill for the town's paternalistic industrialist. Through the adroit use of a turntable, the mill whisked away, the young women fled its gates and made their way past the men building boats and then scattered into the amusement park. The turntable continued to spin and the various attractions of the park flew by, the spinning conveying the giddiness of the young people on their free night. To cap the sequence, the cast assembled the carousel horse by horse in front of us, lights in the walls of the theater flashed sympathetically, and Billy's flirtation with Julie began. Instantly recognized as a classic piece of staging, this new opening established the fluidity of the rest of the evening, which was enhanced by the late Kenneth MacMillan's impassioned choreography of the ballet and Jane Elliott's staging of the other dance sequences—all in all, a stunning production of a difficult work.

The National Actors Theater stumbled with two of their three offerings this year. Clifford Odets's *The Flowering Peach*, a retelling of the story of Noah directed by Martin Charnin (who in collaboration with Richard Rodgers wrote the lyrics to *Two by Two*, the unsuccessful musical version of this play), came across as labored whimsy, even with the assets of Eli Wallach and Anne Jackson as the Biblical couple. As a number of critics commented, artistic director Tony Randall would have probably flourished as one of the corrupt town bureaucrats in Gogol's *The Government In-*

ABE LINCOLN IN ILLINOIS—Sam Waterston *(left)* in the title role, with Peter Maloney, John Newton and J.R. Horne in the revival of Robert E. Sherwood's Pulitzer Prizewinning play

spector. Instead, he played the leading role of the imposter, which more appropriately would have been played by an anarchistic, improvisational spirit like Michael Keaton or Nathan Lane. That production's director and company's artistic advisor, Michael Langham, was, however, responsible for staging NAT's one clear success, *Timon of Athens*, about which more later. And our historian, Thomas T. Foose, clears up some of the confusion around the title of the Gogol play, which so often appears under its other name, *The Inspector General*: "There has always been a split between London and New York on the title. In London, in nearly all cases, the play was called *The Government Inspector*, but in America the play has nearly always been called *The Inspector General* (that was the title of Danny Kaye's loosely-adapted 1949 film version). The National Actors Theater may have preferred the British usage, since they were using Adrian Mitchell's British translation, first used by the the National Theater at the Olivier January 31, 1985."

To admire a writer is not necessarily to be enthusiastic about all of his or her works. I didn't much care for Harold Pinter's *No Man's Land* in its original New

York run with Ralph Richardson and John Gielgud, and I can't say that the new production at the Roundabout, directed by David Jones (director of the fine film version of *Betrayal*) and starring Jason Robards and Christopher Plummer, made me like it any better. Robards's conversational style, so beautifully suited to American naturalism, seemed a mismatch with the purposefully arch and precise Pinter rhythms. Plummer fared much better as the seedy poet hoping to ingratiate himself to the wealthy host into whose house he has insinuated himself. But, except for a high comic passage in the second act when the two fall into an extended reverie over shared memories of events that may or may not have happened, this strikes me as an airless room of a play, written by an author who didn't particularly care whether it communicated much more than an atmosphere of literate menace.

Scott Ellis's second production for the Roundabout was his non-musical debut in New York, a revival of William Inge's *Picnic*. Like *110 in the Shade*, the musical he revived a couple seasons back, the central action concerns a young woman who is torn between a sexy drifter and a more conservative suitor; both stories are played against the background of a picnic. In *110 in the Shade* (based on N. Richard Nash's play *The Rainmaker*) the leading lady, Lizzie, is described as "plain" but sharp as a tack. *Picnic*'s Madge is the most beautiful girl in town and barely made it out of high school. Starbuck of *110* is full of imagination and has a spark of the heroic in him; Hal in *Picnic* has a certain animal magnetism but is only slightly more appetizing than Billy Bigelow, having vague good intentions but insufficient character to resist the weakest of temptations. One of the problems of staging the play is how to make the audience care for these two pretty but dim and heedless people who, once their looks are gone, will have little to sustain or recommend them. Ashley Judd and Kyle Chandler worked conscientiously but weren't able to achieve this.

On the other hand, the performances in what must be acknowledged as the easier supporting roles were first rate. Ellis had the benefit of a group of fine actresses spanning several generations, from young Angela Goethals (as Millie, Madge's brainy younger sister), to Debra Monk's repressed school teacher Rosemary, to Polly Holliday as Madge and Millie's mother, to Anne Pitoniak as Helen Potts, the elderly neighbor still awake to romantic possibility. Larry Bryggman did equally well as the small-town shopkeeper Rosemary has decided is her last hope. The physical production was graced with a handsome set by Tony Walton and intensely romantic lighting by Peter Kaczorowski. Some critics, while praising the production, dismissed Inge's play as a second-rate contraption that has little to say to contemporary audiences. The audience I was in hung breathlessly on every word and gesture.

Also at the Roundabout, Gerald Gutierrez got a delicious performance out of the ever-reliable Nancy Marchand in Peter Shaffer's dated but still funny *Black Comedy*. Neither had much luck with the companion piece, *White Liars*. Gutierrez brought his impressive skills at choreographing large ensembles to the Lincoln Center production of Robert Sherwood's *Abe Lincoln in Illinois*. The skills were not enough to offset the two-dimensionality of the writing of the supporting characters, but it offered Sam Waterston the opportunity to do virtuoso work in dramatizing the evolution of Lincoln's character, showing a rawness and vulnerability this usually reserved actor has seldom displayed before. It was thrilling, too, to see John Lee Beatty cut loose and do a series of sets on such a large scale, greatly abetted by Beverly Emmons's lighting.

If Lincoln Center producer Andre Bishop is correct in saying that *Abe Lincoln* was the most popular play his company has produced, part of the reason probably had to do with its clarity of dramatic line and intent. No such clarity was to be seen in another Lincoln Center revival, that of Jane Bowles's *In the Summer House*, which marked JoAnne Akalaitis's return to the New York stage after her abrupt forced departure from the Joseph Papp Public Theater. As usual, Akalaitis summoned up arresting images, but in this case the sense of the play was hard to discern. It didn't help that Akalaitis staged many of the scenes with such large distances between the characters that Frances Conroy and Dianne Wiest found themselves compelled to shout what was meant to be conversational dialogue.

Our choice of Donald Margulies's *The Loman Family Picnic* as one of the Best Plays of 1989-90 was not universally greeted as a wise one. It had disappeared shortly after its opening at Manhattan Theater Club's second stage was greeted by a scathing review from the New York *Times*. A season or two later, Margulies's *Sight Unseen* was produced to great acclaim (and was also named a Best Play). This encouraged the Manhattan Theater Club to undertake a new production of *Loman* on the mainstage this season. In its second turn at bat, this darkly funny view of the terrors of an "ordinary" Jewish family in Brooklyn in the 1960s was greeted with nearly universal appreciation, including by the New York *Times* (which assigned a different critic to cover it). Peter Friedman, who created the role of the aggressive Scoop Rosenbaum in *The Heidi Chronicles*, reaffirmed his versatility with his performance as Scoop's antithesis, the despairing, defeated Herbie. Christine Baranski has made nervous Jewish ladies a specialty; her ferocious comedic gifts gave Doris's flirtation with madness a particular poignancy, making one laugh and wince at the same time. Manhattan Theater Club Artistic Director Lynne Meadow did herself proud as both producer and director with this production.

J.B. Priestley's 1945 drama *An Inspector Calls* was given an eye-opening staging. As Bernard Herrmann's soundtrack music for Alfred Hitchcock's *Vertigo* blared from the speakers, the curtain went up on a spectacular set depicting a blitz-blasted London road dominated by a large doll's house on stilts representing the home of a wealthy family. As the rich family celebrated a newly-announced engagement inside, outside on the rain-swept cobblestones the silent children of the working class alternated between playing and staring.

In due time, a mysterious man entered from the audience with the news that a young woman has committed suicide and he's there to question the family on how their behavior has contributed to her death. (The script strongly hints that the questioner, named Inspector Goole, is some kind of heavenly agent or a physical embodiment of social conscience.) Of course, it turns out that every one of them—father, mother, son, daughter and daughter's fiancee—played some part in the dead girl's

MEDEA—Tim Oliver Woodward and Diana Rigg as Jason and Medea in a scene from the revival of Euripides's tragedy

downfall. At the climax of this production, the elegant house suddenly lurched on its stilts, wires shorted out in a display of sparklers and anything not nailed down came spilling out of the dining room and onto the street, representing, I suppose, what has happened to the rich family's smug, well-ordered existence and previously unexamined assumptions. And then an army of oppressed humanity showed up and stood in silent witness.

The stage pictures were wonderful, no question, and Ian MacNeil's bold set design and Rick Fisher's expressionistic lighting certainly deserved to be the talk of the season. But all this theatrical magic was mustered in the service of a play that is pretty heavy-handed in its mission to lecture to the audience about the necessity of putting aside class differences and embracing the human family. Somehow, I don't think Priestley intended his script to be staged so that it would be this kind of fun to watch. It was as if director Stephen Daldry were saying, "Hope you don't mind having to sit through the moralizing too much. Hold on, another neat effect will be along in a minute." Rosemary Harris and Philip Bosco are always worth watching, but here they were given very little opportunity to demonstrate the scope of their abilities, imprisoned in archetypes of the Selfish Rich. Kenneth Cranham bullied grimly as the Inspector, sometimes addressing the audience directly with the more overt polemics. Jane Adams registered most strongly as the daughter experiencing some stirring moral awareness.

You have reason to put on *Medea* when you have a Medea. In Diana Rigg, the producers had a formidable one. Working with a new translation by Alistair Elliot of Euripides's play, Rigg played her as a woman who simultaneously was confronting overwhelming emotional pain and marveling at and rather enjoying the insights the pain made possible. But this was no exercise in star showcasing; director Jonathan Kent had the benefit of a very strong supporting cast. Tim Oliver Woodward was reminiscent of Sean Connery as Jason, going a long way toward explaining why Medea fell for him during his days on the Argo. Janet Henfrey was a Nurse who hummed like a sympathetic tuning fork to her terrifying mistress. Judith Paris, Jane Loretta Lowe and Nuala Willis sang the parts of the women's chorus in an *a cappella* score by Jonathan Dove; some of these passages rivalled those offered by the best of this season's musical attractions. In addition, set designer Peter J. Davison's metallic vision of Medea's courtyard provided a dramatic jolt at the play's climax: several of the plates which formed the wall suddenly fell away, banging and clattering, held from smashing to the ground by heavy chains. As the startling din echoed through the theater, we were offered the vision of Medea, wearing her blood-stained clothes, her back turned to Jason, looking forward into a mass of swirling clouds. It was enough to make your heart jump out of your chest, which is undoubtedly what Kent and Davison intended.

Thomas T. Foose's notes on this Greek classic recall other times when *Medea* was done on Broadway because they had a Medea: Judith Anderson in 1947 (with John Gielgud as Jason and Florence Reed as Nurse), Irene Papas in 1973 and Zoe Caldwell in 1982 (with Judith Anderson as Nurse and Mitchell Ryan as Jason). These notes also recall "odd or unusual" proliferations of the Euripides play during the 1980s, including a black *Medea* by the New Federal Theater, adapted by Ernest Ferlita, a Jesuit priest; "one of Charles Ludlam's rip-offs" at the Ridiculous; an all-male version in Japanese by the Toho Company; a Pan Asian Repertory staging with Asian performers, one of whom doubled as Jason and Creon; and a single performance at the Little Theater of a version adapted and directed by Eugenie Leontovich.

Some of Shakespeare's most difficult plays were featured in major stagings this year. As mentioned above, the National Actors Theater produced *Timon of Athens*, with Brian Bedford making vivid and distinct Timon's two faces—the first, the generous host and friend, the second, the raging misanthrope embittered by the ingratitude of erstwhile companions. Michael Langham's production for the Lyceum's proscenium, featuring incidental music by Duke Ellington, was justly acclaimed, though I thought it was better suited to the three-quarters-round stage of the Tom Patterson Theater of Ontario's Stratford Festival where I first saw it in 1991.

An import from the other celebrated Stratford, the Royal Shakespeare Company's production of *The Winter's Tale*, played a widely acclaimed brief engagement at the Brooklyn Academy. Much was made of designer Anthony Ward's use of balloons as a continuing motif, and they went some distance toward unifying this schizophrenic tale of jealousy and redemption; balloons delivered exposition, decorated parties, offered a mode of transportation and represented testicles in a rustic dance. Adrian Noble directed a cast of RSC stalwarts—John Nettles as a tortured Leontes, Suzanne Burden as an aggrieved Hermione, Gemma Jones serving as the court's moral gyroscope as Paulina, and Mark Hadfield, a bit reminiscent of Jonathan Pryce, embodying the spirit of mischief as Autolycus. I admired everyone's work and particularly enjoyed the high spirits of the festive second half; but, as immaculately produced as this was, I missed the depth of feeling which marked James Lapine's haunting production starring Mandy Patinkin for the New York Shakespeare Festival a few seasons back.

At the Festival, Steven Berkoff's staging of Richard II (retitled by Berkoff *The Tragedy of Richard II*) required the actors to pose endlessly like large marionettes to the accompaniment of a relentless score of percussion and wan tunes played on a synthesizer. Andre Braugher gave substantial evidence he could make a good account of Bolingbroke, given half a chance. Michael Stuhlbarg made an improbably young and innocent Richard; though I wasn't taken by this interpretation, he would seem to be a very promising candidate for the pious Henry VI. Carole Shelley worked her usual magic as the Duchess of York pleading for her son's life. This is one of Shakespeare's most subtly written plays. Properly given, it crackles with irony, despair and elegance. It was not properly given here.

The Festival's Central Park offerings at the Delacorte earlier in the season presented happier interpretations. It began with a *Measure for Measure* starring the Festival's associate director Kevin Kline as the Duke under Michael Rudman's direction. Set on a Caribbean island and featuring much outright slapstick on Kline's part, the production was so relentlessly cheerful and sunny that the strong work by

Lisa Gay Hamilton as Isabella and Andre Braugher as Angelo seemed to be intrusions rather than in the service of the central moral conflict of the play. (Braugher seems to be getting cast for his ability to smolder, which he does very well. Maybe the Festival would be so good as to cut him a break and let him try his hand at comedy?)

Whether by happenstance or intention, the other Shakespeare the Festival presented in the summer also featured a dramatic resolution which comes through a would-be seducer being tricked into sleeping with the woman he has abandoned. The production of this play, *All's Well That Ends Well*, was a triumph, one of the high points of the Festival's ongoing Shakespeare Marathon. Stewart Laing, who designed the sets and costumes, used the Delacorte in a new fashion, building a long, narrow stage framed by doors at either end and housing a gallery seating some members of the audience above and behind the action. Given the narrowness of the stage, and the lack of upstage openings, the blocking was made up of alternating waves of action spilling out from first one side of the stage and then the other. Director Richard Jones (best known in New York for his production of *La Bête*) also experimented with staging scenes in counterpoint—at one point, two characters played a dialogue across a table which simultaneously represented a bed in which two others were making love. The two performers playing the play's moral opposites, Michael Cumpsty as the rogue Parolles and Joan MacIntosh as the wise Countess of Rousillon, made the strongest impressions. But this was less a showcase for individual performances than a unified vision of an enchanted world unto itself. There were few moments this season as stirring as the celebration of Helena's cure of the King of France, accompanied by Jonathan Dove's magical score and augmented by glitter raining down from the hands of those in the gallery.

A GENERATION AFTER *MY FAIR LADY*—Noel Harrison (Rex's son, *left*) pays a visit to Julian Holloway (Stanley's son) backstage at the Virginia Theater, where Julian was playing the role of Alfred P. Doolittle which his father created in the original production starring Noel's father as Henry Higgins

Offstage

The League of American Theaters and Producers reported that the 1993-94 season was another record year for Broadway income. The League's figures claim that Broadway ticket sales brought in over $356 million, up 9 percent from the $327.7 million gross that itself established a record last season. There was also an increase in the number of new Broadway productions, 37 this season by their count (42 by ours) as opposed to last season's 33 (we listed 37). The gross for touring productions was approximately $687.7 million (compared to last season's $621 million), bringing the total gross of Broadway shows to well over the $1 billion mark.

It's a matter of speculation how much higher the figures might have gone had it not been for an unusually hard winter. Along with much of the country, New York was hit with a seemingly endless succession of snowstorms. Having purchased tickets in advance, many hardy souls braved the weather, but last-minute walk-up business was severely hit. There were few people out on the street *to* be struck by the impulse to buy a ticket.

Changes in the critical staff at the New York *Times* signaled a shift in the theatrical winds. Frank Rich left his position as first-string critic for a column on the op-ed page. He discussed his years in the hot seat in an emotion-laden memoir for the

Times Sunday magazine that generated a fair amount of controversy. Robert Brustein, critic and artistic director of Boston's American Repertory Theater, attacked Rich for mischaracterizing his record in supporting minority artists. The Dramatists Guild's president, Peter Stone, refuted Rich's portrait of him as an old Broadway hand out of touch with the needs of younger dramatists; noting that the Guild's Council is mostly made up of writers younger than he, Stone observed that, if these members thought he was out of touch, they wouldn't continue to re-elect him to his post. In an article for the *New York Magazine*, Mimi Kramer (a former critic for *The New Yorker*) assessed Rich's tenure, comparing passages from his reviews to those of critics from previous generations to support her affirmation that he had cast off the critic's traditional pose of self-effacement in favor of a highly personal style designed to call attention to himself. My opinion? Though I thought his assertion that he wielded no power disingenuous, I believe future readers will find his vivid and impassioned descriptions of the plays and players of the 1980s and early 1990s to be of enormous value. Critics shouldn't be judged by whether one agrees with them, but by whether they elevate the dialogue on the art they cover. There is no doubt in my mind that Rich did this.

There was other movement among the critical staff at the *Times*. Longtime second-string critic Mel Gussow shifted from critical duties to reportage and interviews, former Sunday critic David Richards moved to the first-string position, former *New Yorker* staff writer Ben Brantley took the second-string position, and former film critic and sometime playwright Vincent Canby moved to the Sunday post.

The 42nd Street Redevelopment Project renamed their renewal project 42nd Street Now!, offering a revised plan for the hoped-for rejuvenation of the area involving rehabilitation of some of the buildings for use as legitimate theaters. The plan received a public boost from the announcement by the Walt Disney Company that, with the aid of a $21 million low-interest government loan, it would take over and refurbish the 91-year-old New Amsterdam Theater on 42nd Street. The company intends to use it as a platform from which to launch legitimate projects designed to cater to family audiences. In a sense, the production of *Beauty and the Beast* at the Palace was a preview of coming attractions. Disney didn't skimp in its entrance into the Broadway arena; *Beauty and the Beast* was capitalized at nearly $12 million, a record.

Of course, those who gamble big risk losing big. By the time Dutch producer Joop Van Den Ende got around to closing *Cyrano: The Musical*, his company was estimated to have lost $12 million, also a record; though, as *TheaterWeek*'s Ken Mandelbaum noted, if Van Den Ende had thrown in the towel earlier, the damage might have been only $7 million. Because of cancelled performances of *Millennium Approaches* and delayed previews of *Perestroika*, the capitalization of the second part of *Angels in America* reportedly topped $3 million. *The Kentucky Cycle* cost its brave producer David G. Richenthal $2.2 million. The visually elaborate *An Inspector Calls* transferred from London for $1.7 million, *Laughter on the 23rd Floor* cost $1.2 million, *Wonderful Tennessee* cost $750,000 and *Broken Glass* came in for

$700,000. Off Broadway, David Rabe's *Those the River Keeps* opened on a $400,000 investment, which it lost. Sherry Glaser's solo show, *Family Secrets*, opened for $300,000 and paid its investors in less than four months. Claudia Shear's solo show, *Blown Sideways Through Life*, also recouped its $230,000 capitalization swiftly. After its off-off-Broadway run at the Vineyard Theater, Edward Albee's *Three Tall Women* transferred to a commercial off-Broadway run for $264,000, where it immediately began posting healthy numbers in the wake of its nearly unanimous acclaim. *Annie Warbucks*, which had originally been prepped for a Broadway production for $5 million, opened off-Broadway in a stripped-down version for $1 million, most of which was lost (though the producers affirmed their belief that a tour and the stock and amateur rights would ultimately put profit into their investors' pockets).

Disney was not the only Hollywood presence in theater this year. The many millions lost on *The Red Shoes* and *The Best Little Whorehouse Goes Public* came from Universal (which had had better luck with its earlier investment in *The Best Little Whorehouse in Texas*). Steven Spielberg's company, Amblin Entertainment, gave a large chunk of cash to Playwrights Horizons to subsidize new writing in return for the right to have first look at the screen potential of material developed there. And film producer Scott Rudin was one of the major backers of *Passion*.

Meanwhile, patterns familiar from movie and TV production were echoed in some of the new arrangements designed to generate new "product" for the theater. James Lapine, who has directed and undertaken librettist duties with composer-lyricists Stephen Sondheim and William Finn, was engaged (as Jeremy Gerard put it in *Variety*) to "set up shop on the Shubert lot" in return for a first look at whatever he might generate. Jujamcyn has a similar deal in place with director Jerry Zaks.

Movies and TV have always generated showbiz gossip; this year a lot of journalistic ink was expended on theater gossip focussing on the troubles of incoming shows. The issue of who was going to play Norma Desmond when the Andrew Lloyd Webber-Christopher Hampton-Don Black musical version of *Sunset Boulevard* opens on Broadway next season achieved the dimensions of a soap opera. Patti LuPone, whose contract guaranteed the New York role and who opened in the London production, received mixed reviews from the New York press that covered her. Glenn Close, who opened the Los Angeles company, received better notices. Though for months the producers were staunch in their denial of the rumors that LuPone would be dropped, ultimately she was indeed dropped in favor of Glenn Close, her contract being bought out for an amount reportedly large enough to capitalize a Broadway play.

Twilight: Los Angeles, 1992 first made a national reputation in its run in L.A. under the direction of Emily Mann. The production then had a run at the McCarter Theater, the artistic director of which is Emily Mann. The producers guiding *Twilight* to New York were staunch in their denial of rumors that Mann would be dropped in favor of George C. Wolfe, the artistic director of the Joseph Papp Public Theater where *Twilight* was to have its next engagement, but when it opened there, Wolfe's name had indeed replaced Mann's in the credits.

Rehearsals and previews for *Passion* and *Perestroika* were similarly the subject of a lot of journalistic speculation, story after story being leaked by so-called insiders on the dire trouble they were in. Nor did playing out of town shield a developing show from sniping by the press. Before it made its way to New York, *Times* columnist Bruce Weber had shared with his readers news of *Broken Glass*'s troubles in New Haven, including its mixed critical reception. The unfavorable review of *The Kentucky Cycle* from Washington *Post* critic Lloyd Rose was mentioned in several pre-opening feature stories on that show, including a long piece in *The New Yorker*. I can't help believing that these reports inhibited advance ticket sales. Once upon a time, New York media observed an unspoken understanding that they wouldn't report critically on shows finding their legs in out-of-town tryouts. No such courtesy is observed today.

Theatergoers continued to dig deeply into their pockets for the hot attractions. At season's end, *The Phantom of the Opera* was charging the same for some of its rear mezzanine seats as seats in the orchestra—$65! *Carousel*, too, cost $65. Next season's production of another Hammerstein classic, *Show Boat*, began selling tickets for $75, and advance seats for *Sunset Boulevard* are being sold for $70. This is still shy of the $100 mark set by *Miss Saigon* in the early days of its run. *The Kentucky Cycle* charged $100, but that bought two evenings of theater.

The Dramatists Guild made progress in its objective to have its standardized contract accepted by the country's leading LORT theaters. Though the Guild was unable to negotiate an overall agreement with the theaters, its contract has been used at about two-thirds of these theaters on an individual basis. The Guild has also formed a committee to look into putting forward a new standardized contract for both commercial and non-commercial venues off Broadway, where most of the action is for new straight plays in New York.

The League of American Theaters and Producers negotiated a new four-and-one-half-year contract with Local 802 of the Musicians' Union. The chief point in contention was the minimum size of orchestras required for musicals. When the dust settled, the ten largest theaters were still required to employ 24 to 26 players. Minimums at smaller theaters were reduced. Health benefits and salaries were increased.

In addition to directing the second part of *Angels in America* and re-staging Anna Deavere Smith's *Twilight: Los Angeles, 1992*, George C. Wolfe also had his hands full restructuring the New York Shakespeare Festival, where he had been installed as artistic director the previous season after the board ousted founding producer Joseph Papp's chosen successor, JoAnne Akalaitis. Wolfe's plan is to have each of the spaces in the company's Lafayette Street building dedicated to a specific kind of work—one for developmental work, one for classical productions, one for solo shows, one for large-scale works and so on. Wolfe has also brought in a new literary staff, headed by Morgan Jenness, a veteran of the Papp years, to develop new works both at the Public and in concert with developmental companies around the country.

Another non-profit company, Circle in the Square, lacked the wherewithal to produce anything this season. According to Jeremy Gerard in *Variety*, the company was $1.4 million in debt, had cut back to a staff of five and still owed subscribers two shows from past seasons.

At the end of the season, the various prizes and nominations for prizes raised the usual rumpus. The Tony nominators bent over backwards to avoid giving a nomination to *The Best Little Whorehouse Goes Public*, preferring to fill one of the four slots in the "best book" category with a nomination for *A Grand Night for Singing*, a revue with no book at all. Many were surprised that *Carousel*'s Billy Bigelow, Michael Hayden, was not nominated. Nor did the critically-praised Amy Irving of *Broken Glass* get an acting nomination. (This did not prevent Miss Irving from graciously co-hosting the Tony broadcast with Anthony Hopkins. Less graciously, Jackie Mason, angered that he was not invited to appear on the broadcast, returned his Tony for *The World According to Me*. He insisted this was on a point of principle, though what the principle was escaped the world according to everyone else.) The Tony administrators further decided that separate awards for revivals for plays and musicals would be given, instead of having them compete in a single category.

Much comment was made about the play that was critically acclaimed to be one of the best—if not *the* best—of the season, *Three Tall Women,* being ineligible for a nomination for the Tony Award by virtue of being produced off Broadway. Many took this to be all the proof that was necessary that by celebrating only Broadway the Tony has scant serious meaning as an award for theatrical excellence. Edward Albee had plenty of compensation, what with winning the Pulitzer Prize and the New York Drama Critics Award as well as a career-achievement Obie Award.

The Pulitzer Prize was apparently given with some confusion. Some of the members of the drama jury reportedly voted under the impression that last season's award to *Millennium Approaches* was also meant to include *Perestroika*, making the second part of Kushner's epic ineligible. There was also some debate as to whether Anna Deavere Smith's text for *Twilight: Los Angeles, 1992*, having been created by editing transcripts of interviews, should be eligible for a writing award. In any case, the runners-up were Terrence McNally's *A Perfect Ganesh* and a regional offering, *Keely and Du*, written by the mysterious author who hides under the pseudonym of Jane Martin, which won the 1993 American Theater Critics Award for an outstanding new script produced in cross-country theater.

The New York Drama Critics refused to give an award to a new musical this season, which was viewed as a snub to *Passion*, which won the Tony for the best musical, best score and best book and picked up the Drama Desk Awards for musical, music, lyrics and book. Both Tony and Drama Desk prizes also went to Donna Murphy, Boyd Gaines, Jeffrey Wright, Jane Adams, Jarrod Emick, Audra Ann McDonald, Stephen Daldry, Nicholas Hytner, Kenneth MacMillan and the revival of *An Inspector Calls* in their respective categories. *Perestroika* also won awards from both organizations for new play and Stephen Spinella for leading performance by an actor. *Angels in America* thus became the first work to win *two* Tonys for best play, and Spinella became the first actor to win two Tonys for playing the same role. (Last year, Spinella won a Tony for featured actor; Ron Leibman won the leading actor prize. Leibman was not nominated this season.) The Tony and the Drama Desk citations for best actress in a play and best revival of a musical were different, however. Myra Carter won the Drama Desk for off-Broadway's *Three Tall Women* and Diana Rigg the Tony for *Medea* (marking the third time the leading lady in a production of *Medea* has won the Tony; Judith Anderson and Zoe Caldwell preceded her). The Tony went to *Carousel* and the Drama Desk to *She Loves Me.*

In addition to citations for Broadway excellence, the Tonys gave a special lifetime achievement award to Jessica Tandy and Hume Cronyn in recognition of their extraordinary careers together and separately. The annual Tony for a regional theater went to the McCarter Theater; among the delegation accepting this award was Emily Mann, who, in addition to directing the version of *Twilight* that played her theater, staged a wonderfully deft production of Joyce Carol Oates's wise comedy on the perils of idealism, *The Perfectionist.* (This, incidentally, was the funniest new play I saw this season.)

Despite winning only one Tony Award (for Ann Hould-Ward's costumes), *Beauty and the Beast* was the big winner the day after the broadcast, setting an all-time box office record for one-day sales—$1,296,722. Many of the Tony losers folded swiftly, including *Broken Glass*, *She Loves Me*, *Sally Marr . . . and Her Escorts* and *Twilight.*

As mentioned above, *Sunset Boulevard* and *Show Boat* are scheduled to open on Broadway next season. *Show Boat*, of course, is a revival, and *Sunset Boulevard* is an adaptation of an old movie which itself deals with a figure obsessed with the past. Whether next season there will be much work that offers a substantial view of the present is something only the future will tell.

A GRAPHIC GLANCE

1993-94
Drawings
By Hirschfeld

Lynn Redgrave haunted by Michael Redgrave in *Shakespeare for My Father*

A GRAPHIC GLANCE

1993-94
Drawings
By Hirschfeld

Lynn Redgrave haunted by Michael Redgrave in *Shakespeare for My Father*

Edward Albee

Michael Damian as Joseph in this season's revival of *Joseph and the Amazing Technicolor Dreamcoat*

Philip Bosco, Kenneth Cranham and Rosemary Harris in *An Inspector Calls*

Peter Michael Goetz, Tony Randall and Lainie Kazan in *The Government Inspector*

Stacy Keach, brandishing the Bible, is surrounded by Gregory Itzin, Scott MacDonald, Ronald Hippe, Ronald William Lawrence, Katherine Hiler, John Aylward, Jeanne Paulsen and Tuck Milligan in *The Kentucky Cycle*

Above, Joan Rivers as Sally Marr in *Sally Marr . . . and Her Escorts; on opposite page,* Nigel Hawthorne as George III in *The Madness of George III*

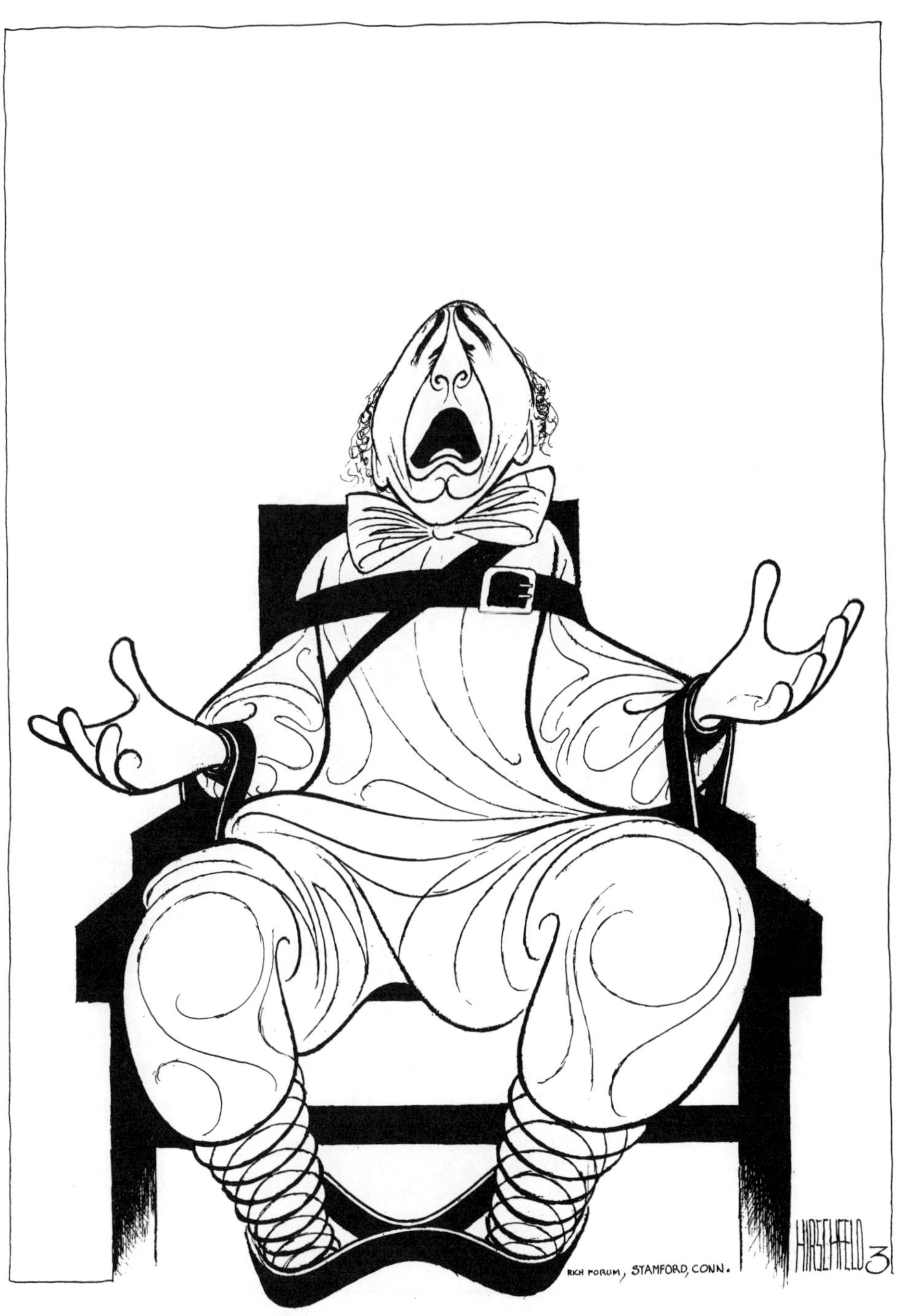
RICH FORUM, STAMFORD, CONN.
HIRSCHFELD 3

As Hirschfeld
Saw Them

On opposite page, above left, Spalding Gray in *Gray's Anatomy; below left,* Irene Worth in *Irene Worth's Portrait of Edith Wharton. On this page, above,* Brian Bedford in *Timon of Athens; right,* Bill Van Dijk as Cyrano in *Cyrano: The Musical*

Kali Rocha, sun bathers, Alina Arenal, Frances Conroy, Liev Schreiber, Dianne Wiest and Jaime Tirelli in *In the Summer House*

NINA
HIRSCHFELD 3

Christopher Plummer and Jason

Robards in *No Man's Land*

Andre Braugher, Lisa Gay Hamilton, Blair Underwood and Kevin Kline in a *Measure for Measure* transposed to a Caribbean island in the 20th century

Julian Holloway, Melissa Errico, Richard Chamberlain, Paxton Whitehead and Dolores Sutton, with spectators at the Ascot races *in background,* in this season's revival of *My Fair Lady*

HIRSCHFELD 3

Miriam Healy-Louie and Michael Cumpsty in *All's Well That Ends Well*

Sam Waterston in the title role of *Abe Lincoln in Illinois*

W

The venerable George Abbott, co-author of the book of *Damn Yankees,* looks over Jarrod Emick, Bebe Neuwirth and Victor Garber performing in the revival of his musical

Gabriel Olds, Sada Thompson, Peter Frechette, Justin Kirk *(in wheelchair),* Andrew Robinson, Victor Slezak, Stephen Pearlman, Andrea Marcovicci and Lisa Eichhorn in *Any Given Day*

HIRSCHFELD 3

On opposite page, Eli Wallach and Anne Jackson in *In Persons; above,* Ashley Judd and Kyle Chandler in the revival of *Picnic*

Jon Marshall Sharp, Sandra Brown, Michael Hayden and Sally Murphy in the revival of *Carousel*

HIRSCHFELD 5

Nina

J.K. Simmons, Stephen Mailer, Randy Graff, Lewis J. Stadlen *(lying on floor),* Nathan Lane, Mark Linn-Baker, John Slattery, Ron Orbach *(kneeling)* and Bitty Schram in *Laughter on the 23rd Floor*

On opposite page, Rosie O'Donnell in the revival of *Grease; above,* Marin Mazzie and Jere Shea in *Passion*

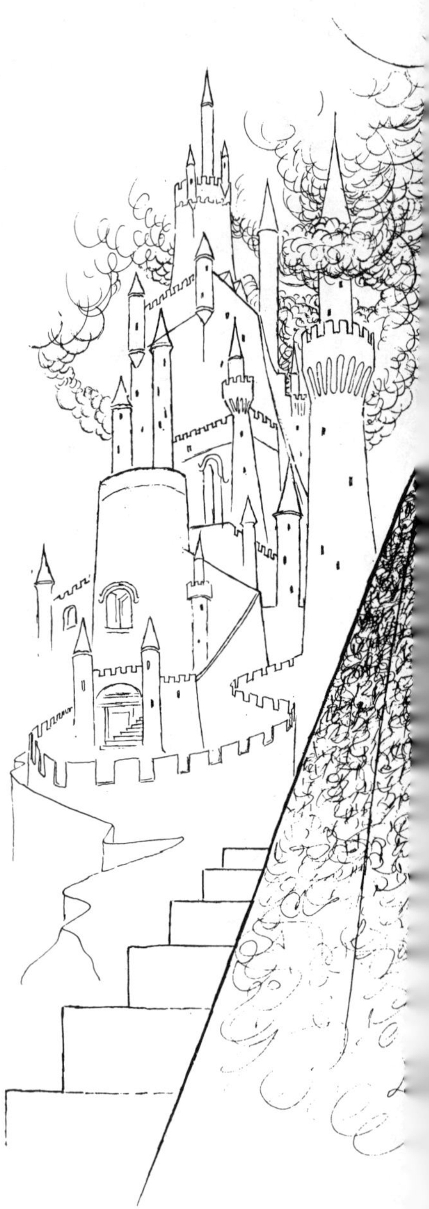

Robert Goulet, Patricia Kies and Steve Blanchard in *Camelot*

HIRSCHFELD 12

Harve Presnell, Kathryn Zaremba and leaping orphans Missy Goldberg, Natalia Harris, Elisabeth Zaremba and Ashley Pettet in *Annie Warbucks*

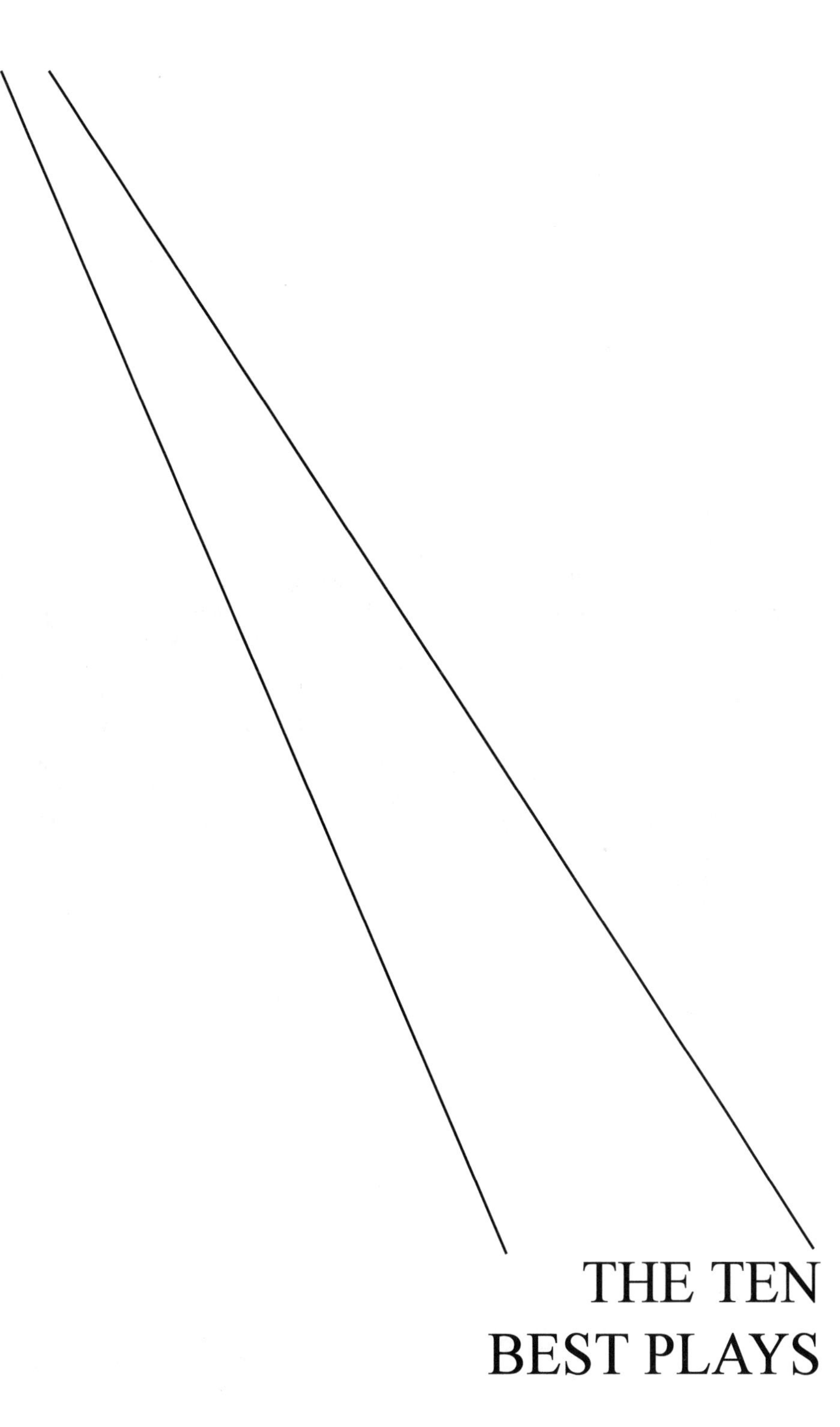

THE TEN BEST PLAYS

Here are the details of 1993–94's Best Plays—synopses, biographical sketches of authors and other material. By permission of the playwrights, their representatives, publishers, and others who own the exclusive rights to publish these scripts in full, most of our continuities include substantial quotations from crucial/pivotal scenes in order to provide a permanent reference to style and quality as well as theme, structure and story line.

In the case of such quotations, scenes and lines of dialogue, stage directions and descriptions appear *exactly* as in the stage version or published script unless (in a very few instances, for technical reasons) an abridgement is indicated by five dots (. . . . .). The appearance of three dots (. . .) is the script's own punctuation to denote the timing of a spoken line.

A PERFECT GANESH

A Play in Two Acts

BY TERRENCE McNALLY

Cast and credits appear on page 443

TERRENCE McNALLY was born in St. Petersburg, Fla., November 3, 1939 and grew up in Corpus Christi, Texas. He received his B.A. in English at Columbia where in his senior year he wrote the varsity show. After graduation he was awarded the Harry Evans Travelling Fellowship in creative writing. He made his professional stage debut with The Lady of the Camellias, *an adaptation of the Dumas story produced on Broadway in 1963. His first original full-length play,* And Things That Go Bump in the Night, *was produced on Broadway in 1965 following a production at the Tyrone Guthrie Theater in Minneapolis.*

McNally's short play Tour *was produced off Broadway in 1968 as part of the Collision Course program. In the next season, 1968–69, his one-acters were produced all over town;* Cuba Si! *off Broadway in the ANTA Matinee series;* Noon *on the Broadway program* Morning, Noon and Night; Sweet Eros *and* Witness *off Broadway that fall, and in early winter* Next *with Elaine May's* Adaptation *on an off-Broadway bill that was named a Best Play of its season.*

McNally's second Best Play, Where Has Tommy Flowers Gone?, *had its world premiere at the Yale Repertory Theater before opening on Broadway in 1971. His third,* Bad Habits, *was produced OOB in 1973 by New York Theater Strategy, directed then and in its off-Broadway and Broadway phases in the 1973–74 season by Robert Drivas. His fourth,* The Ritz, *played the Yale Repertory Theater as* The Tubs *before opening on Broadway January 20, 1975 for a run of 400 performances. His fifth,* It's Only a Play, *was produced in a pre-Broadway tryout under the title* Broadway, Broadway *in 1978 and OOB under the new title by Manhattan Punch Line in 1982. It finally arrived in the full bloom of an off-Broadway production—and Best Play designation—January 12, 1986, for 17 performances at Manhattan Theater Club, which also produced his sixth Best Play,* Lips Together, Teeth Apart, *June 25, 1991 for 406 performances.*

McNally's seventh Best Play, the book for the musical Kiss of the Spider Woman *with a John Kander-Fred Ebb score, took a circuitous route to Broadway. After a 1990 tryout in the short-lived New Musicals Program at SUNY Purchase, N.Y. and a Toronto production, it went on to an award-winning London staging in 1992 before reaching Broadway May 3, 1993, just in time to win last season's Critics best-musical award and the Tonys for book, score and show. His eighth Best Play, this season's* A Perfect Ganesh, *was put on by Manhattan Theater Club June 27 for 124 performances.*

Other notable McNally presentations in one of the most active and successful playwriting careers in his generation have included Whiskey *(1973, OOB); the book for the John Kander-Fred Ebb musical* The Rink *(1984, Broadway);* The Lisbon Traviata *(1985, OOB; 1989, off Broadway at MTC);* Frankie and Johnny in the Clair de Lune *(1987, off Broadway at MTC for 533 performances); sketch material for MTC's musical revue* Urban Blight, *1988; in 1989,* Prelude and Liebestod *and* Hope *OOB and* Up in Saratoga *in regional theater at the Old Globe in San Diego; and in 1990, a revival at MTC of his* Bad Habits. *McNally adapted his own* The Ritz *and* Frankie and Johnny *for the movies and is the author of a number of TV plays, including the 1991 Emmy Award-winning* Andre's Mother. *He has been the recipient of Obies, Hull-Warriner Awards (for* Bad Habits *and* The Lisbon Traviata*); fellowships from CBS, Rockefeller and two from the Guggenheim Foundation; and a citation from the American Academy of Arts and Letters. He lives in Manhattan and has served as vice president of the Dramatists Guild, the organization of playwrights, composers, lyricists and musical book writers, since 1981.*

The following synopsis of A Perfect Ganesh *was prepared by Jeffrey Sweet.*

Time: Now. Or very recently.

Place: India, the United States, points in between and in the characters' minds

ACT I

Scene 1

SYNOPSIS: As lights come up on *"a blinding white"* set, we meet Ganesha. *"He has an elephant's head. His body is covered in gilt."* He proclaims himself happy and introduces himself. He is a Hindu god—"before any venture is taken, it is Ganesha who is invoked and whose blessings are sought. Once asked, always granted. I am a good god. Cheerful, giving, often smiling, seldom sad. I am everywhere." Right now, he is in the International Departures terminal of an airport awaiting the arrival of two women who are going to take a trip together. He tells how one of them, Katharine, before joining her friend Margaret for a lift to the airport, kissed her husband George goodbye. "She was on her way to India," says Ganesha. "He would never see her again."

Margaret Civil, a lady in her late middle age, enters and begins to wrangle with the Man, who in this scene is playing an Air India employee at the ticket counter. (This Man plays someone different in every scene.) Margaret tells the Man she is there to check in herself and her friend Katharine Brynne for the flight to Bombay. The flight apparently is very crowded, as many Indians are flying back to their country for the feast of Hali. The Man, attempting to have a little fun with her, tells her that the flight is 48 hours, not the 18 she is expecting. She isn't amused. He apologizes. It *is* 18 hours, and he has a boring job, so sometimes he makes these little efforts to entertain himself. He begins to search through his computer.

Katharine enters, loaded down with luggage and an assortment of portable electronic stuff. "O for a muse of fire," she cries out. That's what she says when words fail her, and she expects words will fail her a lot in India. Margaret wishes she would subdue herself, and she advises Katharine that she should always have her passport handy. Katharine is evidently the enthusiast of the pair, Margaret the worrier. The women board the plane. The Man exits. Katharine returns—she's forgotten her flight bag. Though it sits onstage, she can't see it, nor can she see Ganesha, who is standing there. He apparently has the power to render himself invisible. Katharine returns to the plane without her bag. The Man (now playing a thief) picks up the flight bag, extracts from it the stuff he wants and tosses aside the rest.

Scene 2

Margaret and Katharine are in the first class cabin, each wearing a headset. Margaret is watching a movie with some degree of dismay ("After all that and they're still going to make love!"), while Katharine listens to a motivational tape ("I choose to be happy"). They hit turbulence. Margaret is concerned. Katharine is not. She asks the Man (playing a Steward) to assure her friend that they will not crash. He obliges, making a joke implying that the imminent dinner service will be a disaster of another sort. Margaret doesn't appreciate the joke. The Man observes, "People think Indians are humorless. They think we're funny but they think we're humorless." The Man moves on.

The turbulence continues to upset Margaret. Katharine, on the other hand, likes it. "It lets me know we're really up there. If it gets too quiet and still, I worry the engines have stopped and we're just going to plummet to the earth." Margaret notices something Katharine is carrying and asks about it. Katharine tells Margaret it's a whistle her husband George gave her. If she runs into trouble in India, she's supposed to blow it to summon help. Just who is supposed to help is another question.

More turbulence. Katharine holds Margaret's hand to comfort her. She remembers something that happened when she and George and Margaret and her husband Alan went to the West Indies.

KATHARINE: . . . . . We were swimming in front of the hotel. A small, single-engine plane had taken off from the airport. The engine kept stalling. No one moved. It was terrifying. That little plane just floating there. No sound. No sound at all. Like a kite without a string. I don't think I've ever felt so helpless.

MARGARET: I remember.

KATHARINE: Finally, I guess the pilot made the necessary adjustments, the engine caught and stayed caught and the little plane flew away, as if nothing had happened, and we finished swimming and played tennis, and after lunch you bought that Lalique vase I could still kick myself for letting you have.

MARGARET: You've envied me that piece of Lalique all these years? It's yours.

KATHARINE: I don't want it.

MARGARET: Really, I insist, Kitty. I think I only bought it because I knew you wanted it. That, and I was mad at Alan for some crack about how I looked in my new bathing suit. The plane's stopped jiggling. Smooth as glass now.

KATHARINE: I've thought about that little plane a lot. Maybe we were helpless. Maybe we weren't responsible. Maybe it wasn't our fault. But what kept that plane up there? God? A god? Some Benevolence? Prayer? Our prayers? I think everyone on that beach was praying that morning in their particular way. So maybe we aren't so helpless. Maybe we are responsible. Maybe it is our fault what happens. Maybe, maybe, maybe.

MARGARET: Do you want to give me my hand back?

KATHARINE: I'm sorry. Thank you. Did I do that? I *was* holding tight! I'm sorry.

(She kisses Margaret's hand.) . . . . . I keep thinking about Walter.

MARGARET: Why would you do that to yourself?

KATHARINE: I can't help it.

MARGARET: Well, stop. Stop right now. Think about something else. Think about the Taj Mahal. Think about India.

They talk some about the history of the construction of the Taj Mahal. Margaret hopes that it's not a disappointment like the Eiffel Tower, which for Margaret, when she saw it, lacked "resonance." Katharine continues to think about Walter. "Nothing will ever get my mind off Walter."

"A light comes up on Ganesha. He is sitting on the wing. He wears a leather flight jacket and an aviator's white silk scarf which blows wildly in the rushing wind we can suddenly hear. He waves to Katharine." Katharine sees him, though what she thinks she sees is an angel. Margaret refuses to look. The Man (playing an Aging Hippy) drifts up from Tourist Class and enters into a dialogue with Katharine about angels. Margaret doesn't take to him. He gets the idea. "You have cruel eyes," he tells her. "They're filled with hate. I mean that nicely. I mean that sincerely." He tells Katharine that Margaret "needs a good purge in the Ganges" and heads back to Tourist Class.

Katharine assures her friend that she doesn't have cruel eyes. Margaret insists she's not upset and goes back to watching her movie.

Ganesha turns to the audience and sighs over the thoughtless cruelty. "We are the ones who are powerless," he confides. "We can only sigh and shake our heads. There's a serenity in being a god but very little power. We gave it all to you." Meanwhile, Katharine has gone back to her motivational tape. Tears stream down Margaret's face while she watches the movie.

Katharine's son Walter (played by the Man) joins Ganesha on the wing. He is bleeding from the beating that killed him.

GANESHA: Mrs. Civil is inconsolable. You must have heard what happened.

MAN: It served her right.

GANESHA: Look at her. I hate to see a woman cry.

MAN: I don't like Mrs. Civil. Mrs. Civil didn't like me. Let her cry her stone-cold heart out. Mrs. Civil was a bitch. Is. Is a bitch. I'm the was.

GANESHA: Your words are like daggers, Walter. They cause me such pain.

MAN: Different people sing from different charts, old man.

GANESHA: Not half so old and hard as you.

KATHARINE: "I choose to be happy. I choose to be loving. I choose to be good."

GANESHA: Your mother's been thinking about you again.

MAN: I'd like her to stop. I'd like her to forget all about me.

GANESHA: There will never come that day. She loves you. You're her son.

MAN: That's not love. It's guilt that's become a curse. She should have loved me not just for falling down and scraping my knee when I was a little boy but for standing tall when I was a young man and telling her I loved other men. She should have loved me when my heart was breaking for the love of them. She should have loved me when I wanted to tell her my heart was finally, forever full with someone—Jonathan!—but I didn't dare. She should have loved me the most when he was gone, that terrible day when my life was over.

KATHARINE *(has taken off her headset but will be drawn into the scene):* "I choose to be happy. I choose to be loving. I choose to be good."

MAN: Instead you waited. You waited until one night, I was coming home, no! to our "apartment" as you always put it; "Two men can't have a 'home,' Walter;" maybe I had a little to much to drink, certainly a lot too much pain and anger to bear—

KATHARINE: I didn't know.

MAN: A car whizzes by. Voices, young voices, scream the obligatory epithets: "Fag. Queer. Cocksucker. Dead from AIDS queer meat."

GANESHA: Oh dear, oh dear!

MAN: I make the obligatory Gay Nineties gesture back. *(He gives the finger.)* Die from my cum, you assholes!

GANESHA: Oh dear, oh dear!

MAN: The car stops. The street is empty. Suddenly this part seems obligatory, too. Six young men pile out.

KATHARINE: Black! All of them black!

MAN: No, mother! All of them you!

Walter remembers how the six, armed with chains and bats and a putter, took turns beating him. He was left lying in the street. The young men piled back into their car. The car turned around and started for him. It swerved at the last moment, only missing his head by inches. "What I figure is this: they were gonna run me over, but at the last second one of them grabbed the wheel. So they weren't a hundred percent animal. One of them had a little humanity. Just a touch. Maybe. If my theory's right, that is. But that's when you waited to love me, mama." He tells Katharine she should let him go. She says she can't. He was her favorite. "You were mine," he tells her, "we killed each other." She wants him to kiss her. He doesn't want to. "You will," she says, and returns to her headset. Walter leaves.

Margaret's movie is over. She makes a derisive comment about happy endings. She sees Katharine is crying and attempts to comfort her.

Ganesha steps in here to give us some details about India, illustrating with a map he had pulled down. He points to his birthplace, Kerala. "How I was born is a very interesting story," he tells us. "Some say I was created out of a mother's loneliness. Some say I was the expression of a woman's deepest need. I say: I don't know. What child does?"

Scene 3

Outside customs at the Bombay airport, the Man (as an Indian Porter) is hauling Katharine and Margaret's luggage on a dolly. Katharine's cassette player is missing,

Dominic Cuskern as Ganesha in Terrence McNally's *A Perfect Ganesh*

and she's upset. Ganesha, playing a tour guide, steps forward to meet them and escort them to the hotel. In Hindi, Ganesha tells the sullen Porter to return the cassette player. The Porter refuses. In response to Margaret's request for a translation, Ganesha tells her that the Porter is going to check with the lost and found and will bring it to their hotel if it's been returned. Ganesha offers to tell them about Bombay, but Margaret is too tired right now. She heads for the hotel.

Katharine, in an "O for a muse of fire!" mode, refuses to allow a missing cassette player to dampen her enthusiasm. She issues herself an injunction: "Look. Attack things with your eyes. See them fiercely. Listen. Hear everything, ignore nothing. Smell. Breathe deeper than you've ever dared. Experience. Be. But above all, remember. Carve adamantine letters in your brain: 'This I have seen and done and known.' Amen. No, above all, *feel!* Take my heart and do with it what you will."

Ganesha now steps forward, and, with the aid of a chart, tells a story about his mother, Parvati, having her privacy in the bath disturbed by her husband Shiva. "Parvati covered herself in shame, she had no prestige now, but she was angry, too. Some say she decided then and there she must have a gana of her own. A gana is someone obedient to our will and our will alone. No woman had ever had a gana of her own." And, so, gathering saffron paste from her own body, she formed it into her gana—a son. And that is how Ganesha was born.

Scene 4

This scene dissolves out of the previous one. We are in Margaret and Katharine's hotel room. Ganesha, playing a Mr. Vintakar, has just finished telling them about Lord Ganesha's birth and now responds to questions about India. He assures Margaret that she'll be able to handle Indian poverty, which is different from American poverty. "Your poverty is angry. Ours is not. In India, poverty is not an emotion. It's a fact." Of course, the lot of women in India is not cheery, what with traditional immolations and such. But now that India is a democracy, perhaps there is some hope for the ladies. He'll return the next morning to tell them more about Lord Ganesha. "You have so many gods!" says Katharine. "Keeping them straight! Vishnu, Parvati, Ganesh! He sounds like a Jewish food."

A Waiter (played by the Man) enters with two Cokes (not the Diet Pepsis the ladies ordered). The Waiter cannot understand the women's English, and the women cannot understand the Waiter's Hindi, which is probably a good thing because, though he's smiling, he's telling Mr. Vintakar that they are "Jew Christian old whores with white saggy skin" and offering to fuck them if he gets proper compensation. Vintakar and the Waiter exchange testy words, but always smiling, so that the women think everything is going pleasantly. The Waiter and Vintakar exit.

Margaret tells Katharine that she was embarrassed when Katharine said "gracias" to the Indian waiter and compared an Indian god to Jewish food. Katharine thinks that her intentions were understood and no offense was taken. Margaret presses on, telling Katharine that if they're going to continue to keep company, Katharine should try for a little more cultural sensitivity. This sets Katharine off. She doesn't care for being chastised. Margaret may order her family about, but Katharine refuses to take it. "I'm me. You're you. Respect the difference or go home." Margaret blames Katharine's outburst on attending New Age lectures about "nurturing your Inner Child." And they squabble some more, until finally they simply decide to call a halt to it. As different as their temperaments are, and even if they get on each other's nerves, the irreducible truth is that they are best friends.

Margaret goes into the bathroom (where she's immediately appalled by a large waterbug). Katharine goes out onto the balcony and gets into a conversation with Harry (a young man played by the Man) who is on an adjoining balcony. In the ensuing dialogue we discover that, like Katharine, Harry is travelling with a companion. Harry's middle name is the same as Katharine's son's was. Harry is gay, too. Harry is a physician who cannot heal himself. (The implication is he has AIDS.) They share their enthusiasm for the opening speech from *Henry V,* beginning "O for a muse of fire." Harry learns Katharine's son is dead. He expects he'll see Walter soon; he promises to say hi for her. Harry's companion, Ben (played by Ganesha), comes out onto the balcony, concerned that Harry will catch cold in his bare feet. They retreat into their room.

Margaret joins Katharine on the balcony. It is just before dawn, and the view is dim. They look down on the plaza. It seems to be moving. Katharine says it's people sleeping. Wall-to-wall people. Katharine thinks it's beautiful. Margaret is sure the people themselves don't. She disappears into the room.

A Japanese man named Toshiro (played by Ganesha) appears on another adjoining balcony while Katharine sings to herself the song that was Walter's favorite, "Blow the Wind Southerly." Toshiro introduces himself. He passed through customs at about the same time she did and overheard her name. He gently asks why she is crying. She denies that she is. He presses her on why she chose to come to India.

KATHARINE: I came to India because I didn't want to go to some mindless resort in the Caribbean with our two husbands for the ninetieth year in a row, and the children and the in-laws and the cats and the dogs and the turtles are all out of the house or dead or married, and no one is especially depending on me right now. This is my turn.

GANESHA: Why India?

KATHARINE: Why not?

GANESHA: Why not the Grand Canyon? Why not Niagara Falls? Why not Disneyland? Why India?

KATHARINE: I heard it could heal . . . . .

GANESHA: What part of you needs healing, Mrs. Brynne? . . . . . You think it is only your heart that is broken. May I be so bold as to suggest it is your soul crying out in this Indian dawn. Hearts can be mended. Time can heal them. But souls . . . ! Tricky, tricky business, souls. I wish you well. You've come to the right place.

He exits. Margaret now appears again, having changed into a nightgown. Katharine continues to be fascinated by the living human carpet in the plaza. She wants to go down, to experience it. She asks Margaret to join her, but her friend refuses. "What if there are lepers down there?" Katharine says she hopes there are, and she disappears.

Now Toshiro's wife (played by Ganesha in a kimono) appears on a balcony and starts a conversation with Margaret. Through the air vents that connect the bathrooms, she heard Margaret cry out. What's wrong? Opening up to the Japanese woman, Margaret tells her that there is a lump in her breast. Every time she touches it, it's grown larger. No, Katharine doesn't know and doesn't need to. Katharine has enough troubles. Margaret knows she's perceived as "a bossy bitch." Katharine has always had love given to her freely, but "I've always had to work at it. I had my big chance and blew it." Her big chance was her firstborn child, a little boy named Gabriel. One day, when they were on a Greenwich Village street, Margaret tried to clean his face. The little boy angrily resisted and ran away from her and straight into the path of a car. He was killed. He was four years old. The driver of the car was a black woman who, though not at fault, was so devastated by the accident she showed up at the funeral service. In the middle of the service, tears streaming down her face, the woman began to hum and then to sing, "Swing Low, Sweet Chariot." The minister stopped speaking as she sang.

Margaret doesn't understand why she has told Toshiro's wife—a stranger—this. She has never told anybody about Gabriel. She and her husband Alan never talk about it. They moved, had two more children, started a new life. Toshiro's wife sees that Margaret is shivering and puts the kimono over her shoulders. "It's not warranted, such kindness," says Margaret.

The lights pick up Katharine in the street, walking among the sleeping people with Harry. She is ecstatic. He is nervous. On the balcony, Ganesha (still playing Toshiro's wife) tells Margaret that Harry and Ben will soon die. "Must they?" Margaret asks. "Yes," says Ganesha.

Below, Katharine asks Harry if he's been to Elephanta Island yet. Harry says yes, and he was a little disappointed. "They're Buddhist. I came to India for the Hindu stuff." Harry looks up and sees that Margaret and Toshiro's wife are watching them. The two pairs wave, but there's no chance they can hear each other.

Katharine and Harry continue to make their way through the plaza. Katharine says, "People probably think I'm your mother." "I'm sure my own mother wishes you were," replies Harry. The people in the plaza are beginning to wake around them, as Harry and Katharine exchange their dreams of India. Harry's is that somehow he and Ben will get well. Katharine's is to be engulfed by India, devoured by it, become a part of it.

KATHARINE: It's a terrifying dream, but I have to walk through it. It's a dream of death, but purgation and renewal, too.

A light has come up on Ganesha sitting on the ground in a beggar's attitude. As Katharine moves toward him, the Man will recede as she leaves him behind.

Look!

Ganesha takes off his elephant's head. It is the first time we have seen his face. He is a leper. He is hideous.

When I was a very young woman I wrote something in my diary that I've never wanted anyone to know until now. This was before George. Before Walter. Before any of them. This is what I wrote, Harry.

Harry is gone by now.

"Before I die, I want to kiss a leper fully on the mouth and not feel revulsion. I want to cradle an oozing, ulcerous fellow human against my breast and feel love. Katharine Mitchell."

Ganesha has opened his arms to her, half-begging, half-inviting her to come to him.

That's why I've come to India. I don't think I can do it, Harry.

She turns to him for support. He isn't there.

Harry? Harry?

MARGARET *(waving wildly):* Kitty, come up now! It's getting light!

KATHARINE: Harry, where are you? Oh God, if he's fallen somewhere in this crowd. Harry!

The sounds of India are getting louder and louder. It is the roar of a vast multitude, the tumult of humanity. It is more like a vibration than a sound. Ideally, we will all feel it as well as hear it.

MARGARET: Kitty! Look up here! I'm calling you!

KATHARINE: Harry! Please! Don't do this! Where are you! Margaret!

MARGARET: She can't hear me. Something's wrong. Just come up now!

Katharine begins to blow on the whistle George gave her.

Kitty! Kitty! Kitty!

KATHARINE: Please, someone, help!

MARGARET: I can't hear you . . . Kitty, Kitty . . .

KATHARINE: I've lost someone, a young man, he's not well, he may have fallen.

She blows and blows the whistle, as Margaret continues to call down from the balcony. The roaring is almost unendurable. Ganesha claps his hands together. Once and all the sounds stop. Twice and the others all freeze. The third time and all the lights snap off. Curtain.

ACT II

Scene 1

In a room in the Lake Palace Hotel in Updaipar, Mr. Bismas, the hotel manager (played by the Man) enters carrying fruit and jokes with Mrs. Jog, a cleaning lady (played by Ganesha). They find the jokes uproarious, but, as Ganesha acknowledges to us, some humor doesn't travel well to other cultures. Mrs. Jog remarks that Margaret is being sick in the bathroom. "Tell me, Mrs. Jog," says Mr. Bismas, "would you fly halfway around the world and spend all your husband's money, just to heave your guts up for a fortnight in a country you have no way of understanding?"

A pale Margaret emeges, and an ebullient Mr. Bismas presents her with the fruit and proudly opens her window to display the magnificent view of the city and the lake, shining in the sunlight. He cheerfully tells her, "The Moghuls used to tie their prisoners to stakes and sew their eyelids open and make them look at the water until they went blind or mad or both . . . . . I hope you will find that very little of that cruelty remains." He turns from her to threaten Mrs. Jog (in Hindi) for having had the effrontery to correct him on something minor. If she wants to keep her job, she must never correct him again, "Especially in front of a woman."

Katharine sails in, crying, "Offamof!" She is exhilarated by the view out the window and by the city in general. ("Offamof" is Katharine's new, shorthand way of saying, "O for a muse of fire!") Mr. Bismas and Mrs. Jog leave. While Katharine displays the bargains she's picked up shopping, Margaret expresses her disapproval that, while bantering with Mr. Bismas, Katharine used the word "tits." Katharine shrugs the objection off, saying, "I'm just your basic white trash."

And Katharine tells things about her past that Margaret never knew—that Katharine's father was a postal worker and her mother took in ironing. She met her husband George when she and a friend crashed a dance at the Westchester Country Club: "Barbara Stanwyck was my role model." She was a damn good dancer. When George asked her where she went to college, she told the truth and said she didn't, she was a dental assistant. They had a wonderful time. She asked to borrow his class ring from Yale, went to the washroom to show it to her friend and lost it down the drain when she was washing her hands. "What do you tell a man you've just met two hours ago at a dance you crashed when you've lost his senior class ring? You don't tell him very much, Maggie. You sleep with him on the first date and you say 'I do,' after you make sure he asks you to bury him on the third. I mean, marry him. I can't believe I said that. Bury him." She shows Margaret one of the things she picked up shopping, a small carved figure of Ganesha.

While Margaret looks at it, an "unbloodied" Walter (played by the Man) appears and asks his mother to dance the fox trot with him. He wishes Katharine had told him the story she just told Margaret. "We might have become friends over a story like that." Margaret, in the meantime, is examining the figure of Ganesha.

MARGARET: What's that around his waist? A snake! A cobra. And one of his tusks is broken.

Lights up on Ganesha. He is on a platform and holds his broken tusk in his right hand.

GANESHA: I broke it off one night and threw it at the moon because she made me angry by laughing at me.

KATHARINE: You still don't know how to hold a woman.

MAN: You mean like this?

He pulls her to him, hard and close.

Is this how you mean?

She slaps him.

KATHARINE: I'm sorry. I'm sorry.

MAN: No, you're not.

MARGARET *(approaches him):* May I cut in?

MAN: Thank you. *(They begin to dance.)* Do I know you?

MARGARET: No, Gabriel.

KATHARINE: Break her heart, the way you did mine. I hate you. I hate both of you!

MAN: Who are you?

MARGARET: Never mind. I just want to dance with you. I have always wanted to dance with you.

GANESHA *(to Katharine):* Join me. With worshippers at my feet I dance my swaying dance. Come, join us!

KATHARINE: Who are you?

GANESHA: I am Ganesha, a very important god in India. Don't laugh. Just because I'm fat and have the head of an elephant doesn't mean that I'm not a god of great influence and popularity. They call me "The Lord of Obstacles." I am good at overcoming problems and bringing success to people. I am also known as a god of wisdom and wealth.

MARGARET: You're a wonderful dancer.

MAN: Thank you.

MARGARET: I'm not. You don't have to say anything.

MAN: I wasn't going to. Hang on!

This time he will whirl her wildly.

MARGARET: Oh, Gabriel! *(They are gone.)*

Katharine asks Ganesha more about himself. "Because I'm a god, I don't have to look or do things thc way ordinary people do." Something he proves by example: "The world is full of opposites which exist peacefully side by side." Impressed by this idea, Katharine wants to take Ganesha back to Connecticut, only she wonders if he comes in a more compact, transportable form. Ganesha says he will check.

Margaret and the Man dance on again. *"Katharine watches them. Man whispers something in Margaret's ear. She throws her head back and laughs."*

KATHARINE: May I cut in?

MARGARET: No.

MAN: I'm sorry. *(They dance away from her.)*

MARGARET: Was that terrible of us?

MAN: Terribly! You're very beautiful.

MARGARET: Thank you.

MAN: For your years.

MARGARET: Did you have to say that?

MAN: Are you happy? *(He stops dancing.)*

MARGARET *(wanting to resume):* Yes. No. I don't know. Does it matter? Are you? Please, don't look at me like that.

He kisses her.

MAN: You should be happy.

MARGARET: I can't be.

MAN: I never knew what hit me. *(He snaps his fingers.)* Like that.

He goes. Lights up on Ganesha. He approaches Katharine with a small carving of himself.

GANESHA: Is this small enough, excellent lady?

He hands it to Katharine.

I come key-ring and necklace pendant size, too, but when I get that small I only come in plastic, and you lose all the detail.

KATHARINE: Excuse me, did you say "I?" "I only come in plastic?"

GANESHA: Oh, Lordy, no! That would be blasphemy.

Katharine is pleased with the small carving and buys it and a second like it from Ganesha (who apparently is now playing the man who sold it to her). The flashback over, she is in the hotel room with Margaret (who has recovered from her dysentery), again, giving her one of the figures. Margaret reads the inscription: "I'm happy and I want people to be happy, too."

Katharine is sorry that because of illness Margaret has missed many of the sights. Katharine speaks of looking up at the Towers of Silence, watching vultures dive down to the bodies she knew were placed on the Towers' tops. "When I go, that's what I want done, Margaret. Just leave me out on the pier at the Greenwich Yacht Club and let the seagulls go to work." She is glad Margaret likes her Ganesha. Margaret wants to know why Ganesha has the head of an elephant, but the train noises from the approaching scene make it impossible for Katharine to hear the question.

Scene 2

Margaret and Katharine are riding on *"the Palace on Wheels, India's legendary luxury train."* The Man plays an American husband they've met on the train. Katharine is trying to keep her spirits up, though she is having painful cramps, probably from eating fruit. Margaret says that Katharine has become "besotted" with Ganesha. The husband says that this is common. He became a Genashaphile himself on his first trip. Perhaps later he will tell them about how Ganesha got the elephant's head, though it is a "dreadful story." He tells the ladies he's here on a repeat visit to India. His wife, Kelly, had been with him until after they went to Benares to watch the bodies being burned on ghats. He had thought that watching this would somehow help him cope with his fear of death. It didn't. It just scared him, and it deeply upset Kelly. Then, for no reason they could glean, an old man, a "wretched figure in rags," threw himself on her. Kelly ended up rolling in the mud, gripped in the old man's embrace. The police finally came and took the old man away. But that was it for Kelly and India. She felt she would never be clean again. She hopped on a plane for Boston. He didn't go with her. "We don't have that sort of marriage," he explains. Anyway, he thinks India is something you ultimately have to experience solo.

As a porter (played by Ganesha) brings tea, the train is plunged into darkness. Apparently they have just entered a very long tunnel. The husband is about to tell the story of Ganesha's head, when Margaret makes a startled cry. As the porter lights a lamp for them, Margaret insists that in the dark someone put a hand on her breast. The husband declares that he didn't do it. The porter, not understanding English, can only sense Margaret's agitation, not its cause. He thinks perhaps Margaret is afraid of the tunnel. He says that Ganesha will protect her. Margaret comments ironically, "I suppose Ganesha fondled my breast." Katharine thinks Margaret is blowing up out of proportion whatever happened: "Next we'll be having the Marabar Caves incident." The porter hears this and apparently recognizes the phrase from E.M. Forster's *A Passage to India* and takes off, afraid that he is to be accused.

Katharine and Margaret begin to squabble, Katharine remarking that they "can't go around accusing people because we feel superior to them." Katharine begins to articulate her guilt about the economic and social inequity they are witnessing. The husband takes this as his cue to leave; he played this dialogue already with his wife.

Margaret is still shaken up. "There is evil in the world, Katharine," she says, and she just was on the receiving end of some of it. Katharine asks if she wants to cut the trip short, but Margaret says no. The train emerges from the tunnel earlier than expected, and now they look out on views of India that, as Margaret comments, people might have seen centuries before. But for once Katharine is not in a rapturous mood. Looking out the window, she wonders, "What makes it India and not Danbury? We travel, but we don't go anywhere. I'm stuck right here. The earth spins, but I don't."

Ganesha, playing the Supervisor, stops in. He heard that there was trouble. Margaret chooses not to complain. The Supervisor leaves.

MARGARET: I wish I could be a better friend to you, Kitty, and vice-versa. I don't know what stops me.

KATHARINE: Thank you for not making an issue about your breast.

MARGARET: It's that good Yankee breeding, don't you know. It's all in the genes, and we all have these marvelous cheekbones and talk like Katharine Hepburn. We're both the same age, and we're from the same background—

KATHARINE: Or so you thought!

MARGARET: Our husbands make approximately the same living. We're both mothers.

KATHARINE: You never lost a child.

MARGARET: Well, that's true.

KATHARINE: Nothing compares to losing a child. No, nothing compares to losing that particular child. Why couldn't it have been his brother or Nan or one of her kids or George even? Do you think God will strike me dead for saying something like that?

MARGARET: Of course not.

KATHARINE: I think maybe He should. Every time the phone rang I dreaded it being him and him saying, "Mom, I've got it. I've got AIDS."

MARGARET: You want to talk about it?

KATHARINE: What is there to say? Who the hell are you to tell me there's evil in the world? You think some little brown man touched your tit in a tunnel. I'm surprised the world didn't spin off its access! I know what one, two, three, four, five, six—

count 'em: six!—African-Americans did to my son at two-thirty in the morning at the corner of Barrow and Greenwich. They get off (Walter was a faggot after all!) and I don't even get to say "nigger!" I know there's evil. I'm not so sure there's any justice.

MARGARET: I wish I could comfort you.

KATHARINE: I wish you could, too . . . . .

MARGARET: May I put my arm around you?

KATHARINE: I'd rather you wouldn't.

Margaret puts her arm around her.

MARGARET: You don't have to say anything. Sshh! Sshh! I'm not going to say anything.

KATHARINE: Thank you for that, at least.

MARGARET: You're not alone, Kitty. I'm here. Another person, another woman, is here. Right here. Breathing the same air. Riding the same train. Looking out the window at the same timeless landscape. You are not alone. Even in your agony.

KATHARINE: Thank you.

MARGARET: I love you. I love you very much. "Offamof."

KATHARINE: What?

MARGARET: "Offamof."

KATHARINE: Oh, yeah. "Offamof!"

Ganesha steps forward to inform the audience that, at the same time Margaret and Katharine are watching the scenery slide past their train, Katharine's husband is dying in a car accident. Katharine will not learn of his death until they return home.

And now Ganesha is a guide, Mr. Tandu, who welcomes them to his village. He is going to take them to a puppet show.

Scene 3

Mr. Tandu hands Katharine a book. "In India we participate in theater." Katharine's part is to read the narration for the puppet show they are watching, the story of how Ganesha got the head of an elephant. The narration tells of how Shiva, angry that Ganesha barred the way to Shiva's wife, Parvati, attacked Ganesha and cut off his head.

But something has happened during the show. While Margaret has been enjoying the performance as a tale, Katharine has begun to see it on a different level. The puppets are being manipulated by the Man, playing Walter. The death of Ganesha she views as the death of her son. The Man uses language Walter used earlier in talking about the assault that killed him.

MAN: I stayed on my feet a remarkably long time, Mama. I was sort of proud of me.

KATHARINE *(looking back to the book):* Where does it say that?

MAN: "Mother, see how I serve you."

KATHARINE: He's not following the script.

GANESHA: And down he fell.

KATHARINE: Why me, Mr. Tandu?

GANESHA: Again, why not you, Mrs. Brynne? As the boy lay dying, Shiva realized what he had done.

KATHARINE: Shiva, not I! *(She abruptly stands up.)*

MARGARET: Where are you going?

GANESHA: You must hear the story to its end, Mrs. Brynne.

KATHARINE: I know how it ends. In a New York hospital. Twenty minutes before I got there.

GANESHA: No, it ends in reconciliation, renewal and rebirth.

KATHARINE: Tell it to Mrs. Civil.

She hands the playbook to Tandu and goes.

MARGARET: I think your story upset Mrs. Brynne.

GANESHA: Perhaps she needed upsetting, Mrs. Civil.

Mr. Tandu (Ganesha) hands Margaret the book, and they continue. Shiva begs Parvati's pardon. Parvati says she will forgive, but " . . . my son must regain his life, and he must have an honorable status among you." Shiva sends a follower out to fetch back the head of the first living creature he encounters. That head turns out to belong to a one-tusked elephant. Shiva has it fixed onto the boy's body, brings him back to life and makes Ganesha the chief of all of his ganas and "worthy of worship forever."

Margaret declines the offer of another story. Her friend Katharine seemed upset by this one. Perhaps it's because it dealt with the death of a son. She leaves to find Katharine, as Mr. Tandu and the puppeteer muse on the oddness of these ladies and the culture from which they come.

We pick up on Margaret and Katharine as they make their ways through the streets and are privy to their private thoughts. Katharine has had her fill of India. The puppet-show tale of Ganesha only made her more aware of the gulf between the Indian myth and her life. Parvati had her son reborn and returned to her; Katharine lost hers. Parvati was honored, her forgiveness was sought; the men who murdered Katharine's son didn't ask for forgiveness, and she hasn't been honored. "I have my anger and nothing more. No love. No love at all."

Margaret is struck afresh by how dependent she's become on her husband. Travelling with Katharine has been harder than she'd anticipated, hard because part of her has wanted to open up about Gabriel. "It would have been such a tiny leap across that void between two people. 'I lost a son too, Kitty.' Six little words, and I couldn't do it. 'I lost a son too, Kitty.' Kitty!"

Katharine is walking with a young Indian boy (played by Ganesha). Margaret has started talking to a Dutch tourist (played by the Man). Their conversations play in counterpoint. Katharine and the boy are getting along, though they don't understand each other. Margaret is supplying most of the conversation with the tourist, talking about a Rembrandt painting she loves called "Woman Bathing." (*"A bolt of blue fabric is rolled across the white floor of the stage. It is a river.")* Margaret and Katharine end up on opposite sides of the river. They wave to each other. Katharine is very taken by the boy and begins tickling him. Margaret remembers that the last time she stood in front of the Rembrandt (which is in the National Gallery in London) she overheard an older man say to a younger female companion, "No one wants me anymore. I've had my day. It's gone now." What particularly upset her was that he said it not caring that he was being overheard by Margaret. Margaret heads back to the hotel for drinks with the manager. Katharine waves but prefers to stay for now with the boy. Time passes. He lies with his head in her lap.

KATHARINE: My little brown *bambino.* My nutmeg *Gesu.* What color is your skin? Coffee? That's not right either. What color is mine? Not white. Where do words come from? What do they mean?

GANESHA: Walter.

KATHARINE: What? I thought you said "Walter."

GANESHA: Walter.

KATHARINE: You did! You did say "Walter."

GANESHA: Walter.

KATHARINE: Walter must be a word in Hindi, then! Yes? Tell me, what does it mean, Walter?

GANESHA *(laughing merrily):* Walter! Walter!

He suddenly throws his arms around her and holds her tight.

KATHARINE: Does it mean "laughter?" It means something joyful! Something good. It must! Walter! Walter! (*She puts her hands to her mouth and calls across the lake.*) Walter! Walter!

There is an echo. "Walter! Walter!" There is a silence as the echo dies away.

It's gone.

GANESHA: Why have you stopped smiling?

She kisses him fiercely.

KATHARINE: Stay this way forever. When you grow up, I won't like you. I will hate you and fear you because of the color of your skin—just as I hated and feared my son because he loved men. I won't tell you this to your face, but you will know it, just as he did, and it will sicken and diminish us both.

GANESHA: Why are you looking at me so intently? What do you want to see?

KATHARINE: I came here to heal, but I can't forgive myself. Maybe if I shout out the names of my fear and hatred of you across this holy river they will vanish, too, just as "Walter" did. Faggot. Queer. The words keep sticking.

And she and the boy shout out "Faggot! Queer!" The echoes float back. She escalates the intensity with which she shouts out these epithets, finally building to the point where she can shout out "NIGGER!" She breaks down as the echoes continue.

Zoe Caldwell (Katharine Brynne), Dominic Cuskern (Ganesha), Fisher Stevens (Man) and Francis Sternhagen (Margaret Civil) in *A Perfect Ganesh*

She asks for Walter to forgive her. Now Ganesha cradles her as Walter (played by the Man) appears, waves to Katharine, blows her a kiss, and then disappears. "Foolish woman," says Ganesha. "You were holding a god in your arms." Another transition: Ganesha is now a Boatman. Margaret enters, calling, "We're coming!" accompanied by a Guide (played by the Man).

Scene 4

Margaret, Katharine and the Guide, an American expatriate named Norman Tennyson, are on the Ganges River in a small skiff piloted by Ganesha. As they sail through the mist of early morning, Tennyson tells them that Varanasi, the city they are in, is a particularly holy place and that to die there is a guarantee of going straight to heaven. He tells them about the ghats—"steps which lead down to the river, from which pilgrims make their sin-cleansing dip in the Ganges." There are a hundred of these. Two of them are burning ghats, where bodies are cremated. Katharine listens attentively, but Margaret is distracted by the fact that their boat keeps bumping into dead things—a rat, a cow, a baby. This is too much for her.

MARGARET: Please, can we get home?

KATHARINE: I thought I would be more appalled by all this.

MAN: Thought or hoped? Some people come to Varanasi to find their hearts have completely hardened. It's a terrible realization.

MARGARET: What are we supposed to do? I can't accept all this. My heart and mind would break if I did. And yet I must. I know it.

KATHARINE: Everything in and on this river seems inevitable and right. Something dead, floating there.

MARGARET: It's a dog.

KATHARINE: That old woman with the sagging breasts bathing herself oblivious to us.

MARGARET: She's lovely.

KATHARINE: Even us in our Burberry raincoats. We all have a place here. Nothing is right, nothing is wrong. Allow. Accept. Be.

MARGARET: Yes.

They alight from the skiff. The women are going to go shopping. Katharine is hoping to find a figure of Ganesha that meets her needs. She has bought a number of them, but she's still looking for the right one: "A perfect Ganesh."

Scene 5

In the hotel room, Margaret is showing Katharine the lump on her breast. No, Margaret doesn't want to cut the trip short. She still wants to see the Taj Mahal. She'll tend to her breast when she gets back. Margaret thanks Katharine for confiding in her. Katharine doesn't know if she'll tell her husband. "It would give him one more reason to work late." His biggest reason has been to visit the divorced girlfriend he's set up in a condo. Margaret is not supposed to know about her. "What happens to women? Who are we? What are we supposed to do? What are we supposed to be? Men still have all the marbles. All we have are our children, and sooner or later we lose them."

From their balcony, they look down on a leper (played by the Man). Katharine hasn't been able to put her intention into action. To go down to a leper, to hold him, to kiss him on the lips, "as I could never kiss my son for fear of terrifying him how much I loved him." Yesterday she tried but couldn't manage it. Instead, she gave the leper 50 rupees and one of the figures she'd purchased. The gesture gave her no peace (though the man was able to eat the best meal of his life). Katharine feels the trip was a failure. "You're too hard on yourself," says Margaret. "You can't save the world." "I can't even save myself," admits Katharine. Nor has she been successful in finding her perfect Ganesh, though, as Ganesha now states, all are perfect, and he displays a rich assortment of figures of various sizes and made of various materials. Katharine gives Margaret one of her favorite figures. Margaret and Katharine embrace and kiss. They will visit the Taj Mahal and return home.

Scene 6

And now they are at the Taj Mahal, completely dazzled. "Do you think this is why we exist?" says Margaret. "To create this?" As they share this vision of paradise, *"Ganesha draws a filmy gauze drape across the stage. It is the first time the stage has been 'closed' the entire evening."*

Ganesha tells of the women's return and being met at the airport with the news of the death of Katharine's husband. "Vacations can end abruptly like this," says Ganesha. "Trips have a way of going on. Mrs. Civil and Mrs. Brynne's visit to India was of the second variety."

He pulls the gauze back again. We now have a view of the two ladies' Connecticut bedrooms. As Margaret gets into one of the twin beds on her side of the stage (the other is occupied by her husband Alan), she sees a postcard on her pillow that Alan (played by the Man) has left for her. It came from India while she was gone. Alan says he's glad she's back and turns out his light.

Margaret phones Katharine and tells her about the postcard. Addressed to both of them, it's from Ben, one half of the gay couple they met on the balcony of the hotel. Margaret reads its message.

MARGARET: "Dear Girls, (all right, *ladies!*) welcome home! Hope you had a wonderful trip and didn't have to use that police whistle again. Did you see the Taj Mahal? Didn't you die just a little? Thanks for all your kindness. Harry is still in the hospital here but doing well. We're both hanging in there. What else are you gonna do? Love, Ben." Guess who the postcard's of? Your favorite, Ganesha. A perfect Ganesh. I'll bring it over tomorrow. Are you sure you're okay?

KATHARINE: I'm fine.

MARGARET: I love you.

KATHARINE: Thank you.

MARGARET: You're supposed to say, "I love you, too."

KATHARINE: I love you, too, Margaret.

MARGARET: Good night, Kitty.

KATHARINE: Good night.

They hang up. They each are sitting on the edge of their beds. Katharine begins to sing/hum "Blow the Wind Southerly." The Man has begun to snore. Margaret looks at him, then at the postcard and begins to sing/hum "Swing Low, Sweet Chariot." At exactly the same time, i.e., simultaneously, the two women get into bed and under the covers. Ganesha appears between them. He takes off his elephant's head. His face is gilded, and he is revealed as a handsome man. He bends over Margaret and kisses her. She stops singing and sleeps. Then he bends over Katharine and kisses her. She, too, stops singing and sleeps.

Ganesha sings "Good Night, Ladies" to them, then pulls the curtain closed and bids us goodnight and disappears. Alan is still snoring. *Curtain.*

THE MADNESS OF GEORGE III

A Play in Two Acts

BY ALAN BENNETT

Cast and credits appear on page 452

ALAN BENNETT was born at Armley, Leeds, May 9, 1934 and was educated at Leeds Modern School and Exeter College, Oxford. As an actor, he took his first bows in the Oxford Theater Group's revue Better Late *at the Edinburgh Festival in August 1959 and again at Edinburgh in 1960 in the revue* Beyond the Fringe *of which, like the other members of its cast, Bennett was co-author. This hit show took him as a performer to his first professional appearance in London in 1961 and to New York October 27, 1962 for its 667-performance Broadway run and a special New York Drama Critics Circle citation.*

Bennett's acting career continued in the London theater, and his playwriting blossomed with Forty Years On *(October 1968 at London's Apollo Theater with Bennett in the role of Tempest). His other works for the stage have included* Getting On, Habeas Corpus *(1973 in London; November 25, 1975 on Broadway for 95 performances),* The Old Country, Enjoy, Kafka's Dick, Single Spies: An Englishman Abroad *and National Theater productions of* A Question of Attribution *(1988) and an adaptation of Kenneth Grahame's* The Wind in the Willows *(1990, 1991 and 1993).*

Bennett's The Madness of George III *opened at the National on November 28, 1991 with Nigel Hawthorne creating the title role, in a production which was remounted for an American tour which included the Brooklyn Academy of Music Sep-*

tember 23, 1933 for a limited 17-performance engagement, winning its author his first Best Play citation. In addition to his stage writings and appearances, Bennett has written extensively for the large and small screens in England, where he continues to reside.

The following synopsis of The Madness of George III *is based on the version performed on tour in the U.S. An ending to the final Windsor scene in the published version, transporting the action in imagination to the 20th century and revealing that George III was suffering from a metabolic disorder called porphyria (a name derived from the color of diseased urine) which recurred later in his life, was cut on tour and is not included in our synopsis.*

Time: 1788-89

ACT I

Windsor

SYNOPSIS: At a ceremony introducing King George III, Queen Charlotte, the Prince of Wales and Duke of York, government members Pitt and Dundas, the Lord Chancellor, Thurlow, and a number of pages and equerries, the King is assaulted by a woman with a grievance. The King, unhurt, urges leniency on those who hustle her away.

PRINCE OF WALES: I rejoice, papa, that you are unharmed.

QUEEN: The son rejoices. The Prince of Wales rejoices. Faugh!

DUKE OF YORK: Me too, pa. God Save the King and so on.

QUEEN *(embracing him but looking at the Prince of Wales):* And he is fatter. Always fatter.

KING: Fatter because he is not doing, what, what? Do you know England, sir?

PRINCE OF WALES: I think so, sir.

KING: You know Brighton, Bath—yes, but do you know its mills and manufactories? Do you know its farms? Because I do.

There are subdued groans from the two brothers, who have had this lecture before.

I have made them my special study. I've written pamphlets on agriculture.

DUKE OF YORK: Yes, sir.

KING: Pigs, what.

PRINCE OF WALES: Yes, father.

KING: Stock. Good husbandry. Do you know what they call me?

PRINCE OF WALES: What do they call you, father?

KING: Farmer George. And do you know what that is?

PRINCE OF WALES: Impertinence?

KING: No, sir. Love.
QUEEN: Affection.
KING: It is admiration, sir.
QUEEN: Respect.
KING: What are your hobbies, sir?
PRINCE OF WALES: Hobbies?
QUEEN: Fashion
KING: Furniture. Do you know what mine are? Learning. Astronomy.
QUEEN: The heavens are at his fingertips.
KING: It is not good, sir, this idleness. That is why you are fat. Do not be fat, sir. Fight it! Fight it!

The King dismisses his sons and turns to speak to William Pitt, "*a long, unbending figure in early middle age.*" The King reminds his Prime Minister that their destinies are linked. The King chose Pitt for the office, and "Anything happens to me you'll be out, what, what, and Mr. Fox will be in." Thurlow comes in to report that they plan to examine the poor woman who attacked the King to see if she's mad.

As the King is helped with taking off his coat, there is a moment when his speech is impeded, but it passes.

Westminster

Church bells have been ringing to celebrate the King's escape from danger, while Burke, Sheridan and Fox—Pitt's Whig opponents—enter, grudgingly admitting that they wouldn't want anything to happen to the King, but . . . The Royal Family, with 15 children, is popular, Fox admits, and it's not this individual King he loathes, it's the idea of royalty itself: "And if a few ramshackle colonists in America can send him packing, why can't we?" In the meantime, Fox intends to send himself packing, with his mistress, on a year's trip to get away from the British political arena dominated by Pitt and his Tories.

Windsor

Pitt enters carrying a dispatch box for the King to read and sign at a portable desk. An equerry, Captain Fitzroy, instructs a new equerry, Greville, in his duties: "His Majesty does nothing by halves. If he is fond of a thing, be it Handel or mutton and potatoes, by God he will have it whenever occasion permits. His mode of life is simple, and he is harnessed to routine." The job is not "the liveliest of situations," Fitzroy admits.

The King advises Pitt that he should marry and have children. Then he astonishes Pitt with his detailed knowledge of the family connections of a minor appointment.

KING: What's happened to Fox?
PITT: He's abroad at present, sir.

Pictured here is Nigel Hawthorne in the title role of *The Madness of George III* before (above, with Selina Cadell as Queen Charlotte) and during (*below,* with Clive Merrison as Dr. Willis) his "madness" brought on by an illness supposed to be porphyria

KING: We must hope he stays there. Such a dodger. And too many ideas. Not like you, Mr. Pitt. You don't have ideas. Well, you have one big idea: balancing the books. And a very good idea to have, what, what? The best. And one with which I absolutely agree, as I agree with you, Mr. Pitt, on everything apart from the place we mustn't mention.

He gives Pitt a sidelong look. Pitt says nothing.

We didn't see eye to eye over that, but we agreed to draw a veil over it. And I'm only mentioning it now just to show that I haven't mentioned it. You know where I mean, what?

PITT: Yes, sir.

KING: The colonies.

PITT: They're now called the United States, sir.

KING: Are they? Goodness me! Well, I haven't mentioned them. I prefer not to, whatever they're called. The United States.

There is a momentary hesitation on the words "United States," as if the King finds them difficult to articulate. Noted by the pages and the equerries and also by Pitt, it quickly passes.

Pitt advises His Majesty to take neither the colonies' loss nor the opposition of the Whigs personally. He and the King then exit, but the King returns almost immediately in his dressing gown and is conducted by the Queen's Mistress of the Robes, Lady Pembroke (the Duke of Marlborough's daughter), into the presence of the Queen, who is in bed, knitting. Their marital relationship is friendly as well as intimate, calling each other "Mr. King" and "Mrs. King."

The King complains of feeling unwell, as though something he ate at supper was disagreeing with him. He is speaking of Pitt to the Queen—"Cold fish, Pitt. Never smiles. Works though, oh yes. Never stops. Drinks, they say. But then they all drink. His father went mad. Doesn't show any sign of that."—when he is seized with a sharp pain in the stomach and cries out. The doctor—Sir George Baker—is summoned, but by the time he arrives and discusses protocol with Greville (Can he ask the King direct questions in order to determine what's wrong with him?) the King is feeling much better and complains only about the laxative Baker sent over. He ignored instructions, greatly overdosed himself and suffered the consequences.

Baker takes the King's pulse and finds it too rapid, suggests His Majesty is working too hard. The King and Queen decide to take a holiday in a fashionable watering place, Cheltonham.

Westminster

Pitt, Dundas and Thurlow hear a report from Fitzroy, Greville and Baker on His Majesty's situation and condition. The King's behavior at Cheltonham has seemed odd: rising at the crack of dawn and asking to be taken on a tour of the cathedral, overdoing the drinking of the therapeutic waters. Pitt dismisses this as normal holiday behavior, but Baker adds that he believes the King to be really ill with colic, sweats, pains in the legs—possibly gout or rheumatism.

After the doctor and attendants exit, Pitt comments that he doesn't believe the King is really ill.

PITT: Baker makes out he is so that when in due course he recovers, Baker gets the credit. I've done the same myself. Before we came in I said the nation was sick, deliberately predicted national bankruptcy, so that when the economy recovered, prosperity was put down to me. No, he is not ill.

THURLOW: Well, I don't like it. Though there was a mysterious illness once before, in your father's time. Government was at a standstill.

DUNDAS: It was of no consequence.

THURLOW: It was of no consequence because he recovered.

PITT: It was of no consequence because the Prince of Wales was then a child of three. It was of no consequence because Mr. Fox and his friends were not perched in the rafters waiting to come in. We consider ourselves blessed in our constitution. We tell ourselves our Parliament is the envy of the world. But we live in the health and well-being of the Sovereign as much as any vizier does the Sultan.

THURLOW: And the Sultan orders it better. He has his son and heir strangled.

Carlton House

Fitzroy is reporting on the King's condition to the Prince of Wales, his physician Dr. Richard Warren, the Duke of York, Sheridan and Burke. Dr. Warren takes a grave view of the King's symptoms, which might lead to madness or death. They consider recalling Fox from his vacation but decide it might be unseemly to appear too eager for change. The Prince muses, "A son who must — reluctantly — shoulder the responsibilities of a sick—who knows, possibly a dying—father—that is hardly self-seeking . . . . . A necessary duty; a task unshirked. No joy in it. No joy at all. Windsor would have to be entirely altered, of course. It's impossible as it is."

Windsor

At 4 a.m. the King decides it's time to get up and grows angry at being unattended. The pages Papandiek, Fortnum and Braun try to pacify and dress him, but the clothes cause his skin to itch and burn. The Queen, Lady Pembroke, Greville and Dr. Baker come in and see that the King is not himself but is being driven by a series of impulses, one of which causes him to embrace and kiss Lady Pembroke (the Queen advises her to ignore this). The pages exit, but Fortnum soon returns with a glass chamber pot which he exhibits to everyone, showing that the King's urine is dark blue, nearly purple.

Baker, who is getting ready to bleed the King, declares, "Whether a man's water is blue or not is neither here nor there." Fitzroy adds, "Well, there's one blessing. At least he's stopped all the what-whatting."

Windsor

Pitt is informed by Dundas that Fox is on his way back to Parliament, which will probably be recalled. Pitt contemplates telling the King that he must not be ill, he is leaving important papers unsigned and endangering the government: "That is the best medicine."

Thurlow comes in with the news that the stock market is falling. Baker, ejected from the sick room by an angry King, admits to the others that he has sold some of his stocks, which may have started a rumor, i.e. that he, Baker, the King's doctor, believes that the King is dying.

The pages come in with the document-signing equipment, followed by the King, "*legs bandaged and moving very slowly.*"

KING *(peering about him)*: Mr. Pitt? Mr. Pitt? You see us suddenly an old man.

GREVILLE: Will Your Majesty not sit down?

Fitzroy heaves a sigh of disapproval.

KING: The King never sits when seeing his ministers. Sits, no. Shits though, yes. They say I soiled my small clothes this morning. It is not true. Or it may be true. My flesh is on fire. I must quench it whatever way comes to hand. Dundas, yes? *(Peers.)*

DUNDAS: Your Majesty.

KING: The Scots one. Thurlow?

THURLOW: Your Majesty.

KING: Father was Rector of Ashfield. Brother's Bishop of Durham. Shaggy fellow. Yes. Why do you look at me? Do not look at me. I am the King. Speak, speak.

PITT: Perhaps I can lay before Your Majesty some of the more urgent papers awaiting Your Majesty's signature.

KING *(motions for them)*: Mr. Pitt, I do not see so well. There is not mist here?

PITT: No, sir.

KING: Oh, my aching brain. What is this? *(Looking at the paper.)* America, is it?

PITT: No, sir. It is a warrant for the most urgent expenditure. I beg Your Majesty to sign it.

KING: America is not to be spoken of, is that it?

PITT: For your own peace of mind, sir. But it is not America. It is a warrant for—

KING: Peace of mind! I have no peace of mind. I have had no peace of mind since we lost America. Forests, old as the world itself, meadows, plains, strange delicate flowers, immense solitudes. And all nature new to art. All ours. Mine. Gone. A paradise lost. The trumpet of sedition has sounded. We have lost America. Soon we shall lose India, the Indies, Ireland even, our feathers plucked one by one, this island reduced to itself alone, a great state mouldered into rottenness and decay. And they will lay it at my door. What is this I am reading? It *is* America. The words fly ahead of me. I cannot catch them in the mist.

PITT: If Your Majesty would trust me, it would assist your ministers immeasurably if Your Majesty would just sign the warrants. It is most urgent, I assure you.

KING: But I have to read them. I do not sign anything I do not read. I might be signing my own deposition. Is that why you are gathered?

THURLOW: No, sir. We are your loyal servants, sir. In your present frame of mind …

KING: What do you know of my mind? Or its frame? Something is shaking the frame; shaking the mind out of its frame. I am not going out of my mind; my mind is going out of me.

The King begins to scratch himself or even to take off some of his clothes.

Pitt begs the King to sign his papers, but the King refuses and departs. Pitt takes one of his recurrent swigs from his hip flask, declares that he doesn't believe the King is really mad and plans to exhibit him to the public in some manageable way so that they will see he is still able to reign.

Windsor

The King—looking somewhat disheveled, with visible body sores—and Queen are attending a Handel concert at court in the presence of their courtiers. After the music stops, the King goes down the lined-up company to acknowledge them, ordering Fitzroy to kick his leg to prove that he has no pain there so his illness can't be the gout as Baker supposes. When the King comes to the Prince of Wales, the Prince introduces him to Dr. Warren, his personal physician.

KING: He is personal physician to half of London. Well, you are not my physician, sir. No man can serve two masters.

WARREN: I am a servant of humanity, sir.

KING: Yes, and how much does humanity pay you? How much does humanity pay him, eh, Greville? You should tell your patient the Prince that he is too fat. Don't slouch, sir. Well, I am old and infirm. I shall not trouble you long.

PRINCE OF WALES: I wish you good health, father.

KING: Wish me, wish me? You wish me death, you plump little partridge.

PRINCE OF WALES: Hush, sir.

KING: Hush? Hush? You dare to keep the King of England from speaking his mind?

The King turns away from the Prince, then suddenly turns back and launches himself on him; there is turmoil as King and Prince fall struggling to the floor, the King's hands at the Prince's neck.

Greville and the pages pull the King to his feet and take him away, as the Queen declares to her son, "We know your game. Monster!" The Prince's doctor, Warren, comments, "Wholly demented, sir. A palsy of the brain." The Prince observes to Pitt that it won't be long now before they will be sharing the burdens of government. The court has separated into two factions—Whigs and Tories—with the Prince in the middle, resolved now to take over his sick father's responsibilities and to place Warren side by side with Baker in taking care of the King, even hinting that he might find it necessary to separate the Queen from the patient. Pitt objects, demanding that the government ministers exercise the right of approval on any measures taken and adding, "I must point out, sir, that His Majesty has frequently expressed his desire never to be separated from the Queen." The Prince replies, "She puts wrong ideas into his head" and is resolved to see them separated, as he and the Duke of York exit with their followers. The Pitt contingent leaves shortly afterwards.

The King enters, followed by the Queen, Lady Pembroke and attendants. The King is under the delusion that the water level is rising and they must rescue the children, including little Octavius, one of their offspring who has died.

QUEEN: Hush, sir, you are talking.

KING: I know I am talking. Do not tell me I talk. I follow my words. I run after them. I am dragged at locution's tail. This ceaseless discourse precedes me wherever I go. Telling me I talk! I have to talk in order to keep up with my thoughts. I thought he had taken you.

QUEEN: Who, sir?

KING: The other George. The fat one. You were not in my bed. I thought you had deceived me with the son.

QUEEN: Sir!

KING: Still, Elizabeth comes to my bed, don't you Elizabeth?

He embraces Lady Pembroke and clasps her to him. This is too much for the Queen.

QUEEN: Leave us! Leave us. You too, Elizabeth. And you, and you. All of you, out, all of you, out.

All leave, still, even though the King is a distracted wreck, bowing and backwards.

Now talk away.

KING: Tell me, which of us do you prefer? He sneaks into your bed, I know. Well, do not flatter yourself, madam. He has many women. You are just one and not even the first. Fancy, his mother is not even the first of the son's women, think of that. The fat hands. That young belly. Those plump thighs. The harlot's delight.

QUEEN: Be *still,* sir. For pity's sake. Listen, George. Hear me.

She holds his mouth closed to stop his babble.

Do you think you are mad?

KING: I don't know. I don't know. Madness isn't such torment. Madness is not half-blind. Madmen can stand. They skip! They dance! And I talk. I talk. I hear the words so I have to speak them. I have to empty my head of the words. *Something* has happened. *Something* is not right. Oh, Charlotte.

Fitzroy comes in with Lady Pembroke, interrupting. The Prince of Wales has issued orders that the Queen and the contents of her apartment be moved—in fact her belongings have already been transferred. The now-docile King is escorted away by Fitzroy. The Prince enters with Dr. Warren and confirms his orders to the Queen: "While you are together there will be no peace . . . . . In his current frame of mind

His Majesty does not seem to care for you. His affections do not that way tend." The Queen calls, "Fiend! Monster!" at the Prince and the doctor as they depart.

Westminster

Drs. Baker and Warren confer with a third, Dr. Lucas Pepys, on the King's condition. Pepys is an expert on "the anfractuosities of the human understanding." Asserting that "I've always found the stool more eloquent than the pulse," Pepys requests a sample of the King's. The doctors, joined by Thurlow, discuss the King's delusion that London is being flooded with rising water. They recommend various remedies, finally agreeing that he must be blistered "to draw the humors from the brain."

Windsor

Dr. Warren and his blistering equipment are ready when the King enters, sees it, tries to flee but is overwhelmed by the pages and forced to submit, bound and helpless, to having heated cups pressed against his already agonizingly sensitive skin.

Carlton House

The Prince, the Duke, Sheridan and Burke are joined by Fox, who has returned from his vacation and learns that the King, while still alive, is no better. The Prince adds, "Nor likely to be, now that Warren's on the case."

The Whig faction is planning to take over the government by winning a few undecided seats—meanwhile, they must be patient and not seem overeager. As for Pitt, Fox says, "We must hustle him out, and once out he'll never crawl back in."

Westminster

Dundas and Thurlow promise an appointment to Sir Selby Markham's son-in-law in order to pin down Sir Selby's vote after next week's debate. Sir Boothby Skrymshir comes in with his nephew with a similar request and is reassured, for the same reason (and Sir Boothby controls three other votes beside his own). Pitt enters after the supplicants leave and expresses his own frustration.

PITT: . . . If only he could sign his name.

THURLOW: We can delay no longer. As Lord Chancellor, I must draw up a bill appointing the Prince of Wales Regent. There is no alternative.

PITT: Very well, but take your time.

DUNDAS: For all our sakes. Once it's passed we will be out of a job.

PITT: Meanwhile, before the vote of confidence, Parliament should examine the doctors.

THURLOW: Well then, you will lose the vote. They'll say the King is mad.

PITT: He is not mad. I will not have that word used.

THURLOW: In the House, no—but here, between ourselves, Goddammit.

PITT: Here, or in the House, or anywhere. I do not admit the thought.

THURLOW: Then why let the physicians be examined? They will all agree.

PITT: Do you think so? Three doctors, each with his reputation to make, and they will all say the same thing? What if they were lawyers?

THURLOW: Oh, very well. *(Going.)* But he is mad, dammit.

DUNDAS: When your father was ill, what form did it take?

PITT: Why? What has that got to do with it? My father was mad, that was the form it took. *(Pause.)* But not this form. Not this form at all.

Windsor

Fitzroy is reporting to Pitt on the King's condition—"He talks filth, the slops of his mind swilling over"—when the King himself enters with the pages, Greville and the writing kit. The King tries to talk to Pitt but keeps getting stuck on a syllable or a word, repeated like a broken record. Greville advises Pitt to forget protocol and interrupt His Majesty, it's the only way of reaching him.

PITT: I saw Your Majesty last week. I left some urgent papers.

KING: Yes. Remember, remember. Remember you. Little boy. Father old. Mad once. Not mad, though, me. Not mad-mad-mad-mad. Madjesty majesty. Majust just nerves nerves nerves sss.

He hisses into silence, but every silence costs him an immense effort, shaken as he is by unspoken speech.

PITT: Yes, sir. It will pass.

Pitt hands the King a paper, but it goes unread and unremarked.

Parliament resumes tomorrow, sir.

KING: Parliament, Parliament . . . Do nothing nothing nothing nothing Pitt Pitt Pitt do—nothing nothing. I am not mad mad mad . . . Can't see can't see mist mist missed Queen missed her, oh missed her Queen, gone, gone, gone . . .

PITT: The doctors thought it best, sir.

KING *(instantly more agitated).* Doc doc doc doctors doctorturers doctormentors doctalk doctalk talk talk talk talk . . .

The King is howling helplessly, and he seizes Greville's hand and puts it over his mouth. He is perhaps shitting himself too, because as Greville helps him out of the room the King clutches his dressing-gown behind him, a despairing and incontinent wretch.

Westminster

Addressing the House, Pitt tells of his visit to His Majesty and his symptoms, which Pitt considers minor. The doctors are to be questioned, he says. Fox tries to bring up the subject of the succession but is shouted down.

Westminster

Dr. Warren tells a committee chaired by Pitt, with Dundas, Fox, Burke and Sheridan present, that he believes the King is suffering from incurable delerium. Drs. Baker and Pepys agree. But the doctors under questioning begin disagreeing about the details of the King's symptoms and finally on the nature of the disease itself and the chances for a cure.

When Parliament's vote takes place, the Tories have a majority of 30. Instead of being gratified, Pitt observes, "Not enough. I saw the King again this afternoon. He did not know me. I was mistaken. He is mad. The next vote will be not so easy. We are finished."

Windsor

Acting on information from Lady Pembroke, Pitt calls in another physician, Dr. Willis, who cured Lady Pembroke's mother-in-law and is known for "particular skill in the treatment of intellectual maladies." Willis has studied the King's symptoms and is at a loss to identify the disease—he's never seen anything like it before. But he assures Pitt, "Oh, I can cure him. I'm just not sure what from." Willis will require total authority over the King and access to him at all times.

The Queen comes in to assure the new doctor that the King is not mad, and Willis assures her in turn that he will cure the King. Greville enters after the Queen leaves and in his turn is informed that Willis will begin his cure by exercising the King like a horse to break his royal rigidity, and that the doctor has no intention of being handicapped by the observance of any protocol.

The King enters, talking non-stop about the sea and its disappointing color, while circling Willis and examining him. *"His legs are bandaged, and a stained cloth is tied round his middle like a nappy. Nevertheless he is still wearing the ribbon of the Garter."* Willis informs the King unceremoniously that he has a hospital in Lincolnshire, that he has come "to alleviate some of the inconveniences from which Your Majesty suffers." The doctor begins by taking hold of the King's shoulder—to the consternation of pages and equerries—and then making him fall to the floor and remain sitting there while Willis talks to him.

WILLIS: You can control your utterance, sir, if you would. I believe you can be well if only you will.

KING: Do not look at me. I am not one of your farmers.

WILLIS: Your Majesty must behave, or endeavor to do so.

KING: *(still struggling):* Must, must? Whose must? Your must or my must? No must. Get away from me, you scabby bumsucker.

PAPANDIEK: Easy, sir, easy.

KING: *(as they try to get him up):* No, no. Leave me, boys. Let me sit upon the ground and tell . . . tell-tell-tell-tell . . . tell this lump-headed fool to shut his gob box. You spunk-splasher, you Lincolnshire lickfingers . . . . .

The pages attempt to pacify the King, to no avail. Willis decides that the time has come to take complete charge.

Willis opens the door, and three of his servants, grim-faced and in leather aprons, wheel in the restraining chair, a wooden contraption with clamps for the arms and legs and a band for the head. The sight of the restraining chair momentarily silences the King.

KING: When felons were induced to talk they were first shown the instrument of their torture. The King is shown the instrument of his to induce him not to talk. Well, I won't, I won't. Not for you and all your ding boys.

The King begins abusing them again, with a torrent of obscenity, as, quietly at first, but growing louder as the scene comes to its climax, we hear Handel's Coronation Anthem, Zadok the Priest. *One servant thrusts aside the protesting pages while the other two lift the King up and amid the ensuing pandemonium manhandle him into the restraining chair.*

You clap-ridden shit-sack. See them off, boys! See them off! *(As he is hauled to the chair.)* Goddam you, I'll have you all thrashed for this! Horse-whipped. Lie off, you rascals. Lie off.

FITZROY: This is unseemly, sir. Who are these bully boys?

GREVILLE: You have no business, sir. His Majesty is ill.

FITZROY: I must inform His Royal Highness. This is a scandal.

GREVILLE: Call off your dogs, sir. Who are these barkers?

WILLIS: If the King refuses food he will be restrained. If he claims to have no appetite he will be restrained. If he swears and indulges in meaningless discourse he will be restrained. If he throws off his bedclothes, tears away his bandages, scratches at his sores, and if he does not strive every day and always towards his own recovery, then he must be restrained.

Willis's men stand back from the King, and we see that he has been strapped into the chair, feet and arms clamped, his head held rigid by a band round his forehead.

KING *(howling):* I am the King of England.

WILLIS: No, sir. You are the patient.

The Coronation Anthem finally reaches its climax and bursts forth in the chorus of Zadok the Priest, *as the King struggles, howling, in the chair, with Willis's men lined up behind him. Fortnum slips in with the chamber pot. He holds it up for examination by the unheeding Fitzroy, his shadow big upon the wall, the music still at full volume as the curtain falls.*

ACT II

Windsor

Drs. Warren and Baker are concerned about Dr. Willis—who now resides here at Windsor, while the others must travel out every day—dominating the treatment of the King.

When Willis enters with a daily report stating that the King had a good night's sleep, the others refuse to issue it. Instead, they once again prescribe purging, emetic and blistering. Warren recommends a change of scene to the Palace of Kew. Willis doesn't object, though he asserts, "I would have him in Lincolnshire if I had my way. He would be on the mend there in no time."

The King is brought in for a session of blistering administered by Braun, which is sheer torture. Willis calls a halt to this cruel treatment, aware that this will cause the King to be thankful to him and possibly obey him. The King babbles on about America and about Lady Pembroke's charms, two subjects which—Willis reminds him—are forbidden to him. Willis lays down the law to his patient: if the King will make an effort to control himself to the point of showing some improvement, he may even be granted a visit from the Queen at Kew. But if he continues to be unruly, he will be restrained—a point which Willis makes clear by having the attendants fit the King into a straitwaistcoat.

Carlton House

The Prince of Wales's entourage watches him having his portrait painted while they discuss the political situation. Sheridan warns that even if the Regency is declared by Parliament, Pitt will take steps to restrict the Prince's ability to hand out appointments to his followers.

PRINCE OF WALES: But if I can't give anyone jobs, who will support me anyway?

SHERIDAN: That's the purpose of it. To tie your hands.

PRINCE OF WALES: Tie my hands?

DUKE OF YORK: I say, that's not fair. Can the fellow do that?

BURKE: It's hard to say what he can and can't do. There is no exact precedent. Of course the Revolution of 1688 established the principle that . . .

FOX: Oh, do be quiet. This is politics, not principle.

PRINCE OF WALES: The King's hands were never tied, so why mine? I'm not having it.

FOX: There can be no question of it. When you are declared Regent it must be with full powers to dismiss Pitt and appoint . . . whomsoever you choose in his place.

BURKE: Charles!

FOX: Of course as Whigs we've always maintained the opposite, that the power of the Crown *should* be restrained, but these are extraordinary circumstances.

PRINCE OF WALES: They are. I'm a good fellow, for a start. My father wasn't ... isn't.

Anthony Calf (Fitzroy), Iain Mitchell (Sheridan), Julian Rhind-Tutt (Duke of York), Nick Sampson (*seated,* Prince of Wales) and Robert Swann (Dr. Warren) in *The Madness of George III* by Alan Bennett

And I'm a Whig too, and for the best of reasons. My father ruled me like he did the Bostonians, and now this is my tea-party. Restrictions indeed.

The Prince adopts a noble pose for Hoppner, the painter, as Sir Boothby Skrymshir arrives with his nephew, his favor-seeking and his four votes. The Prince promises to remember him when the time comes. While Sheridan counts the votes they think they can depend on, Fitzroy comes in with the information that the King doesn't seem to be getting any better under the new treatment. The Lord Chancellor, Thurlow, has accompanied Fitzroy and comes in with the news that Pitt is mightily discouraged at the situation.

FOX: . . . How are we to recompense you for this invaluable intelligence and for your . . . defection?

THURLOW: Defection, no. Administrations come and go. As I see it, the function of the Lord Chancellor is to provide continuity.

BURKE: There are no precedents which would justify that, particularly if we go back to . . .

FOX: What's your price?

THURLOW: To remain on the Woolsack.

PRINCE OF WALES: You shall, I promise you.

THURLOW: Thank you, sir, and were I to offer advice I would say that the present situation calls for the utmost delicacy.

PRINCE OF WALES: Oh yes. Quite agree. The utmost.

THURLOW: Everything will come to you in due course. Your Highness has but to wait . . .

PRINCE OF WALES: Wait! Wait! My life has been waiting. I want to be doing, not dangling. I endeavor to cultivate languor, but it is hard to be languid when the throne of England is pending. To be heir to the throne is not a position; it is a predicament. People laugh at me. What must I do to be taken seriously? I tell you, sir, to be Prince of Wales is not becoming to a gentleman.

Fox, Duke of York, Fitzroy, all leave with the Prince of Wales, as Hoppner cleans up.

THURLOW: Yes. It takes character to withstand the rigors of indolence. Do we need Fox?

SHERIDAN: We need the Prince, and they come as a set. But I know what you mean. Fox despises me because I trim and count heads. He is the great Whig, you see, and I just the manager. Still, I must put up with that, for his friends will vote with him though he coalesce with the devil. But it's fiddling work.

THURLOW: Why do you not stick to the theater?

SHERIDAN: Debt. Company. A game. A club.

THURLOW: So, your support is growing.

SHERIDAN: Yes. The next vote will be close. Well?

THURLOW: I am not ready yet.

Kew

In this bleak setting, with the furniture under dust sheets and the King in the restraining chair, Willis is exerting his authority—"I've had enough of this foolishness"—and won't let the Queen visit the King until he returns to his senses.

Pitt comes in for his usual Tuesday visit, even though this is Christmas Day. He is told by Willis that cold and tomblike Kew, a summer palace, isn't a healthy environment for an invalid. "I wonder the Prince of Wales does not appreciate that," Willis comments, though *"it is plain the Prince appreciated it only too well."*

The King insists on standing up to meet Pitt eye to eye and tells him of his fear that they have killed the Queen. Pitt assures him this isn't true. The King then mentions Lady Pembroke's attractions, a subject which always angers Willis—"It is filth"—and causes him to order the straitwaistcoat as punishment. And in a matter of protocol—whether or not Pitt may take his leave without the King's permission—Willis overrules His Majesty, embarrassing even Pitt.

But before Pitt leaves, he urges Willis to hurry with his promised cure, or it may be too late. Willis assures Pitt that the King is getting better. After Pitt departs, Willis orders the attendants to line up in front of the King.

WILLIS: I wish to remind Your Majesty, in the presence of your attendants, of your contract.

KING: What contract? There is no contract. I am King of England. I signed no contract . . . but I am contracted. I am shrunk. I signed no contract but I am not as majestic as I deserve by reason of damage sustained, whereby my right to be free was abstracted and constrained and I was locked up in this cage-weather and hear myself constantly promenaded in your figures of speech . . .

WILLIS: . . . Namely, if the King indulges in meaningless discourse, he will be restrained. If he struggles or strikes his attendants, he will be restrained. But if he indulges in filth or obscene talk, makes improper allegations against the Queen and Dr. Willis . . . or entertains lascivious thoughts about Lady Pembroke, or any lady, then this is what you must do.

Willis suddenly gags the King in full flow.

GREVILLE: No!

FITZROY: I will do no such thing.

PAPANDIEK: Nor me.

WILLIS: You will do it, because there is no more disrespect in it than turning off a tap. If this putrid discourse eased the King's mind of its poisons, then no, one would not turn it off. But it is not like that. All men, even ministers of religion, nurture such thoughts, but they do not infect our talk, because discretion and decorum filter them out. It is that filter His Majesty refuses to operate, must learn to operate again. And until he does . . . and we must hope, Your majesty, it is *soon* . . .

Willis breaks off when Warren and Pepys arrive. They receive the day's bulletin and look over the situation. Warren's conclusion that what is needed is another session of blistering leaves the King struggling against his bonds.

Westminster

In Parliament, Burke is in the midst of an oration favoring the Prince of Wales. Meanwhile Pitt, Willis and Dundas are conferring re today's medical bulletin—Pitt causes Willis to rewrite it to give a more optimistic impression, otherwise the Tories may lose the forthcoming vote, expected to be close.

On the floor of the House, the Whigs decry Pitt's optimistic bulletin and argue that it is time for Parliament to pass a bill conferring the royal authority to the Prince of Wales, because of the King's incapacity. Pitt promises to introduce such a bill "In due course . . . . . It is still being drafted."

Westminster

Thurlow, Pitt and Dundas confer privately—the desired bill is ready, with many constraints on the Prince. The Tories still have a majority of ten. Thurlow declares,

"That won't last long. You've lost the battle. You must present the bill. The Prince must be made Regent. *(Cheerfully.)* These things happen. The King is not going to recover."

Pitt fears that the Prince will lock the King away, mad or sane, never to be seen again, but he promises to present the bill the following week. A footman enters and presents Thurlow with a hat which was left at the Prince's apartment. Thurlow denies it's his, but it has his coat of arms stamped on it, and he's forced to accept it—demonstrating clearly to the others why, as Pitt remarks, "He has never been on the losing side yet."

Windsor

The King, in his restraining chair, is having a game of cards with Greville and Papandiek. Baker is just leaving, but before he exits the King interrupts his card game to tell Baker he has a secret mission for him.

KING: I want you to hand over Gibraltar to Spain and see if you can get Minorca in return. Do you think you could do that?

BAKER: I'm a physician, sir.

KING: Then you should have no difficulty. Good afternoon. My go, is it?

Baker shakes his head at Willis and goes out.

WILLIS: I have been watching you for a while, sir.

KING & PAPANDIEK: Snap!

KING: So you should. That's what they pay you for.

WILLIS: I have been watching you, but with a new eye.

KING: A new eye? Dear me. A new eye. And what does this new eye spy?

WILLIS: The nonsense that you talk is no longer helpless nonsense. Your improprieties are deliberate, sir, intentional. You enjoy them. They are uttered knowing you have the license of a disturbed mind.

KING: I am the King. I say what I want.

ALL: Snip, snap, snorum.

WILLIS: You are playing a game, sir.

KING: I know. Snap.

WILLIS: No, sir, not snap.

He snatches up the cards and stops the game. Fitzroy hustles Greville and Papandiek from the table.

You are playing a game with me, sir. Well, enough of it. If you choose you can behave.

The King tauntingly puts his feet on the table. Willis fixes him with his gaze, and somewhat shamefacedly the King removes them.

Willis orders the King to recite the names of his children. The King obeys but leaves out the name "George," and Willis makes him utter the Prince's name. The King begins to shake and stutter when Willis repeats the names of the American colonies, so Willis orders Papandiek to strap His Majesty into his chair, but the King knocks Papandiek down. And despite the Prince's wishes, Willis has ordered a visit to the King by the Queen.

The Queen comes in. The King turns his head away and won't look at her.

QUEEN: Your Majesty. Have you nothing to say to me, sir?

KING *(sotto voce):* Say, madam? What is there to say? We were married for twenty-eight years, never separated even for a day, then you abandon me to my tormentors. Ingratitude, that is what I say. *(Loudly, so that Willis can hear.)* It does me good to see you, my dear.

QUEEN: The doctor said it was for your good, sir.

KING *(sotto voce):* My good? What do they know of my good? *(Loudly.)* This is a good little woman. The best. *(Sotto voce.)* He's an old fool. I can't see what you see in him. *(Starts talking quickly in German.) Du blöde Kuh. Er ist nur ein Pfarrer. Du bist eine Hure und eine Schlampe.*

WILLIS: What is His Majesty saying?

KING: Oh, do they not speak German in Lincolnshire then? . . .

The King continues speaking to the Queen in German, telling her there's a woman he likes better than her. Willis classes this as one of the King's obscenities and waves the gag at him threateningly. But the Queen pushes Willis away and tells her husband of the pending bill to make the Prince of Wales Regent. This information, which the King has not had before, shocks him into a fit. Against the King's will, Willis escorts the Queen from the room.

KING: . . . No. Do not leave me. Do not leave me. My skin burns like it used to. Fetch the waistcoat. *(He begins to rave.)* Oh, but the son. The father pushed aside, put out, put away. Ruled out. The father not dead even. Fetch the waistcoat. Fetch it.

Papandiek looks for permission to Greville, who nods, so fetches it for the King, who puts it on.

Fasten it. Fasten it.

Willis returns, as the King stands in front of Greville, then Papandiek, wanting their help in fastening it.

Greville, Arthur. Braun.

WILLIS: No, leave it.

KING: But it frets my guts out like it used to.

WILLIS: You are the master now. Time was when you could not be induced to wear it. Now you must cast it off.

KING: Greville, Arthur, Fitzroy . . . It is stronger than I am.

WILLIS: Control it, sir. Control it. Fight it, sir. Fight it.

The King struggles and fights, almost as if he were having a fit. Gradually the fit passes, and the King droops exhausted, and the waistcoat falls from him.

Now, sir. Call your dissipated spirits home.

The King picks up the waistcoat and hands it to Braun, then takes Willis's hand and kisses it.

KING: Oh, thank you, sir.

WILLIS: Now there is another whom you have offended, whom you struck just now.

KING: Papandiek.

WILLIS: You must ask his forgiveness.

PAPANDIEK: No.

GREVILLE: His Majesty must not.

KING: Forgive me. Give me your pardon.

Papandiek kisses the King's hand.

WILLIS: No.

GREVILLE: This is his *page.*

WILLIS: No matter. He must be broken as a horse is broken.

KING *(takes Papandiek's hand):* Arthur . . .

He kneels before Papandiek and kisses his hand.

Carlton House

Fitzroy moves from the previous scene into this one, where the Prince of Wales and his entourage are making plans for establishing the Regency as soon as the bill passes—important matters like commissioning a Regency medal and ordering a new throne. Burke wants the Prince to consider a number of Parliamentary measures, but the Prince waves him away. The Prince is looking forward to paying his debts and making his policies: "To me, style is the thing. The King has never had any style. From now on, style is going to be everything."

Fox too is reluctant to tackle Burke's measures, such as abolition of slavery and government reform, right away; they have time, they'll probably be in office for the next ten years. But Sheridan senses that "Something is not right. The Prince is about to be made Regent. The Government is on its last legs. We have won. Where is Thurlow?"

Windsor

Thurlow is visiting the King, who is discovered reading *King Lear* aloud with Willis and Greville (Willis chose this play because some of its elements parallel the King's situation). Thurlow joins in, taking the part of Cordelia.

The King and Thurlow exit together, the King quoting the line, "Pray you now, forget and forgive; I am old and foolish." Willis resolves to get in touch with Pitt immediately to tell him of his patient's improvement. Even the King's urine has resumed its normal state.

Westminster

Pitt has received a letter from Willis about the King's recovery, but he doesn't believe it and expects imminent defeat on the Regency Bill in Parliament by 40 or 50 votes. Pitt regrets what is certain then to happen to both his country and his King. As Dundas comments, "Even if he did recover and found Fox his minister, he would go mad all over again."

To their surprise, they receive a visit from Thurlow, who blurts out the news.

THURLOW: . . . I 've been with His Majesty and have had two hours' uninterrupted conversation with him.

DUNDAS: Oh God, you mean he's talking again?

THURLOW: No, dammit. Well, yes. But not fifty to the dozen, and not nonsense either. He's actually a damned clever fellow. Had me reading Shakespeare. Have you read *King Lear?* Tragic story. Of course, if that fool of a messenger had just got that little bit more of a move on, Cordelia wouldn't have been hanged, Lear wouldn't have died, and it would all have ended happily . . . which I think would have made a much better ending. Because as it is, it's so damned tragic . . .

DUNDAS: Lord Chancellor . . .

THURLOW: The point is, the King is better.

PITT: Better than he was?

THURLOW: No. Better in every respect. Improved out of all measure. The "what what" is back. The "hey hey." He is his old self.

Thurlow hastens to explain his own behavior, his aim "to withdraw myself, so far as I could, from any allegiance to party or faction." Pitt bears Thurlow no malice for his vacillating loyalty but hurries off to Parliament with Dundas. Thurlow is left talking to himself: "Next to the King, I reverence the Prince of Wales," in their proper order, now and in the future. Thurlow's conscience is clear.

Windsor

The King, *"wigged again and in his court uniform,"* receives the Queen, accompanied by Lady Pembroke, with Willis suggesting that the time has come for His Majesty to dismiss his other physicians. Greville ushers in Baker, Warren and Pepys.

WARREN: Did Your Majesty pass an untroubled night? Was there sweating?

KING: I'm sorry. Did someone speak?

GREVILLE: Dr. Warren enquired whether Your Majesty had passed a comfortable night, sir.

KING: The King passed an excellent night, but to quiz him on the matter is a gross impertinence. And Greville?

GREVILLE: Your Majesty.

KING: There was no sweating.

PEPYS *(who has found the chamber pot under the restraining chair):* The stool is good. A model of its kind. May I congratulate Your Majesty on another splendid stool.

KING *(vehemently):* No, you may not.

PEPYS *(still not understanding):* Oh. Well, it is very good.

He shows it to an equally furious Warren. Pause

QUEEN: Do it, George.

KING: Yes. Well, will there he anything more, gentlemen?

WARREN: Perhaps we might have a little general conversation with Your Majesty?

QUEEN: What about?

KING: Yes. What about?

WARREN: Oh . . . topics.

QUEEN: Do it, George.

KING: No. That will be all, gentlemen.

WARREN: All? All?

KING: Yes, all, you fashionable fraud. Go and blister some other blameless bugger, what, what.

The King gets up and himself shows the door to the disconcerted doctors.

QUEEN *(clapping her hands):* Sir!

KING: And Baker?

BAKER: Sir?

KING: Backwards, Baker, backwards.

The King is delighted at his own boldness, kisses the Queen and picks her up and whirls her around.

WILLIS: Well done, sir. Full marks.

KING: Yes. And you can go too, Willis.

WILLIS: I don't think so, sir. Not quite yet.

KING: No? Horse not broken yet, is that it? But the day is coming, I promise. What? Lincolnshire shall see you soon. The wolds are agog.

Fitzroy announces the arrival of the Prince of Wales and the Duke of York—two hours late for their appointment with the King. But the King refuses to become agitated, promises to "strike a note of reconciliation." He is angry at their lateness—which was probably deliberate—but manages to control himself. He tells them he means to have this family a model that the nation can look upon as an example. The Prince protests that he wants something to do, and the King replies, "Do? Well, follow in my footsteps, that is what you should do, and forget all this furniture. Style never immortalized anybody."

The King dismisses Duke and Prince, characterizing the latter after he has gone as "a feckless, weak, irresolute, lying, contemptible wretch." The next visitor is Pitt, who brings the King a paper which nearly sets him off into a state of agitation: the doctors' bill at 30 guineas a visit, plus traveling expenses: "They would make a man pay for his own execution."

As for Willis, Pitt has promised him an annuity for his important service to the King, though the King argues that time, not doctors, cured him. He is suddenly taken with a need to vomit and moves quickly from the room. Willis admits to Pitt that he put emetic in the King's breakfast to make him believe he is still somewhat dependent on medical attention, for a time at least.

The King returns (he finds it curious that he is taken with these seizures, though otherwise he feels perfectly well). His next visitor is the Skrymshir nephew (whose uncle controls four votes) still seeking the appointment as Steward of the Newbury Market. This time the King signs his paper, and gives it to the young man along with some advice: "The cow is the one with horns and the pig is the one with the little curly tail." Sir Boothby's arm comes out to pull his nephew out of the King's presence.

KING: . . . What of Europe, Mr. Pitt? Nobody has talked of that yet.

PITT: Nothing of moment, sir. There have been some minor disturbances in Paris, and the mob broke open the Bastille.

KING: The Bastille? The terror is in the word. It is no different from the prison I have been in these last few months.

PITT: Mr. Fox got very . . . inspired, but order seems to have been restored. I do not think we have much to fear from France in this decade.

KING: We shall meet at the Thanksgiving Service in St. Paul's. I must thank God for my recovery. And so must you, Mr. Pitt. So must you. What, what. As for the future, Mr. Pitt, you are not to disagree with me on anything, what? My mind is not strong enough to stand it.

It should not be clear if the King is serious or trying it on.

PITT: I will do my duty, sir.

The King departs as Braun and Papandiek enter to be paid off by Greville—having seen "Majesty in its small clothes," they are both being dismissed despite Papandiek's devotion to the King. After they go, Fitzroy, now a colonel, advises Greville that though he was kind to the King during his illness, "a blind eye" will serve Greville better than kindness in future service to His Majesty.

Lady Pembroke arrives to conduct the King to the Queen's bedchamber. The King has heard about some of the things he said about her during his illness, including the implication that he and Lady Pembroke were lovers. The King wonders if there was ever any truth to this and learns to his regret that he has always treated Lady Pembroke like a respected sister. Lady Pembroke withdraws, and once again the King finds the Queen in bed, knitting.

KING: My dear.

QUEEN: How is Your Majesty this evening, sir?

KING: Oh, better, madam. So much better. Better and better. Do not be nervous. I have missed you, madam.

QUEEN: Yes, sir.

KING: There is something about you . . .

QUEEN *(letting down her hair):* I am grey now, sir. Grey as an old mouse.

KING: Oh well. It is no matter.

QUEEN: I have lost what little share of beauty I once possessed.

KING: Still, you're a good little pudding.

QUEEN: When you were ill, it was said by some that had you led a . . . a normal life . . . it might not have happened.

KING: A normal life?

QUEEN: Other women, sir.

KING: Kicked over the traces, you mean, hey! No life is without its regrets. Yet none is without consolations. You are a good little woman, Mrs. King. And we have been happy, have we not?

QUEEN: Yes, Mr. King, we have.

KING: And shall be again. And shall be again.

The King begins to stutter on the last phrase, so that we are left with the sense that the future may not be quite as trouble-free as it appears.

St. Paul's

Willis assures the King and Queen, now dressed for a formal appearance, that he'll be there at the cathedral for the ceremony in case it proves too taxing for the King.

Willis has laid his hand on the King's arm. The King looks at it, and Willis removes it.

KING: You may tell Dr. Willis that the ceremony will not be such a burden as the want of ceremony has been. And do not look at me, sir. Presume not I am the thing I was. I am not the patient. Be off, sir. Back to your sheep and your pigs. The King is himself again. God save the King.

Willis is escorted out as the King and Queen go slowly up the steps, accompanied by Handel and attended by the company. They are met at the door of St. Paul's by the Archbishop of Canterbury who blesses the newly recovered monarch, and the King raises his hat to the crowds as the curtain falls.

THE KENTUCKY CYCLE

A Play in Nine Episodes

BY ROBERT SCHENKKAN

Cast and credits appear on pages 423-5

ROBERT SCHENKKAN was born in 1953 in Chapel Hill, N.C., where his father was helping to set up an educational TV operation at the University of North Carolina. He grew up in Austin and graduated from the University of Texas in 1975, then going on to Cornell for his MFA in theater arts in 1977. He had long since decided on a life in the theater, aiming eventually to act, write and direct. Even before graduating from Texas he had achieved professional status as an actor with an Equity card, and he was limbering up his writing talent with short stories and poetry.

Schenkkan's first play of record was Derelict, *produced February 12, 1982 at the Studio Arena Theater in Buffalo for 32 performances. New York's Ensemble Studio Theater (of which he is still a member) put on his* The Survivalist *in its 1983 one-act play festival and was the site of one of the early readings of* The Kentucky Cycle *material. New Dramatists (of which he is still a member and which also staged an early* Cycle *reading) produced his* Heaven on Earth *May 20, 1988, and WPA Theater repeated that script off off Broadway in October 1989 after it had been done that summer at the O'Neill Conference.*

Schenkkan began to write The Kentucky Cycle, *a saga comprising nine one-act plays, with* Tall Tales *(play #6) in 1985, as a wedding gift for his wife, Mary Ann Dorward. There followed* Masters of the Trade *(play #1, 1988),* The Courtship of Morning Star *and* The Homecoming *(#2 and #3, 1988) and* Ties That Bind, God's

Great Supper, Fire in the Hole, Tablesalt and Greed *(later retitled* Which Side Are You On) *and* War on Poverty *(Nos. 4, 5, 7, 8 and 9, 1989). The* Cycle *was given the largest-ever Fund for New American Plays grant and was presented in various stages of development from New York and Washington to Seattle and Los Angeles, where it was awarded the 1992 Pulitzer Prize, and PEN Center/West Literary Award and the Los Angeles Drama Critics Circle Award for the best play of its season. It arrived on Broadway November 14, 1993, winning its author his first Best Play citation.*

Schenkkan is also the winner (for Heaven on Earth*) of a Beverly Hills Theater Guild-Julie Harris playwriting contest. His play* Tachinoki, *about the internment of Japanese Americans during World War II, was mounted at the Ensemble Studio Theater in Los Angeles, and he has been working on a new play entitled* Handler. *He and his wife, with two children, live in Los Angeles.*

The Kentucky Cycle *was presented in two parts, each the size of a full-length play, with five of the self-contained one-acts in Part I and four in Part II. With the approval of the author, we are representing his work in the Best Plays presentation with all of* Masters of the Trade *and most of* Tall Tales*—the opening plays of each of the two parts—and an abbreviated synopsis of the others.*

PART I

Masters of the Trade

1775. Early morning, an hour before daybreak. Somewhere in eastern Kentucky. A small clearing in a thick forest. A creek flows nearby.

Earl Tod sits hunched over in front of a dying fire. He dozes, wrapped in a filthy blanket and cradling a rifle. Forest sounds fade in. Beat. A wolf howls in the distance. Beat.

Suddenly, Tod's head snaps upright. Slowly, almost imperceptibly, he moves his hands down the stock, locating the trigger. He calls out a greeting in Cherokee.

TOD: *O si yo!*

There is no answer. He swings the gun up. There is an unmistakable Scottish brogue in his voice as he calls out.

You can step out into the light now wi' your hands up and tell me your name, or I'll put a bullet into ya from here and you can die unburied and nameless. It's all the same to me.

Beat. Out of the dark, a large, squarely built white man in tattered buckskins limps cautiously forward, his hands up. He speaks with a heavy Irish accent.

MICHAEL: The name is Rowen. Michael Rowen. And I have to be tellin' ya, sure but your hospitality is nuthin' much to brag about.

TOD: What do ye want?

MICHAEL: A place by the fire. Somethin' to break me fast. I haven't eaten for two, mebbe three days now.

TOD: What happened?

MICHAEL: Well, after all that terrible trouble at Zion, I said to meself, "Michael, me boy, it's time you were movin' on." And so I packed up me things and headed into the mountains—"whence cometh my strength." *(Beat.)* Psalm 121? "I lift up mine eyes unto these hills, whence cometh my strength." Are you familiar with the Scriptures, sir?

TOD *(remains silent, his gun pointed at Michael):* I know "An eye for an eye."

MICHAEL: Ahh, an Old Testament man, are ya? A fellow after me own heart. The New Testament, it's . . . it's a little watery, now isn't it?

TOD: You didn't finish your story. What happened to you?

MICHAEL: Couple o' days ago, I ran into a catamount. Scared me horse so, he bolted off into a ravine carryin' everythin' I owned, includin' me rifle.

TOD: Bad luck.

MICHAEL: The devil's own! Course, I can't say I blame me horse, poor creature. When I seen that cat, I was off and runnin' meself, with about as much direction. I took a fall, knocked meself silly, ass over teacup, and turned this ankle in the bargain! Been wanderin' ever since. Real glad to see your fire.

TOD: Then why didn't ye just step up, 'stead of sneakin' in?

MICHAEL: Well, after Zion, I wasn't sure but ye might be Indians. *(Beat.)* Listen, Mr. . . . . uh . . . ?

No response.

It's been very nice to chat with ya, but do ya suppose I could finish this conversation with me arms down and me belly full?

TOD: Warm yourself.

Michael drops his hands and limps to the fire. Tod turns quickly and strikes Michael a blow with the stock of his gun. Michael drops. Tod stands over him and searches his body for weapons. He finds a small knife in one boot and drops it in disgust. Michael moans. Tod crosses over to the other side of the fire. He tosses a canteen and a small leather pouch into the dirt in front of Michael.

MICHAEL: *(gasping, as he catches his breath):* Son of a bitch!

TOD: There's water, and pemmican in the bag.

MICHAEL: Son of a bitch.

TOD: Can't take no chances. Not with Cherokee and Shawnee runnin' about. Renegades runnin' wi' 'em.

MICHAEL *(struggles to sit up):* You seen Indians?

TOD: Party o' bucks all painted up. Headin' northwest seven days ago.

MICHAEL *(swallowing some water and digging into the pemmican):* Shawnee?

TOD: Cherokee.

MICHAEL: Probably part of the same group what attacked Zion.

TOD: What happened to Zion?

MICHAEL: Ya don't know? Terrible thing. Tragic.

TOD: You're the first man I've run into since I left Boonesboro two months ago.

MICHAEL: White man.

TOD: What?

MICHAEL: First *white* man you've seen. You saw those Cherokee bucks a week ago. *(Beat.)* What're ya doin' out here? You a trapper?

TOD: You didn't answer my question.

MICHAEL: Oh, Zion. Terrible. About a hundred Cherokee savages attacked the settlement a week ago. Wiped it out. Man, woman and child.

TOD *(pointedly):* 'Cept you.

MICHAEL: I wasn't there. On me way back from Boonesboro, me horse threw a shoe, bless his soul, slowed me down and saved me life. I was in time to watch the massacre. Not take part.

TOD: You're a very lucky man.

MICHAEL: With a very unlucky wife. And two children even more unlucky.

Beat.

TOD: That's hard.

MICHAEL *(shrugs):* May their souls rest comfortably in the arms of the Lord.

TOD: Amen.

MICHAEL: I've no way to repay your hospitality but this . . .

He reaches into his back pocket. Tod starts and lowers his gun, cocked. Michael freezes.

I've nothin' more dangerous in me back pocket than a small flask of poteen. With your permission?

Tod nods. Michael pulls the flask out.

You're a nervous man, Mr. . . . . ?

TOD *(ignoring the implied question):* These are nervous times.

MICHAEL: That they be. When no man dare be sure of his neighbor and a white man'd ride with the murderin' red savages 'gainst his own kind. Nervous times. *(Beat.)* I'd toast the health of my host and saviour, if I knew his name.

Beat.

TOD: Tod. Earl Tod.

MICHAEL: Mr. Tod, sir, your health. Like the Good Samaritan, ya have restored life to this poor wayfarer.

He drinks, then hands the flask to Tod.

TOD: Ye saw renegades at Zion?

MICHAEL: Well, I wasn't close enough to be sure, ya understand, but . . . uh, when did ya ever hear of Indians carryin' rifles?

TOD: Christ!

MICHAEL: I counted near a dozen rifles. Mebbe more. *(Beat.)* They all looked new.

Tod drinks.

Ah well, way of the world, eh, Mr. Tod? I mean, we been sellin' 'em everythin' else. It was bound to happen sooner or later. And one man's profit . . . is just another man's dead wife.

Tod throws the flask back to Michael.

TOD: When there's light enough, I'll show ye where ye are. Give ye some water and jerky. Even with your ankle bad, should make Boonesboro in a week. Little less.

MICHAEL: You in trade, Mr. Tod?

TOD: What I do is none of your damn business.

Beat.

MICHAEL: I meant no offense, to be sure, Mr. Tod. It's just that I find meself in your debt, sir, and I always pay me debts. I've friends in Boonesboro might be useful to a man like yourself, if he's in trade.

TOD: That's kind of ye. But what little tradin' I do, just keeps me in what I needs. Nothin' more.

MICHAEL: Aye, but that's the real question now, innit, Mr. Tod? What is it a man needs?

TOD: Meanin'?

MICHAEL: One man's needs are another man's luxuries. Take yourself, now. What brings you to Kentucky, Mr. Tod?

TOD: Room. And quiet. And it don't look like I'm goin' to get much of either this mornin'.

MICHAEL *(grinning):* It's a beautiful country, now, innit? *Look* at the size of them trees. Sure but that's the King of Oaks there. And the water in that creek is so sweet, and so *clear,* b'God but you could read the date off a shilling on the bottom of it.

TOD: If you had one to throw in.

MICHAEL: Oh, no trouble there! It's a grand land of opportunity, it is, with plenty of scratch to be made for those with an itch! All that, and enough room for a man to stretch out and lose himself entirely. Become somethin' new. Somethin' different. A new *man.* That's what we're makin' here in Kentucky, Mr. Tod. New men. *(Beat.)* Meself, I came by way of Georgia. Brought over indentured, don't ya know. Only, me and me master disagreed over the length of me service.

TOD: And?

MICHAEL: And then there was this terrible accident, and the poor man up and died. Very sudden-like.

TOD *(laughs in short, sharp barks):* Sad!

MICHAEL *(laughing):* Yes! It was all very sad! Tell me, Mr. Tod, don't you worry 'bout sharin' all this lovely space of yours with them savages?

TOD: They don't bother me.

MICHAEL: They don't?

TOD: I leave them alone, they leave me alone.

MICHAEL: Is that a fact? You have an understandin' then, do ya, you and them?

TOD: I wouldna call it that.

MICHAEL: What would you call it? A deal, maybe? Ah, but I forgot, you're not a tradin' man, are ya? *Ha dlv digalowe?*

TOD: What . . . what is that?

MICHAEL: Cherokee. As you well know. *Ha dlv digalowe?* Where are the rifles?

TOD: I don't know what you're talkin' about.

MICHAEL: That was a Cherokee greetin' you called out when I first stumbled onto your campfire. Where *are* the rifles, Mr. Tod?

TOD *(stands up nervously, pointing his gun at Michael):* I don't know what you're talkin' about.

MICHAEL: The rifles them Cherokee had at Zion. They come from you, didn't they? *(Beat.)* Where's the rest?

Tod cocks his rifle.

Don't be stupid as well as greedy, Mr. Tod. Ya don't think I walked in here unarmed, *alone?*

A noise offstage. Tod whirls and fires. As he does so, Michael leaps up and screams.

DON'T KILL HIM!

A single shot rips out of the darkness. Tod falls. Beat. A thin, nervous young man (Sam) emerges from the woods, holding a rifle.

SAM: That him?

MICHAEL: Yes, you little shit—that *was* him.

Sam walks over to the body. He drops his rifle, kneels down and begins to pummel the corpse with both his hands, with increasing ferocity.

SAM: You bastard! *You bastard!* YOU BASTARD!

Michael strides over and hauls the young man roughly to his feet.

He killed my family! He kilt 'em!

Michael slaps him across the face several times and then drops him to his knees with a blow to the stomach.

MICHAEL: And mine! And everyone else's! And now he's *dead,* you little shit! I told you not to kill 'im! *(Beat. With great disgust.)* Now wipe your face and shut up.

SAM *(crying):* He killed my Sarah!

MICHAEL: Piss on your Sarah!

He grabs the young man and throws him to the ground.

You little turd! Them shots will have every Indian in two miles down on us.

SAM *(blanching in terror):* Cherokee?

MICHAEL: Well, who do you think dear Mr. Tod was waitin' for? The blessed St. Christopher? So unless you want to join your precious Sarah in the hereafter, you shut your mouth and do as I say. Now bring our packs in.

Sam staggers off into the woods. Michael searches Tod's body closely, removing and keeping a knife. He discovers a gold watch, which when opened plays a bright tune. He pockets it. He then searches through Tod's belongings, with increasing urgency and finally frustration.

Damn! Damn it!

Sam returns with two heavy leather packs, which he drops by the fire.

SAM: What's wrong?

MICHAEL: I can't find anything! Not flints, powder, bullets or muskets. I don't know—mebbe he buried it somewhere. Worried, were you, Mr. Tod, 'bout the good word of our red brothers?

Michael starts rummaging through one of the packs. He pulls out a worn, red blanket. He looks at it oddly for a moment, then tosses it to Sam.

Cover 'im up.

SAM: Why?

MICHAEL: You're developin' an annoyin' habit, Samuel, of questionin' me. Just do as I say and we'll both live longer. Now cover him up!

Sam obeys.

How much powder and shot have you got, Sam?

SAM: I don't know. Mebbe two horns and a quarter-pound of shot.

MICHAEL: Get it out.

SAM: You think we'll have to make a fight of it?

MICHAEL: I'm hopin' we can work out a trade.

SAM: What?

MICHAEL: Get out what you've got!

Sam starts to comply, but before he can move, four figures emerge from the woods, surrounding them. They are Cherokee warriors, dressed simply in buckskins, but beautifully painted. They all carry rifles. One of the men steps forward. Unnerved, Sam tries to reach for his gun.

Be still, for the love of Christ!

Sam freezes, as every rifle is lowered at him. Two of the Indians—Taskwan and Dragging Canoe—openly contemptuous of the white men before them, converse in Cherokee.

DRAGGING CANOE: *Gago yunsti na anisgaya?* (Who are these men?)

Taskwan shrugs.

TASKWAN *(to Michael): Tod di nah?* (Where is Tod?)

MICHAEL: Greetings to my Cherokee brothers.

TASKWAN: Who are you?

MICHAEL *(surprised):* You speak English?

TASKWAN: It is easier than hearing you butcher Cherokee. I am Taskwan. Who are you?

MICHAEL: Friends.

TASKWAN: Whose friends?

MICHAEL: We could be yours.

TASKWAN *(indicating Tod's body):* Was he a "friend"?

Michael says nothing.

Your friendship is very hard.

DRAGGING CANOE: *Tod is unihlv?* (Have they killed Tod?)

TASKWAN: *Hu tle gi.* (Uncover the body.)

One of the warriors pulls the blanket off Tod. Taskwan steps over and looks into his face.

Vs kidv. (It is him.)

Beat.

DRAGGING CANOE: *Dida luga.* (Kill them.)

The warriors raise their rifles. Michael and Sam tense.

MICHAEL: We can still do business!

DRAGGING CANOE *(gestures for the warriors to hold): Gado adi?* (What does he say?)

MICHAEL: You need us!

Beat. Dragging Canoe gestures to his warriors, and they lower their guns.

DRAGGING CANOE: *Wiga wo ni hi.* (Let him speak.)

MICHAEL: Ya had a deal, right, with Tod? Guns for pelts—right? But how much powder and lead did the bastard give ya? Huh? Not enough, I bet. Not nearly enough.

SAM: What are ya doin', Michael?

MICHAEL: Shut up, boy! So, we'll step in for Mr. Tod, see. Here. Here's a good-faith gesture.

He starts to move toward Sam's pack. The warriors shift uneasily.

Easy, lads! Call 'em off, Taskwan.

Taskwan gestures.

That's it. Here now.

Pawing through Sam's pack, he pulls out two powder horns and a small deerskin bag, which he lays out grandly on the red blanket.

See here. Two horns of black powder and a half-pound of the king's own finest lead! And I'll throw them blankets in too. Fine wool, both of 'em!

TASKWAN: And?

MICHAEL: And? When the moon is full again, we meet you here, by that oak, with ten times that, twenty times . . . whatever ye want.

TASKWAN: How much?

MICHAEL: Twenty pelts per horn. Ten for a quarter-pound of shot. And none of your junk, mind ya! Good skins! Clean cuts!

DRAGGING CANOE: *Gado adi?* (What is he saying?)

TASKWAN *(smiling): (In Cherokee:* Powder and shot just as Tod promised us. Only they are less greedy.)

MICHAEL: You need us, Taskwan! Without us, those muskets are just expensive firewood!

DRAGGING CANOE: *(In Cherokee:* I trust them less than Tod. They stink of fear, and the tall one lies.)

TASKWAN: *(In Cherokee:* Remember Zion, Dragging Canoe? The guns brought us a great victory. But one town burned is nothing to them. Unless we stop them now, they will cover this land and scatter our people as we drove off the Shawnee. For this we need guns. Guns need powder. Powder needs them.)

DRAGGING CANOE: *(In Cherokee:* So be it. What of Tod, though?)

TASKWAN: *Hawa.* (Yes.) *(Turns to Michael.)* We accept your offer.

MICHAEL: Now you're talkin', me friend!

TASKWAN: Old debts before new business, my "friend." He is dead who was a brother to my people, and his blood debt is unpaid.

Pause.

MICHAEL: As you will.

Magically, his knife is out, and in one, swift, brutal motion he slams the blade into Sam's stomach. Sam drops to his knees, a look of incredulity laced with pain spreading across his face.

SAM: Michael?

He collapses on the ground. Michael turns and ceremoniously drops the knife on the blanket with the other trading goods.

MICHAEL: He killed Tod. He's dead. We're even.

DRAGGING CANOE: *Gadousti inage ehnai ni hi?*

MICHAEL: What'd he say?

TASKWAN: He says, What kind of animal are you?

MICHAEL: A necessary animal. Tell him. "A necessary animal!"

TASKWAN: He understands. We will meet you here in one month. Twelve more rifles. Powder and shot for all.

MICHAEL: Two hundred pelts per gun.

TASKWAN: That is more than Tod wanted.

MICHAEL: You can still trade with Tod.

TASKWAN: I could kill you.

MICHAEL: You could. *(Beat. He extends his hand.)* Deal?

Taskwan looks at it in distaste but takes it. When he tries to turn away, Michael holds him.

Just one more thing. I want me some land. Much as a man can walk around in one day, and your word that me and mine is safe on it.

DRAGGING CANOE: *(In Cherokee:* What does he say?)

TASKWAN: *(In Cherokee:* He wants land.)

All the warriors laugh.

No one owns this land. It cannot be "given."

MICHAEL: Is that what you said when you drove the Shawnees off it?

TASKWAN: This land is cursed. We hunt on it, but no tribe lives here.

MICHAEL: I'll take me chances.

DRAGGING CANOE: *(In Cherokee:* It is a dark and bloody land. You cannot live here.)

MICHAEL: What'd he say?

TASKWAN: He says you will find this a dark and bloody land.

MICHAEL *(to Dragging Canoe):* I'll take me chances. *(He turns back to Taskwan.)* Your word.

TASKWAN: You live here, it is not the Cherokee you need fear.

He gestures to the powder, shot and blankets.

(In Cherokee: Take them. We go.)

The warriors gather up the blankets and exit. Dragging Canoe doesn't move. He remains staring at Michael.

(In Cherokee: We go!)

They exit. Michael stands for a moment, breathing hard, a look of triumph on his face. Sam moans.

MICHAEL: Ah, Samuel, you were more use to me than I could ever imagine. How can I ever repay you?

SAM *(faintly):* Water.

MICHAEL: Water? By all means, Samuel!

He lifts Sam up tenderly, crouching behind, half-supporting him and helping him to sip at the canteen.

SAM: Am I goin' to die?

MICHAEL: Oh, I should think so, Samuel. Otherwise, I should have to order you off my land. *(Laughs.)* "My land." Oh, there's a grand sound to that, isn't there? Course, if you and Mr. Tod want to stay here, permanent-like, make yourselves useful—fertilize me corn, mebbe—that'd be all right too! *(He laughs.)*

SAM: They'll kill you.

MICHAEL: Who? The Cherokee? Oh no, Sam. Quite unlike their white brothers, they keep their word, they do. *(Beat.)* And even if they didn't, this lot will. I've seen to that.

SAM: What?

MICHAEL: Them blankets, Sam—they're *poxed.* Salvaged them from that Cutter family in Zion—them whose baby girl died of the pox three weeks ago. Remember? Sweet child. Hair like corn silk. *(Beat.)* Indians has thin blood. Pox'll cut through them like a hot knife through butter. *(Beat.)* So you see, Sam, you can rest easy now. Zion's been revenged after all. *(Beat.)* Sam? *(Beat.)* Sun's comin' up, lad. *(Beat.)* New day for a new land.

Beat. Fade to black. Forest sounds hold for five beats and the fade.

The Courtship of Morning Star

Scene 1: A year later, 1776, in summer, Michael Rowen, age 35, has built a rude pole cabin on his eastern Kentucky land, and he is bringing—or rather, dragging—home a woman. She is Morning Star, a dark-complexioned, pockmarked 16-year-old Cherokee, hands bound and cursing Michael every step of the way. Michael throws her on the floor of the cabin. *Blackout.*

Scene 2: The next morning, Star is the first to awake and tries to slip away but finds herself bound to Michael. She seizes a log to brain him. Michael dodges, wrests it from her and laughs. *Blackout.*

Scene 3: That evening, Michael prepares a wooden bowl of food which Star at first disdains, then devours ravenously. Michael tries to communicate with her by telling her his name and learning that hers is Knox Sanale—Morning Star in Cherokee. After supper Michael takes her in his arms and tries to woo her, but the first chance she gets, she pushes the bowl into his face and flees, with Michael after her. *Blackout.*

Scene 4: Star is stirring an iron pot while Michael tells her about himself in words which of course she cannot understand. He killed his first man—a helpless Englishman who had taken a tumble while hunting—in Ireland when he was seven years old. "But there was no sport innit," Michael confesses, "blood's just the coin of the realm, and it's important to keep strict accounts and pay your debts. That's all." Now that he's a man of fertile property, what he wants most is an heir. Star's ankle is wrapped in a bloody bandage, and Michael assures her that he cut her tendon cleanly—she'll always have a limp, but now she can't run away from her duty to bear him a son. "Gimme a daughter, and I'll leave it on the mountain for the crows," he finishes. *Blackout.*

Scene 5—Star's Vision: Star is downstage facing the audience while a double for her is upstage gripping the bedposts, occasionally screaming with pain, in labor. Star recalls a joyful autumn celebration of her tribe at which Laughing Eagle paid her significant attention. But the following day, she remembers, blisters appeared, and the Red Death played havoc with her family and tribe, killing faster than the few able-bodied people could do the burying. At first, Star hated the life in her womb, but gradually came to realize that the baby would be *hers,* and that the two of them would then have "*One* heartbeat, and *one* thought, and that is DEATH TO HIM!" The double's screams become more frequent, and then the cry of a baby is heard. In her imagination, Star raises her newborn son up the audience, commenting, "He is born with teeth." *Blackout.*

Scene 6: Star rocks her baby and sings a Cherokee warrior song as a lullaby. Michael resents the sound of the Cherokee words, reminding Star that the newborn is a Rowen, not a savage. But when Star offers Michael the baby to hold, Michael seems strangely afraid of him and *"disturbed by forces he has set in motion but doesn't understand."* Star laughs at Michael's fear. *Slow fade to black.*

The Homecoming

Scene 1: Sixteen years later, on a late morning in 1792, Michael's son Patrick rests on his haunches on a high ridge with a long view, sampling the soil with his hand. He is joined by 16-year-old Rebecca Talbert, *"slender and attractive in a blunt and unaffected manner."* Rebecca thinks this might be a good place for their house after they get married; Patrick is concerned about her standing there, silhouetted against sky, an easy target, though there have been no Indians in these parts in five years.

Patrick learns to his surprise that his mother, Star, has been a frequent visitor at the neighboring Talbert place after first having been called there to practice her famous healing powers on Rebecca's ailing father. But Rebecca has sensed that Star has hostile feelings toward her for some reason. And Rebecca has expected Patrick to speak to his father about their getting married, but so far Patrick has neglected to do this. When Rebecca suggests that they just run off, Patrick exposes his innermost feelings with the exclamation, "I AIN'T LEAVIN' THIS LAND! It's mine!"

Patrick promises to speak to Michael as soon as his father gets back from his trip to Louisville. He always brings back a special present for Star from these trips, and maybe he's late in returning from this one because he's arranging an extra special gift.

Patrick reveals to Rebecca that he once had a baby sister, but Michael said she was sickly and took her away. "Star had beaded this piece of buckskin for her so fine, it looked like she pinned all the stars in the sky to it. He wrapped the baby up innit and took her away, and we never saw her agin." Star doesn't even know where the baby is buried, though Patrick has looked for the grave often enough without finding it.

Rebecca must get home with a basket of huckleberries for her father, before her brother Jeremiah gets curious about where she is and what she's doing. Patrick spies a flash reflected from metal on the trail far below. Assuming it's his father coming home, he promises to speak to Michael about their marriage tonight. "I love you," Patrick declares, and disappears before Rebecca can reply. *Fade out.*

Scene 2: In the front yard of the Rowen house (which now has several rooms and a porch) Patrick hands his day's catch—two rabbits—to his mother, who accuses him of wasting time dallying with Rebecca instead of tending to his chores. Patrick reminds Star that she too is friendly with the Talberts, a regular visitor in fact. Star admits that she conducts healing sessions with Rebecca's father Joseph—and anyone else who'll pay her—as a stake for Patrick to buy his own land some day.

Patrick admits he wants to marry Rebecca and suggests his father should ask for the Talbert bottom land as a dowry—it would increase Michael's holding by about a third, and all of it will come to Patrick some day. Star indicates she's not so sure of this—she dreams about a woman of Michael's in Louisville and suggests he might have another family there. Michael hates Patrick—Star reminds her son—because Michael fears him. Patrick is now bigger and stronger than Michael. "He will never give you your rightful share of this land," Star tells him, "*Your* land. Not till you bury him in it."

Michael, arriving with a full pack, greets his family with the news that Kentucky has now achieved Statehood. And he has remembered to bring an important gift. He whistles, and in comes a young black woman, hands manacled, face bruised, carrying a large pack. She is a Guinea princess he has bought for $30 and intends to use to breed field hands, obviously with himself as the father.

Surprisingly, Star approves of this plan and prepares a warm bath for her husband. Michael is only too glad to step into a tub after laying aside the pistol which he carries on a lanyard around his neck. As Star proceeds to wash Michael, she informs him that their son Patrick "has his eye on that Talbert girl." Patrick adds that he has his eye on Talbert land also, and Michael challenges Patrick either to persuade Rebecca's father to part with some of it or go westward and acquire some land of his own in the wilderness as Michael did before him. Michael indicates that he has plans for the Rowen land that don't include Patrick in any important way. Almost hysterically infuriated by his father's attitude, Patrick finally demands: "DOES IT COME TO ME OR DON'T IT?" Michael replies, "I'd sooner give it to my slaves, first! I'd sooner the forest covered my fields than turn them over to some half-blooded, half-witted, droolin' excuse for a man! You were *never* my son."

Star deliberately puts lye soap in Michael's eyes, backs away and tells Patrick to help his father. Patrick draws his knife and stabs his father repeatedly until Michael lies motionless, bleeding his life out.

Star assures Patrick that Michael would have killed him some day if Patrick hadn't acted first. She suggests that they can bury him, and no one will ever know how he died. The black woman has seen what happened, but she wouldn't dare tell. At this moment, however, Rebecca and her father Joe Talbert emerge from the woods. Realizing what has happened, Joe levels his rifle at Patrick and sends Rebecca to fetch the gun on the porch. Star's first thought is that she and Joe are free now to join each other, as apparently they had planned. But Joe tells her, "We didn't talk about nothin' like this, Star. You was just to walk away. That's all. There warn't s'posed to be no killin'."

Star tries to explain how "wicked" Michael was—buying a female slave with intent to breed her himself. Joe doesn't deny it but can't overlook murder. Star is afraid they'll just hang Patrick because he's half-Cherokee and killed a white man. Joe insists that they must follow where the law leads—otherwise they'll all be savages like Michael. Star warns Joe that she's as guilty as Patrick and will go with him to share his fate. She reminds Joe that she once saved his life and asks for her son's life now in return. Apart from the legal aspect, however, Joe doesn't trust Patrick and feels he'd "spend the rest of my life lookin' over my shoulder" if he let Patrick go. Star swears on her life and Patrick swears that Joe would be safe, so—reluctantly—Joe agrees that Patrick can leave, but without his rifle.

Patrick moves as though to bury his father. When he kneels down to pick up Michael's clothes, he seizes Michael's discarded pistol, turns, and fires at Joe, exclaiming, "This is *my* land! *Rowen* land! I ain't leavin'!" As Joe drops, Star, appalled at the death of her lover, vows vengeance on Patrick, who points out that the only witnesses against him are a squaw, a black slave and Rebecca, who won't be able to testify against him as his wife. He orders Star off his land, forces Rebecca into the house and, after finding the key and unlocking the manacles on the black slave—whose name is Sallie—directs her to start digging a grave for Michael down by the old oak tree. As for Joe, he's "not for buryin'," he tells her. As she leaves, Patrick finds the gold watch among Michael's effects. He asks for his father's blessing as the lights fade to black.

Ties That Bind

In 1819, in the front yard of the well-kept Rowen homestead, two young men are wrestling, while a third, Ezekiel "Zeke" Rowen, 19, sits on the porch reading his Bible. In the wrestling, Jesse Biggs, 26, a black slave, clearly has the upper hand over Zachariah "Zach" Rowen, 17—like Zeke the son of Patrick Rowen, now age 43, as Jesse is the son of the slave Sallie. Zeke admonishes the other two for wrestling on

Sunday, but they keep at it anyway. Zach casts aspersions on a girl Zeke is courting, Joleen, which brings Zeke off the porch in anger—so that when Patrick enters he sees his two sons wrestling, pulls them apart and orders them to get spruced up. Patrick expects visitors on business from the Circuit Court. "We give 'em a handshake first, 'fore we show 'em a club," Patrick declares while instructing the boys to load and stack their rifles just inside the front door.

Judge Jim Goddard *("a fat man in a black coat, tie and hat ... one leg is wooden below the knee")* comes on with two well-armed deputies. He is soon followed by *"a tall, slender, expensively dressed man"* carrying a strongbox under his arm. Jesse and Sallie enter with a jug of whiskey Patrick has ordered for his visitors, who soon get down to business. As the Judge states, they are here to proceed with the issue of Patrick's bankruptcy. Having taken out loans to buy an additional 300 acres of land to add to the original 39 Rowen acres, Patrick is now unable to pay the bank his debt because a changeover in the meantime from paper money to hard cash has disrupted his economy and collapsed the price of corn. Many like him are in the same fix following the upheaval of the war of 1812 (in which Patrick fought at New Orleans), and the government is taking steps to relieve the situation, but in the meantime the man with the strongbox—Mr. Jeremiah—has bought Patrick's debts from the bank and has taken steps to have them paid.

The land which Patrick bought for $987 is now worth in the new money only $477, so it's obvious that Mr. Jeremiah is going to take everything Patrick owns, land included, and then some, to discharge the debt. Patrick warns the Judge that they'll have to kill him and his two boys before they'll let go of the land. The Judge's reply is, "While it would grieve the court to see things come to such a state, there is always that possibility, of course."

But Mr. Jeremiah doesn't want Patrick's life, he wants everything Patrick owns, and he is counting up the value of the Rowen assets with a very sharp pencil. When it comes to the slaves, Mr. Jeremiah allows $220 off the debt, but Sallie begs Patrick not to sell Jessie, finally coming out with, "YOU BE SELLIN' YOUR OWN BROTHER!" The boy is not her husband John Biggs's child, but Michael Rowen's. Zach too begs his father not to sell Jesse, but Patrick's view is, "I'm not sellin' no brother, I'm just sellin' a *slave,*" and when Zach persists, Patrick knocks him down.

With the house, the gold watch, his mules, his tools and everything else, Patrick still comes up $13.20 short. He makes a final plea.

PATRICK: . . . . This here . . . this land . . . it's all I ever knowed. All I ever wanted. I know . . . . . know ever foot of this place. I bet if you was to blind me and take me somewheres on it, anywheres, I could tell you where we was just by the smell and the taste of the dirt. I could do that. I did a wrong thing, here. I see that. And the law don't smile on no poor man when he do wrong. But my boys . . . they didn't do nuthin'. You gonna toss me off'n this land, well, you gotta right to do that, but I'm askin' you to think of your own family . . . . . and let my boys stay on. I'm beggin' you . . .

(Beat.)

JEREMIAH: Do it.

PATRICK: Do . . . ?

JEREMIAH: Beg me.

JUDGE: Mr. Jeremiah—really, sir, this is . . . !

JEREMIAH: Shut up! *(Beat.)* Beg me.

PATRICK *(sinks slowly to his knees):* I'm begging you.

JEREMIAH: Mr. Jeremiah.

PATRICK: Mr. Jeremiah.

JEREMIAH: Sir . . .

PATRICK: Sir . . .

JEREMIAH: Don't throw me off my land.

PATRICK: Don't throw me off my land.

Jeremiah agrees to let the Rowens stay on as sharecroppers keeping one-fourth of what they raise, and he'll carry the money Patrick still owes at ten percent interest. The Judge declares the case settled, but Mr. Jeremiah has one more matter to deal with here. He signals, and what appears to be a short man limps onto the scene. It turns out to be Star Rowen in disguise. She has come back to witness Patrick, her lover's killer, being humbled. And Jeremiah reveals that he is Jeremiah Talbert, revenging himself on Patrick for killing his father Joe and taking away his sister Rebecca (she died in childbirth). Jeremiah's final word to Patrick and the boys is, "Two weeks from today, I spect to see all you Rowens over at what used to be the Talbert homestead. Your daddy knows the way, boys. You're gonna build your Uncle Talbert a new house. With a *big* porch. And ever morning I get up I'm gonna sit on my big porch and drink a big cup of coffee and watch you Rowens workin' my land."

Jeremiah departs, followed by the Judge and all others except Patrick and the two boys. Zach is quick to go get his rifle and, in spite of his father's urgent pleas, leave home in the opposite direction from the Judge and the others—he wants no part of the sharecropper's life. Zeke assures Patrick, however, that he means to stay here and, no matter how long it takes, get their land back and their vengeance on the Talberts. In Zeke's arms, Patrick weeps to think that he has lost his son Zach, but Zeke advises him, "Got to be stone . . . . . Then we gonna settle up." *Slow fade to black.*

God's Great Supper

Forty-two years later, in 1861, at the Rowen household, Jed Rowen, 28, tells of a bad dream he has about his father Ezekiel Rowen's impassioned preaching, and Jed's stuffing himself at a church social, urged to eat by the famous William Clarke Quantrill, with gaunt women reciting names until they get to Jed's—and then Jed wakes up.

Stacy Keach and Tuck Milligan as father and son in a scene from Robert Schenkkan's *The Kentucky Cycle*

Patrick Rowen, 85, blind, sits on the porch of the Rowen cabin while his son Ezekiel ("Zeke"), 61, sits leaning against a post. A ten-year-old boy carrying a bundle under his arm runs in and whispers into the cabin, "Jed," but he is grabbed and frightened to tears by Zeke. Joleen Rowen, Zeke's wife, comes out to see what the fuss is about.

Jed Rowen comes in, hoe in hand, and finds that his little friend and next-door neighbor, ten-year-old Randall Talbert, has been scared by too strong a ribbing from the grownups. Randall has come over to tell Jed that his father has joined up with the Confederate Army, and the boy wishes he could come over here and live with the

Rowens. Jed assures Randall he'd be welcome here, but his father would be angry if he found out Randall was even visiting the Rowens, let alone living with them.

Richard Talbert, 39 (Jeremiah's son), comes in dressed in *"a new and rather garish Confederate lieutenant's uniform, topped by a wide-brimmed hat with an enormous plume."* He is indeed angry to find his son Randall at the Rowens and punishes the child by striking his hand with a riding crop, ordering him, "Don't you shame me in front of these people. You're a Talbert! These people work for your daddy, and someday they are gonna work for you. Now how're these people gonna look up to you if you cry?"

Richard strikes Randall again, and the boy runs off with his bundle, without crying. Zeke resents Richard's patronizing attitude, but Jed is deferential, conciliatory, respectful, waiting to hear the purpose of Richard's visit.

Richard Talbert has come over to persuade Jed Rowen to join his troop, promising to provide slaves to bring in the Rowen crop and five cents a week off the Rowen debt for every week Jed serves under him. Furious, Zeke forbids his son to accept this offer, but Jed defies his angry father and promises to join Richard, who is leaving the next day.

But when Richard departs, Jed, Zeke and Joleen have a good laugh at the Talberts' expense. They staged their father-and-son quarrel for Richard's benefit, so that Jed can ride out with Richard's troop unsuspected of any hostile intent, and at the first good opportunity—perhaps during the confusion of battle—settle the score with the Talberts by killing Richard.

Suddenly they realize that Randall Talbert has been hiding under the porch. Zeke wants to silence Randall, but Jed goes through a blood-brother ceremony with the boy and is sure that Randall won't tell his father anything he has heard. The boy departs, as Zeke warns his son, "Ain't no point gettin' too fond of Randall, Jed. Make your mind up to it—we gonna kill 'em all."

"The lights fade to a single spot on Jed," who tells the audience they rode out the next day and ran into Yankee soldiery. Richard is wounded, and Jed helps him off the field. They manage to make their way onto a crowded barge for a river crossing. Halfway across, Jed pushes Richard overboard and watches him sink to the bottom as the vessel continues on its way to the other shore.

Jed meets and follows a group of men who've decided to join up with William Clarke Quantrill and his raiders in their merciless approach to war, killing Union soldiers in cold blood and even sacking Lawrence, Kansas and murdering civilians. The Union army finally manages to scatter the raiders, and Jed heads home with a half dozen other Quantrill men, arriving on the day they are burying his grandfather Patrick.

Jed finds that his father plans to raid the Talbert place the next day and wipe out everyone, family and slaves, to get even once and for all. Jed tries to persuade Zeke not to do this, but Zeke is determined.

When the raid took place (Jed explains to the audience), the Talberts took refuge in their house: "They saw us comin' a course . . . . . Those walls were thick, but I hadn't studied under Quantrill for nothin'." Jed had one of his Quantrill cronies set fire to the house and then they picked off every man who came running out, while Zeke preached at the top of his lungs, "Come and gather for God's great supper to eat the flesh of all men, slave and free, great and small."

Zeke gave orders to let the black Biggs family escape, but he hitched Richard Talbert's younger brother Stephen to a plow to work salt into the Talbert fields before they killed him. Jed tried to arrange for Randall to escape and begged his father to let the child go, but Zeke killed Randall, commenting, "What good does it do to crush the snake if you don't kill its young?" But Jed insisted they let the two Talbert girls, Rose Anne and Julia Anne, go free after the Quantrill men had finished with them.

As Jed begins to bury Randall, his dream of the gaunt, name-reciting women (they are the Talbert girls) and Zeke's impassioned preaching returns to his thoughts. "In my dreams it's always spring," he tells the audience, "and the first, dark shoots reach up through the soil towards me and mine. Whole fields of decay. Fields of appetite. Spring. *(Beat.)* And then the harvest." *He pours the dirt onto Randall's grave. The lights fade out. Blackout. Curtain.*

PART TWO

Tall Tales

NARRATOR: Tall Tales. The year is 1885. The Rowen farm in the hills of eastern Kentucky, in Howsen County, near the Shilling Creek. Tall Tales.

1885. Summer. The prologue and epilogue happen approximately 35 years later.

Prologue

A young girl, Mary Anne Rowen, kneels by a creek and arranges her hair. Standing off to one side is the woman she will become in 35 years. The adult Mary Anne watches her younger self and speaks to us.

ADULT MARY ANNE: Spring usta explode in these mountains like a two-pound charge of black powder hand-tamped down a rathole. After months of gray skies and that damp mountain cold what bores into your bones like termites in a truckload of wood, it's your dogwood trees that finally announce what everythin's been waitin' for. First thing some morning, you might see a single blossom hangin' there, light pink, the color of a lover's promise . . . if lies had a color. And then later that afternoon, damned if that bud ain't been joined by a hunnert of his brothers and sisters all sittin' round, chattin' each other up, Sunday-go-to-meetin' style. Course, dogwood's just the beginnin'. The spark what lights the fuse for spring, that's the azaleas. When they get to goin', you'd swear somebody'd scattered a whole handful of lit matches across those hills. Bible story is how old man Moses talked to a burnin' bush. But for my money, he was just conversin' with a scarlet azalea in full bloom. Story just got a little expanded in the retellin' . . . the way stories do. Fella once told me a story, said these ain't no real mountains here at all—that if you stood high enough, you could see it was all just one big mound that had been crisscrossed and cut up into so many hills and valleys by the spring runoff, that it just looked like mountains. Leastways, that was his story. Only, I don't put no truck in stories no more.

Scene 1

The light fades out on the adult Mary Anne and comes up on the younger Mary Anne. A man, JT Wells, enters and stands quietly behind her. Smiling, he watches for a moment, then picks up a pebble and tosses it over her shoulder and into the water. She turns, startled.

JT: Friend. I'm a friend.

MARY ANNE: Shouldn't sneak up on a body like that!

JT: No, you're quite right, young lady. I shouldn't have. And under any other circumstances, my rudeness would meet your harshest disapprobation.

MARY ANNE: Huh?

JT: You'd a right to be pissed off. But the fact of the matter is, if you hadn't been in mortal danger just now, I probably would've walked right on by, 'stead of savin' your life.

MARY ANNE: My life?

JT: Well, your immortal soul at least.

MARY ANNE: How you figure that?

JT: Why, starin' into that stream like that. I've heard it said from them that knows, that the devil himself hides his bleak heart in the muddy bottom of slow-movin' pools, just like this.

MARY ANNE *(a little uncertain):* You're just foolin'.

JT: Would that I were, ma'am. But 'tis a widely known fact that the Father of Lies often assumes the shape of an *ictalurus punctatus* and—

MARY ANNE: A what?

JT: Channel catfish.

MARY ANNE: You use more twenty-five-cent words when a nickel word would do than any man I ever met.

JT grimaces, mimes being shot by an arrow, pulls it out and hands it to Mary Anne.

JT: I think this is yours.

Both laugh.

Where was I? Oh yeah . . . And thus disguised, he lies in wait for an innocent virgin to come along.

MARY ANNE: Devil hafta wait a might long time for one of those in these parts.

JT: Well, he's a mighty patient fella, the devil is.

They both laugh.

MARY ANNE: There *is* an old catfish in this crick.

JT: Oh yeah?

He sits close beside her and they both look into the stream.

MARY ANNE: I ain't never seen him, but my daddy has. Almost caught him onct. So's Tommy, but I think he was lyin'.

JT: That your brother?

MARY ANNE: Naw, he's my boyfriend.

JT moves away slightly.

Leastways, *he* thinks he is.

JT moves back.

JT: Mighty pretty here.

MARY ANNE: Yeah.

Both are quiet for a moment.

I jist love them old trees. Specially that oak there. That's my favorite.

JT: That's a beaut all right.

MARY ANNE: Folks around here call that the Treaty Oak, 'cause my great-great-grandaddy, Michael Rowen, that's where he bought this land from the Injuns.

JT: That a fact?

MARY ANNE: That's what my daddy says. I don't think there's a tree in these hills comes close to touchin' it for size. Leastways, I ain't never seen one. When I was a kid, I used to think that tree was all that kept the sky off my head. And if that tree ever fell down, the whole thing, moon and stars and all, would just come crashin' down. I think sometimes how that tree was here way before I was born and how it'll be here way after I'm gone, and that always makes me feel safe. I think this is just about my favoritest spot in the whole world. Not that I seen a lot of the world, but my daddy took me to Louisville onct when I was six. You ever been there?

JT: Well, it just so happens I was in Louisville three weeks ago.

MARY ANNE: Yeah? I bet you been a whole heap of places, way you talk 'n' all.

JT: Oh, I been here and there.

MARY ANNE: Where?

JT: Well, places like . . . Atlanta.

MARY ANNE: You been to Atlanta, *Georgia!?*

JT: Hell, that ain't nothin'. I been to *New York City!*

MARY ANNE *(almost inarticulate with wonder and envy):* Nooooo.

JT: Yes, ma'am I have. And lived to tell the tale.

MARY ANNE: What's it like?

JT: Well, I tell you, it's . . . it's pert near indescribable. It's hundreds of buildings, each and every one taller'n that ole granddad oak of yours. "Skyscrapers." That's what they call 'em. Sky*scrapers.* Clawin' up at the very fabric of heaven, threatening to push old Jesus Christ himself off his golden throne! And not more'n two months ago, I's standin' in the top a one of them golden towers, and John D. Rockefeller himself shook me by this hand.

MARY ANNE: No.

JT: Yes ma'am, he did. And me, just a poor boy outta Breathitt County. Said to me, he said, "JT, you've got a future here," and then he clapped me on the back! Imagine that—the richest man in the country—the Standard Oil king himself—standin' no further from me than you are now.

Beat.

MARY ANNE *(shyly):* Is that your name?

JT *(still lost in reverie):* Huh?

MARY ANNE: JT. I was wonderin' what your name was.

JT: Oh lord, isn't that just like me? Here I get to jawin' so much I clean forgot to introduce myself. JT Wells at your service. The JT stands for Just Terrific. And who do I have the honor of speaking to?

MARY ANNE *(mumbling, embarrassed):* Mary Anne Rowen.

JT: Say what?

MARY ANNE: Mary Anne Rowen. *(Quickly.)* Most folks just call me Mare, though.

JT: "Mare"? Well, I don't know. Don't seem right somehow. I mean, isn't that what you call a horse or something? "Mare"? That's not a proper name for a pretty thing like you. Let me see here. Mary Anne. You know what your name is in Spanish?

MARY ANNE: No.

JT *(savoring it):* Mariana.

MARY ANNE *(delighted):* Yeah?

JT: Now, that sounds about right, don't it? Got all the right colors in it and everything. Mariana.

MARY ANNE: Mariana. *(She giggles.)*

Beat.

JT: Mariana.

He moves closer to her. There is a noise offstage. Both turn, startled, as a teenage boy steps out of the underbrush, cradling a shotgun loosely under one arm.

MARY ANNE *(flustered):* Oh. Hi, Tommy. Umm . . . JT, this is Tommy Jackson. Tommy, this is—

TOMMY: "Just Terrific" Wells. Yeah, I heard.

JT: Ah, the boyfriend, yes? Well, it's a rare pleasure to make your acquaintance, young man. You're a very lucky fellow . . .

He starts toward Tommy, hand outstretched, but stops when the boy shifts his gun.

. . . but I guess you know that.

TOMMY *(laconically):* I been told.

JT: Yes, well . . .

MARY ANNE: Be nice, Tommy.

TOMMY: Like you were?

MARY ANNE: We weren't doin' nothin'.

TOMMY: Not yet anyways.

JT: Now Mr. Jackson, I think there's just a little misunderstanding here . . .

TOMMY: Take another step, Mr. "Just Terrific," and I'm gonna misunderstand a hole the size of a butternut squash in the middle of your chest.

MARY ANNE *(moving between them):* Now damn it, Tommy, you just put that gun up right now, you hear me? Right this minute. Or I ain't never gonna speak to you again, as long as I live!

TOMMY *(grudgingly obeying):* Well, what's he doin' here, huh? Answer me that!

MARY ANNE: Well, I'm sure I don't know, Mr. High and Mighty—why don't you just ask him yourself? You ever think of that? No, I guess not. I guess some people been up the creek and outta town so long that they plum forgot their manners. Mr. Wells, would you be good enough to tell this poor, ignorant hillbilly what you'd be doin' in these parts?

JT *(grinning):* Well, now, that'd be a real pleasure, Miss Rowen. Fact of the matter is, I'm here to see your daddy.

Stunned silence.

MARY ANNE: My pa?

JT: Well, if your daddy's a Mr. Jed Rowen of Howsen County, Kentucky, currently living up on Shilling Creek, I guess I am. I'm a storyteller!

Blackout. Fast country music, violins and mandolin, fading up and then down into general laughter.

Scene 2

Lights up to reveal the interior of the Rowen house. JT, Mary Anne, Tommy, Jed Rowen and his wife, Lallie, are all seated around a wooden plank table, the remains of a country dinner in front of them.

JT: I tell you, Jed, there ain't nothing like a home-cooked meal. Now, you might think a traveling man like myself, eating at some fancy restaurant every day of the week, is a man to be envied. But there are moments, sir, when I'd trade it all, every green bean almondine and French this and French that for a piece of cob-cured country ham and red-eyed gravy like I had tonight.

LALLIE: It was all right then?

JT: All right? Ma'am, the President doesn't eat better'n this in the White House!

LALLIE: Mare, I'll get the coffee, you clear the men's plates and then get yourself somethin' to eat.

MARY ANNE: I'm not hungry, Ma.

LALLIE: What's wrong with you, girl?

MANY ANNE: Nothin'. Just not hungry.

JED: Leave the child alone, Lallie. She's too busy feastin' her eyes and fillin' her ears to pay much attention to her belly.

Tommy laughs.

Pity one can't say the same for you, Tommy Jackson

Tommy shuts up. Both women bustle around.

JT: You sure a mighty fortunate man, Jed.

JED: How you figure that, JT?

JT: Because, sir, you got the one thing a man needs to live a life worth livin'.

JED: That bein'?

JT: Your independence. You're not beholden to any man for anything on your . . . how many acres would you say you have?

JED: Oh . . . 'bout three, four hunnert acres.

JT: On your three hundred-odd acres here in the middle of God's country, you're a virtual king. Republican nobility.

JED: Republican?

JT *(quickly correcting his error):* Figure of speech, Jed. What I mean to say is, you and the people like you, your neighbors, they're what makes this country great! I take it you served in the "Glorious Cause," sir?

MARY ANNE: My daddy was a hero—he fought with Quantrill!

JED *(warning):* Now, Mary Anne . . .

MARY ANNE: Well, you did!

JT: Is that a fact?

MARY ANNE: My daddy saved Quantrill's life!

JT: Isn't that somethin'!

MARY ANNE: That was in Lawrence, Kansas. Tell him, Daddy.

JED: It wasn't really all that much . . .

LALLIE: Go on, Jed.

TOMMY: Go on, Mr. Rowen . . .

MARY ANNE: See, they was trapped in this house in Lawrence, and the Yankees had set it on fire, and—

JED: MARY ANNE! *(Beat.)* JT's the storyteller here; you gonna put the poor fella out of work.

JT: What was he like, Quantrill? I mean, you hear so many different things.

LALLIE: He was a real gentleman. That's what Jed always said—isn't that right, Jed?

JED: Well . . . I guess he was a lot of different things to different people, but . . . he always treated me square. Maybe, Mr. JT, you'd like a drop of somethin' a mite stronger than coffee, to settle your stomach?

JT: Well, sir, I'm not ordinarily a drinkin' man, you understand, but as this is a special occasion, I'd be honored to raise a glass with you.

JED: Mare, you get down that ole mason jar and a couple of glasses.

LALLIE: Now, Jed, you promised . . .

JED: I know what I'm doin', Lallie . . .

LALLIE: But you know your stomach can't take it, Jed.

JED *(warning):* Lallie . . .

LALLIE: You go ahead, but don't you be wakin' me up in the middle of the night with them terrible dreams of yours!

JED: I said, I know what I'm doin', woman!

Lallie gives him a withering look as Mary Anne returns with mugs and the jar. Jed folds.

Well, hell, get me a pitcher of buttermilk then.

Lallie smiles and exits, returning quickly with a pitcher. Jed pours a clear liquid out of the jar into two mugs. Then, sorrowfully, he pours buttermilk into one of the half-filled mugs.

Terrible thing to do to good corn liquor. *(Looking at JT.)* I don't suppose you'd care to . . .

JT *(straight-faced):* Ordinarily yes, but I'm tryin' to cut back on the buttermilk.

JED: So was I.

JT: To your health.

JED: Mud in your eye.

They drink.

JT: Oh Lord, that is the elixir of the gods. Pure liquid Kentucky.

JED: Heaven in a mason jar.

TOMMY: Mr. Rowen, you spect I might have some?

JED: Well, sure, Tommy—help yourself, boy . . . *(To JT with a wink as Tommy reaches over)* . . . to the *buttermilk!*

General laughter, to Tommy's embarrassment.

JT: Well, I want to thank you good folks for havin' me in like this, but I know there's nothin' free in this life, so I reckon it's time to sing for my supper, as it were.

Murmurs of approval and enthusiasm.

JED: Mr. JT, afore you get to spinnin' us a yarn, maybe you could say a word or two 'bout what's goin' on out in the world.

JT: Well, sir, we got us a new President, of course—fella named Grover Cleveland.

JED: Cleveland? Who's he?

JT: Democrat.

LALLIE: Praise be to God!

JED: A Democrat! Lord, we waited long enough for that! Lallie, pour us another round—this is cause for celebration!

TOMMY: Where's he from?

JT: New York.

JED: New York? New York? Hell, I ain't drinkin' to no *Yankee* Democrat! What they gonna hand us next—Christian sodomites?

LALLIE: Jed!

TOMMY: What's a sodomite?

LALLIE: Never you mind!

JED: Read your Bible, boy.

TOMMY: Is that the fella who's so helpful and all?

MARY ANNE: That's Samaritan.

JED: O Lord, this is why us folks in the mountains don't miss the world out there: the news is always *bad.*

JT: Well, I got one piece of news I think you'll like.

JED: It ain't likely.

JT: Ulysses S. Grant died four weeks ago.

JED: Dead!?

TOMMY: Hot damn!

LALLIE: Tommy Jackson, you watch your language in this house!

JED: Well, I'll be damned!

LALLIE: Very likely, Jed Rowen—you and Tommy Jackson both for your blasphemous ways!

JED: Oh, hush up, woman—it's just words. Way I always understood it, Lord don't care what you say, it's what you do. What'd he die of?

LALLIE: "Thou shalt not take the Lord's name in vain."

JED: Lallie, as much sin as there is in eastern Kentucky, I don't think the Lord'll notice some bad language.

LALLIE: "Not a sparrow shall fall but what *He* won't see it."

JED: ENOUGH! Tommy, pour everybody some corn liquor, and I think we'll skip the buttermilk this round! *Now,* JT, maybe you'd favor us all with that story you promised.

JT: Well, sir, it'd be a privilege.

JT proceeds to entertain them with a series of very tall tales, the first one about a coon hunting incident in which JT and a companion find themselves trapped between a grizzly bear and a rattlesnake with only one shell left in the gun. The gun explodes, killing both bear and snake without harming the shooter and bringing down a flock of geese flying over, while a coon falls out of a tree, dead of fright.

The listeners applaud, except for Tommy, who sneers at the tallness of this tale. This puts JT in mind of a story about "the Montages and the Caplets" and a star-crossed love affair, with someone named Tommy as Juliet's betrothed, the third side of a love triangle. When in the tomb scene Juliet awakes to find Tommy and her lover struggling, Juliet bashes in Tommy's head with a shovel. The lovers then depart and live happily ever after.

Tommy, already jealous of JT's attentions to Mary Anne, attacks JT. Jed intervenes and orders Tommy out of the house. Tommy wants to take his rifle with him, but Jed refuses to let him have it until he cools off. Jed empties the gun and Tommy departs.

The others call for another story. JT tells them of a time Jesus Christ paid a visit to Kentucky and found doors shut in his face until "an old couple name of Baucis and Philomen" invited him into their shack to partake of their simple hospitality. Jesus caused all the inhospitable Kentuckians to be swallowed up by the earth but offered to grant Baucis and Philomen a wish. Their wish was never to be separated, but to die together. When their time came, hand in hand, "They were changed into two big old oak trees standin' side by side for all eternity. And as the wind blows through their leaves," JT finishes, "it says one thing over and over, throughout all eternity—and that is, 'I love you.' "

LALLIE *(quiet):* I like that story.

JED: AMEN.

They smile at each other.

JT: You know, you folks been so kind to me 'n' all, I'd sure like to be able to do somethin' for you in return. I mean, when you see a family like this one, so close, so full of love for each other 'n' all, it just makes you think: What if . . . ?

Beat.

JED: What if?

JT: What if, God forbid, somethin' should happen to one of you? I mean, we can't all be as lucky as Baucis and Philomen and count on the Lord callin' us at the same time, can we? And in the unpleasant event of your absence, you'd sure want your wife and child looked after proper now, wouldn't you?

JED: Well, sure.

JT: Course you would. But how's a man to do that? You sure wouldn't want to rely on the Jacksons or the rest of your neighbors now, would you?

JED: No, sir.

JT: It's a problem for sure. But one for which, I'm happy to say, there is a solution.

JED: What's that?

JT: I have been empowered by certain parties to purchase the mineral rights from far-sighted Christian gentlemen like yourself.

Beat.

JED: My mineral rights?

JT: Yes sir.

JED: Oh. Well . . . uh . . . what exactly are we talkin' about here, JT?

JT: Well, "mineral rights" is just a twenty-five-cent word for rocks, actually.

JED: Rocks? You mean somebody wants to buy the rocks offa my land?

JT: That's it exactly. The people I represent will pay you *fifty cents an acre* for the right to haul off all mineral and metallic substances and combinations of the same. In your case, countin' your three-hundred-odd acres—

JED: Three hunnert and fifty-seven acres.

JT *(smiling):* That'd be about a hundred and seventy-nine dollars in cold, hard American cash.

Stunned silence.

JED: Let me get this straight, JT—I been breakin' my back diggin' rocks outta my damn fields so I could plow for nigh onto forty years, and now there are people willin' to pay me money for the same privilege?

JT: What can I tell you, Jed, 'cept there's a fool born every day. Here, you read it for yourself, it's all down there in black and white.

He pulls out a contract from his jacket and hands it to Jed, who inspects it awkwardly, too embarrassed to admit he can't read.

(Gently.) Light's kinda bad in here—maybe you'd like me to go over it for you.

JED: Can't do nothin' with these old eyes of mine.

JT: Essentially, this says that for the sum in question, you, the owner, pass over the title to the minerals underlying your land with all the usual and ordinary mining rights. It says all that a lot longer, but that's what it boils down to.

JED: And that's all there is to it?

JT: That's all.

JED: Well, that sounds easy, don't it! Where am I supposed to sign?

JT: Right here.

Jed picks up the pen.

LALLIE: Jed, I don't feel right about this.

JED: What don't you feel right about, Lallie?

LALLIE: This land been in your family back before anybody can remember, and I don't think you oughta be sellin' it.

JED: You heard him, Lallie—I ain't sellin' the land, I'm just sellin' the mineral rights.

LALLIE: I don't think you oughta be sellin' any part of it, even them rocks.

JED: Lallie, I know what I'm doin' here.

JT *(smiling):* I understand your feelings, ma'am, 'bout the land, and as a mountain boy I share' em, but I don't think any of your family'd begrudge you makin' a livin' off your land. What's important is the *land,* that it *stays* in your family.

LALLIE: That's right, but . . .

JT: Now think about it. Everybody knows with corn, couple of bad seasons back to back and you might have to sell a piece of your land—all of it maybe—just to get by. But with all that *money,* folks, that one hundred and seventy-nine dollars, you're covered. You got somethin' to fall back on.

JED: Man's gotta point, Lallie.

JT: And why not make your life a little easier right now, Lallie? You know—get a new stove, maybe. A new dress for your daughter. A new—

LALLIE: We don't need things. We got everything we need.

JED: Lallie . . .

JT: I tell you what. I don't usually do this, but you folks been so nice to me 'n' all, maybe I could see my way to, say . . . sixty cents an acre.

Beat.

JED *(smiling):* Seventy-five cents.

LALLIE: Jed!

MARY ANNE: Daddy!

JED: Hush up, now! JT and I are talkin' business now, and he knows as well as I do, you can't let your personal feelin's get in the way of business—can you, JT?

JT *(smiling evenly):* No sir, that's a fact. *(Beat.)* Seventy-five huh? Well . . . I reckon I might could see my way to seventy-five.

JED: Good enough for me.

LALLIE: It ain't right, Jed—ain't enough money in the world gonna—

JT: Jed, if your wife doesn't want you to do this, maybe we oughta just forget the whole thing . . .

JED: I make the decisions for this family, JT, and *I say that's fine! (Beat.)* Now, where do I sign?

JT: Right here.

Jed picks up the pen and looks the document over again.

JED: Just outta curiosity, JT, what exactly are those "usual and ordinary mining rights" you were talking about?

JT *(picking his way carefully):* That means they can excavate for the minerals . . . uh, build a road here and there, if necessary—long as they don't disturb you, of course. Use some of the local water . . .

JED: Hold it right there! You never said anything before about cuttin' across my land or taking my water!

LALLIE: Uh-huh.

JT: That was understood, Jed. I figured a man of your experience knew how these things worked.

JED: Nope! No way! Ain't no way anybody's gonna build a road over my land!

JT: Look, Jed, I promise you, I swear to God, you'll hardly know they're there! They gonna be real careful with your land.

JED: You want my mineral rights, that's one thing. But I just can't see my way to all that other stuff. Roads and water—no sir! *(Beat.)* 'Less you're willin' to go a whole 'nother quarter per acre.

JT: What?

JED: A dollar an acre and she's yours!

JT: Hell, Jed, you can practically *buy* land in these parts for that!

JED: Then you do it! Course I thought you wanted the mineral rights to a *particular* piece of land. *Mine.*

JT: You tryin' to cut my throat, Jed?

JED *(innocently):* Why no, JT—but you did start out by sayin' how you wanted to do me and mine a favor.

Beat. Both men are breathing a little hard. JT finally manages a smile.

JT: Jed Rowen, I hope you won't take this the wrong way if I tell you I ain't never met anybody like you. You, sir, are one tough son of a bitch.

JED *(smiling):* I'd consider that a compliment. We doin' business?

JT: Yeah, we're doin' business.

JED: Dollar an acre?

JT: Dollar an acre.

JED: Where do I sign?

He picks up the pen and then puts it down again.

JT: I ain't goin' any higher, Jed!

JED *(embarrassed):* Ain't the money, JT. I don't know how to sign my name.

JT *(relieved):* All you do is touch the pen and make your mark. An X or whatever.

Jed signs.

And here's a bank draft for—

JED: Three hundred and fifty-seven dollars!

JT: Now, you just take this draft to the bank—any bank, anywhere. That little paper's as good as gold.

Jed examines the paper with great respect. JT leans over the table.

I'm gonna ask you a favor, Jed, man to man. I'd appreciate it if you wouldn't mention this price to your neighbors—least not till after I been around and had a crack at 'em. Make my job a little easier, you know?

JED: I understand, JT. When it comes to business, everybody got his own lookout.

JT: Ain't that the truth. *(Beat.)* Well, I sure want to thank you folks for your hospitality, but I better be goin'.

MARY ANNE: Can't you stay the night, JT?

JED: Sure would't be any trouble.

JT: No, I better be movin'.

JED: Suit yourself.

JT: Could use some direction gettin' back to the road, though.

MARY ANNE: I'll take him, Pa.

JED: All right, she'll see you down there. I'd do it myself, but I'd probably get us both lost!

They laugh.

JT: Thanks again for everything, Lallie. I'll dream of your red-eye gravy.

LALLIE: You're welcome.

JT: Jed? Take care of youself, sir.

JED: Don't you worry 'bout me.

JT: No sir, I guess I won't.

JT and Jed laugh.

JED: Mary Anne, it ain't all *that* far down there. Don't you be too long gettin' back.

MARY ANNE: I won't, Daddy.

Mary Anne and JT walk out of the house and into the woods. Night sounds and shadows surround them.

Scene 3

MARY ANNE: Where you goin' next?

JT: Oh, just down the road a piece.

MARY ANNE: You think you ever come back through here?

JT: Not likely.

MARY ANNE: Lucky you.

JT: Seems like a real pretty place to me, Mary Anne.

MARY ANNE: It's *borin'*. It's always the same. I'd love to do what you do—travel around, meet folks, see new places.

JT: Maybe my life isn't quite as glamorous as you might think.

MARY ANNE: No?

JT: No.

MARY ANNE: I don't know. *(She stops.)* Wanta trade?

JT *(laughs):* No. *(Beat.)* Come on, Mary Anne, let's get goin'.

MARY ANNE: Couldn't we just stop for a minute? Keep walkin' like this we get to that old road in no time.

JT: Well . . . maybe just a minute.

They sit.

MARY ANNE: Sure is a mighty fine moon tonight.

JT: Pretty.

MARY ANNE: Sometimes I get so restless on a night like this, I get up, sneak outta the house and walk through the woods all by myself. Feels like I'm swimmin' through the moonlight, like a big old lake.

JT: Long time ago, all this was under water, you know.

MARY ANNE: When was that?

JT: Thousands and thousands of years ago.

MARY ANNE: What happened?

JT: Somebody pulled the plug.

MARY ANNE *(laughs):* No, really!

JT: Nobody knows. Things change, that's all. One time there was an ocean, now there isn't. One time there weren't any mountains here, now there are. *(Beat.)* Course, these aren't really mountains, you know?

MARY ANNE: No?

JT: This is Cumberland Plateau. Big, flat-topped rise of land. It's the water, year after year, thousands of years, cutting canyons and gulleys, just makes it seem like mountains.

MARY ANNE: Gosh.

JT: Ain't nothin' what it really seems . . . not even mountains. *(Beat.)* Let's get goin'.

Mary Anne doesn't move.

I can't take you with me, Mary Anne.

MARY ANNE: Why not?

JT: 'Cause . . . Because this is where you belong, swimming in this damn Kentucky moonlight, on these mountains that ain't mountains. Now let's go.

MARY ANNE: I ain't showin' you where the road is 'less you kiss me first.

JT: What? You really are your father's daughter!

MARY ANNE: One kiss—what'd it hurt?

JT: Nothing. Except I couldn't promise you there'd be only the one.

MARY ANNE: That'd be all right too.

JT *(kneels in front of her):* You sure this is what you want?

MARY ANNE: Just kiss me, JT.

He does.

JT: It won't change my mind.

MARY ANNE: I know.

She kisses him again and then slides down to the ground, pulling him with her. Tommy enters with a drawn knife. JT sees him and half gets up.

TOMMY: I said I wouldn't forget you.

Tommy throws himself at JT, who flips him over. Tommy slashes at JT, cutting him on the shoulder. JT grabs him, and they both go down. Tommy comes up on top. He kneels over JT and tries to push the knife into his face. JT holds him off but is clearly weakening.

JT: Help me! Help me!

Mary Anne, who has watched the whole thing in mute horror, now comes to life. She kicks Tommy hard in the side. He rolls over and loses the knife. JT begins to kick and pummel the boy savagely. He winds up over Tommy and smashes the boy's head into the ground.

MARY ANNE: Stop it! Stop it! You're gonna kill him! Stop it!

She pushes JT off Tommy, who is now bloody and unconscious. JT holds his cut arm.

JT: The son of a bitch cut me!

MARY ANNE: You coulda kilt him!

JT: He came at me with a *goddamn knife!* Oh, the little son of a bitch cut me!

MARY ANNE: Lemme see.

JT: Son of a bitch!

MARY ANNE: It ain't bad.

JT *(pulls away from her angrily):* Son of a bitch! *(Beat.)* You saved my life.

MARY ANNE: I guess.

JT: How come?!

MARY ANNE: I need a reason?

JT: How come?!

MARY ANN *(simply):* I love you.

Beat.

JT: This doesn't change anything. I can't take you with me.

MARY ANNE: I know.

JT: Will you stop being so goddamn understanding about everything! Goddamn hillbillies! I could cut your hearts out with a rusty razor, but as long as I smiled and told another story, you'd just sit there happy as pigs in shit! Oh Lord, I can't do this no more. I can't do this.

He is sobbing, his head in her lap.

MARY ANNE: Can't do what?

JT: Everything I ever told you, it's all lies! All of it! *(Laughs.)* Your poor old pa, thinking he's slick as goose shit—*a dollar an acre!* What a joke! Oh, he really got me, he did, burned my ass, your old man! There he is, sitting on top of maybe fifteen, twenty thousand *tons* of coal an acre!

MARY ANNE: What's coal?

JT: Oh, nothin', little hillbilly, just "rocks," that's all. Millions of dollars worth of "rocks" which your daddy just sold me for a lousy buck! *Millions!* Oh, he's slick, he is, the poor dumb son of a bitch!

MARY ANNE: You're lyin'!

JT: That ain't even the worst of it! You ain't seen what they do. "I swear, Jed, I promise they be real careful with your land." Oh, yes sir, they're careful—careful not to miss a trick. First they come in here and cut down all your trees—

MARY ANNE: No!

JT: Listen to me, God damn it! First, they cut down *all* your trees. Then they cut into the land, deep—start huntin' those deep veins, diggin'em out in their deep mines, dumpin' the crap they can't use in your streams, your wells, your fields, whatever! And when they're finished, after they've squeezed out every nickel, they just move on. Leaving your land colder and deader'n that moon up there.

MARY ANNE: It ain't so!

JT: The hell it ain't!

MARY ANNE: If that's true, how can you do it? How can you do that to your own people? You a hillbilly just like my daddy, just like me!

JT: I ain't no hillbilly!

MARY ANNE: You said you was a boy off the creek, just like—

JT: That was a long time ago! Now I'm whoever I say I am. I'm JT Wells, and I invent myself new every day, just like the stories I tell!

MARY ANNE: Don't matter what you call yourself— you still one of us, that's the truth!

JT: *Truth?* Hell, woman, there ain't no such thing. All there is is *stories!*

MARY ANNE *(frightened but unsure why):* What're you sayin'?

JT: Sure. Everybody got his stories. Your *daddy* got his stories. Civil War hero, right? Rode with that "gentleman" Quantrill, right? Shit! Quantrill was a thief and a murderer, and when he died folks danced in the streets!

MARY ANNE: My daddy was a hero!

JT: Course he was! And he's the son of heroes, right? Pioneer stock! That ain't the truth! He's the son of thieves, who came here and slaughtered the Indians and took their land!

MARY ANNE: We bought this land from the Indians under that oak tree fair and square!

JT: Well, sure you did! And the people I work for, those Standard Oil people, they bought this land "fair and square" too. And you think they'll sleep any worse at night than your pa does? When they come here, maybe they'll cut the heart out of that old oak you love so much—

MARY ANNE: NO!

JT: —and they'll ship it off to New York where somebody'll cut it into a fine banker's desk and swivel-back chair for Mr. Rockefeller himself! You think when he sits his skinny ass down on that polished surface he gonna be thinkin' about some poor hillbilly girl whose heart got broke in the process? You won't be part of *his story,* Mary Anne! And when I finish my job for him, I won't be part of his story either! See, he'll give some money to a school or something, and grateful people will call him a hero, a great man, a real *Christian!* And *that* story is the one that'll survive—he'll see to that. While the other story, the one where he's just a thief, that'll fade away. That's your "truth."

MARY ANNE: That ain't . . . you're wrong . . . it ain't just stories . . . !

JT: That's how somebody like me can do what he does! I just tell people the stories they want to hear. I say what people want me to say, and I am whatever they want me to be.

MARY ANNE: Then what's left?

JT: Of what?

MARY ANNE: At the end of the day, when you're by yourself—who are you?

He shrugs.

Why'd you kiss me back there?

Beat.

JT *(right in her face):* Tell me what you want to hear, and I'll tell you why I kissed you.

She slaps him. Beat. Tommy moans and moves slightly.

Take your boyfriend home, little hillbilly. At least he fights for what he believes in . . . thinks he believes in. At least he thinks he believes in something. Take him home and marry him and live happily ever after.

JT . . . . . pulls Jed's contract out of his pocket and puts it in her hand.

Here. I owe you one. Tear it up. Tell Jed to tear his bank note up, too.

JT exits. Mary Anne sobs and moves to Tommy. The lights fade down on her and come up in a single spot on the adult Mary Anne. Again, she contemplates her younger self while she speaks to the audience.

Epilogue

ADULT MARY ANNE: I told my pa what JT said . . . and Pa said it was a lie. That JT was lyin'. That he'd beat JT in the deal and that JT was just tryin' to get out of it now, tryin' to get his money back. I asked Pa about Quantrill and Kansas, and he said I'd just have to make my own mind up about that. That I could believe him, believe my own daddy, or I could believe this stranger. And if I chose JT—well, here was the contract, and I could tear that up too. I didn't tear it up. I didn't want to believe JT, and so I chose not to. Like he said, I guess, people believe what they want to believe. And he was right, of course. Probably the only time in his life JT Wells told the truth, and he wasn't believed. And people say God ain't got a sense of humor. They came a couple of years later, just like he said they would, and they cut down all of the trees, includin' my oak. I was right about it holdin' up the sky, 'cause when they chopped it down, everythin' fell in: moon 'n' stars 'n' all. Spring's different now. Without the trees, you get no color; no green explosion. And you got nothin' to hold the land down neither. What you get is just a whole lotta rain, movin' a whole lotta mud. I try to tell my boy, Joshua, what it was like, so he'll know, so it won't be forgotten, but he just looks at me and laughs. "Mama's telling stories again," he says. *(Pause.)* Maybe I am.

Lights fade slowly out.

Fire in the Hole

Scene 1: A large metal coal tipple looms over the wasteland that Howsen County,

Jeanne Paulsen as Mary Ann Rowen Jackson (*center background,* arms outstretched), Ronald Hippe as her son Joshua (*center foreground,* on men's shoulders) and members of the company in a scene from *The Kentucky Cycle*

Kentucky has become in 1920 in the neighborhood of the Blue Star Mine. Mary Anne Rowen's husband, Tommy Jackson, works in the mine. Of their five sons, only one—Joshua, ten years old—survives. But he is sick with the same sort of fever that took their other children in this barren land, one by one, winter by winter.

While Mary Anne nurses Joshua, we see the miners working one of the tunnels and hear Tommy's comment, "We're cuttin' these Goddamn pillars too fine." As he strikes a match to blow a charge, there is a large explosion in which one of the men is trapped and killed despite Tommy's urgent efforts to save him.

A stranger, Abe Steinman, appears and asks Mary Anne if she can provide him with a place to stay (she'll have to ask her husband). Meanwhile, another explosion in the mine is felt. Andrew Talbert Winston, the man in charge, enters and orders everybody out of the damaged gallery.

A doctor visits Joshua and diagnoses typhoid, but Mary Anne can't afford the necessary medicine. Abe Steinman puts up the money, calling it payment for room and board in advance. When Tommy gets home he agrees to let Abe—who wants a job as a miner at Blue Star—stay on as a boarder.

Scene 2: Andrew Talbert Winston interviews Abe for a job—"Blue Star don't need no troublemakers"—and decides to take him on, partly because Tommy pretends Abe is his cousin. Abe then steps outside, giving Andrew the opportunity to suggest to Tommy—who is badly in need of money—that Andrew would pay well for certain kinds of information about what's going on among the miners.

Scene 3: Abe, now a boarder at the Jacksons, helps Mary Anne with taking care of Joshua and advises her to boil his drinking water—that's what's making him so sick. Mary Anne guesses that Abe is an organizer, come "to bring trouble in here," and Abe admits it. Tommy comes home, drunk, learning that Joshua's fever has broken.

Scene 4: After a drunken brawl in a bar, Tommy listens to Abe suggest that perhaps they ought to start fighting the company for better conditions, instead of taking it out on each other.

Scene 5: At the Rowen house where the Jacksons live, Abe tells Mary Anne and convalescing Joshua a story about fearless Mother Jones defying gunmen while organizing the Paint Creek Mine. It's a true story, Abe declares, and Mary Anne answers him, "I may be nothin' but a dumb hillbilly, but even I know there ain't no such thing as truth."

Scene 6: At the Jacksons, Abe whittles while telling Joshua—who'll be 12 years old next April—how Mother Jones finished the job of setting up a union in defiance of superior force. Abe tries to give Joshua a pamphlet to read, but Tommy comes in and takes it away from him.

Scene 7: Tommy gives the preacher $3 to obtain a false birth certificate—over Mary Anne's protest—saying that Joshua is 14 years old and thus employable in the mine. Mary Anne doesn't want her son to be a miner at all, she wants a better life for him—better than Tommy has been able to provide, she finally admits, and Tommy knocks her down. When Abe intervenes, Tommy orders him to leave the house. Abe goes, after reassuring Mary Anne that efforts to unionize the mine will continue.

Scene 8: Joshua, his affidavit accepted by the mine boss, gets into a coal car with the other miners and disappears into the dark tunnel.

Scene 9: While Tommy and Joshua are eating their lunch, there is a "coal bump" signaled by a large explosion. Abe, Tommy and Joshua manage to get out, but others are trapped. Tommy admits to Abe that the explosion probably happened because "Company cut the pillars too fine . . . just picked away so much coal that there weren't nothin' left to hold up the mountain." Abe, a veteran of many other coal camps, attempts to persuade Tommy that they must do something to make conditions better. While Andrew reads off the names of the missing men, Tommy admits he doesn't know how to go about it. Abe does, and he warns Tommy that after they organize they'll need guns to fight off the scabs. Mary Anne gives Tommy the gold Rowen watch for the wherewithal to buy weapons.

Scene 10: Abe and Tommy meet with Cassius Biggs—miner, bootlegger and black descendant of the slave Sallie—in search of guns. Cassius pretends he doesn't deal in guns, while his wife Sureta observes that the company plans to bury her brother, a black man, separate from the white miners who were killed in the blast. But Abe has approached Cassius so respectfully that Cassius and Sureta decide to join Abe's union.

Scene 11: The union has struck, the mine is shut down and the miners are assembled at night in a tent city at the edge of town, in "a holler near the tracks." At the sound of a train approaching at this time of night, Abe warns the others to douse their lights and get down. As the train comes by, *"a machine gun opens up and rakes the camp."* Cassius orders the others to help him rip up the tracks and promises that the strikers will get the guns they need soon.

Scene 12: The next day, Tommy confers with Andrew, who blames the strike on outside agitators. Andrew informs Tommy that the company plans to call in the army, with tanks. All Tommy wants now is to restore the situation as before, with his old job back; what Andrew wants is information: "A name and a place." Tommy gives it to him—Cassius Biggs and Abe Steinman will meet at the area of the Treaty Oak the next night, to obtain guns—after Andrew has given his word to Tommy that no harm will come to anyone.

When Andrew's company men attack the rendezvous the next night, they execute Abe in cold blood (to Tommy's horror), though Cassius manages to get away. Joshua has been standing in the shadows, has seen what happened and knows his father betrayed them all. The next morning, Tommy tries to blame Cassius for the ambush, but Joshua reveals the truth, and the others haul Tommy away. Cassius, knowing now that the army is coming, gives up and declares the strike ended.

Mary Anne has other ideas—she is a Rowen, she declares, no longer a Jackson—and she has come too far to quit now. The other women line up with her in a protest march which the men finally join. When they arrive at the tipple, the company men flee in fear, throwing down their weapons. Threatening to blow up the entire mining operation with dynamite they've brought with them, the women force Andrew to sign a contract establishing the union.

In spite of everything, Joshua misses his father, but Mary Anne reassures him that the union is his family now. She stands at the highest part of the area and cries "UNION!", arms upraised. *Blackout.*

Which Side Are You On?

Thirty-four years later, in November 1954, Joshua Rowen, 44, is president of United Mine Workers District 16. He is speaking to a large crowd of unemployed miners in their Blue Star Mine union hall, assuring them that if they stick together they'll come through these hard times, leading them in the chant, "Union! Union! Union! Union!"

Scene 1: At the Rowen house, Scotty Rowen (Joshua's son) is dressed in a Marine Corps uniform. His mother, Margaret, pours another of the many drinks she has obviously had this evening, to celebrate her son's homecoming. Scotty is looking forward to going to work for the union.

Scene 2: The next evening at a party at the union hall, Joshua announces Scotty's appointment as field representative for District 16. James Talbert Winston, 43, owner of the Blue Star Mine, a guest at the party, makes a brief speech thanking Scotty for his service to his country in Korea. And Franklin Biggs, 44, prosperous businessman and descendant of Sallie, rises to toast a welcome home to Scotty. Before the festivities come to an end, Franklin has had a quiet word with Josh's secretary Lana about a business arrangement, and Joshua and James have equally quietly set up a date to discuss the new contract.

Scene 3: The next night at their private rendezvous at the union hall, Joshua complains about scheduled layoffs, and James argues that it's part of John L. Lewis's industry-wide policy of cooperation between labor and management. Franklin joins them, complaining that the planned layoffs look "selective" to him, and he wants them based on seniority, not color. The three men wheel and deal—Joshua gets a reduced percentage of layoffs, James gets a little extra time to solve a safety problem of dust in the mine shafts, and Franklin gets the concessions for the new hospital being built, etc. They agree that their conversation must remain strictly private. Joshua promises to submit the new contract to the presidents of the union locals.

Scene 4: Scotty gets a rare chance to talk to his father when he and Joshua meet at a bar. Scotty is worried about his father's apparent neglect of his mother; about the layoffs proposed in the new contract; about refusal of pensions in certain cases; about safety conditions in certain cases. Joshua admits that the pension fund has turned out to be underfunded but suggests that Scotty just do what he's told instead of trying to protect his men. This reminds Scotty of Korea, following orders he knew to be wrong, and he doesn't think he can go along with it now.

Scene 5: A week later in the union hall, Joshua is waiting to hear how the district presidents will react to the new contract. They file in to a meeting and complain about the layoffs, not accepting the current recession in the mining industry as an excuse. Scotty also comes to the meeting; and when he hears the president of the Blue Star union also complain about the dust problem, Scotty departs, over his father's protests, to pull the men out of the dangerous mine at once.

The presidents depart after reluctantly agreeing to present the new contract to their men. Joshua calls Franklin and summons him to help deal with Scotty's wildcat strike at Blue Star. James comes in complaining to Joshua that they had a deal. Joshua is powerless to go through with it now and advises James to shut the mine down and hose down the dust, as he should have done long before. James plans to use force to eject the miners, who would otherwise remain at the tipple to prevent other workers from going into the mine. Joshua suddenly understands that his son Scotty is right, and he refuses to cooperate with James. A moment or two later, there is a tremendous explosion. The dust in the mine has exploded, and as rescue crews go to work, James and Joshua argue about who should take the blame. Franklin reminds them that they are all in this together, and James agrees: "We might as well be smart about it."

A moment after Joshua learns that Scotty was down in the mine with the men and is missing, Margaret Rowen appears, drunk and accusing Joshua of killing Scotty. James and Franklin go out to face the reporters, stressing that everything possible will be done for the trapped men. When Joshua—spokesman for the miners themselves—appears, the reporters belabor him with questions. What he tells them is, "Blue Star has always been a safe and responsible operation with a good record. What this . . . tragedy says to me is that one thing we all know but nobody likes to admit . . . and that is . . . that mining is a dangerous business and . . . we just have to live with this." Not his son Scott Rowen, though—Scott's name is read out among the missing and presumed dead as the lights go to black.

The War on Poverty

Twenty-one years later, in the spring of 1975, at the site of the original Rowen homestead near the now-vanished Treaty Oak, *"The Shilling Creek is now full of silt and garbage and abandoned cars and only occasionally rouses itself in memory of its former glory during one of those torrential thunderstorms that sometimes batter the plateau. The surrounding fields, heavily timbered and mined and then abandoned, have also accumulated their share of refuse over the years; but if you look closely, you can see that the land is slowly regenerating itself."* The creek is the subject of a recurrent dream of 65-year-old Joshua Rowen (he tells the audience, alone in a spotlight), in which his son Scotty and mother and father are shouting to him from the far bank, but Joshua can't make out the words or cross over to them.

The lights come up on the area, where two men are digging a hole, from which one of them pulls a piece of buckskin. As they are examining it, bullets strike the dirt around them. They run off and are soon replaced by Franklin Biggs and Joshua Rowen, who fired the shots to emphasize that this is private property. The intruders were grave robbers searching for Indian relics.

James Talbert Winston joins the other two. They've come here in the fog to look over this piece of land as a possible asset, at a time when the mines are shut down and the hospital project is dead. On the way here, Joshua had noticed a huge tree stump which reminded him of the stories his mother used to tell him about what this area was like before the mines came. James tells them of the prospective buyer for the land hereabouts, Consolidated, whose mining scoops eat up 60 cubic yards at a bite, take out every bit of coal and leave a flat pasture behind—and there are no dangerous mine tunnels and coal dust.

James leaves Joshua and Franklin alone to discuss the potential sale. Joshua is haunted by the way things have gone in this community, remembering the day when they unsealed the Blue Star Mine and one of the men handed him Scotty's gold watch—the Rowen watch. Franklin agrees, things have gone bad, but there is nothing they can do about it now.

James comes back with the piece of buckskin the grave robbers had dropped. Looking into the hole, he discovers and brings out a deerskin bundle with beautiful beadwork, wrapping the very well preserved body of a baby girl, the kind of relic that fetches a very high price these days. James immediately thinks of the money it will bring. Joshua is so adamantly opposed to selling this that he picks up his rifle and orders James at gun point to put down the little body.

> *Beat. James puts the baby down on the ground. He never takes his eyes off Joshua. Joshua picks up the baby.*

FRANKLIN: Okay, Joshua, put the gun down.

Joshua lowers the gun but doesn't put it down.

JAMES: You are outta your fuckin' mind, Joshua, you know that? You know what this is about, don't ya, Franklin? Hell, we all know what this is really about, don't we? I'm s'posed to be the bad guy here. It was all my fault, right, Joshua? Bullshit! You're just as guilty for what happened as I am, and you are just gonna have to live with it.

JOSHUA: I'm tryin', James.

JAMES *(backs off):* We can do this land without you, you know? It'll take a little longer, but I can just get a court order.

James exits.

JOSHUA: I know he can make this work without me, Franklin, but he can't do it without *you.* Don't let him do it.

FRANKLIN: It ain't gonna make no difference, Joshua.

JOSHUA: We gotta try, don't we?

FRANKLIN *(slowly picks up his things):* I'll think about it.

He exits in the opposite direction of James. Beat. Joshua moves to the grave and kneels down. He carefully rewraps the baby in her buckskin shroud. He starts to lay her in the grave and then stops.

JOSHUA: It's cold down there, baby. It's so cold.

He takes off his jacket and wraps it around her. He pauses. He removes a leather thong from around his neck. Tied to it is the now battered and tarnished Rowen family gold watch. He holds it up to the sunrise and looks at it. Then he tucks it into the coat wrapped around the infant. He lays her in the grave. He shoves the dirt in with his bare hands. Finished burying her, he rocks back on his heels, his head bowed.

Behind him . . . . . unseen by Joshua, the ground erupts. Pushing up through the soil are the figures of those we have watched live and struggle and die over this ground.

The figures of Star *("reunited with her baby at last"),* Joe Talbert and his daughter Rebecca, Sallie Biggs and her son Jessie, Richard Talbert and his son Randall, Jed, Scotty and Mary Ann Rowen and Tommy Jackson appear. A wolf's howl is heard, Joshua grabs his rifle but calls the animal "You big, beautiful son of a bitch." The figures from the past watch Joshua fire into the air and yell joyfully, "RUN, YOU SON OF A BITCH! RUN! RUNNNNNNNN!" *Blackout. Curtain.*

LAUGHTER ON THE 23RD FLOOR

A Play in Two Acts

BY NEIL SIMON

Cast and credits appear on pages 427-8

NEIL SIMON was born in the Bronx, N.Y. on July 4, 1927. After graduating from DeWitt Clinton High School he managed to find time for writing while serving as a corporal in the USAAF, 1945-46. Writing soon became his profession without the formalities of college (except for a few courses at New York University and the University of Denver). His first theater work consisted of sketches for camp shows at Tamiment, Pa., in collaboration with his brother Danny. He became a TV writer, supplying a good deal of material for Sid Caesar (Caesar's Hour) *and Phil Silvers* (Sergeant Bilko), *an experience on which* Laughter on the 23rd Floor *is based.*

On Broadway, Simon contributed sketches to Catch a Star *(1955) and* New Faces of 1956. *His first Broadway play was* Come Blow Your Horn *(1961), followed by the book of the musical* Little Me *(1962). His next play, the comedy* Barefoot in the Park *(1963) was named a Best Play of its season, as was* The Odd Couple *(1965). Neither of these had closed when the musical* Sweet Charity, *for which Simon wrote the book, came along early in 1966; and none of the three had closed when Simon's* The Star-Spangled Girl *opened the following season in December 1966—so that Simon had the phenomenal total of four shows running simultaneously on Broadway during the season of 1966-67. When the last of the four closed that summer, they had played a total of 3,367 performances over four theater seasons.*

Simon immediately began stacking another pile of blue-chip shows. His Plaza Suite *(1968) was named a Best Play of its year. His book of the musical* Promises,

Promises *(1968) was another smash and his* Last of the Red Hot Lovers *(1969) became his third show in grand simultaneous display on Broadway (and fourth Best Play).* Plaza Suite *closed before* The Gingerbread Lady *(1970, also a Best play) opened, so that Simon's second stack was "only" three plays and 3,084 performances high.*

There followed The Prisoner of Second Avenue *(1971, a Best Play),* The Sunshine Boys *(1972, a Best Play),* The Good Doctor *(1973, a Best Play) and* God's Favorite *(1974). There was no new Neil Simon play on Broadway the following year because he was moving himself and his family from New York to California, partly for personal reasons and partly to base himself closer to his screen activities. Movies or not, by April 1976 he had* California Suite *ready for production at Center Theater Group in Los Angeles en route to the Eugene O'Neill Theater—which for a time he owned—in June 1976 as his 15th Broadway script and ninth Best Play.*

To continue: Simon's tenth Best Play was Chapter Two, *also produced at Center Theater Group before coming to New York in December 1977. He wrote the book for* They're Playing Our Song, *the long-run musical with a Marvin Hamlisch score and Carole Bayer Sager lyrics. His 11th Best Play,* I Ought To Be in Pictures, *went the California-to-New-York route in 1980. His shortest-run New York play,* Fools *(1981), survived for only 40 performances, and an attempt to revise and revive* Little Me *in 1982 also fell short of expectations, with only 36 performances. But Simon came roaring back in 1983 with the first of three semi-autobiographical works,* Brighton Beach Memoirs *(the Critics Award winner), with the character "Eugene Jerome" standing in for Simon as an adolescent growing up in Brooklyn. This popular hit was still running when its sequel, the Jerome-in-the-Army Best Play* Biloxi Blues *opened in March 1985, both taking the California-to-New York route. The third play in the series was* Broadway Bound, *about Jerome's efforts at gag writing for radio in collaboration with his brother, which came in from a Washington, D.C. tryout to New York on December 4, 1986 as—let's see—its author's 24th Broadway script and 13th Best Play.*

Prior to his third in the Jerome series was a revised version of The Odd Couple—*sex-changed so that the two leading characters were women instead of men as in the original version—produced on Broadway in June 1985. After* Broadway Bound *came* Rumors *for 531 Broadway performances beginning in November 1988. It had tried out at the Old Globe Theater in San Diego, as did Simon's next play,* Jake's Women—*but he withdrew the latter after a week of tryout performances in March 1990. But the beat went on with* Lost in Yonkers *which arrived on Broadway February 21, 1991 after tryouts at the North Carolina School of the Arts in Winston-Salem and the National Theater in Washington, D.C.—Simon's 27th produced playscript, 14th Best Play and first Pulitzer Prize winner, also winning its author the 1991 Tony Award as the season's best play. While* Lost in Yonkers *was still in the midst of its 780-performance run,* Jake's Women *began its 245-performance Broadway engagement March 24, 1992. He adapted his 1977 film* The Goodbye Girl *into a musical which opened on Broadway March 4, 1993 for 188 performances. And now here is Simon's*

29th script and 15th Best Play, Laughter on the 23rd Floor, *which opened on Broadway November 22, 1993 after original performances at Duke University in Durham, N.C.*

Simon wrote the screen plays for his own Barefoot in the Park *(in its time the longest-runner at Radio City Music Hall),* the Odd Couple *(which broke that record the following year),* Plaza Suite, The Prisoner of Second Avenue, the Sunshine Boys, California Suite, Chapter Two, I Ought To Be in Pictures, Brighton Beach Memoirs, Biloxi Blues *and* Lost in Yonkers *plus* The Out-of-Towners, The Heartbreak Kid, Murder by Death, The Goodbye Girl, The Cheap Detective, Seems Like Old Times, Only When I Laugh, Max Dugan Returns *and* The Slugger's Wife.

Simon's many honors and accolades have included Tony Awards every ten years: the 1965 Tony as author of The Odd Couple, *a special 1975 Tony for his overall contribution to the theater and the 1985 best-play Tony for* Biloxi Blues. *He received the Sam S. Shubert Award in 1968, Writers Guild motion picture awards in 1968, 1970 and 1975 and numerous Tony, Emmy and Oscar nominations—and two years ago Broadway's Alvin Theater was renamed the Neil Simon in his honor. He is a member of the Dramatists Guild and the Writers Guild of America and divides his time between New York and Los Angeles. He has been thrice married, with two daughters by his first wife.*

Too much of Laughter on the 23rd Floor*'s wealth of verbal humor, with its group of gag-writers vieing to top each other throughout the play, would be squandered in a complete synopsis of the script. To do* Laughter on the 23rd Floor *reportorial justice without giving away most of its punch lines, therefore, we represent it here with one complete scene (following a description of the characters): the Act I appearance of Max Prince, star of the play's TV show and of the play itself, plus the last two pages of Act I, selected by the* Best Plays *editor with the approval of the author.*

Time: 1953

Place: An office on the 23rd floor of a building on 57th Street, New York City

The Writers' Room of *The Max Prince Show,* a TV variety series, is a single large area with two distinct spaces: the writing area with typewriter on a metal top desk, sofa and assorted chairs (including a large one for Max) at left; and a more informal area at right with coffee maker, an assortment of snacks, magazines, reference books, etc. The room is lined with windows upstage, and there is a door at each end, the one at right the entrance from outside and at left the door to Max's private office.

On a Monday morning in March, a few minutes before 10 a.m., the members of Max Prince's comedy writing staff begin to arrive. They are the following:

Lucas Brickman, *"about mid-20s, wearing a tweed jacket, scarf, gloves and a cap."* The first to arrive, he serves as a narrator explaining what is going on here and that he's the newest member of the staff, this being only the second week of his four-week trial contract.

Milt Fields, *"wears a black cape over a sports jacket, a bow tie and a black beret."* He is acutely aware that the bread on his family's table depends on his making Max Prince laugh, and he is continually trying, with one-liners, and even dressing to this purpose.

Val Skolsky, *"in an old, worn topcoat over a somber suit and tie. He is the senior member of the staff. An emigrant from Russia when he was 12, he still carries his accent."* The other writers, of whom he is *"the most politically aware,"* take every opportunity to make good-natured fun of the way he talks.

Brian Doyle, *"wears a rumpled dark tweed jacket with baggy pants,"* balding but with marks of an ongoing hair transplant, *"Irish, about 29, a heavy smoker . . . . . with a biting sense of humor as caustic as his outlook on life."* He's always on the brink of selling a screen play to a large Hollywood studio.

Kenny Franks, *"neatly dressed, sports jacket, tie, raincoat, tortoise shell framed glasses. He is surely the most sophisticated of the lot."*

Carol Wyman, *"about 28, with a strong and quick defense system that comes with being the only female writer on the staff."* This morning she is particularly concerned about the growing influence of McCarthyism.

The writers are beginning to worry because Max is already half an hour late for this Monday morning meeting, when Helen, Max's secretary, phones to say that Max has just arrived and is on his way up.

> *The door opens. Max Prince enters. He is in his early 30s. He wears a trench coat over a gray double breasted suit, black shoes, a white shirt and tie. He appears to be taller than he is because he exudes great strength. His strength comes more from his anger than from his physique. He dominates a room with his personality. You must watch him because he's like a truck you can't get out of the way of. He is quixotic, changing quickly from warm, infectious laughter to sullen anger. He is often monosyllabic, offering a word or two to convey his thoughts. Today is not a good day for Max. He storms across the room almost oblivious to them.*

VAL: Oh, just talking about you, Max. We were saying the response to Saturday's show was unbelievably good. Maybe the best ever.

CAROL: I got at least twenty phone calls.

MILT: I made ten myself, that's how good it was.

MAX *(paces angrily):* Any reports on the show?

VAL *(a little bewildered):* Yes, Max. Unbelievably good. Maybe the best ever.

MAX *(still pacing):* What did they say?

VAL: . . . They said unbelievably good. Maybe the best ever.

MAX: Mug.

He hangs up his trench coat.

LUCAS: What?

MAX: Mug.

VAL *(to Lucas):* Mug. He wants coffee in his mug. No cream, four sugars.

LUCAS: Oh right, Max.

He quickly goes to get the coffee.

MAX: Did we get any more memos from NBC?

VAL: What?

MAX: Memos! Memos! They love to send memos.

VAL: No, Max. No memos.

MAX *(mocks acting hurt):* No memos? They skipped a day without memos? They're saving them so they can memo me to death. They'll bury me in a folded memo in the Mount Memo Cemetery in Memo Park, New Jersey.

LUCAS *(comes back with coffee):* Here's your coffee, Max. Be careful. It's very hot.

MAX *(he takes cup and then drinks it all down without stopping):* WHOOOOOOOOH . . . that was hot.

VAL: You shouldn't drink hot things so fast, Max.

MAX: No. It's good. Boils the blood.

CAROL: You want an aspirin, Max?

MAX: Took a bottle at home.

BRIAN: Well, a bottle of aspirin should clear it up.

CAROL: Did you get any sleep last night, Max?

MAX: Oh, yeah. Slept like a bear.

KENNY: Those bear sleeps are great, heh, Max? You wake up in April, May, you feel like a million.

Max laughs and unzips his pants, taking them off over his shoes. Holding his pants and jacket he crosses to the door and yells out.

MAX: HELEN! I'M READY!!

HELEN'S VOICE: Coming, Max.

MAX *(to others):* We work today. Lotsa work. I want to do a great show this week. NO!! Not a great show. The best. Best show we ever did, you hear?

MILT: Sure, Max. It's always good to change it once in a while.

Max is standing in his shirt, shorts, socks, shoes and garters. Helen enters. She is an attractive secretary, late 20s. Max hands her the coat and pants.

MAX: Dry cleaned and pressed.

HELEN: Like always, Max.

MAX: But you have to say it. Otherwise they just put it on a hanger and send it back. And check my pockets, I don't want any keys pressed.

HELEN: Yes, Max. Oh, Mr. Revere of NBC sent you a big pile of memos.

Nathan Lane as Max Prince in *Laughter on the 23rd Floor*

Helen goes out with his suit, closes the door. Max crosses to his rack, gets his trench coat, puts it on.

MAX: Ohhhhkay! . . . Oh, yeah. Yes, sir . . . They started, we'll finish . . . Bingo Bango Bingo.

They all look at each other.

VAL: Who's that, Max?

MAX: I just said. Bingo Bango Bingo. What do I have to do, spell it out? NBC.

Does the sound of NBC's chimes.

Bing—bang—bing! . . .

Removing a cigar from decanter.

They want to put the screws into me, you hear?

KENNY: What's up, Max?

MAX: What's up? What's not down is up. . . What's up could be down, what's down could be up. You understand?

KENNY: Certainly. It's Newton's Theory of Obscurity, isn't it?

MAX *(lights his cigar):* They want to cut the show down to an hour.

CAROL: An *hour?*

VAL: Us?? We're number one show in the country. Maybe two, three the worst.

MAX: Cutting us down. Bingo Bango Bingo.

KENNY: Can't you reason with these people, Max?

MAX: What people? NBC is not a people. They're not like us. They wear black socks up to their necks. Crew neck socks . . . They come home from work and before dinner, they dance with their wives . . . They put up wallpaper in their garages . . . You can't talk to them.

KENNY: Then what is it they want?

MAX: All right.

He holds up his cigar.

What is this I'm smoking?

They all look at each other.

BRIAN: I'll take a chance, guys. *(To Max.)* A cigar?

MAX: Wrong.

BRIAN: Damm. I thought I had it.

MAX *(to Brian):* To *us* it's a cigar. To them it's power. To them it's control. To them it's grabbing our testicles and *squeezing* them.

He grabs them and squeezes, grimacing in pain. Max then turns to Carol and squeezes.

You understand?

Lucas and Milt look towards Carol.

MILT *(aside to Carol):* I'll explain what that feels like later.

VAL: Forgive me, Max. I don't mean to interrupt. Let me see if I can understand . . . The cigar is a phallic symbol, i.e. the penis . . . i.e., the penis is power, i.e., the penis is control. Right?

MAX *(nods):* I ee I ee oh!

KENNY: So NBC is using their power to control us, right, Max? To do what?

MAX: To cut out my HEART! They want to cut the budget, save money. He says the show is too sophisticated. Too smart, he says. My own sister, my own brother, two people who never graduated from *spelling,* understand every word. The big money sponsors want out, he says. What do they sell? Raisins? Macaroni? Cream cheese? People who eat and chew can't understand this program? . . . Who does he think we're playing for, dogs and cats?

CAROL: Can't they just say that, Max? "From now on you've got an hour, and that's it?"

MAX: They can say what they want. They can sit in their offices with their camel hair carpeting, hitting golf balls into their toilet bowls . . . eating their little salmon ball wedgies for lunch . . . let 'em. But I've got a plan.

CAROL: What's the plan, Max?

MAX: Okay. Close the doors.

LUCAS *(looks):* The doors are closed, Max.

Max leans forward in his chair. Motions to them to lean in. They all do.

MAX: When the Thracians fought the battle of the Modena Heights in 354 B.C., outnumbered by a hundred thousand men, what did Cyclantis, the greatest military mind in all of history, decide to do?

They all look at each other again.

MILT *(to Carol):* Was Cyclantis the giant with the big eyes?

VAL: Will you let the man finish? . . . What did Cyclantis do, Max?

MAX: He sent out one hundred women, old, young, whatever . . . placed them ten miles apart in a— in a— *(Makes circle with his finger.)*

KENNY: A circle?

MAX *(nods):* A circle . . . covering two hundred miles. Then in the dead of night, each of the hundred women lit a—lit a—*(Makes upward hand gesture.)*

VAL: An umbrella?

MAX: A *torch.* Big torches . . . An umbrella? The enemy saw the torches all around them, thought they were surrounded, threw down their arms and sounded surrender. Y'hear? The surrounded sounded surrender . . . and that's what we're going to do.

MILT: Get a hundred women with torches and surround Rockefeller Center?

Val glares at him.

I'm just asking. I was never *in* the army.

BRIAN: I say we just kill the fuckers.

MAX: You got it.

KENNY: Can you tell us *exactly* what NBC did, Max?

MAX: They sent me their Declaration of War. In the mail. Delivered to the house where my wife and children sleep. There's going to be blood spilled. Oh, yes. But not in my house. Their palaces will crumble and their kings will fall and their wheat fields will be scorched.

MILT *(aside to Carol):* NBC has wheat fields?

KENNY: Let me ask you, Max. Is it NBC who's been sending you the threatening letters?

MAX: Who told you about that?

KENNY: You did. Last night. You called me, remember?

MAX: I called *you?*

KENNY: Yes.

MAX: Last night?

KENNY: Right.

MAX: That was you?

KENNY: I swear.

MAX: It didn't sound like you.

KENNY: I tried my best, Max.

MAX: You sounded foreign to me. Spanish maybe.

VAL: That was my maid from Peru.

MAX: She was at Kenny's house?

VAL: No. In *my* house. You called me after you called Kenny.

MAX: I never spoke to you.

VAL: No. I was at the theater.

MAX: I called you at the theater?

VAL: No. You called me at my house. I went to the theater. In the Village. The Peach. The Pear. The Plum.

LUCAS: The Cherry Lane.

VAL: The Cherry Lane. Thank you.

MAX *(to Lucas):* You were with Val?

LUCAS: No. I was at home. With my wife.

MAX: I called you at home?

LUCAS: No. Not me. Val wanted to know what theater he went to, and I told him.

MAX: Val called you to ask what theater he was in?

LUCAS: No. He already came home. He asked me this morning.

MAX: I didn't even know you were married.

LUCAS: Well, this is the first time we ever talked.

MAX *(holds his head):* I can't remember anything. I think somebody's drugging me, I swear to God.

VAL: Well, Max, that brings up another delicate subject.

MAX: I fell asleep the other night with my eyes open. I thought I was dreaming about a ceiling.

VAL: In the first place, Max, you know we all love you.

MAX: Sometimes I go in the kitchen in the middle of the night, get a hammer and smash walnuts. Why would I do that?

KENNY: I think Freud says that's a symptom of fear.

MAX: Why? I'm not afraid of walnuts . . . You want to hear the worst part?

CAROL: I thought we did, Max.

MAX: When I eat, I can't tell the difference between steak and fish any more. Why is that? *(He is near tears.)*

BRIAN: Where did they catch your steak, Max?

Max glares at Brian. Brian looks away.

MAX *(to Val):* What was the delicate subject?

VAL: Well, it's just that we feel for your own good, Max, for your own health, for your family's well being . . .

MAX: I don't want to hear my fortune. I just want to hear the delicate subject.

KENNY: We don't think those pills you take before you leave here at night are good for you, Max.

MAX *(confused):* What pills?

VAL: The pills, Max. That you take before you go home.

MAX: I take pills? What are you talking about? Those tranquilizers? They're prescription. Two little pills.

KENNY: *Little* pills? We could play nine innings of soft ball with one pill.

MAX: I hardly take them. Once a week.

BRIAN: You take them once a week every night, Max.

MAX: They're harmless. Carol, remember you weren't feeling well one night? I gave you half a pill. Did anything happen?

CAROL: I don't remember. I slept for nine days.

KENNY: It's not just the pills. It's the four jiggers of scotch you take to wash them down. Pills and liquor don't mix, Max. Or Max, mix, however you want.

MAX: I gotta sleep. If I don't sleep, who's gonna protect my family from them?

CAROL: NBC is threatening your family?

MAX: They're threatening my show. My show is my life. If they threaten my life, they threaten my family. You want to hear the letter they sent me? You want to know what they said, word for word for word?

MILT: Go ahead, Max. The doors are still closed.

MAX *(leans back in his chair, looks at his cigar):* . . . They said . . . "Give the people shit."

They all look at each other.

CAROL: The president of NBC said that?

MAX: You heard me. "Give the people shit."

BRIAN: You mean as a gift?

CAROL: Why would he say that, Max?

MAX: Because—they can make money on shit. A pot full. Drive up to Connecticut, they got big Tudor shit houses wherever you look, that's why they invented television. They put shit on for people to watch, they advertise shit, the people run out and buy the shit, their kids break the shit, so they buy them more shit, and the shit moguls go to France in the summer, and the poor people stay here and watch more shit . . . That's why I got a letter saying, "Give the people shit."

MILT *(aside to Carol):* Isn't that what Marie Antoinette said?

CAROL *(swatting Milt):* Why do you always talk to *me?* Annoy somebody else once in a while.

KENNY: Let me take a whack at this. For four years in a row we sweep the Emmy Awards. Every critic in the country loves us. But suddenly television is expanding. They're going into the midwest, the south. Different kinds of audience. They want to watch quiz shows, bowling, wrestling, am I right?

MAX *(nods):* If you got shit, shovel it over.

KENNY: So they want to cut us to an hour. Don't make the shows too esoteric. Too smart. Don't do takeoffs on Japanese movies, Italian movies.

MAX: Feed a horse hay, what are you going to get?

CAROL: You don't even have to say it, Max.

KENNY: So it's not only cutting the half hour, it's the kind of show they want us to do.

VAL: Can't we talk to them, Max?

MAX: Talk? No! No talk! Fight! We fight them on the sea, we fight them on the beaches. Or we'll get the bastards in an alley in Brooklyn somewhere. Remember

Ron Orbach (Ira), J.K. Simmons (Brian), Lewis J. Stadlen (Milt), Mark Linn-Baker (Val), John Slattery (Kenny) and Stephen Mailer (Lucas) in a scene from Neil Simon's comedy

what Churchill said? "Never have so many given so much for so long for so little for so few for so seldom . . ."

He nods to the others . . . then Max crosses to the coffee table and pours water into a paper cup. He carries it back, then sips it.

CAROL: My God! This ties up with everything that's going on in this country today. The censorship. The blacklisting. It's Senator McCarthy publicly disgracing a man like General George Marshall.

MAX *(spitting out water): What??* What did he say about Marshall?

CAROL: You didn't hear? It was on the radio all morning.

MAX *(crushes the paper cup, water erupts):* What'd he say? I want to hear it exactly. Say it slowly, I don't want to miss a word.

Max crosses to his chair, takes a final sip from his crushed cup and puts it on the table.

CAROL: Joe McCarthy accused General George Marshall, a five star General of the Army, of being a member of the Communist Party.

Max squeezes the arm of his chair so tightly, a piece breaks off. He gets up, so angry, we can see the veins in his neck.

MILT *(aside):* Somebody trade places with me

Max moves around, seething.

VAL: We know how you feel, Max. We feel the same way.

MAX: You feel the same way I do? . . . I don't think so. Would you like to know how I feel? Ask me. Ask me how I feel about McCarthy.

CAROL: Don't ask him, Val. I'm afraid to see.

MAX: You don't want to see, don't look. *(To Val.)* Ask me how I feel.

VAL: We can already *see* how you feel, Max.

MAX *(to Val):* Not yet. When you ask me, then you'll see . . . *Ask me!!*

Max's hand beckons strongly to be asked. Kenny, who sits between Max and Val, turns slowly to Val.

VAL: How do you feel about McCarthy, Max?

MAX: Thank you.

He turns and smashes his fist through the wall. His hand remains in the hole.

There! That's how I feel.

CAROL: Oh, my god!

VAL: Are you all right, Max?

BRIAN: Someone go in the other room and see how McCarthy is.

MAX: They want me to give them shit? There! I gave them shit.

VAL: Can you get your hand out, Max?

MAX: *LEAVE IT THERE!!* Get a knife. Cut it off. Send it in a box to that no-good bastard. Let him know what I think of him.

CAROL: Someone get his hand out. It could be broken.

Max pulls it out. It is still in a fist.

MAX *(calls out):* HELEN!! GET IN HERE!! *(To Carol.)* Called him a Communist, heh? *(He looks around.)* I want to hit something. Something big. Something expensive.

MILT: There's a bank across the street, Max.

HELEN *(rushes in):* Yes, Max?

MAX *(points):* You see this hole? Don't touch it. Leave it there. Call up a framer. No. Call Tiffany's. I want that hole framed in their *best* silver. And underneath I want a plaque. Gold! And on the plaque I want engraved, "In honor of General George Marshall, Soldier, Statesman, slandered by that son of a bitch, McCarthy."

HELEN *(writes this down):* I'm not sure that Tiffany's would print that, Max.

MAX: You pay 'em enough, they'll print it.

HELEN: Yes, Max.

She rushes out. Brian, who has exited stage left, sticks his head through the hole in the wall.

BRIAN: I think this could be a National Monument. Like Monticello.

MAX *(an idea hits him):* OKAY!! OKAY, I GOT THE SKETCH FOR THIS WEEK'S SHOW.

KENNY: What is it, Max?

MAX: I want to be the Statue of Liberty. I want to wear a long gown down to my toes.

VAL: I like that.

MAX: With big sandals. And a tiara. With a torch and a book. I want to be painted green. With bird shit on my shoulders from the pigeons. And I'm standing on this box that says, "Give me your poor, your hungary, your sunburned, your toothless . . ." whatever they got there.

MILT: We'll look it up.

VAL: God dammit, dot's funny, Max.

KENNY: And what happens?

MAX: She gets subpoenaed. To Washington. She comes in the courtroom, the bottom of her dress is dripping wet from the harbor. With codfish in her hair.

He "squeezes" water out of an imaginary bottom of dress.

LUCAS: This is terrific.

MAX: And he's sitting up there looking at her. Senator Joseph McNutcake.

KENNY: *McNutcake?* . . . We can't say that, Max. Not on the air.

MAX: You don't think it's funny?

KENNY: Yes, it's funny. I don't think eight years in jail would be funny. You can't say McNutcake.

MAX *(thinks):* How about McBirdbrain? . . . McFruithead? . . . McFahrblungett. It means crazy in Yiddish, he'll never understand it.

VAL: Someone'll tell him.

MAX: So we do nothing? Is that what you all want to do? Nothing?

MILT: I don't think having a long life is nothing, Max.

MAX: Where I grew up, we took care of bullies. There was a big fat shlub in my class. We called him Tank Ass. He used to steal my sister's lunch. One day I put a rock in her sandwich. That taught him.

CAROL: He bit into it?

MAX: He ate it. The whole rock. He had to start wearing iron underwear. We gotta do *something,* guys. I got a knot in my stomach that's blocking my pituitary canal.

VAL: We feel the same as you, Max.

MAX: No, you don't, you don't know how I feel.

MILT *(to Val):* Don't ask him. It'll look like Swiss cheese in here.

MAX: I'm not lying down. I'm not doing nothing. We gotta make some kind of stand, like Spartacus in the war against the Byzantimums.

VAL: So what do you suggest we do, Max?

MAX: We quit. We tell them to keep their show and put on shit seven days a week. We walk out of here in single file, our hands up in the air like the heroes of Bataan . . . We're off the air as of today. No show Saturday!! . . . That's what Patrick Henry said.

VAL: He said no show Saturday?

MAX *(glares at him):* "Give me liberty or give me death."

KENNY: If we walk, Max, they'll sue us.

MAX: Listen, are we together or not? Because if someone here doesn't want to quit, I don't want him here. He can leave.

MILT: That'll show him, Max.

MAX: I'm calling them now. *(He crosses to the phone.)* I'm telling them our decision is immediate, unanimous and conclusionary.

He picks up the phone.

Helen, get me NBC. *(Hand over the mouthpiece.)* I just want to know if we're agreed.

VAL: Is it possible to talk first, Max?

MAX: Yes, it's possible, but it's not gonna happen. Listen, we have to stick together on this. Otherwise I'm going to ask everyone to leave the room and I'll have a closed vote. You'll vote yes, then it's closed.

MILT: Think of it this way, Max. If we go off the air, isn't there a good chance they'll find someone *else* who doesn't mind giving them shit?

MAX: Someone else's shit isn't mine . . . Do you know who said that?

CAROL: Tell us, Max. We'll get it wrong.

MAX: It's in the Bible. You have to look for it.

BRIAN: Someone else's shit isn't mine is in the Bible, Max? Where?

MAX: Bottom of page 162. You think I memorized the whole Bible, for crise sakes?

KENNY: Max, it's a dumb idea. You've worked your whole life for this show. You think ABC or CBS are any different? They have corporate minds, Max. If they could get a TV set to turn out sausages, we'd all be pigs instead of writers. They're not interested in culture. Maybe if Van Gogh and Goya were wrestlers, they'd put them on Friday nights. But if we quit, Max, they win. We give up an hour and a half to *Miss America* and *Beat the Clock* . . . We stay, Max. We do what we've been doing for years. Only we do it better. And we keep doing it. And you know why, Max? Because maybe we'll never have this much fun again in our entire lives.

Silence. Max hangs up the phone and sits.

MAX: . . . I served under General Marshall in the war. We were together in the European front.

MILT: I thought you were in the navy, Max. Playing in a band.

MAX *(slowly looks at Milt):* . . . He came to a dance I played in London. He was fox trotting ten feet away from me. I played a saxophone solo in his honor.

HELEN *(comes in):* He's on the phone, Max. Mr.—you know. NBC. He's waiting.

MAX *(rising):* I'll take it up in my office.

Helen leaves. Max crosses to the door.

We're not pulling down our flag. I will not break my sword over my knee for anyone. When the Roman legions, led by Augustus the Fourth, fled in defeat, he came back to win on Novembus the Fifth.

He thinks about that, wonders if he got it right, nods and leaves.

The seventh member of the writing team, Ira Stone, *"all energy with a touch of brilliant madness,"* comes in. He carries hypochondria to extremes. His imagined illnesses are the butt of the others' jokes. Ira boasts that he could write all of next week's show by himself and collects a stack of typewriter paper. But he has left the room when Max comes in again.

KENNY: How'd the call go with NBC, Max?
MAX *(sits):* The call with NBC?

He lights his cigar.

The call with NBC went fine.
VAL: Everything's all right?
MAX: It's fine.
CAROL: It all got settled?
MAX: It got settled fine.
BRIAN: Was anything decided?
MAX: Fine was decided. We decided fine.
VAL: No problems?
MAX: We had *some* problems, but we fined them out.
VAL: That sounds fine to me, Max.
KENNY: You want to give us any details, Max? Any changes?
MAX: Changes? Let me see! . . . Oh, yes. They're cutting us back to an hour. This year is fine, next year is an hour. Next year they cut the budget. Next year they want approval of the sketches. Next year they put an observer on the show. That's all. That's the only changes. Minor stuff.

He looks at his cigar. They can see he is controlling an explosion.

CAROL: And that's fine with you, Max?
MAX: No. That's fine with *them. Them* is fine. We is not so fine yet. But we'll see. We'll wait. We'll think. We'll plan. And then we'll be fine.
LUCAS: What is the observer going to do, Max?
MAX: The observer? He's going to observe. *(He gets up.)* He'll be around the show observing the coffee, the cream cheese, the potato chips. Maybe he'll come up here and observe us working, observe Ira coming in late. *(He crosses to the telephone. He is standing behind the sofa.)* Maybe he'll observe me getting upset that he's observing me, and then he'll observe me taking the fucking *telephone* and smashing it on the fucking floor.

In a fury, Max hurls the phone to the floor. He grimaces, whimpers softly and then continues. Obviously, he has hit his foot with the phone.

Or . . . *(He steps away, limping on the foot that was hit.)* . . . if the observer is not through observing, maybe he can observe me putting my fist through his *fucking face!*

Max punches another hole in the wall, right next to McCarthy's hole.

And then they'll take him away for surgery, and he'll observe the hospital for a while. But right now I'm fine . . . Lucas, when Helen comes back, tell her to call Tiffany's again . . . Just a simple frame with a gold plaque underneath saying, "Fine." *(He sits.)* So. What have we got for this week's show?

The door suddenly opens, and Ira comes back with a stack of paper.

IRA: What, am I crazy?

He throws the entire stack of paper up in the air.

Write a whole show myself? Get outa here! *(He looks at Max.)* How you doing, Max?

MAX: Fine. Just fine.

He calmly crosses his legs and puffs on his cigar. Curtain. End of Act I.

Act II takes place in the same room with the same characters seven months later, as Max and his writers struggle to come up with comedy ideas for their hour-long TV variety show, while they fight their inevitably losing battle to keep the show on network air. When the end finally comes, Max faces it with a joke: ". . . They didn't believe that Hannibal could cross a thousand miles over the Alps on elephants. They said the elephants would all freeze and die. And you know what Hannibal said? . . . He said, 'Not if they *run* all the way.' *(He breaks up laughing.)* Come on. Let's celebrate."

Lucas sums up as follows: "I would have followed Max to the ends of the earth . . . But the earth went off the air on June First . . . And we all went our separate ways . . . Some up, some down, some struggled, some had more babies, and one, like Brian, died much too young . . . Helen went to law school, and God knows what happened to her . . . But the most wonderful and incredible thing *did* happen . . . On the very last day of the very last show of the season, the newspapers announced that the United States Senate voted 67 to 22 to censure Joseph McCarthy for conduct unbecoming a Senator. His days were numbered . . . That night Max took us all out to dinner, and he was so unbelievably funny, the tears ran down our faces, and only some of it was from laughter."

ANGELS IN AMERICA, PART II: PERESTROIKA

A Play in Five Acts

BY TONY KUSHNER

Cast and credits appear on page 428

TONY KUSHNER was born in Manhattan July 16, 1956, but his mother and father, both professional musicians, soon moved the family to Lake Charles, La., where the playwright-to-be grew up. His first memories of the theater were of his mother acting in amateur productions. When he came to New York for college at Columbia, he went to the theater almost every night. He received his B.A. in 1978 and went on to N.Y.U. for its graduate program in directing, getting his M.F.A. in 1984. At that time directing was "doable," Kushner felt, but "I never imagined I could write a play that was worth anything. It was unattainable." Such didn't turn out to be the case. The Eureka Theater Company in San Francisco produced his first play, A Bright Room Called Day, *in 1985 (it arrived at the Public Theater in New York January 7, 1991 for 14 performances). And Kushner's adaptation of Corneille's* L'Illusion Comique *provided him with his New York debut OOB at the New York Theater Workshop October 27, 1988 and has since been produced in regional theater venues including Hartford, Conn. and Berkeley, Calif.*

Angels in America *was commissioned through a special projects grant from the NEA. Its first version was a 250-page, six-act script workshopped at the Mark Taper Forum (it is now a two-parter,* Millennium Approaches *and* Perestroika.*) The two* *parts premiered at Eureka in 1991, winning the Fund for New American Plays/ Kennedy Center, Joseph Kesselring and Bay Area Theater Critics Awards.* Millennium Approaches *then moved on to London's National Theater, winning the Evening Standard Award as the season's best new play. In November 1992, both parts of* Angels in America *(subtitled* A Gay Fantasia on National Themes) *were produced at the Mark Taper Forum and won the 1993 Pulitzer Prize as well as the Los Angeles Drama Critics Award. The New York Drama Critics followed suit, voting the* Millennium Approaches *segment of* Angels in America *the best new play of the season after it opened on Broadway May 4, 1993. Kushner's first Best Play citation soon followed, as did the best-play Tony Award. Part II of* Angels in America, *entitled* Perestroika, *opened on Broadway November 23, 1993, running in repertory with Part I and winning its author his second Best Play citation and his second best-play Tony.*

Kushner, who lives in Brooklyn, has been additionally honored by a 1990 Whiting Foundation Writers Award as well as playwriting and directing fellowships from the New York State Foundation for the Arts and Council on the Arts and the National Endowment for the Arts.

Place: New York City and elsewhere

ACT I: Spooj, January 1986

Scene 1

In the Kremlin's Hall of Deputies, the Oldest Living Bolshevik, Aleksii Antedilluvianovich Prelapsarianov, is discoursing on the sad difference between the ideal and the reality of any proposed change.

> *A tremendous tearing and crashing sound, the great red flag is flown out, and lights come up on the same tableau as at the close of* Part I, Millennium Approaches: *Prior Walter (Louis's abandoned boyfriend, worked occasionally as a club designer or caterer) cowering in his bed, which is strewn with the wreckage of his bedroom ceiling; and the Angel (the Continental Principality of America; she has magnificent gray steel wings), in a gown of surprising whiteness, barefoot and magnificent, hovering in the air facing him.*

ALEKSII: Then we dare not, we *cannot,* we MUST NOT move ahead!
ANGEL: Greetings, Prophet. The Great Work begins. The Messenger has arrived.
PRIOR: Go away.

Scene 2

Late the same night that *Millennium Approaches* ended, Louis Ironson, who works at the Court of Appeals, brings home Joe Pitt, a Court of Appeals chief clerk, to his apartment in "Alphabetland" (the Lower East Side). Louis was Prior Walter's lover but left him when he could not bear to live with the deteriorating effects of AIDS which began to show in and on Prior. This is Joe Pitt's first homosexual encounter after having left his wife Harper—so Louis must take careful initiative toward their having sex.

Scene 3

Harper Pitt *("an agoraphobic with a mild valium addiction and a much stronger imagination")* dreams herself in Antarctica with Mr. Lies, an imagined travel agent. To enhance her dream environment, she's appropriated a small pine tree from Prospect Park, though Mr. Lies reminds her there are no trees in Antarctica. Harper's husband Joe materializes in her dream, wrapped in Louis's bedsheet and protesting that he never fell out of love with Harper. Harper invites him to come back to her, but in the middle of his adventure with Louis he can't. The flashing lights of a police car end the flow of Harper's imagination.

Scene 4

Joe's mother, Hannah Pitt, has sold her house in Salt Lake City and moved to New York (after learning in *Millennium Approaches* that her son Joe is a homosexual and has left his wife). Hannah has taken up residence in the Pitts's Brooklyn apartment. She receives a phone call from the police: Harper has been picked up in Prospect Park with a pine tree she has apparently chewed down. Harper isn't crazy, Hannah assures the police, and she leaves to pick Harper up.

Scene 5

Later that same night, Prior awakens after a lustful dream and phones Belize *("a former drag queen and a former lover of Prior's; a registered nurse")* to suggest that he join him. Prior adds, "I'm scared. And also full of, I don't know, joy or something. Hope." But Belize is too busy right now.

At the hospital, Henry, Roy Cohn's doctor, has come to get his famous patient admitted to the AIDS section as a liver cancer patient (Cohn does not want to admit he has AIDS), where Belize is the duty nurse.

Scene 6

Roy Cohn (a successful New York lawyer and unofficial power broker, now facing disbarment and dying of AIDS) is in his hospital bed, sick and very scared. Belize enters with the IV drip.

ROY: Get outta here you, I got nothing to say to you . . .
BELIZE: Just doing my . . .
ROY: I want a white nurse. My constitutional right.

BELIZE: You're in a hospital, you don't have any constitutional rights.

He begins preparing Roy's right arm for the IV drip, palpating the vein, disinfecting the skin, etc.

ROY *(getting nervous about the needle):* Find the vein, you moron, don't start jabbing that Goddamned spigot in my arm till you find the fucking vein or I'll sue you so bad they'll repossess your teeth, you dim black motherf . . .

BELIZE *(had enough, very fierce):* Watch. Yourself. You don't talk that way to me when I'm holding something this sharp. Or I might slip and stick it in your heart. If you have a heart.

ROY: Oh I do. Tough little muscle. Never bleeds.

BELIZE: I'll bet. Now I've been doing drips a long time. I can slip this in so easy you'll think you were born with it. Or I can make it feel like I just hooked you up to a bag of Liquid Drano. So you be nice to me, or you're going to be one sorry asshole come morning.

ROY: Nice.

BELIZE: Nice and quiet.

He puts the drip needle in Roy's arm.

There.

ROY *(fierce):* I *hurt.*

BELIZE: I'll get you a painkiller.

ROY: Will it knock me out?

BELIZE: I sure hope so.

ROY: Then shove it. Pain's . . . nothing, pain's life.

BELIZE: Sing it, baby.

ROY: When they did my facelifts, I made the anesthesiologist use a local. They lifted up my whole face like a dinner napkin, and I was wide awake to see it.

BELIZE: Bullshit. No doctor would agree to that.

ROY: I can get anyone to do anything I want. For instance: Let's be friends. *(Sings.)* "We shall overcome . . ." Jews and coloreds, historical liberal coalition, right? My people being the first to sell retail to your people, your people being the first people my people could afford to hire to sweep out the store Saturday mornings, and then we all held hands and rode the bus to Selma. Not me of course, I don't ride buses, I take cabs. But the thing about the American Negro is, he never went Communist. Loser Jews did. But you people had Jesus, so the reds never got to you. I admire that.

BELIZE: Your chart didn't mention that you're delusional.

ROY: Barking mad. Sit. Talk.

BELIZE: Mr. Cohn, I'd rather suck the pus out of an abscess. I'd rather drink a subway toilet. I'd rather chew off my tongue and spit it in your leathery face. So thanks for the offer of conversation, but I'd rather not.

Belize starts to exit, turning off the light as he does.

ROY: Oh for Christsake. Whatta I gotta do? Beg? I don't want to be alone.

Belize stops.

Oh how I fucking *hate* hospitals, *nurses,* this waste of time and . . . *wasting* and weakness . . . . .

Cohn asks Belize, who has obviously seen a great number of AIDS cases, what his chances are. Belize tells him frankly that he is probably going to die soon.

ROY: Hah. I appreciate the . . . the honesty, or whatever . . . If I live I could sue you for emotional distress, the whole hospital, but . . . I'm not prejudiced, I'm not a prejudiced man.

Pause. Belize just looks at him.

These racist guys, simpletons, I never had any use for them—too rigid. You want to keep your eye on where the most powerful enemy really is. I save my hate for what counts.

BELIZE: Well. And I think that's a good idea, a good thing to do, probably. *(Little pause; with great effort and distaste.)* This didn't come from me, and I *don't* like you, but let me tell you a thing or two: They have you down for radiation tomorrow for the sarcoma lesions, and you don't want to let them do that, because radiation will kill the T-cells, and you don't have any you can afford to lose. So tell the doctor no thanks for the radiation. He won't want to listen. Persuade him. Or he'll kill you.

ROY: You're just a fucking nurse. Why should I listen to you over my very qualified, very expensive WASP doctor?

BELIZE: He's not queer. I am. *(Winks at Roy.)*

ROY: Don't wink at me. You said a thing or two. So that's one.

BELIZE: I don't know what strings you pulled to get in on the azidothymidine trials.

ROY: I have my little ways.

BELIZE: Uh-huh. Watch out for the double blind. They'll want you to sign something that says they can give you M&Ms instead of the real drug. You'll die, but they'll get the kind of statistics they can publish in the *New England Journal of Medicine.* And you can't sue, 'cause you signed. And if you don't sign, no pills. So if you have any strings left, pull them, because everyone's put through the double blind, and with this, time's against you, you can't fuck around with placebos.

ROY: You hate me.

BELIZE: Yes.

ROY: Why are you telling me this?

BELIZE: I wish I knew.

Pause.

ROY *(very nasty):* You're a butterfingers spook faggot nurse. I think . . . you have little reason to want to help me.

BELIZE: Consider it solidarity. One faggot to another.

Belize snaps his fingers, turns, exits. Roy calls after him.

ROY: Any more of your lip, boy, and you'll be flipping Big Macs in East Hell before tomorrow night!

A beat. He picks up his bedside phone.

And get me a real phone, with a hold button, I mean look at this, it's just one little line, how am I supposed to perform bodily functions on *this?*

He thinks a minute, picks up the receiver, clicks the hang-up button several times.

Yeah, who is this, the operator? Give me an outside line. Well then dial for me. It's a medical emergency darling, dial the fucking number or I'll strangle myself with the phone cord. 202/733-8525. *(Little pause.)* Martin Heller. Oh, hi Martin. Yeah, I know what time it is, I couldn't sleep, I'm busy dying. Listen Martin, this drug they got me on, azido-methatalo-molamoca-whatchamacallit. Yeah. AZT. I want my own private stash, Martin. Of serious Honest-Abe medicine. That I control, here in the room with me. No placebos, I'm no good at tests, Martin, I'd rather cheat. So send me my pills with a get-well bouquet, PRONTO, or I'll ring up CBS and sing Mike Wallace a song: the ballad of adorable Ollie North and his secret Contra slush fund.

He holds the phone away from his ear: Martin is excited.

Oh, you only *think* you know all I know. *I* don't even know what all I know. Half the time I just make it up, and it *still* turns out to be true! We learned that trick in the Fifties. Tomorrow, you two-bit scumsucking shitheel flypaper insignificant dried-out little turd. A nice big box of drugs for Uncle Roy. Or there'll be seven different kinds of hell to pay.

He slams the receiver down.

Scene 7

In a split scene taking place over the course of three weeks, Joe and Louis are in bed in Alphabetland while Hannah and Harper, in her nightdress, are in the Pitt apartment in Brooklyn. Hannah informs Harper that she's sold her house in Salt Lake City, so presumably she's come here to stay.

Louis and Joe are having sex, Joe now unreservedly enjoying it.

Hannah, dressed for a job she has obtained at the Mormon Visitor's Center, listens to Harper describing her Antarctic fantasy. Hannah suggests that Harper come to work with her at the Mormon Center.

As the days pass, Joe and Louis, in bed, discuss politics, Joe on the conservative side, Louis on the liberal—and they continue to have sex.

One morning at 5 o'clock, Hannah (she goes to work early to open the Center) has persuaded Harper to join her and is helping Harper get dressed to go out.

Joe and Louis discuss Louis feeling guilty for having left his sick lover, Prior, and Joe at peace with no bad dreams at having left his wife Harper. They comfort each other affectionately.

JOE *(very softly):* Louis? Louis? Louis? I love you.

Harper appears.

HARPER: Don't worry, I'm not really here. I have terrible powers. I see more than I want to see. Maybe I'm a witch.

JOE: You're not.

HARPER: I could be a witch. Why not? I married a fairy.

JOE: Please, Harper, just go, I . . .

LOUIS *(waking from a drowse):* Joe . . . ? Are you O.K.?

JOE: Yeah, yeah, I . . . I have a screwy stomach. It's nothing.

HARPER *(simultaneously):* Talk softer, you're keeping him awake. Why am I here? You called me.

JOE: I didn't . . .

HARPER: You called me. Leave me alone if you're so Goddamned happy.

JOE: I didn't call you.

HARPER: *THEN WHY AM I HERE?*

Pause. They look at each other.

To see you again. Any way I can. You're a liar. You do so have dreams. Bad ones. OH GOD I WISH YOU WERE . . . No I don't. DEAD. Yes, I do.

LOUIS: Joe?

HARPER: You can't save him. You never saved anyone. Joe in love. Isn't it pathetic.

JOE: What?

HARPER: You're turning into me.

JOE: GO.

She vanishes.

LOUIS: What's . . .

JOE: Night chills. Nothing. I just can't sleep.

Curtain.

ACT II: The Epistle, February 1986

Scene 1

Three weeks later, Belize and Prior have just attended the funeral of a friend. Belize is well and brightly dressed, while *"Prior is dressed oddly: a great long black coat and a huge, fringed, matching scarf, draped to a hoodlike effect. His appearance is disconcerting, menacing and vaguely redolent of the Biblical . . . . . This is his costume . . . . . it stays fundamentally corvine, ragged and eerie."*

Prior has been looking and acting strangely, Belize observes, ever since the night of Prior's dream about the Angel. It wasn't a dream, it was real, Prior believes, and the experience has changed him: "I've been given a prophecy. A book. Not a *physical* book, or there was one but they took it back, but somehow there's still this book. In me. A prophecy."

Scene 2

Three weeks earlier, Prior remembers, he was lying in bed amid the wreckage of his ceiling, with the Angel hovering above. Prior ordered the Angel to go away, but the Angel remained, repeating a message about the Great Work beginning.

Ellen McLaughlin as the Angel and Stephen Spinella as Prior Walter in Tony Kushner's *Perestroika*

ANGEL: I I I I
Am the Bird of America, the Bald Eagle,
Continental Principality,
LUMEN PHOSPHOR FLUOR CANDLE!
I unfold my leaves, Bright Steel,
In salutation open sharp before you:
PRIOR WALTER
Long-descended, well-prepared . . .

PRIOR: No. I'm not prepared for anything, I have lots to do, I . . .

ANGEL *(with a gust of music):*
American Prophet tonight you become,
American Eye that pierceth Dark,
American Heart all Hot for Truth,
The True Great Vocalist, the Knowing Mind,
Tongue-of-the-Land, Seer-Head!

PRIOR: Oh, shoo! You're scaring the shit out of me, get the fuck out of my room. Please, oh please . . .

ANGEL: Now: Remove from their hiding place the Sacred Prophetic Implements.

Little pause.

PRIOR: The *what?*

ANGEL: Remove from their hiding place the sacred Prophetic Implements. *(Little pause.)* Your dreams have revealed them to you.

PRIOR: What dreams?

ANGEL: You have had dreams revealing to you . . .

PRIOR: I haven't had a dream I can remember in months.

ANGEL: No . . . dreams, you . . . Are you sure?

Something is apparently amiss, but the Angel consults her invisible sources and is told that the Sacred Implements are buried under the tiles in the kitchen. An offstage explosion raises some dust. Prior goes out to see what it was and returns with an ancient leather suitcase. He takes out a pair of spectacles made of rocks instead of lenses, puts them on, sees something terrible he doesn't want to look at and tears them off. Prior then *"removes a large book with bright steel pages from the suitcase,"* as the Angel tells him, "Heaven here reaches down to disaster and in touching you touches all of Earth." She gives him back the spectacles to put on, and after Prior does so he is taken with intense sexual desire, which he satisfies in company with the multi-sexual Angel.

"The sexual politics of this are *very* confusing," Prior comments to Belize, who is observing this scene from close by, a listener to whom a story about a past incident is being told.

PRIOR: God, for example, is a man. Well, not a man, he's a flaming Hebrew letter, but a male flaming Hebrew letter.

ANGEL: The Aleph Glyph. Deus Erectus! Pater Omnipotens!

PRIOR: Angelic orgasm makes protomatter, which fuels the Engine of Creation. They used to copulate *ceaselessly* before . . . Each angel is an infinite aggregate myriad entity, they're basically incredibly powerful bureaucrats, they have no imagination, they can *do* anything but they can't invent, create, they're sort of fabulous and dull all at once.

ANGEL: Made for His Pleasure, We can only ADORE: Seeking something New . . .

PRIOR: God split the World in Two . . .

ANGEL: And made YOU:

PRIOR & ANGEL: Human Beings: Uni-Genitaled: Female. Male.

ANGEL:

In creating You, our Father-Lover unleashed
Sleeping Creation's Potential for Change
In YOU the Virus of TIME began!

PRIOR: In making us, God apparently set in motion a potential in the design for change, for random event, for movement forward.

ANGEL:

YOU *Think!* And You *IMAGINE!*
Migrate, Explore, and when you do . . .

PRIOR: As the human race began to progress, travel, intermingle, everything started to come unglued. Manifest first as tremors in Heaven.

ANGEL:

Heaven is a City Much Like San Francisco.
House upon house depended from Hillside,
From Crest down to Dockside,
The green Mirroring Bay.

PRIOR: And there are earthquakes there, or rather, heavenquakes.

ANGEL:

Oh Joyful in the Buckled Garden,
Undulant Landscape Over Which
The Threat of Seismic Catastrophe hangs:
More beautiful because imperiled.
POTENT: yet DORMANT: the Fault Lines of Creation!

BELIZE: So human progress . . .

PRIOR: Migration. Science. Forward Motion.

BELIZE: . . . shakes up Heaven.

ANGEL:

Paradise itself Shivers and Splits,
Each day when You awake, as though WE are only the Dream of YOU.
PROGRESS! MOVEMENT!
Shaking *HIM:*

BELIZE: God.

The Angel explains further that God, bored by paradise and fascinated by humanity, left the heavenly hosts on April 18, 1906—the day of the San Francisco earthquake—and disappeared, they know not where. Things must return to the way they were before God vanished, the Angel declares, so human progress must stop.

ANGEL *(softly):*
Forsake the Open Road:
Neither Mix Nor Intermarry: Let Deep Roots Grow:
If you do not MINGLE you will Cease to Progress:
Seek Not to Fathom the World and its Delicate Particle Logic:
You cannot Understand, You can only Destroy,
You do not Advance, You only Trample.
Poor blind Children, abandoned on the Earth,
Groping terrified, misguided, over
Fields of Slaughter, over bodies of the Slain:
HOBBLE YOURSELVES!
There is No Zion Save Where You Are!
If you Cannot find your Heart's desire . . .
PRIOR: In your own backyard . . .
ANGEL, PRIOR & BELIZE: You never lost it to begin with.
ANGEL *(coughs):*
Turn back. Undo.
Till HE returns again.
PRIOR: Please. Please. Angel or dream, whatever you are . . .
BELIZE: It's a dream, baby . . .

PRIOR: Whatever you are, I don't understand this visitation, I don't understand what you want from me, I'm not a prophet, I'm a sick, lonely man, I . . . What are you? Did you come here to save me or destroy me? Stop. Moving. That's what you want. Answer me! You want me dead.

Pause. The Angel and Prior look at each other.

ANGEL: YES. NO. NO. *(Coughs.)* YES. This is not in the Text. We *deviate* . . . No more.

She picks up the Book.

PRIOR: *I. WANT.* You to go away. I'm tired to death of being done to, walked out on, *infected,* fucked over and *now* tortured by some mixed-up, irresponsible angel, some . . . Leave me alone.

The Angel warns Prior that he cannot escape her or his role as a prophet, now or in the future. She presses the book against his chest, making him, as she says, "Vessel of the BOOK," then ascends, taking the book with her, leaving Prior and Belize as they were in the previous scene in front of the funeral home, with Prior recounting this experience to Belize. Belize insists it wasn't really an angelic visitation, it was only a dream.

PRIOR: Then I'm crazy. The whole world is, why not me? It's 1986, and there's a *plague,* half my friends are dead, and I'm only thirty-one, every Goddamn morning I wake up and I think Louis is next to me in the bed, and it takes me long minutes to remember . . . that this is *real,* it isn't just an impossible, terrible dream, so maybe yes I'm flipping out.

BELIZE *(angry):* You better not. You better fucking not flip out. This is not dementia. And this is not real. This is just you, Prior, afraid of the future, afraid of time. Longing to go backwards so bad you made this angel up, a cosmic reactionary. But there's no angel. You hear me? For me? I can handle anything but not this happening to you.

PRIOR: Maybe I am a prophet. Not just me, all of us who are dying now. Maybe we've caught the virus of prophecy. Be still. Toil no more. Maybe the world has driven God from Heaven, incurred the angels' wrath.

ANGEL'S VOICE:

Whisper into the ear of the World, Prophet,
Wash up red in the tide of its dreams,
And billow bloody words into the sky of sleep.

PRIOR: I believe I've seen the end of things. And having seen, I'm going blind, as prophets do. It makes a certain sense to me.

ANGEL'S VOICE: FOR THIS AGE OF ANOMIE: A NEW LAW!

PRIOR: And if I hate Heaven, my only resistance is to run.

ANGEL'S VOICE:

Delivered this night, this silent night, from Heaven,
Oh Prophet, to You.

Curtain.

ACT III: Borborygmi, February 1986

Scene 1

In his hospital bed strewn with papers, a week later, Roy is now in considerable pain from time to time but still able to fight the disbarment proceedings in phone conversations. Ethel Rosenberg appears and sits in a chair by the bed. Belize comes in with medication, but Roy now has his own medicine, locked in a small icebox at the foot of his bed. Roy tosses Belize the key, and Belize opens the box to find it full of bottles of AZT, when only about 30 other people in the U.S. are able to obtain this drug.

BELIZE: If you live fifty more years you won't swallow all these pills. *(Pause.)* I want some.

ROY: That's illegal.

BELIZE: Ten bottles.

ROY: I'm gonna report you.

BELIZE: There's a nursing shortage. I'm in the union. I'm real scared. I have friends who need them. Bad.

ROY: Loyalty I admire. But no.

BELIZE *(amazed, off guard): Why?*

Pause.

ROY: Because you repulse me. *"WHY?"* You'll be begging for it next. *"WHY?"* Because I hate your guts, and your friends' guts, that's *why.* "Gimme!" So Goddamned entitled. Such a shock when the bill comes due.

BELIZE: From what I read, you never paid a fucking bill in your life.

ROY: *No one* has worked harder than me. To end up knocked flat in a . . .

BELIZE *(overlapping):* Yeah, well things are tough all over.

ROY *(continuous, over Belize):* And you come *here* looking for *fairness*? *(To Ethel.)* They couldn't *touch* me when I was alive, and now when I am dying they try this.

He grabs up all the paperwork in two fists.

Now! When I'm a . . . *(Back to Belize.)* That's fair? What am I? A dead man! *(A terrible spasm, quick and violent, he doubles up.)* Fuck! What was I saying, Oh God I can't remember any . . . Oh yeah, dead. I'm a Goddamn dead man.

BELIZE: You expect *pity*?

ROY *(a beat, then):* I expect you to hand over those keys and move your nigger ass out of my room.

BELIZE: What did you say.

ROY: Move your nigger cunt spade faggot lackey ass out of my room.

BELIZE *(overlapping, starting on "spade"):* Shit-for-brains filthy-mouthed selfish motherfucking cowardly cocksucking cloven-hoofed pig.

ROY *(overlapping):* Mongrel. Dinge. Slave. Ape.

BELIZE: Kike.

ROY: *Now* you're talking!

BELIZE: Greedy kike.

ROY: Now you can have a bottle. But only one.

Belize tosses the keys at Roy, hard. Roy catches them. Belize takes a bottle of the pills, then another, then a third, and leaves. As soon as he is out of the room Roy is wracked with a series of spasms; he's been holding them in.

GOD, I thought he'd never go! *(To Ethel.)* So what? Are you going to sit there all night?

ETHEL: Till morning.

ROY: Uh huh. The cock crows, you go back to the swamp.

ETHEL: No, I take the 7:05 to Yonkers.

ROY: What the fuck's in Yonkers?

ETHEL: The disbarment committee hearings. You been hocking about it all week. I'll have a look-see.

ROY: They won't let you in the front door. You're a convicted and executed traitor.

ETHEL: I'll walk through a wall.

She starts to laugh. He joins her.

ROY: Fucking SUCCUBUS! Fucking bloodsucking old bat!

He picks up the phone, punches a couple of buttons and then puts the receiver back, dejectedly.

The worst thing about being sick in America, Ethel, is you are booted out of the parade. Americans have no use for sick. Look at Reagan: He's so healthy he's hardly human, he's a hundred if he's a day, he takes a slug in his chest, and two days later he's out West riding ponies in his PJs. I mean who does that? That's America. It's just no country for the infirm.

Scene 2

Later the same day, Harper is sitting in the Diorama Room (a little theater with curtains drawn) of the Mormon Visitor's Center, surrounded by bags of snacks and cans of soda. Hannah shows Prior in and sits him down, then goes out to get the show started. Harper introduces herself to Prior as a flawed Mormon especially interested in the Diorama because one of the talking dummies bears an uncanny resemblance to her husband Joe, and Prior in turn identifies himself as an "angelologist."

The Diorama begins, depicting a Mormon family with covered wagon on their way west from Missouri to Salt Lake; a Mother, Daughter, two Sons and a Father (Joe, not a dummy) who urges his dummy family to be brave as they follow their Lord to a promised Zion. To the Father's encouraging message—which she's obviously heard many times before—Harper adds her own cynical comments: "They drag you on your knees through hell and when you get there the water, of course, is undrinkable. Salt. It's a Promised Land, but what a disappointing promise!"

The Father starts to tell a tale about a Mormon prophet in 1823, when Louis appears in the Diorama and begins to argue religion with Joe. Prior is shocked at Louis's appearance ("I must be delirious"). Harper assures him that Louis is merely a "little creep" who intrudes on the Diorama every day but has nothing to do with the Mormon adventure story. Prior calls to Louis, who almost hears him; but then Louis and Joe exit, and Harper pulls the curtain on the show.

Hannah enters, sees that Prior is in emotional distress and pulls open the curtain on the Diorama, to which the Father dummy has now been restored. Hannah orders Harper to clean up the mess she has made with her snacks, then exits. "Imagination is a dangerous thing," Prior sums up their curious experience with the Diorama, leaving Harper to imagine what it might be like if the Mormon Mother stepped down and Harper joined the Mormon Father, Joe, on the trip West.

Scene 3

Sitting on the Jones Beach dunes late that same winter afternoon, Louis describes the homosexual experience to Joe as "Exploration across an unmapped terrain." Joe professes that he loves Louis, but Louis assures him that what he feels isn't love but "just the gay virgin thing." And Louis is somewhat surprised to learn that Joe is a Mormon.

JOE: . . . . . I am in love with you. You and I, fundamentally we're the same. We both want the same things.

LOUIS: I want to see Prior again.

Joe stands up, moves away.

I miss him, I . . .

JOE: You want to go back to . . .

LOUIS: I just . . . need to see him again. *(Little pause.)* Don't you . . . You must want to see your wife.

JOE: I do see her. All the time. *(Pointing to his head.)* In here. I miss her, I feel bad for her, I . . . I'm afraid of her.

LOUIS: Yes.

JOE: And I want more to be with . . .

LOUIS: I have to. See him. It's like a bubble rising up through rock, it's taken time, I don't know, the month in bed and the . . . Love is still what I don't get, it . . . never seems to fit into any of the schematics, wherever I'm going and whatever I've prepared for I always seem to have forgotten about love. I only know . . . It's an unsafe thing. To talk about love, Joe. Please don't look so sad. I just. I have to see him again. Do you understand what I . . .

JOE: You don't want to see me any more. Louis. Anything. Whatever you want. I can give up anything. My skin.

Joe is wearing a Mormon temple garment as underwear, which he regards as a second skin, and he begins to take it off to demonstrate his commitment to Louis. Louis stops him, and as Joe lets Louis help him put it back on, Joe advises Louis that "Sometimes self-interested is the most generous thing you can be . . . . . Think about what you need. Be brave. And then you'll come back to me."

Scene 4

Louis and Joe remain onstage as the scene shifts to that night in Roy's hospital bedroom. Belize comes in to check on his patient, who is under the heavy influence of morphine given him to reduce his pain. Roy wants to know what it might be like after death, and Belize describes a heaven "like San Francisco," a partly broken down, weedy, trashy citylike environment with "everyone in Balenciaga gowns with red corsages, and big dance palaces full of music and lights and racial impurity and gender confusion," with mulatto gods. Ethel Rosenberg comes in as Belize advises Roy to go to sleep.

Scene 5

"Night. At the Brooklyn Heights Promenade. Everyone from the previous two

scenes remains onstage," as the Mormon Mother from the Diorama describes to Harper how people change: "Well, it has something to do with God, so it's not very nice," a bloody and painful process.

Prior appears, at home, sick, swallowing some pills, when the phone rings. It's Louis on the phone, telling Prior, "I want to see you."

Curtain.

ACT IV: John Brown's Body, February 1986

Scene 1

A day later, in a split scene, Louis is sitting on a park bench and Joe is visiting Roy in his hospital room. Reflecting on his life, Roy, growing ever sicker, remarks that it wasn't the money he was after, it was the power, "the moxie." At Roy's request, Joe kneels by the bed and Roy puts his hand on Joe's head, giving him a blessing.

Prior enters and sits on the bench, as far as he can from Louis.

PRIOR: Oh, this is going to be so much worse than I'd imagined.

LOUIS: Hello.

PRIOR: Fuck you, you little shitbag.

LOUIS: Don't waste energy beating up on me, O.K.? I'm already taking care of that.

PRIOR: Don't see any bruises.

LOUIS: Inside.

PRIOR: You are one noble guy. Inside. Don't flatter yourself, Louis. So. It's your tea party. Talk.

LOUIS: It's good to see you again. I missed you.

PRIOR: Talk.

LOUIS: I want to . . . try to make up.

PRIOR: Make up.

LOUIS: Yes. But . . .

PRIOR: Aha. But.

LOUIS: But you don't have to be so hostile. Don't I get any points for trying to arrive at a resolution? Maybe what I did isn't forgivable, but . . .

PRIOR: It isn't.

LOUIS: But I'm trying to be responsible. Prior. There are limits. Boundaries. And you have to be reasonable. Why are you dressed like that?

Little pause.

PRIOR: You were saying something about being reasonable.

LOUIS: I've been giving this a lot of thought. Yes, I fucked up, that's obvious. But maybe you fucked up too. You never trusted me, you never gave me a chance to find my footing, not really, you were so quick to attack and . . . I think, maybe just too much of a victim, finally. Passive. Dependent. And what I think is that people do have a choice about how they handle . . .

PRIOR: You want to come back. Why?

LOUIS: I didn't say I wanted to . . .

Pause.

PRIOR: Oh . . . No, you didn't.

LOUIS *(softly, almost pleading):* I can't. Move in again, start all over again. I don't think it'd be any different.

Little pause.

PRIOR: You're seeing someone else.

LOUIS *(shocked):* What? No.

PRIOR: You are.

LOUIS: I'M NOT. Well, occasionally a . . . he's a . . . just a pickup, how do you . . .

PRIOR: Threshold of revelation. Now: Ask me how I know he's a Mormon.

Pause. Louis stares.

Is he a Mormon? *(Little pause.)* Well, Goddamn. Ask me how I knew.

LOUIS: How?

PRIOR: Fuck you. I'm a prophet. *(Furious.) Reasonable? Limits?* Tell it to my *lungs*, stupid, tell it to my lesions, tell it to the cotton-woolly patches in my eyes!

LOUIS: Prior, I . . . haven't seen him for days now . . .

PRIOR: I'm going, I have limits too.

Prior starts to leave. He has an attack of some sort of respiratory trouble. He sits heavily on the bench. Louis starts to go near him. Prior waves him away. Prior looks at Louis.

You cry, but you endanger nothing in yourself. It's like the idea of crying when you do it. Or the idea of love.

In Roy's hospital room, Joe is letting Roy know that he has left his wife and has formed an attachment to a man. This distresses Roy so much that he sits up, pulls the IV out of his arm, getting blood on Joe's shirt as he orders Joe to return to Harper. Belize enters, sees what has happened and bandages Roy's arm. As Joe leaves, Belize advises him to change and get rid of that shirt without touching the blood on it.

Prior complains to Louis, "There are thousands of gay men in New York City with AIDS, and nearly every one of them is being taken care of by . . . a friend or by . . . a lover who has stuck by them through things worse than my . . . So far. Everyone got that, except me. I got you. Why? What's wrong with me." Prior doesn't want Louis to come back unless his feelings—his pain—are clearly visible. Prior exits.

Roy is explaining the importance of lawyers—"the High Priests of America"—when he suffers an acute spasm and Ethel Rosenberg returns to his bedside, almost feeling sorry for him.

Scene 2

The next day, Prior and Belize visit Joe at his office in the Hall of Justice, Brooklyn, to learn for themselves what Louis's new lover is like. Prior sees that Joe looks very much like the dummy in the Mormon Diorama, as Harper had told him. Prior confuses Joe by seeming to know his wife, and Joe becomes even more bewildered when he recognizes Belize as Roy's nurse. Joe corners them and tries to find out what they're doing here. They manage to get away by pretending that Prior is a mental patient with business here at the Hall and Belize is his nurse.

Scene 3

The next day, Louis is sitting in a tunnel near the Bethesda Fountain in Central Park, sheltered from the late February cold and rain. Belize joins him, and they discuss Prior, Louis believing that he's becoming a bit strange. Belize arouses Louis's resentment when he informs him that he and Prior had visited Joe the day before to check him out. And Louis is even more upset to learn that Joe is not the "very moral man" Louis had thought him, but, as Belize puts it, "Roy Cohn's buttboy." Louis can hardly believe this, he considers Roy "the polestar of human evil . . . . . the worst human being who ever lived."

Stephen Spinella and Kathleen Chalfant (Hannah Pitt) in *Perestroika*

Louis believes Belize may be telling him this story because Belize is in love with Prior himself and wants to hurt Louis, but Belize categorically denies this and tells Louis, "Big Ideas are all you love. 'America' is what Louis loves." Belize challenges Louis to come to hospital room 1013 with him: "I'll show you America. Terminal, crazy and mean."

Scene 4

That same day at the Mormon Visitor's Center, Joe has come to see his mother, Hannah, telling her that he means to get Harper back and that he wishes he'd never phoned Hannah about the change in his life (in *Angels in America, Part I)* and that she had not left Salt Lake City to come and live here. Joe leaves just as Prior, arriving, notices him and guesses that Hannah is his mother. Hannah wonders how Prior happens to know Joe.

PRIOR: My ex-boyfriend, he knows him, *now*—I wanted to warn your son about *later,* when his hair goes and there's hips and jowls and all that . . . human stuff, that poor slob there's just gonna wind up miserable, fat, frightened and *alone* because Louis, he can't handle bodies.

HANNAH *(a beat):* Are you a . . . homosexual?

PRIOR: Oh, is it *that* obvious? Yes. I am. What's it to you?

HANNAH: Would you say you are a typical homosexual?

PRIOR: Me? Oh, I'm *stereotypical.* What, you mean like am I a hairdresser or . . .

HANNAH: Are you a hairdresser?

PRIOR: Well, it would be *your* lucky day if I was, because frankly . . . I'm sick. I'm sick. It's expensive. *(He starts to cry.)* Oh shit, now I won't be able to stop, now it's started. I feel really terrible, do I have a fever? *(Offering his forehead, impatiently.) Do I have a fever?*

HANNAH *(hesitates, then puts her hand on his forehead):* Yes.

PRIOR: How high?

HANNAH: There might be a thermometer in the . . .

PRIOR: Very high, very high, could you get me a cab, I think I want . . . *(He sits heavily on the floor.)* Don't be alarmed, it's worse than it looks, I mean . . .

HANNAH: You should . . . Try to stand up, or . . . let me see if anyone can . . .

PRIOR *(listening to his lungs):* Sssshhh. Echo-breath, it's . . . *(He shakes his head "no good.")* I . . . overdid it. I'm in trouble again. Take me to St. Vincent's Hospital, I mean, help me to a cab to the . . .

Little pause, then Hanna exits and reenters with her coat on.

HANNAH: Can you stand up?

PRIOR: You don't . . . Call me a . . .

HANNAH: I'm useless here.

She helps him stand.

PRIOR: Please, if you're trying to convert me this isn't a good time.

Distant thunder.

HANNAH: Lord, look at it out there. It's pitch-black. Storm's coming in. We better move.

They exit. Thunder.

Scene 5

In the stormy late afternoon of the same day, Joe finds Harper coatless, hatless and shoeless at the railing of the Promenade in Brooklyn Heights. Joe shelters her with an umbrella and tells her he's come back to her and will take her home. Harper's reaction is, "Oh, I know . . . . . let's go home."

Scene 6

At night at St. Vincent's Hospital, Emily, a nurse, is examining Prior in Hannah's presence and observes that he has lost eight pounds. Emily orders Prior to stay where he is and goes out. Prior admits to Hannah that ever since the Angel's visitation he has run himself down with "this ice-cold, razor-blade terror." Hannah understands visions and tells Prior of the Mormon angel who appeared to their prophet, Joseph Smith: "His desire made prayer. His prayer made an angel. The angel was real. I believe that." Prior doesn't.

PRIOR: . . . . . I'm sorry, but it's repellent to me. So much of what you believe.

HANNAH: What do I believe?

PRIOR: I'm a homosexual. With AIDS. I can just imagine what you . . .

HANNAH: No you can't. Imagine. The things in my head. You don't make assumptions about me, Mister; I won't make them about you.

PRIOR *(a beat, he looks at her, then):* Fair enough.

HANNAH: My son is . . . well, like you.

PRIOR: Homosexual.

HANNAH *(a nod, then):* I flew into a rage when he told me, mad as hornets. At first I assumed it was about his . . . *(She shrugs.)*

PRIOR: Homosexuality.

HANNAH: But that wasn't it. Homosexuality. It just seems . . . ungainly. Two men together. It isn't an appetizing notion, but then, for me, men in *any* configuration . . . well, they're so lumpish and stupid. And stupidity gets me cross.

PRIOR: I wish you would be more true to your demographic profile. Life is confusing enough.

Little pause. They look at each other.

You know the Bible, you know . . .

HANNAH: Reasonably well, I . . .

PRIOR: The prophets in the Bible, do they . . . ever refuse their vision?

HANNAH: There's scriptural precedent, yes.

PRIOR: And what does God do to them? When they do that?

HANNAH: He . . . Well, He feeds them to whales.

They both laugh. Prior's laugh brings on breathing troubles.

Prior shows Hannah his lesions, and her reaction is that it's just cancer, a part of being human, and that he shouldn't be afraid of the Angel. Prior hears the thunder, suspects the Angel is coming (he is sure of it when he begins to feel sexually aroused). He asks Hannah to keep watch while he sleeps.

Scene 7

That same night, Harper and Joe are in bed, Harper accusing Joe of keeping his eyes closed during sex so that he can imagine a male lover. Harper also imagines a lover during sex with anyone except Joe—to her, he is real.

Joe decides to get up, get dressed and go out. Harper demands that he look at her and tell her what he sees. He does, and his reply is *"Nothing."* Harper thanks him for telling the truth and tells him "Goodbye" as he exits.

Scene 8

Later that night, Joe comes in to Louis's apartment where Louis is reading a series of judge's decisions which were in fact written by Joe. To Louis they seem ultra-conservative, particularly one which dealt in a rather left-handed way with a gay soldier's discharge and pension: "This is an important bit of legal fag-bashing, isn't it? They trusted you to do it. And you didn't disappoint." Joe pleads that "It's law, not justice, it's power," causing Louis to wonder whether Joe has ever had sex with his mentor Roy Cohn. This brings the two men to name-calling and blows. Soon Louis is on the floor, bleeding, and reproaching a very contrite and apologetic Joe.

Scene 9

Later that night in a hospital bed rigged up with heavy support facilities, Roy tells Ethel Rosenberg that he is finally on the way out, but he has managed to retain his credentials as a lawyer to the very last. Ethel gloats: she has been monitoring the disbarment hearings, and the panel's Executive decided to push Roy's disbarment through.

ETHEL: They won, Roy. You're not a lawyer any more.

ROY: But am I dead?

ETHEL: No. They beat you. You lost. (Pause.*)* I decided to come here so I could see could I forgive you. You who I have hated so terribly I have borne my hatred for you up into the heavens and made a needlesharp little star in the sky out of it. It's the star of Ethel Rosenberg's Hatred, and it burns every year for one night only, June Nineteen. It burns acid green. I came to forgive, but all I can do is take pleasure in your misery. Hoping I'll get to see you die more terrible than I did. And you are, 'cause you're dying in shit, Roy, defeated. And you could kill me, but you couldn't ever defeat me. You never won. And when you die all anyone will say is: better he had never lived at all.

Roy addresses Ethel as though she were his mother. He asks her to sing for him, which she does. Afterwards she takes a close look at him and decides, "That's it."

Belize enters, goes to bed.

BELIZE: Wake up, it's time to . . . Oh. Oh, you're . . .

ROY *(sitting up violently):* No I'm NOT! I fooled you, Ethel, I knew who you were all along. I can't believe you fell for that ma stuff, I just wanted to see if I could finally, finally make Ethel Rosenberg sing! I WIN! *(He falls back on the bed.)* Oh fuck, oh fuck me, I . . . *(In a very faint voice.)* Next time around: I don't want to be a man. I wanna be an octopus. Remember that, O.K.? A fucking . . . *(Punching an imaginary button with his finger.)* Hold. *(He dies.)*

Curtain.

ACT V: Heaven, I'm in Heaven, February 1986

Scene 1

Very late that same night in Prior's hospital room there appear Hebrew letters in flames, with the sound of trumpets. The Angel enters, dressed in black. Hannah, who had supposed Prior's vision to be more dreamy and metaphorical than real, is terrified. But she remembers that the way to deal with angels is to wrestle with them and declare, "I will not let thee go except thou bless me." Reluctantly, Prior grapples with the Angel, and he manages to get the upper hand.

PRIOR: I . . . will not let thee go except thou bless me. Take back your Book. Anti-Migration, that's so feeble, I can't believe you couldn't do better than that, free me, unfetter me, bless me or whatever, but I will be let go.

ANGEL *(taking to the air, trying to escape, a whole chorus of voices):*

I I I I Am the
CONTINENTAL PRINCIPALITY OF AMERICA, I I I I
AM THE BIRD OF PREY I Will NOT BE COMPELLED, I . . .

There is a great blast of music and a shaft of white light streams in through the blue murk. Within this incredibly bright column of light there is a ladder of even brighter, purer light, reaching up into infinity. At the conjunctions of each rung there are flaming alephs.

ANGEL: Entrance has been gained. Return the Text to Heaven.

PRIOR *(terrified):* Can I come back? I don't want to go unless . . .

ANGEL *(angry):*

You have prevailed, Prophet. You . . . Choose.
Now release me.

I have torn a muscle in my thigh.

PRIOR: Big deal, my leg's been hurting for months.

He releases the Angel. He hesitates. He ascends. The room is instantly plunged into near darkness. The Angel turns her attention to Hannah.

HANNAH: What? What? You've got no business with me, I didn't call you, you're *his* fever dream, not mine, and he's gone now and you should go too, I'm waking up right . . . NOW!

Nothing happens. The Angel spreads her wings. The room becomes red hot. The Angel extends her hands toward Hannah. Hannah walks towards her and kneels. The Angel kisses her on the forehead and then the lips—a long, hot kiss.

ANGEL: The Body is the Garden of the Soul.

Hannah has an enormous orgasm as the Angel flies away to the accompanying glissando of a baroque piccolo trumpet.

Scene 2

Prior visits Heaven (which looks something like San Francisco after an earthquake) carrying the Book of the Anti-Migratory Epistle and dressed in prophet robes. Harper is there, sitting on a crate, not dead but full of Valium. She can't stay here with Prior, she is ready to face reality now, which includes giving up Joe. She's learned that what energizes human beings, causing them to migrate like the Mormons or indulge in creative activities, is "Devastation . . . Heartbroken people do it, people who have lost love." Harper disappears, and the scene changes to the Hall of the Upper Orders (looking a lot like the San Francisco City Hall), where the Angel awaits Prior.

Scene 3

In Roy's hospital room at 2 a.m., Roy lies dead and Belize welcomes Louis, whom he has summoned to smuggle the AZT out of the hospital before it's confiscated. Belize chose Louis because Louis is Jewish, and Belize also wants someone to say Kaddish for Roy. Louis can hardly bring himself to do this for someone whom he detested in life, but he finally does so, helped out by Ethel Rosenberg. Ethel and Louis alternate the phrases, but they both end with the same one: "You sonofabitch."

Scene 4

At the same hour, Joe returns to his Brooklyn apartment to await Harper, but Roy appears to him, kisses him on the mouth and then exits with the parting comment, "You'll find, my friend, that what you love will take you places you never dreamed you'd go." At this point Harper joins Joe in the apartment, telling him she's been with a friend in paradise.

Scene 5

(Editor's Note: The introduction to this scene in the published version was omitted from the stage presentation.)

In a Council Room in Heaven, the Angel introduces Prior to her colleagues, Continental Principalities, who wonder if there's anything wrong with the Book, causing Prior to want to return it.

AUSTRALIA: What's the matter with it?

PRIOR *(a beat, then):* It just . . . It just . . . We can't just stop. We're not rocks—progress, migration, motion is . . . modernity. It's *animate,* it's what living things do. We desire. Even if all we desire is stillness, it's still desire *for.* Even if we go faster than we should. We can't *wait.* And wait for what? God . . .

Thunderclap.

God . . .

Thunderclap.

He isn't coming back. And even if He did . . . if He ever did come back, if He ever *dared* to show His face, or His Glyph, or whatever, in the Garden again . . . if after all this destruction, if after all of the terrible days of this terrible century He returned to see . . . how much suffering His abandonment had created, if He did come back you should *sue* the bastard. That's my only contribution to all this Theology. Sue the bastard for walking out. How dare He.

Pause.

ANGEL: Thus spake the Prophet.

PRIOR *(starting to put the Book on the table):* So thank you . . . for sharing this with me, but I don't want to keep it.

OCEANIA *(to the Angel of America):* He wants to live.

PRIOR: Yes. I'm thirty years old, for God's sake.

Softer rumble of thunder.

I haven't *done* anything yet, I . . . I want to be healthy again. And this plague, it should stop. In me and everywhere. Make it go away.

AUSTRALIA:

Oh We have tried.
We suffer with You but
We do not know. We
Do not know how.

Prior and Australia look at each other.

EUROPA:

This is the Tome of Immobility, of respite, of cessation.
Drink of its bitter water once, Prophet, and never thirst again.

Prior puts the Book on the table. He removes his prophet robes, revealing the hospital gown underneath. He places the robe by the Book.

PRIOR: I . . . can't. I still want . . . My blessing. Even sick. I want to be alive.

ANGEL:

You only think you do.
Life is a habit with you.
You have not *seen* what is to come:
We *have:*
What will the grim Unfolding of these Latter Days bring?
That you or any Being should wish to endure them?
Death more plenteous than all Heaven has tears to mourn it,
The slow dissolving of the Great Design,
The spiraling apart of the Work of Eternity,
The World and its beautiful particle logic
All collapsed. All dead, forever,
In starless, moonlorn onyx night.

The generator begins to fail, the lights to dim.

We are failing, failing,
The Earth and the Angels.
Look up, look up,
It is Not-to-Be Time.
Oh who asks of the Orders Blessing
With Apocalypse Descending?
Who demands: More Life?
When Death like a Protector
Blinds our eyes, shielding from tender nerve
More horror than can be borne.
Let any Being on whom Fortune smiles
Creep away to Death
Before that last dreadful daybreak
When all your ravaging returns to you
With the rising, scorching, unrelenting Sun:
When morning blisters crimson
And bears all life away,
A tidal wave of Protean Fire
That curls around the planet
And bares the Earth clean as a bone.

PRIOR: But still. Still. Bless me anyway. I want more life. I can't help myself. I do. I've lived through such terrible times, and there are people who live through much, much worse, but . . . You see them living anyway. When they're more spirit than body, more sores than skin, when they're burned and in agony, when flies lay eggs in the corners of the eyes of their children, they live. Death usually has to *take* life away. I don't know if that's just the animal. I don't know if it's not braver to die. But I recognize the habit. The addiction to being alive. We live past hope. If I can find hope anywhere, that's it, that's the best I can do. It's so much not enough, so inadequate, but . . . Bless me anyway. I want more life.

Prior begins to exit. The Angels, unseen by him, make a mystical sign. He turns again to face them.

And if He returns, take Him to court. He walked out on us. He ought to pay.

Scene 6

(Editor's Note: Scenes numbered 6 and 7 in the published version were omitted from the stage presentation and from this synopsis.)

Belize is in the hospital room the next day to welcome Prior back to the world as he slips into bed. Emily enters to inform Prior that his fever has broken. Hannah comes in and out (she has slept in a chair at Prior's bedside all night, suffering strange dreams). Louis comes in showing the bruises of having been in the fight with Joe but bringing the shoulder bag full of AZT. Belize presents it to Prior who voices his suspicions about side effects and isn't sure that he's going to take the AZT pills. After Belize exits, Louis declares, "Prior, I want to come back to you."

Scene 7

That same morning, in a split scene, Louis and Prior are in the hospital room as before, and Joe and Harper are seen in the Brooklyn apartment. Harper wants Joe's credit card, and that's all she wants from him, though Joe begs her to come back to him. She takes the card, advising, "Get lost. Joe. Go exploring." She gets her Valium stash from the sofa, gives Joe two pills and exits.

Likewise, in the hospital room, Louis admits that he failed Prior but loves him still. Prior admits he loves Louis too—"But you can't come back. Not ever. I'm sorry. But you can't."

Scene 8

Louis and Prior are still visible, as is Joe, alone in Brooklyn. Harper is seen on a night flight to San Francisco, describing what she could see from this great height: "Souls were rising, from the earth far below, souls of the dead, of people who had perished, from famine, from war, from the plague, and they floated up, like skydivers in reverse, limbs all akimbo, wheeling and spinning. And the souls of these departed joined hands, clasped ankles and formed a web, a great net of souls, and the souls were three-atom oxygen molecules, of the stuff of ozone, and the outer rim absorbed them, and was repaired. Nothing's lost forever. In this world, there is a kind of painful progress. Longing for what we've left behind, and dreaming ahead. At least I think that's so.

Curtain.

Epilogue: Bethesda, February 1990

Prior *("heavily bundled, he has thick glasses on and supports himself with a cane"),* Louis, Belize and Hannah are sitting around the Bethesda Fountain in Central Park, Louis and Belize discussing the end of the Cold War, Hannah reading the

New York *Times,* Prior trying just to enjoy the bright sunny day, the pleasant environment and his favorite angel, Bethesda. At Prior's request, Louis tells the story of Bethesda, how she once landed in the Temple area of Jerusalem and touched the earth with her foot. A fountain of healing waters sprang up there and flowed until the Romans destroyed the Temple. Hannah declares that when the Millennium comes the fountain will flow again and "We will all bathe ourselves clean."

Prior observes, "The fountain's not flowing now, they turn it off in the winter, ice in the pipes. But in the summer it's a sight to see. I want to be around to see it. I plan to be. I hope to be. This disease will be the end of many of us, but not nearly all, and the dead will be commemorated and will struggle on with the living, and we are not going away. We won't die secret deaths anymore. The world only spins forward. We will be citizens. The time has come. Bye now. You are fabulous creatures, each and every one. And I bless you: *More Life.* The Great Work Begins."

Curtain.

ALL IN THE TIMING

A Program of Six One-Act Plays

BY DAVID IVES

Cast and credits appear on pages 467-9

DAVID IVES was born in 1950 in Chicago, where his father worked for Standard Oil. A high school teacher encouraged his interest in writing, and he received his B.A. at Northwestern University in 1971. Much later—in 1984—he got his M.F. A. in playwriting at Yale Drama School, but long before that he was an oft-produced playwright. At age 22, thanks to a grant from the Office of Advanced Drama Research, his Canvas *was produced in Los Angeles and a year later off off Broadway at Circle Repertory. OOB productions of his works followed each other in quick succession during the 1970s:* Saint Freud *(1975),* Borders *(1977),* The Conversion *(1978). In 1983 he was playwright-in-residence at the Williamstown, Mass. festival, which produced his* Lives and Deaths of the Great Harry Houdini.

Following Yale Drama School, Ives "started liking what I was writing" and came up with Money in the Bank *(1986, New Dramatists),* Words, Words, Words *(1987, Manhattan Punch Line),* Sure Thing *and* Seven Menus *(1987, New Dramatists),* The Red Address *(1988, New Dramatists),* Ancient History *(1989, Primary Stages),* Mere Mortals *and* Variations on the Death of Trotsky *(1989, New Dramatists),* Philip Glass Buys a Loaf of Bread *(Manhattan Punch Line, 1990),* Foreplay, or The Art of the Fugue *(Manhattan Punch Line, 1991) and* Long Ago and Far Away *(1993, Ensemble Studio Theater). In the course of these productions, others also started liking what Ives was writing, including* Best Plays *OOB critic Mel Gussow who called* Sure

Thing *"a mirthful compendium of conversations" and later noted Ives's "continuing nimbleness with language and theatrical technique."*

Not until this season, however, have any of Ives's plays received the full-fledged off-Broadway staging that makes them eligible for selection as a Best Play. That situation was happily remedied with the opening February 17 of All in the Timing, *a collection of six Ives one-acters including the abovementioned* Sure Thing; Words, Words, Words; Philip Glass Buys a Loaf of Bread, *and* Variations on the Death of Trotsky, *plus the New York premiere of* The Philadelphia *and the world premiere of* The Universal Language. *This program won its author his first Best Play citation and the Outer Critics Circle's 1993-94 John Gassner Playwriting Award. He makes his home in New York City, and his next play,* Don Juan in Chicago, *is to be produced there at Primary Stages in the 1994-95 season.*

Sure Thing

Betty, in her late 20s, is sitting reading at a cafe table at which there is also an empty chair. Bill, also in his late 20s, approaches.

BILL: Excuse me. Is this chair taken?
BETTY: Excuse me?
BILL: Is this taken?
BETTY: Yes it is.
BILL: Oh. Sorry.
BETTY: Sure thing.
A bell rings softly.
BILL: Excuse me. Is this chair taken?
BETTY: EXCUSE me?
BILL: Is this taken?
BETTY: No, but I'm expecting somebody in a minute.
BILL: Oh. Thanks anyway.
BETTY: Sure thing.
A bell rings softly.
BILL: Excuse me. Is this chair taken?
BETTY: NO, but I'm expecting somebody very shortly.
BILL: Would you mind if I sit here till he or she or it comes?
BETTY *(glances at her watch):* They seem to be pretty late . . .
BILL: You never know who you might be turning down.
BETTY: Sorry. Nice try, though.
BILL: Sure thing.

But the bell rings again and again, changing lines and segments of dialogue along with the characters' actions and attitudes, so that Bill is soon sitting at the table with

Betty and getting acquainted, discussing the book she is reading (a Faulkner novel). Appreciation of Faulkner is "all in the timing of when you read him," Bill observes more than once, and indeed so is their relationship, which varies from bell to bell but seems to be getting more and more friendly.

They mention the possibility of going to a movie or taking the Concorde to Paris. Each of them may have recently ended an important affair and may be lonely. When Betty asks Bill whether he has some "weird political affiliation," the bell starts ringing in almost staccato rhythm.

BILL: Nope. Straight-down-the-ticket Republican.

Bell.

Straight-down-the-ticket Democrat.

Bell.

Can I tell you something about politics?

Bell.

I like to think of myself as a citizen of the universe.

Bell.

I'm unaffiliated.

Nancy Opel and Robert Stanton in *Sure Thing*

BETTY: That's a relief. So am I.

BILL: I vote my beliefs.

BETTY: Labels are not important.

BILL: Labels are not important, exactly. Like me, for example. I mean, what does it matter if I had a two-point at—

Bell.

—three-point at—

Bell.

—four-point at college, or if I did come from Pittsburgh—

Bell.

—Cleveland—

Bell.

—Westchester County?

BETTY: Sure.

BILL: I believe a man is what he is.

Bell.

A person is what he is.

Bell.

A person is . . . what they are.

BETTY: I think so too.

There's a festival of Woody Allen movies just up the street, and it seems they both are Woody Allen fans. They have other characteristics in commen, they gradually discover.

BILL: Do you still believe in marriage in spite of current sentiments against it?

BETTY: Yes.

BILL: And children?

BETTY: Three of them.

BILL: Two girls and a boy.

BETTY: Harvard, Vassar and Brown.

BILL: And will you love me?

BETTY: Yes.

BILL: And cherish me forever?

BETTY: Yes.

BILL: Do you still want to go to the movies?

BETTY: Sure thing.

BILL & BETTY: *Waiter*

Blackout. Curtain.

Words, Words, Words

Three monkeys—Milton, Swift and Kafka (a female monkey)—dressed in *"the sort of little-kid clothes that chimps wear in circuses"* are typing away on three machines. When not actually typing, however, they behave as monkeys, swinging on a tire-swing, pounding their chests, etc. Swift reads what he's just typed: "Ping drobba fft fft fft inglewarp carcinoma" and is rather pleased with it. The others also like it.

SWIFT: But do you think it's *Hamlet?*

MILTON: Don't ask me. I'm just a chimp.

KAFKA: They could've given us a clue or something.

SWIFT: Yeah. Or a story conference.

MILTON: But that'd defeat the whole purpose of the experiment.

SWIFT: I know, I know, I know. Three monkeys typing into infinity will sooner or later produce *Hamlet.*

MILTON: Right.

SWIFT: Completely by chance.

MILTON: And Dr. David Rosenbaum up in that booth is going to prove it.

SWIFT: But what *is Hamlet?*

MILTON: I don't know.

SWIFT *(to Kafka):* What is *Hamlet?*

KAFKA: I don't know.

Swift thinks the whole experiment is stupid. Milton points out that the sooner they finish the job, the sooner they'll get out of this cage. Milton has been hard at work on his typewriter and reads them what he has come up with: "Of Man's first disobedience, and the fruit/Of that forbidden tree whose mortal taste/Brought death into the—". "It really sings," Swift comments, "but is it Shakespeare?" The rest of Milton's day's work goes, "—whose mortal taste/Brought death into the blammagan/Bedsocks knockwurst tinkerbelle." Milton agrees with Swift that it needs work.

A light comes on, and the three monkeys immediately assume the "See no evil, hear no evil, speak no evil" pose. The light goes off, and they relax, Kafka presents her day's work: "K.K.K.K.K.K.K.K.K.K.K.K.K.K.K." After twenty lines of this, she suffered writer's block.

The monkeys pass the time complaining about their captivity, putting on an act that causes cigarettes to be lowered into their cage, discussing the possibility of luring Dr. Rosenbaum into their cage so they can get some sort of revenge, occasionally coming up with stray segments from *Hamlet.*

SWIFT: . . . . . You two serfs go back to work. I'll do all the thinking around here. Swifty—revenge! *(He paces, deep in thought.)*

MILTON: "Shtuckelschwanz hemorrhoid." Yeah, that's good. *That is good. (Types.)* "Shtuckelschwanz . . ."

KAFKA *(types):* Act One, Scene One. Elsinore Castle, Denmark . . .
MILTON *(types):* . . . hemorrhoid.
KAFKA *(types):* Enter Bernardo and Francisco.
MILTON *(types):* Pomegranite.
KAFKA *(types):* Bernardo says, "Who's there?"
She continues to type Hamlet *as the lights fade.* Curtain.

The Universal Language

The setting is a classroom furnished with desk, chairs and a blackboard on which is written "he, she, it" and below that "arf." Around the upper part of the wall is written "wen, yu, fre, fal, fynd, iff, heven, waitz" which will be revealed as representing the numbers one to eight. There is a knock on the door at right. When no one replies, Dawn *("late 20s, plainly dressed, very shy, with a stutter")* enters tentatively and looks around the room, taking in the strange words.

Another door at left opens and Don *("about 30, charming and smooth")* appears. Don greets Dawn with "Velcro!", apparently in the same strange language as the inscriptions. It is intended to mean "Welcome!", but Dawn doesn't know that yet.

DAWN: Excuse me?
DON: Velcro! Bell jar, Froyling! Harvard*yu?*
DAWN: H-h-h-how do you d-d-d-do, my n-n-name is—*(Breaks off.)* I'm sorry. *(She turns to go.)*
DON: Oop, oop, oop! Varta, Froyling! Varta! Varta!
DAWN: I'm v-very sorry to b-b-bother you.
DON: Mock—klah*too bod*dami *nik*to! *Ven*trica! Ventrica, ventrica. Police!
DAWN: Really—I think I have the wrong place.
DON: Da *rrrroong*platz? Oop da-doll! Du doppe da *rekt*platz! Dameetcha play*zeer. Com*intern. Police. Plop da chah.
DAWN: Well. J-just for a second.
DON *(cleaning up papers on the floor):* Squeegie la mezza. *(He points to the chair.)* Zitz?
DAWN: No thank you. *(She sits.)*
DON: Argo. Bell jar, Froyling. Harvardyu?
DAWN: "Bell jar?"
DON: Belljar. Bell. Jar. Bell*jar!*
DAWN: Is that "good day"—?
DON: Ding! "Bell jar" arf "good day." Epp—Harvardyu?
DAWN: Harvard University?
DON: Oop! Harvard*yu?*
DAWN: Howard Hughes?
DON: Oop. Har*vard*yu?

DAWN: Oh! "How *are* you."

DON: Bleeny, bleeny! Bonanza bleeny!

DAWN: Is this Thirty East Seventh?

DON: Thirsty oyster heventh. Ding.

DAWN: Suite Six-Six-Two?

DON: Iff-Iff-Yu. Anchor ding.

DAWN: Room B?

DON: Rimbeau.

DAWN: The School of Unamunda?

DON: Hets arf dada Unamunda Ka*ka*-day*mee.* Epp vot kennedy *doop*feryu?

DAWN: Excuse me . . . ?

DON: Vot. Kennedy. Doopferyu?

DAWN: Well. I s-saw an ad in the n-newspaper.

DON: Video da klip enda peeper. Epp? Knish?

DAWN: Well it says— *(She takes a newspaper clipping out of her purse.)* "Learn Unamunda, the universal language."

DON: "Lick Unamunda, da linkwa looniversahl!"

A banner unfurls which says just that.

DAWN: "The language that will unite all humankind."

DON: "Da linkwa het barf oonide*vair*sify alla da peepholes enda voooold!"

Dawn raises her hand.

Quisling?

DAWN: Do you speak English?

DON: "English" . . . ?

DAWN: English.

DON: Ah! John*cleese!*

DAWN: Yes. John*cleese.*

DON: John*cleese.* Squeegie, squeegie. Alaska, iago parladoop johnclease.

DAWN: No johncleese at all?

DON: One, two, three worlds. "Khello. Goombye. Rice Krispies. Chevrolet." Et cinema, et cinema. Mock—votsdy beesnest, bella Froyling?

It seems that after reading the ad, Dawn thought she might like to be one of the first to learn the universal language, but she's not sure, she wants to know more about it. Don asks for her "klink"—her name—and eventually learns it along with the fact that she is 28 and her occupation is that of word processor. Don in his turn tells her his name is Don Finninneganegan and informs her he's translating Shakespeare into Unamunda. Since much of this information is communicated in that language, Dawn is surprised at how easy it seems to learn its rudiments. But when Dawn inquires how much the lessons will be, Don states in perfect English, "Five hundred dollars." This is a lot of money to Dawn, but she believes that "Language is the opposite of loneliness. And if everybody in the world spoke the same language, who would ever be lonely?", and maybe she wouldn't stutter in Unamunda and make people laugh at her, as she does in English. She decides to take the course.

Don and Dawn go through the Unamunda pronouns, the parts of the body, etc., until the lesson takes on a rhythm so that they are chanting, even dancing together. The verbiage comes to a verse-like climax, and *"They collapse in a sort of post-coital exhaustion as the lesson ends."* It has been a wondrous experience for Dawn, ecstatic, stutterless. Henceforth she'll speak nothing but Unamunda. She gets her purse and offers Don all the money she has with her as part payment for the lesson, promising to bring the rest tomorrow.

DON: I'm sorry, but I—I c-c-can't take your money.

DAWN: Da parla johncleese?

DON: Actually, yes, I do speak a little johncleese.

DAWN: Mock du parla par*foom!*

DON: Well, I've been practicing a lot. Anyway, I-I-I-I don't think I mentioned that the first lesson is free.

DAWN: Mock ya *vanta* pago.

DON: But I don't *want* you to vanta pago.

DAWN: Votsda mattress? Cheer! Etsyuris!

DON: I can't take it.

DAWN: Porky?

DON: Because I can't.

DAWN: Mock porky?

DON: Because it's a fraud.

DAWN: Squeegie?

DON: Unamunda. It's a fraud.

DAWN: A froyd . . . ?

DON: A *sigismundo* froyd.

DAWN: Oop badabba.

DON: It's a con game. A swindle. A parla trick.

DAWN: No crayola.

DON: Believe it, Dawn! I should know—I invented it! Granted, it's not a very *good* con, since you're the only person who's ever knocked at that door, and I'm obviously not a very good con *man,* since I'm refusing to accept your very attractive and generous money, but I can't stand the thought of you walking out there saying, "Velcro belljar harvardyu" and having people laugh at you. I swear, Dawn, I swear, I didn't want to hurt you. How could I? How could anybody? Your beautiful heart . . . It shines out of you like a beacon. And then there's me. A total fraud. I wish I could lie in any language and say it wasn't so, but . . . I'm sorry, Dawn. I'm so, so—sorry.

DAWN: Vot forest?

DON: Will you stop?!

DAWN: Unamunda arf da linkwa looniversahl!

DON: But you and I are the only peepholes in the vooold who speak it!

DAWN: Dolby udders! Dolby udders!

DON: Who? What others?

DAWN: Don, if you and I can speak this linkwa supreemka, anybody can. Everybody *will!* This isn't just any language. This isn't just any room! This is the Garden of Eden. And you and I are finding names for a whole new world. I was so . . .

DON: Happy. I know. So was I.

DAWN: Perzakto.

DON: I was happy . . .

DAWN: And *why?*

DON: I don't know, I . . .

DAWN: Because du epp ya parla da dentrical linguini.

DON: Okay, maybe we speak the same language, but it's nonsense!

DAWN: Oop.

DON: Gibberish.

DAWN: Oop.

DON: Doubletalk.

DAWN: The linkwa you and I parla is ama*mor,* Don.

DON: Ama*mor* . . . ?

DAWN: Unamundamor. Yago arf amorphous mit du.

DON: Amorphous . . . ?

DAWN: Polymorphous.

DON: Verismo?

DAWN: Surrealismo.

DON: But how? I mean . . .

DAWN: Di anda di destiny, Don.

DON: Are you sure?

DAWN: Da pravdaz enda pudding. *(Points around the walls at the numbers.)* "When you free fall . . . "

DON: "Find if . . . "

DAWN: "Heaven . . . "

DON: "Waits."

DAWN: Geronimo.

DON: So you forgive me.

DAWN: For making me happy? Yes. I forgive you.

DON: Yago arf . . . spinachless.

DAWN *(holds out her hand):* Di anda.

DON *(holds out his):* Di anda.

DAWN: Da palma.

DON: Da palma.

They join hands.

DAWN: Da kooch.

They kiss.

DON: Yago arf amorphous mit du tu.

They are about to kiss again, when the door at right opens, and a young man looks in.

YOUNG MAN: Excuse me. Is this the school of Unamunda?

DON & DAWN *(look at each other, then):* Velcro!

Blackout. Curtain.

Philip Glass Buys a Loaf of Bread

Philip Glass, the composer, is at the counter of a bakery asking the baker for a loaf of bread. Two women, about to exit from the bakery, pause as one of them recognizes the composer.

1ST WOMAN: Isn't that Philip Glass?

The 2d Woman turns and looks.

2D WOMAN: I think it is.

BAKER: Can I help you, sir?

GLASS: Yes. I need a loaf of bread, please.

BAKER: Just a moment.

1ST WOMAN: It's time now.

2D WOMAN: Yes. Let's go.

But she doesn't move. Glass turns and looks at her. Their eyes meet.

BAKER: Do you know that woman, sir?

A bell rings.

After the sound of the bell, the above dialogue is repeated with the words thrown back and forth among the characters as a verbal takeoff on the rhythms and repetitions typical of Glass's music, as in the following sample:

1ST WOMAN	2D WOMAN	GLASS	BAKER
Philip	Philip	Philip	Philip
need	need	need	need
bread	bread	bread	bread
loaf	loaf	loaf	loaf
		do I need a	
loaf of bread	loaf of bread		loaf of bread
		can I need a	
loaf of bread	loaf of bread		loaf of bread
		can I *know* a	
loaf of bread	loaf of bread		loaf of bread
			I need bread
I know	I know	I know	
I know	I know	I know	
			I need bread

I know	I know	I know	
I know	I know	I know	
			I need bread
I know	I know	I know	
I know	I know	I know	
		Isn't *that* a loaf of bread?	

In the course of this exercise, Glass admits that he has indeed met one of the women. The bell rings again, and the scene returns to ordinary dialogue.

BAKER: Do you know that woman, sir?
GLASS: Yes. I loved her once.
1ST WOMAN: What's the matter?
2ND WOMAN: Nothing. Nothing.
The two women go out.
GLASS: I also need some change.
The Baker points to a sign which reads "No Change." Blackout. Curtain.

The Philadelphia

Al *("California cool; 20s or 30s")* is seated at a table in a restaurant near the Daily Specials board. He negotiates with the waitress for a dish of pickled pig's feet, and she exits as Mark *("20s or 30s, looking shaken and bedraggled")* enters and sits at the table with his friend Al. Absolutely everything has gone wrong with Mark's day from the moment he woke up this morning: no aspirin in the drug store, no *Daily News* at the newsstand, no pastrami at the deli, and the taxi driver wouldn't take him where he wanted to go.

AL: Don't panic. You're in a Philadelphia.
MARK: I'm in a what?
AL: You're in a Philadelphia. That's all.
MARK: But I'm in—
AL: Yes, physically you are in New York. *Meta*physically you are in a Philadelphia.
MARK: I've never heard of this!
AL: You see, inside of what we know as reality there are these pockets, these black

holes called Philadelphias. If you fall into one, you run up against exactly the kinda shit that's been happening to you all day.

MARK: Why?

AL: Because in a Philadelphia, no matter what you ask for, you can't get it. You ask for something, they're not gonna have it. You want to do something, it ain't gonna get done. You want to go somewhere, you can't get there from here.

MARK: Good God. So this is very serious.

AL: Just remember, Marcus. This is a condition named for the town that invented the *cheese steak.* Something that nobody in his right mind would willingly ask for.

MARK: And I thought I was just having a very bad day . . .

AL: Sure. Millions of people have spent entire lifetimes inside a Phildelphia and never even knew it. Look at the city of Philadelphia itself. Hopelessly trapped forever inside a Phildelphia. And do they know it?

MARK: Well, what can I do? Should I just kill himself now and get it over with?

AL: You try to kill yourself in a Philadelphia, you're only gonna get hurt, babe.

Wait it out, Al advises Mark, it will pass. The waitress enters to tell Al there was a phone message for him that he has been fired from a job he loves. Al shrugs this off—he is in a Los Angeles, he explains to Mark, and everything that happens to him is euphoric in some way. If he's lost his job in the garment center, he'll write a movie script about it and sell it to Hollywood.

Al explains that in order to get what he wants for lunch, Mark must order the opposite. He must brush off the waitress to get her to wait on him (he does) and manages to maneuver a Budweiser and hamburger by convincing her they're the last things he wants.

When the waitress brings Al's order, it turns out to be a cheese steak instead of pig's feet. Obviously, Mark has pulled Al out of his Los Angeles into Mark's Philadelphia, and Al is furious. He realizes he must do something about having lost his job, and he exits in search of a phone (having asked for one, in his Philadelphia, he is obviously told there is none in the restaurant).

MARK: I don't know. It's not that bad in a Philadelphia.

WAITRESS: Could be worse. I've been in a Cleveland all week.

MARK: A Cleveland? What's that like?

WAITRESS: It's like death, without the advantages.

MARK: Really? Care to stand?

WAITRESS: Don't mind if I do.

MARK: I hope you won't reveal your name.

WAITRESS: Sharon.

MARK *(holds out his hand):* Goodbye.

WAITRESS: Hello.

They shake.

MARK *(indicating the cheese steak):* Want to starve?

WAITRESS: Don't mind if I do.

She picks up the cheese steak and starts eating.

MARK: Yeah, everybody has to be someplace . . . *(Leans across the table with a smile.)* So.

Black. Curtain.

Variations on the Death of Trotsky

The setting is Trotsky's study in Mexico, with desk and chair, mirror, doorway at left and windows upstage through which can be glimpsed lush tropical foliage. *"A large wall calendar announces that today is August 21, 1940 . . . . . Trotsky is sitting at his desk, writing furiously. The handle of a mountain-climber's axe is sticking out of the back of his head,"* with the blade embedded in his skull.

Mrs. Trotsky, *"grandmotherly and sweet,"* enters with an encyclopedia and reads from it: "On August 20th, 1940, a Spanish Communist named Ramon Mercader smashed a mountain-climber's axe into Trotsky's skull in Coyoacan, a suburb of Mexico City. Trotsky died the next day." The date on the encyclopedia is 1992. Trotsky admits that he is Trotsky, this is their home in Coyoacan and they have a gardener named Ramon Mercader. Asking what day this is, Trotsky is told it is August 21.

TROTSKY: Then I'm safe! That article says it happened on the 20th, which means it would've happened yesterday.

MRS. TROTSKY: But Leon . . .

TROTSKY: And I'd be dead today, with a mountain-climber's axe in my skull.

MRS. TROTSKY: Um—Leon . . .

TROTSKY: Will the capitalist press never get things right?

He resumes writing.

MRS. TROTSKY: But Leon . . . isn't that the handle of a mountain-climber's axe, sticking out of your skull.

TROTSKY *(looks in the mirror):* It certainly does look like one . . . And you know, Ramon was in here yesterday, telling me about his mountain-climbing trip. And now I think of it, he was carrying a mountain-climber's axe. I can't remember if he had it when he left the room . . .

MRS. TROTSKY: But Mexico City is on a plateau.

TROTSKY: So Ramon may have been lying.

MRS. TROTSKY: Yes.

TROTSKY: Unless he was rappelling in and out of town.

MRS. TROTSKY: Which is possible.

TROTSKY: But I've never seen him in climbing spikes or crampons.

MRS. TROTSKY: Neither have I.

Pause. Trotsky considers all this.

TROTSKY: Did Ramon report to work today?

Daniel Hagen in *Variations on the Death of Trotsky*

Trotsky dies, falling face forward onto his desk. A bell rings. Trotsky resumes writing . . . . .

"No one is safe. Force must be used. And the revolution of the proletariat against oppression must go on forever, and forever . . . . ."

Continuing his conversation with his wife, Trotsky reminds her that his recurrent fear is of an ice pick, not an axe, and he feels he's "outsmarted destiny" by forbidding the presence of an ice pick in his house. From his desk drawer he takes a skull which he bought and owns, therefore it's "Trotsky's skull," therefore it will serve as a decoy for anyone wishing to bury a weapon in it.

Mrs. Trotsky finally makes her husband realize that he has an axe coming from his skull and is scheduled—according to the encyclopedia—to die today (he has already died several times in the course of their conversation but comes to life again when the bell rings). At least he has until midnight, he believes. He asks his wife to summon Ramon, which she does.

TROTSKY *(to Ramon):* Ramon, did you bury this mountain-climber's axe in my skull?

RAMON: I did not bury it, sir. I *smashed* it into your skull.

TROTSKY: Excuse me?

RAMON: You see? You can still see the handle.

MRS. TROTSKY: It's true, Leon. The axe is not entirely out of sight.

RAMON: So we cannot say "buried," we can only say "smashed," or perhaps "jammed"—

TROTSKY: All right, all right. But *why* did you do this?

RAMON: I think I read about it in an encyclopedia.

TROTSKY *(to audience):* The power of the printed word!

RAMON: I wanted to use an icepick, but there weren't any around the house.

TROTSKY: But why? Do you realize who I am? Do you realize that you smashed this axe into the skull of a major historical figure? I helped run the Russian Revolution! I oversaw the troops as Commissar! I fought Stalin! I was a major political theorist! Why did you do this? Was it political disaffection? Anti-counterrevolutionary backlash?

RAMON: Actually—it was love, Senor.

MRS. TROTSKY: It's true, Leon.

She and Ramon join hands.

I'm sorry you had to find out this way.

TROTSKY: No

MRS. TROTSKY: Yes.

TROTSKY: No.

RAMON: Si!

TROTSKY: Oh God! What a fool I've been!

He dies. Bell.

Why did you really do this, Ramon?

RAMON: *You* will never know, Senor Trotsky.

TROTSKY: This is a nightmare!

RAMON: But luckily for you—your night will soon be over.

Trotsky dies. Bell.

TROTSKY: All right, Ramon. Thank you. You may go.

Before Ramon leaves, Trotsky promises to look at the nasturtiums today if he can find the time. He apologizes to his wife for being so often distracted by political affairs that he wasn't the husband he should have been, and Mrs. Trotsky in her turn apologizes for shortcomings.

TROTSKY: Sometime, for everyone, there's a room that you go into, and it's the room that you never leave. Or else you go out of a room, and it's the last room that you'll *ever* leave. *(He looks around.)* This is my last room.

MRS. TROTSKY: But you aren't even here, Leon.

TROTSKY: This desk, these books, that calendar . . .

MRS. TROTSKY: You're not even here, my love.

TROTSKY: The sunshine coming through the blinds.

MRS. TROTSKY: That was yesterday. You're in a hospital, unconscious.

TROTSKY: The flowers in the garden. You, standing there. . .

MRS. TROTSKY: This is yesterday you're seeing.

TROTSKY: What does that entry say? Would you read it again . . . ?

MRS. TROTSKY: "On August 20th 1940, a Spanish Communist named Ramon Mercader smashed a mountain-climber's axe into Trotsky's skull in Coyoacan, a suburb of Mexico City. Trotsky died the next day."

TROTSKY: It gives you a little hope about the world, doesn't it? That a man could have a mountain-climber's axe smashed into his skull, and yet live on for one whole day . . . ? Maybe I'll go look at the nasturtiums.

Trotsky dies. The garden outside the louvered window begins to glow. Lights fade. Curtain.

THREE TALL WOMEN

A Play in Two Acts

BY EDWARD ALBEE

Cast and credits appear on pages 469-70

EDWARD FRANKLIN ALBEE was born March 12, 1928 in Washington, D. C. Two weeks after his birth he was adopted by a branch of the Keith-Albee theater family. He attended several schools including Rye Country Day, Lawrenceville, Valley Forge Military Academy and Choate, and he spent a year and a half in 1946-47 at Trinity College. His occupations during his 20s included a three-year stint as a Western Union messenger until, in 1958, at 30, he wrote his first play, The Zoo Story, *which went on to production in German in West Berlin in 1959, followed by stagings at the Actors Studio and in a Vernon Rice Award-winning off-Broadway presentation in 1960. Other Albee plays produced off Broadway (not trying to count the countless revivals) have been* The Sandbox *(1960),* Fam and Yam *(1960),* The American Dream *(1961, winner of a Foreign Press Association Award),* The Death of Bessie Smith *(1961),* Bartleby *(a one-act opera in collaboration with James Hinton Jr. and William Flanagan, based on a Herman Melville story)—and now, after a long and hugely successful Broadway playwriting career,* Three Tall Women, *Albee's sixth Best Play, which had its world premiere in June 1991 at the English Theater in Vienna, its American premiere in regional theater at River Arts, Woodstock, N.Y. and its New York City premiere February 13 at the Vineyard Theater for 29 off-off-Broadway performances before moving on to a full-fledged off-Broadway run April 5, winning the 1994 Pulitzer Prize and Critics Award.*

Albee made his commanding Broadway debut with Who's Afraid of Virginia Woolf?

(1962), a Best Play of its season and the winner of the New York Critics Award, and in 1966 a successful movie. His four subsequent Best Plays on Broadway were Tiny Alice *(1964),* A Delicate Balance *(the 1966 Pulitzer Prize winner),* Seascape *(the 1975 Pulitzer Prize winner) and the short-lived but long-shadowed* The Lady From Dubuque *(1980). Albee's Broadway canon has also included three more originals—the program of one-acters* Box *and* Quotations From Chairman Mao Tse-Tung, *(1968),* All Over *(1971) and* The Man Who Had Three Arms *(1983)—and five adaptations:* The Ballad of the Sad Cafe *(1963, from a novella by Carson McCullers),* Malcolm *(1966, from a novel by James Purdy), a musical adaptation of Truman Capote's* Breakfast at Tiffany's *which closed in tryout in 1966),* Everything in the Garden *(1966, based on a play by Giles Cooper) and* Lolita *(1981, from Vladimir Nabokov's novel). Albee plays produced in other venues have included* Counting the Ways *and* Listening *at Hartford Stage Company in 1977 and OOB in 1979,* Finding the Sun, Walking, Marriage Play *(under its author's direction at the Alley Theater, Houston in 1992),* The Lorca Play *and* Fragments (A Concerto Grosso).

Albee has acquired additional distinction as a director of his own, Samuel Beckett's and others' works; as a producer with Richard Barr and Clinton Wilder of many important new plays introducing talented new playwrights; and as the artistic director of Lincoln Center's 1980-81 program of one-acters at the Mitzi E. Newhouse Theater (among them Jeffrey Sweet's Stops Along the Way). *He is a member of the Dramatists Guild, PEN American, The American Academy of Arts and Letters (which awarded him its Gold Medal in Drama in 1980) and the Theater Hall of Fame, and he serves as president of the International Theater Institute USA and the Edward F. Albee Foundation. He lives in New York City and Long Island.*

Place: A "wealthy" bedroom, French in feeling

ACT I

SYNOPSIS: A bed with a bench at its foot is set between two windows on the upstage wall. Archways give entrance to the room left and right. At rise, three women are seated, one on the bench and one in each of light armchairs left and right. They are identified as A, *"a very old woman; thin, autocratic, proud, as together as the ravages of time will allow,"* well appointed and dressed in nightgown and dressing gown; B, *"looks rather as A would have at 52,"* the old woman's paid companion, plainly dressed, strong and active despite the crippling effect of some spinal or orthopedic disorder; and C, *"looks rather as B would have at 26,"* an attractive blonde representative of A's lawyer, here on business and smartly dressed in a tailored suit. A breaks the silence with a comment that is apparently *"an announcement from nowhere."*

A: I'm ninety-one.
B *(pause):* Is that so?
A *(pause):* Yes.
C *(small smile):* You're ninety-*two.*
A *(longer pause; none too pleasant):* Be that as it *may.*
B *(to C):* Is that so?
C *(shrugs, indicates papers):* Says so here.
B *(pause; stretching):* Well . . . what does it matter?
C: Vanity is amazing.
B: So's forgetting.
A *(general):* I'm ninety-one.
B *(accepting sigh):* O.K.
C *(smaller smile):* You're ninety-*two.*
B *(unconcerned):* Oh . . . let it alone.
C: No! It's important. Getting things . . .
B: It doesn't matter!
C *(sotto voice):* It does to *me.*

Pause.

A: I know because he says you're exactly thirty years older than I am; I know how old I am because I know how old *you* are, and if you ever forgot how old you are, ask me how old *I* am, and then you'll know. *(Pause.)* Oh, he's said that a lot.

C suggests that "he" might be wrong, but A denies any such possibility ("he" is her son who comes to visit his mother on occasion). And A is no longer interested in her age but now wonders what day of the week this is.

C *(to A):* What day do you *think* it is?
A *(confusion):* What day is it? What day do I . . . ? *(Eyes narrowing.)* Why, it's today, of course. What day do you *think* it is!? *(Turns to B; cackles.)*
B: Right on, girl!
C *(scoffs):* What an answer! What a dumb . . .
A: Don't you talk to me that way!
C *(offended):* Well! I'm sorry!
A: I pay you, don't I? You can't talk to me that way.
C: In a way.
A *(a daring tone):* What!?
C: Indirectly. You pay someone who pays me, someone who . . .
A: Well; there; you see? You can't talk to me that way.
B: She isn't talking to you that way.
A: What?
B: She isn't *talking* to you that way.

A starts to cry, out of self-pity, and then continues because she hates herself for

Jordan Baker (C), Marian Seldes (B) and Myra Carter (A)
in an Act I scene from Edward Albee's *Three Tall Women*

crying. The crying fit tapers off after a while, and soon A is again joking with B and displaying her resentment of C in little ways.

A begins fretting because she has to go to the bathroom, and B attends to her, helping A out of her chair *("We discover A's left arm is in a sling, useless").* A shuffles offstage with B's help, complaining that B is hurting her. Alone, C mutters to herself, "Why can't I be nice?"

B comes back and lets C know that A occasionally loses control of her bodily functions first thing in the morning but won't hear of wearing a diaper. B declares, "It's downhill from sixteen on! For all of us!", wishing that six-year-olds could grasp the idea that from the minute they are born they are dying.

A hobbles in, pretending that she is about to fall and can't see her chair (C has been sitting in it in A's absence and is now forced to move). B gets A resettled comfortably.

A *(to B):* You can't just leave me in there like that. What if I fell? What if I died?

B *(considers it; calm):* Well . . . if you fell I'd either hear you or you'd raise a racket, and if you died what would it matter?

A *(pause; then she laughs; true enjoyment):* You can say that again! *(Is amused at seeing C not amused.)* What's the matter with you?

C *(small silence, until she realizes she's being talked to):* Who!? Me!?

A: Yes. You.

C: What's the *matter* with me?

B *(amused):* That's what she *said.*
A: That's what I *said.*
C *(panicking a little):* What are you all doing—ganging up on me?
B *(to A):* Is that what we're doing?
A *(enjoying it greatly): May*be!
C *(to defend herself):* There's *nothing* the matter with me.
B *(sour smile):* Well: . . . you just *wait.*
A: What did she say?
B: She says there's nothing the matter with her—Miss Perfect over there.
C: I didn't *say* that; that's not what I . . . !!
A *(to B; sincere):* Why is she *yelling* at me!?
B: She's *not.*
C: I'm *not!*
B: *Now* you are.
A: You see!? . . . . .

Plaintively, A wishes this was one of her son's visiting days. It isn't, B assures her, which sours A's disposition: "You all want something," she accuses them. Her mother taught her and her sister that they'd have to be resolute and make their own way in the world, dealing with men. "Sis couldn't do it," A remembers. "That's too bad. *I* could; *I* did. I met him at a party, and he said he'd seen me before. He'd been married twice—the first one was a whore, the second one was a drunk." He invited A to go riding with him, and she did, though up to then she didn't ride. It took her only six weeks to land him. After their marriage, horses were a very important factor in their lives—they owned a stable, she went riding every day and their horses won all sorts of prizes.

"We won because we were the best," A declares. "Of course," C remarks under her breath. "Be decent," B advises C. "Oh, she'll learn," A finishes.

Their stable was famous, A remembers. She never rode in the championships herself, but she knew all the judges. A had never learned to ride when she was a child because "You rode if you were a farmer or if you were rich," and her family was neither—her father designed and made furniture. "I wasn't rich until I got married," A recalls, but she came to love horses and riding them: *"He* would go with me—not all the time. Sometimes I would go off alone, or with the dog, part way, never too far from the stable . . . . . I had my jodhpurs and my coat and my switch and my derby hat. I always rode in all my costume. Never go out except you're properly dressed, I always say. I'd drive the station wagon from the house—I loved to drive. I was good at it. I was good at everything; I *had* to be; *he* wasn't."

A's train of thought is interrupted by a sudden need to return to the bathroom. In A's absence, C wants to know what happened to her arm. "She fell and broke it," B explains. "It didn't heal. Mostly they don't at that age. They put pins in it, metal pins; the bone disintegrates around the pins, and the arm just hangs there. They want to take it off," but even though it hurts, A won't let them. She goes to the doctor in the city once a week to have it checked, and she always tells him it feels much better.

There is the sound of glass breaking offstage, and A comes back, happily telling the others that she deliberately broke a glass in the sink. When B gets A resettled, C explains that she's come from the lawyer's office (someone named Harry was A's lawyer, but he's been dead for 30 years and his son has taken over). It seems that A hasn't signed any of the papers the lawyer sent over, and her affairs are in a mess. B prods A with a reference to the "I'll get to it" pile.

A: I don't know *what* you're talking about.

C *(to B):* Papers? Checks?

B *(broad):* Oh . . . lots of stuff.

A *(adamant):* There's *nothing!*

C *(to B):* What *is* there? What *is* it?

B *(to A, patiently):* You have a drawer full; the bills come and you look at them, and some of them you send on and they get paid, and some of them you say you can't remember and so you don't send them, and . . .

A *(defiant):* Why would I send in a bill for something I never ordered?

B *(shuts eyes briefly):* And they send you your checks—to sign? To pay bills? And some of them you sign because you remember what they were for, but some of them—some of the checks—you can't remember?

A: I *what!?*

B *(smiles tolerantly):* . . . you don't remember what they're for, and so you don't sign them, and you put them in the drawer.

A: So?

B *(shrugs):* These things pile up.

C: I *see;* I *see.*

A: Everybody out there's ready to rob me blind. I'm not made of money, you know.

B *(laughs):* Yes, you *are. (To C.)* Isn't she?

C *(smiles):* More or less.

A *(conspiratorially):* They'd steal you blind if you didn't pay attention: the help, the stores, the markets, that little Jew makes my furs—what's her name? She's nice. They all rob you blind if you so much as turn your back on them. All of them!

C: We've asked you: let all your bills come to us; we'll know what to do; let me *bring* you your checks every month; I'll stay here while you sign them. Whatever you like.

A *(a superior smile, but hesitant around the edges):* None of you think I can handle my own affairs? I've done it for . . . when he was so sick I did it all; I did all the bills; I did all the checks; I did everything.

C *(gentle):* But now you don't *have* to.

A *(proud):* I didn't have to then: I *wanted* to. I wanted everything to be *right;* and I do now; I still do!

C: Well, of *course* you do.

B: Of *course* you do.

A *(ending it; superior):* And so I'll handle my own affairs, thank you.
C *(defeated; shrugs):* Well; certainly.
B: And *I'll* watch you *pretend* to handle them.

A reminisces about a gunshot wound her husband suffered in a hunting accident. It became infected in those days before antibiotics and almost killed him until she took him to Arizona and baked him in the sun for six months so that the wound finally healed. She learned to ride a Western saddle and met a movie star there, wife of a studio head, with eyes of different colors, one blue, one green. A has difficulty remembering the star's name but finally comes up with Norma Shearer, married to Irving Thalberg.

A continues with her memories—her parents were "strict but fair," insisting on polite behavior and cleanliness as "proper young ladies." Then, abruptly, she changes the subject.

A *(to B):* How much did you steal?
B *(not rising to it):* When?
A: Whenever.
B *(drawling):* Well, I waited until you were asleep . . .
A: I never sleep.
B: . . . until you were pretending to be asleep, and then I went into the silver closet and took down all the big silver bowls, and I stuck them up under my skirt, and I waddled out into the hall . . .
A: Joke about it if you want to. *(A sudden fit of giggles.)* You must have looked *funny!*
B *(playing along):* Well, I suppose.
A: Waddling out like that; you probably clanked, too.
B: Yes; I'm sure I did. Clank, clank.
A *(hoots):* Clank, clank! *(Notices C isn't amused; tough.)* You don't think *any*thing's funny, do you?
C: Oh, yes; I'm just trying to decide what I think's really the most hilarious—unpaid bills, anti-semitism, senility, or . . .
B: Now, now. Play in your own league, huh?
C *(miffed):* Well! I'm *sorry!*

A complains that her friends are all dead or have moved away, she never sees them any more. B reminds A that she doesn't enjoy their company any more anyway. A agrees but feels that somehow that's wrong: "Isn't it a contract? You take people as friends and you spend time at it, you put effort in, and it doesn't matter if you don't like them any more—who likes anybody any more?—you've put in all that time, and what right do they have to . . . to . . ."

But now A is thinking of her sister who was younger and brighter than A but a drunk. When they got out of school they shared a little apartment in the city, looking for jobs, wearing each other's clothes and enjoying the company of young men, but not sharing them. A "liked . . . wilder men" than her sister. Her sister cared little for sex but finally, almost 40, married an Italian, to whom A refers as a "wop." To C's exasperation, A uses degrading terms for various other minorities. B explains to C, "It doesn't *mean* anything. It's the way she learned things."

A remembers that her sister was "tall and pretty" and everything came easily to her. A was "tall and handsome" (the natural compression of her spine has since cost her some of her height) and had to work hard for what she got. "I liked a good time, but I had my eye out" for the right man, A recalls. Her sister's husband was a dentist with no gift for handling money. The thought of money sends her off again on suspicion that everyone around her is stealing from her (she spends every cent of her income on chauffeur, cook, nurses, companion, etc. and could probably use more), but she soon returns to memories of her husband. He was short and had one glass eye, the original having been removed after being hit by a golf ball. She is suddenly distressed because she can't remember which eye was glass and because her memory seems to be leaving her, but B comforts her, "I think you remember everything; I think you just can't bring it to mind all the time." C observes, "Isn't salvation in forgetting?"

A loved her husband, and his frequent gifts to her of jewelry included pearls and a two-inch-wide diamond bracelet. They were undressing in their separate bathrooms after a party (A recalls). A was naked except for her jewelry which she hadn't yet taken off, and her husband walked in naked.

A: . . . . . We were naked a lot, early on, pretty early on. All that stopped. *(Pause.)* Where am I?

B: In your story?

A: What?

B: In your story. Where are you in your story?

A: Yes; of course.

C: You're naked at your dresser, and *he* walks in, and *he's* naked, too.

A: . . . as a jaybird, yes! Oh, I shouldn't *tell* this!

B: Yes! Yes, you should!

C: Yes!

A: Yes? Oh . . . well, there I was, and I had my big powder puff, and I was powdering myself, and I was paying attention to *that.* I knew he was there, but I wasn't paying attention. "I have something for you," he said, "I *have* something for you." And I was sitting there, and I raised my eyes and looked in the mirror and . . . no! I can't tell this?

B & C *(silly schoolgirls; ad lib):* Yes, yes; tell, tell. Tell us! Yes! Tell us!

A: And I looked, and there he was, and his . . . his pee-pee was all hard, and . . . hanging on it was a new bracelet.

C *(awe):* Oh, my God!

B smiles.

A: And it was on his pee-pee, and he came close, and it was the most beautiful bracelet I'd ever seen; it was diamonds, and it was wide, so wide, and . . . "I thought you might like this," he said. "Oh my goodness, it's so beautiful," I said. "Do you want it?" he said. "Yes, yes!" I said, "Oh goodness, yes!" *(Mood shifts a little toward darkness.)* And he came closer, and his pee-pee touched my shoulder—he was short, and I was tall, or something. "Do you want it?" he said, and he poked me with it, with his pee-pee, and I turned, and he had a little pee-pee. Oh, I shouldn't say that; that's terrible to say, but I *know.* He had a little . . . *you* know . . . and there was the bracelet on it, and he moved closer, to my face, and "Do you want it? I thought you might like it." And I said "No! I can't *do* that! You *know* I can't *do* that!", and I couldn't; I could *never* do that, and I said, "No! I can't do that!" And he stood there for . . . well, I don't know . . . and his pee-pee got . . . well, it started to go soft, and the bracelet slid off, and it fell into my lap. I was naked; deep into my lap. "Keep it," he said, and he turned, and he walked out of my dressing room.

Long silence; finally she weeps slowly, conclusively.

B comforts A, who asks to be helped into bed. C tries to help but manages to hurt A's arm. C apologizes to both A and B for not being any good at helping: "I can't pro*ject.*" B advises her, "Well, think of it this way: if you live long enough, you won't have to; you'll be there."

In bed, A's thoughts are muddled between the past, when she hated being taller than the boys in her class, and the present, when she feels she is being robbed by everyone and neglected by her son, who never comes to see her (B reminds A that her son *does* visit her regularly, bringing flowers or chocolates). A rambles on about tending her invalid husband, her sister's drinking, her mother's having to come to live with her, her son's leaving home. A shudders slightly, then becomes silent and motionless. B checks and decides A has suffered a stroke but is still alive. B tends sympathetically to unconscious A before calling the doctor, while C exits to call A's son. *Curtain.*

ACT II

A dummy with a life mask of the actress playing A is propped up in bed, with a breathing mask connected to life support facilities. B and C enter, moving gracefully and dressed smartly, observing that there has been no change in the condition of the motionless figure on the bed.

C is now a glamorous young woman and B is a handsome matron—the fact is, they are A as she was in her 20s and 50s instead of the other people, the companion and lawyer's representative, they portrayed in the previous act. C doesn't even want to think about growing into the aged and infirm woman in the bed. B accepts the aging process more tranquilly, noting that everyone has to die of something, and a stroke is better than having your throat cut by thieves (but that didn't happen, since they survived into old age).

While B and C are chatting about living wills, A enters, an elderly but still wholly active woman in a beautiful lavender dress. *"She is thoroughly rational during this act. B and C are not surprised to see her."*

A: . . . . . Any change?

B: No, we're . . . just as we were; no change.

A: I wonder how long *this'll* go on. I hope it's quick. What's-her-name took six years; not a move, not a blink, hooked up, breathed for, pissed for.

B: Do I know her?

A: No; after your time, so to speak.

B: A *ha.*

A: A lot of money—a *lot.* The kids—hah! Fifty the youngest—the "kids" disagreed. They wanted to see the will first, the lawyer wouldn't *show* it to 'em, they came down on both sides—*kill* her off! *Keep* her going! Not pretty.

C *(really beside herself):* Stop it! Stop it!

A *(to a naughty child): Grow . . . up.*

B *(smiles):* She will; she does.

A: Well; yes; of course. And so do *you.*

C is adamantly unwilling to age into what is lying in the bed—nor, for that matter to become B. To the audience, as though talking to herself, C says she is a good girl of 26 with a pleasant life in an apartment with her sister, with an eye out for the right man, and with a good job as a model in "the fanciest shop in town" (matronly B wouldn't want it to be known that she once worked as a model). But both A and B remember that there was method in C's madcap life, "A little calculation; a little design."

C protests again that she's a good girl—if not a virgin—attractive to men, especially to a muscular young athlete whom she dated often and who liked to dance.

C: . . . . . We were dancing—slowly—late, the end of the evening, and we danced so close, all . . . pressed, and . . . we were pressed, and I could feel that he was hard, *that* muscle and sinew, pressed against me while we danced. We were the same height, and he looked into my eyes as we danced, slowly, and I felt the pressure up against me, and he tensed it, and I felt it move against me.

B *(dreamy):* Whatever is *that,* I said.

A: Hmmmmmmmm.

C: Whatever is *that,* I said. I *knew,* but whatever is that, I said, and he smiled, and his eyes shone, and it's me in love with you, he said. You have an interesting way of showing it, I said. Appropriate, he said, and I felt the muscle move again, and . . . well, I knew it was time; I knew I was ready, and I knew I wanted him—whatever that *meant*—that I wanted *him,* that I wanted *it.*

B *(looking back; agreeing):* Yes; oh, yes.

A: Hmmmmmmmmmm.

Myra Carter and Marian Seldes in an Act II scene from *Three Tall Women*

C: Remember, don't give it away, Mother said; don't give it away like it was nothing.

B *(remembering):* They won't respect you for it, and you'll get known as a loose girl. *Then* who will you marry?

A *(to B):* Is that what she said? I can't remember.

B *(laughs): Yes* you can.

C was finally persuaded to go to the man's place to make love, and she remembers that "It was wonderful." But even at 26 she "couldn't do . . . you know: the thing he wanted . . . I just *couldn't:* I *can't.*" A and B advise C not to worry any more about it.

B remembers that C will meet her future husband two years later, when she's 28, remaining married for almost 40 years ("Yes, but the last *six* aren't much fun," A adds). C met him at a dance where he was dancing with her sister but looking at her. B remembers that the main reason she married the little man with one eye was that he looked a little like a penguin and made her laugh, and that she was "more or less" faithful to him.

C *(some panic):* Why would I marry him if I'm going to cheat on him?

A *(smiles):* Why would you marry him if he's going to cheat on *you?*

C: I don't *know!*

B: Calm down; adjust; settle in. Men cheat; men cheat a *lot.* We cheat *less,* and we cheat because we're lonely; men cheat because they're men.

A: No. We cheat because we're bored, sometimes. We cheat to get back; we cheat because we don't know better; we cheat because we're whores. *We* cheat for *lots* of reasons. Men cheat for only one—as you say, because they're men.

C: *Tell* me about him!

A: Don't you want to be surprised?

C: No!

B: You've seen him, or . . . he's seen *you.* I don't think you've met him. He's something of what they call a playboy—at least in *my* time, not yours. He's rich—or his father is—and he's divorcing his second wife; she's just plain bad; the first one drank; still does.

Moreover he is a great dancer, has a good tenor voice and likes tall women. He was dating a tall comedienne, but C took him away from her. About this time, their father died of heart failure, while their mother lived on and 20 years later moved in with B. "She becomes an enemy," A recalls, and she survived for 17 more years, resenting A's comfortable life and happiness.

B's father-in-law liked her and wanted a grandson, and B and her husband obliged him. As A and B speak of their son, *"He appears in the archway, stands stock still, stares at 'A' on the bed."* B's reaction to his presence is immediate anger, ordering him out of the house, but of course he doesn't hear her or know that A, B and C are there (except for the motionless figure on the bed). He sits on a chair beside the sick woman and holds her hand sympathetically, while C remarks that he is handsome and A that "He never loved us, but he came back." B remembers how her son packed his things one day and left home, not to return (A adds) until he learned that his mother had suffered a heart attack, not returning even for his father's funeral. He never came back to see B, but he did start coming to see A, as she remembers, "He comes; we look at each other, and we both hold in whatever we've been holding in since that day he went away. You're looking well, he says; and you too, I say. And there are no apologies, no recriminations, no tears, no hugs; dry lips on my dry cheeks; yes, that. And we never discuss it? Never go into why? Never go beyond where we are? We're strangers; we're curious about each other; we leave it at that." But B remains adamant—it was she the son walked out on, and "I'll *never* forgive him." A agrees, but 20 years later, lonely, she started receiving his visits without offering him forgiveness.

C *(to A):* How did we change? *(To the son.)* How did I change?

The son strokes A's face, shudders a little.

B: Don't bother yourself. He *never* belonged.

C *(enraged):* I don't believe it!

B *(furious):* Let it *alone!*

C: No! How did I *change?* What *happened* to me!?

A *(sighs):* Oh, God.

C *(determined):* How did I *change!?*

B *(sarcasm; to the audience):* She wants to know how she *changed.* She wants to know how she turned into *me.* Next she'll want to know how I turned into *her. (Indicates A.)* No; I'll want to know *that; maybe* I'll want to know that.

A: Hahh!

B: Maybe *(To C.)* You want to know how I changed?

C *(very alone):* I don't know. *Do* I?

B: Twenty-six to fifty-two? Double it? Double your pleasure, double your fun? Try *this.* Try *this* on for size. They *lie* to you. You're growing up, and they go out of their way to hedge, to qualify, to . . . to evade; to avoid—to *lie.* Never tell it how it is—how it's *going* to be—when a half truth can be got in there. Never give the alternatives to the "pleasing prospects," the "what you have to look forward to." God, if they did the streets'd be littered with adolescent corpses! Maybe it's better they don't.

A *(mild ridicule):* They? *They?*

B: Parents, teachers, all the others. You *lie* to us. You don't tell us things change—that Prince Charming has the morals of a sewer rat, that you're supposed to *live* with that . . . *and* like it, or give the ap*pear*ance of liking it. Chasing the chambermaid into closets, the kitchen maid into the root cellar, and God knows *what* goes on at the stag at the Club! They probably nail the whores to the billiard tables for easy access. Nobody *tells* you any of this . . . . . No wonder one day we come back from riding, the horse all slathered, snorting, and he takes the reins, the groom does, his hand touching the back of our thigh, and we notice, and he notices we notice, and we remember that we've noticed him before, most especially bare chested that day heaving the straw, those arms, that butt. And no wonder we smile in that way he understands so quickly, and no wonder he leads us into a further stall—into the fucking *hay,* for God's sake—and down we go, and it's revenge and self pity we're doing it for until we notice it turning into pleasure for its own sake, for *our* own sake, and we're dripping wet, and he rides us like we've seen in the pornos, and we actually scream, and then we lie there in the straw—which probably has shit on it—cooling down, and he tells us he's wanted us a lot, that he likes big women, but he didn't dare, and will he get fired now? . . . . .

At first she didn't have him fired, but then she did, "because it's dangerous not to, because it's a good deal I've got with the penguin." In the meantime, B was busy protecting herself and her husband against a hostile mother-in-law, trying to help her sister and her mother, trying to straighten out the son who hates her and was caught "doing it with your niece-in-law *and* your nephew-in-law the same week!" Finally the anger between mother and son reached a crisis when the son mentioned the stable groom, touched her hair and remarked, "I thought I saw some straw." Then he packed his bag and went out of her life.

A tells C, "How you got to *her* is one thing; how you got to me is another." There were good times and bad in the process, B remembers. A dwells on the day she and her husband rode out on hunters; she never trusted hunters in general and the one she was riding in particular. The horse shied at a fence in the mist, and A took a bad fall.

A: Damned cast weighed a ton! And you know what I thought about most?

B *(remembering):* Who he's doing it with; who's he got cornered in what corner, what hallway, who he's poking his little dick into.

A: That he might leave us, that he might decide to get one isn't broken.

C *(awe):* What kind of man *is* this?

A *(to C):* Man-man.

B *(to C):* Man-man.

C: How was this happy time? Good times, you said?

B *(to C):* Oh, well, we proved we were human. *(To A.)* No?

A *(to B):* Of course. *(To C.)* We were fallible. Once you fall—whether you get up or not—once you fall, and they see it, they know you can be pushed. Whether you're made of crockery and smash into pieces, or bronze and you clang when you topple, it makes no never-mind; it's the plinth is important.

B *(to C):* To translate . . .

C: Thank you.

A *(sweet smile):* Thank you.

B: To translate . . . you can go around fixing the *world,* patching everything up—*everyone*—and they're *grate*ful to you—grudgingly, but grateful—but once you fall yourself, prove you're not quite as *much* better than they are than they thought, then they'll *let* you go right on doing everything for them, fixing the world etcetera, but they won't hate you quite so much . . . because you're not perfect.

A *(very bright):* And so everything's *better.* Nice and better. Doesn't that make it a good time? He *doesn't* leave you for something else; he's sweet and gives you a big diamond ring, and you don't have to get back up on a hunter any more. Doesn't that make it a happy time?

C is still resolved not to turn into either A or B. As for the big diamond, A has long since sold it, along with most of her other jewelry, to supplement her income. The fakes with which she's replaced it serve her perfectly well.

Asked by B how it was when her husband was dying of cancer, A sums up, "terrible!" and describes the relentless onslaught of the disease, leading to pain and death.

A sits on the bed, on the side opposite her son (and for these moments he seems to be able to hear her and respond with gestures). She remembers a premonition she once had of dying in a hospital; in fact she had been dead for an hour when her son came in bringing her her favorite flowers. The chauffeur and maid were in the room, watching, as her son came in: "You stopped and you *thought. (Loathing.)* I *watched* you *think!* And your face didn't change. *(Wistful.)* Why didn't your face ever change? And there you were, and you thought, and you decided, and you walked over to the bed, and you touched my hand, and you bent down, and you kissed me on the forehead—for them! They were there, and they were watching, and you kissed me for *them!"*

The son *"looks at her once more, shudders, weeps,"* then returns to his affectionate concentration on the figure lying motionless in the bed. C is still determined never to become A, and A sees that B also denies her. What upsets C the most is the thought that at 26 her happiest times are behind her, and she begs the others to reassure her that this isn't so. B obliges, telling C that, to her, now is the happiest time, the peak of life's mountain, "Old enough to be a *little* wise, past being *really* dumb," with a view in both directions of time and a lot of the worst of it gone through and finished.

No, A declares to B and C (and to the audience), the happiest moment is when "the greatest woes subside, leaving breathing space, time to concentrate on the greatest woe of all—that blessed one—the end of it," when you begin to observe yourself in the third person coping with the increasingly challenging physical problems of daily life.

A: . . . . . I can think about myself that way, which means, I suppose, that that's the way I'm *living*—beside myself, to one side. Is that what they mean by that? I'm beside myself? I don't think so. I think they're talking about *another* kind of joy. There's a difference between knowing you're going to *die* and *knowing* you're going to die. The second is better; it moves away from the theoretical. I'm rambling, aren't I.

B *(gently; face forward):* A little.

A *(to B):* Well, we *do* that at ninety, or whatever I'm supposed to be, I mean, give a girl a break. *(To the audience again now.)* Sometimes when I wake up and start thinking about myself like that—like I was watching—I really get the feeling that *I am dead,* but going on at the same time, and I wonder if she can talk and fear and . . . and then I wonder which has died—me, or the one I think about. It's a fairly confusing business. I'm rambling. *(A gesture to stop B.)* Yes, I know! I was talking about . . . what: coming to the end of it, yes. So. There it is. You asked, after all. That's the happiest moment.

A looks to C and B, puts her hands out, takes theirs.

When it's all done. When we stop. When we can stop

Curtain.

TWILIGHT: LOS ANGELES, 1992

A Series of Monologues in Two Parts

BY ANNA DEAVERE SMITH

Credits appear on pages 433-4 and 463

ANNE DEAVERE SMITH was born in 1950 in Baltimore, where her father was self-employed in the coffee and tea business. She trained as an actress, receiving her M.F. A. from the American Conservatory Theater after graduating from Beaver College, and she became interested in "writing roles for multi-cultural casts and different representations of people in gender than we traditionally have seen." In 1991 the Los Angeles Theater Center produced her play Piano, *which won her the Drama League Award in Playwriting.*

Meanwhile, Smith was developing a series of character studies she called On the Road: A Search for American Character, *verbatim interviews performed in character as monologues "meant to capture the personality of a place by attempting to embody its varied population and varied points of view in one person—myself. Often, the shows are built around a specific controversial and timely event or series of events." Such was the case with the one-woman show in which Smith made her professional stage debut as both actress and playwright at the Joseph Papp Public Theater December 1, 1991 as an item in George C. Wolfe's* Moving Beyond the Madness: A Festival of New Voices. *Much of it concerned the tragic Crown Heights confrontation in Brooklyn—material created expressly for this staging. When presented as a separate program at the Public May 12, 1992 under the title* Fires in the Mirror, *it won its author her first Best Play citation, plus a special Obie Award and*

Drama Desk, Lucille Lortel and George and Elisabeth Marton Awards and the Kesselring Prize. This season another section of her On the Road *creations—*Twilight: Los Angeles, 1992*—was presented at the Public Theater March 23, Smith's second Best Play, bringing her a special New York Drama Critics citation "for unique contribution to theatrical form" and moving on to Broadway April 17 for an extended run.* Twilight *was commissioned by the Center Theater Group/Mark Taper Forum in Los Angeles, premiered there in June 1992 and concerns events and attitudes surrounding the Rodney King verdict and subsequent violence including the Reginald Denny beating.*

Other sections of Smith's On the Road *have included* Hymn, *in collaboration with Judith Jamison, for the Alvin Ailey American Theater;* Identities, Mirrors and Distortions *for the Bay Area Playwrights Festival;* From the Outside Looking In: San Francisco, 1990 *for the Eureka Theater;* Fragments: On Intercultural Performance *for the Rockefeller Conference Center, Bellagio, Italy;* Black Identity and Black Theater *for Crossroads Theater;* Gender Bending *for Princeton University; and material for The National Conference of Women and the Law. Smith is a fellow of Radcliffe College's Bunting Institute, and she holds the Ann O'Day Maples Professorship of the Arts at Stanford University. She lives in San Francisco.*

SYNOPSIS: *Twilight: Los Angeles, 1992* is a series of more than 40 characterizations enacted in a solo but multi-faceted performance of monologues derived from the subject's own words. In each case these words bear directly or indirectly on the causes, results and personal impact of the rioting and looting in Los Angeles following the "not guilty" verdict in the first trial of the four police officers accused of beating up Rodney King.

Among the interviewees are representatives of the famous—such as Mayor Tom Bradley, victim Reginald Denny, Police Chief Daryl F. Gates, director Peter Sellars, Senator Bill Bradley, publisher Otis Chandler—the involved—such as jurors and victims of violence (notably an expectant mother whose unborn child was wounded by a bullet)—and the bystander, sometimes anonymous, in many variations and points of view. In order to represent the probing and powerful Smith work as effectively and comprehensively as possible in the space of a Best Play citation, instead of sketching in all the characterizations we here present four of the staged episodes in their entirety

No Justice, No Peace, Part I

PAUL PARKER *(chairperson, Free the LA Four Plus Defense Committee):*

So it's just a PR type of program.
Gates knew that the police were catching a lot of flak
and he

also caught a lot of flak from being at a benefit
banquet,
um, the time when the rebellion
was comin' down,
jumpin' off.
It just goes to show more or less the extremes that he went to just to
get these brothers.
And when they came for my brother Lance more or less,
they sent out two SWAT teams simultaneously,
one to my brother's and my fiancee's residence and one to my mom's.
They basically had *America's Most Wanted* TV cameras there.
Saying he was a known gang member,
a big head honcho drug dealer in the underground world for the last
two years,
he owns two houses,
things of this nature,
and here my brother went to college for four years,
he's been working in a law firm as a process server.
They basically paraded him around in the media,
saying we got the gunman, we got this guy.
They accused him of attempted murder, of shootin' at Reginald Denny,
um, with a shotgun. They said he
attempted to blow up some gas pumps
and my father got shot in the streets eleven years ago
over a petty robbery,
and Van de Kamp,
and their attitude was "We don't want to bring your family
through the trauma and drama,
just stir up some more trouble."
They basically feel that if it's a black-on-black crime,
a nigger killin' a nigger,
they don't have no problem with that.
But let it be a white victim,
oh,
they gonna . . . they gonna go
to any extremes necessary
to basically convict some black people.
So that's more or less how . . .
really what made me bitter
and I said well, I ain't gonna stand for this,
I'm not gonna let you
just put my brother's face around world TV headline news,
CNN world span,

and just basically portray him as a negative person.
I'm not gonna let you do that.
So that's more or less when I just resigned from my job,
more or less quit my job, and I just took it on.
And like I said, I been in law enforcement for a while, I been in the army for six years
I been doin' a lot of things.
So I just decided I'm not gonna let my brother, my one and only brother, go down like that, my one and only brother,
my younger brother, so I decided to take this on full-time
and I was voted in as being chairperson of the Free the LA Four Plus Defense Committee
and I been workin' for all the brothers ever since.

A Weird Common Thread in Our Lives

REGINALD DENNY:

Every single day
I must make this trip to Inglewood—no problem—
and I get off the freeway like usual,
taking up as much space as I can in the truck.
People don't like that.
Because I have to.
That little turn onto Florence
is pretty tricky,
it's really a tight turn.
I take two lanes to do it in
and
it was just like a scene
out of a movie.
Total confusion and chaos.
I was just in awe.
And the thing that I remember most vivid—
broken glass
on the ground.
And for a split second I was goin'
check this out,
and the truck in front of me—
and I found out later—
the truck in front of me,
medical supplies goin' to Daniel Freeman!

He laughs.

Kind of a
ironic thing!
And the, uh,
the strange thing was
that what everyone thought was a fire extinguisher
I got clubbed with,
it was a bottle of oxygen,
'cause the guy had medical supplies.
I mean,
does anyone know
what a riot looks like?
I mean, I'm sure they do now.
I didn't have a clue of what one looked like
and
I didn't know that the verdict had come down.
I didn't pay any attention
to that,
because that
was somebody else's problem
I guess I thought
at the time.
It didn't have anything to do with me.
I didn't usually pay too much attention of what was going on in
California
or in America or anything
and, uh,
I couldn't for the life of me figure out what was goin on.
Strange things do happen on that street.
Every now and again police busting somebody.
That was a street that was never . . .
I mean it was always an exciting . . .
we,
lot of guys looked forward to going down that street
'cause there was always something going on, it seemed
like,
and the cool thing was I'd buy those cookies
from
these guys
on the corner,
and I think they're uh,
Moslems?
And they sell cookies
or cakes,

Anna Deavere Smith in a scene from her *Twilight: Los Angeles, 1992*

the best tasting stuff,
and whatever they were selling that day,
and it was always usually a surprise,
but it was very well known
that it was a good surprise!
Heck, a good way to munch!
But when I knew something was wrong was when they bashed in the right window of
my truck.
That's the end of what I remember as far as anything
until five or six days later.
They say I was in a coma,
And I still couldn't figure out,
you know,
how I got here.
And

It was quite a few weeks after I was in the hospital
that they even let on that there was a riot,
because the doctor didn't feel it
was something I needed to know.
Morphine is what they were givin me for pain,
and it was just an interesting time.
But I've never been in an operating room.
It was like . . .
this is just . . .
I 'member like in a movie
they flip on the big lights
and they're really in there.
He laughs.
I was just goin' "God"
and seein' doctors around with masks on
and I still didn't know why I was still there
and next thing
I know I wake up a few days later.
I think when it really dawned on me
that something big might had happened
was when important people wanted to come in and say hi.
The person that I remember that wanted to come in and see me,
the first person that I was even aware of who wanted to see me,
was Reverend Jesse Jackson,
and I'm just thinkin':
not this guy,
that's the dude I see on TV all the time.
And then it was a couple days later that
Arsenio Hall came to see me
and he just poked his head in, said hello,
and, uh,
I couldn't say nothin' to him.
And then, about then I started to, uh,
started to get it.
And by the time I left Daniel Freeman I knew what happened,
except they wouldn't let me watch it on TV.
I mean they completely controlled that remote control thing.
They just had it on a movie station.
And if I hadn't seen some of the stuff,
you know, of me doin' a few things after everything was done,
like climbing back into the truck,
and talking to Titus and Bobby and Terry and Lee—
that's the four people

who came to my rescue.
you know—they're telling me stuff that I would never
even have known.
Terry
I met only because she came as a surprise guest visit to the hospital.
That was an emotional time
How does one say that
someone
saved
my life?
How does a person,
how do I
express enough
thanks
for someone risking their
neck?
And then I was kind of . . .
I don't know if "afraid" is the word,
I was just a little,
felt a little awkward meeting people
who
saved me.
Meeting them was not like meeting
a stranger,
but it was like
meeting a
buddy.
There was a weird common thread in our lives
That's an extraordinary event,
and here is four people—
the ones in the helicopter—
and they just stuck with it,
and then you got four people
who seen it on TV
and said enough's enough
and came to my rescue.
They tell me
I drove the truck for what? About a hundred or so feet.
The doctors say there's *fight* or *flight* syndrome.
And I guess I was in *flight!*
And it's been seventeen years since I got outta high school!
I been drivin semis,
it's almost second nature,

but Bobby Green
saw that I was gettin' nowhere fast and she just jumped in and
scooted me over
and drove the truck.
By this time
it was tons of glass and blood everywhere,
'cause I've seen pictures of what I looked like
when I first went into surgery,
and I mean it was a pretty
bloody mess.
and they showed me my hair,
when they cut off my hair
they gave it to me in a plastic bag.
And it was just
long hair and
glass and blood.
Lee—
that's a woman—
Lee Euell,
she told me
she just
cradled me.
There's no
passenger seat in the truck
and here I am just kind of on my knees in the middle of the floor
and, uh,
Lee's just covered with blood,
and Titus is on one side,
'cause Bobby couldn't see out the window
The front windshield was so badly broken
it was hard to see.
And Titus is standing on the running board telling Bobby where to go,
and then Terry
Titus's girlfriend,
she's in front of the truck
weaving through traffic,
dodging toward cars
to get them to
kind of move out of the way,
to get them to clear a path,
and next stop was
Daniel Freeman Hospital!
Some day when I,

uh,
get a house,
I'm gonna have one of the rooms
and it's just gonna be
of all the riot stuff
and it won't be a
blood-and-guts
memorial,
it's not gonna be a sad,
it's gonna be a happy room.
It's gonna be . . .
of all the crazy things that I've got,
all the,
the
love and compassion
and the funny notes
and the letters from faraway places,
just framed, placed,
framed things,
where a person will walk in
and just have a good old time in there.
It'll just be
fun to be in there,
just like a fun thing,
and there won't be
a color problem
in this room.
You take the toughest
white guy
who thinks he's a bad-ass
and
thinks he's better than any other race in town,
get him in a position where he needs help,
he'll take the help
from no matter who the color of the guy across . . .
because he's so self-
centered and -serving,
he'll take it
and then
soon as he's better
he'll turn around
and rag on 'em.
I know that for a fact.

Give me what I need and shove off.
It's crazy, it's nuts.
That's the person I'd like to shake and go,
"Uuuh,
you fool,
you selfish little shit"—
those kind of words.
"Uhhh man, you *nut.*"
Pause and intense stare, low key.
I don't know what I want.
I just want people to wake up.
It's not a color, it's a person.
So this room,
it's just gonna be
people,
just a wild place,
it's gonna be a blast.
One day,
Lord
willing, it'll happen.

No Justice, No Peace, Part II

PAUL PARKER:
Because Denny is white,
that's the bottom line.
If Denny was Latino,
Indian, or black,
they wouldn't give a damn,
they would not give a damn.
Because
many people got beat,
but you didn't hear about the Lopezes or the Vaccas
or the, uh, Quintanas
or the, uh,
Tarvins.
You didn't hear about them,
but you heard about the Reginald Denny beating,
the Reginald Denny beating,
the Reginald Denny beating.
This one white boy
paraded all around

this nation
to go do every talk show there is,
get paid left and right.
Oh, Reginald Denny,
this innocent white man.
But you didn't hear nuthin' about all these other victims
until the day of the trial came.

Mimicking dorky voice.

"Well, this is more than about Reginald Denny. This is about several people. Many people got beat up on the corner."
So the bottom line is it, it, it's
a white victim, you know, beaten down by some blacks.
"Innocent."
I don't see it on the innocent tip,
because if that's the case,
then we supposed to have some empathy
or some sympathy toward this one white man?
It's like well, how 'bout the empathy and the sympathy
toward blacks?
You know, like I said before, we innocent. Like I said,
you kidnapped us,
you raped our women,
you pull us over daily,
have us get out of our cars, sit down on the curb,
you go through our cars,
you say all right,
take all our papers out, go through our trunk,
all right,
and drive off,
don't even give us a ticket.
You know we innocent,
you know where's our justice,
where's our self-respect,
but, hey, you want us to feel something toward
this white man, this white boy.
I'm like please,
it ain't happenin' here,
not from the real brothers and sisters.
That white man,
some feel that white boy just better be glad he's alive,
'cause a lot of us didn't make it.
They caught it on video.
Some brothers beatin' the shit out of a white man.

And they were going to do everything in their power to convict these brothers.
We spoke out on April 29.
Hoo *(Real pleasure.)*
it was flavorful,
it was juicy.
It was, uh,
it was good for the soul,
it was rejuven . . .
it was . . .
Count four, he sighs.
It it it was beautiful.
I was a cornerback
and I ran some track
and played football,
everything.
I been all off into sports since I was five.
It was . . .
it was bigger than any . . . any type of win I've been involved in.
I mean, we been National Champions,
Golden State League.
I been . . .
I have so many awards and trophies,
but, um, it's it's nothing compared to this.
They lost seven hundred million dollars.
I mean basically you puttin' a race of people on notice.
We didn't get to Beverly Hills but
that doesn't mean we won't get there,
you keep it up.
Um,
they're talkin' about "You burned down your own neighborhoods."
And I say, "First of all,
we burned down these Koreans in this neighborhood."
About ninety-eight percent of the stores that got burned down were Korean.
The Koreans was like the Jews in the day
and we put them in check.
You know, we got rid of all these Korean stores over here.
All these little liquor stores.
You know, we got rid of all that.
We did more in three days than all these
politicians been doin' for years.
We just spoke out.

We didn't have a plan.
We just acted and we acted in a way that was just.
Now we got some weapons, we got our pride.
We holdin' our heads up and our chest out.
We like yeah, brother, we did this!
We got the gang truce jumpin' off.
Basically it's
that you as black people ain't takin' this shit no more.
Even back in slavery.
'Cause I saw *Roots* when I was young.
My dad made sure. He sat us down
in front of that TV
when *Roots* came on,
so it's embedded in me
since then.
And just to see that aye aye.
This is for Kunta.
This is for Kizzy.
This is for Chicken George.
I mean,
it was that type of thing,
it was some victory.
I mean it was burnin' everywhere.
It was takin' things and nobody was tellin' nobody.
It wasn't callin' 911.
"Aww they are takin'."
Unh-unh, it was like "Baby go get me some too."
"I'm a little bit too old to move but get me somethin'."
You know, I mean, it was the spirit. I mean, actually today
they don't know who . . . who . . . who . . .
You know, they only got these . . .
What?
Eight people.
Eight people
out of several thousand?
Um. *(Real mock disappointment.)*
Um, um,
they lost.
Oh.
Big time.
No Justice No Peace.
That's just more or less, I guess you could say, my motto.
When I finally get my house I'm gonna have just one room set aside.

It's gonna be my No Justice No Peace room.
Gonna have up on the wall No Justice,
over here No Peace,
and have all my articles
and clippings and, um,
everything else.
I guess so my son can see,
my children can grow up with it.
Know what Daddy did.
You know, if I still happen to be here,
God willin',
they can just see what it takes
to be a strong black man,
what you gotta do for your people,
you know.
When God calls you, this is what you gotta do.
You either stand
or you fall.
You either be black
or you die
and *(Exhale.)*
you know, with No Justice No Peace
it . . . it's,
you know, um,
I guess you might say it's fairly simple,
but to me it's pretty, um,
not complex,
but then again it's deep,
it's nothin' shallow.
It basically just means if there's no justice here
then we not gonna give them any peace.
You know, we don't have any peace.
They not gonna have no peace,
a peace of mind,
you know,
a physical peace,
you know, body.
You might have a dent . . . a dent in your head from now on in life.
It might not be you
but it may be your daughter.
You know, somewhere
in your family
you won't have no peace.

You know, it . . . it's that type of thing.
Without doing, say, justice,
if I don't do what I'm doing,
when I do
happen to die,
pass away,
I won't be able to really rest,
I won't have no peace,
'cause I didn't do something in terms of justice.
I'm one brother
doing the work of
one brother
and
I just do that,
the best I can do.
It's educational.
It's a blessing.
It's a gift from God.

Swallowing the Bitterness

MRS. YOUNG-SOON HAN *(former liquor store owner):*
Until last year
I believed America is the best.
I still believe it.
I don't deny that now
because I'm victim,
but
as
the year ends in '92
and we were still in turmoil
and having all the financial problems
and mental problems.
Then a couple months ago
I really realized that
Korean immigrants were left out
from this
society and we were nothing.
What is our right?
Is it because we are Korean?
Is it because we have no politicians?
Is it because we don't

speak good English?
Why?
Why do we have to be left out?
She is hitting her hand on the coffee table.
We are not qualified to have medical treatment.
We are not qualified to get, uh,
food stamp
She hits the table once.
not GR
Hits the table once.
no welfare
Hits the table once.
Anything.
Many Afro-Americans
Two quick hits.
who never worked
One hit.
they get
at least minimum amount
One hit.
of money
One hit.
to survive
One hit.
We don't get any!
Large hit with full hand spread.
Because we have a car
One hit.
and we have a house.
Pause six seconds.
And we are high taxpayers.
One hit. Pause fourteen seconds.
Where do I finda (sic) justice?
Okay, black people
probably
believe they won
by the trial?
Even some complains only half right?
justice was there.
but I watched the television
that Sunday morning,
early morning as they started.
I started watch it all day.

They were having party and then they celebrated,
all of South-Central,
all the churches.
They finally found that justice exists
in this society.
Then where is the victims' rights?
They got their rights.
By destroying innocent Korean merchants . . .
They have a lot of respect,
as I do,
for
Dr. Martin King?
he is the only model for black community.
I don't care Jesse Jackson.
But
he was the model
of nonviolence.
Nonviolence?
They like to have hiseh (sec) spirits.
What about last year?
They destroyed innocent people.

Five second pause.

And I wonder if that is really justice

And a very soft uh after "justice," like "justicah," but very quick.

to get their rights
in this way.

Thirteen-second pause.

I waseh swallowing the bitternesseh,
sitting here alone
and watching them.
They became all hilarious

Three-second pause.

and, uh,
in a way I was happy for them
and I felt glad for them.
At leasteh they got something back, you know.
Just let's forget Korean victims or other victims
who are destroyed by them.
They have fought
for their rights

One hit simultaneous with the word "rights."

over two centuries

One hit simultaneous with "centuries."

and I have a lot of sympathy and understanding for them.
Because of their effort and sacrificing,
other minorities like, Hispanic
or Asians,
maybe we have to suffer more
by mainstream.
You know
that's why I understand,
and then
I like to be part of their
'joyment.
But . . .
That's why I had mixed feeling
as soon as I heard the verdict.
I wish I could
live together
with eh (sic) blacks,
but after the riots
there were too much differences.
The fire is still there—
how do you call it?—
igni . . .
igniting fire.

She says a Korean phrase phonetically "Dashi yun gi ga nuh."

It's still dere.
It canuh
burst out anytime.

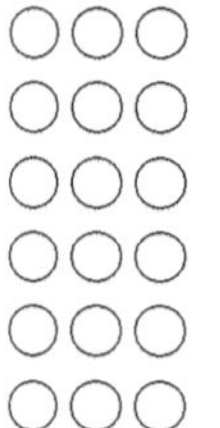

PASSION

A Musical in 15 Scenes

BOOK BY JAMES LAPINE

MUSIC AND LYRICS BY STEPHEN SONDHEIM

BASED UPON THE FILM *PASSIONE D'AMORE* DIRECTED BY ETTORE SCOLA AND THE NOVEL *FOSCA* BY I.U. TARCHETTI

Cast and credits appear on page 438

JAMES LAPINE (book) was born in 1949 in Mansfield, Ohio, where his father was a sales representative. He was educated at Franklin & Marshall (B.A. in history, 1971) and the California Institute of the Arts (M.F.A. in design, 1973). After a year in New York he landed a job in 1975 as a graphics designer for Yale Drama School and their magazine Yale Theater. *For some years he had been interested in writing, and while at Yale he adapted Gertrude Stein's three-page poem* Photograph *for the stage, directing it in New Haven and in its Obie Award-winning production in 1977 off Broadway at The Open Space in Soho.*

The following year Lapine wrote and directed Twelve Dreams *for production off off Broadway by Lyn Austin's Music Theater Group. His* Table Settings *was pro-*

duced OOB in 1979 under its author's direction in workshop at Playwrights Horizons, which then presented it in a full-scale 264-performance off-Broadway production January 14, 1980, its author's first Best Play. The following season he collaborated with William Finn on the musical March of the Falsettos, *launching it into a 268-performance off-Broadway run. In late 1981 he directed a revised version of* Twelve Dreams *off Broadway at New York Shakespeare Festival and staged that group's* A Midsummer Night's Dream *in Central Park the following summer and* The Winter's Tale *at the Public Theater in 1989.*

The felicitous Lapine-Sondheim collaboration first surfaced when Lapine directed a production of Sunday in the Park With George *(book, James Lapine; music and lyrics, Stephen Sondheim) in workshop at Playwrights Horizons and opening on Broadway, May 2, 1984 for 604 performances, Lapine's second Best Play, winning its authors the 1983-84 Critics Award as the season's best musical and the 1984-85 Pulitzer Prize. The collaboration continued with Lapine's direction of a regional theater revival of Sondheim's 1981 musical* Merrily We Roll Along *at the La Jolla, Calif. Playhouse and again with great distinction with the book and direction of the Broadway musical* Into the Woods *November 12, 1987 at the Martin Beck Theater, Lapine's third Best Play, Critics Award and the Tony best-book winner. His fourth best-play accolade came not with Sondheim but in a return to collaboration with William Finn on the off-Broadway musical* Falsettoland *(1990) as co-author of the book and director of the show, which was revived the following year on a Broadway program with* March of the Falsettos, *Lapine directing. This season, again in collaboration with Sondheim, he receives his fifth Best Play citation for* Passion *as well as the best-book Tony.*

Lapine has also directed the feature films Impromptu *and* Life With Mikey. *He lives in New York City.*

STEPHEN SONDHEIM (music, lyrics) was born March 22, 1930 in New York City. The Oscar Hammerstein IIs were family friends, and it was under Hammerstein's influence and guidance that young Sondheim became interested in the theater and was induced to write a musical for his school (George School, a Friends school in Bucks County, Pa.). At Williams College he won the Hutchinson Prize for musical composition. After receiving his B.A. he studied theory and composition with Milton Babbitt. He wrote scripts for the Topper *TV series and incidental music for the Broadway productions of* Girls of Summer *(1956) and* Invitation to a March *(1961).*

It was as a lyricist that Sondheim first commanded major attention, however. He'd written a show called Saturday Night *which never made it to Broadway; but Arthur Laurents remembered it, liked the lyrics and took steps to bring Sondheim into collaboration on the great* West Side Story *(1957) as its lyricist. Sondheim then wrote both music and lyrics for the hit show* A Funny Thing Happened on the Way to the Forum *(1962) and* Anyone Can Whistle *(1964), as well as for his five straight Best Plays and Critics Award winners directed by Harold Prince:* Company *(1970),* Follies *(1971),* A Little Night Music *(1973, winning Sondheim his third straight*

Tony Award as best composer and lyricist), Pacific Overtures *(1976) and* Sweeney Todd, the Demon Barber of Fleet Street *(1979, and another best-score Tony). Prince also directed the 1981 Broadway musical adaptation of the George S. Kaufman-Moss Hart play* Merrily We Roll Along *with Sondheim music and lyrics.* Sunday in the Park With George *(1984) was the composer-lyricist's sixth Best Play, seventh Critics Award and first Pulitzer Prize winner.* Into the Woods *(1987) became his seventh Best Play, eighth Critics Award winner and fourth Tony-winner for its score, and now* Passion, *which opened April 28, wins him his eighth Best Play citation (far more than any other composer-lyricist) and the Tonys for best musical, book and score in what has certainly been and continues to be one of the most distinguished American musical theater careers ever.*

Other major Sondheim credits include the lyrics for Gypsy *(1959) and* Do I Hear a Waltz? *(1965), additional lyrics for the 1974 revival of* Candide *(still another Sondheim-Prince winner of the Critics Award, the chronological sixth in Sondheim's long line). Anthology programs of his work have included* Side by Side by Sondheim *on Broadway in 1977 and, off Broadway,* Marry Me a Little *(1981) and* Sondheim—Putting It Together *(1993). He also wrote the incidental music for the play* Twigs, *the movie script for* The Last of Sheila *in collaboration with Anthony Perkins, the scores of the movies* Stavisky *and* Reds, *the music and lyrics for Burt Shevelove's adaptation of Aristophane's* The Frogs, *staged in the Yale University swimming pool, and songs for the TV production* Evening Primrose.

Sondheim is an ex officio member of the council of the Dramatists Guild, the professional association of playwrights, composers, lyricists and librettists, and served as its president from 1973 to 1981, during which period it greatly expanded services to its members. He was elected to the American Academy and Institute of Arts and Letters in 1983, and he lives in New York City.

Time: 1863

Place: Milan and a remote military outpost

Scene 1

SYNOPSIS: The sound of drums reaches a climax, as does the lovemaking of Clara and Giorgio. Relaxing in the bed, passion for the moment spent, they assure each other that true happiness has grown from a relationship which began with a chance meeting in the park.

BOTH *(sing):*
. . . . Just another love story,
That's what they would claim.

Another simple love story—
Aren't all of them the same?

CLARA *(sings):*

No, but this is more,
We feel more!

BOTH *(sing):*

This is so much more—!

Beat. Smiling at each other.

Like every other love story.
Some say happiness
Comes and goes.
Then this happiness
Is a kind of happiness
No one really knows.

GIORGIO *(sings):*

I thought I knew what love was.

CLARA *(overlapping; sings):*

I'd only heard what love was.

GIORGIO *(sings):*

I thought it was no more than a name
For yearning.

CLARA *(sings):*

I thought it was what kindness became.

GIORGIO *(sings):*

I'm learning—

CLARA *(sings):*

I thought where there was love there was shame.

GIORGIO *(sings):*

—That with you—

CLARA *(sings):*

But with you—

BOTH *(sing):*

—There's just happiness.

CLARA *(sings):*

Endless happiness . . .

Their joy is to be short-lived, however, because Giorgio, an army officer, has been transferred from the city to an outpost. They promise to write each other daily while he's away. Clara tries to dress, but Giorgio, studying details of her beauty to record them vividly in his memory, draws her back into bed.

Scene 2

Seated around the table in the officers' mess are Col. Ricci ("*a rather taut gentle-*

Marin Mazzie (Clara) and Jere Shea (Giorgio) in the Stephen Sondheim-James Lapine musical *Passion*

man who carries the weight of his position with authority and ease"), Lt. Torasso ("*a man often given to laughter and opera singing*"), Maj. Rizzolli ("*a sober, straight-arrow type*"), Lt. Barri ("*a veterinarian with a love of gambling and not much else*") and Dr. Tambourri ("*a somewhat aloof and distinguished older officer*"). They are chatting with the cook (Sgt. Lombardi) about the food, when a woman's scream offstage causes them to pause in their conversation, briefly. They continue without acknowledging the scream.

Giorgio enters and is introduced to the others by the Colonel as "Captain Bachetti." As they discuss Giorgio's act of heroism in a skirmish with the Russian infantry, Giorgio's mind wanders to a letter exchange with Clara.

Clara enters to the side of the stage, singing from a letter she holds.

CLARA *(sings):*

Clara . . .

GIORGIO *(sings):*

Clara . . .
I cried.

CLARA *(sings):*

I cried.

BOTH *(sing):*

Imagine that—
A soldier who cries.

CLARA *(sings):*

I had to hide my eyes
So the others on the train
That carried me away from you—
Would think I was asleep.

Giorgio's reverie of Clara reading his letter is broken by the sound of *"elegant Chopinesque piano music"* being played offstage, upstairs.

DOCTOR: That's Signora Fosca playing.

COLONEL: My cousin. I have no family, and neither does she. She is in such poor health, it's a continual worry.

DOCTOR: That's her place setting, but she stays in her room most days. Perhaps soon she'll be well enough to join us for a meal.

RIZZOLLI: She eats like a sparrow.

Torasso lets out an involuntary laugh, which is immediately stopped by a cold stare from the Colonel.

TORASSO *(sober):* My apologies, sir. The comparison struck me as funny. A sparrow seems to eat more than Signora Fosca. A pity it is . . .

COLONEL *(to Giorgio):* My cousin loves to read—it's her only passion, really. I can't find enough books for her.

GIORGIO: I also love to read. I've brought a few of my favorite books. I'd be most happy to lend them to Signora Fosca, though I can't promise they will appeal to her.

COLONEL: She's been given to reading military handbooks. I've no doubt she will welcome anything in print!

Pvt. Augenti enters to distribute mail. A letter to Giorgio returns his thoughts to Clara. His thoughts are broken by a scream from upstairs which is ignored by all but him. The Colonel explains that they have become accustomed to these outbursts from the reclusive Fosca and that Giorgio, too, will become inured to her sounds.

The scene changes with the sound of snare drums. Outdoors, Giorgio is reviewing troops, as Clara reads one of his letters, in which he complains that life here at the Brigade is a hell shared with "pompous little men." The Doctor enters, and their conversation turns to talk of Fosca. The Doctor explains that she is young, in her late 20s, but "a kind of medical phenomenon, a collection of ills." Giorgio asks whether she might be the Colonel's lover, but the Doctor sets him straight: "No, I'm afraid Signora Fosca's fragile physical state prevents her from being anyone's lover."

The scene segues back to the mess hall, where Giorgio joins a group for breakfast. Fosca, as usual, hasn't come to the table, and her place setting is removed. When the others exit, Giorgio takes out Clara's latest letter, and reads it, imagining they are making love, as *"Fosca, in silhouette, appears descending a long staircase behind a semi-transparent wall."* She comes into the room carrying books. *"She walks with an uncertain gait and, as she turns from the shadows, revealing herself, we discover that she is an ugly, sickly woman: incredibly thin and sallow, her face all bones and nose, her hair pulled tightly back."* When Giorgio sees Fosca, he is *"momentarily stunned."* His vision of Clara disappears, as Fosca speaks to him in a voice that is *"lovely and elegant, but melancholy."* She has come to thank Giorgio (who introduces himself) for lending her his books.

FOSCA: I so enjoyed the novel by Rousseau.
GIORGIO: It's wonderful. My favorite, really.
FOSCA: The character of Julie is a great mystery.
GIORGIO: You should have kept the book longer to meditate over.
FOSCA *(sings, her moods changing rapidly):*
I do not read to think.
I do not read to learn.
I do not read to search for truth,
I know the truth,
The truth is hardly what I need.

I read to dream.

I read to live
In other people's lives.
I read about the joys
The world
Dispenses to the fortunate,
And listen for the echoes.
Fiercely.
I read to live,
To get away from life!
Calmer.
No, Captain, I have no illusions.
I recognize the limits of my dreams.
I know how painful dreams can be
Unless you know
They're merely dreams . . . . .

Fosca sings of a flower that combines nectar with poison which dooms the incautious butterfly. "If you have no expectations, Captain/You can never have a disappointment," she finishes and then ceases talking about herself and comments on the gardens, the town, and the ruined castle which she particularly likes to visit. Giorgio tells her he hasn't seen a garden or a flower since he arrived. Abruptly, she leaves him, only to return quickly carrying a small bunch of flowers which she presents to Giorgio. She takes him to the window to point out the local greenhouse. Funereal drums are heard. Giorgio calls her attention to a hearse drawn up by the greenhouse to get flowers to decorate a casket. Fosca, upset by this image, involuntarily collapses with a cry. Giorgio calls the Doctor, who comes with Attendants to carry Fosca off.

Giorgio writes to Clara, trying to describe Fosca's wretchedness and his own embarrassment in "Listening to all that self pity." A formation of soldiers marches the action into the next scene.

Scene 3

Giorgio is strolling in the garden with Fosca, as Clara sings from his last letter. Fosca apologizes for her behavior when last they met. She confides, "I rather think I'd welcome dying. It's everything that follows that I dread. Being shut up in a coffin, smothered in the earth, turning into dust. These images send me into a state of terror."

Giorgio suggests that Fosca might seek pleasure in helping others. "Pity is nothing but passive love . . . . . dead love," Fosca replies scornfully.

GIORGIO: There is no absolute happiness in anyone's life, Signora. The only happiness we can be certain of is love.

FOSCA: What do you mean?

CLARA *(sings):*

The garden filled with you . . .

FOSCA: Are you speaking of friendships? Family?

GIORGIO: I'm speaking of a superior kind of love—

CLARA *(sings):*

And all that I could do,

GIORGIO: —the kind between two people.

CLARA *(sings):*

Because of you,
Was talk of love . . .

FOSCA: Two people . . .

GIORGIO: Yes.

Giorgio sings to Fosca, as Clara continues to sing the letter.

CLARA & GIORGIO *(sing):*

Love that fills
Every waking moment,
Love that grows
Every single day,
Love that thinks
Everything is pure,
Everything is beautiful,
Everything is possible . . . . .

FOSCA: Yes, I've read about that love, but you speak of it as one who lives it.

Music stops. She stumbles slightly; Giorgio goes to aid her, but she pulls herself away.

I don't feel well. I must go back.

Music resumes.

GIORGIO: I'm sorry.

FOSCA: You can be incredibly cruel, Captain.

GIORGIO: Cruel?

FOSCA *(sings):*

To speak to me of love . . . . .

You with all your books,
Your taste,
Your sensitivity,
I thought you'd understand.

The others—well,
They're all alike.
Stupidity is their excuse,
As ugliness is mine.
But what is yours?

I've watched you from my window.
I saw you on the day that you arrived.
Perhaps it was the way you walked,
The way you spoke to your men—
I saw that you were different then.
I saw that you were kind and good.
I thought you understood.

Intensely.

They hear drums,
You hear music,
As do I.
Don't you see?
We're the same,
We are different,
You and I are different.
They hear only drums . . . . .

Fosca continues in song, begging Giorgio to be her friend. Taking her hand, he promises friendship. They head back toward the castle.

Scene 4

Giorgio and Clara, corresponding by mail, stand on opposite sides of the stage speaking lines from their letters about Giorgio's fears of Fosca. Clara admires him for offering friendship to this unfortunate soul, but both agree he must be careful to define the relationship, as Fosca might long for a more intimate one. "Keep your distance," Clara advises, and they profess over and over again their love for one another.

Giorgio and Clara exit. The scene changes to the mess hall as Fosca comes in, reading a letter of her own she's written to Giorgio. Apparently Giorgio has been making himself scarce recently, greatly affecting Fosca: "Did you know your absence would upset me? I wish that I could strike you from my mind and heart. But I can't, Giorgio. You may disappear, but I will not." She slips the letter near the plate at Giorgio's place at the dinner table.

Giorgio comes in and responds to his fellow officers' queries as to his absence that he'd chosen to go on maneuvers with his troops these past three days. He discovers Fosca's letter and, realizing it's from her, slips it into his pocket as she looks on. When Giorgio reaches across the table for some salt, Fosca grabs his hand, whispering, "I've missed you so." She clings to his hand under the table when he tries to withdraw it. Abruptly, Giorgio asks the Colonel for five days' leave to go to Milan on urgent business, and the Colonel reluctantly grants his request. When Torasso comments, "By this time tomorrow, you'll probably be in the arms of some young beauty," Fosca lets go of Giorgio's hand and *"dissolves into herself"* while the others continue conversing, and the lights slowly fade to black.

Scene 5

In the early morning, Giorgio, suitcase in hand, is on his way to the train. Fosca appears and stands in his way. When he protests, she seizes his hand and *"presses it to her breast, then throws herself around him planting kisses over his face and neck."* Giorgio tries to free himself.

GIORGIO: . . . . . What will people think if they see this display?

FOSCA: What does it matter if they see me? What do I care if the world knows how I feel? I adore you!

She drops to the ground and wraps herself around his legs.

Is that something I should be ashamed of? Is that something I should hide? I'm no fool. I know you don't feel the same towards me. But one loves a dog, an animal. What can I do to get you to love me—a human being such as yourself.

She begins to weep.

GIORGIO *(trembling):* Get up, Signora, please. I beg you.

He helps her up.

Compose yourself. Calm down. You see that I must leave right away. I am touched by your affection. It flatters me greatly. My mind races with a thousand thoughts.

FOSCA: Tell me your thoughts.

GIORGIO: Really, I must go.

FOSCA: Write me.

GIORGIO: Fine. I will write you.

FOSCA: Promise.

GIORGIO: Yes, I promise.

FOSCA: Tomorrow.

GIORGIO: Tomorrow. Go. I want no one to see you here.

In a split scene with Fosca in her drawing room on one side of the stage and Giorgio joining Clara in their bedroom, Fosca receives the promised letter from Giorgio. Singing in a trio, Fosca reads, "My heart belongs to someone else," while Clara and Giorgio express their love in the most ardently romantic terms. Fosca reads, "There is nothing between us. Nothing," as Clara and Giorgio are locked in a passionate embrace. *"Fosca, stone-faced, remains alone in her drawing room."*

Scene 6

Returned from leave, Giorgio calls on Fosca. She thanks Giorgio for his letter and expresses herself "mortified" for letting her emotions rule her judgement, but then she refers at once to Giorgio's leave for the sole purpose of visiting "my rival." Giorgio admits that this is so.

FOSCA: . . . . . And you will go back soon?

GIORGIO: Whenever I can. As soon as possible.

FOSCA: If you get another leave.

GIORGIO: Naturally.

FOSCA: Perhaps I could put in a word to my cousin. It all depends on him. Help from me might serve you well. Of course, a negative word . . .

GIORGIO: Place more value on your dignity. Don't offend your own pride, Signora.

FOSCA: We each deal with our pride as best we can. You love this woman very much?

GIORGIO: I wrote you . . .

FOSCA: Is she beautiful?

GIORGIO: An angel.

FOSCA: Then why don't you marry her?

GIORGIO *(uncomfortable):* She is already married.

FOSCA: Ah ha! And you respect her?

GIORGIO: Respect has everything to do with love.

FOSCA: That's not true, but it hardly matters. And is your angel also a mother?

GIORGIO: Let's stop torturing each other. It's humiliating and unworthy of us. I find your sarcasm most distasteful.

FOSCA: I have many flaws, Captain.

GIORGIO: Our situation has been well-defined. Let's not discuss the subject again.

FOSCA: That's what I would like.

GIORGIO: Good. I hope we have no more occasion to speak of ourselves.

FOSCA: You can also hope that we will not see each other again.

GIORGIO: That may be the best course of action.

FOSCA: You may go now, Captain. I have more important things to do.

While the company of soldiers sings of "This Godforsaken place/This sterile little town," Clara reads a letter from Giorgio telling her that Fosca has virtually disappeared from his life. Even in her absence he's found himself hating her, and he must try to suppress such feelings.

Giorgio is summoned by the Doctor, who tells him, "Signora Fosca has taken a turn for the worse. She is mortally ill," and all because Giorgio has rejected her love. She has confided her situation to the Doctor, who explains that Fosca is letting herself die. The least Giorgio can do, the Doctor contends, is visit Fosca at her sick bed and implore her to choose life.

GIORGIO: . . . . . It is improper. The Colonel would never allow it.

DOCTOR: You needn't worry. I have made all the arrangements.

GIORGIO: She knows of this business?

DOCTOR: You cannot imagine what this has cost her. You are a good-looking young man. Beauty is something one pays for, the same as goodness, another quality you embody. Please go to her now.

GIORGIO: And if I go, what next? What will she ask of me tomorrow or next week? You speak of what her feelings have cost her—but what have they cost me?

DOCTOR: I can imagine how difficult this is for you. But she is dying, and you have only to give her words. Words that will make her well. What is the cost of a few words when a life hangs in the balance?

Fade to black.

Scene 7

Fosca's sickroom is lit by a single candle as Giorgio enters and takes her outstretched hand. She greets him with a little cry; she never believed he would visit her. She insists that he make himself comfortable and sit by her side. Reluctantly, he obeys, and she brings the candle close to his face to study it, singing "God, you are so beautiful/Come, let me see you in the light/No, don't look at me/Let me look at you/I feel better in the dark."

Giorgio declares, "Your kindness makes you beautiful," and Fosca places his hand on her heart to feel its beating.

FOSCA: My heart says it loves you, Giorgio.

She places her hand on his chest.

What does your heart say?

GIORGIO *(beat):* It says it loves you, Fosca.

FOSCA: Like a . . . friend?

GIORGIO: Tonight it loves you as you wish.

He withdraws his hand and she does likewise.

FOSCA: Thank you, Giorgio. I so wanted to forget you. To think that I could! I wanted to die without seeing you—

GIORGIO: I am here to tell you you'd be happier living.

Giorgio urges her to sleep and promises to stay by her side while she sleeps. But as

Fosca drops off, it's Clara of whom Giorgio dreams. When Fosca awakes, she questions Giorgio about his career (his father was an officer and he's following in his footsteps) and gets him to say "Giorgio and Fosca . . . Fosca and Giorgio"—music to her ears. But in answer to her questions, he begins to tell of Clara before declaring, "It will be getting light soon." Fosca asks him to write her a letter before he goes, which she will dictate. Obligingly, he goes to her desk, picks up a pen and begins, as she instructs him, "My Dearest Fosca."

FOSCA *(sings):*
I wish I could forget you,
Erase you from my mind.
But ever since I met you,
I find
I cannot leave the thought of you behind.
Quickly, as Giorgio looks up.
That doesn't mean I love you . . .
GIORGIO *(writing, sings):*
That doesn't mean I love you . . .
FOSCA *(sings):*
I wish that I could love you . . .
Giorgio stops writing.
Please.
Giorgio resumes writing after a brief pause . . . . .
(Sings):
. . . . . For now I'm seeing love
Like none I've ever known,
A love as pure as breath,
As permanent as death,
Implacable as stone . . . . .

I don't know how I let you
So far inside my mind,
But there you are and there you will stay.
How could I ever wish you away?
I see now I was blind.

And should you die tomorrow,
Another thing I see:
Your love will live in me.

(As music fades.) I remain always . . . your Giorgio . . . . Please bring it to me. Thank you, Giorgio. Do you have sisters?

GIORGIO: Yes.

FOSCA: Do you kiss them goodbye?

GIORGIO: On occasion.

FOSCA: Kiss me goodbye the way you do them.

Giorgio quickly gives her a peck on the forehead.

No, like you kiss her.

Fosca suddenly pulls Giorgio to her and embraces him like a lover.

(Agitated.) Now go! Thank you, Giorgio. Quickly! Run!

Giorgio runs from the room. There is a moment of calm and then Fosca screams.

Soldiers sing of Fosca's wretchedness and despair as the scene ends.

Scene 8

The men are playing pool and commenting on Fosca's unhappy state in sarcastic terms. Over to one side, Giorgio challenges the Doctor about the need for him to visit Fosca. The Doctor replies, "You have done a brave thing, now it is over." When Giorgio exits, the men remark on his standoffish behavior and imply that he'll be made a Major by summer if he continues his attentions to the Colonel's unfortunate cousin.

Giorgio strolls with the Colonel, who thanks him for helping Fosca and talks of her past. Simultaneously, Fosca writes Giorgio telling him of her childhood from her perspective. The Colonel remembers: "I was a young man when my parents died, and Fosca's mother and father welcomed me into their house whenever I was on leave." Fosca grew up lonely, with doting parents (they appear in a reenactment of Fosca's childhood) who told her she was beautiful. She believed them and at 17 she met a handsome Austrian count. "I was amazed to see the Count take such an interest in my cousin," the Colonel remarks. Fosca too had her suspicions, but love blinded her. So she married Count Ludovic of Austria, and he soon gambled away her dowry and spent long periods of time away from her, traveling. Then one day a woman approached Fosca on the street, identified herself as Ludovic's mistress and told Fosca that Count Ludovic was a fraud who in fact spent his time with her when supposedly he was traveling.

MISTRESS *(sings):*

He calls himself a count,
But he's not.
He's never had a title in his life.
He doesn't have a title,
But he does have a wife
And a child
In Dalmatia.

FOSCA: No, you must be mistaken.

MISTRESS: Oh, yes. *(Sings.)*

He only wants to bleed you.
Until the day he doesn't need you,

I warn you he'll abandon you
As he abandoned her
And me,
And countless others, I've no doubt.
I'm telling you, the man was born without
A heart.

Starts away, turns back.

You fool . . .

Exits, music continues under.

FOSCA: I confronted him with this information, and he made no attempt to deny it.

LUDOVIC *(shrugging pleasantly, sings):*

. . . . . We merely made a little bargain, did we not?
And we got
Exactly what we bargained for.

The music becomes a waltz.

You gave me your money, I gave you my looks
And my charm
And my arm.
I would say that more than balances the books.
Where's the harm?
Now it's through.
If women sell their looks,
Why can't a man
If he can?
Besides, the money wasn't even yours,
It belonged to those ridiculous old bores,
Your parents . . . . .

Ludovic goes on to tell Fosca, "You are no beauty, I fear," and suggests they part "by mutual consent," of course with bills unpaid. Fosca returned home (the Colonel continues) to find her parents "impoverished and in poor health." She suffered a decline in health and her first attack of convulsions. The Colonel sought out Ludovic to punish him, but could never find him. It wasn't long before Fosca's mother and father died, and her cousin the Colonel took her under his protection. He blames himself for not having intervened to prevent Ludovic from taking advantage of Fosca; but he persuaded himself, "As long as she seems happy, why interfere?"

COLONEL *(sings):*

. . . . . The enemy was love,
Selfishness really, but love.
All of us blinded by love
That makes everything seem possible.

You have to pay a consequence

Jere Shea and Donna Murphy as Giorgio and Fosca in a scene from *Passion*

For things that you've denied.
This is the thorn in my side.
Music continues under, as Mistress reappears.

MISTRESS *(sings):*
As long as you're a man,
You're what the world will make of you.
Mother, Father reappear.

MISTRESS, MOTHER *(sing):*
Whereas if you're a woman,
You're only what it sees.
Ludovic reappears.

COLONEL, FATHER, LUDOVIC *(sing):*
A woman is a flower
Whose purpose is to please.

ALL *(except Giorgio and Fosca; sing):*
Beauty is power
Longing a disease . . .

Scene 9

Giorgio is outdoors far away from camp reading his latest letter from Clara. She longs to share a sunrise with him; she has found a gray hair which she has pulled out and is sending to him. "Time is now our enemy," Clara finishes.

Fosca surprises him, willfully intruding on Giorgio's privacy and accusing him of avoiding her since her recovery. Giorgio doesn't want to hold a conversation with Fosca, but she persists, even asking him to kiss her. When he refuses, *"She takes his hand and kisses it."*

GIORGIO *(sings, agitated):*

Is this what you call love?
This endless and insatiable
Smothering
Pursuit of me,
You think that this is love?
Softly, attempting to control himself.
I'm sorry that you're lonely,
I'm sorry that you want me as you do.
I'm sorry that I fail to feel
The way you wish me to feel,
Growing in anger.
I'm sorry that you're ill,
I'm sorry you're in pain,
I'm sorry that you aren't beautiful.
Evenly.
But yes, I wish you'd go away
And leave me alone! . . . . .

This is an obsession (Giorgio continues in song), not love, which is an emotion which must be nurtured into slow and tender growth. Fosca's attentions are a curse, and Giorgio is beginning to fear for his soul. A clap of thunder interrupts his diatribe. Fosca turns to go but faints with a cry. It begins to rain. Reluctantly, Giorgio goes to her, covers her with his coat and carries her off as the lights fade to black.

Scene 10

The soldiers discuss the Giorgio-Fosca relationship, and they decide he'll be made Major sooner than they thought.

In his sleep, Giorgio struggles with dreams of Fosca. When he wakes, the Doctor is at his side, and Giorgio informs him, "She was dragging me down into the grave with her. She was hugging me. Kissing me with her cold lips. Those thin arms pulling me, drawing me, like icy tentacles."

It seems that Giorgio has become sick after carrying Fosca home. The Doctor has decided to put Giorgio on sick leave and send him to Milan when he's well enough to travel. "This place can get to us all," he warns.

Scene 11

Clara sings of how much she's looking forward to being with Giorgio for the 40 days of his leave, as Giorgio, wrapped in a blanket, enters a train compartment and prepares for the journey to Milan. To his utter exasperation, he is joined by Fosca, who means to accompany him to Milan, ostensibly to help him recover.

FOSCA: . . . . . I'll keep my distance . . . stay out of your path. But I can be nearby. I can be there quietly waiting.

GIORGIO: And this you think will make me love you?

FOSCA: No. No, I am doing this because *I* love *you.*

GIORGIO: Well, my heart feels nothing for you. How many times must you hear this?

FOSCA: This has nothing to do with your heart. This has to do with your eyes—what you see. If I were beautiful, if there were ample flesh on my bones, if my breasts were large and full, if I were soft and warm to your touch—you would feel otherwise.

GIORGIO: No. Your appearance is no excuse for the way you behave. My feelings toward you are a result of your relentlessness. Your constant selfishness and insensitivity.

FOSCA: I'm sorry. No one has ever taught me how to love. I know I feel too much. I often don't know what to do with my feelings. You understand that, Giorgio. Don't you?

GIORGIO *(slowly):* Fosca. Face the truth. Please. You have to give me up.

FOSCA *(sings):*

Loving you
Is not a choice,
It's who I am.

Loving you
Is not a choice
And not much reason
To rejoice,

But it gives me purpose,
Gives me voice,
To say to the world:

This is why I live.
You are why I live . . . . .

She would die for him if necessary, Fosca insists and challenges him to state that Clara would do likewise. Fosca offers to move to another compartment. Giorgio informs her that they are getting off at the next stop and he will take her back. As Fosca shivers in the cold, Giorgio wraps her in his blanket.

The lights fade, and when they come up again, Giorgio is back at the post talking to the Doctor, telling him, "You know her, and you know there is no way I could have acted differently" and reproaching him with the question, "Why did you bring this woman into my life?" To help Fosca, the Doctor replies, not having realized it would turn out like this. His other patient, Giorgio, now intends to return to Milan, but only for four days, not 40. This runs counter to the Doctor's wish to send Giorgio away for his own good, and he hints that he could have him transferred permanently if he does not obey. Giorgio doesn't want this, he feels it's his duty to stay here and help Fosca. "Don't you understand, Captain? No one can help her," the Doctor tells him. They exit, as the soldiers enter and gossip about Giorgio and Fosca.

Scene 12

In Milan, a delighted Clara sings to Giorgio that her husband will travel to Rome for three days so that they can go into the country for the night and perhaps share a sunrise. But Giorgio informs her that he is here for only a short visit, not the expected 40 days. Clara is afraid he is sacrificing himself for this other woman, and Giorgio tries to explain his commitment. Fosca, having no other friends, has thrown herself into Giorgio's life and is at his mercy. "I didn't ask for this power," he tells Clara, "she bestowed it upon me, but somehow it carries responsibilities that I can't seem to shed."

Giorgio turns the tables on Clara with the proposal that she leave her husband: "Let's have a life together." Clara responds that this is impossible, she would lose her child.

CLARA: Where would we go? How would we live?

GIORGIO: We would manage.

CLARA: We are not two people who could ever just "manage." We have to carve out a life for ourselves around our present obligations. We have no choice.

GIORGIO: We have a choice.

CLARA: Yes, I suppose that's true, Giorgio. Just as you have chosen to forgo your sick leave.

He is surprised by her remark. They look at one another awkwardly.

I've often wondered if you would love me as much if I were free.

GIORGIO: I would. You know I would. I love you.

CLARA: And I love you. *(Beat.)* You're not coming back, are you?

GIORGIO: I'll be back, Clara. I'll be back. Let's stop this talk. Let's enjoy our four days together.

Scene 13

At a Christmas party for the officers and household staff, Fosca is playing the piano. Giorgio appears, and Augenti comes in with a stack of mail which he distributes. Fosca and Giorgio are left alone to share a moment before he receives a perfumed letter. She backs off as the Colonel announces he has just received orders to transfer Giorgio from this Brigade outpost to headquarters immediately. The Colonel, angry, believes Giorgio has arranged for this transfer, but Giorgio seems surprised. Impulsively, Fosca throws herself into Giorgio's arms with the exclamation, "My love, don't leave!" Realizing what she has done in front of everyone, Fosca, embarrassed, screams and runs offstage.

The Colonel dismisses the gathering, and as he and the Doctor follow Fosca he commands Giorgio to wait for him. As Giorgio stands stunned, he remembers his letter from Clara and opens it. Clara appears and sings to Giorgio that she's noticed a significant change in him, he's not the man she knew before, then telling him that her heart is still his: "When my son is older, when he goes off to school, there is the chance for us to be together. I will make the sacrifice you ask of me then. Please understand why I can't now. Will you wait for me, Giorgio? Can we have back what we once had? I have to know. We both have to know."

GIORGIO *(looking at the letter, sings):*
Is this what you call love? . . . . .
This logical and sensible
Practical arrangement—
CLARA *(overlapping, sings):*
We can have that happiness—
GIORGIO *(sings):*
—This foregone conclusion—
CLARA *(sings):*
—Once again!
GIORGIO *(sings):*
—You think that this is love?
His voice rising.
Love isn't so convenient.
Love isn't something scheduled in advance,
Not something guaranteed
You need
For fear it may pass you by.
You have to take a chance,
You can't just try it out.
What's love unless it's unconditional?

Love doesn't give a damn
About tomorrow,
And neither do I! . . . . .

Clara continues (in song) hopeful that their love can be restored, but Giorgio finally sings, "What we have is nothing . . . nothing."

Clara disappears when the Colonel enters, holding the "letter" Giorgio wrote at Fosca's dictation, which the Colonel has discovered in Fosca's room. The Colonel accuses Giorgio of taking advantage of Fosca's weakness. Giorgio replies, "You don't know your cousin. She is not a child. She is not just a sick person. Signora Fosca is as responsible for her actions as I am for mine." But the Colonel insists that Giorgio has abused his trust and dishonored his house, and he demands satisfaction—a duel the following day. The Doctor tries to intervene with an explanation of this affair, but neither Giorgio nor the Colonel will listen to him. They agree to meet the following morning, and that Fosca is to know nothing of this business.

The Colonel exits. Giorgio tells the Doctor, "Whatever the outcome of this duel, I'll never see her again. Arrange for me to meet her tonight as you did before." The Doctor protests that Fosca is too ill ever to be anyone's lover and calls Giorgio's request "madness."

Scene 14

Giorgio enters Fosca's room, telling her he had nothing to do with being transferred, and that his relationship with Clara has come to an end.

FOSCA *(beat):* I'm sorry.

GIORGIO *(surprised):* Sorry? I thought you would be pleased.

FOSCA: There was a time when I would have welcomed that news, but I realize I don't wish you to be unhappy. I don't wish to see you sad.

GIORGIO: I feel so much . . . but I'm not really sad.

FOSCA: I thought you loved Clara?

GIORGIO: I did love Clara. I did, but . . . *(Sings, quietly at first.)*

No one has ever loved me
As deeply as you.
No one has truly loved me
As you have, Fosca.

Love without reason, love without mercy,
Love without pride or shame.
Love unconcerned
With being returned—
No wisdom, no judgement
No caution, no blame . . .

No one has ever known me
As clearly as you.
No one has ever shown me
What love could be like until now:

Not pretty or safe or easy,
But more than I ever knew.

Love within reason—that isn't love.

And I've learned that from you.

Music continues under. He sees her trembling.

Are you cold?

FOSCA: No, I'm afraid.

GIORGIO: Of what?

FOSCA *(sings):*

All this happiness,
Coming when there's so little time.
Too much happiness,
More than I can bear.

Music continues under.

I pray for the strength to enjoy it. Tomorrow you will leave. This is the only time I have. *(Beat.)* You do love me, don't you?

GIORGIO: Yes, I love you.

FOSCA: Say it again.

GIORGIO: I love you.

FOSCA: Once more.

GIORGIO: I love you. Be calm. Strong. I am yours.

FOSCA: This isn't a dream.

GIORGIO: This isn't a dream.

She begins to lead him towards the bed.

We can't.

FOSCA: To die loved is to have lived.

They kiss. Fosca becomes weak, and Giorgio carries her to the bed. He is about to leave when she pulls him on to the bed and into an embrace as the music builds and the lights fade.

The lights come up on the duelling ground, where the principals and their aides take up their positions. As Torasso counts, the Colonel and Giorgio step off ten paces, then turn and fire. The Colonel staggers for a moment, then falls to the ground and is immediately attended to by the men. *"Suddenly, Giorgio lets out a high-pitched howl—a cry that could only be reminiscent of Fosca's—as lights fade to black."*

Scene 15

A Nurse delivers a box and letter to Giorgio, who is seated at a desk. They are from the Doctor. Now that the Doctor has heard that Giorgio's "nervous condition has improved," he writes him that Fosca died three days after the night they were together. She knew nothing of the duel. The Colonel, though seriously wounded, recovered. The Doctor has enclosed some of Fosca's personal belongings and a letter she wrote to Giorgio just before she died.

Going through the items summons up memories of the past—the Officers, Clara, Count Ludovic, the Colonel. Giorgio reads Fosca's letter aloud, in song.

GIORGIO *(sings):*
. . . . . Strange, how merely
Feeling loved,
You see things clearly.
Fosca's voice slowly begins to be heard from offstage.
Things I feared,
Like the world itself,
I now love dearly . . . . .
GIORGIO & FOSCA *(sing):*
. . . . . Everything seems right,
Everything seems possible,
Every moment bursts with feeling.

Why is love so easy to give
And so hard to receive?
FOSCA *(sings):*
But though I want to live,
I now can leave
With what I never knew:
I'm someone to be loved.
GIORGIO *(sings):*
I'm someone to be loved.
FOSCA *(sings):*
And that I learned from you.
ALL *(sing):*
I don't know how I let you
So far inside my mind,
But there you are, and there you will stay.
How could I ever wish you away?
I see now I was blind.
FOSCA *(sings):*
And should you die tomorrow,
Another thing I see:
GIORGIO *(sings):*
Your love will live in me . . .
FOSCA *(sings):*
Your love will live in me . . . . .

Giorgio, Fosca and the others repeat this line again and again, until finally the others exit, *"Fosca last, leaving Giorgio alone at his desk as the lights fade to black." Curtain.*

SUBURBIA

A Play in Two Acts

BY ERIC BOGOSIAN

Cast and credits appear on page 465

ERIC BOGOSIAN was born in Boston April 24, 1953, the son of an accountant. His college years were equally divided between the University of Chicago and Oberlin, to which he transferred after two years and from which he received his B.A. in theater in 1976. A year later, in New York City, he founded the dance program known as The Kitchen, which he ran until 1981. He had always wanted to write, however, and he kept at it with stage vehicles for his own performances. In July 1982, New York Shakespeare Festival workshopped Bogosian's Men Inside *and* Voices of America, *solo pieces which he performed and which were repeated in September of that year. His next, a collection of mostly sinister characters written and acted by Bogosian and entitled* Fun House, *was put on in workshop by New York Shakespeare, then moved to full off-Broadway independent production Sept. 29, 1983 for 70 performances.*

From then on, every Bogosian project has made an exceptional mark. His fourth writing-and-solo-performing presentation of a variegated assortment of characters, Drinking in America, *became his first Best Play in American Place production January 19, 1986 for 94 performances and winning both Drama Desk and Obie Awards. His first conventionally constructed play,* Talk Radio, *was one of the highlights of its season in New York Shakespeare production May 28, 1987 for 210 performances and later won the Berlin Film Festival's Silver Bear after it was made into a motion picture starring its author. His fifth writing-and-solo-performing collection of char-*

acters, Sex, Drugs, Rock & Roll, *was presented February 8, 1990 for 103 performances in independent off-Broadway production, collected his second Best Play citation and a special Obie Award and was revived for another 36 off-Broadway performances in the fall of that year. Bogosian's third Best Play is* SubUrbia, *presented May 22 by Lincoln Center Theater (which had previously showcased him in its summer Serious Fun festivals under the titles* An American Chorus *in 1989 and* Dog Show *in 1992). And another of these collections of characters written and acted by Bogosian,* Pounding Nails in the Floor With My Forehead, *played 83 off-Broadway performances this season starting February 3.*

Bogosian has been the recipient of National Endowment and New York State Arts Council grants. He is married, lives in New Jersey and once described his ambition as "to continue writing, for actors other than myself."

The following synopsis of SubUrbia *was prepared by Sally Dixon Wiener.*

ACT I

SYNOPSIS: The setting is basically the sidewalk area of a 7-Eleven convenience store which is set at an angle. There is a low wall downstage and a high rear wall upstage over which four large lights loom. Exits are right and left. The interior of the convenience store is mostly visible, with the usual ads and merchandise displays—cigarettes, soda, sunglasses, junk food, film, more cigarettes. On the curbing of the store there is a cement bench. There are two pay telephones. Partially visible around the corner of the store is a dumpster. A trash container is near the door of the store, but the set is littered with cans and other trash. A pair of old sneakers is on the curbing also, along with two dilapidated hockey sticks, and downstage there is a boombox.

A blast of rock music in the darkness precedes the start of the play (and occurs periodically to indicate scene changes). The light finds Tim, 20, short-haired, athletic build but a burned-out look, his clothes disheveled, sitting smoking and drinking beer, leaning against the metal upright supporting one of the telephones. The music changes as Buff, on roller blades, and Jeff come on from stage right with slices of pizza. Both are 20. Buff is a cherubic, sturdy, long-haired blond human yo-yo in a tie-dye sleeveless top and grungy pants. Jeff is a more delicate piece of work, dark-haired, handsome, but equally messy-looking. Buff off-handedly greets Tim, and it's obvious that this is the place, in this suburb called Burnfield, where they all hang out. And it's obvious, too, that from inside the store Norman, 20, the well-groomed, nicely-dressed Pakistani proprietor, is keeping an eye on the proceedings outside as he eats with a spoon from a big plastic bowl. Also watching, not comfortable with the situation, is his sister Pakeeza, a pretty young woman who wears traditional Pakistani dress. Norman speaks English, but his sister speaks only Urdu.

Jeff thinks he could live on pizza and beer. "Vegetables, minerals, cheese and pepperoni. All four food groups, man," Buff believes. The pizza's hot, and Jeff burns himself taking a bite. The pizza drops on the ground. He swears vehemently, throws it into the trash container, goes inside the 7-Eleven and gets a package of Oreos and a six-pack. He puts money on the counter and comes out, followed by Norman, who insists he is still owed 20 cents. Jeff pays him, and Norman goes inside. Tim resents Norman's attitude and suggests that someone should "crack his dot-head with a baseball bat."

BUFF: I went in there yesterday, he was practicing the Pledge of Allegiance. Boning up for the big test.

TIM: That's depressing.

JEFF: He's from a Third World country. I respect him for that.

TIM: Spare me that Third World shit.

JEFF: That's what you call it.

TIM: I've been to the Third World, man. It smells like you wiped your ass and made a country out of the paper. The people are dog-eating, monkey-faced greaseballs.

Buff sits and removes his skates, exchanges them for his sneakers.

JEFF: He's a human being. You gotta give him that.

TIM: Only thing I gotta give him is a one-way ticket back to greaseball land.

JEFF: He wants to be like us.

TIM: Good luck. Eat an ice cube over there, you get the shits for a week.

JEFF: Those places are screwed up 'cause we fuck them up.

TIM: Who's "we"?

JEFF: The American Empire. The Air Force. You. Me.

TIM: The gooks did it to themselves, pal. You have no idea, fucking chaos on a stick.

BUFF: But like, isn't he from Arabia or some shit like that? You're not a gook if you're from Arabia, man.

JEFF: He's from India. The whole family's from India. India and Saudi Arabia aren't even the same continents, jerky!

TIM: The C.O.s used to give us that shit. "Don't confuse the Thai with the Filipino. It offends them. Don't confuse the Chinese with the Vietnamese." Bullshit. They're all the same. Subhuman.

Jeff remarks that Buff's pizza would be enough to feed a family in India or Turkey. Buff wonders if Federal Express would get it there in eatable condition. It could be life or death for some Bangladeshi, Jeff insists. Buff is upset. He ought to be, Jeff insists, everybody should be. When Hitler was "greasing the Jews" people didn't want to be upset. It's his duty to be upset, but Jeff doesn't believe it makes any difference because things don't change. In 50 years they will be dead, and new people will be having beer and pizza here, unaware that they'd been here. In another 50, another bunch, and generation after generation wondering what they were doing on this planet.

Steve Zahn (Buff), Josh Hamilton (Jeff), Tim Guinee (Tim) and Firdous E. Bamji (Norman, *in store*) in Eric Bogosian's *SubUrbia*

JEFF: SARAJEVO! HAITI! ARMENIA! *(Pacing.)* You ever watch the news, Buffman? There's a world outside this tar pit of stupidity. This cauldron of spiritual oatmeal. It's the end of the world, man—no ideas, no hope, no future. The fucking apocalypse. You don't even know what "apocalypse" means, do you, Buff-cake?

BUFF: Of course I do, man. It was a movie. I saw it. Vietnam. Martin Sheen. Marlon Brando. Surfing. Snails crawling on razor blades. "This is the end . . . " Dum-dum-dum. "My only friend, the end . . ."

Incongruously, Tim raises his voice almost sermonlike. Buff continues to sing under.

TIM: "And in those days shall men seek death and shall not find it; and shall desire to die, death shall flee from them." Saint John the Disciple wrote Apocalypse. Check your Bible.

BUFF: My mom bought this toilet paper with Bible sayings printed on it, but I told her like if the Pope came by and had to take a shit we'd all get excommunicated and sent to hell.

JEFF: Yeah, yeah, it's all a big joke. It's because of the Pope that the world is crawling with starving people. Ever heard of the slums of Rio?

TIM: What about Calcutta?

JEFF *(not getting the reference):* Huh?

TIM: Pope doesn't have much pull in India.

JEFF: Well, that's an exception.

TIM: What about China? About a billion starving people there in China.

JEFF: So what's your point?

TIM: What's *your* point?

JEFF: Forget it. I'm just saying . . .

TIM: Yeah?

JEFF: Things are fucked up and no one cares.

TIM: Things are fine with me. How are things with you, Buff?

BUFF: Excellent.

The talk turns to Fred Pierce—"the best running back we *ever* had" according to Tim—now reported by Buff to be gay. Pierce is in the hospital with AIDS, according to Buff's mother. And she was praying for him. This reminds Jeff of the best teacher he ever had, who died of alcohol poisoning. "A loser," Tim recalls, "too delicate." One of the sort of people who become statistics. "The stupid, the delicate, the weak. Like Pierce." That hasn't anything to do with being stupid, Jeff argues. Lots of geniuses were homosexual. Sometimes Jeff wishes he were, to make life more simple. They get laid more, and you're more free than if you're with only one person and having to worry about what they think and want, he rationalizes.

Tim sees this as Jeff having trouble with his lady, whose name is Sooze, and figures Jeff's problem is that she's too good for him. When a woman's vocabulary is bigger than the man's he shouldn't be with her. Buff wonders how Sooze's friend Bee-Bee is. She has a nice smile. He should ask her himself, Jeff tells Buff.

BUFF: I'm at work yesterday, bitch comes in, orders a twelve-inch pie with extra cheese, so I asked her if she wanted me to like carry it out to the car . . . right? Bitch is obviously in heat. Says "Yes" right away. So I carry the pie out to her car. We smoke a J, she blows me, we eat the pizza, I chase it with a beer. Smoke, babe, slice, brew—all four bases—fucking home run, man . . . . .

JEFF: Buff, your ability to fantasize is only exceeded by your ability to lie.

BUFF: Untrue, Jeffster. Last week I picked up two nymphets at the Sound Garden concert. Two on one. I swear. You can ask them. I got their numbers.

Jeff grabs an imaginary prick and jerks it up and down.

TIM: Fuckin' Pierce. I knew something was wrong with him. Must have been why we blew the playoffs.

Jeff has gone to the telephone and is talking to his girl friend Sooze. Tim's finished another beer, and Buff turns the boombox on. Norman comes out of the 7-Eleven. He doesn't want them there, but they ignore him. Norman turns off the boombox. They're just talking, Buff says, turning it on again. It's private property, Norman insists, and his customers complain. Buff claims they are his customers, and they're not complaining. Buff and Tim slam dance. Norman turns the music off again. Meanwhile, Jeff winds up his phone conversation. Pakeeza finally succeeds in getting her brother Norman to come back into the 7-Eleven to talk on their portable phone.

Jeff explains he was talking to Sooze and she might be coming by, to wish him happy birthday, his birthday is this week. Jeff's been leaning over tying his shoelace, and Buff grabs him and begins "humping him" while singing "Happy Birthday," and a mock fight is in progress as Bee-Bee enters. She does have a nice smile, and dark hair, a nice figure and drab sweatshirt and jeans. Not interested in their fighting, she lights a cigarette.

BUFF: Hi, Bee-Bee.

BEE-BEE: What did Sooze say, is Pony coming?

JEFF: I don't know.

Buff gives Bee-Bee a big smile and sidles up to her.

BUFF: Wanna beer?

BEE-BEE: No thanks. I don't drink. What did she say? Did she talk to Pony?

TIM: "Pony?" "Pony?" You mean that geek who played folk music at the senior prom? What's his name, Neil Moynihan?

BUFF: Pony's band, Dream Girl's, been on the road opening for Midnight Whore. Stadiums, man! So, Pony's coming by here?

BEE-BEE *(to Tim):* Didn't you see their video on MTV?

TIM: I shot my TV.

BUFF: So, Pony's coming by?

JEFF: And anyway, now he's back, and I thought maybe we'd get together tonight. And, you know, talk. That's all. No big deal. Me, him and Sooze . . .

TIM: Uh-huh. You wanted to get together with your close friend, Pony, the rock star? Sure, I understand. You want us to leave?

JEFF: No. We're gonna go someplace or something.

BEE-BEE: We are?

JEFF: She told him to come here. Fuck.

BUFF: Pony's coming?

JEFF: Don't ask me, ask Sooze.

Tim encourages Jeff to have time alone with Pony, but Jeff doesn't care about it that much. He didn't think that well of Pony's music. They were friends, though, and Sooze is eager to see Pony. They all want to, Buff adds.

Sooze, an attractive young woman wearing an outfit with a tiny skirt and badly torn black mesh tights and—at the moment—a blond fright wig, enters and performs a routine she has devised, an aggressive statement which goes in part, "Bang your head, blow your nose, run down the street, suck a hose/Chew my lips, eat some shit, eat a stick of dynamite and blow yourself to bits . . . . . "

JEFF: Is that suppose to be about me?

SOOZE: Slides go with it. Behind me.

BEE-BEE: It's called "Burger Manifesto: Part I—The Dialectical Exposition of Testosterone." Isn't that a great title?

JEFF: I said, is that suppose to be about me?

SOOZE: Why is everything about you, Jeff?

JEFF: Not everything. This. I *am* the man in your life.

SOOZE: "Man"?

JEFF: Yeah, "man," male, significant other, whatever the fuck I am.

SOOZE: It's a piece!

Jeff walks away.

(To Tim.) So, do you think it's good?

BEE-BEE: It's great.

BUFF: Yea, cool.

TIM: It needs work. But it has promise. So when do we get to see the completed opus?

SOOZE: I'm not actually doing it anywhere. I'm composing it as part of my application to the School of Visual Arts . . . in New York.

She knows nobody in New York but, she announces with a look at Jeff, the worst that could happen is, she could starve to death. Jeff ridicules her—she's all set to go because a community college conceptual artist with a mid-life crisis told her she's talented. He's a site specific performance studies instructor, Sooze corrects him, and had shows in New York and has been reviewed by Artforum. Sooze, put out by Jeff's deprecating attitude, suggests "Let's just stick our thumbs up our ass and twirl!". Tim applauds. Sooze wants to communicate, get people to think about things—sexual politics, military-industrial complex, racism. Jeff calls idealism "middle-class bullshit" and professes he's honest but can't seem to articulate what he stands for. Status quo, according to Sooze, who seeks her validation from Tim, who once also left town.

TIM: I did. I expanded my horizons. I served my country, and I saw the world. I sowed my wild oats. And now I'm back. I've gained wisdom, and now I'm back. Go, you have my blessing, child. Say hi to Jack Kerouac if you see him out there . . . . .

SOOZE: I can't wait till Pony gets here. Have a conversation with a human being.

JEFF: Since when did you get this big affection for the guy? You didn't even know him in school.

SOOZE: Of course I did! He sat right behind me in study hall. All we did was talk. He called *me,* remember?

JEFF: You used to make fun of him.

SOOZE: I did not. Now you're lying.

JEFF: If you love him so much, why didn't you go see him play?

SOOZE: Because you didn't want to pay for tickets.

JEFF: There's a limit, Sooze. I'm not going to pay twenty bucks to see Neil Moynihan play in a band I helped start!

SOOZE: He's always been a nice guy, and I like him.

JEFF, TIM & BUFF: He's a geek.

Buff is fiddling with one of the hockey sticks.

BUFF: I'm a *video* artist, man. I been making these tapes. I ripped off a camcorder up at the mall, and I've been making these tapes. I thought, it could be, you know, something I *do*. I sent one in to America's Funniest Home Videos.

TIM: Buff, the post-modern idiot savant! He will outdo us all!

When Sooze turns on the boombox, Norman comes out of the 7-Eleven with a broom. He's going to call the police. They're trespassing. Buff figures his cousin Jerry could show up if Norman does call the police, and Buff will report that cigarettes are being sold to minors.

Norman keeps urging them to leave. It's his property. The argument gets nastier, and so do the epithets. When Norman turns away to go back into the store, Tim blocks his way. Sooze wants Jeff to intervene, and then she tries to. Norman pushes Tim aside and Tim pushes back. Norman stumbles. When Jeff does try to separate the two, Buff pulls Jeff away, claiming "the dude" wants to fight. Norman has his broomstick, and Tim takes Buff's hockey stick, claiming that if his adversary wants to be American he ought to learn a sport. "This is called hockey." Tim whams into Norman's broom, and Norman falls. Tim won't let him get up and prods him as Pakeeza appears with a gun aimed at Tim.

Norman finally persuades Pakeeza to return inside. The others have backed off, but Tim has held his ground, urging Pakeeza to shoot. She will be sorry about this and ought to kill him while she has a chance, he warns her. He also warns Norman, "I can find you anytime." Jeff tries to apologize—it was a misunderstanding, Tim was drunk—and Jeff wants Norman to know that he, personally, is on Norman's side.

Later in the evening, *"The lights over the wall are on, but the 7-Eleven is closed and dark."* The boombox is on, and Bee-Bee is dancing when Buff comes on and sits nearby, nodding his head to the music. When the music stops, Bee-Bee asks Buff what his video is about. It isn't about anything, but on it he has things from television, the Jetsons and "some shit blowing up" he saw on the news. He also videotaped his mother when she was praying, and a cloud that "looks excellent on the tape." He sees the video as his head. Everything is in there that he sees. Now he wants to get inside the 7-Eleven at night with the camera and then add music to it. He's also tape-recorded their group talking but can't seem to recall Bee-Bee saying anything at the time. She can see the video anytime, though.

It seems Bee-Bee is a nurse's aide at the local hospital. Buff suggests that's "a total bummer," but Bee-Bee likes it. Most of the patients know when she's helping them. She mentions Fred Pierce. There was a birthday party for him last week, he was 22, but he'll die soon. Bee-Bee likes talking to him, he's funny, says things like "Watch out or I'll bleed on you." Buff assumes his imminent death must bother Bee-Bee. It does, but "It's a lot worse for him," she guesses. He needs her, and she needs him.

Right now she's waiting for Pony, wondering if he'll have a stretch limo. Buff asks if she'd like to go out in the back into the woods. "We could smoke a dube," he suggests. Bee-Bee says she doesn't do drugs, but she'll go. She takes the boombox, and they go off. Tim comes on, climbs onto the dumpster and gets up onto the roof of the 7-Eleven with a six-pack. He drains a beer, throws the empty down. *"Only the smoke from his cigarette is visible."*

Jeff and Sooze come on arguing about the incident earlier with Norman. Jeff insists he would have somehow stopped it if he'd really thought something very bad was about to happen. He pulls Sooze into an embrace and suggests they go to the van. It doesn't appeal to Sooze. "Moldy old blankets, beer cans . . . there's enough stuff stuck to the floor to open a sperm bank!" She just wants to be held while they're waiting for Pony.

SOOZE: I went by my sister's this afternoon.

JEFF: Yeah.

SOOZE: Jerry was outside lighting the barbecue, and Debbie's in the kitchen making macaroni salad. I'm watching the baby in his crib, and Jerry Junior's playing with his truck on the floor, and I suddenly felt like I couldn't breathe.

JEFF: Because of the kids.

SOOZE: I don't know. They're great kids. I love them. I do. But it all seems so pathetic. And Debbie's my sister and she's like this stranger. She acts like I'm a kid. Like she's mature and I'm not. Like she knows something I don't.

JEFF: Because you're smart enough not to get married when you're two years out of high school.

SOOZE: I guess.

JEFF: Because you're smart enough not to get knocked up two times in three years.

SOOZE: You're right.

JEFF: Don't compare yourself with your sister. You're completely different! You have a life. You're going to school. You're an artist, she's a housewife married to a guy who puts up aluminum siding.

Sooze reveals she's heard about a sublet in New York that's available at a price she can handle. She wants Jeff to come too. He doesn't see any point to it. Sooze wonders what he wants to do. Nothing, it seems. He's taking one community college course and "barely holding down a job packing boxes," Sooze points out. His job is not who he is, Jeff insists, and he needs nothing. All he wants is to "make something that shatters the world." If he can't, he doesn't want to do anything. He wonders about her goal.

SOOZE: . . . . . My goal is to make art.

JEFF: Why can't you do that here? What's wrong with here? How is something else better?

SOOZE: Why should I stay, Jeff? So I can sit next to you and watch the lights change while you bitch about Burnfield? So we can talk about dead high school teachers? So I can spend the rest of my life guessing what it would be like to be a real artist? So you and I can fuck while your parents are out having dinner at The Sizzler? I mean what are we doing? You and me?

JEFF: I don't know. I just want us to be happy. You got this thing about leaving, about New York. I want you to stay. I don't want you to go away. Who will I talk to? Who will I hang out with? Who will I make love to?

SOOZE: Jeff.

JEFF: Who will I dream with?

SOOZE: You don't have any dreams.

Buff comes on, and Sooze goes off to get beer. Buff calls a friend on the pay phone, waking him up. He wants him to get dressed and come down there because he knows he has just bought some weed. The friend is not going to come, and Buff is annoyed. He talks with Jeff and begins fantasizing about Pony in his stretch limo—with a television, mini-bar, coke and a naked babe. "That's the rock star thing." Jeff points out that the amount of partying you can do has its limits. Buff disagrees. When he finds Jeff doesn't have any grass he leaves with Bee-Bee, who has come back on, to go to his friend's house.

Jeff is alone when Pony arrives at last. Pony, a soft-spoken *"chunky, long-haired kid,"* greets Jeff and embraces him. They open beers, and Pony looks out and waves. It's the limo the record company makes Pony use: "It's dumb, I know." Jeff explains Sooze went for refreshments. Pony's pleased to hear she and Jeff are still together. He looks around, noting that nothing has changed. He's only been gone a year, Jeff reminds him. Jeff's seen Pony's album at the mall. They're getting good placement now, Pony relates, and have sold more than 90,000 units. But it is not a wild life, he has to confess. The road is hard work. "The road is hell. Airport-hotel-show, airport-hotel-show . . . . . "

Erica, Pony's press aide, comes on with a cellular telephone and *"sits primly on the bench."* She is beautiful, dark and sexy, with a sophisticated hair-style and makeup and wears a tight cut-out crop top, bell bottoms and boots. She has a beeper and a day-runner. When she finishes her phone conversation, Tony introduces Erica and Jeff to each other. Pony seems disappointed Jeff and the others had not come to the show and Jeff claims Sooze "screwed up the tickets." Jeff reveals he has dropped out of college for the most part, is rethinking his value system and is doing some writing.

Jeff should try writing some songs, Pony thinks, recalling for Erica that Jeff wrote a funny piece in high school about his dick.

JEFF: But so, you think I should?
PONY: What?
JEFF: Write? Because I have. Written some things. You know.
PONY: Songs?
JEFF: They could be songs.
PONY: Yeah? You should show 'em to me.
JEFF: No.
PONY: Really.
JEFF: Now?
PONY: Maybe later.
A beat.
JEFF *(relaxing, smile):* Hey.
PONY: Hey, you know?
JEFF *(chatty):* I'm thinking, he's out there, he's touring, he's a big deal now. MTV. Stadiums. And then you show up and you're just Pony.
PONY: I'm just Pony, man.
JEFF: Now that I'm thinking about it, it *would* be interesting to do something together.
PONY: It would.
JEFF: Yeah. *(Suddenly serious.)* You're doing good work, man.
PONY *(serious):* So are you, man.
JEFF: Maybe I'll stop by the house and get the songs later.
PONY: You should.

Sooze returns, pleased to see Pony and the limo. She's never seen a black limo before. Pony wants to know about her painting. And performance art, Sooze adds. Sooze tells Pony she's contemplating going to New York. He approves—he still has some drawings of hers. Buff interrupts the conversation by bursting in, hoping the police aren't after him. His entrance rouses Tim on the roof, who wonders what happened. Bee-Bee, who followed Buff on, explains Buff's friend's mother called the cops because Buff was climbing the drain-pipe to his friend's room to get some pot. He did get it, Buff allows.

Buff wants to know all about Pony's lifestyle and about Erica, the publicist for the band, hired by the record company to take care of interviews. Pony had just been doing an interview, and she'd expressed interest in seeing Burnfield. "We hear all about Burnfield," Erica confirms.

Jeff asks if Pony tells "how we started the band." Pony recalls Jeff came by only once and played the harmonica, before they were really a band, before Danny signed them. Jeff claims it was more than once. Tim wants to know who Danny is. Danny David is the band's manager, Sooze says. It sounds like a Jewish name to Tim.

Tim puts an arm around Erica's shoulder and wonders, since she "came by to see how the other half lives," what she thinks. Erica likes it, finds it "different."

Tim goes to Pony.

TIM: What do they interview you about?

PONY: There's this benefit for Somalia we're going to do. And you know . . . my work . . .

TIM: Your "work?" What do you tell them about "your work?"

PONY: I explain the message of my songs: "Tear down the walls, find honesty, reach out to another naked human being, help the revolution." How I write it, get my ideas, you know.

TIM: How do you get your ideas?

SOOZE: Leave him alone, Tim.

TIM: I want to know! I'm curious. How do you get your ideas?

Pony smiles.

SOOZE: Tim's jealous. He wants to have ideas too.

TIM: Yea, I'm jealous. I'm jealous of Jew-loving faggots who do benefits for starving niggers.

Tim sits with his back to the wall and closes his eyes.

Pony is strumming his guitar as Buff talks to Erica. He can't believe she's just Pony's publicist. What else is she? he wonders. Erica asks Pony to describe their relationship. He calls it mother-daughter. Buff wants to know if she is available—"in a horizontal and wet way." Sooze is upset at Buff's objectifying Erica. Tim terms it Buff having "verbal intercourse." Erica seems to find Buff funny.

Jeff changes the subject by asking Pony if he's staying at his mother's house. That is a hassle, it is revealed, so Pony stays at the Four Seasons. Tim goes off, mocking Pony and exchanging smiles with Erica on the way out.

The band is going to do a new album, and Buff offers to do the video. Pony takes him seriously and asks him if he has a reel—"Like something I can see?" Pony's also serious about having Sooze do the new album cover. Sooze is afraid they would not let her do what she wants, but he assures her he gets final approval. Sooze is pleased. Pony seems happy to be hanging out with them. It's good because they are real, have a sense of humor, "live your lives." On the road everybody thinks of nothing but scoring chicks, and Danny only talks about money. Buff assures Pony jokingly that they are "above all that."

PONY: No, I mean, when we were driving out here, I told George, the driver, to roll the windows down, just so I could smell the air. The smell of freshly cut grass . . . great! I could see into the picture windows of the houses. Families watching TV, eating dinner, guys drinking beer. It's . . . the suburbs! They don't call it the American dream for nothing.

Pony takes a break from his rhapsody and receives blank stares.

JEFF: Who's "they?"

PONY: This afternoon I went by the old mall and just walked around by myself. I just wanted to be alone and get, you know, that old mall feeling.

SOOZE: What's that?

Pony strums the guitar.

PONY: You know, safety, security. I've been trying to write something about this. But . . . it's new. Na . . . never mind.

BUFF: Come on, play it, man.

SOOZE: Play it!

BUFF: FREE CONCERT!!

PONY *(starts song with difficulty; sings):*

I get up in the morning and I go to work
I have a car . . . lawn and a TV, my boss is a jerk
My kids are good, my wife is sane
When I wake up tomorrow gonna do it all again . . .
You might think there's nothing to it,
The truth is hard to see
To be a man invisible is a remarkable thing to be.
I went out on the highway there was a big jam
A family had died inside their mini-van
There was a back-up, you know it went for miles

Babette Renee Props (Erica) with Tim Guinee (Tim) in *SubUrbia*

But as bad as it was, it was gone after awhile
You might think there's nothing to it,
And the truth is hard to see
To be a man invisible is a remarkable thing to be.

Jeff asks Pony whether Pony is "the man invisible." He is an artist, Pony asserts, an artist being someone who watches life and comments on it. Jeff insists he does the same thing, so why is Pony special? The difference is that Pony is communicating his thinking to people with his music, Pony believes. He cites the old cliche, "If a tree falls in the forest, and no one's there to hear it, does it make a sound?" Jeff argues that it doesn't mean the tree isn't artistic if it isn't cut down. Jeff argues for the sake of arguing, Sooze points out. As Tim returns with more beer, Erica somewhat reluctantly reveals in reply to questioning that she's from Bel-Air.

TIM *(pause):* You rich?

ERICA: Not really. Middle class.

TIM: Me too. Middle class.

ERICA: Maybe upper middle class.

TIM: Yeah. So your Dad's a big deal, huh?

ERICA: He thinks so.

TIM: You love him a lot, he bought you a BMW for your birthday but finally you had to move out and get your own place.

Erica doesn't say anything as Tim holds a hand over her head and shuts his eyes, speaks like a mind-reader.

Your parents hate your smoking. You didn't tell them about your abortion. You know your dad's having an affair with somebody at work. You used to be bulemic, but now you're over it. You have a subscription to *Vanity Fair*. You have a personal trainer. You've been seeing the same therapist for years. You have your nails done by a professional.

BUFF: What's he doing, man?

TIM: You Jewish?

ERICA: My dad. Not my mom. I know. You hate Jews.

TIM: I never said that. I just like to know who I'm dealing with.

ERICA: Well now that you know what you're dealing with, what are you going to do about it?

Meanwhile Bee-Bee has gone off unnoticed with the boombox. Pony begins strumming and sings for Sooze who smiles at him when the song ends. Jeff kicks over the trash container. He would have gone to the concert if he'd wanted to hear Pony sing, he tells him, and he continues berating him. Pony plays it cool—he's sorry if Jeff doesn't like his stuff. That isn't it, Jeff tries to explain. Jeff knows that things are "fucked up beyond belief," and he knows he personally has nothing new to say about it, has no answer, no "message." Pony starts to speak. Jeff swings at him and hits the wall, hurting his hand.

BUFF *(cheery):* Hey, man, chill!

Buff hands Jeff a beer. Jeff looks at the beer like he's never seen one before.

JEFF: "The man invisible."

PONY *(diplomatic):* Hey, man, I'm sorry if I said something wrong.

JEFF: It's OK. It's not you. It's this sidewalk. This cell. This void. You know?

The group is mystified by Jeff's rant. He makes no sense.

PONY: No, look, I come here and I'm so used to everyone kissing my ass I think I'm a fucking star, and I'm sorry if I'm full of attitude.

Pony puts his arm on Jeff's shoulder.

JEFF: It's not you. It's not anybody. It's me.

PONY: Hey, man, it's OK!

Pony locks eyes with Sooze as he massages Jeff's shoulders.

JEFF: I have no brain. No eyes. The blind leading the blind. FUCK!

Pony suggests they all go in the limo to get something to eat. Chinese take-out, Sooze says. Jeff wants them to bring it back, but he's finally persuaded to go with them to get it. Sooze calls, unsuccessfully, for Bee-Bee. Pony asks Erica if she's coming, but a look from her seems to be a silent signal to him she's not.

When Erica and Tim are alone, she admits he was correct about everything except the car. It was a Porsche. He knows a lot about her. She doesn't know anything about him. What kind of music does he like? "Military marching bands," he jokes. He tells her about his time in the Air Force mopping floors, filling gas tanks, kissing officer ass. On kitchen duty he chopped off the tip of his little finger and was "home free" three days later. They did sew it back on, and they give him a disability check every month. The lesson he learned was "Shut up and stay where you belong. Learn your place or lose your place." It seems neither of them are happy. Erica is "Go to the gym. Eat the yogurt . . . . . Check the Voice-Mail." If she feels anything it's "mild expectation." She hopes for the unexpected. She thinks Tim is nice, and sweet.

TIM: You think you and I are alike, Erica?

ERICA *(thinks):* Deep down. Way down.

TIM: It's a mistake to think that.

ERICA: We can still talk. It's nice to talk.

TIM: It's "nice" to do a lot of things.

ERICA: That's what I mean.

TIM: You don't understand me. What I'm saying here.

ERICA *(seductive):* I want to understand.

TIM: I'm not a "nice man." I'm not a "sweet."

ERICA: That's OK, I like tough.

TIM: Oh yeah?

ERICA: Yeah. If I didn't I'd be in a limo right now with a bunch of kids. Looking for Chinese food.

Tim looks at her. There is fear in his eyes.

TIM: You don't know.

ERICA: No?

TIM: No.

Erica is right up to him now, hands behind her back, offering herself to him, challenging him.

ERICA: So teach me a lesson.

They kiss. The kissing becomes animated, strenuous, awkward. Tim is aggressive, but then Erica returns the aggression. Tim breaks away.

TIM: Whoaaa . . .

Tim looks her in the eyes.

You sure about this?

Erica nods her head. She takes Tim by the hand, and he leads her off. Curtain.

ACT II

Later, as Jeff comes on, Bee-Bee is sitting, back to the wall, smoking with the boombox beside her. An unopened bottle of Jack Daniels is in front of her. *"She watches the bottle as if it were something alive, about to speak to her."* At the other end of the wall Tim is curled up, asleep. Jeff turns off the boombox and proudly reports he's walked here from the Center. He hasn't walked that far since junior high, it seems, and it has energized him. Bee-Bee missed the limo ride, but it was "disgusting and stupid," Jeff admits. He tries unsuccessfully to wake Tim. He sees the bottle and asks if he can have some. Bee-Bee doesn't mind. Jeff feels that somehow everything has changed, become clear and makes sense now because of the 20-minute walk. He asks Bee-Bee if she's familiar with the saying "This too shall pass." She is. She hears it in group.

BEE-BEE: Rehab. Outpatient. I have to go once a week. It's kinda like AA.

JEFF: Oh yeah, you had to go to Highgate. You stole a car or something.

BEE-BEE: Or something.

JEFF: How long were you in there?

BEE-BEE: Ninety days. But now I just go once a week. I'm rehabilitated, see?

Jeff swigs from the bottle.

JEFF: You shouldn't drink, then. Are you gonna drink?

BEE-BEE: No. Yes. Maybe. Fuck.

JEFF: That would suck if you had to go back . . . to rehab.

BEE-BEE: It would suck big time. I'd kill myself first.

JEFF: Is it really bad?

BEE-BEE: It was hell with windows. So noisy, I always had a headache. Smelly. Shit on the walls. There were kids my age sucking their thumbs, wetting their pants. Most of us were there because of drugs, but you wanna know something funny? There were more drugs inside that place than I ever saw on the outside. A kid from my floor shot up cough medicine, had convulsions right in front of me.

Her parents had put her there after she'd stayed out all night once and after she'd broken the VCR when she was drunk and out of control. She had thought her parents loved her. Her parents tried to help her, Jeff reminds her. "That's one way of looking at it," Bee-Bee retorts. And now she doesn't drink.

Jeff admits that he was feeling "pretty down" before. Then when they were in the limo it occurred to him that they were "getting off" on the experience of riding around in a car five feet longer than most other cars. That's when he got out. He admits he was jealous of Pony. Bee-Bee can understand that. Pony is "rich and famous," he has everything, and Jeff has nothing. As Jeff was walking he could see that Pony is stuck in the limo, with autographs and interviews, and has to comply with his manager's orders. But freedom is all there is. Jeff used to worry about making a wrong move. Now he's not sure there is a right move. No one's really different, he's decided, and that makes him free, because he can do anything if he doesn't care about the result. He doesn't need money, nor even a future. He could knock his teeth out or poke his eyes out and still be alive, "strip naked and fart in the wind." He'd know he was doing something real, at least. Bee-Bee's face is expressionless, she is so down, but Jeff doesn't see this.

JEFF: . . . . . It's all about fear. And I'm not afraid any more. Fuck it!

Jeff starts disrobing. Bee-Bee watches him flatly. She absent-mindedly takes the bottle and drinks.

Because anything is possible. It is night on the planet Earth, and I am alive, and someday I will be dead. Someday, I'll be bones in a box. But right now I'm not. And anything is possible. And that's why I can go to New York with Sooze. Because each moment can be what it is. I'm on the train going there, I'm living there, I'm reading a newspaper, I'm walking down the street. There is no failure, there is no mistake. I just go and live there, and what happens, happens.

Jeff is down to his underwear.

So at this moment, I am getting naked. And I'm not afraid! FUCK FEAR! FUCK MONEY! I WILL GO TO NEW YORK AND I WILL LIVE IN A BOX. I WILL SING WITH THE BUMS. I WILL STARVE BUT I WILL NOT DIE. I WILL LIVE. I WILL TALK TO GOD!

Jeff has another swig from the bottle. Neither he nor Bee-Bee notice that Norman has come on. His sister felt he should check the store. She thought Jeff and his friends might break the windows. Jeff remarks that that's stupid. "You're standing there in the middle of the street with your penis sticking out, and you're calling my sister stupid?" Norman comments. Jeff begins to dress and tries again to wake Tim. Bee-Bee still sits motionless, smoking and looking down at the ground.

NORMAN: We had a servant in Karachi who took to drinking. She died a beggar.

JEFF: Just because I'm having a couple of shots of Jack Daniels doesn't mean I'm an alcoholic.

NORMAN: Uh-huh.

JEFF: What do you mean you had a servant? You were poor.

NORMAN: We were not poor. In fact, some cousins of mine are very wealthy. And also in fact, at one point we had a cook, a gardener, and I had a personal tutor. How do you think I learned to speak English so well? Or do you ever think about anything?

JEFF: So why did you come here if you had it so fucking great?

Tim stirs. Norman stubs out his cigarette.

NORMAN: We used to have a shop in South Hall. London. England.

JEFF: I know where London is.

NORMAN: Lots of trouble from the blacks. They would come in stealing things. I would argue with them. Then they came one night and burnt our shop to the ground. I thought it would be different here.

JEFF: We're not like them.

NORMAN: Let me give you some advice. You seem like a smart guy. This is not for you. This, what you are doing with your life. You know?

JEFF: Thanks for the advice, but you really wouldn't understand what's going on with me.

NORMAN: Very complicated.

JEFF: That's right.

NORMAN: Complicated or not, life moves on, eh?

Norman is concerned about Bee-Bee, but Jeff assures him she's fine, that they're all fine. If that's so, why don't they go home? Norman wonders. And take their friend, too, or Norman might sweep him up with the trash. Norman goes off.

Bee-Bee is trying to talk to Jeff. "The days just keep coming . . . " But does it make any difference if you live them or not? she wonders. Jeff's attention is not really engaged. He's concentrating on waking up Tim, as Sooze and Pony come on with bags of Chinese food and more six-packs. Sooze is solicitous about Bee-Bee, and she's sorry Jeff didn't enjoy the ride. No, Jeff tells her, he is sorry, but he was tired of listening to the demo tape, and he had a chance to do some important thinking on the walk back.

Buff, who threw up out of the limo's window, roars on singing loudly and hopping around. Unnoticed, Tim picks up the Jack Daniels and gets up to the roof of the 7-Eleven via the dumpster. Buff grabs up a pint of fried rice, talking and spitting rice as he eats, ingesting the whole pint. Just as quickly, he vomits it up, rolls onto his back and groans. Pony doubts the driver will take him home in the limo, so Jeff offers to take him. Jeff and Buff go off.

There is no place like Burnfield, Pony laughs. It's the "pizza and puke capital of the world," Sooze remarks. She takes Pony behind the store and faces into the darkness. When she was little there were only woods where the condos are now, and a big stream and a pond; who knows where the stream is now. Pony gets more food and sits up on the dumpster, as Sooze tells him about the brother she had. He had Down's syndrome, and they called him "Mikey," like the little boy in the commercials who would eat anything. He would walk down here in the afternoons and be given a doughnut by a lady who worked in the bakery. Then one cold winter the bakery closed. "No more nice lady. No more doughnuts." But Mikey came anyway, looking for her, and then there was the day he didn't come home. They found him in the spring. He seemed to have fallen through the ice and gotten sucked under, downstream. Sooze claims she's over it, it's been ten years, but her mother isn't. She just watches the home shopping network and drinks. Sooze never sees her dad.

"I hate it here," she declares. She wants to get away, like Pony. "Away" is not always great, Pony warns her. He wouldn't want to come back, but he does get homesick. And it can be a hard life. He does it for the work, to protect the work. Sooze thinks it has to be fun. Pony agrees, but it's hard, too, being pressured to write new material. He'll write a song, and they ask, "But what will the video look like?"

SOOZE: Or the album cover.

PONY: Or the album cover. *(Smiles at her.)* Sometimes I try to remember why I left in the first place. I think about people. I wonder what they're doing. I thought about you. A lot.

SOOZE: Uh-huh.

PONY: I did.

SOOZE: Yeah, when you called, I thought, there's a name from the past.

PONY: Or a name from the future.

Pause. Tension.

I mean, we'll be working on the cover, right?

Voices off.

SOOZE: I know what you're saying.

PONY: You do?

Sooze has made a decision, although she doesn't look happy about it. Pony has stopped eating.

SOOZE: I like you too, Pony.

Sooze walks up to Pony, takes his hand . . . . . She looks him in the eye.

My mother has a saying: "Don't write any checks you can't cash."

PONY: Sooze . . .

Jeff has returned, with Buff, who wouldn't let Jeff take him home. Buff has a large lawn gnome he has appropriated somewhere and is settling his stomach with a beer. Tim has come down from the roof and is eating. He wants to know if Sooze enjoyed

Zak Orth (Pony), Martha Plimpton (Sooze) and Josh Hamilton (Jeff) in *SubUrbia*

the limo ride. She did. Pony wonders where Erica is. Tim claims she was tired. He'd called a cab for her, and she went to the hotel. Pony goes off to the limo, promising to be back shortly. Jeff tries to talk to Sooze. Tim is discussing eating dog in Thailand and a restaurant that served live monkey brains, and Sooze moves away from him.

Pony comes back. He got no answer when he called Erica's beeper. She'd said she might go have a drink, Tim recalls. He doesn't know where, maybe the bar at the hotel. Pony thinks he should go and see if Erica's all right. Sooze asks Pony to give her a ride. A ride in the back seat is Tim's interpretation. It isn't Tim's business, Pony points out. To Tim it is, if Pony's "fucking my best friend's girlfriend." When Tim gets in his face Pony warns him that if he hits him his lawyer will "drop an assault charge" on him. Jeff is confused. Is Sooze leaving with Pony for a ride, or going away, or to his hotel—so she can do an album cover? Is she telling Jeff something? Sooze doesn't know.

JEFF: So, what about us?
SOOZE: What about us? I'm moving away, you're staying here.
JEFF: Maybe.
SOOZE: Oh now it's maybe? You think I'm with somebody else so now it's maybe?

JEFF: No!

SOOZE *(marveling):* Wow. Wow. You're unbelievable.

JEFF: I was thinking.

SOOZE: I bet.

JEFF: Hey, you know what? Do what you want! Go with him.

Pony puts on his diplomatic smile.

PONY: Hey, man. We're just going for a ride.

BUFF: In the limo!!

JEFF: Oh yeah?

PONY: Yeah. That's all.

TIM: What's your lawyer's number? Gimme his number. I'll call him right now!

Pony meets Sooze's eyes. Grabs her hand.

PONY: Come on, Sooze. Let's go.

SOOZE: Bye, Jeff.

Jeff has turned away, disgusted.

JEFF: Just go!

SOOZE: What?!

JEFF: Just go!

Sooze goes right up into Jeff's face, almost in tears.

SOOZE: You really suck, you know that?

JEFF: Go.

Pony and Sooze leave. Jeff's knees buckle under him, and he ends up sitting next to Tim on the curb.

Bee-Bee is in the shadows as Tim brings out the Jack Daniels and proposes a toast to womanhood. Jeff insists he's not jealous of Pony and that he doesn't want Sooze the way she is now. Tim calls him a coward, saying he's got "think" confused with "fear." Jeff disagrees. He understands something now, and it isn't a big deal. Sooze can't help herself, and Pony can't help himself, either, Tim rationalizes. Jeff doesn't know what to do. Tim will lend him his .45, and he should blow Pony's brains out: "Kill him or kill her." "Kill me," Jeff suggests, but Tim doesn't think Jeff has the guts.

As Tim starts to leave, Jeff asks what went on between him and Erica. "Nothing" Tim reports. They'd gone to the van, things were "hot and heavy" and he'd looked down at her and was "filled with disgust." He got up, and she hung on him, urging him to come back and would not let go. "And I hit her." How many times did he hit her? Jeff wonders. *"Tim turns and looks at Jeff. The last true believer in the mythology of Tim."* Tim tells Jeff that he'd hit her until she wasn't moving, believes she is still back there and suggests Jeff go look. Tim's going home, he has "a hard day of drinking tomorrow."

Jeff wants to know why Erica isn't moving. Tim goes off, asking him if he has the guts to go and see for himself. Jeff starts toward the back, then stops and surveys the mess. He begins to collect the Chinese food containers but gives it up and walks back behind to look at the van. Bee-Bee picks up the bottle of Jack Daniels and drinks.

It is morning. The 7-Eleven is open, and Pakeeza is at the counter. Norman is outside clearing up, unaware that Jeff is sitting around the corner behind the store. Buff has come on, found change in the coin returns of the pay telephones and bought a package of Devil Dogs, which he eats as Norman works. Buff crumples the paper and drops it, then quickly retrieves it, apologizing to Norman, and aims it accurately at the trash container. Norman says it's OK, that he should enjoy himself. Buff is glad. When Norman gets his engineering degree and is swimming in his swimming pool, it will be "very fucking OK," Norman informs Buff. He'll have his degree in two more years, and they'll sell the store and move.

Buff sees Jeff, who admits he's been there all night. Buff goes into the 7-Eleven to get coffee for them, and to flirt with Pakeeza, and Jeff goes to the telephone to report "a crime." He doesn't want to tell them his name. It isn't in progress. It already happened. He didn't exactly see it and didn't have anything to do with it. He agrees to hold on, but when Buff comes out he hangs up. Jeff has something to tell Buff, if Buff will promise not to tell anybody else. It's serious, Jeff warns. "Last night," he begins, but Buff interrupts to apologize for not sticking up then for Jeff. It seems Sooze had stayed at the hotel all night, it's revealed. They all had, according to Buff. "It was party time." But Buff had talked with Pony's manager about the video. Jeff tries to interrupt, but Buff goes on about the video, and then interrupts Jeff again with, "And guess who showed up?"

JEFF: No. *Wait a second.* I have to tell you this. Tim . . .

BUFF *(concentrating):* Yeah, Tim.

JEFF: No, Tim . . . Tim . . . is in trouble . . .

BUFF: I know, man.

JEFF: You know?

BUFF: Yeah, that's what I'm trying to tell you. That chick Erica . . .

JEFF: They're looking for her?

BUFF: No, man! She showed up! And we had this great time together. I stayed in her room last night. What can I say?

JEFF: You saw Erica last night at the hotel?

BUFF: Yeah, all of her, man.

JEFF: Buff, stop making shit up. It didn't happen.

BUFF: Sure it did.

JEFF: Erica's in the back, in the van.

Jeff pulls Erica's hand-held computer from his pocket.

Yeah, I mean, look, I found this on the path back there. Her computer thing. She's in the van. I didn't have the guts to look. She's dead.

BUFF *(panicked):* She's dead?

JEFF: Tim confessed to me last night. He was with her last night.

BUFF: Tim?

JEFF: Killed her.

BUFF: Bullshit!

JEFF: It's true.

BUFF: Total and utter bullshit. Look!

Erica is coming on, *"fresh, up, smiling, happy,"* calling "Good morning!" She and Buff kiss, continue embracing and looking at each other. She claims she is "burnt out" from "playing with something very hot." She sees Jeff and is glad he found the computer. She'd thought she'd lost it.

Buff explains he's to show his video to Pony's manager, and, if he gets the gig, Erica will teach him to surf. Erica assures Jeff that Pony had a "nice time" last night and looks forward to seeing Jeff's songs. "Tell Pony to fuck himself," Jeff snaps. Erica cheerfully agrees to do that and goes off to wait in the limo for Buff.

Tim lied to Jeff, Buff states. Tim had pleaded with Erica to stay. She had laughed about it. Tim had done "this whole macho thing on her head and then got pissed off because she wouldn't suck his limp alcoholic dick." She told Buff about it, saying Tim cried when "he couldn't get it up." Tim comes on with a six-pack and sits and begins drinking. Buff says goodbye to Jeff and goes off.

Tim asks Jeff if he was right about Sooze staying with Pony last night. Jeff is concentrated on the fact that Tim lied to him. Tim tosses it off—Jeff will buy anything, he's so gullible and gutless. Jeff points out that he'd stayed up all night trying to plan how he could protect his best friend with some lie so he would not go to jail. If that's the case, Jeff's an idiot, Tim claims. "Because I care about you?" Jeff asks. Tim observes that Jeff didn't even "have the guts to look." No, it's Tim who's gutless, Jeff retorts, "a gutless, drunken loser. *A line has been crossed. Tim looks up with weary eyes,*" admitting that he's a drunk and a loser, but not gutless. Then why is he drinking at 10 o'clock in the morning? Jeff wonders. The little Jewish princess had laughed at Tim. He's sick of being laughed at, by pilots, by people with money, by "these greaseballs." He is sure that after "that brown bitch"—Pakeeza—aimed the gun at him yesterday, she and "Mohammed" had laughed about him. He pulls out a Colt .45.

JEFF: Go home. Stop drinking. Go home and sleep it off.

TIM: What should I sleep off, Jeff? My life? I should go home and go to sleep and when I wake up, what will I be? A pilot? A superbowl quarterback? Maybe a rock star? I don't think so.

JEFF: Just go home.

TIM: This is my home.

JEFF: What good does it do to start this? They never hurt you.

TIM: Sure they have. Every day! They hurt me every day, with their attitude. Who the fuck do they think they are? I was born here. I had a life! They took it from me.

JEFF: They're people. They have feelings.

TIM: What about my feelings. What about my FUCKING FEELINGS?

Tim stands up, still holding the gun.

THEY COME OVER HERE AND THEY KNOW ALL THE ANSWERS! AND THEY KNOW SHIT! WELL, I'M THE NEW TEACHER!

Norman hears Tim shouting, comes around and sees him with the gun. Tim warns Norman he'll shoot him if he calls the police. Norman isn't going to call the police. Tim suggests he call his sister and get her to fight his fights for him. Tim aims his gun at Norman. Norman reaches behind his back. He has Pakeeza's .38 in his waistband and he takes it out and aims it at Tim.

NORMAN: Go ahead, big man.
TIM: You fucking nigger.
NORMAN: Why do you call me names? I never hurt you. I'm just working here.
TIM: That's the problem.

Jeff steps between them, blocking line of fire.

JEFF: Tim, wait a minute. *(To Norman.)* What *is* your name?
NORMAN: What do you care?
JEFF: Maybe if we knew names, you know, things wouldn't get like this. My name is Jeff.
NORMAN: Norman.
JEFF: Norman what?
NORMAN: My name is Nazeer Chaudhry. Norman is . . . just a name.
JEFF: Nazeer! What's that, Indian?
TIM: Jeff, shut the fuck up!
NORMAN: Pakistani. Karachi is in Pakistan.
JEFF: You know, I wanted to ask you last night, Nazeer. You like living in America?
NORMAN: It's not a choice of whether I like it or not. I'm here.
TIM: Why don't you ask him if you can work in his store?
JEFF: Tim . . .
TIM: You have no respect for yourself.
NORMAN: Get off my property now.
TIM: You gonna shoot me?

Tim backs up, hitches himself onto the dumpster and stands up on it. Norman says he'll call the police. Tim tells him to go ahead. Norman urges Jeff to get Tim to come down. Jeff tries. Jeff is a coward—he doesn't go anywhere with cowards, Tim announces. Tim climbs onto the roof, gesturing and shouting. Pakeeza comes out. Tim aims at Norman, but something on the roof attracts his attention, and he seems to collapse. He calls to Jeff to come up. Norman goes on telling him to get off his roof. Tim gets down on his knees, out of sight for a moment, then stands. He isn't holding his gun any longer; he is holding Bee-Bee in his arms. He calls again to Jeff, and Norman wails, "See what happens?"

Tim climbs down with Bee-Bee over his shoulder and lays her down gently. Assuming she is drunk, Norman asserts that this situation has nothing to do with him.

Tim claims it has everything to do with Norman. It's his roof, and it's his problem.

Tim calls from the pay telephone for an ambulance, reporting that Bee-Bee has overdosed, then rages that Norman is going to be sorry he ever showed his face in Burnfield. Bee-Bee has no pulse, Jeff reveals. Tim tells Jeff to stay there and watch Norman, then exits, saying he thinks someone is at the liquor store who might have a truck. Pakeeza goes back into the 7-Eleven.

NORMAN: This has nothing to do with me. You know. She went up by herself. I tell them over and over, don't go on the roof. How is she?

JEFF: She's dead.

Jeff crumples over her body, silently crying.

NORMAN: Oh God! Oh God! See what happens? On my roof! See what happens? Oh God! The police are coming. My sister called the police. It's not too late. She's not dead. They will come and take care of her. I'm going inside. Oh God!

Norman goes into the store.

You people are so stupid!

He comes out again.

What's wrong with you?! You throw it all away! You just throw it all away, like savages! What do you think is going to happen? What do you think? Oh, God! Oh, God!

Norman goes into the store, leaving Jeff alone with Bee-Bee. Sirens can be heard approaching. Curtain.

Special Citation

AMERICAN ENTERPRISE

A Play With Songs in Two Acts

BY JEFFREY SWEET

Cast and credits appear on page 470

JEFFREY SWEET was born in Boston May 3, 1950, but before the end of that decade his family moved to Evanston, Ill., near Chicago, where his father worked in public relations for the University of Chicago. Sweet went to school and high school in Evanston and "began writing as soon as I learned to make block letters" in first or second grade. By age 11 he was distributing his short stories in a mimeographed magazine, and by age 13 he was writing sketches for the stage. He was drawn to New York City for college at N.Y.U. and his M.F.A. degree in 1971, the same year that he had his first New York production, the musical Winging It *off off Broadway at St. Clements.*

In the 1970s and 1980s, Sweet branched out into journalism and criticism as the reporter for the playwrights' magazine The Dramatists Guild Quarterly, *then succeeding Otis L. Guernsey Jr. in the critical function of the* Best Plays *series beginning with the 1985-86 volume. In this capacity he has made a maximum effort to see all of a season's Broadway and off-Broadway productions and some off off Broadway in order to form his opinions of the best plays, performances and craft contributions in his annual review of a New York theater year. Few if any other first-string*

New York critics cover a whole theater season in anywhere near the breadth that Sweet does, or for that matter with the depth of experience that comes from being a participant as well as an observer.

Meanwhile, Sweet's playwriting career has progressed apace with contributions to the 24-performance 1977 off-Broadway revue The Present Tense; *off-off-Broadway productions of* Porch *at the Encompass Theater in 1978 and* The Value of Names *at the Vineyard Theater June 1, 1989 for 39 performances (after its debut in 1982 at the Actors Theater of Louisville, which commissioned it, a nomination for that year's ATCA citation and several regional productions); and* Ties, *produced in Chicago at the Victory Gardens and later as a TV special. This season's* American Enterprise *(which includes some traditional and some original songs) was mounted by the New York State Theater Institute in Troy on March 13 and transferred to New York City April 13 for a limited engagement of 15 performances at St. Clements, the site of its author's New York stage debut 23 years before. The play's previous history and accolades are described in the Editor's Note below.*

Sweet is the author of two books on the theater: Something Wonderful Right Away, *an oral history of the improvisational group Second City (published by Limelight Editions) and* The Dramatist's Toolkit, *on writing for the theater (published last year by Heinemann). For television he wrote the award-winning adaptation of the play* Pack of Lies *and has won the Writers Guild of America Award and an Emmy nomination for his work on daytime dramas. Sweet projects in the works for the future include a play,* With and Without, *and a musical,* I Sent a Letter to My Love, *with music by Melissa Manchester who also collaborated on the lyrics, to be produced in New York by Primary Stages with Patricia Birch, who staged* American Enterprise, *directing. Sweet has received an NEA Fellowship in Literature, and he is a member of the Dramatists Guild, a former member of the Tony nominating committee and a frequent lecturer on playwriting and other theater topics. He lives in New York City, as does his son Jonathan.*

EDITOR'S NOTE: Of course Jeffrey Sweet, the associate editor of this volume, had nothing whatever to do with this special Best Play citation of his American Enterprise. *There have been plenty of others to cite it for him. As a raw script, it was awarded a Kennedy Center-American Express Fund for New American Plays grant, with which it was produced in Chicago by the Organic Theater March 6, 1991. On the basis of that production it was nominated by Richard Christiansen, drama critic of the Chicago* Tribune, *for an American Theater Critics Association citation. ATCA's play-reading committee thereupon selected it as one of 1991-92's three outstanding new scripts in cross-country theater, as reported with a sample scene from the play in* The Best Plays of 1991-92. *And this season's off-Broadway production by the New York State Theater Institute won its author a nomination for the Outer Critics Circle's prestigious 1993-94 John Gassner Playwriting Award.*

Sweet's script is special not only as a viable 18-character play in a small-cast era, but also in the size of its reach. To leave American Enterprise *out of Best Play consideration would be untrue to this volume's function as a reference to the best the theater has to offer, and the undersigned's single-handed special citation of it pushes no other playwright's work off our 1993-94 ten Best Plays list. Part living-newspaper account of George M. Pullman's career and part folk-tale accented with songs, it is exceptionally theatrical as it dramatizes a major problem in our society, past and present: namely, the agonies of reconciling totally free capitalist activity with the compassionate concerns of democracy. With certain conviction and great pleasure, we salute* American Enterprise *for its entertaining treatment of a major theme.*

OTIS L. GUERNSEY Jr.

Time: The latter half of the 19th century

Place: The city of Chicago

ACT I

Prologue

SYNOPSIS: In a setting composed of a series of platforms and a few objects of furniture suggesting a men's club, an office, a union hall, a public square, etc., etc., against a backdrop of what might be a multi-windowed factory wall, an Ensemble is gathered with a choral director for the song "Shall We Plant a Tree?" An author's note to the play explains, "In this form, actors alternate between playing characters and stepping outside those roles to narrate their characters' actions in the third person . . . . . whenever lines are assigned to the Ensemble, they are intended to be distributed among individual members of the Ensemble . . . This is not to be an occasion for choral speaking."

ENSEMBLE *(sings "Shall We Plant a Tree?"):*
Neighbors, shall we promise now
Someday under spreading bough
We'll know joy only peace can endow?
Shall we plant a tree? . . . . .

This is the story of a man who had good intentions. And how those intentions led him to try a noble experiment. And how that experiment didn't exactly lead where he hoped. This is the story of an American enterprise.

Sings.

Though we hail from separate parts,
Common purpose gathers our hearts.
This is where the future starts.
Shall we plant our tree?
Yes, we'll plant our tree!

Scene 1

The Ensemble and Cyrus McCormick with his reaper and Marshall Field with his merchandise establish Chicago in mid-century as a place where fortunes are to be made by men with the right ideas. George M. Pullman wants to be one of them—he's designed a comfortable, even luxurious railroad car to make rail travel an easygoing pleasure instead of a dirty, noisy uncomfortable experience. He tries to persuade a Railroad Owner to give his Pullman Palace Car a trial run between Chicago and Springfield, Ill. The Railroad Owner is interested in this car which, Pullman tells him, has "Twice the number of wheels, springs, shock absorbers. Cushioned seats that convert into real beds with clean sheets and pillow cases. Result: a smooth ride, a luxurious sleeping experience . . . . . The railway car that makes travel a pleasure."

But the Railroad Owner's Assistant, measuring the prototype car, finds that it is two feet wider than the space allowed for standard cars at the station platforms. Pullman knew this when he designed the car, commenting, "You have saws." But the Railroad Owner has no intention of cutting two feet off his platforms and advises Pullman, "If you ever build a practical version of this, do let me know." Stubborn Pullman maintains, "I have built what I intended," so the deal is off.

While his new car stands unused on a siding, Pullman adamantly refuses to make the slightest compromise with its design. Businessmen at the Chicago Club call him "pigheaded." Pullman explains to the audience that he won't budge because he knows he's right, just as he was right when he said he could raise the Tremont Hotel eight feet without disturbing anything in it—and did so, with 1,200 men operating jack-screws.

On April 15, 1865, the Ensemble reminds the audience, President Abraham Lincoln died, and his body began its solemn journey home to Springfield. By the time the train reached Chicago, Mrs. Lincoln was on the verge of collapse from the ardors of the trip.

Pullman steps forward, locates Mrs. Lincoln beyond the proscenium.

PULLMAN: Mrs. Lincoln, may I offer you the use of my car?

RAILROAD OWNER *(turns to Assistant):* Where do we keep the saws?

ASSISTANT: The saws?

RAILROAD OWNER: The saws. The goddamn saws, goddamn it.

ASSISTANT: All of the platforms?

RAILROAD OWNER: Between here and Springfield.

ASSISTANT: But we can't do that.

RAILROAD OWNER: Would you like to tell that to Mrs. Lincoln?

Railroad patrons, including Mrs. Lincoln, find that the new car is marvellously comfortable. The enthusiastic letters pour in, expressed by members of the Ensemble all speaking at once. The success of the car and Pullman's fortune are assured.

Scene 2

At the Chicago Club the Club Attendant comments, "A strike in Baltimore has touched off demonstrations and violence," handing a copy of a newspaper to the members, who voice their concerns about the current labor situation, even suggesting that the government and the army should step in.

PULLMAN: You wouldn't need a militia if they didn't think of you as the enemy.

3D BUSINESSMAN: I like the way you say "you."

1ST BUSINESSMAN: I didn't know that you had resigned from the club, George.

PULLMAN: Have you ever seen the sort of neighborhood where the workers we employ live? Have you been to the First Ward?

3D BUSINESSMAN: Oh, George—

PULLMAN: The ugliness, the relentless filth. A bar every third building to take their money and ravage their minds. Brothels to corrupt their morals and spread disease. The air stinks with death and despair. If this were your life, how much affection would you have for a system that places you there?

1ST BUSINESSMAN: That's right—I personally drove every one of them there and put a bottle in his hands.

PULLMAN: When I built my first sleeping car, I was told I was crazy. Putting in carpeting, fresh linen—they said the passengers would destroy it. In point of fact, people behave better in my cars than they do in their own homes.

1ST BUSINESSMAN: I assume there's a point to this.

PULLMAN: The more artistic and refined a man's external surroundings—

1ST BUSINESSMAN *(finishing Pullman's sentence):*—the nicer person he is.

PULLMAN *(finishing the sentence his way):*—the better and more refined the man. If we put our men into a decent environment, we won't need an army.

1ST BUSINESSMAN: I have to hand it to you, George. You've sure solved that.

3D BUSINESSMAN: Now, now.

1ST BUSINESSMAN: No, really, why didn't we think of it before? All we need for peace and harmony is to give everyone his own personal Pullman car.

PULLMAN *(coolly):* Good afternoon, gentlemen. *(He rises.)*

3D BUSINESSMAN: Oh now, George—you must cultivate a sense of humor.

PULLMAN: I am not aware of being deficient in that regard.

In 1880, after building thousands of railroad cars, Pullman addresses a stockholder's meeting to describe the prospering company's new venture. The factory is to be expanded to construct and service all manner of railroad cars, and around it will be built a model town to house not only the workers and their families but the executives as well. It will include a hotel, stables and market, plus an Arcade with shops, a library and even a theater. Pullman explains that in return for their investment the stockholders will benefit from the services of "clean, sober, healthy and consequently happy" workers whose output will increase and who will not strike.

This is not philanthropy, Pullman emphasizes: "People will work in our factories.

We will pay them fair market rates. They will live in the town. They will pay us fair market rent. The company will make a profit on both enterprises. Both the company and the workers will prosper. Far from being philanthropy, it is a system designed to make philanthropy unnecessary. By doing good, we will do well. Call it an experiment in enlightened capitalism."

A couple of stockholders express their misgivings, but Pullman overrides them and goes ahead with his Utopian experiment, acquiring 4,000 acres and employing a young architect, Beman, to design it. As it is being finished, Beman suggests a name for the town—his own. Pullman decides that they should combine their two names, the first syllable of Pullman's and the second syllable of Beman's, commenting, "And they say I have no sense of humor."

At the opening ceremony for the town of Pullman a huge generator (the Corliss Engine) is on display, and the Presbyterian minister, Rev. E.C. Oggel, points out with satisfaction that there's no bar, brothel or gaming room in the place. The Ensemble recites many public statements of praise for this project. On a Saturday afternoon, Pullman strolls with his daughter Florence through the town, observing its happy citizenry.

ENSEMBLE: And on Sundays, there are free concerts in the park featuring performers drawn from the ranks of the Pullman workers.

THREE MEN *(sing "Porters on a Pullman Train," music by Michael Vitali and lyrics, c. 1890, by Charles D. Crandall):*

We need no introduction.
You can see who we are—
Porters on a Pullman train,
Standing at the platform of the sleeping
Car—
Ready, quick and willing to explain,
Explain where you're located.
But we must be remunerated.
Don't forget a friendly tip.
We think you oughta give us a quatah
For then you'll have a very pleasant trip . . . . .

Now a Woman of the town steps forward.

WOMAN *(sings "Leave a Light"):*

Oh leave a light
To guide me back.
Oh leave a light so bright
That when I'm lost
And so alone
I can raise my eyes
And find my way back home,
And find my way back home.

Erol K.C. Landis (Hopkins), Marshall Factora (Wickes) and John Romeo (George M. Pullman) in Jeffrey Sweet's *American Enterprise*

Oh leave a light
So I can see.
Oh leave a light for me . . . . .

The 1st and 2d Businessmen observe from seats in the Chicago Club. The following is played over underscoring.

2D BUSINESSMAN: Beautiful.
1ST BUSINESSMAN: I suppose.
2D BUSINESSMAN: What's bothering you?
1ST BUSINESSMAN: Nothing.
2D BUSINESSMAN: Are you upset that he's made a success of it?
1ST BUSINESSMAN: Every honeymoon comes to an end.
2ND BUSINESSMAN: A worm in every apple, hunh? I feel sorry for you.
1ST BUSINESSMAN *(referring to Pullman):* I feel sorry for *him.*

The music comes to an end. Pullman and Florence applaud and exit as the next scene begins.

Scene 3

A job applicant, J. Patrick Hopkins, is checked out for vices (none), hired and sent to the lumber yard. The other lumber yard workers wish he could play the cornet—they have a band, but their cornet player has been fired for using "offensive language" like "union and organize." Hopkins isn't musical, and anyway he is not long for the lumber yard. He rises quickly through the ranks to storekeeping, timekeeping and then is summoned to an interview with Pullman, who seems to know everything about him, even the title of a book overdue at the library. Pullman takes the opportunity to inform Hopkins that a determined man may rise without a formal education; Hopkins has had none, and neither did Pullman, who began work at age 14 as a $40-a-year clerk. And Hopkins is surprised and gratified to learn that he is to be made the company's paymaster.

Pullman's Secretary interrupts the interview to tell Pullman his son is here to see him.

PULLMAN: Did we have an appointment?

SECRETARY: No.

PULLMAN: I'm busy.

SECRETARY: Do you want me to tell him that?

PULLMAN: Tell him he's being paid for a full day's work, and I expect him to do it. If he wants to see me, he should make an appointment like everybody else.

Junior has entered during the last of this.

JUNIOR: Thanks, Pop. Nice to know you're willing to treat me as well as everybody else.

PULLMAN: I didn't invite you in.

JUNIOR: You cancelled the contract with Fleischer.

PULLMAN: Yes.

JUNIOR: The contract I negotiated.

PULLMAN: We can get the linen from Nickerson and Company for half what Fleischer's asking.

JUNIOR: Not according to Nickerson's price list.

PULLMAN: You don't rely on the price list. We're dealing in bulk. If you had bothered to contact Nickerson directly—

JUNIOR: The point is, I set up a purchase, and you cancelled it.

PULLMAN: Because I arranged for better terms.

JUNIOR: Don't you care what this makes me look like?

PULLMAN: What does it matter what Fleischer thinks?

JUNIOR: Not just Fleischer. The others in my department. They all know about it.

PULLMAN: I wish you were as concerned about my good opinion as you are about theirs.

JUNIOR: How am I supposed to command any respect if you undercut me?

PULLMAN: George, as you can see, I am in a meeting. You will oblige me by returning to your desk.

JUNIOR *(after a beat, to Hopkins):* Excuse me.

Junior exits with the Secretary, as Pullman comments, "I'm afraid my son has a few problems to—sort out." Hopkins accepts the new job as paymaster and dons a jacket and tie, befitting his new position.

Scene 4

Jackson, a lecturer, books Pullman's Market Hall and starts to put up handbills. After a short conference with Pullman and the Superintendant, the Agent then informs Jackson that the lecture has been cancelled. Getting in to see Pullman about the cancellation, Jackson is told that the word "monopoly" appears on his handbill and that Pullman forbids discussion of the labor question here. Jackson's plea that his lecture is on constitutional, not labor, issues falls on deaf ears.

But Jackson has already sold tickets, a crowd has gathered at the Market Hall, and the Agent is forced to pretend that the event is cancelled because of repairs to the structure. Arriving on the scene, Hopkins sizes up the situation and orders the Agent to open the doors to the Hall, declaring that he will take the responsibility for overruling Pullman's instructions. Later, Pullman confronts him.

PULLMAN: I was under the impression I gave an order.

HOPKINS: It wasn't a very good lecture.

PULLMAN: That's not the issue, Pat. Did I or did I not give an order?

HOPKINS: Yes, sir.

PULLMAN: And are you or are you not in my employ?

HOPKINS: Yes, sir.

PULLMAN: If you are willing to enjoy the benefits of this company, you must show some responsibility to it, and to me.

HOPKINS: I understand, sir. But there was a large crowd. Cancelling the lecture wouldn't have made them very happy.

PULLMAN: There are sufficient resources in this town to make them happy without wasting their time and money on crackpot speeches.

HOPKINS: If I'd known it would upset you—

PULLMAN *(irritated):* I'm not upset. I am disappointed. *(A beat. More controlled.)* This town works because there is a system. Perhaps the reason for everything in this system is not evident to you, but I ask you to trust that there is indeed a reason for all of it. Upset the equilibrium, and you invite chaos.

HOPKINS: Yes, sir.

Pullman takes Hopkins's youth and inexperience into account and decides that what Hopkins needs is a business of his own to manage. With Pullman's backing, Hopkins opens a store in the Arcade selling clothing and utensils, at the same time holding his position as paymaster. The business is a great success, and soon Hopkins is one of the town's most affluent citizens. "Nothing like a little success to reinforce the correct values," Pullman observes.

Junior resents his father's favoring Hopkins and, one day while drunk, tells him so. Pullman is angry, but Florence intervenes and calms them down.

Pullman introduces Hopkins to his colleagues at the Chicago Club and arranges for his election as a member.

MALE ENSEMBLE *(sings "It's a Trust"):*
In this world
Prosperity comes to few
But it came to you
And me,
And me,
And me.
But there's
Something else that goes hand in hand
You must understand
You must see . . . . .

It's a trust.
God's bounty is a trust,
This great and good fortune he's sent you.
Make a solemn vow
A solemn vow
To be the best kind of rich you know how.
To be the best kind of rich you know how.

Scene 5

The Roman Catholic members of the Pullman community (of which Hopkins is one) and their Priest are negotiating for a site on which to build a church. Meanwhile, Richard T. Ely of *Harper's Magazine* arrives to do an article on the town of Pullman and is shown around by Pullman Vice President Thomas Wickes. One of Ely's questions is about where in town Pullman himself lives. He doesn't live here, Wickes explains, but on Prairie Avenue in Chicago proper; when he comes here he has a suite in the hotel. "The town was built to help elevate the character of his employees. Mr. Pullman does not need to live here," Wickes remarks. Wickes expects Ely to leave after his guided tour, but Ely decides to stay on and inquire how the workers feel about this Utopian experiment. As Ely strolls away, Wickes orders the Foreman to keep an eye on the writer, which the Foreman does.

Ely approaches the Priest and comments on the impressive church which is part of the Pullman complex.

PRIEST: The stone was hauled all the way from New England.
ELY: Very handsome.

PRIEST: It's too bad nobody uses it.

ELY: The residents of Pullman—they're not concerned with spiritual matters?

PRIEST: Oh yes, only none of the denominations here can afford to rent it. The Pullman Company is determined to make a profit on it.

ELY: A profit on the church?

PRIEST: My congregation is planning to build a church on Pullman property outside of the town. We should take possession of the deed shortly. Uh, you won't mind a little advice, Mr. Ely?

ELY: Anything you think might be helpful, Father.

PRIEST: Put away the notebook. If the men see you writing in it, they may think you're reporting to management. You're not likely to learn much that way.

A woman circulating a petition shows it to Ely, declaring that Pullman is a fine place to live in many respects but could do with some changes (unspecified) which are the subject of her petition.

As Ely sits and begins to write his article, copies of the magazine appear, and when they are distributed to various characters, including Pullman, Ely recites from it: "Though built near Chicago, the town has been designed by its namesake to be independent of that city. Consequently, it is governed not by the democratically-determined will of the residents but by George M. Pullman himself. The books in the library are books Pullman chooses, the lessons taught in the schools are those he endorses, the businesses are those he approves. In designing his model town, Mr. Pullman has diminished the residents from citizens to serfs. Mr. Pullman hopes his community to serve as an example for other companies to follow. A patriotic American must reply God forbid. We must not embrace the gilded cage as a substitute for personal liberty."

Hopkins encounters the Priest and learns that because the Priest was seen talking to Ely, Pullman will withhold the deed for the church land unless the Priest is reassigned elsewhere, and the Priest is leaving town. Hopkins casts a sharp look in Pullman's direction, then seeks out the woman with the petition and signs it. The Foreman has seen this, reports it to Pullman and soon Hopkins is summoned into the presence. Pullman has a copy of the petition but is trying to believe that someone forged Hopkins's name. The petition asks that the town of Pullman be incorporated into the city of Chicago, which would weaken Pullman's personal influence over the community. Pullman blames all this on the Democrats. Hopkins informs him that not only is he a Democrat but he signed the petition. Pullman raised Hopkins to his present prominent status (Pullman reminds him), and Hopkins musn't openly oppose company policy, whatever private opinions he may hold.

HOPKINS: Sir, I am very mindful of all that you have done for me. I'm very grateful.

PULLMAN *(interrupting):* Which is why you signed that petition.

HOPKINS: The two are not connected.

PULLMAN: Don't you have any idea of the plans I have for you?

Hopkins has no idea what Pullman means. Pullman proceeds rather stiffly.
I'm in my sixties. In good health, thank God, but some day somebody else will have to run this company. My son has demonstrated no particular aptitude, so it's logical I should look for somebody who does. This is what you put at risk.

HOPKINS *(simply):* And what do you require of me? A promise I'd never do anything you wouldn't?

PULLMAN: Assurances that the company would hold to the principles on which it was founded.

HOPKINS: And if I don't subscribe to those principles?

PULLMAN *(flaring):* You damn well should. They're what put you where you are. Who were you? What were you? A young man with little education, no money and no prospects. You started here in the lumber yard, and now look at you. This system has worked for you. It is a gesture of the purest perversity to try to dismantle it.

HOPKINS: I don't see it that way.

PULLMAN *(a plea):* Haven't you got the sense to bend?

HOPKINS: Mr. Pullman, you are a man of principle. It is one of the reasons why people respect you. Why *I* respect you. What you have built you have built without compromising your principles.

PULLMAN: Yes, well?

HOPKINS: How much respect would you have for me if I were to compromise mine?

PULLMAN *(a beat, then):* Please clean out your desk before the end of the day.

Despite an oration against it by the Rev. Oggel, the proposition for the town of Pullman to become part of Chicago passes. Eugene V. Debs comes onto the scene with a new idea for labor activity in the railroad business. Instead of grouping themselves by individual crafts—motormen, conductors, linemen in their individual unions—all railroad workers of all descriptions must organize in one body, the American Railway Union.

Scene 6

Chicago wins the competition among cities to become the site of the Columbian Exposition, leading Pullman to comment, "Now we will show the world what we can do."

A sheet is pulled as if to unveil a statue. Underneath is a soloist dressed as Columbus.

SOLOIST *(sings "The Columbian Exposition"):*

Four hundred years ago
More or less,
Christopher Columbus
Stood on the brink of a new world.
Four hundred years have passed
And just like him,

Here we stand
On the brink of a new world.

Female Soloist, also extravagantly attired, enters and joins in.

SOLOISTS *(sing):*

But you don't have to set to sea to see it,
Nor sail away to foreign shore
Just hurry to the city of Chicago
To see what lies in store!

ENSEMBLE *(sings):*

Come and see tomorrow at the fair!
Come and see the
Bright and gleaming future that is shimmering
There!
A Mr. Otis says
Why climb up stairs
When you can use his new
Invention?
Cordially he
Welcomes you to come and ride
The elevator
Won't you kindly step inside
It will sweep you off the ground
And lift you to the sky . . . . .

The song describes others of the Fair's marvels, and Pullman invites visitors to tour his facilities. Mayor Carter Harrison rises to speak.

HARRISON: . . . . . This Exposition has been a celebration of Chicago's audacity. Chicago has chosen a star, has looked upward to it, and knows nothing she cannot accomplish.

ENSEMBLE *(applauds):* With the sound of applause still in his ears, the Mayor goes home for lunch. A madman shoots him dead—

Harrison tumbles forward and disappears into the Ensemble.

—A special election is held to finish the Mayor's term. And the winner is—

HOPKINS: At the age of 35, J. Patrick Hopkins is the Mayor of the city of Chicago.

PULLMAN: Including the town of—the neighborhood of Pullman.

A moment as Hopkins and Pullman look at each other. Then Hopkins's supporters raise him onto their shoulders and carry him off, leaving Pullman alone on a quiet stage. A beat. Pullman looks after him for a second, then turns away. He holds his position as the lights fade. Curtain.

ACT II

Scene 1

The end of the Exposition marks the beginning of a business depression in 1893. Mayor Hopkins opens public buildings as sleeping accommodations for the homeless. Even the Pullman Company is affected and finds it necessary to cut wages by 25 percent across the board. When the Supervisor announces this cut, he is asked whether the rents in Pullman will also be cut. The Supervisor has no instructions on that.

On payday one of the repairmen, Stephens, receives $.07 for his two weeks' work—$9.07 minus $9 rent. When Stephens demands the rest of it, the Supervisor orders the Paymaster to give it to him and at the same time fires him. Behind Stephens in the pay line, Clayton, a carpenter, makes no objections.

A grievance committee is admitted to Pullman's office. Their spokesman, Heathcote, explains that with the wage cut "There is no way for me and my family to keep head above water. I am here in the hope that, as reasonable men, we might be able to work something out." Pullman is willing to discuss this with Heathcote as an individual, but not as a representative of all the other workers. "It is in your interest to keep this plant open," Heathcote argues, but Pullman presents him with the facts: every Pullman car now being manufactured is being sold at a loss to the company and the stockholders, "Nevertheless I continue to secure contracts. Why? To keep the factory gates open. To keep you gainfully employed, to keep this town alive. Management is making sacrifices," and Pullman expects some sacrifice from the workers in their turn. But how are they to live until prosperity returns? Jennie, a stitcher, wants to know. Pullman doesn't have an answer to that, and the committee departs.

WICKES: You handled them well, sir.

PULLMAN: Handled? All I did was tell them the truth. You should have greater faith in the power of reason.

Pullman exits. Wickes turns to Supervisor, gives him a look. Supervisor nods.

HEATHCOTE: The next morning, members of the grievance committee are informed—

FOREMAN:—there is no longer sufficient work to warrant your continued employment.

PULLMAN *(returning, to Wickes):* You what?

WICKES: I had them dismissed, of course.

PULLMAN: That was not my intention.

WICKES: Would you like me to rehire them?

A beat.

PULLMAN: No, we can't do that. It would appear that we did so under compulsion.

HEATHCOTE: In protest, three thousand workers put down their tools and walk off the job.

JENNIE: The machinery lumbers to a halt.

CLAYTON: Inside the plant, all is still.

Scene 2

Wickes explains to reporters that the company won't suffer much from having the shops idle at this time, as to some extent they've been keeping them open only to create employment. The Rev. Oggel is discredited when it is discovered that the anti-strike sermon he preached was paid for by Pullman. To raise some money, the strikers hold a dance. The band strikes up a popular song of the period.

FEMALE SOLOIST *(sings "Maggie Murphy," music and lyrics by Ned Harrington and Dave Braham c. 1880):*

On Sunday night, 'tis my delight
And pleasure don't you see
Meeting all the girls and all the boys
That work downtown with me.
There's an organ in the parlor
To give the house a tone,
And you're welcome ev'ry evening
At Maggie Murphy's home.

Present at the dance are Mayor Hopkins (who has let the strike committee use a room in his store, which he continues to operate), Heathcote as spokesman for the strikers and Eugene V. Debs, who is in town for a railroad union convention. Debs assures the strikers that "This strike is going to be won. If it takes months it will be won." Debs plans to have the union issue a statement of support, but Heathcote asks for more than that: he wants the railroad workers of all crafts to boycott any line that carries a Pullman car, and he intends to suggest it to the convention. Debs is reluctant to take any such drastic action. He fears loss of public support and suggests arbitration. Heathcote doubts that Pullman would agree to arbitration. Debs asks him to hold off until Pullman at least has the opportunity to turn it down, and Heathcote gives his word to do so.

HOPKINS: A few days later, Mayor Hopkins enters the Chicago Club. *(To Pullman.)* Mr. Pullman.

PULLMAN: Mr. Mayor.

HOPKINS: This is an extremely painful situation. You must know the affection most of the workers hold for you. They are well aware of all you have done for them in the past.

PULLMAN: Indeed.

HOPKINS: No good can come of a prolonged strike—either for them or for you. There is still a chance of ending this business. If you would agree to arbitration before a panel of neutral observers—

PULLMAN: Do you know I was just thinking—

John T. McGuire III, Joel Aroeste, Gerard Curran and Michael Steese as Chicago Club members singing "It's a Trust" to new member Hopkins (Erol K.C. Landis, back to camera) in a scene from *American Enterprise*

HOPKINS: Sir?

PULLMAN: I was the one who nominated you for membership in this club. *(Gets up.)* Good day. *(He turns away from Hopkins.)*

Scene 3

Arbitration having been refused, Heathcote once again approaches Debs at the 1894 American Railroad Union Convention. Debs can't prevent Heathcote from taking his issue to the floor for a vote of the members, but he fears that "If we take on this fight, in six months there will *be* no American Railway Union."

Heathcote delegates Jennie to describe the Pullman workers' situation to the convention. Nervously at first but gaining confidence, she tells them that at one time she was earning $2.25 a day—"very good wages for a girl"—but was getting only $.80 a day at the time of the strike. The workers have even been forbidden to supplement their food supply by fishing in the Pullman lake. "However, they did tell us that we're free to pick through the hotel's garbage for whatever food a customer might not have been able to finish. So we come to you."

A Delegate rises to move that the union declare a boycott on Pullman Palace Cars. The motion is seconded and carried unanimously.

Debs doesn't look particularly happy, but his course of action is determined.

ENSEMBLE *(sings "Step by Step," a traditional Irish song, c. 1800s):*

Step by step the longest march
Can be won, can be won
Many stones can form an arch
Singly none, singly none.
And by union, what we will
Can be accomplished still.
Drops of water turn a mill,
Singly none, singly none . . . . .

Scene 4

The officers of the country's major railroads meet and are told by Pullman, "The issue is a simple one: Who is to run our businesses—we who have founded and developed them or the people we employ? I submit that this is the essence of the contest in which we find ourselves."

One of the businessmen at the meeting, Harahan, feels that Pullman not only acted on his vision of a model town and went ahead and built it, but also, mistakenly, went further and tried to design the sort of people he wanted to live in it, people in his own image. "Now," Harahan concludes, "he's got himself a town full of people who are just as pigheaded as he is . . . . . I think they deserve each other."

The Railroad Officials discuss the situation and decide that their best bet is to invoke a law forbidding interference with the delivery of U.S. mail. By putting mail and Pullman cars on the same train, they could prevent the strikers from stopping it. Pullman tries to make some further suggestions, but the others dismiss him with "You are irrelevant . . . . . You have blundered into this situation. Now, it so happens that we may be able to use your blunder to our advantage. The fact that we do so, though, has nothing to do with any personal regard or respect for you. We do not work for you, nor are any of us so unlucky as to live in your town. We do not have to listen to your philosophy. So, in future, why don't you spare yourself and us the bother of your presence?" *(A beat; Pullman turns away.)*

Scene 5

SOLOIST *(sings "The Pullman Strike," music by Lewis Hall, lyrics by William M. Delaney, c. 1894):*

Near the city of Chicago
Where the bosses hold full sway
The working men of Pullman
Are battling for fair play
But Pullman would not listen
To the working men's appeal
And scorned their mute advances,
Nor sympathy did feel.

Pullman is at home in the evening, with his daughter Florence. As she goes off to bed, George Junior comes home. Junior is faintly surprised when his father seems to want his company. Junior fetches them both drinks, hears that his father has had a hard day, with his railroad colleagues rejecting his advice. Junior sympathizes, but their conversation is interrupted by the sound of breaking glass—someone has thrown a rock through the parlor window. The Pullmans turn their backs and order a heavy guard around the house while the strike lasts.

Scene 6

Debs admonishes the striker who threw the rock, "A man who will destroy property or violate the law is not a friend but an enemy to the cause of labor!" But when the cause languishes, per a U.S. Circuit Court injunction against interfering with mail trains enforced by federal troops, violence erupts in the railroad yards, people are killed and many of the Exposition structures are destroyed by fire. A Federal Marshal informs Debs, "I have a warrant for your arrest." Hopkins declares, "The strike is over," and Pullman says, "The Pullman Company reopens its doors."

Scene 7

The Pullman residents appeal to Illinois Gov. John Peter Altgeld for help in preventing starvation. Altgeld inquires of Pullman what he expects to do about the situation but receives no reply, so comes to Pullman to see for himself. Pullman absents himself, and Wickes offers to guide Altgeld through the facilities. Altgeld prefers the company of Hopkins, Heathcote and Jennie on his tour, and he witnesses first hand the suffering that is taking place. He tells Pullman by mail that "No matter what caused this distress, it must be met . . . . . Six thousand people are suffering for want of food, four-fifths of them women and children. I am now compelled to take those steps I feel necessary," as Pullman in his noncommital reply to Altgeld seems unwilling or unable to do anything whatsoever to relieve the suffering. Altgeld's first move is to appeal to the public for contributions of money and goods. Public reaction includes the Ensemble's judgement, "Pullman represents a tide in industrial feudalism which must be beaten back. It is a disgrace!" The aid pours in from all over the nation. Pullman has no comment.

Scene 8

Pullman is appearing before three Commissioners in a hearing ordered by President Cleveland, during most of which he *"stays calm and courteous, as if he sees his task to be to patiently explain a civics lesson to slightly rude boys."* Commissioner Worthington reminds Pullman that he refused arbitration, and Pullman explains that he did so on the principle that a person has the right to manage his own property.

WORTHINGTON: Well, for the sake of argument, let's suppose that a board of arbitration had examined the matter and had said, "Yes, we accept your statement that you're losing money; but with a body of workmen that have been with you some time, you ought to divide with them a little, give them at least enough to live on.

PULLMAN: The wage question is settled by the law of supply and demand.

WORTHINGTON: Supply and demand. Fair market.

PULLMAN: That is the system under which we live. In this particular case, a mutual sacrifice had to be made. The Pullman Company had to use its profits as a cushion so as to underbid and thus win contracts it would not have ordinarily won, and the men had to work a little harder and at the new wages as they had been adjusted.

WORTHINGTON: Who adjusted these wages?

PULLMAN: They were fixed between the shop managers and the men. The men were to work at a reduced scale.

WORTHINGTON: And had the men agreed to work at these reduced wages?

PULLMAN: A scale of wages was presented to them. They continued to work.

WORTHINGTON: That's not what I asked. Had they agreed?

PULLMAN: Wouldn't you regard it as agreement if they were at work?

WORTHINGTON: Lack of food might compel a man to work at a lower wage.

PULLMAN: I would have been very glad to pay the men higher wages if business conditions had so warranted.

Worthington points out that the Pullman Company has been phenominally successful, now worth 36 times is original capitalization, with dividends ranging from eight to 12 percent, earning almost $3 million in a depression year. Pullman did not and does not see fit to share these profits with any but the stockholders. Nor did he reduce the wages of the officers or the superintendants and foremen, lest the company lose them.

WORTHINGTON: You might reduce your own perhaps, but not theirs.

PULLMAN: I might.

WORTHINGTON: Did you reduce your own?

PULLMAN: Did I—?

WORTHINGTON: Did you reduce your own salary?

A beat.

PULLMAN: No.

WORTHINGTON: You did not.

PULLMAN: I did not.

WORTHINGTON: You don't consider that it might have been a gesture that would have been appreciated by your employees?

PULLMAN: I don't consider that it would have made any significant difference to the financial situation of the company.

WORTHINGTON: I see. That will be all.

PULLMAN: I don't feel that I need to justify to you—

COMMISSIONER WRIGHT: Thank you, Mr. Pullman.

The Commission's report blames the strike and its "consequent loss of property, wages and life" on Pullman and his company's policy.

Pullman remains seated while the Commissioners exit. Hopkins steps forward to protest that much of what happened was indeed not Pullman's fault; much of it was the fault of a depression under a Democratic administration in Washington whose policies Pullman, a devout Republican, never supported. Hopkins goes on, "To saddle him with the responsibility for the unfortunate events of this past summer is scapegoating, pure and simple." He calls Pullman "one of our greatest citizens" and declares, "I most heartily regret any part I may have inadvertently played in this travesty. Effective immediately, I resign the office of the Mayor of the city of Chicago."

The lights change, and now Pullman, still seated, is at his home. *"We should gradually realize that he has been dreaming this reconciliation,"* which was purely and simply a figment of his wishful thinking and emotional distress. The dream figure of Hopkins disappears.

A Servant brings Pullman a lap desk so that he may write out a letter to his newborn grandson, endowing a bed in St. Luke's Hospital in his name, wishing him a successful life and advising him, "Remember that good actions speak louder than do spoken words." As he hands back the desk to the Servant, Pullman winces from sudden and severe chest pain and is helped offstage.

ENSEMBLE: The doctor arrives too late to be of any assistance.

1ST CITIZEN: Had he been better known, he would have been better liked.

2ND CITIZEN: He did a great deal of good, even if he was not thoroughly understood by a part of the public

3D CITIZEN: He loved his town as he loved his children.

JUNIOR: One of his children discovers a measure of his father's love when the will is read.

ENSEMBLE: "Inasmuch as my son has never developed a sense of responsibility, I am compelled to limit provisions for his benefit."—Nevertheless, George Pullman Jr. is heard to remark that he intends to visit his father's grave regularly.

JUNIOR: Yeah, with my dog.

Florence gives Junior a sharp look. Junior turns away.

REPORTER: Eugene Debs, no longer imprisoned for his part in the strike, is asked for comment.

DEBS: Mr. Pullman would not arbitrate. Now he is on an equal footing with those who worked for him.

The Female Soloist begins a reprise of "Leave a Light," over which the following is played.

ENSEMBLE: Special precautions are taken to prevent any possible interference with the remains by those who disagreed with him in life. The body is placed in a mahogany casket. The casket is secured within a sheath of tar paper. The tar paper is surrounded by a layer of asphalt. And the asphalt is sealed within a block of steel-reinforced concrete the size of a drawing room. It takes two days to fill in the grave.

HOPKINS: And so George Pullman lies undisturbed for the ages.

"Leave a Light" ends. Blackout. Curtain.

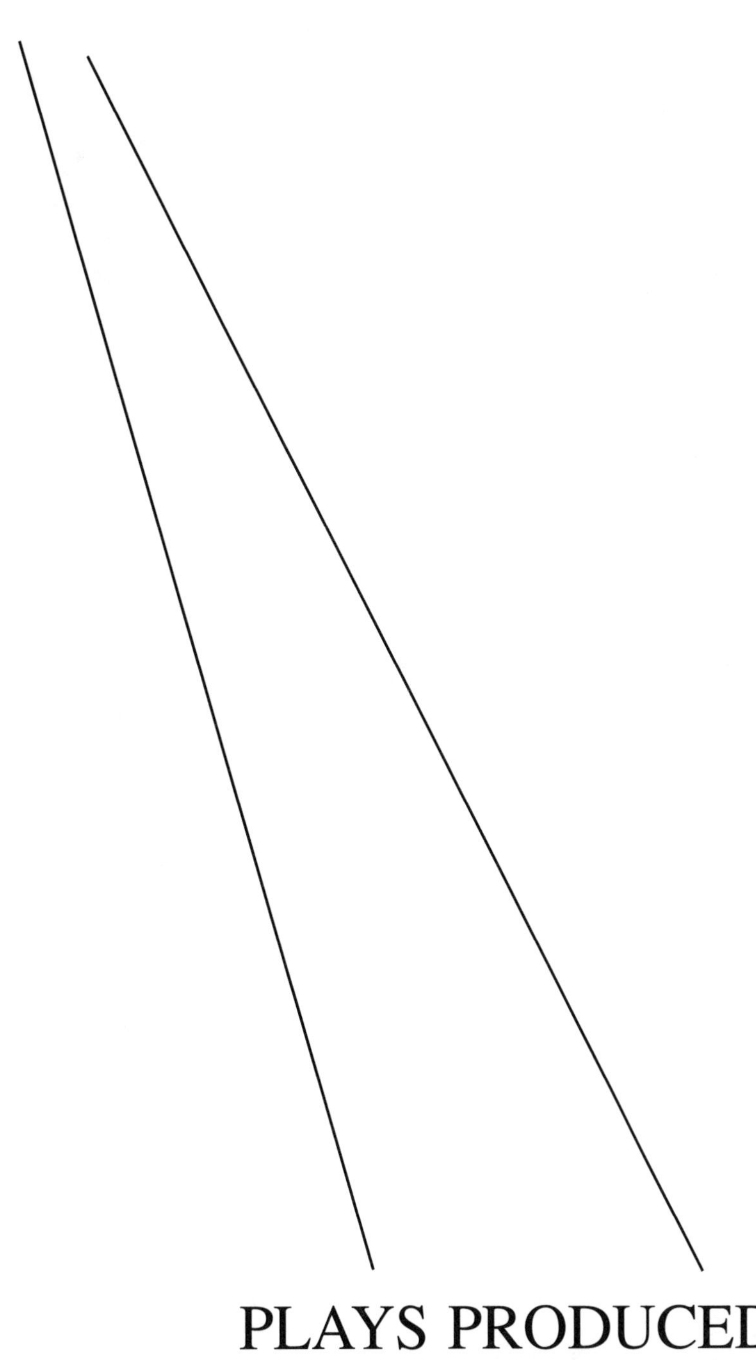

PLAYS PRODUCED IN NEW YORK

PLAYS PRODUCED ON BROADWAY

Figures in parentheses following a play's title give number of performances. These figures do not include previews or extra non-profit performances. In the case of a transfer, the off-Broadway run is noted but not added to the figure in parentheses.

Plays marked with an asterisk (*) were still in a projected run June 1, 1994. Their number of performances is figured through May 31, 1994.

In a listing of a show's numbers—dances, sketches, musical scenes, etc.—the titles of songs are identified wherever possible by their appearance in quotation marks (").

HOLDOVERS FROM PREVIOUS SEASONS

Plays which were running on June 1, 1993 are listed below. More detailed information about them appears in previous *Best Plays* volumes of appropriate years. Important cast changes since opening night are recorded in the Cast Replacements section of this volume.

***Cats** (4,862). Musical based on *Old Possum's Book of Practical Cats* by T.S. Eliot; music by Andrew Lloyd Webber; additional lyrics by Trevor Nunn and Richard Stilgoe. Opened October 7, 1982.

***Les Misérables** (2,949). Musical based on the novel by Victor Hugo; book by Alain Boublil and Claude-Michel Schönberg; music by Claude-Michel Schönberg; lyrics by Herbert Kretzmer; original French text by Alain Boublil and Jean-Marc Natel; additional material by James Fenton. Opened March 12, 1987.

***The Phantom of the Opera** (2,650). Musical adapted from the novel by Gaston Leroux; book by Richard Stilgoe and Andrew Lloyd Webber; music by Andrew Lloyd Webber; lyrics by Charles Hart; additional lyrics by Richard Stilgoe. Opened January 26, 1988.

***Miss Saigon** (1,310). Musical with book by Alain Boublil and Claude-Michel Schönberg; music by Claude-Michel Schönberg; lyrics by Richard Maltby Jr. and Alain Boublil; additional material by Richard Maltby Jr. Opened April 11, 1991.

The Will Rogers Follies (963). Musical with book by Peter Stone; music by Cy Coleman; lyrics by Betty Comden and Adolph Green. Opened May 1, 1991. (Closed September 5, 1993)

***Crazy for You** (952). Musical with book by Ken Ludwig; co-conceived by Ken Ludwig and Mike Ockrent; inspired by material (in the musical *Girl Crazy*) by Guy Bolton and John McGowan; music by George Gershwin; lyrics by Ira Gershwin. Opened February 19, 1992.

***Guys and Dolls** (888). Revival of the musical based on a story and characters by Damon Runyon; book by Jo Swerling and Abe Burrows; music and lyrics by Frank Loesser. Opened April 14, 1992.

Jelly's Last Jam (569). Musical with book by George C. Wolfe; music by Jelly Roll Morton; lyrics by Susan Birkenhead; musical adaptation and additional music by Luther Henderson. Opened April 26, 1992. (Closed September 5, 1993)

Falsettos (487). Revival of the musicals *March of the Falsettos* and *Falsettoland;* book by William Finn and James Lapine; music and lyrics by William Finn. Opened April 29, 1992. (Closed June 27, 1993)

Someone Who'll Watch Over Me (232). By Frank McGuinness. Opened November 23, 1992. (Closed June 13, 1993)

Fool Moon (207). Comic performance program created by Bill Irwin and David Shiner. Opened February 25, 1993. (Closed September 5, 1993)

The Goodbye Girl (188). Musical with book by Neil Simon; music by Marvin Hamlisch; lyrics by David Zippel. Opened March 4, 1993. (Closed August 15, 1993)

***The Sisters Rosensweig** (501). Transfer from off Broadway of the play by Wendy Wasserstein. Opened October 22, 1992 off Broadway where it played 149 performances through February 28, 1993; transferred to Broadway March 18, 1993.

***The Who's Tommy** (461). Musical with book by Pete Townshend and Des McAnuff; music and lyrics by Pete Townshend; additional music and lyrics by John Entwistle and Keith Moon. Opened April 22, 1993.

***Blood Brothers** (456). Musical with book, music and lyrics by Willy Russell. Opened April 25, 1993.

Skakespeare for My Father (272). One-woman performance by Lynn Redgrave; conceived and written by Lynn Redgrave. Opened April 26, 1993. (Closed January 2, 1994)

***Kiss of the Spider Woman** (450). Musical based on the novel by Manuel Puig; book by Terrence McNally; music by John Kander; lyrics by Fred Ebb. Opened May 3, 1993.

***Angels in America, Part I: Millennium Approaches** (260). By Tony Kushner. Opened May 4, 1993 and was joined in repertory by *Angels in America, Part II: Perestroika* in previews October 20, 1994 and regular performances November 23, 1994.

PLAYS PRODUCED JUNE 1, 1993–MAY 31, 1994

Radio City Music Hall. Schedule of three programs. **Jesus Was His Name** (18). Multimedia spectacle conceived by Robert Hossein; adapted by Alain Decaux; produced in cooperation with Denise Petitdidier. Opened June 2, 1993. (Closed June 15, 1993) **Radio City Christmas Spectacular** (183). Spectacle originally conceived by Robert F. Jani. Opened November 12, 1993. (Closed January 8, 1994) **Radio City Easter Show** (25). Spectacle conceived by Patricia M. Morinelli and William Michael Maher; *The Glory of Easter* pageant originally produced by Leon Leonidoff. Opened March 27, 1994. (Closed April 10, 1994) Produced by Radio City Music Hall Productions, Scott Sanders executive producer (for *Jesus Was His Name*), Deet Jonker executive producer (for *Christmas Spectacular* and *Easter Show*), David J. Nash producer (for *Christmas Spectacular*), Howard Kolins producer (for *Easter Show*) at Radio City Music Hall.

JESUS WAS HIS NAME

Jesus .... Jean-Marie Lamour   Thomas .... Vincent Lo Monaco

Matthew .... Luciano Baldelli
Judas .... Thierry Charpiot
James .... Pascal David
James, Son of Alphaeus ..... Nicholas Hocquenghem
Andrew .... Laurent Huon
Simon Peter .... Jean-Pierre Lecloarec
John .... Pascal Mengelle
Thaddaeus .... Pascal Montel
Philip .... Philippe Moyssan
Simon, Called The Zealot .... Touhami Ouildamar
Bartholomew .... Serge Papiernik

Others: Jean Antolinos, Carole Babin, Alain Berlioux, Bernard Bouche, Isy Chautemps, Isabelle Cote, Jean-Philippe Daguerre, Gilles Dargere, Serge Deban, Veronique Deluy, Valerie Deranlot, Mostafa Derif, Corinne Devaux, Valerie Dreano, Martine Duffas, Phil Fanelli, Christine Gagnepain, Gerard Galy, Agnes Gaudin, Charles Ginvert, Mehdi Hamani, Ani Hamel, Eric Henon, Nathalie Hermann, France Herve, Eric Jansen, Benoit Jarde, Frederique Lachkar, Nathalie Loubens, Nathalie Markevitch, Stephane Moncuit, Virginie Patou, Valerie Pelegatti, Jacques Perez, Michele Perrin, Nicolas Pissaboeuf, Yann Peyra, Sandrine Pommelet, Catherine Quiniou, Noelle Rivas, Didiler Rochelmagne, Jean-Claude Scionico, Caryl Senneville, Patrice Studer, Fatiha Tafraoui, Eliane Varon, Philippe Villiers, Didier Wolff.

Directed by Robert Hossein; choreography (Dance of Salome and Peter's Betrayal), Micha Van Hoecke, Luce Francois; scenery, Francois Comtet, Francis Robin; costumes, Sylvie Poulet, Martine Mulotte; harmonization, Guy Dirigo; 1st assistant director, Stephane Prouve; 2d assistant director, Guillaume Lagorce; producers, Eliot Weisman, Eric Weisman, Levon Sayan, Ed Micone, Patricia Kellert; stage manager, Joseph Farese; press, Rose Polidoro-Taylor, Jay Winuk, Aileen Krikoryan, Kevin Brockman, Annie Fort.

The story of Jesus Christ told with 70mm wide screen (on which all of the dialogue is spoken) synchronized with live actors. A foreign play previously produced at the Palais des Sports, Paris, in October 1991 and in Worcester, Mass. April 6, 1993 at the beginning of a 31-city tour including this New York limited engagement.

RADIO CITY CHRISTMAS SPECTACULAR

Scrooge; Santa;
Narrator .... Charles Edward Hall
Bob Cratchit .... Arte Phillips
Scrooge's Nephew .... Michael Berglund
Marley's Ghost .... Michael McGowan, Jeff Elsass
Ghost of Christmas Past .... Stephanie Michels, Carol Lee Meadows Mitchell
Ghost of Christmas Present .... Jim Osomo, Steve Campanella
Mrs. Cratchit .... Bonnie Lynn
Belinda Cratchit .... Suzanne Phillips
Sarah Cratchit .... Fabiana Furgal, Genevieve LaBean
Peter Cratchit .... Chris Boyce, Robert Fidalgo
Tiny Tim .... Joey Cee, Travis Greisler
Poultry Man .... Raymond C. Harris, David Robertson

Elves:
Tinker .... Elena Gilden
Thinker .... Phil Fondacaro
Tannenbaum .... Michael J. Gilden
Bartholemew .... Kristoffer Elinder
Thumbs .... Leslie Stump
Understudies .... Steve Babiar, Marty Klebba

Skaters: Marina Kulbitskaya, Alexander Esman, Elisa Curtis, Kevin Day.

The New Yorkers: Carol Bentley, Michael Berglund, Kim Culp, John Dietrich, Frank DiPasquale, Carolyn Doherty, Bryon Easley, Lisa Embs, Kevin Gaudin, Nanci Jennings, Keri Lee, Bonnie Lynn, Michelle Mallardi, Joanne Manning, Erich McCall, Rod McCune, Sharon Moore, Michael O'Donnell, Jim Testa, David Wood.

Dancers: Barbara Angeline, Todd Bailey, Jean Barber, Joe Bowerman, Steve Campanella, Jeff Elsass, Raymond C. Harris, Terry Lacy, Mary MacLeod, Marty McDonough, Michael McGowan, Stephanie Michels, Joan Mirabella, Carol Lee Meadows Mitchell, Jim Osorno, Arte Phillips, Suzanne Phillips, David Robertson.

The Rockettes: Pauline Achillas, Carol Beatty, Kiki Bennett, Heather Berman, Julie Branam, Eileen Collins, Linda Deacon, Mary Lee DeWitt, Joanne DiMauro, Susanne Doris, Dottie Earle, Debi Field, Debbie Freeman, Prudence Gray, Leslie Guy, Susan Heart, Cheryl Hebert, Connie House, Stephanie James, Jennifer Jiles, Joan Peer Kelleher, Pam Kelleher, Dee Dee Knapp-Brody, Luann Leonard, Judy Little, Setsuko Maruhashi, Mary Francis McCatty, Patrice McConachie, Julie McDonald, Lori McMacken, Mary McNamara, Laraine Memola, MarQue Munday, Beth Woods Nolan, Rosemary Noviello, Carol Paracat, Jill Perin, Rene Perry, Angela Piccinni, Kerri Quinn, Rosemary Rado, Madeline Reiss, Linda Riley, Mary Ellen Scilla, Genia Sherwood, Jane Sonderman, Terry Spano, Pam Stacey, Katherine Steers, Katherine Stroud, Darlene Wendy.

Orchestra: Don Pippin conductor; Bryan Louiselle associate conductor; Mary L. Rowell concertmaster; Andrea Andros, Carmine DeLeo, Joseph Kowalewski, Julius J. Kunstler, Nannette Levi, Susan Lorentsen, Samuel Marder, Holly Ovenden violin; Barbara H. Vaccaro, Richard Spencer viola; Frank Levy, Sarah Carter cello; Dean Crandall bass; Kenneth Emery flute; Gerard J. Niewood, Richard Oatts, John M. Cipolla, Joshua

Siegel, Kenneth Arzberger reeds; George Bartlett, Nancy Freimanis, French horn; Richard Raffio, Zachary Shnek, Hollis Burridge trumpet; John D. Schnupp, Thomas B. Olcott, Mark Johansen trombone; Andrew Rogers tuba; Thomas J. Oldakowski drums; Mario DeCiutiis, Maya Gunji percussion; Anthony Cesarano guitar; Susan Nason, Henry Aronson piano; Jeanne Maier harp; George Wesner, Robert Maidhof, Fred Davies organ.

Co-director and choreographer, Linda Haberman; co-director and production stage manager, Howard Kolins; musical direction and vocal arrangements, Don Pippin; scenery, Charles Lisanby; lighting, Ken Billington; choreography and staging for "We Need a Little Christmas," "Carol of the Bells," "A Christmas Carol" and Santa's Toy Fantasy, Scott Salmon; choreography for Christmas in New York, Marianne Selbert; original choreography and staging restaged by Violet Holmes and Linda Lemac; producer/director of Rockettes, Penny DiCamillo; costumes for "Carol of the Bells," "We Need a Little Christmas," Santa's Toy Fantasy and gowns and Rockette costumes for Christmas in New York, Pete Menefee; assistant choreographers, Dennis Callahan, John Dietrich; assistant musical director, Bryan Louiselle; associate lighting designer, Jason Kantrowitz; associate producer, Giles Colahan; stage managers, Andrew Feigin, Mimi Apfel, Cathy Blaser, Travis DeCastro, Doug Fogel, Janet Friedman, Robin Rumpf; press, Annie Fort.

Special Credits: Writing—*Charles Dickens' A Christmas Carol* (play) by Charles Lisanby. Music—"Silent Night" arrangement by Percy Faith. Design—original costume designer, Frank Spencer. Original music—"Sing a Little Song of Christmas," music by Don Pippin, lyrics by Carolyn Leigh; "What Do You Want for Christmas," music by Larry Grossman, lyrics by Hal Hackady. Original orchestrations—Elman Anderson, Michael Gibson, Don Harper, Arthur Harris, Phillip J. Lang, Dick Lieb, Don Pippin, Danny Troob, Jonathan Tunick, Jim Tyler. Dance music arrangers—Marvin Laird, Mark Hummel. Musical routines—Tony Fox, Bob Krogstad, Don Pippin, Don Smitth. Santa film score arrangement—Bryan Louiselle.

61st edition of the Music Hall's Christmas show, starring the Rockettes and presented without an intermission.

SCENES AND MUSICAL NUMBERS: Herald Trumpeters. Scene 1: "We Need a Little Christmas"—Rockettes, Company. Overture—Radio City Music Hall Orchestra. Scene 2: *The Nutcracker; A Teddy Bear's Dream.* Scene 3: The Parade of the Wooden Soldiers—Rockettes. Scene 4: *Charles Dickens' A Christmas Carol.* Scene 5: Christmas in New York—New Yorkers, Rockettes, Orchestra, Company. Scene 6: Ice Skating in the Plaza. Scene 7: Santa's Toy Fantasy—Santa, Elves. Scene 8: "Carol of the Bells"—Rockettes, Company. Scene 9. *The Living Nativity* with *One Solitary Life* ("Silent Night," "O Little Town of Bethlehem," "The First Noel," "We Three Kings," "O Come All Ye Faithful," "Hark, the Herald Angels Sing")—Company; Jubilant ("Joy to the World")—Organ, Company.

RADIO CITY EASTER SHOW

Rabbit .... Gregg Burge
Tortoise .... James Darrah

Dancers: Todd Bailey, Bryon Easley, Jeff Elsass, Christiane Farr, Jennifer Frankel, Kevin Gaudin, Mary MacLeod, Carol Lee Meadows Mitchell, Sharon Moore, Elizabeth Mozer, Arte Phillips, Tom Porras, Vincent Sandoval, David Scala, Rebecca Sherman, Maria Torres.

Singers: Michael Berglund, Judith Daniel, James Darrah, John Dietrich, Carolyn Doherty, Keith Locke, Joan Mirabella, Clarence Sheridan, David Wood, Suzanne Van Johns.

The Rockettes: Pauline Achillas, Linda Beausoleil, Kiki Bennett, Julie Branam, Eileen Collins, Joanne DiMauro, Susanne Doris, Dottie Earle, Debbie Freeman, Prudence Gray, Susan Heart, Cheryl Hebert, Connie House, Stephanie James, Jennifer Jiles, Joan Peer Kelleher, Pam Kelleher, Dee Dee Knapp-Brody, Luann Leonard, Judy Little, Setsuko Maruhashi, Patrice McConachie, Mary McNamara, Loraine Memola, MarQue Munday, Beth Woods Nolan, Rosemary Noviello, Carol Paracat, Kerri Pearsall, Jill Perin, Kerri Quinn, Rosemary Rado, Linda Riley, Trina Simon, Terry Spano, Pam Stacey, Katherine Steers, Darlene Wendy.

Singer/dancer Swings: Barbara Angeline, Jim Osorno.

Princess Tenko Company: Noboru Ochiai illusion manager; Yukari Imai personal assistant; Shoichi Sawamura, Shusaku Umetsu, Komei Mori magic assistants; Joan Spina, Chris Giordano musical staging.

Orchestra: Don Pippin conductor; Bryan Louiselle assistant conductor; Mary L. Rowell concertmaster; Andrea Andros, Carmine DeLeo, Joseph Kowalewski, Julius J. Kunstler, Nannette Levi, Susan Lorentsen, Samuel Marder, Holly Ovenden violin; Barbara H. Vaccaro, Adria Benjamin viola; Frank Levy, Sarah Carter cello; Dean Crandall bass; Kenneth Emery flute; Gerard J. Niewood, Richard Oatts, John M. Cipolla, Joshua Siegel, Kenneth Arzberger reeds; George Bartlett, Nancy Freimanis, French horn; Richard Raffio, Zachary Shnek, Hollis Burridge trumpet; John D. Schnupp, Thomas B. Olcott, Mark Johansen trombone; Thomas

Oldakowski drums; Mario DeCiutiis, Maya Gunji percussion; Anthony Cesarano guitar; Jeanne Maier harp; Susanna Nason, Henry Aronson piano; Robert Wendel keyboard; George W. Wesner III organ.

Directed and choreographed by Linda Haberman; original production directed and choreographed by Scott Salmon; musical direction and vocal arrangements, Don Pippin; scenery and costumes, Erté; lighting, Ken Billington, Jason Kantrowitz; co-costume designers, Eduardo Sicangco, Jose Lengson; orchestrations, Michael Gibson, Dick Lieb, Glenn Osser, Jim Tyler; dance music arrangements, Gordon Lowry Harrell, Mark Hummel, Marvin Laird, Ethyl Will; producer/director Rockettes, Penny DiCamillo; associate musical director, Bryan Louiselle; additional material, Stuart Ross; *The Glory of Easter* lighting, Billy B. Walker; additional costumes, Pete Menefee; *The Glory of Easter* restaging, Linda Lemac; assistant choreographer, Dennis Callahan; *The Glory of Easter* vocal solo recording, Marilyn Horne; production stage manager, Andrew Feigin; stage managers, Mimi Apfel, Doug Fogel, Robin Rumpf, Tom Aberger.

Original Music Credits: "Put a Little Spring in Your Step," music and lyrics by Jeffrey Ernstoff; "I Know," music by Larry Grossman, lyrics by Hal Hackady.

Special Music Credits: "Put on Your Sunday Clothes," music and lyrics by Jerry Herman; "Friends," music by Larry Grossman, lyrics by Hal Hackady; "La Cage aux Folles," music by Jerry Herman, arranged by Gordon Lowry Harrell.

1994 edition of the Music Hall's Easter production including the pageant *The Glory of Easter* first presented in 1933.

ACT I, Prologue: *The Glory of Easter*—Company. Overture—Radio City Music Hall Orchestra. Scene 1: Pure Imagination. Scene 2: "Put a Little Spring in Your Step"—Rabbit, Singers, Dancers, Rockettes in Happy Feet. Scene 3: Yesteryear—Company (1890s Easter Parade). Scene 4: I'd Rather Lead the Band—Rabbit, Orchestra. Scene 5: With Gershwin—Singers, Dancers, Orchestra, Rockettes (George and Ira Gershwin musical numbers).

ACT II, Scene 1: Rockettes Easter Parade—Rabbit, Rockettes. Scene 2: Hats—Dancers. Scene 3: Princess Tenko—Princess Tenko Company (magic show). Scene 4: "Dancing in the Dark"—Rockettes (laser show). Scene 5: Friends—Rabbit, Tortoise. Scene 6: Rainbow Follies—Finale, Company.

***Roundabout Theater Company.** 1992-93 season concluded with ***She Loves Me** (332). 30th anniversary revival of the musical based on a play by Miklos Laszlo; book by Joe Masteroff; music by Jerry Bock; lyrics by Sheldon Harnick. Produced by Roundabout Theater Company, Todd Haimes artistic director, Gene Feist founding director, at Criterion Center Stage Right. Opened June 10, 1993.

Ladislav Sipos ..... Lee Wilkof
Arpad Laszlo ..... Brad Kane
Ilona Ritter ..... Sally Mayes
Steven Kodaly ..... Howard McGillin
Georg Nowack ..... Boyd Gaines
Mr. Maraczek ..... Louis Zorich
1st Customer ..... Tina Johnson
2d Customer ..... Kristi Lynes
3d Customer ..... Trisha Gorman
4th Customer ..... Cynthia Sophiea
5th Customer ..... Laura Waterbury
Amalia Balash ..... Judy Kuhn
Keller ..... Nick Corley
Headwaiter ..... Jonathan Freeman
Busboy ..... Joey McKneely

Ensemble: Bill Badolato, Peter Boynton, Nick Corley, Trisha Gorman, Tina Johnson, Kristi Lynes, Joey McKneely, Cynthia Sophiea, Laura Waterbury.

Orchestra: David Loud conductor, synthesizer; Todd Ellison associate conductor, synthesizer; Bruce Doctor percussion; Phil Granger trumpet; Rick Prior, Frank Basille woodwinds; Elliot Rosoff violin; Bob Renino bass.

Understudies: Mr. Freeman—Bill Badolato; Messrs. McGillin, Gaines—Peter Boynton; Mr. Wilkof—Nick Corley; Miss Kuhn—Mary Illes; Miss Mayes—Kristi Lynes; Mr. Kane—Joey McKneely; Swings—Mary Illes, Mason Roberts.

Directed by Scott Ellis; musical staging, Rob Marshall; musical direction, David Loud; scenery, Tony Walton; costumes, David Charles, Jane Greenwood; lighting, Peter Kaczorowski; sound, Tony Meola; orchestrations, Frank Matosich Jr., Don Walker; musical coordinator, Seymour Red Press; casting, Pat McCorkle/Richard Cole; production stage manager, Kathy J. Faul; stage manager, Matthew T. Mundinger; press, Boneau/Bryan-Brown, Adrian Bryan-Brown, Susanne Tighe.

Time: 1934. Place: Budapest. Act I: In and around Maraczek's Parfumerie, a morning in June through an evening in early December; Cafe Imperiale, later that evening. Act II: Hospital, the next day; Amalia's apart-

Above left, Judy Kuhn and Boyd Gaines in the revival of the Masteroff-Bock-Harnick musical *She Loves Me; above right,* Jason Graae and Lynne Wintersteller in the Rodgers & Hammerstein revue *A Grand Night for Singing; right,* Ashley Judd and Kyle Chandler in a scene from the revival of William Inge's *Picnic*

ment, later the same day; in and around Maraczek's Parfumerie, later that evening to December 24.

She Loves Me was originally produced on Broadway 5/23/63 for 301 performances and was namd a Best Play of its season. Its only previous New York revivals of record were by Equity Library Theater 5/18/69 for 15 performances and in a concert version at Town Hall in the 1976-77 season. The present production suspended performances at the Roundabout 8/1/93 and resumed at the Brooks Atkinson Theater 10/7/93.

Diane Frantantoni replaced Judy Kuhn 9/28/93. Danny Cistone replaced Brad Kane 3/1/94. Dennis Parlato replaced Howard McGillin 5/31/94.

ACT I

Overture .... Orchestra
"Good Morning, Good Day" .... Arpad, Sipos, Ritter, Kodaly, Georg
"Sounds While Selling" .... Georg, Sipos, Kodaly, Three Customers
"Days Gone By" .... Maraczek
"No More Candy" .... Amalia
"Three Letters" .... Georg, Amalia
"Tonight at Eight" .... Georg
"I Don't Know His Name" .... Amalia, Ritter
"Perspective" .... Sipos
"Goodbye, Georg" .... Clerks, Customers
"Will He Like Me?" .... Amalia
"Ilona" .... Kodaly, Sipos, Arpad
"I Resolve" .... Ritter
"A Romantic Atmosphere" .... Headwaiter, Busboy, Patrons
(orchestration by David Krane)
"Dear Friend" .... Amalia

ACT II

Entr'acte .... Orchestra
"Try Me" .... Arpad
"Where's My Shoe?" .... Amalia, Georg
"Vanilla Ice Cream" .... Amalia
"She Loves Me" .... Georg
"A Trip to the Library" .... Ritter
"Grand Knowing You" .... Kodaly
"Twelve Days to Christmas" .... Carolers, Shoppers, Clerks
Finale .... Amalia, Georg

Camelot (56). Revival of the musical based on T.H. White's *The Once and Future King;* book and lyrics by Alan Jay Lerner; music by Frederick Loewe. Produced by Music Fair Productions, Inc. at the Gershwin Theater. Opened June 21, 1993. (Closed August 7, 1993)

Sir Dinadan .... Richard Smith
Sir Lionel .... Virl Andrick
Merlyn; Pellinore .... James Valentine
Arthur .... Robert Goulet
Sir Sagramore .... Cedric C. Cannon
Lady Anne .... Jean Mahlmann
Guenevere .... Patricia Kies
Nimue .... Vanessa Shaw
Lancelot .... Steve Blanchard
Dap .... Newton R. Gilchrist
Mordred .... Tucker McCrady
Tom of Warwick .... Chris Van Strander

Ensemble: Virl Andrick, Steve Asciolla, Greg Brown, Cedrick C. Cannon, Ben Starr Coates, William Thomas Evans, Newton R. Gilchrist, Lisa Guignard, Theresa Hudson, Brian Jefferey Hurst, Donald Ives, Ted Keegan, Karen Longwell, Jean Mahlmann, Raymond Sage, Barbara Scanlon, Vanessa Shaw, Richard Smith, Verda Lee Tudor, Kimberly Wells.

Swings: Tina Belis, Michael J. Novin.

Orchestra: John Visser musical director, conductor; Milton Granger associate conductor, synthesizer; Dominic De trumpet 1; Bud Burridge trumpet 2; Dale Kirkland trombone 1; Nathan Durham bass trombone; Glen Estrin, French horn 1; Kathy Canfield, French horn 2; Helen Campo flute, piccolo; William Shadel clarinet; Mitchell Estrin B-flat and E-flat clarinets; David Kossoff oboe, English horn; George Morera bassoon; Pattee

Cohen harp; Joseph Russo bass; Yuval Waldman concertmaster; Paul Woodiel violin 2; Nina Simon violin 3; Lesa Terry violin 4; Judy Witmer viola 1; Richard Spencer viola 2; Jennifer Langham cello 1; Marisol Espada cello 2; Kenneth Canty drums, percussion.

Understudies: Mr. Goulet—Richard Smith; Miss Kies—Barbara Scanlon; Mr. Blanchard—Brian Jefferey Hurst; Mr. Valentine (Merlyn)—Newton R. Gilchrist; Mr. Valentine (Pellinore)—Steve Asciolla; Mr. McCrady—Ted Keegan; Messrs. Van Strander, Cannon—Michael J. Novin; Mr. Smith—William Thomas Evans; Mr. Andrick—Ben Starr Coates; Miss Mahlmann—Theresa Hudson; Miss Shaw—Verda Lee Tudor; Mr. Gilchrist—Raymond Sage.

Directed and choreographed by Norbert Joerder; original production directed by Moss Hart; scenery supervision and lighting, Neil Peter Jampolis; costume supervision and additional design, Franne Lee; sound, Tom Morse; executive producer, Shelly Gross; casting, Sherie L. Seff; production stage manager, Martin Gold; stage manager, John C. McNamara; press, Jeffrey Richards Associates, William Schelble.

The last major New York revival of *Camelot* took place on Broadway 11/15/81 for 48 performances.

The list of scenes and musical numbers in *Camelot* appears on pages 345-6 of *The Best Plays of 1980-81*.

***Lincoln Center Theater.** Schedule of three programs (see note). **In the Summer House** (24). Revival of the play by Jane Bowles. Opened August 1, 1993. (Closed August 22, 1993) **Abe Lincoln in Illinois** (40). Revival of the play by Robert E. Sherwood. Opened November 29, 1993. (Closed January 2, 1994) ***Carousel** (74). Revival of the musical based on the play *Liliom* by Ferenc Molnar, as adapted by Benjamin F. Glazer; book and lyrics by Oscar Hammerstein II; music by Richard Rodgers; presented by arrangement with The Royal National Theater, Cameron Mackintosh and The Rodgers & Hammerstein Organization. Opened March 24, 1994. Produced by Lincoln Center Theater under the direction of Andre Bishop and Bernard Gersten at the Vivian Beaumont Theater.

IN THE SUMMER HOUSE

Gertrude Eastman Cuevas .... Dianne Wiest
Molly .... Alina Arenal
Mr. Solares .... Jaime Tirelli
Mrs. Lopez .... Alma Martinez
Frederica .... Karina Arroyave
Esperanza .... Mary Magdalena Hernandez
Alta Gracia .... Carmen De La Paz
Quintina .... Carmen Rosario
Arturo .... Arturo Vera
Lionel .... Liev Schreiber
Figure Bearer .... Robert Castro
Vivian Constable .... Kali Rocha
Chauffer; Photographer .... James Puig
Mrs. Constable .... Frances Conroy
Inez .... Sheila Tousey

Understudies: Misses Arenal, Hernandez, De La Paz, Rosario, Tousey—Lisa Benavides; Mr. Tirelli—James Puig; Miss Martinez—Carmen Rosario; Miss Arroyave, Mr. Vera—Carmen De La Paz; Messrs. Schreiber, Castro, Puig—John Freeman; Miss Rocha—Katie Finneran.

Directed by JoAnne Akalaitis; music, Philip Glass; scenery, George Tsypin; costumes, Ann Hould-Ward; lighting, Jennifer Tipton; sound, John Gromada; casting, Daniel Swee; production stage manager, Mireya Hepner; stage manager, Mark Dobrow; press, Merle Dubuskey, Susan Chicoine.

Time: The early 1950s. Act I, Scene 1: Gertrude Eastman Cuevas's garden on the coast, Southern California. Scene 2: The beach, one month later. Scene 3; The garden, one month later. Act II, Scene 1: The Lobster Bowl, ten months later, before dawn. Scene 2: The same, two months later, afternoon. Scene 3: The same, a few hours later.

The most recent New York revival of record of *In the Summer House* took place off Broadway 3/25/64 for 15 performances.

ABE LINCOLN IN ILLINOIS

Mentor Graham .... George Hall
Abe Lincoln .... Sam Waterston
Ann Rutledge .... Marissa Chibas
Ben Mattling .... Nesbitt Blaisdell
Judge Bowling Green .... David Huddleston
Ninian Edwards .... Robert Westenberg
Joshua Speed .... Robert Joy
William Herndon .... David Aaron Baker
Elizabeth Edwards .... Ann McDonough
Mary Todd .... Lizbeth Mackay
Jimmy Gale; Willie Lincoln .... Jeffrey Stern
Aggie Gale .... Charlotte Maier
Gobey .... Bo Rucker
Stephen A. Douglas .... Brian Reddy

Trum Cogdal .... Ralph Buckley
Jack Armstrong .... Barton Tinapp
Bab; Kavanaugh .... Charles Geyer
Feargus; Cavalry Captain .... Kevin Chamberlin
Jasp; Jed .... John Michael Gilbert
Seth Gale .... Tom Wiggin
Nancy Green .... Joan MacIntosh
Tad Lincoln .... Cameron Boyd
Robert Lincoln .... P.J. Ochlan
Crimmin .... Peter Maloney
Barrick .... John Newton
Sturveson .... J.R. Horne
Phil .... Reese Madigan

Soldiers, Townspeople: Nesbitt Blaisdell, Robert Burke, Ralph Buckley, Kevin Chamberlin, Marissa Chibas, Bob Freschi, Jason Fuchs, John Michael Gilbert, J.R. Horne, Robert Jiminez, Joan MacIntosh, Reese Madigan, Charlotte Maier, Peter Maloney, David Manis, John Newton, Michelle O'Neill, Bo Rucker, Carol Schultz, Barton Tinapp, Tom Wiggin.

Citizens of New Salem and Springfield: Allan Benjamin, Melanie Boland, Scott Breit Bart, Duane Butler, Stacie Chaiken, Bill Corcoran, Constance Crawford, Richard DeDomenico, Ralph Feliciello, Ralph Friar, Bill Galarno, Jeff Stuart Janus, Spencer Leuenberger, Marilyn McDonald, Nell Wade.

Understudies: Messrs. Hall, Blaisdell, Huddleston—John Newton; Mr. Waterston—David Manis; Misses Chibas, Maier—Michelle O'Neill; Messrs. Westenberg, Joy, Geyer (Kavanaugh)—Robert Burke; Messrs. Buckley, Reddy—J.R. Horne; Messrs. Tinapp, Wiggin—Charles Geyer; Messrs. Geyer (Bab), Kevin Chamberlin (Feargus), Maloney, Madigan—Bob Freschi; Messrs. Gilbert (Jasp), Ochlan, Chamberlin (Cavalry Captain)—Reese Madigan; Misses MacIntosh, McDonough—Carol Schultz; Mr. Baker—John Michael Gilbert; Miss Mackay—Charlotte Maier; Mr. Stern—Cameron Boyd; Mr. Boyd—Jason Fuchs; Mr. Rucker—Robert Jiminez; Messrs. Newton, Gilbert (Jed)—Ralph Buckley; Mr. Horne—Kevin Chamberlin.

Directed by Gerald Gutierrez; scenery, John Lee Beatty; costumes, Jane Greenwood; lighting, Beverly Emmons; original music, Robert Waldman; sound, Guy Sherman/Aural Fixation; casting, Meg Simon; production stage manager, Michael Brunner; stage manager, Jane E. Neufeld; press, Merle Debuskey, Susan Chicoine.

Act I (In and about New Salem, Ill. in the 1830s), Scene 1: Mentor Graham's cabin, late at night. Scene 2: New Salem, the Fourth of July. Scene 3: Bowling Green's house, a year or so later. Act II (In and about Springfield, Ill. in the 1840s), Scene 4: The law office of Stuart and Lincoln, a summer's afternoon five years later. Scene 5: The Edwards house, later that evening and six months later. Scene 6: The law office, New Year's Day. Scene 7: On the prairie at New Salem, two years later. Scene 8: The parlor of the Edwards house, a few days later. Act III (In and about Springfield, Ill. in 1858-1861), Scene 9: A speaker's platform, 1858. Scene 10: The Lincoln home, spring of 1860. Scene 11: Lincoln campaign headquarters in the Illinois State House, the evening of Election Day, November 6, 1860. Scene 12: The railroad station at Springfield, February 11, 1861.

The most recent major New York revival of record of *Abe Lincoln in Illinois* was by the Phoenix Theater off Broadway 1/21/63 for 40 performances, with Hal Holbrook in the title role.

CAROUSEL

Carrie Pipperidge .... Audra Ann McDonald
Julie Jordan .... Sally Murphy
Mrs. Mullin .... Kate Buddeke
Billy Bigelow .... Michael Hayden
Policeman; Peter Bentley Jr. .... Tony Capone
Policeman; Cyrus Hamlin .... Taye Diggs
David Bascombe .... Robert Breuler
Nettie Fowler .... Shirley Verrett
Enoch Snow .... Eddie Korbich
Jigger Craigin .... Fisher Stevens
Captain; Principal;
Hudson Livermore .... Brian d'Arcy James
Heavenly Friend; Jenny Sanborn .... Lauren Ward
Starkeeper; Dr. Seldon .... Jeff Weiss
Louise .... Sandra Brown
Fairground Boy .... Jon Marshall Sharp
Enoch Snow Jr.; Orrin Peesley .... Duane Boutté
Robert Allen .... Steven Ochoa
Hannah Bentley .... Cindy Robinson
Abbie Chase .... Natascia A. Diaz
Charles "Chip" Chase .... Alexies Sanchez
Jonathan Chase .... Robert Cary
Virginia Frazer .... Rebecca Eichenberger
Buddy Hamlin .... Devin Richards
Arminy Livermore .... Paula Newsome
William Osgood .... Rocker Verastique
Susan Peters .... Linda Gabler
Myrtle Robbins .... Lacey Hornkohl
Ella Sanborn .... Alexia Hess
Martha Sewell .... Keri Lee
Liza Sinclair .... Endalyn Taylor-Shellman
Penny Sinclair .... Lovette George
Henry Sears .... Jeffrey James
Abner Sperry .... Michael O'Donnell
Ben Sperry .... Glen Harris
Sadie Sperry .... Dana Stackpole

Louise's Friends: Robert Cary, Glen Harris, Steven Ochoa, Michael O'Donnell, Alexis Sanchez, Rocker Verastique. Other Snow Children: Philipp Lee Carabuena, Cece Cortes, Lovette George, Lyn Nagel, Cindy Robinson, Tiffany Sampson, Tse-Mach Washington.

Orchestra; Eric Stern conductor; Lawrence Goldberg associate conductor; Diva Goodfriend-Koven, Charles Wilson, John Siegel, Virgil Blackwell, Ethan Bauch woodwinds; Paul Riggio, Christopher Costanzi, Janet Lantz horns; John Frosk, Darryl Shaw trumpet; Ed Neumeister, David Bargeron trombone; Beth Robinson harp; Susan Evans percussion; Alicia Edelberg, Maura Giannini, Susan Lorentsen, Heidi Stubner, Martha Mott-Gale, Janine Kam-Lal, Blair Lawhead violin; John Dexter, Richard Spencer viola; Matthias Naegele, Beverly Lauridsen, Eileen Folson cello; Richard Sarpola bass.

Understudies: Miss McDonald—Paula Newsome, Lovette George; Miss Murphy—Laureen Ward, Cindy Robinson; Miss Buddeke—Rebecca Eichenberger, Endalyn Taylor-Shellman; Mr. Hayden—Duane Boutté, Tony Capone; Mr. Breuler—Brian d'Arcy James, Devin Richards; Miss Verrett—Rebecca Eichenberger, Paula Newsome; Mr. Korbich—Brian d'Arcy James, Thomas Titone; Mr. Stevens—Taye Diggs, Jeffrey James; Mr. Weiss—Robert Breuler, Devin Richards; Miss Brown—Dana Stackpole, Jennifer Alexander, Donna Rubin; Mr. Sharp—Glen Harris, Alexies Sanchez; Swings—Lisa Mayer, Donna Rubin, Thomas Titone, Reggie Valdez.

Directed by Nicholas Hytner; choreography, Kenneth MacMillan; choreography staged by Jane Elliott; musical direction, Eric Stern; scenery and costumes, Bob Crowley; lighting, Paul Pyant; sound, Steve Canyon Kennedy; orchestrations, William David Brohn; fight direction, David Leong; dance captain, Rocker Verastique; casting, Daniel Swee; production stage manager, Peter von Mayrhauser; stage manager, Michael J. Passaro; press, Merle Debuskey, Susan Chicoine.

This revival of *Carousel*, presented in two parts, was previously produced in London at the Royal National Theater. The last major New York revival of this musical was by New York City Center Light Opera Company on Broadway 12/15/66 for 22 performances.

The list of scenes and musical numbers in *Carousel* appears on pages 378-9 of *The Best Plays of 1966-67*.

Note: In addition to its regular programs, the Lincoln Center Theater's 1993-94 season at the Vivian Beaumont Theater included *Gray's Anatomy* (12), one-man performance by Spalding Gray, written by Spalding Gray, directed by Renee Shafransky, production stage manager Jeff Hamlin, presented on Sunday and Monday evenings 11/28/93-1/3/94, an autobiographical monologue about an eye affliction, with wide-ranging comments on life experiences, most of them observed with humor.

New York City Opera. 1993-94 schedule included revivals of three legitimate stage musicals. **The Student Prince** (13). Book by Dorothy Donnelly; adapted by Hugh Wheeler; music by Sigmund Romberg; lyrics by Dorothy Donnelly. Opened August 17, 1993. (Closed August 28, 1993) **The Mikado** (7). Book by W.S. Gilbert; music by Arthur Sullivan. Opened September 12, 1993. (Closed October 19, 1993) **Cinderella** (14). Book by Oscar Hammerstein II; adapted by Steve Allen and adapted for the stage by Robert Johanson; music by Richard Rodgers; lyrics by Oscar Hammerstein II. Opened November 9, 1993. (Closed November 21, 1993) Produced by New York City Opera, Christopher Keene general director, Donald Hassard managing director of artistic administration, at the New York State Theater.

THE STUDENT PRINCE

Dr. Engel	Louis Otey	Detlef	Gordon Gietz
Count von Mark	David Rae Smith	von Asterberg	Ron Baker
Secretaries	Michael Lockley, Jonathan Guss	Lucas	David Langan
Prince Karl Franz	Michael Rees Davis	Freshman	Steven Raiford
Lutz	James Billings	Kathie	Michele Patzakis
Gretchen	Sandra Ruggles	Grand Dutchess Anastasia	Murial Costa-Greenspon
Ruder	Joseph McKee	Princess Margaret	Michele McBride
Nicholas	Gunnar Waldman	Capt. Tarnitz	Jeff Mattsey
Toni	Jonathan Green	Countess Leyden	Dulce Reyes
Hubert	William Ledbetter		

Lackeys: Steven Raiford, Louis Perry, Edward Zimmerman, Ron Hilley. Girls: Madeleine Mines, Beth Pensiero, Paula Hostetter. Huzzars: James Russell, Michael Lockley, Daniel Shigo, Richard Pearson.

New York City Opera Orchestra (ALL PLAYS): John Pintavalle (concert master), Alicia Edelberg (associate concert master), Yevgenia Strenger (associate concert master), Eric Wyrick (associate concert master), Anne Fryer, Jack Katz, Marina Markov, Martha Marshall, Nancy McAlhany, Junko Ota, Helene Shomer,

Sander Strenger, Fred Vogelgesang first violin; Alan Martin (principal), Heidi Carney, Marshall Coid, Susan Gellert, Yana Goichman, Abram Kaptsan, Kate Light, Martha Mott, Barbara Randall, Helen Strilec second violin; Eufrosina Raileanu (principal), Robert Benjamin, Donald Del Maso, Laurance Fader, Susan Gingold, Warren Laffredo, Jack Rosenberg viola; Robert Gardner (principal), Alla Goldberg, Esther Gruhn, Eleanor Howells, Charles Moss, Bruce Rogers cello; Lewis Paer (principal), Jamie Austria, Joseph Bongiorno, Gail Kruvand bass; John Wion (principal), Janet Arms, Gerardo Levy flute; Janet Arms piccolo; Randall Wolfgang (principal), Livio Caroli, Doris Goltzer, English horn; Charles Russo (principal), Laura Flax, Mitchell Kriegler clarinet; Mitchell Kriegler bass clarinet; Frank Morelli (principal), Cyrus Segal, Bernadette Zirkuli bassoon; Cyrus Segal contra bassoon; Stewart Rose (principal), Katherine Eisner, Sharon Moe, Frank Santonicola, Scott Temple horn; Philip Ruecktenwald (principal), Thomas Lisanbee, Bruce Revesz trumpet; Robert Hauck (principal), James Biddlecome, David Titcomb trombone; Stephen Johns tuba; Francesca Corsi harp; Paul Fein timpani; Howard van Hyning (principal), Michael Osrowitz percussion.

Stage director, Christian Smith; choreography, Donald Saddler; choreography restaged by Jessica Redel; conductor, Scott Bergeson; production, Jack Hofsiss; scenery, David Jenkins; costumes, Patton Campbell; lighting, Gilbert V. Hemsley Jr.; chorus master, Joseph Colaneri; assistant stage director, Beth Greenberg; musical preparation, Robert DeCeunynck; press, Susan Woelzl.

Time: In the golden years. Place: Karlsberg, Germany. Prologue: Garden of the Royal Palace at Karlsberg. Act I: Garden of the Inn of the Three Golden Apples in Heidelberg. Act II: Prince Karl Franz's rooms at the inn, four months later. Act III, Scene 1: The Royal Palace at Karlsberg, three months later. Scene 2: Garden of the Inn of the Three Golden Apples, the next day.

The last major New York revival of record of *The Student Prince* was in Light Opera of Manhattan (LOOM) repertory off Broadway during the 1980-81 season.

MUSICAL NUMBERS, PROLOGUE: "By Our Bearing So Sedate," "Golden Days." ACT I: "Garlands Bright With Glowing Flowers," "To the Inn We're Marching," "Drink! Drink! Drink!", "Come Boys, Let's All Be Gay Boys," "Drink! Drink! Drink!"/"To the Inn We're Marching" (Reprise), "Heidelberg, Beloved Vision of My Heart," "Gaudeamus Igitur," "Golden Days" (Reprise), "Deep in My Heart, Dear," "Come Sir, Will You Join Our Noble Saxon Corps," "Overhead the Moon Is Beaming," "When the Spring Wakens Everything."

ACT II: "Student Life," "Golden Days" (Reprise), "Thoughts Will Come to Me," Finale.

ACT III: Scene 1: Ballet, "Just We Two," "What Memories, Sweet Rose." Scene 2: Finale.

THE MIKADO

Nanki-Poo .... Paul Austin Kelly
Pish-Tush .... Jeff Mattsey
Pooh-Bah .... Joseph McKee
Ko-Ko .... James Billings
Yum-Yum .... Abbie Furmansky
Pitti-Sing .... Sondra Gelb
Peep-Bo .... Frances Pallozzi
Katisha .... Joyce Castle
The Mikado .... Richard McKee

Stage director, Christian Smith; choreographer, Patricia Birch; choreography restaged by Helen Andreyko; conductor, Steven Mosteller; scenery and costumes, Thierry Bosquet; lighting, John Gleason; chorus master, Joseph Colaneri; assistant stage director, Albert Sherman; musical preparation, John Beeson, William Barto Jones, Susan Caldwell.

Place: The town of Titipu. The play was presented in two parts.

The last major New York revivals of record of *The Mikado* took place in the 1986-87 season, on Broadway in the Stratford, Canada Festival production 4/2/87 for 46 performances and off Broadway in Light Opera of Manhattan (LOOM) repertory 8/27/86 for 14 performances.

CINDERELLA

Fairy Godmother .... Sally Ann Howes
Royal Herald .... Ron Baker
Little Girl .... Abigail Mentzer
Cinderella's Stepmother .... Nancy Marchand
Cinderella's Stepsisters:
Joy .... Alix Corey
Portia .... Jeanette Palmer
Cat .... Debbi Fuhrman
Queen .... Maria Karnilova
King .... George S. Irving
Royal Chef .... Jonathan Green
Royal Steward .... John Lankston
Prince .... George Dvorsky
Youngest Fairy .... Stephanie Godino

Cinderella .... Crista Moore Tiara Fairy .... Shawn Stevens
Dog .... Andrew Pacho

Directed and choreographed by Robert Johanson; co-choreographer, Sharon Halley; conductor, Eric Stern; orchestrations, Robert Russell Bennett; scenery, Henry Bardon; costumes, Gregg Barnes; lighting, Jeff Davis; sound, Abe Jacob; chorus master, Joseph Colaneri; children prepared by Mildred Hohner; assistant stage director, Paul L. King; musical preparation, Susan Caldwell.

Act I, Prologue: Public square. Scene 1: The kitchen. Scene 2: Royal dressing room. Scene 3: Back in the kitchen. Scene 4: A magical place. Act II, Scene 1: The palace ballroom. Scene 2: A garden at the palace. Scene 3: The palace ballroom. Scene 4: Back in the kitchen. Scene 5: Garden at the palace. Scene 6: The palace ballroom.

This Rodgers & Hammerstein version of the *Cinderella* tale was originally produced by Richard Lewine and directed by Ralph Nelson for CBS-TV March 31, 1957. Stage versions have been presented at the Palladium in London (1958), the St. Louis Municipal Opera (1961), plus hundreds of other stage productions licensed by the Rodgers & Hammerstein Theater Library. This is its first major New York stage revival.

Three never-before-staged Rodgers & Hammerstein musical numbers were added to the *Cinderella* score for this production: "The Loneliness of Evening" (dropped from *South Pacific*), "My Best Love" (dropped from *Flower Drum Song*) and "If I Weren't King" (discovered among Oscar Hammerstein II's papers).

MUSICAL NUMBERS, ACT I: "The Prince Is Giving a Ball," "In My Own Little Corner," "The Loneliness of Evening," "My Best Love," "Impossible," "The Gavotte."

ACT II: "Ten Minutes Ago," "Stepsisters' Lament," "Waltz for a Ball," "If I Weren't King," "Do I Love You Because You're Beautiful?", "A Lovely Night," Finale.

Roundabout Theater Company. Schedule of five programs. **White Liars & Black Comedy** (38). Revival of two plays by Peter Shaffer. Opened September 1, 1993. (Closed October 3, 1993) **A Grand Night for Singing** (52). Revue of songs with music by Richard Rodgers and lyrics by Oscar Hammerstein II; conceived by Walter Bobbie; presented by special arrangement with Gregory Dawson and Steve Paul. Opened November 17, 1993. (Closed January 2, 1994) **No Man's Land** (61). Revival of the play by Harold Pinter. Opened January 27, 1994. (Closed March 20, 1994) **Picnic** (45). Revival of the play by William Inge. Opened April 21, 1994. (Closed May 29, 1994) And *Hedda Gabler,* revival of the play by Henrik Ibsen, scheduled to open 7/10/94. Produced by Roundabout Theater Company, Todd Haimes artistic director, Gene Feist founding director, at Criterion Center Stage Right.

PERFORMER	"WHITE LIARS"	"BLACK COMEDY"
David Aaron Baker	Tom	
Anne Bobby		Carol Melkett
Keene Curtis		Col. Melkett
Peter MacNicol	Frank	Brindsley Miller
Nancy Marchand	Sophie: Baroness Lemberg	Miss Furnival
Kate Mulgrew		Clea
Brian Murray		Harold Gorringe
Robert Stattel		Schuppanzigh
Ray Xifo		Georg Bamberger

Understudies: Miss Marchand—Sybil Lines; Messrs. MacNicol, (Frank), Baker—Jon Patrick Walker; Mr. MacNicol (Miller)—David Aaron Baker; Misses Bobby, Mulgrew—Meg Chamberlain; Mr. Curtis—Robert Stattel; Messrs. Murray, Stattel, Xifo—Nick Sullivan.

Directed by Gerald Gutierrez; scenery, John Lee Beatty; costumes, Jess Goldstein; lighting, Craig Miller; sound, Douglas J. Cuomo; stunt director, Linwood Harcum; casting, Pat McCorkle, Richard Cole; dialect consultant, Elizabeth Smith; production stage manager, Jay Adler; stage manager, Charles Kindl; press, Boneau/ Bryan-Brown, Susanne Tighe.

WHITE LIARS—Time: 1965, around 5 o'clock in the evening, late September. A foreign play previously produced on Broadway 2/12/67 under the title *White Lies* a curtain-raiser on the program with *Black Comedy,* as on this program.

BLACK COMEDY—Time: 1965, 9:30 on a Sunday night. Place: Brindsley Miller's apartment in South

Kensington, London. A foreign play previously produced on Broadway 2/12/67 for 337 performances on a program with *White Lies* and named a Best Play of its season. This is its first major New York revival.

A GRAND NIGHT FOR SINGING

Victoria Clark
Jason Graae
Alyson Reed
Martin Vidnovic
Lynne Wintersteller

Orchestra: Fred Wells conductor, piano; William Ellison bass; Susan Evans percussion; Annabelle Hoffman cello; Lise Nadeau harp; Albert Regni woodwinds.

Standbys: Rebecca Eichenberger, James Hindman.

Directed by Walter Bobbie; musical direction and arrangements, Fred Wells; scenery, Tony Walton; costumes, Martin Pakledinaz; lighting, Natasha Katz; sound, Tony Meola; orchestrations, Michael Gibson, Jonathan Tunick; musical coordination, Seymour Red Press; additional staging, Pamela Sousa; casting, Pat McCorkle/Richard Cole; production stage manager, Lori M. Doyle.

Collection of 36 Rodgers & Hammerstein song numbers from nine of their Broadway shows, the movie *State Fair* and the TV musical *Cinderella*.

Suzzanne Douglas replaced Alyson Reed 12/14/93.

MUSICAL NUMBERS, ACT I: "Carousel Waltz"/"So Far" (*Allegro*)/"It's a Grand Night for Singing" (*State Fair*)—Company; "The Surrey With the Fringe on Top" (*Oklahoma!*)—Jason Graae; "Stepsisters' Lament" (*Cinderella*)—Lynne Wintersteller, Victoria Clark; "We Kiss in a Shadow" (*The King and I*)—Martin Vidnovic; "Hello, Young Lovers" (*The King and I*)—Company; "A Wonderful Guy" (*South Pacific*)—Alyson Reed; "I Can't Say No" (*Oklahoma!*)—Clark; "Maria" (*The Sound of Music*)—Graae; "Do I Love You Because You're Beautiful? (*Cinderella*)—Wintersteller; "Honey Bun" (*South Pacific*)—Vidnovic, Company; "The Gentleman Is a Dope" (*Allegro*)—Reed; "Don't Marry Me" (*Flower Drum Song*)—Vidnovic, Graae, Wintersteller, Clark; "I'm Gonna Wash That Man Right Outa My Hair" (*South Pacific*)—Reed, Wintersteller, Clark; "If I Loved You" (*Carousel*)—Clark; "Shall We Dance?" (*The King and I*)—Wintersteller, Graae; "That's the Way It Happens" (*Me and Juliet*)—Reed, Graae; "All at Once You Love Her" (*Pipe Dream*)—Vidnovic, Graae; "Some Enchanted Evening" (*South Pacific*)—Company.

ACT II: "Oh, What a Beautiful Mornin' " (*Oklahoma!*)—Vidnovic; "Wish Them Well" (*Allegro*)—Company; "The Man I Used To Be" (*Pipe Dream;* dance arrangements by Wally Harper)—Clark, Reed, Graae; "It Might as Well Be Spring" (*State Fair*)—Wintersteller; "Kansas City" (*Oklahoma!*)—Company; "When the Children Are Asleep" (*Carousel*)/"I Know It Can Happen Again" (*Allegro*)/"My Little Girl" (*Carousel;* from "Soliloquy")—Company; "It's Me" (*Me and Juliet;* dance arrangements by Wally Harper)—Reed, Graae, Vidnovic; "Love, Look Away" (*Flower Drum Song*)—Graae; "When You're Driving Through the Moonlight"/"A Lovely Night" (*Cinderella*)—Clark, Vidnovic, Reed, Graae; "Something Wonderful" (*The King and I*)—Wintersteller; "This Nearly Was Mine" (*South Pacific*)—Vidnovic; "Impossible" (*Cinderella*)/"I Have Dreamed" (*The King and I*)—Company.

NO MAN'S LAND

Hirst .... Jason Robards
Spooner .... Christopher Plummer
Foster .... Tom Wood
Briggs .... John Seitz

Standbys: Mr. Seitz—Kevin McClarnon; Mr. Wood—Robert Carin.

Directed by David Jones; scenery, David Jenkins; costumes, Jane Greenwood; lighting, Richard Nelson; sound, Douglas J. Cuomo; dialect consultant, Elizabeth Smith; stunt consultant, Linwood Harcum; casting, Pat McCorkle/Richard Cole; production stage manager, Jay Adler; stage manager, Charles Kindl.

Place: A large room in a house in North West London. Act I: Summer, night. Act II: Morning.

No Man's Land was produced on Broadway 11/9/76 for 47 performances, following its premiere engagement in London. This is its first major New York revival.

PICNIC

Millie Owens .... Angela Goethals
Helen Potts .... Anne Pitoniak
Hal Carter .... Kyle Chandler
Beano .... W. Aaron Harpold
Rosemary Sydney .... Debra Monk
Alan Seymour .... Tate Donovan
Irma Kronkite .... Audrie Neenan
Christine Schoenwalder .... Charlotte Maier

Madge Owens .... Ashley Judd
Flo Owens .... Polly Holliday
Howard Bevans .... Larry Bryggman

Understudies: Misses Goethals; Judd—Kathryn Fiore; Misses Pitoniak, Neenan, Maier—Mary Fisher; Messrs. Chandler, Harpold, Donovan—Josh Hopkins; Miss Monk—Charlotte Maier; Miss Holliday—Audrie Neenan; Mr. Bryggman—Michael Ouimet.

Directed by Scott Ellis; scenery, Tony Walton; costumes, William Ivey Long; lighting, Peter Kaczorowski; sound, Tony Meola; musical interludes and choreography, Susan Stroman; original music, Louis Rosen; fight direction, David S. Leong; casting, Pat McCorkle; production stage manager, Lori M. Doyle.

Place: A small town in Kansas in the backyard shared by Flo Owens and Helen Potts. Act I: Labor Day, early morning. Act II: Same day, just before sunset. Act III, Scene 1: Early next morning, before daylight. Scene 2: Later the same morning, after sunrise. The play was presented without an intermission.

Picnic was first produced on Broadway 2/19/53 for 477 performances, was named a Best Play and won the New York Drama Critics Award for best American play and the Pulitzer Prize. This is its first major New York revival.

Mixed Emotions (55). By Richard Baer. Produced by Michael Maurer at the John Golden Theater. Opened October 12, 1993. (Closed November 28, 1993)

Chuck .... Vinny Capone
Ralph .... Brian Smiar
Christine Millman .... Katherine Helmond
Herman Lewis .... Harold Gould

Understudies: Miss Helmond—Maeve McGuire; Messrs. Gould, Smiar—Frank Savino.

Directed by Tony Giordano; scenery and lighting, Neil Peter Jampolis; costumes, David Murin; sound, Dan Moss Schreier; casting, Pat McCorkle, Diane Silverstadt; production stage manager, Tom Aberger; stage manager, John F. Weeks; press, Shirley Herz Associates, Miller Wright.

Time: The present. Place: The living room of Christine's apartment, Manhattan. Act I, Scene 1: Thursday afternoon. Scene 2: A few hours later. Scene 3: A few hours later. Act III: Friday morning.

Comedy, a romance in their later years of a widow and widower.

The Twilight of the Golds (29). By Jonathan Tolins. Produced by Charles H. Duggan, Michael Leavitt, Fox Theatricals, Libby Adler Mages, Drew Dennett and Ted Snowdon at the Booth Theater. Opened October 21, 1993. (Closed November 14, 1993)

David Gold .... Raphael Sbarge
Suzanne Gold-Stein .... Jennifer Grey
Rob Stein .... Michael Spound
Phyllis Gold .... Judith Scarpone
Walter Gold .... David Groh

Understudies: Messrs. Sbarge, Spound—Dean Fortunato; Miss Grey—Dani Klein; Mr. Groh—Richard Reicheg.

Directed by Arvin Brown; scenery, John Iacovelli; costumes, Jeanne Button; lighting, Martin Aronstein; sound, Jonathan Deans; production stage manager, Arthur Gaffin; stage manager, Daniel Munson; press, the Pete Sanders Group, Pete Sanders, Ian Rand, David Roggensack.

Time: Early autumn through late winter. Place: New York. The play was presented in two parts.

The emotional and ethical consequences of discovering by means of futuristic high tech that an unborn child will be gay.

Wonderful Tennessee (9). By Brian Friel. Produced by Noel Pearson and The Shubert Organization in association with Joseph Harris in the Abbey Theater Production at the Plymouth Theater. Opened October 24, 1993. (Closed October 31, 1993)

Terry .... Donal McCann
Frank .... John P. Kavanagh
Berna .... Ingrid Craigie
George .... Robert A. Black
Angela .... Catherine Byrne
Trish .... Marion O'Dwyer

Understudies: Messrs. McCann, Kavanagh—Robert Emmet; Mr. Black—Charlie Giordano; Miss O'Dwyer—Maggie Marshall; Misses Byrne, Craigie—Ellen Tobie.

Directed by Patrick Mason; design, Joe Vanek; lighting, Mick Hughes; sound, Dave Nolan, T. Richard

National Actors Theater

Above, Anne Jackson as Esther and Eli Wallach as Noah in the revival of Clifford Odets's *The Flowering Peach; left,* Brian Bedford in the title role of *Timon of Athens*

Fitzgerald; production stage manager, Sally Jacobs; stage manager, Judith Binus; press, Shirley Herz/Sam Rudy.

Time: A very warm day in August, early afternoon. The play was presented in two parts.

Three couples on a trip to a mysterious island, taking with them all the usual problems and frustrations of our times. A foreign play previously produced in Dublin.

National Actors Theater. Schedule of three revivals. **Timon of Athens** (37). By William Shakespeare. Opened November 4, 1993. (Closed December 5, 1993) **The Government Inspector** (37). By Nikolai Gogol; adapted by Adrian Mitchell; American version by Mark Vietor. Opened January 6, 1994. (Closed February 6, 1994) **The Flowering Peach** (41). By Clifford Odets. Opened March 20, 1994. (Closed April 24, 1994) Produced by National Actors Theater, Tony Randall founder and artistic director, Michael Langham artistic advisor, at the Lyceum Theater.

TIMON OF ATHENS

Flavius .... Jack Ryland
Servants to Timon:
Flaminius .... Alec Mapa
Ventidius .... Tim MacDonald
Servilius .... Michael Wiggins
Poet; Representative of Varro's .... Derek Smith
Painter; Representative
of Isidore's .... Jeffrey Alan Chandler
Jeweller .... Alec Phoenix
Merchant .... Jerry Lanning
Lucius .... Michael Lombard
Lucullus .... Tom Lacy
Sempronius.............................. Nicholas Kepros
1st Senator (State) .... Herb Foster
2d Senator (Military) .... Michael Rudko
3d Senator (Church) .... Leo Leyden
Caphis .... Mark Niebuhr
Philotus .... Brian Evaret Chandler
Soldier .... Kevin Shinick
Timon .... Brian Bedford
Old Athenian; 1st Masseur .... Michael Stuhlbarg
Apemantus .... John Franklyn-Robbins
Alcibiades .... Michael Cumpsty
Alcibiades's Officer;
2d Masseur .... Jesse L. Martin
Photographer; Cupid .... Rod McLachlan
Phrynia .... Andi Davis
Timandra .... Annette Helde
Hortensius .... Richard Holmes
Soldier .... Francis Henry

Dancers: Evelyn W. Ebo, Rebecca Sherman, Stevi Van Meter. Bandits: Michael Stuhlbarg, Alec Phoenix, Mark Niebuhr. Citizens: John Dybdahl, Ted Hoffstatter, John Burton Willson. Soldiers, Guests, Citizens: Members of the Company.

Understudies: Mr. Martin—Brian Evaret Chandler; Miss Helde—Andi Davis; Miss Davis—Annette Helde; Messrs. Chandler, Rudko—Richard Holmes; Messrs. MacDonald, Stuhlbarg—Martin Kildare; Mr. Ryland—Tim MacDonald; Mr. McLachlan—Alec Mapa; Mr. Cumpsty—Jesse L. Martin; Mr. Lombard—Rod McLachlan; Messrs. Lacy, Leyden—Mark Niebuhr; Mr. Smith—Alex Phoenix; Messrs. Lanning, Phoenix—Blake Robison; Messrs. Franklyn-Robbins, Kepros—Michael Rudko; Messrs. Niebuhr, Mapa, Wiggins—Kevin Shinick; Mr. Bedford—Derek Smith; Mr. Chandler—Michael Wiggins.

Directed by Michael Langham; original music by Duke Ellington adapted by Stanley Silverman; choreography, George Faison; scenery, Douglas Stein; costumes, Ann Hould-Ward; lighting, Richard Nelson; sound, Keith Handegord; fight staging, B.H. Barry; special effects, Gregory Meeh; executive producer, Manny Kladitis; casting, Liz Woodman; production stage manager, Michael Ritchie; press, John Springer, Gary Springer.

The last major New York revival of *Timon of Athens* was by New York Shakespeare Festival 6/25/71 for 19 performances. The present revival was presented in two parts and, according to a program note, was "originated and nurtured" in essence at the Stratford Festival of Canada.

THE GOVERNMENT INSPECTOR

Police Governor .... Peter Michael Goetz
Anna .... Lainie Kazan
Marya .... Nancy Hower
Mishka .... Kevin Shinick
Avdotya .... Elizabeth Heflin
Judge .... Jack Ryland
Charities Commissioner .... Michael Lombard
Doctor; Rastakovsky .... Leo Leyden
Postmaster .... Michael Stuhlbarg
School Superintendant .... Nicholas Kepros
Nastinka; Sergeant's Widow .... Andi Davis
Dobchinsky .... Jefrey Alan Chandler
Bobchinsky .... Derek Smith
Police Inspector .... Rod McLachlan
Svistunov .... Mark Niebuhr
Pugovitizin .... Alec Phoenix
Dherzimorda; Gendarme .... Jerry Lanning
Ivan Khlestakov .... Tony Randall
Osip .... David Patrick Kelly
Waiter; Chernyayev .... Tom Lacy
Abdulin .... Jesse L. Martin
Panteleyeva .... Tim MacDonald
Locksmith's Wife;
Korobkin's Wife .... Annette Helde
Stepan Korobkin .... Herb Foster
Lyulyukov .... Richard Holmes

Townspeople, Petitioners, Guests: Martin Kildare, Leo Leyden, Rod McLachlan, Mark Niebuhr, Alec Phoenix, Blake Robison, Adrienne Alitkowski, John Dybdahl, Francis Henry, Ted Hoffstatter, Demetria McCain, Bruce Villineau, John Burton Willson.

Understudies: Miss Hower—Andi Davis; Miss Davis—Elizabeth Heflin; Miss Kazan—Annette Helde; Messrs. Lombard, Kepros—Richard Holmes; Messrs. Goetz, Leyden—Martin Kildare; Messrs. Ryland, Martin—Tim MacDonald; Mr. MacDonald—Jesse L. Martin; Messrs. Foster, Lanning—Rod McLachlan; Messrs. Chandler, Lacy (Chernyayev)—Mark Niebuhr; Messrs. Smith, Lacy (Waiter)—Alec Phoenix; Messrs. McLachlan, Shinick, Kelly—Blake Robison; Messrs. Stuhlbarg, Phoenix, Niebuhr—Kevin Shinick; Mr. Randall—Michael Stuhlbarg.

Directed by Michael Langham; scenery, Douglas Stein; costumes, Lewis Brown; lighting, Richard Nelson; music, Stanley Silverman; sound, Dan Moses Schreier; assistant director, Mark Vietor; executive producer, Manny Kladitis; casting, Liz Woodman; production stage manager, Michael Ritchie.

Time: The early 19th century. Place: A small provincial town in Russia. The play was presented in two parts.

The last major New York revival of Gogol's play was by Circle in the Square on Broadway 9/21/78 for 69 performances, under the title *The Inspector General,* which is frequently used.

THE FLOWERING PEACH

Noah .... Eli Wallach
Esther .... Anne Jackson
Japheth .... David Aaron Baker
Shem .... Josh Mostel
Ham .... Steve Hofvendahl
Leah .... Lorraine Serabian
Rachael .... Joanna Going
Goldie .... Molly Scott

Understudies: Mr. Wallach—Marvin Einhorn; Messrs. Mostel, Hofvendahl—David Green; Mr. Baker—

Danny Burstein; Misses Jackson, Serabian—Elaine Kussack; Miss Going—Grace Sadye Phillips; Miss Scott—Kaili Vernoff.

Directed by Martin Charnin; scenery, Ray Recht; costumes, Theoni V. Aldredge; lighting, Richard Nelson; sound, Abe Jacob; original music, Keith Levenson; executive producer, Manny Kladitis; casting, Liz Woodman; production stage manager, Suzanne Prueter.

Time: Then, not now. Act I: Before. Act II: After.

The Flowering Peach was first produced on Broadway 12/28/54 for 135 performances. Its only previous major New York revival was its adaptation by Peter Stone, Richard Rodgers and Martin Charnin as the musical *Two by Two* on Broadway 11/10/70 for 351 performances.

Joseph and the Amazing Technicolor Dreamcoat (231). Revival of the musical based on the Old Testament story; music by Andrew Lloyd Webber; lyrics by Tim Rice. Produced by James M. Nederlander and Terry Allen Kramer in the Andrew Lloyd Webber production at the Minskoff Theater. Opened November 10, 1993. (Closed May 29, 1994)

Joseph .... Michael Damian
Narrator .... Kelli Rabke
Pharaoh .... Robert Torti
Jacob; Potiphar; Guru .... Clifford David
Butler .... Glenn Sneed
Baker .... Bill Nolte
Mrs. Potiphar .... Julie Bond
Apache Dancers .... Tina Ou, Tim Schultheis
Brothers and Wives:
Reuben .... Marc Kudisch
Simeon .... Neal Ben-Ari
Levi .... Robert Torti
Napthali .... Danny Bolero
Issachar .... Bill Nolte
Asher .... Timothy Smith
Dan .... Joseph Savant
Zebulun .... Tim Schultheis
Gad .... Glenn Sneed
Benjamin .... Ty Taylor
Judah .... Gerry McIntyre
Reuben's Wife .... Michelle Murlin
Simeon's Wife .... Mindy Franzese
Levi's Wife .... Jocelyn Vodovoz Cook
Napthali's Wife .... Julie Bond
Issachar's Wife .... Jacquie Porter
Asher's Wife .... Lisa Akey
Dan's Wife .... Sarah Miles
Zebulun's Wife .... Diana Brownstone
Gad's Wife .... Betsy Chang
Benjamin's Wife .... Tina Ou
Judah's Wife .... Susan Carr George

Children's Choirs: The Carolabbe Chorus, La Petite Musicale, Long Island Performing Arts Center Choir, The William F. Halloran Vocal Ensemble.

Orchestra: Patrick Vaccariello conductor; Robert Hirschorn associate conductor, keyboards; Sanford Allen concertmaster; Sylvia D'Avanzo violin; Richard Brice viola; Francesca Vanasco cello; Andrew Sterman flute, clarinet, saxophone; Edward Zuhlke oboe, English horn; Steven Zimmerman, French horn; James Abbott, Grant Sturiale keyboards; Robby Kirshoff, J.J. McGeehan guitars; Hugh Mason bass; Gary Tillman drums; Bill Hayes percussion.

Understudies: Mr. Damian—Ty Taylor, Matthew Zarley; Miss Rabke—Lisa Akey, Susan Carr George, Kelli Severson; Mr. David—Bill Nolte, Glenn Sneed; Mr. Torti—Marc Kudisch, Joseph Savant; Swings—Ron Kellum, Andrew Mackay, Janet Rothermel, Kelli Severson, Gina Trano, Matthew Zarley.

Directed by Steven Pimlott; choreography, Anthony Van Laast; musical direction, Patrick Vaccariello; musical supervision, Michael Reed; scenery and costumes, Mark Thompson; lighting, Andrew Bridge; sound, Martin Levan; orchestrations, John Cameron; assistant to director and choreographer, Nichola Treherne; production stage manager, Jeff Lee; stage manager, J.P. Elins; press, Boneau/Bryan-Brown, Adrian Bryan-Brown, John Barlow.

This production of *Joseph and the Amazing Technicolor Dreamcoat* was originally produced in Los Angeles 2/25/93 and played subsequent engagements on tour before its New York opening. The show's last major New York revival took place on Broadway 1/27/82 for 747 performances. Its list of musical numbers appears on pages 335-6 of *The Best Plays of 1976-77*.

The Kentucky Cycle (34). By Robert Schenkkan. Produced by David Richenthal, Gene R. Korf, Roger L. Stevens, Jennifer Manocherian, Annette Niemtzow, Mark Taper Forum/Intiman Theater Company and The John F. Kennedy Center for the Performing Arts, in association with Benjamin Mordecai, at the Royale Theater. Opened November 14, 1993. (Closed December 12, 1993)

PART I

Masters of the Trade

Earl Tod .... Randy Oglesby
Michael Rowen .... Stacy Keach
Sam .... Tuck Milligan
Taskwan .... Ronald William Lawrence
Dragging Canoe .... John Aylward

Cherokee Warriors: Philip Lehl, Lee Simon Jr., Stephen Lee Anderson, Patrick Page.

Time: 1775, early morning, an hour before daybreak. Place: Somewhere in Eastern Kentucky.

The Courtship of Morning Star

Michael Rowen .... Stacy Keach
Morning Star .... Lillian Garrett-Groag

Time: 1776, summer. Place: A cabin in Eastern Kentucky.

The Homecoming

Patrick Rowen .... Scott MacDonald
Rebecca Talbert .... Katherine Hiler
Star Rowen .... Lillian Garrett-Groag
Michael Rowen .... Stacy Keach
Joe Talbert .... John Aylward
Sallie .... Gail Grate

Time: 1792. Place, Scene 1: A ridge overlooking a vast expanse of mountains and valleys in Eastern Kentucky. Scene 2: Dusk, the front yard of the Rowen house.

Ties That Bind

Patrick Rowen .... Scott MacDonald
Ezekiel Rowen .... Tuck Milligan
Zachariah Rowen .... Ronald Hippe
Sallie Biggs .... Gail Grate
Jessie Biggs .... Ronald William Lawrence
Judge Goddard .... John Aylward
Deputy Grey .... Randy Oglesby
Deputy O'Sullivan .... Michael Hartman
Jeremiah .... Gregory Itzin
Star .... Lillian Garrett-Groag
Guitar Player .... James Ragland

Time: 1819, summer. Place: The Rowen homestead.

God's Great Supper

Jed Rowen .... Tuck Milligan
Ezekiel Rowen .... Stacy Keach
Patrick Rowen .... John Aylward
Joleen Rowen .... Jeanne Paulsen
Richard Talbert .... Gregory Itzin
Randall Talbert .... Ronald Hippe
Rose Anne Talbert .... Katherine Hiler
Julia Anne Talbert .... Lillian Garrett-Groag
Sharecropper #1 .... Randy Oglesby
Sharecropper #2 .... Philip Lehl
Union Colonel .... John Aylward
Rebel #1 .... Patrick Page
Rebel #2 .... Stephen Lee Anderson
Boatman .... Ronald William Lawrence
Tommy Nolan .... Scott MacDonald
Carl Dawkins .... Ronald Hippe
Gus Slocum .... John Aylward
William Clark Quantrill .... Randy Oglesby
Union Soldier #1 .... Michael Hartman
Union Soldier #2 .... Lee Simon Jr.

Church Choir, Mourners, Soldiers: Ensemble.

Time: 1861, early summer. Place: The Rowen cabin, then various places through the border states during the Civil War.

PART II

Tall Tales

Mary Anne Rowen (younger) .... Katherine Hiler
Mary Anne Rowen (older) .... Jeanne Paulsen
J.T. Wells .... Gregory Itzin
Tommy Jackson .... Tuck Milligan
Jed Rowen .... Stacy Keach
Lallie Rowen .... Lillian Garrett-Groag

Time: 1890, summer. Place, Scene 1: The hills of Eastern Kentucky in Howsen County, near the Shilling Creek. Scene 2: The Rowen house.

Fire in the Hole

Mary Anne Rowen Jackson .... Jeanne Paulsen
Tommy Jackson .... Randy Oglesby
Joshua Rowen Jackson .... Ronald Hippe
Doctor; Preacher .... John Aylward
Andrew Talbert Winston .... Gregory Itzin
Mother Jones .... Lillian Garrett-Groag
Cassius Biggs .... Ronald William Lawrence
Sureta Biggs .... Gail Grate
Lucy .... Katherine Hiler
Man in the Woods .... Michael Hartman

Mackie .... Patrick Page
Silus .... Scott MacDonald
Abe Steinman .... Tuck Milligan
Gun Thugs .... Stacy Keach, Patrick Page
Banjo Player .... James Ragland

Miners, Townspeople, Guards: Ensemble.

Time: 1920. Place: The Blue Star Coal camp, mine and environs in Howsen County.

Which Side Are You On?

Joshua Rowen .... Stacy Keach
Scott Rowen .... Scott MacDonald
Margaret Rowen .... Jeanne Paulsen
James Talbert Winston .... John Aylward
Franklin Biggs .... Ronald William Lawrence
Jefferson Biggs .... Lee Simon Jr.
Lana Toller .... Gail Grate
Calvin Hayes .... Tuck Milligan
Chuck .... Stephen Lee Anderson
Mike .... Patrick Page
Greg; Bob Smalley .... Michael Hartman
Stucky .... Randy Oglesby
Sheriff Ray Blanko .... Gregory Itzin

Reporters, Miners, Party Guests: Ensemble.

Time: 1954, early winter. Place: Various locations in Howsen County, Eastern Kentucky, including the Rowen home, a bar and the UMW District #16 Meeting Hall, near the Blue Star Mine.

The War on Poverty

Steve .... Randy Oglesby
Frank .... Tuck Milligan
James Talbert Winston .... John Aylward
Joshua Rowen .... Stacy Keach
Franklin Biggs .... Ronald William Lawrence

Time: 1975, early spring. Place: The original Rowen homestead, near the stump of the Treaty Oak.

Understudies: Mr. Aylward—Michael Hartman; Misses Garrett-Groag, Paulsen—Susan Pellegrino; Miss Grate—Novel Sholars; Miss Hiler—Jennifer Rohn; Mr. Hippe—Philip Lehl; Messrs. Itzin; MacDonald—Patrick Page; Mr. Lawrence—Lee Simon Jr.; Mr. Milligan—Stephen Lee Anderson, Philip Lehl; Mr. Oglesby—Stephen Lee Anderson; Ensemble—Larry Paulsen.

Directed by Warner Shook; scenery, Michael Olich; costumes, Frances Kenny; lighting, Peter Maradudin; original music and sound, James Ragland; fight direction, Randy Kovitz; casting, Pat McCorkle; production stage manager, Joan Toggenburger; stage manager, Tracy Crum; press, Jeffrey Richards Associates.

Violent emotions and conflicts among Kentucky mountian families over two centuries, dramatized in nine episodes, each of them a one-act play, presented in two full programs, the first comprising five episodes with an intermission following *God's Great Supper* and the second comprising four episodes with an intermission following *Fire in the Hole*. Previously produced 6/1/91 at Intiman Theater, Seattle, 2/2/92 at the Mark Taper Forum, Los Angeles, where it was awarded the 1991-92 Pulitzer Prize in drama, and 9/14/93 at Kennedy Center, Washington, D.C.

A Best Play; see page 204.

Any Given Day (32). By Frank D. Gilroy. Produced by Edgar Lansbury, Everett King and Dennis Grimaldi at the Longacre Theater. Opened November 16, 1993. (Closed December 12, 1993)

Mrs. Benti .... Sada Thompson
Carmen Benti .... Andrea Marcovicci
Willis .... Justin Kirk
Gus Brower .... Andrew Robinson
Nettie Cleary .... Lisa Eichhorn
John Cleary .... Victor Slezak
Timmy Cleary .... Gabriel Olds
Eddie Benti .... Peter Frechette
Doctor Goldman .... Stephen Pearlman

Standby: Miss Thompson—Isa Thomas. Understudies: Messrs. Pearlman, Robinson, Slezak—Bill Cwikowski; Misses Marcovicci, Eichhorn—Mary Layne; Messrs. Frechette, Kirk, Olds—Nick Rodgers.

Directed by Paul Benedict; scenery, Marjorie Bradley Kellogg; costumes, Ann Roth; lighting, Dennis Parichy; associate producers, Matt Garfield, David Young; casting, Pat McCorkle; production stage manager, Pamela Singer; stage manager, Brian Kaufman; press, Keith Sherman & Associates, Kevin P. McAnarney, Jim Byk.

Place: The Bronx, New York, west of Grand Concourse. Act I, Scene 1: November 1941, Sunday afternoon. Scene 2: Wednesday, two weeks later. Act II: Fifteen months later, early February 1943, Saturday afternoon.

A prelude to the author's 1965 Pulitzer Prizewinning play *The Subject Was Roses* (which was set in 1946),

ANY GIVEN DAY—Andrew Robinson in one of the year's best performances in a secondary role, with Andrea Marcovicci in the play by Frank D. Gilroy

the new play depicts the roots of tension in the Cleary family and its affiliates, including a stern and clairvoyant matriarch.

Cyrano: The Musical (137). Musical based on the play by Edmond Rostand; music by Ad Van Dijk; book and lyrics by Koen Van Dijk; English lyrics by Peter Reeves; additional lyrics by Sheldon Harnick. Produced by Joop Van Den Ende in association with Peter T. Kulok at the Neil Simon Theater. Opened November 21, 1993. (Closed March 20, 1994)

Man; Capt. De Castel Jaloux ...... Geoffrey Blaisdell
Le Bret .... Paul Schoeffler
Ragueneau .... Ed Dixon
Christian .... Paul Anthony Stewart
De Guiche .... Timothy Nolen
Roxane .... Anne Runolfsson
Valvert .... Adam Pelty
Chaperone .... Joy Hermalyn
Montfleury .... Mark Agnes
Cyrano .... Bill Van Dijk
Cyrano (Wed. eves., Sat. mats.) .... Jordan Bennett
Mother Superior .... Elizabeth Acosta
Novice .... Michele Ragusa

Opera Audience, Cadets, Precieuses, Chefs, Waitresses, Nuns: Elizabeth Acosta, Mark Agnes, Carina Andersson, Christopher Eaton Bailey, James Barbour, Geoffrey Blaisdell, Michelle Dawson, Jeff Gardner, Daniel Guzman, Joy Hermalyn, Bjorn Johnson, Peter Lockyer, Stuart Marland, Kerry O'Malley, Adam Pelty, Tom Polum, Michele Ragusa, Sam Scalamoni, Robin Skye, Tami Tappan, Ann Van Cleave, Charles West.

Orchestra: Constantine Kitsopoulos conductor; Ethyl Will associate conductor, keyboards; Milton Granger keyboards; Jeff Carney bass; Scott Kuney guitar; Lou Oddo, Dean Witten percussion; Neil Balm trumpet; Richard Clark, Nathan Durham trombone; Peter Gordon, Katherine Canfield, French horn; Brian Miller, Lynn Cohen, Richard Shapiro, Donald McGeen woodwinds; Belinda Whitney concert mistress; Rob Shaw violin; Rachel Evans viola; Alvin McCall cello.

Understudies: Miss Runolfsson—Tami Tappan; Mr. Stewart—Peter Lockyer; Mr. Nolen—Geoffrey Blaisdell; Mr. Dixon—Stuart Marland; Mr. Schoeffler—Jeff Gardner; Swings—Ted Keegan, Rose McGuire, Christian Nova.

Directed by Eddy Habbema; musical direction, Constantine Kitsopoulos; scenery, Paul Gallis; costumes, Yan Tax; lighting, Reiner Twebeeke; sound, Rogier Van Rossum; associate set design, Duke Durfee; associate costume design, Marcia K. McDonald; associate lighting design, Brian Nason; associate sound design, Steve Canyon Kennedy; orchestrations, Don Sebesky, Tony Cox; musical coordinator, John Miller; special effects, Gregory Meeh; associate director, Eleanor Fazan; fight director, Malcolm Ranson; executive producer, Robin De Levita; casting, Julie Hughes, Barry Moss; production stage manager, Bob Borod; stage manager, David John O'Brien; press, Merle Frimark, Marc Thibodeau.

Time: 1640. Place: Act I, Paris. Act II, a beseiged camp near Arras, a few months later; then Paris, seven years later.

A foreign production originally staged in The Netherlands. The last major New York revival of the Rostand play was by the Royal Shakespeare Company on Broadway 10/14/84 for 59 performances.

Robert Guillaume replaced Bill Van Dijk 3/8/94.

ACT I

Prologue .... Man, Le Bret, Ragueneau, Ensemble
"Opera, Opera" .... Ensemble
"Aria" .... Montfleury, Cyrano, Ensemble
"One Fragment of a Moment" .... Christian, Roxane
"Confrontation" .... Ensemble
"The Duel" .... Cyrano, Ensemble
"Where's All This Anger Coming From" .... Le Bret, Cyrano
"Loving Her" .... Cyrano, Christian
"A Message From Roxane" .... Chaperone, Cyrano
"Ragueneau's Patisserie" .... Ragueneau, Chefs, Waitresses
"Roxane's Confession" .... Roxane, Cyrano
"What a Reward" .... De Guiche, Le Bret, Ragueneau
"Hate Me" .... Cyrano
"Courage Makes a Man" .... Cadets, Captain
"Cyrano's Story" .... Cyrano, Christian
"A Letter for Roxane" .... Cyrano, Christian
"I Have No Words" .... Christian
"Two Musketeers" .... Cyrano, Christian
"An Evening Made for Lovers" .... Ensemble
"Balcony Scene" .... Roxane, Christian, Cyrano
"Poetry" .... Cyrano, Roxane
"Moonsong" .... Cyrano
"Stay With Me!" .... Ensemble

ACT II

"Every Day, Every Night" .... Cyrano, Christian, Roxane, Cadets
"A White Sash" .... De Guiche, Cyrano, Cadets
"When I Write" .... Cyrano
"Two Musketeers" (Reprise) .... Christian, Cyrano
"Rhyming Menu" .... Roxane, Ragueneau, Ensemble
"Even Then" .... Roxane
"Tell Her Now" .... Christian, Cyrano
"The Evening" .... Cyrano, Cadets
"Even Then" (Reprise) .... Roxane, Cyrano
"The Battle" .... Ensemble
"Everything You Wrote" .... Roxane
"He Loves to Make Us Laugh" .... Nuns, Mother Superior
"A Visit From De Guiche" .... De Guiche, Roxane, Mother Superior
"Opera, Opera" (Reprise) .... Ensemble
"An Old Wound"/"The Letter"/"Moonsong" .... Cyrano, Roxane

***Laughter on the 23rd Floor** (218). By Neil Simon. Produced by Emanuel Azenberg and Leonard Soloway at the Richard Rodgers Theater. Opened November 22, 1993.

Lucas .... Stephen Mailer
Milt .... Lewis J. Stadlen
Carol .... Randy Graff
Max Prince .... Nathan Lane

Val .... Mark Linn-Baker
Brian .... J.K. Simmons
Kenny .... John Slattery
Helen .... Bitty Schram
Ira .... Ron Orbach

Standbys: Messrs. Lane, Orbach—Alan Blumenfeld; Misses Graff, Schram—Alison Martin; Messrs. Linn-Baker, Slattery—Mitchell Greenberg; Messrs. Stadlen, Simmons—Richard Ziman; Mr. Mailer—Allan Heinberg.

Directed by Jerry Zaks; scenery, Tony Walton; costumes, William Ivey Long; lighting, Tharon Musser; associate producer, Ginger Montel; casting, Stuart Howard/Amy Schecter, Jay Binder; production stage manager, Steven Beckler; stage manager, Fredric H. Orner; press, Bill Evans & Associates, Jim Randolph, Sandy Manley.

Place: An office on the 23rd floor of a building on 57th Street, New York City. Act I: March 1953. Act II, Scene 1: Seven months later. Scene 2: Christmas Eve.

An inside look at comedy writers for a New York-based TV variety show, not unlike *Your Show of Shows* or *Caesar's Hour,* on which Neil Simon was employed as a writer in the early years of his career. Previously produced at Duke University, Durham, N.C.

A Best Play; see page 243.

***Angels in America, Part II: Perestroika** (117). By Tony Kushner. Produced by Jujamcyn Theaters and Mark Taper Forum/Gordon Davidson, with Margo Lion, Susan Quint Gallin, Jon B. Platt, The Baruch-Frankel-Viertel Group and Frederick Zollo in association with Herb Alpert at the Walter Kerr Theater. Opened November 23, 1993 in repertory with *Angels in America, Part I: Millennium Approaches.*

Prelapsarianov; Hannah Pitt; Henry;
Ethel Rosenberg;
Rabbi Chemelwitz .... Kathleen Chalfant
Angel; Emily; Mormon Mother ... Ellen McLaughlin
Prior Walter .... Stephen Spinella
Louis Ironson; Sarah Ironson .... Joe Mantello
Joe Pitt .... David Marshall Grant
Harper Pitt .... Marcia Gay Harden
Mr. Lies; Belize .... Jeffrey Wright
Roy Cohn .... Ron Leibman

Council of Principalities: Kathleen Chalfant, David Marshall Grant, Marcia Gay Harden, Ron Leibman, Joe Mantello, Jeffrey Wright.

Understudies: Mr. Leibman—Larry Pine, Matthew Sussman; Mr. Mantello—Matthew Sussman; Messrs. Spinella, Grant—Daniel Zelman; Misses Harden, McLaughlin—Susan Bruce, Beth McDonald; Mr. Wright—Darnell Williams.

Directed by George C. Wolfe; scenery, Robin Wagner; costumes, Toni-Leslie James; lighting, Jules Fisher; original music, Anthony Davis; sound, Scott Lehrer; casting, Meg Simon, Stanley Soble; executive producers, Benjamin Mordecai, Robert Cole; produced in association with the New York Shakepeare Festival; associate producers, Dennis Grimaldi, Marilyn Hall, Ron Kastner, Hal Luftig/126 Second Avenue Corp., Suki Sandler; production stage manager, Mary K Klinger; stage managers, Michael J. Passaro, Maximo Torres, Eric S. Osbun; press, Boneau/Bryan-Brown, Chris Boneau, Bob Fennell.

Place: New York City and elsewhere. Act I: Spooj—January 1986. Act II: The Epistle—February 1986. Act III: Borborgyms—The Squirming Facts Exceed the Squamous Mind, February 1986. Act IV: John Brown's Body, February 1986. Act V: Heaven, I'm in Heaven—February 1986. Epilogue: February 1990. The play was presented in three parts.

Perestroika is Part II of *Angels in America* (subtitled A Gay Fantasia on National Themes) whose Part I, *Millennium Approaches* was produced on Broadway 5/4/93 and was still running when Part II opened. *Millennium Approaches* was named a Best Play of its season and was awarded the Critics and Tony Awards for best play. Parts I and II premiered at the Eureka Theater Company in San Francisco in 1991 and were subsequently produced in November 1992 at the Mark Taper Forum, Los Angeles, where *Millennium Approaches* was awarded the 1993 Pulitzer Prize. *Angels in America* as a whole is a review of modern emotional, intellectual and spiritual crises—particularly the AIDS epidemic—in the hope of a positive future.

F. Murray Abraham replaced Ron Leibman 1/11/94. Susan Bruce replaced Marcia Gay Harden 1/94. Cynthia Nixon replaced Susan Bruce 4/94.

A Best Play; see page 259.

My Fair Lady (165). Revival of the musical based on George Bernard Shaw's play *Pygmalion;* book and lyrics by Alan Jay Lerner; music by Frederick Loewe. Produced by Barry and Fran

Weissler and Jujamcyn Theaters in association with Pace Theatrical Group, Tokyo Broadcasting System and Martin Rabbett at the Virginia Theater. Opened December 9, 1993. (Closed May 1, 1994)

Eliza Doolittle .... Melissa Errico
Freddie Eynsford-Hill .... Robert Sella
Mrs. Eynsford-Hill .... Lisa Merrill McCord
Col. Pickering .... Paxton Whitehead
Prof. Henry Higgins .... Richard Chamberlain
Bystander; Bartender .... Bill Ullman
Hoxton Man .... Bruce Moore
Jamie .... Michael J. Farina
Harry; Prof. Zoltan Karpathy .... James Young
Mrs. Pearce .... Glynis Bell
Butler; Lord Boxington .... Jeffrey Wilkins
Alfred P. Doolittle .... Julian Holloway
Chauffeur .... Michael Gerhart
Mrs. Higgins .... Dolores Sutton
Lady Boxington .... Marnee Hollis
Policeman .... Ron Schwinn
Flower Girl .... Corinne Melançon
Footman .... Ben George
Queen of Transylvania .... Patti Karr
Mrs. Higgins's Maid .... Sue Delano

The "Loverly" Quartet: Jeffrey Wilkins, Bruce Moore, Michael Gerhart, Jamie Mackenzie. Servants: Michael Gerhart, Marilyn Kay Huelsman, Edwardyne Cowan, Corinne Melançon, Meg Tolin.

Orchestra: Burt Collins trumpet I; Laurie Frink trumpet II; Greg Ruvolo trumpet III; Dan Levine tenor trombone; Alan Raph bass trombone; Glen Estrin, French horn; Billy Kerr flute, piccolo; Mitchell Estrin clarinet; Dennis Anderson, English horn, oboe; Steven Boshi bassoon; Ray Kilday bass; David Tancredi drums, percussion; John Mulcahy assistant conductor, synthesizer; Christopher Cardona concertmaster; Alfred Brown viola; Anne Callahan cello.

Understudies: Mr. Chamberlain—Paxton Whitehead; Miss Errico—Meg Tolin, Edwardyne Cowan; Mr. Holloway—James Young; Mr. Whitehead—Jeffrey Wilkins, Bill Ullman; Miss Sutton—Patti Karr; Mr. Sella—Michael Gerhart; Miss Bell—Lisa Merrill McCord; Swings—Newton Cole, Wendy Oliver, John Scott.

Directed by Howard Davies; choreography, Donald Saddler; musical and vocal direction, Jack Lee; scenery based on original designs by Ralph Koltai; costumes, Patricia Zipprodt; lighting, Natasha Katz; sound, Peter J. Fitzgerald; associate producer, Alecia Parker; casting, Stuart Howard, Amy Schecter; production stage manager, Maureen F. Gibson; stage manager, Peter Wolf; press, Richard Kornberg & Associates, Thomas Naro, Barbara Carroll, Don Summa.

The last major New York revival of *My Fair Lady* took place on Broadway 9/18/81 for 119 performances.

The synopsis of scenes and musical numbers in *My Fair Lady* appear on pages 378-9 of *The Best Plays of 1955-56.*

Michael Moriarty replaced Richard Chamberlain 4/8/94.

The Red Shoes (5). Musical with book by Marsha Norman; music by Jule Styne; lyrics by Marsha Norman and Paul Stryker. Produced by Martin Starger in association with MCA/Universal and James M. Nederlander at the Gershwin Theater. Opened December 16, 1993. (Closed December 19, 1993)

Grisha Ljubov .... George De La Pena
Irina Boronskaya .... Leslie Browne
Ivan Boleslavsky .... Jon Marshall Sharp
Livy .... Robert Jensen
Sergei Ratov .... Tad Ingram
Dmitri .... Charles Goff
Boris Lermontov .... Steve Barton
Julian Craster .... Hugh Panaro
Lady Ottoline Neston .... Pamela Burrell
Victoria Page .... Margaret Illmann
(Amy Wilder mat.)
Marguerite .... Jamie Chandler-Torns
Jean Louis .... Scott Fowler
(Don Bellamy mat.)

The Ballet Lermontov: Jennifer Alexander, Anita Intrieri, Don Bellamy, Robert Jensen, Mucuy Bolles, Christina Johnson, Jamie Chandler-Torns, Jeff Lander, Geralyn Del Corso, Christina Marie Norrup, Scott Fowler, Oscar Ruge, Antonia Franceschi, Marie Barbara Santella, Laurie Gamache, Keith L. Thomas, Lydia Gaston, Joan Tsao, Nina Goldman, James Weatherstone, Daniel Wright. Swings: Kellye Gordon, James Hadley, Alexies Sanchez, Catherine Ulissey, Aliceann Wilson.

Orchestra: Katherine Fink, Joshua Siegel, Virgil Blackwell, Eugene Scholtens, Lawrence Feldman, Kenneth Dybisz woodwinds; John Frosk, Richard Raffio trumpet; Santo Russo, David Bergeron trombone; John Clark, Paul Riggo, Janet Lantz, French horn; Elliot Rosoff, Yuri Vodovoz, Paul Woodiel, Blair Lawhead, Maura Giannini violin; John Dexter, Richard Spencer viola; Beverly Laurisden, Eileen Folson cello; Ronald

Raffio bass; Francesca Corsi harp; Bryan Louiselle (assistant conductor), Sande Campbell keyboards; Raymond Marchica, Henry Jaramillo percussion.

Understudies: Mr. Barton—Robert Jensen; Miss Illmann—Amy Wilder; Miss Browne—Laurie Gamache; Mr. De La Pena—Alexies Sanchez; Mr. Panaro—James Weatherstone; Mr. Ingram—Charles Goff; Mr. Sharp—Scott Fowler, Alexies Sanchez; Mr. Goff—Robert Jensen; Miss Burrell—Laurie Gamache; Miss Chandler-Torns—Christina Marie Norrup; Mr. Jensen—Oscar Ruge, James Weatherstone.

Directed by Stanley Donen; choreography, Lar Lubovitch; musical direction and vocal arrangements, Don Pippin; scenery, Heidi Landesman; costumes, Catherine Zuber; lighting, Ken Billington; sound, Tony Meola; ballet and dance music arrangements, Gordon Harrell; music coordinator, Seymour Red Press; orchestrations, Sid Ramin, William D. Brohn; flying, Foy; assistant to choreographer, Ginger Thatcher; casting, Julie Hughes, Barry Moss; production stage manager, Martin Gold; stage manager, Frank Lombardi; press, Frimark & Thibodeau Associates, Marc Thibodeau, Merle Frimark, Erin Dunn, Colleen Brown.

Time: 1921-22. Place: The world of The Ballet Lermontov in London, Paris and Monte Carlo.

Paralleling the story of the 1948 movie of the same title, a ballerina is torn between the demands of romance and the dance, in the process of becoming a star.

ACT I

Scene 1: Covent Garden Opera House—London
Swan Lake .... Irina, Ivan, Grisha, Company
"Impresario" .... Lermontov
Scene 2: Covent Garden Opera House—Lermontov's office
Scene 3: Lady Neston's town house—Mayfair, London
Scene 4: Covent Garden Rehearsal Hall
"The Audition" .... Vicky
"Corps de Ballet" .... Grisha, Company
Scene 5: Julian's hotel room—Paris
"When It Happens to You" .... Julian
Scene 6: Paris Opera House—Lermontov's office
Scene 7: Paris Opera House—on stage
"Top of the Sky" .... Lermontov, Vicky
Scene 8: Paris Opera House—Rehearsal Hall and on stage
Ballet Montage (Swan Lake, Coppelia, Sleeping Beauty, Les Sylphides, Swan Lake) ..... Vicky, Company
Scene 9: Monte Carlo Opera House—Vicky's dressing room
Scene 10: Lermontov's villa—Monte Carlo
"It's a Fairy Tale" .... Lermontov, Julian, Grisha, Sergei, Dmitri
Scene 11: Monte Carlo Opera House—on stage
Scene 12: A restaurant—Monte Carlo
"The Rag" .... Grisha, Company
Scene 13: A promenade—Monte Carlo
"Be Somewhere" .... Julian
Scene 14: Monte Carlo Opera House—on stage
"Am I to Wish Her Love" .... Lermontov, Vicky

ACT II

Scene 1: Monte Carlo Opera House—Vicky's dressing room
Scene 2: Monte Carlo Opera House
The Ballet of the Red Shoes
The Girl .... Victoria Page
The Shoemaker .... Grisha Ljubov
The Young Man .... Jean Louis
Scene 3: Monte Carlo Opera House—on stage/Lermontov's office/backstage
"Do Svedanya" .... Grisha, Sergei, Company
"Miss Page" .... Lermontov
Scene 4: Vicky and Julian's flat—London
"Alone in the Light" .... Vicky
Scene 5: Monte Carlo Opera House—Lermontov's office
"Come Home" .... Lermontov

Scene 6: Vicky and Julian's flat—London/Monte Carlo Opera House—Lermontov's office
"When You Dance for a King" .... Lermontov, Vicky
Scene 7: Monte Carlo Opera House—backstage
Scene 8: Monte Carlo Opera House—Vicky's dressing room
Scene 9: Monte Carlo Opera House—on stage

***Damn Yankees** (103). Revival of the musical based on Douglas Wallop's novel *The Year the Yankees Lost the Pennant;* book by George Abbott and Douglas Wallop; music and lyrics by Richard Adler and Jerry Ross. Produced by Mitchell Maxwell, PolyGram Diversified Entertainment, Dan Markley, Kevin McCollum, Victoria Maxwell, Fred H. Krones, Andrea Nasher, The Frankel-Viertel-Baruch Group, Paula Heil Fisher and Julie Ross, in association with Jon B. Platt, Alan J. Schuster and Peter Breger at the Marquis Theater. Opened March 3, 1994.

Meg Boyd .... Linda Stephens
Joe Boyd .... Dennis Kelly
Applegate .... Victor Garber
Sister .... Susan Mansur
Joe Hardy .... Jarrod Emick
Rocky .... Scott Wise
Smokey .... Jeff Blumenkrantz
Sohovik .... Gregory Jbara
Mickey .... John Ganun
Vernon .... Joey Pizzi
Del .... Scott Robertson
Ozzie .... Michael Winther
Bubba .... Cory English
Henry .... Bruce Anthony Davis
Bomber .... Michael Berresse
Van Buren .... Dick Latessa
Gloria Thorpe .... Vicki Lewis
Betty .... Paula Leggett Chase
Donna .... Nancy Ticotin
Kitty .... Cynthia Onrubia
Photographer; Rita .... Amy Ryder
Welch .... Terrence P. Currier
Lola .... Bebe Neuwirth

Orchestra: Lawrence Feldman, Kenneth Hitchcock, William Meade, Richard Centalonza, Roger Rosenberg reeds; David Stahl, Danny Cahn, Steve Guttman trumpet; Keith O'Quinn, Dale Kirkland trombone; Jack Schatz bass trombone; Ann Yarborough, French horn; Marti Sweet concertmaster; David Niwa, Carlos Villa, Rebekah Johnson violin; Sarah Carter cello; Katherine Easter harp; Ronald Raffio bass; Raymond Marchica drums; Ian Finkel percussion; David Chase associate conductor, piano; Nancy Blair Wolfe keyboard 2.

Standby: Mr. Garber—Patrick Quinn. Understudies: Miss Neuwirth—Nancy Ticotin; Mr. Emick—Michael Berresse, John Ganun; Messrs. Kelly, Latessa, Currier—Scott Robertson; Miss Stephens—Paula Leggett Chase; Miss Mansur—Amy Ryder; Miss Lewis—Robyn Peterman. Swings—Mark Santoro, Robyn Peterman.

Directed by Jack O'Brien; choreography, Rob Marshall; music supervision and vocal arrangements, James Raitt; scenery, Douglas W. Schmidt; costumes, David C. Woolard; lighting, David F. Segal; sound, Jonathan Deans; special effects, Gregory Meeh; orchestrations, Douglas Besterman; dance arrangements, Tom Fay; additional dance arrangements, David Krane; musical coordinator, William Meade; assistant director, Will Roberson; assistant choreographer, Kathleen Marshall; casting, Jay Binder; associate producers, Thomas Hall, Jennifer Manocherian, Jonathan Pilot, Andrea Pines, TDI, Mark Balsam, Meyer Ackerman, Julian Schlossberg, Workin' Man Films, Inc.; production stage manager, Douglas Pagliotti; press, Cromarty & Company, Peter Cromarty, Michael Hartman.

Damn Yankees was originally produced on Broadway 5/5/55 for 1,019 performances. Its only previous New York revival of record was by Equity Library Theater in the 1966-67 season. This 1994 production was originally presented in regional theater at the Old Globe Theater, San Diego.The list of musical numbers in the original production (differing somewhat from that below) appears on pages 413-4 of *The Best Plays of 1954-55*.

ACT I

Overture
"Six Months Out of Every Year" .... Meg, Joe Boyd, Sister, Gloria, Husbands, Wives
"Goodbye, Old Girl" .... Joe Boyd, Joe Hardy
"Blooper Ballet" .... The Senators
"Heart" .... Van Buren, The Senators
"Shoeless Joe From Hannibal, Mo." .... Gloria, The Senators
"Shoeless Joe" (Reprise) .... Gloria, Joe Hardy, Ensemble
"A Little Brains, a Little Talent" .... Lola

DAMN YANKEES—Gregory Jbara, John Ganun, Cory English, Bruce Anthony Davis, Michael Berresse, Dick Latessa, Scott Wise, Jeff Blumenkrantz and Scott Robertson performing one of the numbers in the musical revival

"A Man Doesn't Know" .... Meg, Joe Hardy
"Whatever Lola Wants (Lola Gets)" .... Lola

ACT II

Entr'acte
"Who's Got the Pain?" .... Lola, The Senators
"The Game" .... The Senators
"Near to You" .... Meg, Joe Hardy, Joe Boyd
"Those Were the Good Old Days" .... Applegate
"Two Lost Souls" .... Lola, Applegate
"A Man Doesn't Know" (Reprise) .... Meg, Joe Boyd
Finale: "Heart" (Reprise) .... Company

A Little More Magic (29). Black light performance piece conceived by Diane Lynn Dupuy. Produced by Famous People Players at the Belasco Theater. Opened March 17, 1994. (Closed April 10, 1994)

Keith Albertson
Darlene Arsenault
Gord Billinger

Lesley Brown
Ronnie Brown
Else Buck

Michelle Busby	Paul Edwards
Sandra Ciccone	Greg Kozak
Charleen Clarke	Debbie Lim
Benny D'Onofrio	Thomas O'Donnell
Jeanine Dupuy	Debbie Rossen
Joanne Dupuy	Lisa Tuckwell

Understudies: Sue Ellis, Helen Lee, Jim Stoneburgh, Ginny Young.

Directed by Diane Lynn Dupuy; visual art effects, Mary C. Thornton; lighting, Ken Billington; sound, Tony Meola; narration, Diane Lynn Dupuy; guest celebrity-narrated performances, Ralph Meyers; stage manager, Phil Chart; press, Shirley Herz Associates, Miller Wright, Wayne Wolfe.

Life-size puppets of Elvis Presley, the Beatles, Liberace, etc. and other devices in ultraviolet light rendering the operators invisible, with a recorded score. A foreign (Canadian) troupe in a production presented in two parts.

MUSICAL NUMBERS, ACT I: "A Little More Magic" (Doug Riley); "Operator" (Manhattan Transfer); "Dur Dur d'Etre Bebe" (Jordy); Dying Swan (Camille Saint-Saëns); "Figaro" (Tito Gobbi); "Meow Duet" (Maureen Forrester, Mary Lou Fallis); Aquarium (Camille Saint-Saëns); "If a Tree Falls" (Bruce Cockburn); Beatles Medley (Boston Pops); "Take Five" (Dave Brubeck); "Sing, Sing, Sing" (Benny Goodman); "What a Wonderful World" (Louis Armstrong).

ACT II: "Two Hearts" (Phil Collins); "Proud Mary" (Tina Turner); "Crocodile Rock" (Elton John); "Turn Me Round Polka" (k.d. lang); "Bud the Spud" (Stompin' Tom Connors); Flight of the Bumble Bee (Rimsky-Korsakov); Scheherazade (Rimsky-Korsakov); "A Little More Magic" (Reprise) (Doug Riley); "Jailhouse Rock" (Elvis Presley); "Impossible Dream" (Liberace).

***Jackie Mason: Politically Incorrect** (50). One-man performance by Jackie Mason; created and written by Jackie Mason. Produced by Jill Rosenfeld at the Golden Theater. Opened April 5, 1994.

Design and lighting, Neil Peter Jampolis; sound, Bruce Cameron; production stage manager, Don Myers; press, Zarem, Inc., Robert M. Zarem, Montana Dodel, Andrew Quintero.

Iconoclastic standup comedy reaching into the corners of contemporary life and times.

***Medea** (55). Revival of the play by Euripides; translated by Alistair Elliot. Produced by Bill Kenwright in the Almeida Theater Company production in association with the Liverpool Playhouse at the Longacre Theater. Opened April 7, 1994.

Medea	Diana Rigg	Jason	Tim Oliver Woodward
Nurse	Janet Henfrey	Aegeus	Donald Douglas
Tutor	John Southworth	Messenger	Dan Mullane
Creon	John Turner	Children	Tyler Noyes, Lucas Weisendanger

Women of Corinth: Judith Paris, Jane Loretta Lowe, Nuala Willis.

Understudies: Messrs. Woodward, Mullane—John Woodson; Messrs. Southworth, Turner, Douglas—Mark Hammer; Misses Paris, Lowe, Willis, Henfrey—Tanny McDonald; Children—Blake C. Eastman.

Directed by Jonathan Kent; scenery, Peter J. Davison; costumes, Paul Brown; lighting, Wayne Dowdeswell in association with Rui Rita; music, Jonathan Dove; music associate, Matthew Scott; sound, John A. Leonard; movement, Caroline Pope; production stage manager, Dianne Trulock; press, Philip Rinaldi, Kathy Haberthur, James Morrison, Dennis Crowley, William Schelble.

This Greek tragedy was presented here without intermission in a new translation. Its last major New York revivals of record were in the Japanese language 9/3/86 for 6 performances and in English 5/2/82 for 65 performances with Zoe Caldwell in the title role.

***Twilight: Los Angeles, 1992** (50). Transfer from off Broadway of the one-woman performance by Anna Deavere Smith; conceived and written by Anna Deavere Smith. Produced by Benjamin Mordecai, Laura Rafaty, Ric Wanetik, New York Shakespeare Festival and Mark Taper Forum in association with Harriet Newman Leve, Jeanne Rizzo, James D. Stern, Daryl

Roth, Jo-Lynne Worley, Ronald A. Pizzuti, The Booking Office, Inc. and Freddy Bienstock in the New York Shakespeare Festival production at the Cort Theater. Opened April 17, 1994.

Directed by George C. Wolfe; scenery, John Arnone; costumes, Toni-Leslie James; lighting, Jules Fisher, Peggy Eisenhauer; sound, John Gromada; original music, Wendy Blackstone; projections and video, Batwin + Robin Productions, Inc.; production stage manager, Jane E. Neufeld; stage manager, Jane Gorey; press, Bonneau/ Bryan-Brown, Craig Karpel.

The recent racial strife in Los Angeles, including the Rodney King verdict and Reginald Denny beating, viewed in a series of more than 40 character portrayals by Anna Deavere Smith, the text making use of material adapted by the actress from interviews she conducted with Denny and many others involved as witnesses, police, participants, bystanders, etc. in these events. The work was commissioned by Center Theater Group/ Mark Taper Forum, Gordon Davidson artistic director, and premiered there in June 1993. It was previously produced off Broadway at New York Shakespeare Festival, George C. Wolfe artistic director, 3/23/94 for 13 performances; see its entry in the Plays Produced Off Broadway section of this volume. The play was presented in two parts.

A Best Play; see page 317.

ACT I—Prologue: "Riot" (Chung Lee, president, Korean American Victims Association); "Walking Right" (Ruben Martinez, author/journalist); "Rocked" (Keith Watson, former security guard, co-assailant of Reginald Denny); "Sunset Blvd." (Dorinne Kondo, scholar/anthropologist).

Safe and Sound: "Safe and Sound in Beverly Hills" (Elaine Young, real estate agent); "My Enemy" (Rudy Salas Sr., painter/sculptor); "The Money Train" (Suzanne DePasse, C.E.O. DePasse Productions; former president of Motown); "Broad Daylight" (anonymous young man, former gang member); "The Prom" (Diane Van Iden, Brentwood mother); "Losing a Lot of Blood" (anonymous young woman, former gang member).

No Justice No Peace ("The Story of Latasha Harlins"): "Two Dollars in Her Hand" (Queen Malkah, spokesperson for the Harlins family); "Like a Billard Ball" (Charles Lloyd, attorney for Soon Ja Du); "You Don't Understand" (Jay Woong Yang, liquor store owner).

Control Holds ("The Verdict in Simi Valley"): "Indelible Substance" (Josie Morales, clerk typist, City of L.A.); "Control Holds" (Sgt. Charles Duke, Special Weapons and Tactics Unit, L.A.P.D. Use of Force expert for the defense witness, Simi Valley and Federal Trials); "Your Heads in Shame" (anonymous man juror, first Rodney King trial).

The Social Explosion Rocked: "Butta Boom" (Joe Viola, television writer); "Big and Dreadful Things," Part I (Shelby Coffey II, editor and executive vice president, L.A. *Times*); "Coming From the Church," Part I (Lydia Ramos, reporter); "The Beverly Hills Hotel" (Elaine Young); "Coming From the Church," Part II (Lydia Ramos); "Big and Dreadful Things," Part II (Shelby Coffey II); "Tornado" (Keith Watson); "It's Awful Hard to Break Away" (Daryl Gates, former chief of L.A. Police Department).

Arias: "That's Another Story" (Katie Miller, bookkeeper and acountant); "Godzilla" (anonymous Hollywood talent agent); "To Look Like Girls From Little" (Elvira Evers, general worker and cashier, Canteen Corporation); "National Guard" (Julio Menjivar).

The Park Family: "Kinda Lonely" (Walter Park, store owner, gunshot victim); "To Drive" (Chris Oh, medical student, stepson of Walter Park); "And in My Heart for Him" (Mrs. June Park,wife of Walter Park); "Execution Style" (Chris Oh).

Roar—Fractured Harmony: "The Spirit" (Paul Parker, chairperson, Free the L.A. Four Plus Defense Committee); "It's Coming to Our Area?" (Diane Van Iden); "Roar" (Jessye Norman, opera singer).

Entr'acte: "Twilight," Part I (Homi Bhabha, academic and cultural critic living in London).

ACT II—A Weird Common Thread: "War Zone," Part I (Judith Tur, ground reporter, L.A. *Times*); "No Justice No Peace," Part I (Paul Parker); "War Zone," Part II (Judith Tur); "A Weird Common Thread in Our Lives" (Reginald Denny, semi truck driver); "No Justice No Peace," Part II (Paul Parker).

Here's a Nobody: "Hand Fishin' " (Angela King, aunt of Rodney King); "Front Yard" (Ted Brisenio, police officer acquitted in beating of Rodney King).

What Are You Going to Lose?: "Ask Saddam Hussein" (Elaine Brown, former chairwoman of the Black Panther Party): "What Are You Going to Lose?" (Ruben Martinez); "The Application of the Law" (Bill Bradley, U.S. Senator, D-New Jersey); "The Taiko and the African Drum" (Dan Kuramoto, Jazz Fusion Band leader, Hiroshima); "The Mirror" (Lani Guinier, legal scholar, University of Pennsylvania, and civil rights attorney).

Human Remains: "AA Meeting" (Maria, Juror #7, Federal trial); "Swallowing the Bitterness" (Mrs. Young-Soon Han, former liquor store owner); "Human Remains" (Dean Gilmour, lieutenant, L.A. County Coroner's office); "Twilight," Part II (Twilight Bey, gang member, architect of the Gang Truce).

***Beauty and the Beast** (50). Musical with book by Linda Woolverton; music byAlan Menken; lyrics by Howard Ashman and Tim Rice. Produced by Walt Disney Productions at the Palace Theater. Opened April 18, 1994.

Enchantress	Wendy Oliver	Lumiere	Gary Beach
Young Prince	Harrison Beal	Babette	Stacey Logan
Beast	Terrence Mann	Mrs. Potts	Beth Fowler
Belle	Susan Egan	Chip	Brian Press
Lefou	Kenny Raskin	Mme. de la Grande Bouche (Wardrobe)	Eleanor Glockner
Gaston	Burke Moses	Monsieur D'Arque	Gordon Stanley
Maurice	Tom Bosley	Voice of Prologue Narrator	David Ogden Stiers
Cogsworth	Heath Lamberts		

Three Silly Girls: Sarah Solie Shannon, Paige Price, Linda Talcott.

Townspeople, Enchanted Objects: Joan Barber, Roxane Barlow, Harrison Beal, Michael-Demby Cain, Kate Dowe, David Elder, Merwin Foard, Gregorey Garrison, Jack Hayes, Kim Huber, Elmore James, Rob Lorey, Patrick Loy, Barbara Marineau, Joanne McHugh, Anna McNeeley, Bill Nabel, Wendy Oliver,Vince Pesce, Paige Price, Sarah Solie Shannon, Gordon Stanley, Linda Talcott, Wysandra Woolsey.

Orchestra: Michael Kosarin conductor; Kathy Sommer assistant conductor; Belinda Whitney concertmaster; Cenovia Cummins, Ann Labin, Evan Johnson, George Wozniak, Jean "Rudy" Perrault violin; Caryl Paisner, Joseph Kimura cello; Jeffrey Carney bass; Katherine Fink flute; Vicki Bodner oboe; Alva Hunt, KerriAnn K. DiBari clarinet; Marc Goldberg bassoon; Neil Balm, Tony Kadleck trumpet; Jeffrey Lang, Anthony Cecere, Glen Estrin, French horn; Paul Faulise bass trombone; John Redsecker drums; Joseph Passaro percussion; Stacey Shames harp; Kathy Sommer, Glen Kelly keyboards.

Standby: Mr. Mann—Chuck Wagner. Understudies: Miss Oliver—Kate Dowe, Alisa Klein; Mr. Beal—Gregorey Garrison, Dan Mojica; Mr. Mann—David Elder; Miss Egan—Kim Huber, Paige Price; Mr. Raskin—Harrison Beal, Vince Pesce; Mr. Moses—Merwin Foard, Chuck Wagner; Misses Shannon, Price, Talcott—Kate Dowe, Alisa Klein; Messrs. Bosley, Lamberts, Beach—Bill Nabel, Gordon Stanley; Miss Logan—Joanne McHugh, Sarah Solie Shannon; Miss Fowler—Barbara Marineau, Anna McNeeley; Mr. Press—Linda Talcott; Mr. Stanley—Rob Lorey; Swings—Alisa Klein, Dan Mojica, Joan Barber, Kate Dowe, Gregorey Garrison, Rob Lorey.

Directed by Robert Jess Roth; choreography, Matt West; musical direction and incidental music arrangements, Michael Kosarin; scenery, Stan Meyer; costumes, Ann Hould-Ward; lighting, Natasha Katz; sound, T. Richard Fitzgerald; illusions, Jim Steinmeyer, John Gaughan; prosthetics, John Dods; orchestrations, Danny Troob; musical supervision and vocal arrangements, David Friedman; fight director, Rick Sordelet; musical coordinator, John Miller; dance arrangements, Glen Kelly; casting, Jay Binder; production stage manager, James Harker; stage managers, John M. Atherlay, Pat Sosnow, Kim Vernace; press, Boneau/Bryan-Brown, Chris Boneau, Patty Onagan, Brian Moore.

This musical stage version of the fairy tale was adapted in part from the 1991 Walt Disney animated film and includes its Academy Award-winning score and title song by Alan Menken and the late Howard Ashman, plus additional songs by Menken and Tim Rice, designated with an asterisk * after the title in the listing of musical numbers below.

ACT I

Overture	
Prologue	Enchantress
"Belle"	Belle, Gaston, Lefou, Silly Girls, Townspeople
"No Matter What"*	Maurice, Belle
"No Matter What"* (Reprise)	Maurice
"Me"*	Gaston, Belle
"Belle" (Reprise)	Belle
"Home"*	Belle
"Home"* (Reprise)	Mrs. Potts
"Gaston"	Lefou, Gaston, Silly Girls, Tavern Patrons
"Gaston" (Reprise)	Gaston, Lefou
"How Long Must This Go On?"*	Beast
"Be Our Guest"	Lumiere, Mrs. Potts, Cogsworth, Wardrobe, Chip, Babette, Enchanted Objects
"If I Can't Love Her"*	Beast

ACT II

Ent'racte/Wolf Chase
"Something There" .... Belle, Beast, Lumiere, Mrs. Potts, Cogsworth
"Human Again" .... Lumiere, Wardrobe, Cogsworth, Mrs. Potts, Babette, Chip, Enchanted Objects
"Maison des Lunes"* .... Gaston, Lefou, Monsieur D'Arque
"Beauty and the Beast" .... Mrs. Potts
"If I Can't Love Her"* (Reprise) .... Beast
"The Mob Song" .... Gaston, Lefou, Monsieur D'Arque, Townspeople
"The Battle" .... Company
"Transformation"* .... Beast, Belle
"Beauty and the Beast" (Reprise) .... Company

***Broken Glass** (42). By Arthur Miller. Produced by Robert Whitehead, Roger L. Stevens, Lars Schmidt, Spring Sirkin and Terri and Timothy Childs in association with Herb Alpert at the Booth Theater. Opened April 24, 1994.

Phillip Gellberg .... Ron Rifkin
Margaret Hyman .... Frances Conroy
Dr. Harry Hyman .... David Dukes
Sylvia Gellberg .... Amy Irving
Harriet .... Lauren Klein
Stanton Case .... George N. Martin

Directed by John Tillinger; scenery and costumes, Santo Loquasto; lighting, Brian Nason; sound, T. Richard Fitzgerald; music, William Bolcom; associate producer, Herb Goldsmith; casting, Jay Binder, Terry Fay; production stage manager, Pamela Singer; stage manager, Diane DiVita; press, Bill Evans & Associates, Jim Randolph, Terry M. Lilly.

Time: The last days of November 1938. Place: Brooklyn. The play was presented without an intermission.

The cause of a woman's emotionally-induced paralysis is a mystery: either brought on by the Nazis' *kristallnacht* (hence the play's title) and its aftermath, her domineering husband's tyrannies, or both. Previously produced this season in March at the Long Wharf Theater, Arvin Brown artistic director, New Haven, Conn.

***An Inspector Calls** (40). Revival of the play by J.B. Priestley. Produced by Noel Pearson, The Shubert Organization and Capital Cities/ABC in association with Joseph Harris in the Royal National Theater production, Richard Eyre director, at the Royale Theater. Opened April 27, 1994.

Sybil Birling .... Rosemary Harris
Edna .... Jan Owen
Arthur Birling .... Philip Bosco
Gerald Croft .... Aden Gillett
Sheila Birling .... Jane Adams
Eric Birling .... Marcus D'Amico
Inspector Goole .... Kenneth Cranham
Boy .... Christopher Marquette

Crowd: Joe Ambrose, Judy Baird, Milton Carney, Jenny Conroy, Maryellen Conroy, Mary Ellen Cravens, James Heilman, June Miller, Jimmy Noonan, Connie Roderick, David Sitler, Blaire Stauffer.

Musicians: Terry Farrow conductor, piano; Stephanie Cummins cello; Chuck Olsen trumpet; Jim Baker percussion.

Standbys: Mr. Boscoe—George Morfogen; Mr. Cranham—John Lantz; Messrs. D'Amico, Gillett—Harry Carnahan; Misses Harris, Owen—Catherine Wolf; Miss Adams—Susannah Hoffman; Mr. Marquette—David E. Cantler.

Directed by Stephen Daldry; scenery and costumes, Ian MacNeil; lighting, Rick Fisher; music, Stephen Warbeck; sound, T. Richard Fitzgerald; special effects designer, Gregory Meeh; music coordinator, John Miller; fight direction, B.H. Barry; associate producer, PW Productions, Ltd.; casting, Julie Hughes, Barry Moss; production stage manager, Sally Jacobs; stage manager, Judith Binus; press, Alma Viator, Matt Hagan.

Time: An evening in spring. Place: Brumley, an industrial city in Yorkshire. The play was presented without an intermission.

The American premiere of *An Inspector Calls* took place on Broadway 10/21/47 for 95 performances, after having been staged in Moscow in 1945 and in London in 1946, and it was named a Best Play of its season. The present production is its first major New York revival of record.

The Rise and Fall of Little Voice (9). By Jim Cartwright. Produced by James M. and Charlene Nederlander, Peggy Hill Rosenkranz, Dennis Grimaldi, Pace Theatrical Group, Kevin McCollum, Jon Platt, James L. Nederlander, Leonard Soloway and Michael Codron in the Steppenwolf Theater Company production, Randall Arney artistic director, at the Neil Simon Theater. Opened May 1, 1994. (Closed May 8, 1994)

Mari Hoff .... Rondi Reed
Little Voice .... Hynden Walch
Phone Man; Mr. Boo .... John Christopher Jones
Billy .... Ian Barford
Sadie .... Karen Vaccaro
Ray Say .... George Innes

Studio Musicians: Rokko Jans keyboards; Tom Mendel acoustic and electric bass; Steve Eisen, Paul Mertens reeds; Barbara Haffner cello; Arnold W. Roth violin.

Directed by Simon Curtis; scenery, Thomas Lynch; costumes, Allison Reeds; lighting, Kevin Rigdon; sound, Rob Milburn; action sequences, B.H. Barry; musical direction, June Shellene; technical supervisor, Arthur Siccardi; associate producers, Matt Garfield, Leavitt/Fox Theatricals/Mages, Nick Scandalios; production stage manager, Malcolm Ewen; stage manager, Alden Vasquez; press, Shirley Herz Associates, Sam Rudy.

Time: 1994. Place: A town in northern England. The play was presented in two parts.

Singer with a voice capable of mimicking many different stars such as Barbra Streisand and Judy Garland is exploited by her mother's lover. A foreign play which won the Evening Standard Award for best comedy in 1992 at London's National Theater and had its American premiere in this production at the Steppenwolf Theater Company in Chicago.

***Sally Marr . . . and Her Escorts** (30). Play by Joan Rivers, Erin Sanders and Lonny Price; suggested by the life of Sally Marr. Produced by Martin Richards, Robert Cole, Ron Kastner, Sam Crothers, Dennis Grimaldi, Kenneth B. Greenblatt and 44 Productions at the Helen Hayes Theater. Opened May 5, 1994.

SALLY MARR . . . AND HER ESCORTS—Joan Rivers in her Tony-nominated performance of the title role in a play of which she is also a co-author

Sally Marr .... Joan Rivers
Escort #1 .... Valerie Wright
Escort #2 .... Jonathan Brody
Escort #3 .... Ken Nagy
Voice of Young Lennie .... Jason Woliner

The Band: Tim Weil conductor, keyboard; Aaron Heick reeds; Peter Purpura Brown bass; Joe Damone drums.

Directed by Lonny Price; scenery, William Barclay; production costumes, David C. Woolard; Miss Rivers's costumes, David Dangle; lighting, Phil Monat; original music and orchestrations, Tim Weil; sound, Jan Nebozenko; projection design, Wendall K. Harrington; dance sequences, Lynne Taylor-Corbett; associate producers, Joel Brykman, Kevin Duncan, Randy Finch, Sandra Greenblatt, David Young; production stage manager, Martin Gold; stage manager, Kenneth J. Davis; press, Bill Evans & Associates, Terry M. Lilly, Jim Randolph.

Inspired by the life of Sally Marr, Lenny Bruce's mother, as she strove to establish her own career in show business as a burlesque comic.

***Passion** (26). Musical based on the film *Passione D'Amore* by Ettore Scola and the novel *Fosca* by I. U. Tarchetti; book by James Lapine; music and lyrics by Stephen Sondheim. Produced by The Shubert Organization, Capital Cities/ABC, Roger Berlind and Scott Rudin by arrangement with Lincoln Center Theater at the Plymouth Theater. Opened May 9, 1994.

Clara .... Marin Mazzie
Giorgio .... Jere Shea
Col. Ricci .... Gregg Edelman
Dr. Tambourri .... Tom Aldredge
Lt. Torasso .... Francis Ruivivar
Sgt. Lombardi .... Marcus Olson
Lt. Barri .... William Parry
Maj. Rizzolli .... Cris Groenendaal
Pvt. Augenti .... George Dvorsky
Fosca .... Donna Murphy
Fosca's Mother .... Linda Balgord
Fosca's Father .... John Leslie Wolfe
Ludovic .... Matthew Porretta
Mistress .... Juliet Lambert

Orchestra: Paul Gemignani conductor; Nick Archer associate conductor; Suzanne Ornstein concert mistress; Xin Zhao violin; Sally Shumway viola; Scott Ballantyne cello; Judith Sugarman bass; Dennis Anderson, John Campo, Al Regni, Les Scott woodwinds; Stu Satalof trumpet; Ron Sell, Michael Ishii horns; Nick Archer, Paul Ford keyboards; Thad Wheeler percussion.

Understudies: Mr. Shea—Matthew Porretta, George Dvorsky; Miss Murphy—Linda Balgord, Colleen Fitzpatrick; Miss Mazzie—Colleen Fitzpatrick, Juliet Lambert; Messrs. Aldredge, Wolfe, Dvorsky—Gibby Brand; Mr. Edelman—William Parry; Mr. Porretta—George Dvorsky; Misses Balgord, Lambert—Colleen Fitzpatrick; Messrs. Ruivivar, Groenendaal, Parry, Olson—John Leslie Wolfe; Mr. Dvorsky—Frank Lombardi.

Directed by James Lapine; musical direction, Paul Gemignani; scenery, Adrianne Lobel; costumes, Jane Greenwood; lighting, Beverly Emmons; sound, Otts Munderloh; orchestrations, Jonathan Tunick; associate director, Jane Comfort; casting, Wendy Ettinger; production stage manager, Beverly Randolph; stage manager, Mireya Hepner; press, Philip Rinaldi, James Morrison, Dennis Crowley, Kathy Haberthur, William Schelble.

Time: 1863. Place: Milan and a remote military outpost. The play was presented without intermission.

The obsessive love of a sickly, homely woman for a handsome officer. None of the score is listed as formal musical numbers in the playbill.

A Best Play; see page 336.

The Best Little Whorehouse Goes Public (15). Musical with book by Larry L. King and Peter Masterson; music and lyrics by Carol Hall. Produced by Stevie Phillips and MCA/Universal at the Lunt-Fontanne Theater. Opened May 10, 1994. (Closed May 21, 1994)

Showroom Headliner .... Troy Britton Johnson
Ralph J. Bostick .... Danny Rutigliano
Comedian; President's Hairdresser .... Jim David
I.R.S. Director .... Kevin Cooney
Schmidt; B.S. Bullehit; President .... David Doty
Terri Clark .... Gina Torres
Mona Stangley .... Dee Hoty
Client of the Whorehouse .... Joe Hart
Sam Dallas .... Scott Holmes
Sen. A. Harry Hardast .... Ronn Carroll
Lotta Lovingood .... Pamela Everett

Showroom Patrons: Gerry Burkhardt, Laurel Lynn Collins, Sally Mae Dunn, Tom Flagg, Joe Hart, Don Johanson, Mark Manley, Mary Frances McCatty, Casey Nicholaw, Louise Ruck, William Ryall, Shaver Tillitt,

Jillana Urbina, Richard Vida, Theara J. Ward.

Street Whores: Pamela Everett, Ganine Giorgione, Amy N. Heggins, Lainie Sakakura, Christina Youngman.

Las Vegas Legends: Mary Frances McCatty, Don Johanson, Laurel Lynn Collins, Gerry Burkhardt, Sally Mae Dunn, Theara J. Ward, William Ryall.

Others: Gerry Burkhardt, Laurel Lynn Collins, Sally Mae Dunn, Pamela Everett, Tom Flagg, Ganine Giorgione, Joe Hart, Amy N. Heggins, Don Johanson, Troy Britton Johnson, Mark Manley, Mary Frances McCatty, Casey Nicholaw, Louise Ruck, Danny Rutigliano, William Ryall, Lainie Sakakura, Shaver Tillitt, Jillana Urbina, Richard Vida, Theara J. Ward, Christina Youngman.

Orchestra: Robert Billig conductor; Raymond Beckenstein, Dale Kleps, Edward Zuhlke, Vincent Della-Rocca, Wally Kane woodwinds; Robert Millikan, Larry Lunetta, David Rogers trumpet; John Fedchok, Sonny Russo, Vincent Fanuele trombone; Mary Rowell, Andrew Stein, Paul Woodiel, Melanie Baker violin; Bruce Wang cello; Karl Jurman, Donald Rebic keyboards; Jay Berliner, Steven Bargonetti guitar; John Burr bass; Ronald Zito, James Saporito percussion; Lise Nadeau harp; Susannah Blinkoff, Nancy LaMott, Ryan Perry pit vocalists.

Standbys: Miss Hoty—Lauren Mitchell; Mr. Holmes—J. Mark McVey. Understudies: Messrs. Cooney, Carroll—Joe Hart; Mr. Doty—Danny Rutigliano; Mr. David—Gerry Burkhardt; Miss Torres—Laurel Lynn Collins. Swings: Niki Harris, Vincent D'Elia.

Directed by Peter Masterson and Tommy Tune; choreography, Jeff Calhoun, Tommy Tune; musical and vocal direction, Karl Jurman; scenery, John Arnone; costumes, Bob Mackie; lighting, Jules Fisher, Peggy Eisenhauer; sound, Tony Meola; video, Batwin + Robin Productions; musical supervision and vocal and dance arrangements, Wally Harper; orchestrations, Peter Matz; musical advisor, Robert Billig; musical coordinator, Seymour Red Press; casting, Stuart Howard, Amy Schecter; production stage manager, Arturo E. Porazi; stage manager, Bonnie L. Becker; press, Jeffrey Richards Associates, Kevin Rehac.

Sequel to the 1978 musical *The Best Little Whorehouse in Texas:* The Chicken Ranch's former madam is brought out of retirement to reorganize and run a Las Vegas brothel. The play was presented in two parts.

ACT I

Prologue: The showroom, Las Vegas
"Let the Devil Take Us" .... Las Vegas Legends, Showroom Patrons, Street Whores, Ralph J. Bostick
Scene 1: Conference Room, I.R.S., Washington, D.C.
Scene 2: Cactus Motel, somewhere in Texas
"Nothin' Like a Picture Show" .... Mona
"I'm Leavin' Texas" .... Mona, Texans
Scene 3: In the shadows of the Washington Monument
Scene 4: In the kitchen of the whorehouse, Nevada
"It's Been a While" .... Sam, Mona
Scene 5: The parlor of the whorehouse and Wall Street, N.Y.
"Brand New Start" .... Sam, Mona, Terri, I.R.S. Director, Schmidt, Working Girls, Wall Street Wolves

ACT II

Scene 1: On the information highway
"The Smut Song" .... Sen. A. Harry Hardast
"Call Me" .... Mona, Girls, Couch Potatoes
Scene 2: Air Force One—on the tarmac, LAX
Scene 3: I.R.S. Director's Georgetown home
Scene 4: Sam Dallas's apartment, Washington, D.C.
"Change in Me" .... Sam
Scene 5: An I.R.S. corridor
Scene 6: The hearing
"Here for the Hearing" .... Ladies, Senators
Scene 7: Larry King Live
"Piece of the Pie" .... Mona, Sam, Ladies
Scene 8: Sam Dallas's dressing room, Washington, D.C.
"Change in Me" (Reprise) .... Sam
Scene 9: The Stallion Fields Whorehouse, Nevada
Scene 10: The steps of our nation's Capitol
"If We Open Our Eyes" .... Company

***Grease** (24). Revival of the musical with book, music and lyrics by Jim Jacobs and Warren Casey. Produced in the Tommy Tune production by Barry and Fran Weissler and Jujamcyn Theaters, in association with Pace Theatrical Group and TV Asahi at the Eugene O'Neill Theater. Opened May 11, 1994.

Vince Fontaine	Brian Bradley	Miss Lynch	Marcia Lewis
Danny Zuko	Ricky Paull Goldin	Patty Simcox	Michelle Blakeley
Sandy Dumbrowski	Susan Wood	Eugene Florczyk	Paul Castree
Betty Rizzo	Rosie O'Donnell	Jan	Heather Stokes
Doody	Sam Harris	Marty	Megan Mullally
Frenchy	Jessica Stone	Roger	Hunter Foster
Cha-Cha Degregorio	Sandra Purpuro	Kenickie	Jason Opsahl
Teen Angel	Billy Porter	Sonny Latierri	Carlos Lopez

Straight A's: Clay Adkins, Patrick Boyd, Denis Jones. Dream Mooners: Patrick Boyd, Katy Grenfell. Heartbeats: Katy Grenfell, Janice Lorraine Holt, Lorna Shane. *Grease* Ensemble: Clay Adkins, Melissa Bell, Patrick Boyd, Vincent D'Elia, Katy Grenfell, Ned Hannah, Janice Lorraine Holt, Denis Jones, Addison Metcalf, Lorna Shane.

The High School Band: John McDaniel conductor; Steve Marzullo associate musical director, keyboard; Norbert Goldberg drums; Donald Downs trumpet; Charles Gordon trombone; Timothy Ries saxophone; Alan Cohen guitar; Steven Freeman keyboard 2; Vincent Fay bass; Beth Ravin percussion.

Understudies: Miss Lewis—Patti D'Beck; Miss Blakeley—Melissa Bell; Mr. Castree—Ned Hannah; Miss Stokes—Katy Grenfell; Miss Mullally—Allison Metcalf; Miss O'Donnell—Sandra Purpuro; Messrs. Harris, Porter—Clay Adkins; Mr. Foster—Patrick Boyd; Messrs. Opsahl Bradley, Goldin—Vincent D'Elia; Mr. Lopez—Denis Jones; Miss Stone—Janice Lorraine Holt; Miss Wood—Michelle Blakely; Miss Purpuro—Lorna Shane; Swings—Patti D'Beck, Brian Loeffler, Brian-Paul Mendoza.

Directed and choreographed by Jeff Calhoun; musical direction, John McDaniel; scenery, John Arnone; costumes, Willa Kim; lighting, Howell Brinkley; sound, Tom Morse; vocal and dance music arrangements, John McDaniel; orchestrations, Steve Margoshes; musical coordination, John Monaco; associate choreographer, Jerry Mitchell; associate producer, Alecia Parker; casting, Stuart Howard, Amy Schecter; production stage manager, Craig Jacobs; press, Pete Sanders.

Grease was originally produced on Broadway 2/14/72 for 3,388 performances. This is its first major New York revival.

The list of scenes and musical numbers in *Grease* appears on pages 332-3 of *The Best Plays of 1971-72*.

PLAYS PRODUCED OFF BROADWAY

Some distinctions between off-Broadway and Broadway productions at one end of the scale and off-off-Broadway productions at the other are blurred in the New York Theater of the 1990s. For the purposes of the *Best Plays* listing, the term "off Broadway" is used to distinguish a professional from a showcase (off-off-Broadway) production and signifies a show which opened for general audiences in a mid-Manhattan theater seating 499 or fewer and 1) employed an Equity cast, 2) planned a regular schedule of 8 performances a week in an open-ended run (7 a week for one-person shows) and 3) offered itself to public comment by critics at designated opening performances.

Occasional exceptions of inclusion (never of exclusion) are made to take in visiting troupes, borderline cases and nonqualifying productions which readers might expect to find in this list because they appear under an off-Broadway heading in other major sources of record.

Figures in parentheses following a play's title give number of performances. These figures do not include previews or extra non-profit performances.

Plays marked with an asterisk (*) were still in a projected run on June 1, 1994. Their number of performances is figured from opening night through May 31, 1994.

Certain programs of off-Broadway companies are exceptions to our rule of counting the number of performances from the date of the press coverage. When the official opening takes place late in the run of a play's regularly-priced public or subscription performances (after previews) we count the first performance of record, not the press date, as opening night—and in each such case in the listing we note the variance and give the press date.

In a listing of a show's numbers—dances, sketches, musical scenes, etc.—the titles of songs are identified wherever possible by their appearance in quotation marks (").

HOLDOVERS FROM PREVIOUS SEASONS

Plays which were running on June 1, 1993 are listed below. More detailed information about them appears in previous *Best Plays* volumes of appropriate date. Important cast changes since opening night are recorded in the Cast Replacements section of this volume.

***The Fantasticks** (14,103; longest continuous run of record in the American theater). Musical suggested by the play *Les Romanesques* by Edmond Rostand; book and lyrics by Tom Jones; music by Harvey Schmidt. Opened May 3, 1960.

***Nunsense** (3,513). Musical with book, music and lyrics by Dan Goggin. Opened December 12, 1985.

***Perfect Crime** (2,908). By Warren Manzi. Opened October 16, 1987.

***Tony 'n' Tina's Wedding** (2,062). By Artificial Intelligence. Opened February 6, 1988. (Editor's note: This show fits some but not all conditions of our off-Broadway category, in which it hasn't always been listed. We list it now for information purposes, recognizing the unique place it has made for itself on the New York theater scene.)

***Forever Plaid** (1,794). Musical by Stuart Ross. Opened May 20, 1990.

Beau Jest (1,069). By James Sherman. Opened October 10, 1991. (Closed May 1, 1994)

***Tubes** (1,044). Performance piece by and with Blue Man Group. Opened November 17, 1991.

The Night Larry Kramer Kissed Me (337). One-man performance by David Drake; written by David Drake. Opened June 22, 1992. (Suspended performances January 10, 1993) Reopened February 3, 1993 (Closed June 27, 1993)

Oleanna (513). By David Mamet. Opened October 25, 1992. (Closed January 16, 1994)

Hello Muddah, Hello Fadduh (235). Musical revue with music and lyrics by Allan Sherman; conceived and written by Douglas Bernstein and Rob Krausz. Opened December 5, 1992. (Closed June 27, 1993)

Forbidden Broadway 1993 (288). Musical revue created and written by Gerard Alessandrini. Opened January 12, 1993. (Closed September 19, 1993)

Wrong Turn at Lungfish (145). By Garry Marshall and Lowell Ganz. Opened February 21, 1993. (Closed June 27, 1993)

Jeffrey (365). By Paul Rudnick. Opened March 6, 1993. (Closed January 9, 1994)

Three Hotels (231). By Jon Robin Baitz. Opened April 6, 1993. (Closed October 10, 1993)

Lypsinka! A Day in the Life (46). One-man musical performance by John Epperson; created by John Epperson. Opened May 5, 1993. (Closed June 13, 1993)

Wild Men (59). Musical with book by Peter Burns, Mark Nutter, Rob Riley and Tom Wolfe; music and lyrics by Mark Nutter. Opened May 6, 1993. (Closed June 27, 1993)

Playboy of the West Indies (89). By Mustapha Matura. Opened May 9, 1993. (Closed July 25, 1993)

Later Life (126). By A.R. Gurney. Opened May 23, 1993. (Closed January 2, 1994)

PLAYS PRODUCED JUNE 1, 1993–MAY 31, 1994

Brooklyn Academy of Music. 1992-93 season concluded with **Sheila's Day** (7). By Duma Ndlovu; conceived and created by Duma Ndlovu and Mbongeni Ngema; Ruby Lee role conceived and co-written by Ebony Jo-Ann. Produced by Brooklyn Academy of Music's 651

(King's Majestic Corp.), Mikki Shepard and Leonard Gaines artistic directors, in association with American Music Theater Festival and Houston Grand Opera, in the Crossroads Theater Company production, Ricardo Khan artistic director, at the Carey Playhouse. Opened June 2, 1993. (Closed June 6, 1993)

Stephanie Alston	Annelene Malebo
Terry Burrell	Denise Morgan
Irene Datcher	Tu Nokwe
Thuli Dumakude	La Tangela Reese
Tina Fabrique	Mary Twala
Ebony Jo-Ann	Theara J. Ward

Directed by Mbongeni Ngema; choreography, Thuli Dumakude; scenery, Charles McClennahan; costumes, Toni-Leslie James; lighting, Victor En Yu Tan; vocal arrangement, Irene Datcher, Thuli Dumakude, Mbongeni Ngema, Ebony Jo-Ann, Duma Ndlovu; associate producer, Ken Johnson; production stage manager, Doug Hosney; stage manager, Patreshettarlini Adams; press, Ellen Jacobs, Jennifer Vandestienne.

Time and Place: Perry County, Ala., 1965 and Soweto, Johannesburg, South Africa, 1972. The play was performed without intermission.

Parallel struggles toward liberation by two black women, domestic workers, one in the U.S. and one in South Africa, with interpolations of song and dance—Pentecostal wails, tribal anthems, juke joint blues, Zulu chants. Previously produced in 1992 as part of the National Black Arts Festival.

Manhattan Theater Club. 1992-93 season concluded with **Playland** (24). By Athol Fugard. Opened June 8, 1993. (Closed June 27, 1993) And **A Perfect Ganesh** (124). By Terrence McNally. Opened June 27, 1993. (Closed September 19, 1993) Produced by Manhattan Theater Club, Lynne Meadow artistic director, Barry Grove managing director, at the City Center, *Playland* at Stage II, *A Perfect Ganesh* at Stage I.

PLAYLAND

Martinus Zoeloe .... Frankie R. Faison
Gideon Le Roux .... Kevin Spacey
Voice of "Barking Barney" Barkhuize .... Bill Flynn

Directed by Athol Fugard; scenery and costumes, Susan Hilferty; lighting, Dennis Parichy; sound, David Budries; associate director, Susan Hilferty; associate artistic director, Michael Bush; casting, Nancy Piccone; production stage manager, Sandra Dee Williams; press, Helene Davis, Amy Lefkowitz.

Time: New Year's Eve, 1989. Place: A small travelling amusement park encamped on the outskirts of a Karoo town in South Africa. The play was presented without intermission.

A white and a black actor reveal dark secrets of their past to each other, in a metaphor of life in South Africa. A foreign play previously produced at the Market Theater, Johannesburg and in U.S. regional theater at the La Jolla Playhouse and Alliance Theater.

A PERFECT GANESH

Ganesha .... Dominic Cuskern
Man .... Fisher Stevens
Margaret Civil .... Frances Sternhagen
Katharine Brynne .... Zoe Caldwell

Directed by John Tillinger; movement direction, Carmen de Lavallade; scenery, Ming Cho Lee; costumes, Santo Loquasto; lighting, Stephen Strawbridge; sound, Scott Lehrer; casting, Randy Carrig; production stage manager, Pamela Singer; stage manager, Craig Palanker.

American women touring India discover a new deity in the elephant god Ganesha. The play was presented in two parts.

A Best Play; see page 159.

Prime Time Prophet (54). Musical with book by Randy Buck; music and lyrics by Kevin Connors. Produced by The Prophet Company Limited at the Players Theater. Opened June 10, 1993. (Closed July 25, 1993)

Ginger .... Beth Glover
Max .... Marcus Maurice
B.L.; Tina Rae Tanner .... David Brand
Tim Christy .... Jonathan Hadley
Jennifer McCune .... Janet Aldrich

Musicians: David Wolfson musical director, keyboards; Michael Lipsey drums.

Directed by Kevin Connors; scenery, Don Jensen; costumes, David Robinson; lighting, John Michael Deegan; vocal arrangements, David Wolfson; production stage manager, James Schilling; stage manager, John A. Roff; press, the Pete Sanders Group, Matthew Lenz, David Roggensack.

Satire on evangelical use of television.

ACT I

Scene 1: Hell
"The Devil to Pay" .... Max, Ginger
"Hot Shot" .... B.L.
"The Award" .... Tim
Scene 2: A TV studio
"Saved!" .... Tina, Max, Ginger
"Heavenly Party" .... Tim, Tina, Max, Ginger
"Expect a Miracle" .... Max, Ginger
"Expect a Miracle" (Reprise) .... Tim, Max, Ginger
Scene 3: Tim's dressing room, immediately following
"So Help Me God" .... Jennifer
Scene 4: Tina's dressing room, a week later
"Homesick for Hell" .... Max, Ginger, Tina
Scene 5: The studio, the next morning
"Leap of Faith" .... Tim, Jennifer, Tina, Max, Ginger
"Step Into the Light" .... Tim, Jennifer
Scene 6: Limbo, immediately following
"Diva Supreme" .... Tina, Max Ginger

ACT II

Scene 1: The broadcast
"Tina Seeks Solace" .... Tina, Max, Ginger
Scene 2: Tina's dressing room, immediately following
"Tips From Tina" .... Tina, Jennifer
Scene 3: Limbo, the following week
"Necessarily Evil" .... Tim, Jennifer, Max, Ginger
Scene 4: The broadcast, the following Sunday
"Expect a Miracle" .... Max, Ginger
"How Does She Do It?" .... Max, Ginger
"Tina's Finest Hour" .... Tina
"Armageddon" .... Tina, Company
"Step Into the Light" (Reprise) .... Tim, Jennifer
Epilogue/Finale

Piaf . . . Remembered (175). One-woman performance by Juliette Koka; conceived by Juliette Koka; additional dialogue by Janet Alberti and Milli Janz. Produced by Michael and Barbara Ross at the 45th Street Theater. Opened June 16, 1993. (Closed November 14, 1993)

Musicians: Bill Schimmel accordion; Ron Davis drums.

Musical direction and arrangements, John Marino; lighting and stage manager, Steven Jay Cohen; press, the Pete Sanders Group.

Miss Koka evokes the style and personality of Edith Piaf in selections from her repertory of songs.

MUSICAL NUMBERS: "Padam" (by Norbert Glanzberg and Henri Contet); "Bravo Pour le Clown" (by Louguy and Henri Contet, translated by D. Cohen); "L'Etranger" (by Marguerite Monnet and Robert Malleron, translated by D. Cohen); "L'Accordioniste" (by Michel Emer, translated by D. Cohen); "Mon Dieu" (by Charles

HOWARD CRABTREE'S WHOOP-DEE-DO—Jay Rogers, Peter Morris and Alan Tulin in costumes designed for the musical by Howard Crabtree

Dumont and Michel Vaucaire); "La Foule" (by A. Cabral and Michel Rivgauche); "L'Homme à la Moto" (by Jerry Leiber, Mike Stoller and J. Drejac); "Roulez Tambours" (by Francis Lai and Edith Piaf, translated by D. Marino); "Mon Menage à Moi" (by Norbert Glanzberg and J. Constantin); "La Vie en Rose" (by Louguy and Edith Piaf); "Hymne à l'Amour" (by Marguerite Monnet and Edith Piaf, translated by G. Parsons).

Also: Medley—"Les Trois Cloches" (by J. Villard and B. Reisfeld); "Sous le Ciel de Paris" (by K. Gannon and H. Girau) and "La Goulante de Pauvre Jean" (by Marguerite Monnet and R. Roulaud); "Le Diable de la Bastille" (by Charles Dumont and P. de Lange, translated by D. Marino); "C'Est Toujours la Même Histoire" (by D. White and Henri Contet); "Le Droit d'Aimer" (by Francis Lai and R. Nyel, translated by M. Segwick and Juliette Koka); "A Quoi Ca Sert l'Amour" (by Michel Emer); "Les Blouses Blanche" (by Marguerite Monnet and M. Rivgauche, translated by D. Cohen); "Milord" (by Marguerite Monnet and G. Moustaki); "Non Je Ne Regrette Rien" (by Charles Dumont and Michel Vaucaire, translated by Hal Davis).

Howard Crabtree's Whoop-Dee-Doo! (258) Musical revue conceived, created and developed by Charles Catanese, Howard Crabtree, Dick Gallagher, Phillip George, Peter Morris and Mark Waldrop; songs and sketches by Dick Gallagher, Peter Morris and Mark Waldrop;

additional material by Brad Ellis, Jack Feldman, David Rambo, Bruce Sussman and Eric Schorr. Produced by The Glines, Charles Catanese, John Glines and Michael Wantuck executive producers, and Postage Stamp Xtravaganzas at the Actors' Playhouse. Opened June 29, 1993. (Closed February 20, 1994)

Howard Crabtree
Keith Cromwell
Tommy Femia
David Lowenstein
Peter Morris
Jay Rogers
Ron Skobel
Richard Stegman
Alan Tulin

Directed by Phillip George; musical direction, Fred Barton; additional staging and tap choreography, David Lowenstein; scenery, Bill Wood; costumes, Howard Crabtree; lighting, Tracy Dedrickson; graphic design, Jim Cozby; production stage manager, Michael Henderson; press, William McLaughlin, Tony Origlio Publicity.

The Follies satirized by a gay version.

ACT I

"Whoop-Dee-Doo" .... Howard Crabtree, Jay Rogers, Company
(words by Peter Morris, music by Dick Gallagher)
"Stuck on You" .... Alan Tulin, David Lowenstein, Keith Cromwell
(words by Mark Waldrop, music by Dick Gallagher)
"Teach It How to Dance" .... Peter Morris, Tulin, Lowenstein, Richard Stegman
(words and music by Dick Gallagher)
"Elizabeth" .... Cromwell
(words and music by David Rambo)
"Nancy: The Unauthorized Musical" .... Tommy Femia, Stegman, Lowenstein, Crabtree
(words by Mark Waldrop, music by Dick Gallagher)
"Tough To Be a Fairy" .... Rogers, Tulin, Morris
(words by Mark Waldrop, music by Dick Gallagher)
"Blue Flame" .... Lowenstein
(words and music by Dick Gallagher)
"A Soldier's Musical" .... Company
(words by Peter Morris, music by Dick Gallagher)

ACT II

"It's a Perfect Day" .... Company
(words by Mark Waldrop, music by Dick Gallagher)
"Last One Picked" .... Tulin
(words by Mark Waldrop, music by Dick Gallagher)
"As Plain as the Nose on My Face" .... Lowenstein, Cromwell
(words by Peter Morris, music by Eric Schorr)
"I Was Born This Way" .... Stegman
(words by Peter Morris, music by Dick Gallagher)
"You Are My Idol" .... Company
(words by Peter Morris, music by Brad Ellis)
"The Magic of Me" .... Femia
(by Bruce Sussman and Jack Feldman)
"My Turn to Shine" .... Ron Skobel
(words by Peter Morris, music by Dick Gallagher)
"Less Is More" .... Crabtree, Company
(words by Mark Waldrop, music by Dick Gallagher)

New York Shakespeare Festival Shakespeare Marathon. Schedule of three revivals of plays by William Shakespeare. **Measure for Measure** (17). Opened July 8, 1993; see note. (Closed July 25, 1993) **All's Well That Ends Well** (19). Opened August 5, 1993; see note. (Closed August 29, 1993) **Richard II** (The Tragedy of Richard II) (37). Opened March 31, 1994. (Closed May 1, 1994) Produced by New York Shakespeare Festival, Joseph Papp founder,

George C. Wolfe producer, Jason Steven Cohen managing director, *Measure for Measure* and *All's Well that Ends Well* with the cooperation of the City of New York, David N. Dinkins Mayor, Peter F. Callone speaker of the City Council, Luis R. Cancel Commissioner of Cultural Affairs, Betsy Gotbaum Commissioner of Parks & Recreation, at the Delacorte Theater; *Richard II* at the Anspacher Theater.

MEASURE FOR MEASURE

Duke	Kevin Kline	Friar Peter	John MacKay
Escalus	Helmar Augustus Cooper	Isabella	Lisa Gay Hamilton
Angelo	Andre Braugher	Francisca; A Nun	Charlotte Schully
2d Gentleman	Marc Johnson	Elbow	Ethan Phillips
1st Gentleman	Johnny Garcia	Froth	Ken Cheeseman
Lucio	Ruben Santiago-Hudson	Juliet	Denise Hernandez
Mistress Overdone	Karla Burns	Mariana	Hope Davis
Pompey Bum	Tom Mardirosian	Abhorson	Stuart Rudin
Claudio	Blair Underwood	Angelo's Lieutenant	Stephen Turner
Provost	Peter Francis James	Barnardine	Lanny Flaherty

Ensemble: Brian Barnes, Brigitte Barnett, Ken Cheeseman, John Conlee, Enrique Cruz-DeJesus, Andi Davis, Hope Davis, Stephen DeRosa, Johnny Garcia, Megan Gleeson, Cedric Harris, Caleb Hart, Denise Hernandez, Mercedes Herrero, Marc Johnson, Chris McKinney, Robert Morgan, Ethan Phillips, Stuart Rudin, Charlotte Schully, Annette Stubbins, Stephen Turner, Dina Wright.

Musicians: Steve Sandberg musical director, arranger, keyboards; Jimmy Delgado percussion; Paul Ricci guitar; Bobby Sanabria drums, percussion.

Understudies: Mr. Kline—Stephen Turner; Mr. Braugher—Chris McKinney; Messrs. MacKay, James—Stephen DeRosa; Mr. Underwood—Cedric Harris; Messrs. Santiago-Hudson, Rudin—Marc Johnson; Mr. Phillips—Johnny Garcia; Messrs. Cheeseman, Garcia—Robert Morgan; Messrs. Mardirosian, Cooper—John Conlee; Miss Hamilton—Brigitte Barnett; Miss Davis—Mercedes Herrero; Miss Hernandez—Andi Davis; Miss Burns—Megan Gleeson; Miss Schully—Annette Stubbins; Messrs. Turner, Johnson—Brian Barnes; Mr. Flaherty—Enrique Cruz-DeJesus.

Directed by Michael Rudman; original music and additional lyrics, Andre Tanker; additional songs, Iwan Williams; scenery, John Lee Beatty; costumes, Toni-Leslie James; lighting, Peter Kaczorowski; sound, Tom Morse; choreography, Abdel Salaam; fight direction, Jamie Cheatham; casting, Jordan Thaler; associate producers, Rosemarie Tichler, Kevin Kline; production stage manager, William Joseph Barnes; stage manager, Liz Small; press, Bruce Campbell, Barbara Carroll, James Morrison.

Time: Prior to World War II. Place: A Caribbean Island. The play was presented in two parts.

The last major New York revival of *Measure for Measure* was by Lincoln Center Theater 3/9/89 for 69 performances.

ALL'S WELL THAT ENDS WELL

Countess of Rousillon	Joan Macintosh	Rinalda	Betty Henritze
Bertram	Graham Winton	Lavatch	Rocco Sisto
Lafeu	Henry Stram	Widow Capilet	Patricia Kilgarriff
Helena	Miriam Healy-Louie	Diana	Patrice Johnson
Parolles	Michael Cumpsty	Mariana	Vivienne Benesch
King of France	Herb Foster	Interpreter	Brett Rickaby
Brothers of Dumaine	Mark Deakins, Trellis Stepter	French Gentleman	Michael Stuhlbarg
		Boy	Pierce Cravens

Ensemble: Christopher Michael Bauer, Joel De La Fuente, Enid Graham, Cedric Harris, Steven Liebhauser, Klea Scott, Stephen Turner.

Musicians: Alan Johnson musical director, keyboard; Frank Cassara percussion; Jon Gibson flute, piccolo; Paul Loxtercamp trumpet; Elizabeth Panzer harp.

Understudies: Messrs. Cumpsty, Stram—Christopher Michael Bauer; Misses Henritze, Kilgarriff, Macintosh—Vivienne Benesch; Messrs. Deakins, Stepter—Joel De La Fuente, Michael Stuhlbarg; Misses Healy-Louie, Benesch—Enid Graham; Mr. Stuhlbarg—Cedric Harris; Mr. Winton—Brett Rickaby; Miss

Johnson—Klea Scott; Mr. Cravens—Michael Stuhlbarg; Messrs. Foster, Sisto, Rickaby—Stephen Turner.

Directed by Richard Jones; original music, Jonathan Dove; scenery and costumes, Stewart Laing; lighting, Mimi Jordan Sherin; sound, Tom Morse; movement, Daniel Banks; casting, Jordan Thaler; production stage manager, Ron Nash; stage manager, Lisa Buxbaum; press, Carol R. Fineman, Barbara Carroll, James Morrison.

Place: Rousillon, Paris, Florence, Marseilles. The play was presented in two parts.

The last major New York revival of *All's Well That Ends Well* took place in the Royal Shakespeare Company production on Broadway 4/13/83 for 38 performances.

RICHARD II

King Richard II .... Michael Stuhlbarg
John of Gaunt .... Earl Hyman
Henry Bolingbroke (later Henry IV) .... Andre Braugher
Duke of Norfolk; Earl of Salisbury; Abbot of Westminster ..... Jack Stehlin
Duchess of Gloucester; Duchess of York .... Carole Shelley
Duke of Aumerle .... Patrick Page
Bagot; Sir Stephen Scroop .... Bray Poor
Green; Duke of Surrey; Sir Pierce of Exton .... Boris McGiver
Bushy .... Francis Jue
Duke of York .... Herb Foster
Queen to Richard II .... Elaina Davis
Gaunt's Nurse; Lady Attending Queen .... Drew Richardson
Earl of Northumberland .... Sam Tsoutsouvas
Lord Ross; Lord Fitzwater .... Darryl Theirse
Lord Willoughby; Gardener's Man .... Rene Rivera
Henry Percy; Groom .... Reese Madigan
Lord Berkley .... Daniel Oreskes
Gardener; Keeper .... T.J. Meyers

Courtiers, Marshals, Soldiers, Servants: Francis Jue, Reese Madigan, Boris McGiver, T.J. Meyers, Daniel Oreskes, Patrick Page, Bray Poor, Rene Rivera, Jack Stehlin, Darryl Theirse.

Directed by Steven Berkoff; scenery, Christine Jones; costumes, Elsa Ward; lighting, Brian Nason; music composed and performed by Larry Spivak; casting, Jordan Thaler; production stage manager, Buzz Cohen; stage manager, Ruth Kreshka.

Act I, Scene 1: London, King Richard's palace. Scene 2: London, a room in John of Gaunt's palace. Scene 3: Gosford Green, near Coventry, the lists. Scene 4: The court. Act II, Scene 1: London, a room in Ely-house. Scene 2: The court. Scene 3: The wilds in Gloucestershire. Scene 4: A camp in Wales. Act III, Scene 1: Bolingbroke's camp in Bristol. Scene 2: The coast of Wales. Scene 3: Wales, before Flint Castle. Scene 4: Langley, the Duke of York's garden. Act IV, Scene 1: Westminster Hall. Act V, Scene 1: London, a street leading to the Tower. Scene 2: The Duke of York's palace. Scene 3: Windsor Castle. Scene 4: Windsor Castle. Scene 5: Pomfret Castle. Scene 6: Windsor Castle. The play was presented in two parts.

The last major New York revival of *Richard II* was by New York Shakespeare Festival 6/24/87 for 17 performances.

Note: New York Shakespeare Festival's Shakespeare Marathon is scheduled to continue through following seasons until all of Shakespeare's plays have been presented. *A Midsummer Night's Dream, Julius Caesar* and *Romeo and Juliet* were produced in the 1987-88 season; *Much Ado About Nothing, King John, Coriolanus, Love's Labour's Lost, The Winter's Tale* and *Cymbeline* were produced in the 1988-89 season; *Twelfth Night, Titus Andronicus, Macbeth* and *Hamlet* were produced in the 1989-90 season; *The Taming of the Shrew, Richard III* and *Henry IV, Part 1* and *Part 2* were produced in the 1990-91 season; *Othello* and *Pericles, Prince of Tyre* were produced in the 1991-92 season and *As You Like It* and *The Comedy of Errors* were produced in the 1992-93 season (see their entries in Best Plays volumes of appropriate years).

Annie Warbucks (200). Musical based on the comic strip *Little Orphan Annie;* book by Thomas Meehan; music by Charles Strouse; lyrics by Martin Charnin. Produced by Ben Sprecher, William P. Miller and Dennis Grimaldi by special arrangement with Karen Walter Goodwin at the Variety Arts Theater. Opened August 9, 1993. (Closed January 30, 1994)

Annie Warbucks .... Kathryn Zaremba
Sandy .... Cindy Lou
Oliver Warbucks .... Harve Presnell
Grace Farrell .... Marguerite MacIntyre
Drake .... Kip Niven
Mrs. Pugh; Dr. Margaret Whittleby ... Brooks Almy
Simon Whitehead .... Joel Hatch
The Orphans:
Molly .... Ashley Pettet
Pepper .... Missy Goldberg
Tessie .... Elisabeth Zaremba
Kate .... Rosie Harper
Peaches .... Natalia Harris
Mrs. Sheila Kelly .... Donna McKechnie

Warbucks Accountant; Fletcher;
David Lillianthal; Mr. Stanley .. Michael E. Gold
Warbucks Accountant; Harry; Hobo;
Sen. Arthur I. Vandenberg .... Steve Steiner
Commissioner Harriet Doyle .... Alene Robertson
Miss Clark; Gladys .... Colleen Fitzpatrick
Trainman; Man in Stetson Hat .... J.B. Adams
Hobo .... Jennifer L. Neuland
Alvin T. Paterson .... Harvey Evans
C.G. Paterson .... Jackie Angelescu
Ella Paterson .... Molly Scott
President Franklin Delano
Roosevelt .... Raymond Thorne

Warbucks's Staff: J.B. Adams, Collen Fitzpatrick, Michael E. Gold, Jennifer L. Neuland. White House Aides: J.B. Adams, Brooks Almy, Jennifer L. Neuland. Wedding Guests: J.B. Adams, Colleen Fitzpatrick, Jennifer L. Neuland, Steve Steiner.

Orchestra: Keith Levenson musical director, synthesizer; Andrew Wilder assistant musical director, synthesizer; David Bargeron trombone, tuba; Donald Haviland woodwinds; Jeff Potter drums, percussion; Burt Collins trumpet, flugelhorn.

Standbys: Mr. Presnell—Steve Steiner; Kathryn Zaremba—Missy Goldberg; Misses Robertson, Scott—Brooks Almy; Misses MacIntyre, McKechnie—Colleen Fitzpatrick; Messrs. Thorne, Niven—Michael E. Gold; Messrs. Hatch, Evans—J.B. Adams; Orphans—Alexis Dale Fabricant; Miss Almy—Jennifer L. Neuland; Cindy Lou—Cosmo.

Directed by Martin Charnin; choreography, Peter Gennaro; scenery, Ming Cho Lee; costumes, Theoni V. Aldredge; lighting, Ken Billington; sound, Tom Sorce; orchestrations, Keith Levenson; casting, Sherie L. Seff; associate producers, Amy Miller, Matthew Garfield, David Young, Bulldog Theatrical Productions, Inc., Eve-Lynn Miller; production stage manager, Jeffrey M. Markowitz; stage manager, Jill Cordle; press, Jeffrey Richards Associates, Tom D'Ambrosio, William Schelble.

Sequel to the musical *Annie;* Little Orphan Annie has been adopted by Daddy Warbucks, who must now find a wife within 60 days in order to make the adoption stick.

ACT I

Scene 1: The living room of the Warbucks mansion, Christmas moning, 1933
"A New Deal for Christmas" .... Company
"Annie Isn't Just Annie Any More" .... Annie, Warbucks, Grace, Drake, Staff
Scene 2: Warbucks's study, a moment later
"Above the Law" .... Commissioner Doyle
Scene 3: The balcony outside Warbucks's study, immediately after
"Changes" .... Warbucks, Annie
Scene 4: The orphanage playground in downtown Manhattan, two weeks later
"The Other Woman" .... Orphans
"The Other Woman" (reprise) .... Orphans
Scene 5: The breakfast room of the Warbucks mansion, a month later
Scene 6: The kitchen of the Warbucks mansion, moments later
"That's the Kind of Woman" .... Drake, Annie, Warbucks, Servants
"A Younger Man" .... Warbucks
Scene 7: Commissioner Doyle's office, the NYC Department of Child Welfare, the following Thursday morning
"But You Go On" .... Mrs. Kelly
"Above the Law" (Reprise) .... Commissioner Doyle, Mrs. Kelly
Scene 8: The front hallway of the Warbucks mansion, an hour later
"When You Smile" .... Warbucks, Annie, Orphans
"I Got Me" .... Annie, Orphans
Scene 9: The Pennsylvania Railroad yards, later that night
"I Got Me" (Reprise) .... Annie

ACT II

Scene 1: A sharecropper's cabin in rural Tennessee, six weeks later, April 1934
"Love" .... Ella
"Love" (Reprise) .... Annie, C.G. Paterson
Scene 2: The White House Communications Office, Washington, D.C., late afternoon of the following day
"Somebody's Gotta Do Somethin' " .... Annie, Patersons, Roosevelt, Grace, White House Staff
"Leave It to the Girls" .... Commissioner Doyle, Mrs. Kelly

ANNIE WARBUCKS—Cindy Lou (Sandy), Kathryn Zaremba (Annie) and Harve Presnell (Daddy Warbucks) in a scene from the Thomas Meehan-Charles Strouse-Martin Charnin musical sequel to *Annie*

Scene 3: The top deck of the Staten Island Ferry, the following Saturday night
"All Dolled Up" .... Orphans, Annie, Warbucks, Grace, Roosevelt, Patersons, Staff
"The Tenement Lullaby" .... Mrs. Kelly
"It Would Have Been Wonderful" .... Grace
Scene 4: An art deco suite in the Waldorf-Astoria Hotel, the following Wednesday evening, shortly before 9 p.m.

"Changes" (Reprise) .... Warbucks, Annie
Scene 5: A ballroom in the Waldorf-Astoria, an instant later
"Wedding, Wedding" .... Company
"I Always Knew" .... Annie

A Better Life (23). By Louis Delgado Jr. Produced by Hospital Audiences, Inc. Theater Festival at Theater Row Theater. Opened August 11, 1993. (Closed August 29, 1993)

Marty .... Byron Utley
Norma .... Rachel Follett Avidon
Kelvin .... Lenwood Benitez
Nurse .... Sharon Hope
Howard .... Jeff Ranara
Pat .... Man-ching Lorber
David .... Tom Gerard

Directed by Max Daniels; scenery, Miguel Lopez-Castillo; costumes, Susan Ruddie; lighting, Steven Rust; sound, Mike Sargent; production stage manager, Frank Laurents.

Two hospitalized H.I.V.-positive patients, one a drug addict, explore the common ground of their humanity. Previously produced off off Broadway.

Asylum (32). By Mark Pearce. Produced by Robert Pearce in association with Sigma Theatrical Group at the Hudson Guild Theater. Opened August 17, 1993. (Closed September 12, 1993)

Peter Mathews .... Timothy Greeson
Ann Dailey .... Mary Walter
Jack Dailey .... Michael Wilson
Phil Burroughs .... Jim Ivey
Officer Jameson .... Jerry Ferris
Burglar .... Skip Maloney
Dr. Ream .... Brian Gagné
Janet Opel .... Teresa Ashford
Harry .... Tim Doherty
Nigel .... Francis Fabrizio
Mr. Cross .... Neal Heinze

Understudies: Tom Wade, Marilyn Matarrese, Juliane Dressner, Malik Purley.

Directed by Tim Taylor; scenery, Jean Raveau; costumes, Starr Fisher; lighting, Elizabeth Farshtey; stage manager, Lisa Holzemer.

Time: The present.

A man's life is changed when he comes to believe the Ralph Waldo Emerson statement that the world is an asylum for angels who have lost their minds.

1993 Young Playwrights Festival (24). Program of four one-act plays: *Crystal Stairs* by Kim Daniel, *Five Visits From Mr. Whitcomb* by Carter L. Bays, *Sweetbitter Baby* by Madeleine George and *Live From the Edge of Oblivion* by Jerome D. Hairston. Produced by Young Playwrights, Inc., Sheri M. Goldhirsch artistic director, Brett W. Reynolds managing director, in association with Playwrights Horizons at Playwrights Horizons. Opened September 22, 1993. (Closed October 10, 1993)

Crystal Stairs

Evette .... Stacy Highsmith
Ulis .... Ron Brice
Genesis .... Aleta Mitchell
Boy .... Curtis McClarin

Directed by Mark Brokaw; fight direction, Rick Sordelet; dramaturge, Eduardo Machado; stage manager, Lloyd Davis Jr.

Pregnant teen-ager in conversation with homeless man on a subway car.

Five Visits From Mr. Whitcomb

Tom .... Daniel Jenkins
Mr. Whitcomb .... Robert Stanton
Dr. Benton .... Camryn Manheim
Sheriff .... Paul Bates
Fedeal Agent .... Ramon Melindez Moses

Directed by Michael Mayer; dramaturge, Paul Selig; stage manager, Lloyd Davis Jr.

An innocent in confrontation with an IRS representative.

Sweetbitter Baby

Malina .... Lucy Deakins
Sasha .... Michael Stuhlbarg

Directed by Seret Scott; dramaturge, Victoria Abrash; stage manager, Peter J. Davis.

High school romance goes awry after graduation.

Live From the Edge of Oblivion

Johnas .... Akili Prince
Sir Hoodlum; Frank Tuff;
Mista Say No .... Curtis McClarin
Mista Officer; Reporter;
TV Announcer .... Paul Bates
Bobby D.; Brother Winno .... Ramon Melindez Moses
Hood Mother; Mama;
Mutha Crackhead .... Lisa Louise Langford
Teacher .... Lucy Deakins

Directed by Marion McClinton; dramaturge, Morgan Jenness; stage manager, Peter J. Davis.

ALL PLAYS: Scenery, Allen Moyer; costumes, Caryn Neman; lighting, Pat Dignan; sound, Raymond D. Schilke; casting, Janet Foster.

These four plays were selected from hundreds of entries in Young Playwrights, Inc.'s 12th annual playwriting contest for authors 18 years of age or younger at the time of submission. The program was presented in two parts with an intermission after *Five Visits From Mr. Whitcomb.*

Brooklyn Academy of Music. Schedule of three programs. **The Madness of George III** (17). By Alan Bennett; produced in the Royal National Theater of Great Britain production. Opened September 28, 1993. (Closed October 10, 1993) **Sacrifice of Mmbatho** (Daughter of Nebo) (12). Conceived and written by Hilary Blecher; produced in the Market Theater Company production. Opened March 2, 1994. (Closed March 13, 1994) **The Winter's Tale** (8). Revival of the play by William Shakespeare; produced in the Royal Shakespeare production. Opened April 19, 1994. (Closed April 24, 1994) Produced by Brooklyn Academy of Music, Harvey Lichtenstein president and executive producer, *The Madness of George III* and *The Winter's Tale* at Brooklyn Academy of Music, *Sacrifice of Mmbatho* at the Carey Playhouse.

THE MADNESS OF GEORGE III

The Royal Family:
King George III .... Nigel Hawthorne
Queen Charlotte .... Selina Cadell
Prince of Wales .... Nick Sampson
Duke of York .... Julian Rhind-Tutt
The Royal Household:
Lady Pembroke .... Richenda Carey
Fitzroy .... Anthony Calf
Greville .... William Chubb
Papandiek .... Matthew Lloyd Davies
Fortnum .... William Oxborrow
Braun .... Paul Corrigan
The Government:
William Pitt .... Julian Wadham
Lord Thurlow .... Jeffry Wickham
Henry Dundas .... Simon Scott
Sir Boothby Skrymshir .... Collin Johnson
Ramsden .... Adam Barker
The Opposition:
Charles James Fox .... David Verrey
Richard Brinsley Sheridan .... Iain Mitchell
The Doctors:
Sir George Baker .... Roger Hammond
Dr. Richard Warren .... Robert Swann
Sir Lucas Pepys .... Cyril Shaps
Dr. Francis Willis .... Clive Merrison
Margaret Nicholson .... Richenda Carey
Maid .... Celestine Randall
Footman .... Tony Sloman

Footmen, Courtiers, MPs, Dr. Willis's Assistants: Members of the Company.

Directed by Nicholas Hytner; design, Mark Thompson; lighting, Brian Ridley; original lighting, Paul Pyant; music, Kevin Leeman; sound, Scott Myers; stage manager, Courtney Bryant; press, Boneau/Bryan-Brown, Bob Fennell.

Time: 1788-89.

Study of George III's personality before, during and after an attack of madness apparently caused by the illness called porphyria. A foreign play previously produced in London.

A Best Play; see page 180.

SACRIFICE OF MMBATHO (DAUGHTER OF NEBO)

David Thobela .... Max Ngcobo
Ma Thobela .... Thembi Mtshali
Mmakhudu; Sangoma; Villager .... Baby Cele
Sempethe .... Tshidi Manye
Constance; Sangoma .... Thembi Sambo
Mrs. Nakeni; Sangoma .... Felicia Mahambehlala
Mr. Nakeni .... Sam Phillips
Mr. Komane .... Vuyisile Bojana
Mogase (Chief Sangoma) .... Doris Sihula
Mr. Maponyane;
Court Interpreter .... Henry Faca Kulu
Umthakathi; Villager .... Mpumi Shelembe
Sangoma; Comrade .... Nkosana Mzolo
Comrade .... Peter Mashigo
Old Man .... Norman Ntsiko
Musicians .... Mthandeni Mvelase, Mdudzi Nzuza

Directed by Hilary Blecher; music by Victor N'Toni, Rashid Lanie; choreography, Nomsa Kupi Manaka; scenery adapted from Sarah Roberts design; costumes, Sarah Roberts; lighting, Mannie Manim; vocal coach, Irene Frangs; stage manager, Gabriele Blecher; press, William Murray, Kyrie Mackinnon.

Time: 1991. Place: Nebo and the Supreme Court in Pretoria. The play was presented in two parts.

Based on a documentary video made by Sara Blecher in collaboration with James Mthoba, in a village beset with demonic influences, a father who cannot find a cow for a ritual sacrifice substitutes his daughter. A foreign play commissioned by the Brooklyn Academy of Music and workshopped at the Market Theater in Johnannesburg.

THE WINTER'S TALE

In Sicilia:
Archidamus; Paulina's Steward ... Don Gallagher
Camillo .... Paul Jesson
Polixenes .... Julian Curry
Leontes .... John Nettles
Hermione .... Suzanne Burden
Emilia .... Angela Vale
Lady .... Ruth Jones
Lords .... Richard Long, Guy Williams
Antigonus .... John Bott
Paulina .... Gemma Jones
Gaoler .... David Acton
Cleomenes .... William Haden
Dion .... James Walker
Mariner .... Ian Taylor
Mamillius: David Leslie, Jeremy Levitsky, Peter Munro, Simon Walton.
In Bohemia:
Old Shepherd .... Jeffry Dench
Young Shepherd .... Graham Turner
Autolycus .... Mark Hadfield
Florizel .... Barnaby Kay
Perdita .... Phyllida Hancock
Dorcas .... Emma Gregory
Mopsa .... Stephanie Jacob
Shepherd's Servant .... Jack Waters
Children: Chelsea Stevens, Merin Reyes, Miriem Hess. Other parts played by members of the cast.

Musicians: Peter Standaart flute; Andy Grenci clarinet, saxophone; Gary Bennett bassoon, contrabassoon; Chuck Bumcrot trumpet; George Hoyt trombone; Andy Rogers tuba, sousaphone; Larry Deming violin, mandolin; Tony McVey percussion; Roger Hellyer keyboards.

Understudies: Mr. Nettles—David Acton; Mr. Hadfield—Don Gallagher; Misses Hancock, Jones—Emma Gregory; Mr. Jesson—William Haden; Miss Burden—Stephanie Jacob; Misses Vale, Jacob, Gregory, Mr. Waters—Ruth Jones; Mr. Turner—Richard Long; Messrs. Gallagher, Dench, Acton—Ian Taylor; Miss Jones—Angela Vale; Mr. Bott—James Walker; Messrs. Kay, Haden, Walker—Jack Waters; Messrs. Curry, Taylor—Guy Williams.

Directed by Adrian Noble; scenery and costumes, Anthony Ward; lighting, Chris Parry, recreated for the tour by Mike Gunning; music, Shaun Davey; movement, Sue Lefton; sound, Paul Slocombe, recreated for the tour by Michael McCoy; musical direction, Roger Hellyer; stage manager, Michael Dembowicz; U.S. production stage manager, Mitchell Erickson; U.S. stage manager, John Handy; press, Boneau/Bryan-Brown, Bob Fennell.

The last major New York revival of record of *The Winter's Tale* was in New York Shakespeare Festival's Shakespeare Marathon 3/21/89 for 24 performances. The 1994 production was presented in two parts.

***Blown Sideways Through Life** (213). One-woman performance by Claudia Shear; written by Claudia Shear. Produced by New York Theater Workshop, James C. Nicola artistic director, Nancy Kassak Diekmann managing director, in the 6th annual O Solo Mio Festival at New York Theater Workshop. Opened September 29, 1993 (see note).

Scenery, Loy Arcenas; costumes, Jess Goldstein; lighting, Christopher Akerlind; sound, Aural Fixation; original music, Richard Peaslee; choreography, Nafisa Sharriff; production stage manager, Kate Broderick; press, Richard Kornberg, Don Summa.

An autobiographical piece, adventures and misadventures in and out of 64 jobs. The play was presented without intermission.

Note: After 51 performances at New York Theater Workshop, *Blown Sideways Through Life* transferred to the Cherry Lane Theater January 7, 1994, for an additional commercial run produced by James B. Freydberg, William B. O'Boyle, Sonny Everett, Evangeline Morphos, Nancy Richards and Dori Berinstein.

In Persons (53). Two-actor performance by Eli Wallach and Anne Jackson as themselves; written by various authors (see listing below). Produced by Martin R. Kaufman at the Kaufman Theater. Opened September 30, 1993. (Closed November 14, 1993)

Directed by Martin Charnin; scenery, Ann Keehbauch; lighting, Ken Billington, Jason Kantrowitz; sound, Raymond D. Schilke; music composed and produced by Keith Levenson; production stage manager, Anne Marie Paolucci; press, David Rothenberg Associates.

The husband-and-wife team recounting anecdotes from their careers and personal lives and performing selected scenes, poems and other material. The play was presented in two parts.

Program included selections from *The Waltz of the Toreadors* by Jean Anouilh, *Enid Bagnold's Autobiography, Home Burial* by Robert Frost, poems of Samuel Hoffenstein, *Recuerdo* by Edna St. Vincent Millay, writings by Dorothy Parker, *Harlequinade* by Terence Rattigan, *Luv* by Murray Schisgal, *Life Story* by Tennessee Williams and *Go, Lovely Rose* by Edmund Waller.

Circle Repertory Company. Schedule of five programs. **The Fiery Furnace** (64). By Timothy Mason. Opened October 5, 1993. (Closed November 28, 1993) **Desdemona—A Play About a Handkerchief** (30). By Paula Vogel. Opened November 11, 1993. (Closed December 5, 1993) **A Body of Water** (18) by Jenna Zark, opened February 9, 1994 in repertory with **Escape From Paradise** (18) one-woman performance by Regina Taylor, written by Regina Taylor, opened February 17, 1994. (Repertory closed March 13, 1994) **Moonshot and Cosmos** (32). Program of two monologues by Lanford Wilson; performed by John Dossett and Judith Ivey. Opened May 3, 1994. (Closed May 29, 1994) Produced by Circle Repertory Company, Tanya Berezin artistic director, Abigail Evans managing director, *The Fiery Furnace* at the Lucille Lortel Theater, *Desdemona—A Play About a Handkerchief, A Body of Water, Escape From Paradise* and *Moonshot and Cosmos* at Circle Repertory Theater.

THE FIERY FURNACE

Faith .... Ashley Gardner
Jerry .... William Fichtner
Charity .... Susan Batten
Eunice .... Julie Harris
Louis .... Zach Grenier

Directed by Norman Rene; scenery, Loy Arcenas; costumes, Walter Hicklin; lighting, Debra J. Kletter; sound, Tom Clark; dialect coach, Ralph Zito; production stage manager, Denise Yaney; press, Bill Evans & Associates, Roger Bean, Tom D'Ambrosio.

Place: Chippewa Falls, Wis., the kitchen of a large, old farmhouse. Act I: August 1950, June 1953 and Thanksgiving Day 1956. Act II: New Year's Eve 1963.

As the women in a family strive for various forms of freedom, their lives are endangered by the conscienceless greed of one of the husbands. Previously produced in East Hampton, N.Y.

DESDEMONA—A PLAY ABOUT A HANDKERCHIEF

Emilia .... Fran Brill
Desdemona .... J. Smith-Cameron
Bianca .... Cherry Jones

Directed by Gloria Muzio; scenery, Derek McLane; costumes, Jess Goldstein; lighting, Michael Lincoln; original music and sound design, Randy Freed; fight direction, Rick Sordelet; production stage manager, Fred Reinglas.

Prologue: Ages ago. Time: A week later, on Desdemona's last day. Place: Cyprus. The play was presented without intermission.

Comedy, if Desdomona were in fact the bawd that Iago pretended she was in Shakespear's *Othello*. Previously produced by the Bay Street Theater, Sybil Christopher and Emma Walton co-artistic directors, Stephen Hamilton executive producer, of Sag Harbor, L.I., in conjunction with Circle Repertory.

A BODY OF WATER

Sandy; Malka .... Jodi Thelen
Eddie; Gershon .... Bruce MacVittie
Devi .... Stephanie Roth
Betty .... Maggie Burke
Rabbi Joel Messinger .... Don T. Maseng
Dr. Natalie Carroll .... Nikki Rene

Directed by Carolina Kava; production stage manager, Denise Yaney. Jewish women practice an ancient bathing ritual to bring new meaning to their ordinary lives. The play was presented in two parts.

ESCAPE FROM PARADISE

Directed by Anne Bogart; production stage manager, M.A. Howard. A black woman reviews important events and characters in her past and during a trip to Venice.

BOTH PLAYS: Scenery, Loy Arcenas; lighting, Brian Aldous; costumes, Thomas L. Keller; sound, Darron L. West.

MOONSHOT AND COSMOS

A Poster of the Cosmos

Tom .... John Dossett

The Moonshot Tape

Diane .... Judith Ivey

Directed by Marshall W. Mason; scenery, John Lee Beatty; costumes, Walter Hicklin; lighting, Dennis Parichy; original music, Peter Kater; sound, Donna Riley; production stage manager, Denise Yaney.

In *A Poster of the Cosmos,* a gay man who has lost a lover to AIDS is being interrogated by police. In *The Moonshot Tape,* a slightly tipsy New York writer visiting her home town in Missouri is interviewed by a reporter for the high school paper.

***Family Secrets** (264). One-woman performance by Sherry Glaser; written by Sherry Glaser and Greg Howells. Produced by David Stone, Irene Pinn and Amy Nederlander-Case in association with Harriet Newman Leve and Robert J. Linden at the Westside Theater. Opened October 6, 1993.

Directed by Greg Howells; scenery, Rob Odorisio; costumes, Lorraine Anderson; lighting, Brian MacDevitt; production stage manager, Cathy B. Blaser; press, the Pete Sanders Group, Pete Sanders, Ian Rand, David Roggensack.

Portrayal of five members of a Jewish American family: Father, Mother, Elder Sister, Younger Sister and Grandma. The play was presented without intermission. Previously produced in Los Angeles, San Diego and elsewhere in the U.S.

***Playwrights Horizons.** Schedule of four programs. **Sophistry** (32). By Jonathan Marc Sherman. Opened October 11, 1993. (Closed November 7, 1993) **An Imaginary Life** (33). By Peter Parnell. Opened December 5, 1993. (Closed January 2, 1994) **Avenue X** (48). Musical with concept and book by John Jiler; music by Ray Leslee; lyrics by John Jiler and Ray Leslee. Opened February 21, 1994. (Closed April 3, 1994) ***Moe's Lucky Seven** (18). By Marlane Meyer. Opened May 15, 1994. Produced by Playwrights Horizons, Don Scardino artistic director, Leslie Marcus managing director, at Playwrights Horizons, *Sophistry* at the Studio Theater, *An Imaginary Life, Avenue X* and *Moe's Lucky Seven* at the Anne G. Wilder Theater.

AVENUE X—Performing *a cappella* in this John Jiler-Ray Leslee musical at Playwrights Horizons: Colette Hawley, Keith Johnston, Chuck Cooper, Roger Mazzeo, Harold Perrineau, John Leone, Ted Brunetti, Alvaleta Guess

SOPHISTRY

Whitey McCoy .... Austin Pendleton
Willy .... Steve Zahn
Igor Konigsberg .... Jonathan Marc Sherman
Xavier Reynolds .... Ethan Hawke
Robin Smith .... Calista Flockhart
Quintana Matheson .... Linda Atkinson
Jack Kahn .... Anthony Rapp
Debbie .... Nadia Dajani

Directed by Nicholas Martin; scenery, Allen Moyer; costumes, Michael Krass; lighting, Kenneth Posner; sound, Jeremy Grody; production stage manager, Christopher Wigle; press, Philip Rinaldi, Dennis Crowley.

Professor is accused of sexual harassment of a student. The play was presented in two parts.

AN IMAGINARY LIFE

Matt Abelman .... Chip Zien
Maggs Morris .... Caroline Aaron
Dr. Jeff Portnoy .... Reed Birney
Noah Abelman .... Christopher Collet
Spenser Glick .... Jonathan Walker
Igor Fuchs .... Tim Blake Nelson
Marvin Frappe .... Merwin Goldsmith

Directed by Don Scardino; scenery, Loren Sherman; costumes, Jess Goldstein; lighting, Phil Monat; sound, Raymond D. Schilke; production stage manager, Dianne Trulock.

A playwright confronts a diagnosis of possible cancer by writing an autobiographical play about it and other crises in his life. The play was presented in two parts.

AVENUE X

Pasquale .... Ted Brunetti
Ubazz .... Roger Mazzeo
Chuck .... John Leone
Barbara .... Colette Hawley
Milton .... Harold Perrineau
Roscoe .... Chuck Cooper
Julia .... Alvaleta Guess
Winston .... Keith Johnston

Directed by Mark Brokaw; musical direction and vocal arrangements, Chapman Roberts; choreography, Ken Roberson; scenery, Loy Arcenas; costumes, Ellen McCartney; lighting, Donald Holder; sound, Janet Kalas; fight direction, Rick Sordelet; casting, Janet Foster; production stage manager, Lisa Buxbaum; stage manager, Robert Castro; press, Philip Rinaldi.

Time: 1963. Place: Gravesend, Brooklyn. The play was presented in two parts.

A capella musical about Brooklyn in the 1960s, with its tensions between black and Italian American groups. Previously presented at the 1992 National Music Theater Conference at the O'Neill Theater Center in Waterford, Conn.

MOE'S LUCKY SEVEN

Tiny; Divina .... Jodie Markell
Knuckles .... Steve Harris
Patsy .... Deirdre O'Connell
Moe .... Mark Margolis
Drake .... Barry Sherman
Drew .... Rick Dean
Mokie .... Jefferson Mays
Kurt .... Lanny Flaherty
Benito .... Ismael Carlo
Eggs .... Bruce McCarty
Janine .... Phyllis Somerville
Lon .... Sean San Jose Blackman

Directed by Roberta Levitow; scenery, Rosario Provenza; costumes, Tom Broecker; lighting, Robert Wierzel; original music and sound design, O-Lan Jones; fight direction, Rick Sordelet; casting, Janet Foster; production stage manager, William H. Lang.

Life and love in a sleazy waterfront barroom, with overtones of Adam, Eve and the tempting serpent. The play was presented in two parts.

All That Glitters (5). By Stephan Bullard. Produced by Wallack's Point Productions, Maria Di Dia executive producer, at Theater Four. Opened October 13, 1993. (Closed October 16, 1993)

Clayton Maguire .... Dana Vance
Barbra Reed .... Linda Cook
Baroness Katarina von Oberdorf .... Barbara Gulan
Scooter Goldberg .... Ilene Kristen

Directed by Eleanor Reissa; scenery, Harry Darrow; costumes, Lisa Tomczeszyn; lighting, Tom Sturge; production stage manager, James FitzSimmons; press, Shirley Herz Associates, Sam Rudy.

Comedy of four well-to-do women at a cocktail party, clawing at each other.

Fire in the Rain (11). One-woman performance by Holly Near; written by Holly Near and Timothy Near. Produced by Richard Martini, Albert Nocciolino, Allen Spivak, Larry Magid, Polygram Diversified Entertainment and Center Theater Group/Mark Taper Forum, Gordon Davidson artistic director, at the Union Square Theater. Opened October 14, 1993. (Closed October 24, 1993).

Directed by Timothy Near; musical direction, John Bucchino; scenery, Kate Edmunds; costumes, Marianna Elliott; lighting, Richard Winkler; projections, Charles Rose; sound, Christopher K. Bond; synthesizer orchestration, Derek Nakamoto; original sound effects, Jon Gottlieb; associate producer, Jo-Lynne Worley; production stage manager, Thomas P. Carr; press, Keith Sherman, Jim Byk, Stuart Ginsberg.

Autobiography of the singing star and left-wing activist.

Johnny Pye and the Foolkiller (49). Musical based on the short story by Stephen Vincent Benet; book by Mark St. Germain; music by Randy Courts; lyrics by Mark St. Germain and Randy Courts. Produced by Lambs Theater Company, Carolyn Rossi Copeland producing artistic director, at Lamb's Theater. Opened October 31, 1993. (Closed December 12, 1993)

Johnny Pye .... Daniel Jenkins
The Foolkiller .... Spiro Malas
Suzy Marsh .... Kaitlin Hopkins
Wilbur Wilberforce .... Peter Gerety
Mrs. Miller .... Tanny McDonald
Barber .... Ralston Hill
Bob .... Mark Lotito
Bill .... Michael Ingram
Young Johnny Pye .... Conor Gillespie
Young Suzy Marsh .... Heather Lee Soroka

Musicians: Steven M. Alper, Andrew Lippa keyboards; Steven Machamer percussion.

Directed by Scott Harris; musical staging, Janet Watson; musical director and conductor, Steven M. Alper; scenery, Peter Harrison; costumes, Claudia Stephens; lighting, Kenneth Posner; sound, David Lawson; orchestrations, Douglas Besterman; casting, Pat McCorkle, Richard Cole; production stage manager, David Waggett; press, Boneau/Bryan-Brown, Hillary Harrow.

Time: 1928-1995. Place: Martinsville, U.S.A. and various locations.

Runaway orphan grows up into a father and grandfather, while trying to solve a riddle which will gain him immortality. Previously produced in regional theater at the George Street Playhouse, New Brunswick, N.J.

ACT I

"Another Day" .... Foolkiller, Company
"Goodbye Johnny" .... Young Johnny, Young Suzy
"Shower of Sparks" .... Foolkiller
"Occupations" .... Young Johnny, Young Suzy, Johnny, Suzy, Company
"Goodbye Johnny" (Reprise) .... Johnny, Suzy
"Handle With Care" .... Wilbur, Suzy
"The End of the Road" .... Johnny, Suzy, Foolkiller, Company
"Challenge to Love" .... Johnny, Suzy, Company

ACT II

"The Barbershop" .... Barber, Bob, Bill
"Married With Children" .... Johnny, Suzy, Company
"The Land Where There Is No Death" .... Johny, Young Johnny
"Time Passes" .... Foolkiller, Company
"Challenge to Love" (Reprise) .... Johnny, Suzy
"Never Felt Better in My Life" .... Wilbur, Johnny, Barber, Bob, Bill
"Epilogue (The Answer)" .... Johnny
"The End of the Road" (Reprise) .... Johnny, Foolkiller
Finale .... Company

***Manhattan Theater Club.** Schedule of six programs (see note). ***Four Dogs and a Bone** (240). By John Patrick Shanley. Opened October 31, 1993; transferred to the Lucille Lortel Theater 12/9/93. **The Loman Family Picnic** (62). Revival of the play by Donald Margulies. Opened November 18, 1993. (Closed January 9, 1994) **Day Standing on Its Head** (24). By Philip Kan Gotanda. Opened January 25, 1994. (Closed February 13, 1994) **Three Birds Alighting on a Field** (56). By Timberlake Wertenbaker. Opened February 8, 1994. (Closed March 27, 1994) **The Arabian Nights** (25). By Mary Zimmerman; adapted from *The Arabian Nights: The Book of One Thousand and One Nights*. Opened March 20, 1994. (Closed April 10, 1994) ***Kindertransport** (17). By Diane Samuels; produced by arrangement with the Soho Theater Company, London. Opened May 17, 1994. Produced by Manhattan Theater Club, Lynne Meadow artistic director, Barry Grove managing director, *Four Dogs and a Bone, Day Standing on Its Head* and *The Arabian Nights* at City Center Stage II, *The Loman Family Picnic, Three Birds Alighting on a Field* and *Kindertransport* at City Center Stage I.

FOUR DOGS AND A BONE

Brenda .... Mary-Louise Parker
Bradley .... Tony Roberts
Collette .... Polly Draper
Victor .... Loren Dean

Understudies: Miss Parker—Paula DeVicq, Debra Messing; Miss Draper—Debra Messing, Paula DeVicq; Messrs. Roberts, Dean—Peter Jacobson.

Directed by John Patrick Shanley; scenery, Santo Loquasto; costumes, Elsa Ward; lighting, Brian Nason; sound, Bruce Ellman; casting, Randy Carrig; associate artistic director, Michael Bush; production stage manager, Donna A. Drake; press, Helene Davis, Amy Lefkowitz.

Time: Not long ago. Place: New York City. Act I, Scene 1: A producer's office. Scene 2: A restaurant/bar catering to theatrical clientele. Act II, Scene 1: A makeup trailer on a location film set. Scene 2: A producer's office.

AT MANHATTAN THEATER CLUB—The Lynne Meadow-Barry Grove group's 1993-94 schedule included *Four Dogs and a Bone (above)* by John Patrick Shanley, with Tony Roberts, Loren Dean, Mary-Louise Parker and Polly Draper; and *The Arabian Nights (below)* adapted by Mary Zimmerman, with Faran Tahir, Ramon Melindez Moses *(background),* Bruce Norris *(center),* Enrico Colantoni *(background)* and Jesse L. Martin

Satire on moviemaking, with a New York City focus on a writer, a producer and two actresses.

Peter Jacobson replaced Tony Roberts and Arabella Field replaced Mary-Louise Parker 12/9/93. Adam Arkin replaced Peter Jacobson 1/11/94. Ann Magnuson replaced Polly Draper 1/25/94. Grant Shaud replaced Adam Arkin 5/3/94. Reg Rogers replaced Loren Dean 4/94. Kim Zimmer replaced Ann Magnuson 5/27/94.

THE LOMAN FAMILY PICNIC

Doris .... Christine Baranski
Mitchell .... Jonathan Charles Kaplan
Stewie .... Harry Barandes
Herbie .... Peter Friedman
Marsha .... Liz Larsen

Understudy: Messrs. Kaplan, Barandes—Tristan Smith.

Directed by Lynne Meadow; scenery, Santo Loquasto; costumes, Rita Ryack; lighting, Peter Kaczorowski; sound, Otts Munderloh; fight director, Rick Sordelet; music, David Shire; musical staging, Marcia Milgrom Dodge; orchestrations, Martin Erskine; musical direction, Seth Rudetsky; casting, Randy Carrig, Nancy Piccione; production stage manager, William Joseph Barnes; stage manager, Lisa Buxbaum.

Time: Around 1965. Place: Coney Island, Brooklyn, N.Y. The play was presented in two parts.

The Loman Family Picnic was first produced off Broadway by Manhattan Theater Club 3/20/89 for 16 performances and was named a Best Play of its season. This is its first New York rivival of record.

DAY STANDING ON ITS HEAD

Harry Kitamura .... Keone Young
Lillian .... Kiya Ann Joyce
Joe Ozu .... Stan Egi
Lisa .... Liana Pai
Nina .... Tamlyn Tomita
Mother .... Kati Kuroda
Fisherman .... Glenn Kubota
Sam .... Zar Acayan

Understudies: Messrs. Young, Acayan, Kubota—James Saito; Misses Joyce, Kuroda, Pai—Dawn Saito; Mr. Egi—Zar Acayan; Miss Tomita—Liana Pai.

Directed by Oscar Eustis; scenery, David Jon Hoffmann; costumes, Lydia Tanji; lighting, Christopher Akerlind; sound, John Kilgore, original music, Dan Kuramoto; associate director, Naomi Goldberg; casting, Randy Carrig; production stage manager, Ed Fitzgerald.

Time: The present. Place: The city. The play was performed without an intermission.

The midlife crisis of a Japanese-American law professor.

THREE BIRDS ALIGHTING ON A FIELD

Auctioneer; David; Constantin; Ahmet .... Robert Westenberg
Biddy Andreas .... Harriet Walter
Alex Brendel; Marianne Ryle .... Caitlin Clarke
Jeremy Bertrand; Sir Philip Howard; Russian Priest .... Daniel Gerroll
Julia Roberts; Mrs. Boreman; Yoyo's Mother .... Susan Pilar
Nicola; Gwen Ryle; Jean; Russet; Katerina .... Jill Tasker
Yorgosn Andreas (Yoyo); Mr. Boreman .... Zach Grenier
Lady Lelouche; Fiona Campbell .... Deirdre O'Connell
Stephen Ryle; Mr. Mercer .... Jay O. Sanders

Directed by Max Stafford-Clark; scenery, Sally Jacobs; costumes, Peter Hartwell; lighting, Rick Fisher; sound, Bryan Bowen; casting; Nancy Piccione; production stage manager, Thom Widmann; stage manager, Lisa Iacucci.

Time: The end of the 1980s. Place: London. The play was presented in two parts.

A woman finds herself in the midst of the wheeling-and-dealing art world. Previously produced by the English Stage Company at the Royal Court Theater, London.

THE ARABIAN NIGHTS

Scheherazade .... Jenny Bacon
Perfect Love; Other Woman .... Ellen M. Bethea
Jester; Chief of Police .... Enrico Colantoni
Shahryar; Aziz .... Christopher Donahue
Dunyazad; Aziza .... Kathryn Lee
Prince of Fools; Clarinetist; Boy .... Jesse L. Martin
Jafar; Robber; Sage .... Ramon Melindez Moses
Madman; Abu al-Hasan; Sage .... Bruce Norris

Slave; Girl; Girl in the Garden .... Sara Erde
Jester's Wife; Sympathy .... Julia Gibson
Pastrycook; Sheik; Ishaak .... Denis O'Hare
Harun al-Rashid; Sheik al-Islam .... Faran Tahir

Others: Ellen M. Bethea, Enrico Colantoni, Sara Erde, Julia Gibson, Kathryn Lee, Jesse L. Martin, Ramon Melindez Moses, Bruce Norris, Denis O'Hare, Faran Tahir.

Understudies: Misses Bacon, Bethea, Erde, Gibson, Lee—Karen-Angela Bishop; Messrs. Donahue, Martin, Tahir—Richard Holmes; Messrs. Colantoni, Moses, Norris, O'Hare—David Pittu.

Directed by Mary Zimmerman; scenery, Karen TenEyck; costumes, Tom Broecker; lighting, Brian MacDevitt; casting, Nancy Piccione, Randy Carrig; production stage manager, Diane DiVita; stage manager, Alyssa Hoggatt.

Act I: Opening; The Madman's Tale; The Perfidy of Wives: The Pastrycook's Tale (The Dream), The Butcher's Tale (The Contest of Generosity), The Greengrocer's Tale (The Wonderful Bag, improvised nightly), The Clarinetist's Tale (Abu al-Hasan's Historic Indiscretion). Act II: Sympathy the Learned; The Mock Calipha/Aziz and Aziza; The Confusion of Stories; The Forgotten Melody; Closing.

Selections from the famous tales, rendered in theatrical form. Previously produced by the Lookingglass Theater Company.

KINDERTRANSPORT

Ratcatcher .... Michael Gaston
Eva .... Alanna Ubach
Helga .... Jane Kazmarek
Evelyn .... Dana Ivey
Faith .... Mary Mara
Lil .... Patricia Kilgarriff

Directed by Abigail Morris; scenery; John Lee Beatty; costumes, Jennifer Von Mayrhauser; lighting, Don Holder; original music and sound, Guy Sherman/Aural Fixation; casting, Nancy Piccione; production stage manager, Thom Widmann; stage manager, Brian Kaufman.

Time: The 1980s. Place: An attic in Evelyn's house in an outer London suburb. The play was presented in two parts.

Traumatic aftereffects on someone who, as a child, escaped from Hitler's Germany. A foreign play previously produced by the Soho Theater Company in London.

Note: Manhattan Theater Club also scheduled two programs under the heading New American Musicals in Concert: *The Gig* by Douglas J. Cohen, based on the film by Frank D. Gilroy, 5/17/94-6/5/94 and *The Prince and the Pauper* by Elizabeth Swados, based on Mark Twain's story, 6/14/94-7/3/94.

Trophies (62). By John J. Wooten. Produced Yabadoo Productions at the Cherry Lane Theater. Opened November 1, 1993. (Closed December 26, 1993)

David .... Marc West
Mr. Stone .... John Henry Cox
Mrs. Stone .... Janet Nell Catt
Robert/Bobby .... Mark Irish
Laura .... Christen Tassin

Understudies: Mr. Irish—Bob Bender; Miss Tassin—Beau Dakota Berdahl; Mr. West—R. Ward Duffy.

Directed by John Gulley; scenery, Mark Cheney; costumes, Missy West; lighting, Mark F. O'Connor; sound, Scott Stauffer; original music, David Brunetti; casting, Carol Hanzel, Elsie Stark; executive producers, Andrew C. McGibbon, Steven M. Levy; production stage manager, Geoffrey F. Morris; press, Shirley Herz Associates, Glenna Freedman, Wayne Wolfe.

Son returns home to care for his family after a younger brother suffers a serious accident.

New York Shakespeare Festival. Schedule of ten programs (see note). **The Treatment** (24). By Martin Crimp. Opened November 2, 1993. (Closed November 21, 1993) **The Swan** (32). By Elizabeth Egloff. Opened November 15, 1993. (Closed December 12, 1993) **First Lady Suite** (15). Musical with book, music and lyrics by Michael John LaChiusa. Opened December 15, 1993. (Closed December 26, 1993) **East Texas Hot Links** (38). By Eugene Lee. Opened January 13, 1994. (Closed February 13, 1994) **Irene Worth's Portrait of Edith Wharton** (49). One-woman performance by Irene Worth. Opened January 11, 1994. (Closed February 27, 1994) **The America Play** (22). By Suzan-Lori Parks; co-produced by Yale Repertory Theater, Stan Wodjewodski Jr. artistic director, in association with Theater for a New

Audience, Jeffrey Horowitz artistic/producting director. Opened March 10, 1994. (Closed March 27, 1994) **Twilight: Los Angeles, 1992** (13). One-woman performance by Anna Deavere Smith; conceived and written by Anna Deavere Smith. Opened March 23, 1994. (Closed April 3, 1994 and transferred to Broadway; see its entry in the Plays Produced on Broadway section of this volume) **All for You** (6), one-man performance by John Fleck, written by John Fleck, opened May 4, 1994 in repertory with **Airport Music** (6), two-actor performance by Jessica Hagedorn and Han Ong, written by Jessica Hagedorn and Han Ong, opened May 9, 1994. (Repertory closed May 15, 1994) **Big Momma 'N'Em** (14). One-woman performance by Phyllis Yvonne Stickney; conceived and written by Phyllis Yvonne Stickney. Opened May 26, 1994. (Closed June 5, 1994). Produced by New York Shakespeare Festival, George C. Wolfe producer, Jason Steven Cohen managing director, Rosemarie Tichler and Kevin Kline associate producers, at the Joseph Papp Public Theater (see note).

THE TREATMENT

Jennifer .... Randy Danson
Anne .... Angie Phillips
Andrew .... Daniel Von Bargen
Clifford .... David Margulies
Simon .... Rob Campbell
Police Officer; John (Othello in Central Park) .... Robert Jason Jackson
Waitress; Nicky; Female Movie Star (Emilia in Central Park); Maid; Mad Woman .... Susan Knight
Taxi Driver .... Arthur French

Directed by Marcus Stern; scenery, James Schuette; costumes, Melina Root; lighting, Scott Zielinski; sound, John Huntington, Darron West; original music, John Hoge; featured music, Jane Ira Bloom; fight director, David Leong; casting, Jordan Thaler; production stage manager, Kristen Harris; stage manager, Cathleen Wolfe; press, Carol R. Fineman, James Morrison, Terence Womble, Eugenie Hero.

Time: The present. Place: New York City. Act I: A day in June. Act II: Evening of the same day. Act III: A few days later. Act IV: A year later. The play was presented in two parts.

Black comedy view of Manhattan, with a group of people in the movie-producing world. A foreign play previously produced at the Royal Court Theater, London.

THE SWAN

Dora .... Frances McDormand
Bill .... Peter Stormare
Kevin .... David Chandler

Directed by Les Waters; scenery, James Youmans; costumes, David Woolard; lighting, Ken Posner; original music and sound design, John Gromada; movement/violence, David Leong; casting, Jordan Thaler; production stage manager, Buzz Cohen.

Time: The present. Place: Somewhere in Nebraska. The play was presented without intermission.

Fantasy, a love triangle in which one of the men first appears in the form of a swan.

FIRST LADY SUITE

Eleanor Sleeps Here

Eleanor Roosevelt .... Carolann Page
Lorena Hickok .... Carol Woods
Eleanor's Brother .... David Wasson
Amelia Earhart .... Maureen Moore

Time: 1936, night. Place: Amelia Earhart's Lockheed Electra.

Olio

Bess Truman .... David Wasson
Margaret Truman .... Debra Stricklin

Time: 1950. Place: Christian Democratic Mothers and Daughters Luncheon.

Where's Mamie?

Mamie Eisenhower .... Alice Playten
Marian Anderson .... Priscilla Baskerville
Dwight D. Eisenhower .... David Wasson
Kay Summersby .... Debra Stricklin

Time: 1957. Place: Ike and Mamie Eisenhower's bedroom, the White House.

Olio

Time: 1960. Place: The East Room of the White House.

Over Texas

Evelyn Lincoln .... Carolann Page
Mary Gallagher .... Debra Stricklin
Presidential Aide .... David Wasson
Jacqueline Kennedy .... Maureen Moore
Lady Bird Johnson .... Alice Playten

Time: November 22, 1963. Place: On board Air Force One.

Piano: Alan Johnson.

Directed by Kirsten Sanderson; musical direction, Alan Johnson; choreography, Janet Bogardus; scenery, Derek McLane; costumes, Tom Broecker; lighting, Brian MacDevitt; casting, Jordan Thaler; production stage manager, Liz Small; stage manager, Russell Kaplan.

Imaginary travels and travails of famous women, many of them First Ladies. The play was presented without intermission. Portions previously presented at Ensemble Studio Theater.

EAST TEXAS HOT LINKS

Roy .... Ruben Santiago-Hudson
XL .... Curtis McClarin
Charlesetta .... Loretta Devine
Columbus .... Ed Wheeler
Adolph .... Earle Hyman
Delmus .... Monté Russell
Buckshot .... Bo Rucker
Boochie .... Willis Burks II

Directed by Marion McClinton; scenery, Charles McClennahan; costumes, Toni-Leslie James; lighting, Allen Lee Hughes; sound, Dan Moses Schreier; fight direction, David Leong; casting, Jordan Thaler; production stage manager, Ruth Kreshka; stage manager, Lloyd Davis Jr.

Time: Early summer, 1955. Place: Top o' the Hill Cafe, East Texas. The play was presented without intermission.

Violence finally explodes in a Southern black community hangout. Previously produced in regional theater in Los Angeles and Washington, D.C. and at the Royal Court Theater in London.

IRENE WORTH'S PORTRAIT OF EDITH WHARTON

Scenery, Ben Edwards; lighting, Pat Dignan; stage manager, Riley Cohen.

Irene Worth portrays Edith Wharton and her works in a monologue text taken from Wharton's autobiography and novels.

THE AMERICA PLAY

CAST: Lucy—Gail Grate; A Man, B Man, C Man, Augusta, Asa Trenchard—Tyrone Mitchell Henderson; A Woman, B Woman, C Woman, Florence, Augusta—Adriane Lenox; The Foundling Father as Abraham Lincoln—Reggie Montgomery; Brazil—Michael Potts.

Directed by Liz Diamond; scenery, Riccardo Hernandez; costumes, Angelina Avallone; lighting, Jeremy V. Stein; sound, John Gromada; casting, Wendy Ettinger; production stage manager, Gwendolyn M. Gilliam; stage manager, Shannon Rhodes.

Place: An exact replica of the Great Hole of History. Act I: Lincoln Act. Act II: The Hall of Wonders—A. Big Bang, B. Echo, C. Archeology, D. Echo, E. Spadework, F. Echo, G. The Great Beyond.

Surrealistic kaleidoscope of events in American history with one family at their center. Previously produced in development by Theater for a New Audience, in workshop by Arena Stage, Washington, D.C. and Dallas Theater Center, and in world premiere at Yale Repertory Theater, New Haven, Conn.

TWILIGHT: LOS ANGELES, 1992

Directed by George C. Wolfe; scenery, John Arnone; costumes, Toni-Leslie James; lighting, Jules Fisher, Peggy Eisenhauer; sound, John Gromada; projections and video, Batwin + Robin Productions; presented by arrangement with Center Theater Group/Mark Taper Forum, Gordon Davidson artistic director; production stage manager, William Joseph Barnes.

The recent rascial strife in Los Angeles, including the Rodney King verdict and Reginald Denny beating, viewed in a series of more than 40 character portrayals by Anna Deavere Smith, the text making use of material from interviews she conducted with Denny and many others involved as witnesses, police, participants, etc. in these events. The work was commissioned by Center Theater Group/Mark Taper Forum, Gordon Davidson artistic director, and premiered there in June 1993. The play was presented in two parts.

A Best Play; see page 317.

ALL FOR YOU

Directed by David Schweizer and John Fleck; lighting, Kevin Adams; taped video images, Adam Soch; camera operator, Ryan Hill; boom and grip, Michelle Stevens.

Multimedia performance piece described as "video interactive," with John Fleck exploring such pop phenomena as advertising and show business. Previously produced in workshop at Mark Taper Forum New Works Festival, Los Angeles.

AIRPORT MUSIC

Directing consultation, Laurie Carlos; lighting, Kevin Adams; production stage manager, Keith Jones.

Multimedia performance piece with Jessica Hagedorn and Han Ong exploring the immigrant experience.

BIG MOMMA 'N'EM

Directed by Loni Berry; scenery and costumes, Felix E. Cochren; lighting, Kevin Adams; sound, Carmen Whiip; production stage manager, Trevor Brown.

Phyllis Yvonne Stockney portrays five characters including Big Momma, a healer who helps the other four with their troubles.

Note: In addition to its own programs, New York Shakespeare Festival made available its Estelle R. Newman Theater for the three-program touring repertory of The Acting Company (Zelda Fichandler artistic director, Margot Harley executive director) *The African Company Presents Richard III* (7) by Carlyle Brown, directed by Clinton Turner Davis, opened May 18, 1994; *A Doll's House* (3), revival of the play by Henrik Ibsen, directed by Zelda Fichandler, opened May 20, 1994; and *Twelfth Night* (4), revival of the play by William Shakespeare, directed by Bartlett Sher, opened May 23, 1994 (Repertory closed May 28, 1994). The members of the company included Matt Bradford Sullivan, Shona Tucker, Kelly Taffe, Allen Gilmore, Chuck Patterson, Cedric Harris and Richard Topol.

Note: Among the many auditoria of the Joseph Papp Public Theater, *The Treatment* and *Twilight: Los Angeles, 1992* played the Estelle R. Newman Theater, *The Swan* and *The America Play* played Martinson Hall, *First Lady Suite, Irene Worth's Portrait of Edith Wharton, All for You, Airport Music* and *Big Momma 'N'Em* played the Susan Stein Shiva Theater, *East Texas Hot Links* played the Florence Sutro Anspacher Theater.

***Lincoln Center Theater.** A Festival of New American Plays schedule of three programs. **The Lights** (47). By Howard Korder; presented in the Atlantic Theater Company production, Neil Pepe artistic director, Jeffrey Solis managing director. Opened November 3, 1993. (Closed December 12, 1993) **Hello Again** (65). Musical suggested by the play *La Ronde* by Arthur Schnitzler; book, music and lyrics by Michael John LaChiusa. Opened January 30, 1994. (Closed March 27, 1994) ***SubUrbia** (10). By Eric Bogosian. Opened May 22, 1994. Produced by Lincoln Center Theater under the direction of Andre Bishop and Bernard Gersten at the Mitzi E. Newhouse Theater.

THE LIGHTS

Rose ..... Kristen Johnston
Lilian ..... Kathleen Dennehy
Customer; Woman With Junk; Spectator 1 ..... Ileen Getz
Man in Overcoat; Man 1; Man With Cup; Manager; Scab 2 ..... Steven Goldstein
Kraus; Spectator 4 ..... Todd Weeks
Fredric ..... Dan Futterman
Man in Chair; Scab 3 ..... Leon Addison Brown
Man 2; Spectator 3; Bill; Guard; Scab 1 ..... David Pittu
Speaker; Man With Pants ..... Ray Anthony Thomas
Spectator 2; Waiter 2; Mr. Barry ..... Jordan Lage
Spectator 5; Erenhart ..... Christopher McCann
Man With Camera ..... Andrew Mutnick
Waiter 1; Art ..... Herbert Rubens
Young Waiter; Foreman ..... Neil Pepe
Diamond ..... Jerry Grayson
Passersby ..... Tom Bloom, Robin Spielberg
Others ..... Members of the Ensemble

Understudies: Miss Johnston—Ileen Getz; Misses Dennehy, Getz—Robin Spielberg; Mr. Futterman—Steven Goldstein; Mr. McCann—Tom Bloom; Mr. Grayson—Herbert Rubens; Messrs. Goldstein, Rubens, Lage, Pepe—Andrew Mutnick; Mr. Weeks—David Pittu; Mr. Brown—Ray Anthony Thomas; Mr. Pittu—

Todd Weeks; Mr. Thomas—Leon Addison Brown.

Directed by Mark Wing-Davey; scenery, Marina Draghici; costumes, Laura Cunningham; lighting, Christopher Akerlind; additional music and sound, Mark Bennett; fight direction, David Leong; casting, Daniel Swee; production stage manager, Thom Widmann; stage manager, Eric Eligator; press, Merle Debuskey, Susan Chicoine.

Time: The modern era. Place: A large city. The play was presented in two parts.

Problems of the modern city—drugs, crime, garbage, homelessness, etc. Previously produced by Atlantic Theater Company in regional theater at Burlington, VT.

HELLO AGAIN

Whore	Donna Murphy	Husband	Dennis Parlato
Soldier	David A. White	Young Thing	John Cameron Mitchell
Nurse	Judy Blazer	Writer	Malcolm Gets
College Boy	Michael Park	Actress	Michele Pawk
Young Wife	Carolee Carmello	Senator	John Dossett

Orchestra: David Evans conductor, keyboards; Wayne Abravanel assistant conductor, keyboards; Virginia Benz, French horn; Susan Evans percussion; Jonathan Kass violin, viola; Dale Kleps woodwinds; Matthias Naegele cello.

Understudies: Messrs. White, Park, Mitchell—Roy Chicas; Misses Murphy, Blazer—Pamela Isaacs; Messrs. Parlato, Gets, Dossett—Bob Stillman; Misses Carmello, Pawk—Elizabeth Ward.

Directed and choreographed by Graciela Daniele; musical direction, David Evans; scenery, Derek McLane; costumes, Toni-Leslie James; lighting, Jules Fisher, Peggy Eisenhauer; sound, Scott Stauffer; orchestrations, Michael Starobin; casting, Daniel Swee; production stage manager, Leslie Loeb; stage manager, Michelle Bosch.

Scene 1: The Whore and the Soldier, circa 1900. Scene 2: The Soldier and the Nurse, 1940s. Scene 3: The Nurse and the College Boy, 1960s. Scene 4: The College Boy and the Young Wife, 1930s. Scene 5: The Young Wife and the Husband, 1950s. Scene 6: The Husband and the Young Thing, 1910s. Scene 7: The Young Thing and the Writer, 1970s. Scene 8: The Writer and the Actress, 1920s. Scene 9: The Actress and the Senator, 1980s. Scene 10: The Senator and the Whore, the present and the past. The play was presented without intermission.

Interlocking sexual adventures coming full circle after leaping about among the decades.

SUBURBIA

Tim	Tim Guinee	Bee-Bee	Wendy Hoopes
Buff	Steve Zahn	Sooze	Martha Plimpton
Jeff	Josh Hamilton	Pony	Zak Orth
Norman Chaudry	Firdous E. Bamji	Erica	Babette Renee Props
Pakeeza	Samia Shoaib		

Understudies: Messrs. Guinee, Zahn—Nick Rodgers; Messrs. Hamilton, Orth, Zahn—Jon Patrick Walker; Mr. Bamji—Aasif Mandviwala; Misses Shoaib, Plimpton, Hoopes, Props—Anney Giobbe.

Directed by Robert Falls; scenery, Derek McLane; costumes, Gabriel Berry; lighting, Kenneth Posner; sound, John Gromada; fight direction, David Leong; casting, Daniel Swee, Jean Bacharach; production stage manager, Christopher Wigle; stage manager, Miriam Auerbach.

Young people, bitterly resentful of their empty lives, hanging out in the parking lot of small-town 7-Eleven. The play was presented in two parts.

A Best Play; see page 359.

A Quarrel of Sparrows (15). By James Duff. Produced by Drew Dennett at the Promenade Theater. Opened November 9, 1993. (Closed November 21, 1993)

August Ainsworth	Henderson Forsythe	Angela Mercer	Jan Hooks
Rosanna Ainsworth Jackson	Polly Holliday	Lynn Waters	Andrew Weems
Paul Palmer	Mitchell Lichtenstein	Martin Green	John C. Vennema

Standbys: Miss Holliday—Patricia O'Connell; Miss Hooks—Alison Fraser.

Directed by Kenneth Elliott; scenery, Loren Sherman; costumes, Debra Tennenbaum; lighting, Donald Holder; sound, Aural Fixation; casting, Stuart Howard, Amy Schecter; production stage manager, Allison Sommer; press, Shirley Herz Associates, Sam Rudy, Barbara Carroll.

Time: The present. Place: The living room of August Ainsworth's country house at Sag Harbor on the South Fork of Long Island. The play was presented in two parts.

Comedy, a visiting playwright's vision from God stirs up a household during a weekend on Long Island. Previously produced in regional theater at the Cleveland Play House.

Forbidden Broadway 1994 (62). Created and written by Gerard Alessandrini. Produced by Jonathan Scharer at Theater East. Opened November 11, 1993. (Closed January 2, 1994)

Susanne Blakeslee
Brad Ellis
Brad Oscar
Christine Pedi
Craig Wells

Directed by Gerard Alessandrini; musical direction, Brad Ellis; choreography, Susanne Blakeslee, Craig Wells, Phill George; wigs, Teresa Vuoso; costumes, Alvin Colt, Erika Dyson; production consultant, Pete Blue; associate producer, Chip Quigley; production stage manager, Jim Griffith; press, Shirley Herz Associates, Glenna Freedman.

New "Take-No-Prisoners" edition of the revue sending up popular New York stage attractions amd personalities. The show was presented in two parts. This was the 13th edition of the revue which began in January 1982.

Out Is In (72). One-woman performance by Kate Clinton; written by Kate Clinton. Produced by Virginia Giordano at the Perry Street Theater. Opened December 1, 1993. (Closed January 30, 1994)

Lighting, Traci Renee Klainer; stage manager, Tigre McMullan; press, Boneau/Bryan-Brown, Jamie Morris.
Comedienne commenting on a multitude of topical subjects, including the lesbian life and times.

Greetings! (48). By Tom Dudzick. Produced by Arthur Cantor and Carol Ostrow at the John Houseman theater. Opened December 13, 1993. (Closed January 23, 1994)

Andy Gorski ..... Gregg Edelman
Randi Stein ..... Toby Poser
Phil Gorski ..... Darren McGavin
Emily Gorski ..... Lenore Loveman
Mickey Gorski ..... Aaron Goodwin

Directed by Dennis Zacek; scenery and costumes, Bruce Goodrich; lighting, Deborah Constantine; sound, One Dream; production stage manager, Tom Aberger; press, Arthur Cantor, Beck Lee.

Place: The Gorski household in a working class neighborhood of Pittsburgh, Pa. The play was presented in two parts.

Comedy, New York advertising man brings his Jewish fiancee home to meet his Catholic family. Previously produced in regional theater at the George Street Playhouse, New Brunswick, N.J.

Those the River Keeps (8). By David Rabe. Produced by James B. Freydberg, Kenneth Feld and Dori Berinstein at the Promenade Theater. Opened January 31, 1994. (Closed February 6, 1994)

Susie ..... Annabella Sciorra
Phil ..... Paul Guilfoyle
Sal ..... Jude Ciccolella
Janice ..... Phyllis Lyons

Directed by David Rabe; scenery, Loren Sherman; costumes, Sharon Sprague; lighting, Peter Kaczorowski; fight direction, David Leong; sound, One Dream; associate producers, Thirty-One Productions, Coffee Shop Productions, Jerry L. Cohen, Cheryl Shad; casting, Meg Simon; production stage manager, Jane Grey; stage manager, K. Dale White; press, Boneau/Bryan-Brown, Jackie Green, Jamie Morris.

Act I, Scene 1: A while ago. Scene 2: Later; Scene 3: That night. Act II, Scene I: Three days later. Scene 2: That night.

Ex-con trying to build a new life with a young wife, with having a baby as one of their major goals. Previously produced in regional theater at the McCarter Theater Company, Princeton, N.J. and the American Repertory Theater, Cambridge, Mass.

Smiling Through (14). Musical with book by Ivan Menchell; music and lyrics by various authors (see listing below). Produced by Lois Teich at Theater 4. Opened February 2, 1994. (Closed February 6, 1994)

Mavis Daily .... Vicki Stuart
Arthur; Frank; Norma; Penelope; Announcers .... Jeff Woodman

Orchestra: Tom Fay conductor; Andrew Lippa keyboards; Anthony Tedesco percussion.

Directed and choreographed by Patricia Birch; musical direction and arrangements, Tom Fay; scenery, James Morgan; costumes, Frank Krenz; lighting, Craig Miller; sound, Otts Munderloh; associate director/choreographer, Jonathan Stewart Cerullo; production stage manager, R. Wade Jackson; press, Jeffrey Richards Associates, Carol Van Keuren, Diane Judge.

Act I: London, 1940, the South London Palace of Varieties and other locations. Act II: Four years later, the Bristol Canteen, the Nottingham Canteen and other locations.

Veteran English music hall singer lifts the spirits of her audiences and carries on during World War II. Previously produced by the Pennsylvania Stage Company and the Emelin Theater in Mamaroneck, N.Y.

MUSICAL NUMBERS, ACT I: "Don't Dilly Dally on the Way" (music and lyrics by Charles Collins, Fred W. Leigh and Dick Manning); "Nobody Loves a Fairy" (music and lyrics by Arthur Le Clerq); "Underneath the Arches" (music and lyrics by Bud Flanagan and Reg Connelly); "All Our Tomorrows" (music and lyrics by Jimmy Kennedy); "Wish Me Luck" (music by Harry Parr-Davies, lyrics by Phil Park); "No One Believes . . ." (music and lyrics by Desmond Carter and Noel Gray).

ACT II: "The Deepest Shelter in Town" (music and lyrics by Leslie Julian Jones); "Dancing With My Shadow" (music and lyrics by Harry Woods); "I'm Gonna Get Lit Up" (music and lyrics by Hubert Gregg); "We'll Meet Again" (music and lyrics by Ross Parker and Hughie Charles); "The White Cliffs of Dover" (music by Walter Kent, lyrics by Nat Burton); "A Nightingale Sang in Berkeley Square" (music by Manning Sherwin, lyrics by Eric Maschwitz).

Pounding Nails in the Floor With My Forehead (84). One-man performance by Eric Bogosian; written by Eric Bogosian. Produced by Frederick Zollo, Nick Paleologos, Ron Kastner and Randy Finch at the Minetta Lane Theater. Opened February 3, 1994. (Closed April 24, 1994)

Directed by Jo Bonney; scenery, John Arnone; lighting, Jan Kroeze; sound, Raymond D. Schilke; production stage manager, Robbie Young; press, Philip Rinaldi, Kathy Haberthur.

Collection of Bogosian-created characters illustrating in monologue some of the major ills and annoyances of modern urban life.

Ricky Jay & His 52 Assistants (110). One-man magic show performed by Ricky Jay; written by Ricky Jay. Produced by Second Stage Theater, Carole Rothman artistic director, Suzanne Schwartz Davidson producing director, at Second Stage Theater. Opened February 6, 1994. (Closed May 28, 1994)

Directed by David Mamet; scenery, Kevin Rigdon; lighting, Jules Fisher; consultants, Jim Steinmeyer, Michael Weber; associate producer, Carol Fishman; production stage manager, Matthew Silver; press, Richard Kornberg.

Magic show with some audience participation and running commentary, the "52 assistants" being a deck of cards.

***All in the Timing** (117). Program of six one-act plays by David Ives. Produced by Estragon Productions, Inc. in the Primary Stages Company production, Casey Childs artistic director, at the John Housman Theater. Opened February 17, 1994.

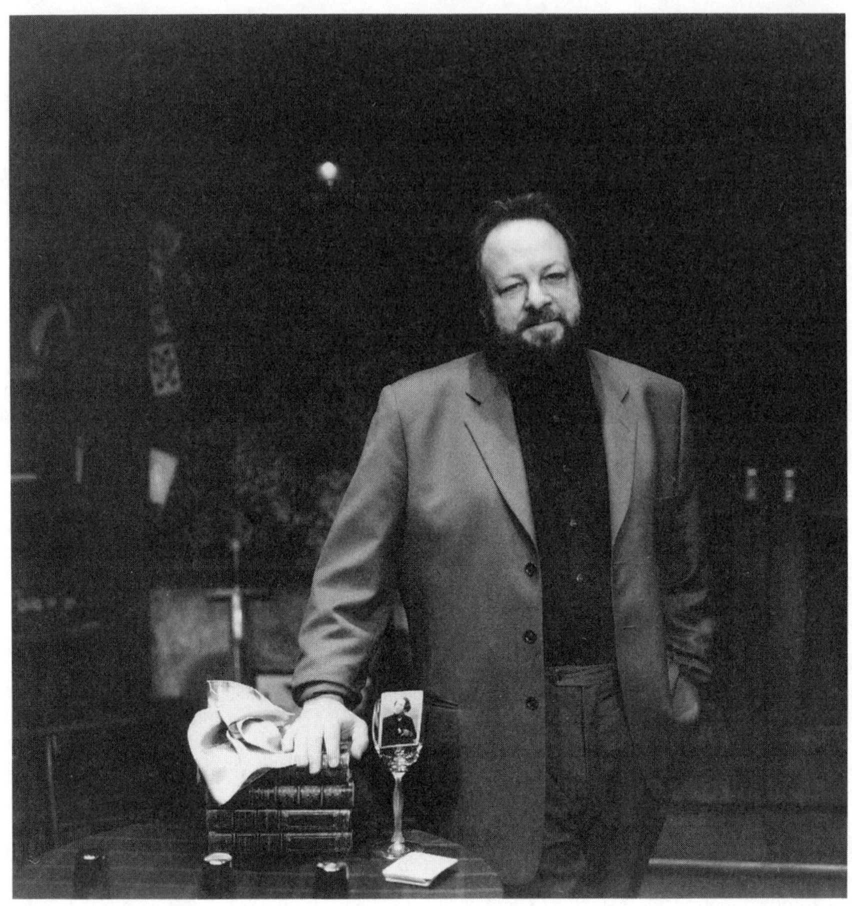

RICKY JAY & HIS 52 ASSISTANTS—Above, Ricky Jay in his magic show

Sure Thing (1988)

Bill .... Robert Stanton
Betty .... Nancy Opel

Time: A rainy night. Place: A cafe. Boy tries to make the acquaintance of girl in a restaurant in many variations, as lines of dialogue are changed over and over again at the sound of a bell as though the play were being rewritten by the actors as it went along.

Words, Words, Words (1987)

Swift .... Robert Stanton
Milton .... Michael Countryman
Kafka .... Nancy Opel

Time: Somewhere in infinity. Place: A lab at Columbia University. Three monkeys are locked in a cage under observation, with three typewriters, presumably on their way to coming up with *Hamlet,* as per the old saying.

The Universal Language (1993—premiere)

Dawn .... Wendy Lawless
Young Man .... Ted Neustadt
Don .... Robert Stanton

Time: The present. Place: A classroom. A student is attempting to learn a universal language—"Unamunda"—a humorous juggling of sounds forming gibberish in which much of this play is written.

Philip Glass Buys a Loaf of Bread (1990)

1st Woman .... Wendy Lawless Baker .... Michael Countryman
2d Woman .... Nancy Opel Philip Glass .... Robert Stanton

Time: Now. Place: A bakery. A verbal parody of the rhythms and repetitions typical of Glass's musical style.

The Philadelphia (1992—New York premiere)

Al .... Ted Neustadt Mark .... Robert Stanton
Waitress .... Wendy Lawless

Time: The present. Place: A restaurant in New York City. Some days everything seems to go impossibly wrong or impossibly right, depending on whether one is, metaphysically speaking, "in a Philadelphia" or "in a Los Angeles."

Variations on the Death of Trotsky (1991)

Trotsky .... Michael Countryman Ramon .... Ted Neustadt
Mrs. Trotsky .... Nancy Opel

Time: August 21, 1940. Place: Trotsky's study in Coyoacan, Mexico. Imaginary conversations about life, death and politics among Trotsky, his wife and his killer on the day of his death.

Directed by Jason McConnell Buzas; scenery, Bruce Goodrich; costumes, Sharon Lynch; lighting, Deborah Constantine; sound, Jim van Bergen; original recorded music, Bruce Coughlin; production stage manager, Christine Catti; press, Tony Origlio Publicity, Stephen Murray, William McLaughlin.

Six one-act comedies written as per the dates opposite the titles above, on a program which premiered off off Broadway at Primary Stages Company 12/1/93 and was subsequently mounted off Broadway 2/17/94. The program was presented in two parts with the intermission following *The Universal Language. Sure Thing; Words, Words, Words; Philip Glass Buys a Loaf of Bread* and *Variations on the Death of Trotsky* were previously produced by The Manhattan Punch Line. *The Philadelphia* was previously produced at the 1992 New Hope, Pa. Performing Arts Festival.

A Best Play; see page 286.

***Stomp** (104). Percussion performance piece created by Luke Cresswell and Steve McNicholas. Produced by Columbia Artists Management, Inc., Harriet Newman Leve, James D. Stern, Morton Wolkowitz, Schuster/Maxwell, Gallin/Sandler and Markley/Manocherian at the Orpheum Theater. Opened February 27, 1994.

CAST: Luke Cresswell, Nick Dwyer, Sarah Eddy, Theseus Gerard, Fraser Morrison, David Olrod, Carl Smith, Fiona Wilkes.

Swings; Everett Bradley, Allison Easter.

Directed by Luke Cresswell and Steve McNicholas; lighting, Steve McNicholas, Neil Tiplady; executive producers, Richard Frankel Productions/Mark Routh; associate producer, Fred Bracken; production manager, Pete Donno; press, Boneau/Bryan-Brown, Jackie Green, Bob Fennell.

British troupe of eight performers who specialize in creating rhythms, not with conventional instruments, but with many of the objects in everyday life. A foreign performance piece previously produced at the Edinburgh Festival in 1991 and elsewhere including a world tour.

***Mort Sahl's America** (64). One-man performance by Mort Sahl; written by Mort Sahl. Produced by Eric Krebs, Bobby Roberts and Roger Paglia at Theater Four. Opened April 4, 1994.

Lighting, Robert Bessoir; sound, Dean Marletta; technical direction, E.F. Morrill; press, David Rothenberg Associates.

Stand-up comedy, comments on politcal, social and other contemporary matters. The show was presented without intermission.

***Three Tall Women** (65). By Edward Albee. Produced by Elizabeth I. McCann, Jeffrey Ash and Daryl Roth in association with Leavitt/Fox/Mages in the Vineyard Theater production, Douglas Aibel artistic director, Barbara Zinn Krieger executive director, Jon Nakagawa managing director, at the Promenade Theater. Opened April 5, 1994.

A .... Myra Carter
B .... Marian Seldes
C .... Jordan Baker
The Boy .... Michael Rhodes

Standbys: Miss Baker—Melissa Bowen; Miss Carter—Lucille Patton; Miss Seldes—Kathleen Butler; Mr. Rhodes—Timothy Altmeyer.

Directed by Lawrence Sacharow; scenery, James Noone; costumes, Muriel Stockdale; lighting, Phil Monat; associate producer, Randall L. Wreghitt; production stage manager, Elizabeth M. Berther; stage manager, Timothy Altmeyer; press, Shirley Herz Associates, Sam Rudy.

Three Tall Women had its world premiere at the English Theater in Vienna, Franz Schafranck producer, in June 1991; its American premiere at River Arts Repertory, Woodstock, N.Y., Lawrence Sacharow producer; and its New York premiere off off Broadway in this production at the Vineyard Theater 2/13/94-3/13/94 for 29 performances. The play was presented in two parts.

A Best Play; see page 302.

American Enterprise (15). By Jeffrey Sweet; songs by Jeffrey Sweet. Produced by The New York State Theater Institute, Patricia Di Benedetto Snyder producing director, at Playhouse 46 at St. Clements Church. Opened April 13, 1994. (Closed April 23, 1994).

George M. Pullman .... John Romeo
J. Patrick Hopkins .... Erol K.C. Landis
George Jr.; Paymaster .... David Bunce
Eugene V. Debs; Beman; Businessman McCormick; Priest .... Gerard Curran
John P. Altgeld; Jackson; Clayton; Porter .... Bernard J. Tarver
Stephens; Harahan; Agent .... Paul Villani
Thomas Wickes; Commissioner; Wright; Porter .... Marshåll Factora
Heathcote; Railroad Owner; Commissioner Worthington .... Joel Aroeste
Jennie Curtis; Florence Pullman .... Erika Newell
Soloists .... Betsy Riley, Kelley Sweeney
Rev. E.C. Oggel; Businessman Field .... John T. McGuire III
Mayor Harrison; Businessman Swift; Delegate Cosgrove; Federal Marshal .... Michael Steese
Railroad Assistant; Porter; Servant .... Jack Seabury
Club Attendant .... Jason W. Bowman
Secretary .... Tracey E. Madison
Ensemble .... Laura Roth, Allison Sharpley
Keyboards/Synthesizer .... Aaron Hagan

Understudies: Messrs. Landis, McGuire—David Bunce; Mr. Curran—Marshåll Factora; Mr. Aroeste—John T. McGuire III; Miss Newell—Kelly Sweeney; Mr. Seabury—Jason W. Bowman; Messrs. Bunce, Bowman—Jack Seabury; Swing—Joseph Quandt.

Directed by Patricia Birch; incidental music (from sources contemporaneous to the play) and vocal arrangements, Michael Vitali; scenery, Richard Finkelstein; costumes, Brent Griffin; lighting, John McLain; sound, Matt Elie; musical direction and additional vocal arrangements, Betsy Riley; production stage manager, Heather J. Hamelin; press, Susan L. Schulman.

Time: The latter half of the 19th century. Place: The city of Chicago. The play was presented in two parts.

Historical play with music giving it the character of a folk tale about the life and character of George M. Pullman, the railroad car manufacturer, and his eventual conflict with his workers during the famous Pullman strike.

A Best Play (special citation); see page 384.

MUSICAL NUMBERS (music and lyrics by Jeffrey Sweet unless otherwise indicated); "Shall We Plant a Tree?"—Soloists, Ensemble; "Porters on a Pullman Train" (music by Michael Vitali, lyrics by Charles D. Crandall, circa 1890)—Porters; "Leave a Light"—Soloist; "It's a Trust"—Pullman, Hopkins, McCormick, Railroad Owner, Oggel, Harrison, Club Attendant; "The Columbian Exposition"—Ensemble; "Maggie Murphy" (music and lyrics by Ned Harrington and Dave Braham, circa 1890)—Soloist; "Step by Step" (traditional Irish song, circa late 1800s)—Ensemble; "The Pullman Strike" (music by Lewis Hall, lyrics by William M. Delaney, circa 1894)—Soloist.

Fallen Angel (32). Rock musical with book, music and lyrics by Billy Boesky; additional musical credits are listed below. Produced by Peter Holmes à Court and Roger Hess in association with Back Row Productions at Circle in the Square Downtown. Opened April 14, 1994. (Closed May 11, 1994)

Will	Jonathan Goldstein	Father; Stu Rosen	George Coe
Luke	Corey Glover	Dr. Bamberger; Alexandra	Susan Gibney
Gretta	Shannon Conley		

The Band: Derek Boshart, Allison Cornell, Van Romaine, Winston Roye.

Understudies: Mr. Goldstein—Billy Boesky; Mr. Glover—Michael McCoy; Misses Conley, Gibney—Amy Correia.

Directed by Rob Greenberg; musical direction, Steve Postell; scenery, David Birn; costumes, Wendy A. Rolfe; lighting, Christopher Akerlind; sound, Tom Clark; murals, Adair Peck; associate producer, Divonne Jarecki; casting, Stephanie Corsalini; production stage manager, Allison Sommers; press, Boneau/Bryan-Brown, Adrian Bryan-Brown, Craig Karpel.

Songwriter's efforts to hold his rock-and-roll band together. Previously produced off off Broadway at La Mama ETC. The play was presented without intermission.

MUSICAL NUMBERS

"Coming and Going" .... Luke, Gretta
(music by Billy Boesky and Steve Postell)
"More Than You Know" .... Gretta
(music by Billy Boesky, Deanna Kirk and Kevin Bents; lyrics by Billy Boesky and Deanna Kirk)
"Falling in Line" .... Luke
"Till I'm Gone" .... Luke, Gretta
(music by Billy Boesky and Steve Postell)
"Southbound Train" .... Gretta
(music by Billy Boesky and Steve Postell)
"Hey Lady" .... Luke
(music by Billy Boesky and Michael McCoy)
"Silo" .... Gretta, Luke
(music and lyrics by Billy Boesky and Josh Klausner)
"Fallen Angel" .... Luke
(music by Billy Boesky and Steve Postell)
"Unveil My Eyes" .... Will
"All Right" .... Company

Hide Your Love Away (42). By Kevin Scott. Produced by the Eclectic Theater Company in association with The Liverpool Production Company and Peter Breger at the Actors' Playhouse. Opened April 19, 1994. (Closed May 29, 1994)

Brian Epstein	Albert Macklin	Clive Epstein	Stephen Singer
Lynne Whelan	Sarah Long	Cilla Black	Amy Hohn
Teddy Baker	Justin Theroux		

Directed by Leonard Foglia; scenery, Michael McCarty; costumes, Markas Henry; lighting, Betsy Finston; sound, One Dream; dialect coach, Ralph Zito; fight director, Rick Sordelet; executive producer, Steven M. Levy; casting, Irene Stockton, Kelly Nugent; production stage manager, Bruce Greenwood; press, Shirley Herz Associates, Miller Wright.

Time: An evening in August 1967. Place: Sitting room used as an office in the home of Brian Epstein on Chapel Street in Belgravia, London.

Subtitled The Ballad of Brian Epstein, a crucial situation in the life of the man who was the manager of the Beatles.

Bring in the Morning (51). Musical based on the writings of young people participating in the "Poets in Public Service, Inc." program; adaptation and lyrics by Herb Schapiro; music by Gary William Friedman. Produced by Jeff Britton in association with Edgar M. Bronfman at the Variety Arts Theater. Opened April 23, 1994. (Closed June 5, 1994)

Sonya	Yassmin Alers	Alicia	Nicole Leach
Roberto	Roy Chicas	Jamal	Shannon Reyshard Peters

Judy .... Imelda de los Reyes
Cougar .... Sean Grant
Lakesha .... Inaya Jafa'n
Inez .... Yvette Lawrence
Mavis .... Raquel Polite
Hector .... Steven X. Ward
Nelson .... Kevin R. Wright

The Band (The Groove Masters): Louis St. Louis conductor, piano; Wayne Abravanel associate conductor, synthesizer; Jeff Porter drums; Steve Mack bass; Bob Rose guitar; Rick Kriska saxophone.

Directed by Bertin Rowser; co-directed and choreographed by Michele Asaf; Musical direction and dance arrangements, Louis St. Louis; scenery and projections, Ken Foy; costumes, Robert Mackintosh; lighting, Ken Billington; orchestrations, Dianne Adams McDowell; additional orchestrations, Michael Gibson; vocal arrangements, Gary William Friedman, Louis St. Louis; sound, Ivan Pokorny, Tom Clark; casting, Stephen Deangelis; production stage manager, Brian Meister; stage manager, Jill Cordle; press, Shirley Herz Associates, Shirley Herz, Miller Wright.

Time: Now. Place: The city of their minds.

Poems, stories and writings expressing the emotions and ideals of young people from age 16 to the early 20s, with music ranging through reggae, rap, gospel and contemporary pop, derived from the project Poets in Public Service, Inc., which sends professional writers to help youngsters express themselves.

ACT I

"Come Into My Jungle" .... Cougar, Company
"Bring in the Morning" .... Alicia, Company
"Let It Rain" .... Judy, Nelson, Sonya, Roberto, Inez, Company
"You (Tu)" .... Inez, Roberto
"Not Your Cup of Tea" .... Judy
"Ghetto of My Mind" .... Cougar
"Funky Eyes" .... Hector
"Another Cry" .... Inez
"I'm on My Way" .... Lakesha, Company
"Never Stop Believing" .... Company

ACT II

"Never Stop Believing" (Reprise) .... Company
"Something Is Wrong With Everyone Today" .... Sonya, Company
"Missing Person" .... Nelson
"The Light of Your" (La Luz de Tu Amor) .... Roberto
"Ghetto of My Mind" (Reprise) .... Cougar
"Hector's Dream" .... Hector, Company
"Trip" .... Jamal
"The Glory of Each Morning" .... Company
"Deliver My Soul" .... Mavis, Lakesha, Company
"I Want to Walk in a Garden" .... Company

Additional rap numbers "Best Kept Secret" and "Awake and a Dream" by Bertin Rowser were inspired by students of Boys Harbor Performing Arts in East Harlem, N.Y.

***Hysterical Blindness** (15). Musical with book by Leslie Jordan; music and lyrics by Joe Patrick Ward. Produced by Dana Matthow at Playhouse on VanDam. Opened May 19, 1994.

CAST: Storyteller (Leslie)—Leslie Jordan; Preacher, Buck, Commerical Director—Matthew Bennett; Miss Bessemer, A.D. #5, Ethyl Mae, Nurse, Sister Shame, Woman at Bus Station—Mary Bond Davis; Pastel Griffin, A.D. #2, Twin #1, Johnny Ruth, Girl With Dog—Terri Girvin; Grandma, Twin #2, A.D. #4, Sister Swope, Therapist—Blair Ross; Grady, A.D. #1, Medical Specialist, Tor, Sit-Com Director—Cordell Stahl; Earl, Clerk at Bus Station, A.D. #3, Master, Stepmonster, Video Clerk—David Titus.

Understudies: Female Roles—Mary Jo McConnell; Male Roles—Robert Roznowski.

Directed by Carolyne Barry; script development, Carolyne Barry; musical direction and vocal arrangement, Joe Patrick Ward; production design, Charles E. McCarry; costumes, Wern-Ying Hwarng; lighting, Phil Monat; musical supervision, Glenn Gordon; sound, Aural Fixation; musical staging, Mark Knowles, associate lighting designer, Archie Wilson; associate producer, Bonnie Loren; casting, Joe Rydell; production stage manager, Sarahjane Allison; press: Springer Associates, John Springer, Gary Springer, Candi Adams, Ann Guzzi.

Trials of a Tennessee Baptist coping with his mother's psychosomatic illness and trying to break into show business.

MUSICAL NUMBERS, ACT I: Prelude (Instrumental)/Long Long Way to Heaven; "Keep Smilin' Through"; "God Loves the Baptist"; "Precious Twins"; "Pessimistic Voices, Part One"; "Pessimistic Voices, Part Two"; "Come Little Children"; "Sing, All Ye Women of the Lord"; "Precious Twins" (Reprise); "Mother, May I Be Forgiven?".

ACT II: "A Prayer for Mama"; "Keep Smilin' Through" (Reprise); "The Hymn of Shame"; Ace's Revelation (Instrumental)/"What a Friend We Have in Jesus" (by George Scriven and C.C. Converse); "I'm Twirling"; "The Trashy Effeminate Hoodlum"; "Just the Way We're Bred"; "Keep Smilin' Through" (Finale); Postlude (Instrumental).

CAST REPLACEMENTS AND TOURING COMPANIES

Compiled by Jeffrey A. Finn

The following is a list of the major cast replacements of record in productions which opened in previous years, but were still playing in New York during a substantial part of the 1993-94 season; or were on a first-class tour in 1993-94.

The name of each major role is listed in *italics* beneath the title of the play in the first column. In the second column directly opposite appears the name of the actor who created the role in the original New York production (whose opening date appears in *italics* at the top of the column). In shows of the past five years, indented immediately beneath the original actor's name are the names of subsequent New York replacements, together with the date of replacement when available. In shows that have run longer than five years, only this season's or the most recent cast replacements are listed under the names of the original cast members.

The third column gives information about first-class touring companies. When there is more than one roadshow company, #1, #2, etc., appear before the name of the performer who created the role in each company (and the city and date of each company's first performance appears in *italics* at the top of the column). Their subsequent replacements are also listed beneath their names in the same manner as the New York companies, with dates when available.

BLOOD BROTHERS

	New York 4/25/93
Mrs. Johnson	Stephanie Lawrence Petula Clark 8/16/93
Narrator	Warwick Evans Adrian Zmed
Mickey	Con O'Neill David Cassidy 8/16/93
Eddie	Mark Michael Hutchinson Shaun Cassidy
Mrs. Lyons	Barbara Walsh
Linda	Jan Graveson Shauna Hicks

CATS

	New York 10/7/82	*National Tour 1993-94*

Alonzo	Hector Jaime Mercado
	  Angelo Fraboni
		William Patrick Dunne
		  MacArthur Hambrick
		  Michael Koetting

Bustopher	Stephen Hanan Jeffrey Clonts	Buddy Crutchfield Bryan Landrine Lee Lobenhofer Richard Poole
Bombalurina	Donna King Marlene Danielle	Wendy Walter Helen Frank Dana D'Amore
Carbucketty	Steven Gelfer Ray Roderick (character eliminated)	(not in tour)
Cassandra	Rene Ceballos Colleen Dunn Amy N. Henning Leigh Webster Sara Henry	Laura Quinn Darlene Wilson Elizabeth Mills
Coricopat	Rene Clemente James Hadley	(not in tour)
Demeter	Wendy Edmead Betsy Chang	N. Elaine Wiggins Patty Everett
Grizabella	Betty Buckley Liz Callaway	Mary Gutzi Jan Horvath Rosemary Loar
Jellylorum	Bonnie Simmons Nina Hennessey	Linda Strassler Lindsay Dyett Patty Gobie
Jennyanydots	Anna McNeely Carol Dilley	Alica C. DeChant
Mistoffeles	Timothy Scott Lindsay Chambers	Christopher Gattelli Vince Pesce Joey Pizzi
Mungojerrie	Rene Clemente Roger Kachel	Gavan Pamer Robert Barry Fleming Todd Lester
Munkustrup	Harry Groener Keith Bernardo	Robert Amirante Kevin McCready Bryan Batt Kevin McCready
Old Deuteronomy	Ken Page Ken Prymus	Jimmy Lockett John Treacy Egan
Plato/Macavity	Kenneth Ard Robb Edward Morris	Taylor Wicker Randy Wojcik Taylor Wicker
Pouncival	Herman W. Sebek Devanand N. Janki	Joey Gyondla Joseph Favalora Joey Gyondla
Rum Tum Tugger	Terrence Mann David Hibbard	David Hibbard Brad Minoff Hunter Foster B.K. Kennelly John Seykell

CRAZY FOR YOU—Karen Ziemba and Carleton Carpenter as daughter and father in the long-run musical

Rumpleteazer	Christine Langner Christine DeVito	Jennifer Cody Maria Jo Ralabate
Sillabub	Whitney Kershaw Jeanine Meyers	Bethany Samuelson Amelia Marshall Lanene Charters
Skimbleshanks	Reed Jones George Smyros	Carmen Yurich Craig Meyer John Scherer Mickey Nugent
Tantomile	Janet L. Hubert Michelle Artigas	(not in tour)
Tumblebrutus	Robert Hoshour Marc Ellis Holland	Tim Hunter Randy Bettis Jay Poindexter Tim Hunter

Victoria	Cynthia Onrubia Kayoko Yoshioka	Tricia Marshall Natasha Davidson Kristie Tice

Note: Only this season's or the most recent cast replacements are listed above under the names of the original cast members. For previous replacements, see previous volumes of *Best Plays.*

CRAZY FOR YOU

	New York 2/19/92	*Dallas 5/11/93*
Polly Baker	Jodi Benson Karen Ziemba 3/15/94	Karen Ziemba Crista Moore
Bobby Child	Harry Groener	James Brennan
Tess	Beth Leavel	Cathy Susan Pyles
Bela Zangler	Bruce Adler	Stuart Zagnit
Irene Roth	Michele Pawk Kay McClelland	Kay McClelland Belle Callaway
Mother	Jane Connell	Lanka Peterson Ann B. Davis
Everett Baker	Ronn Caroll Carleton Carpenter	Carlton Carpenter Al Checco

THE FANTASTICKS

	New York 5/3/60
El Gallo	Jerry Orbach Robert Vincent Smith
Luisa	Rita Gardner Debbie Pavelka
Matt	Kenneth Nelson Richard Roland

Note: Only this season's or the most recent cast replacements are listed above under the names of the original cast members. For previous replacements, see previous volumes of *Best Plays.*

FIVE GUYS NAMED MOE

	New York 4/8/92	*Los Angeles 7/7/93*
Nomax	Jerry Dixon Weyman Thompson 12/92	Kirk Taylor
Big Moe	Doug Eskew	Doug Eskew
Four-Eyed Moe	Milton Craig Nealy	Milton Craig Nealy
No Moe	Kevin Ramsey	Keith Tyrone
Eat Moe	Jeffrey D. Sams	Kevyn Brackett
Little Moe	Glenn Turner	Jeffrey Polk

FOREVER PLAID

	New York 5/20/90
Sparky	Jason Graae Dale Sandish Michael Winther David Benoit Daniel Eli Friedman David Benoit
Smudge	David Engel Greg Jbara John Ganun Tom Cianfichi
Jinx	Stan Chandler Paul Binotto Ryan Perry
Francis	Guy Stroman Drew Geraci 4/15/91 Neil Nash Robert Lambert Drew Geraci

Note: Many out-of-town stagings of *Forever Plaid* were local productions, but casts of two road companies appear in *The Best Plays of 1990-91.*

GUYS AND DOLLS

	New York 4/14/92	*Hartford 9/15/92*
Sky Masterson	Peter Gallagher Tom Wopat 10/12/92 Burke Moses 4/12/93 Tom Wopat	Richard Muenz
Nathan Detroit	Nathan Lane Jonathan Hadary 5/17/93 Jamie Farr 3/15/94	Lewis J. Stadlen David Garrision Philip LeStrange Steve Landesberg
Sarah Brown	Josie de Guzman	Patricia Ben Peterson
Miss Adelaide	Faith Prince Jennifer Allen	Lorna Luft Beth McVey
Nicely-Nicely Johnson	Walter Bobbie Larry Cahn	Kevin Ligon

JEFFREY

	New York 3/6/93
Jeffrey	John Michael Higgins Jeffrey Hayenga
Steve	Tom Hewitt Tony Brown
Darius	Bryan Batt Greg Louganis

Sterling	Edward Hibbert Peter Bartlett

KISS OF THE SPIDER WOMAN

	New York 5/3/93
Molina	Brent Carver Jeff Hyslop Howard McGillin
Warden	Herndon Lackey
Valentin	Anthony Crivello Brian Mitchell
Spider Woman/Aurora	Chita Rivera Vanessa Williams
Molina's Mother	Merle Louise
Marta	Kirsti Carnahan

LES MISERABLES

	New York 3/12/87	*#1 Boston 12/5/87* *#2 Los Angeles 5/21/88* *#3 Tampa 11/18/88*
Jean Valjean	Colm Wilkinson Craig Schulman	#1 William Solo Mark McKerracher #2 William Solo Richard Poole #3 Gary Barker Craig Schulman Frederick C. Inkley
Javert	Terrence Mann Robert Cuccioli	#1 Herndon Lackey Richard Kinsey #2 Jeff McCarthy Tim Bowman #3 Peter Samuel David Masenheimer
Fantine	Randy Graff Andrea McArdle 8/16/93 Susan Gilmour	#1 Diane Frantantoni Anne Runolfsson #2 Elinore O'Connell Kelly Ground #3 Hollis Resnik Alice Ripley Christy Baron Anne Torsiglieri
Enjolras	Michael Maguire Ron Bohmer	#1 John Herrera Christopher Yates #2 Greg Blanchard Craig Oldfather #3 Greg Zerkle Gary Mauer
Marius	David Bryant Craig Rubano	#1 Hugh Panaro Peter Gunter

		#2 Reece Holland John Ruess #3 Matthew Porretta Hayden Adams
Cosette	Judy Kuhn Jennifer Lee Andrews	#1 Tamara Jenkins Kimberly Behlman #2 Karen Fineman Ellen Rockne #3 Jaqueline Piro Barbra Russell
Eponine	Frances Ruffele Sarah Uriarte	#1 Renee Veneziale Susan Tilson #2 Michelle Nicastro Misty Cotton #3 Michele Maika Jennifer Rae Beck Sarah Uriarte Gina Felicia
Thenardier	Leo Burmester Drew Eshelman	#1 Tom Robbins Drew Eshelman #2 Gary Beach #3 Paul Ainsley J.P. Dougherty
Mme. Thenardier	Jennifer Butt Diana Rogers Gina Ferrall	#1 Victoria Clark Rosalyn Rahn #2 Kay Cole Gina Ferrall #3 Linda Kerns Kelly Ebsary

Note: Only this season's or the most recent cast replacements are listed above under the names of the original cast members. For previous replacements, see previous volumes of *Best Plays.*

MILLENNIUM APPROACHES

	New York 5/4/93
Hannah Pitt	Kathleen Chalfant
Roy Cohn	Ron Leibman F. Murray Abraham 1/11/94
Joe Pitt	David Marshall Grant
Harper Pitt	Marcia Gay Harden Susan Bruce 1/94 Cynthia Nixon 4/94
Belize	Jeffrey Wright
Louis Ironson	Joe Mantello
Prior Walter	Stephen Spinella
Angel	Ellen McLaughlin

MISS SAIGON

	New York 4/11/91	*Chicago 10/12/93*
The Engineer	Jonathan Pryce	Raul Aranas

	Francis Ruivivar 8/19/91 Jonathan Pryce 9/30/91 Francis Ruivivar 12/16/91 Herman Sebek Alan Muraoka	
Kim	Lea Salonga Lelia Florentino 3/16/92 Rona Figueroa	Jennie Kwan Jennifer C. Paz (alt.) Jennifer C. Paz Hazel Raymundo (alt.) Melanie Tojio (alt.)
Chris	Willy Falk Sean McDermott 12/16/91 Chris Peccaro Jarrod Emick Eric Kunze	Jarrod Emick Eric Kunze Peter Lockyer

THE PHANTOM OF THE OPERA

	New York 1/26/88	*#1 Los Angeles 5/31/90* *#2 Chicago 5/24/90* *#3 Seattle 12/13/92*
The Phantom	Michael Crawford Jeff Keller Davis Gaines	#1 Michael Crawford Davis Gaines #2 Mark Jacoby Rick Hilsabeck #3 Frank D'Ambrosio Grant Norman
Christine Daae	Sarah Brightman Tracy Shane Laurie Stephenson	#1 Dale Kristien Mary Darcy (alt.) #2 Karen Culliver Laurie Stephenson Rita Harvey (alt.) #3 Tracy Shane Adrienne McEwan Sylvia Rhyne (alt.)
Raoul	Steve Barton Ciaran Sheehan	#1 Reece Holland Ray Saar #2 Keith Buterbaugh Nat Chandler #3 Ciaran Sheehan John Schroeder

Note: Alternates play the role of Christine Daae Monday and Wednesday evenings. Only this season's or the most recent cast replacements are listed above under the names of the original cast members. For previous replacements, see previous volumes of *Best Plays*.

SOMEONE WHO'LL WATCH OVER ME

	New York 11/23/92
Edward	Stephen Rea David Dukes 6/1/93
Adam	James McDaniel Chuck Cooper 3/30/93

Michael	Alec McCowen Michael York 4/6/93	

THE SISTERS ROSENSWEIG

	New York 3/18/93	*Norfolk, VA 1/7/94*
Sara Goode	Jane Alexander Michael Learned 8/16/93	Mariette Hartley
Georgeous Teitelbaum	Madeline Kahn Linda Lavin 8/16/93	Caroline Aaron
Pfeni Rosensweig	Christine Estabrooke Joanne Camp	Joan McMurtrey
Mervyn Kant	Robert Klein Hal Linden 8/16/93 Tony Roberts 1/18/94	Charles Cioffi

THE WILL ROGERS FOLLIES

	New York 5/1/91	*San Francisco 8/25/92*
Will Rogers	Keith Carradine Mac Davis 5/18/92 Larry Gatlin 2/16/93	Keith Carradine Mac Davis Larry Gatlin Mac Davis Larry Gatlin
Betty Blake	Dee Hoty Nancy Ringham 5/18/92	Dee Hoty Danette Cuming
Ziegfeld's Favorite	Cady Huffman Susan Anton 12/9/91 Cady Huffman 1/27/92 Marla Maples 8/3/92 Kimberly Hester 5/4/93 Lisa Niemi 5/27/93	Leigh Zimmerman Dana Leigh Jackson
Clem Rogers	Dick Latessa Mickey Rooney 7/6/93	

THE WHO'S TOMMY

	New York 4/22/93	*Dallas 10/12/93*
Tommy Walker	Michael Cerveris	Steve Isaacs
Captain Walker	Jonathan Dokuchitz	Jason Workman
Mrs. Walker	Marcia Mitzman Laura Dean	Jessica Molaskey
Uncle Ernie	Paul Kandel	William Youmans
Cousin Kevin	Anthony Barrile	Roger Bart
The Gypsy	Cheryl Freeman	Kennya Ramsey
Sally Simpson	Sherrie Scott	Hilary Morse

SHOWS OF OTHER YEARS ON FIRST CLASS TOURS IN 1993–94

ANNIE GET YOUR GUN

	Baltimore 3/2/93
Annie Oakley	Cathy Rigby
Frank Butler	Brent Barrett
Charlie Davenport	Paul V. Ames
Chief Sitting Bull	Mauricio Bustamante
Dolly Tate	KT Sullivan Robin Lusby

CAMELOT

	Detroit 9/8/92
Arthur	Robert Goulet
Guenevere	Patricia Kies
Lancelot	Steve Blanchard
Merlyn	James Valentine
Mordred	Kenneth Boys Tucker McGrady
Nimue	Vanessa Shaw

Note: This production was brought to Broadway, opening 6/21/93.

GREASE

	Wilmington, Del. 1/13/94
Vince Fontaine	Brian Bradley
Miss Lynch	Marcia Lewis
Betty Rizzo	Rosie O'Donnell
Doody	Sam Harris
Kenickie	Jason Opsahl
Frenchy	Jessica Stone
Danny Zuko	Ricky Paull Golden
Sandy Dumbrowski	Susan Wood

Note: This production was brought to Broadway, opening 5/11/94.

HAIR

	Baltimore 2/23/94
Berger	Kent Dalian
Claude	Luther Creek
Dionne	Catrice Joseph
Woof	Sean Jenness
Hud	Henry Shead Jr.
Sheila	Cathy Trien
Jeanie	Ali Zorlas
Crissy	Rochele Rosenberg
Mead	Matthew Ferrell
Hubert	Eric Davis

JESUS CHRIST SUPERSTAR

	Baltimore 12/12/92
Jesus of Nazareth	Ted Neeley
Mary Magdalene	Leesa Richards
Judas	Carl Anderson
Pontius Pilate	Dennis DeYoung
King Herod	Laurent Giroux
Peter	Kevin R. Wright
Caiphas	David Bedella
Simon	Steven X. Ward

JOSEPH AND THE AMAZING TECHNICOLOR DREAMCOAT

	Los Angeles 2/25/93
Joseph	Michael Damian
Narrator	Kelli Rabke
Jacob; Potiphar; Guru	Clifford David
Pharoah	Robert Torti
Butler	Glenn Sneed
Baker	Bill Nolte
Mrs. Potiphar	Julie Bond Mamie Duncan-Gibbs

Note: This production was brought to Broadway, opening 11/10/93.

THE SOUND OF MUSIC

	Baltimore 11/30/93
Maria Rainer	Marie Osmond
Captain Georg Von Trapp	Laurence Guittard
Liesl	Vanessa Dorman
Friedrich	Erik McCormack
Louisa	Laura Bundy
Kurt	Stephen Blosil
Brigitta	Sara Zelle
Marta	Jacy DeFilippo
Gretl	Lisbeth Zelle
Rolf Gruber	Richard H. Blake
Elsa Schraeder	Jane Seaman
Max Detweiler	John Tillotson
Mother Abbess	Claudia Cummings

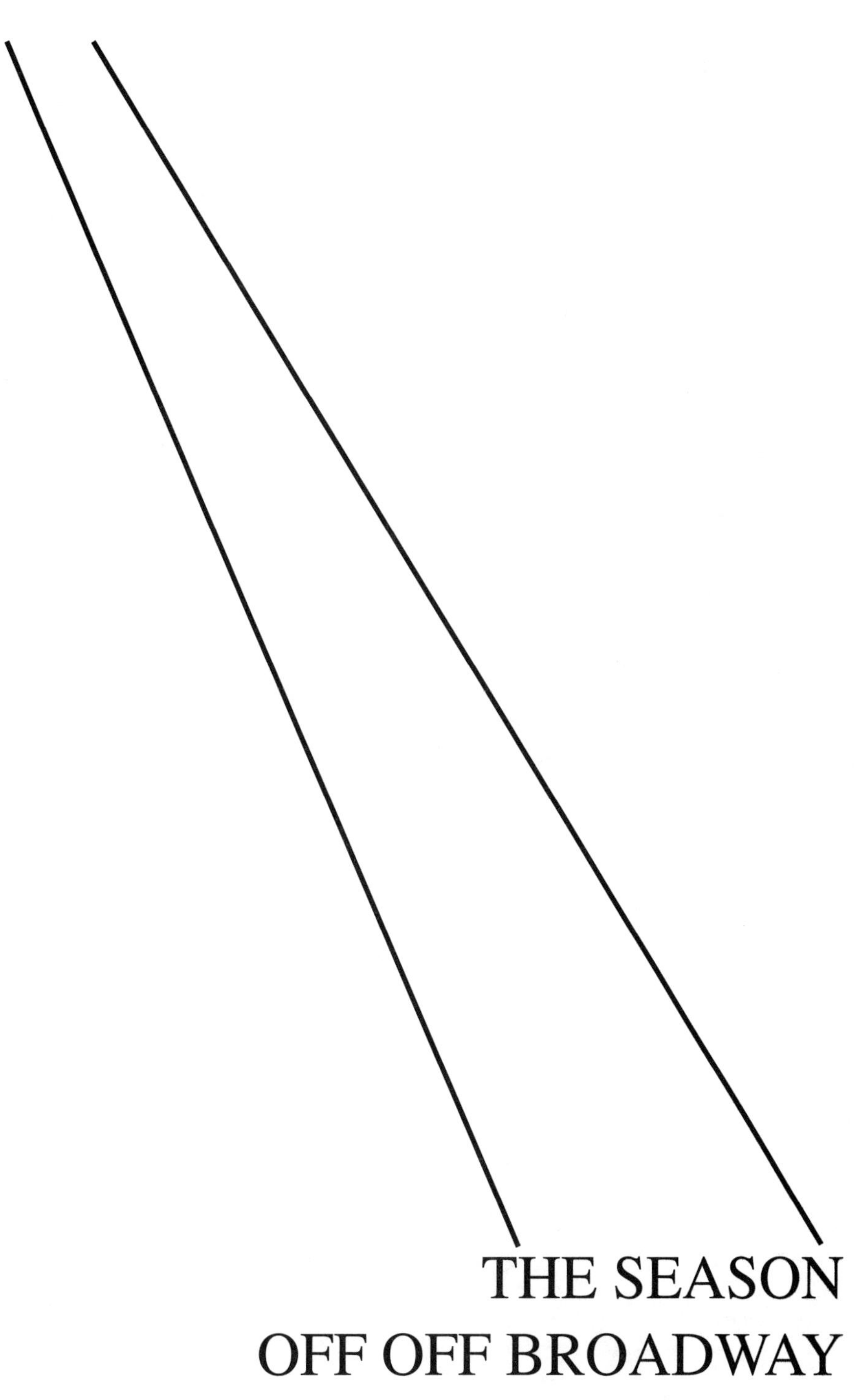

THE SEASON OFF OFF BROADWAY

OFF OFF BROADWAY

By Mel Gussow

OFF OFF Broadway remains the most inclusive area in the American theater, at least partly for economic reasons. Away from union strictures and profit-making motives, the companies can do more for less money and can take more chances. While long-running institutions like La Mama, the Ridiculous Theatrical Company and the Pan Asian Repertory Theater continue to thrive, younger companies are infusing their own vitality—places like the Signature Theater Company and Primary Stages. Increasingly, it is difficult to define the parameters of off off Broadway, especially as shows are moved into extended engagements.

Three years ago, James Houghton initiated the Signature Theater, with the innovative idea of devoting an entire season to a single writer. Romulus Linney and Lee Blessing were first in line. This year the choice was Edward Albee. At the time of Mr. Houghton's selection, Albee was distinctly out of favor in theatrical circles. By the end of the season, at least partly through the efforts of Signature Theater, he was, once again, the most acclaimed playwright in New York.

The series opened with Albee's *Marriage Play,* a deviously comic dialogue about a collapsing marriage, a kind of coda to *Who's Afraid of Virginia Woolf?*. In the play, Tom Klunis and Kathleen Butler warily flayed each other with words. That was followed by a double bill of *Counting the Ways* and *Listening*, a whimsical cartoon paired with an abstraction. Next was a trio of "sand plays"—revivals of *The Sandbox*, one of Albee's earliest works, the monodrama *Box* and the New York premiere of *Finding the Sun*. This anthology was the eye-opener of the series. *Sandbox* was both mirthful and elegiac in its evocation of an American family (in a fine cast, Jane Hoffman, Mommy in the original *Sandbox*, moved up to the role of Grandma). *Box* proved to be Beckettian. *Finding the Sun* was an amusing roundelay about couples uncoupling at the beach. The center of attention was a questing teenager, deftly played by James Van Der Beek. Signature completed the season with *Fragments*, sometimes sardonic journal cuttings in search of a play.

The festival underscored the range and the persistence of the playwright and seemed to complement quite naturally Albee's comeback with *Three Tall Women* in its New York premiere OOB at the Vineyard Theater prior to its off-Broadway run. In other words, Signature performed a valuable service to the playwright as well as to the theater. Next season the company plans to present the work of Horton Foote and, with success, seems likely to secure a new theater for a permanent home.

Under the artistic direction of Casey Childs, Primary Stages has given particular encouragement to playwrights with a linguistic limberness, opening David Ives's *All in the Timing*, and then sending it on for a long run off Broadway. Later, Primary Stages turned to one of its other favorite playwrights, Mac Wellman, with *The Hyacinth Macaw*, a companion play to Wellman's *A Murder of Crows*, previously presented at this theater. Both are phantasmal apocalyptical comedies in which characters are trapped in delusionary nightmares. The acme of *Macaw* was reached by Steve Mellor, delivering a torrential monologue of vivid verbiage. In a change of pace, Wellman was also represented (at Soho Rep) by his variation on *Dracula*, with the title pronounced in three piercing syllables. Cited as an outstanding OOB production, this play is both literate and bloodthirsty in its view of the liveliness of the undead. The staging by Julian Webber was environmental style, surrounding theatergoers with necromantic tableaux. Acted to the hilt, the work featured diabolical performances by Thomas Jay Ryan (in the title role), Christopher McCann, a very vulnerable Julia Gibson and a batty chorus of Vampirettes.

As a directorial conceptualist, the prolific Anne Bogart had a double-barreled festival, with *Marathon Dancing* (a play about the dance craze of the 1930s, with text by Laura Harrington) for the En Garde Arts site-specific troupe, and a fascinating Bogart original, *The Medium*, at the New York Theater Workshop. *The Medium* was a synergistic movement piece inspired by the writings of Marshall McLuhan. On one level, this was 90 minutes of nonstop infotainment as McLuhan lectured the audience, foretelling a life controlled by computers. As with Bogart's *No Plays No Poetry*, a dramatization of Brecht's non-dramatic writings, *The Medium* transformed prose into vibrant theater. In the central role, Tom Nelis created a kinetic portrait of a man apparently ahead of his times.

Earlier in the season, the New York Theater Workshop offered Claudia Shear a stage for her circuitous saga of a careering life, *Blown Sideways Through Life*, and then moved the show into a long-running off-Broadway engagement. Among other monologuists filling off-off stages was Danny Hoch with *Some People*, the voices of New York (at Performance Space 122). *Frustration (Frustra-azioni)* was a smell-a-rama abattoir as monologue written and performed by Dario D'Ambrosi at La Mama.

The indefatigable Richard Foreman has been pursuing an idiosyncratic course for 25 years, channeling his diaristic thoughts into quirky, electronically enhanced self-documentations. This year's *My Head Was a Sledgehammer*, cited as an outstanding OOB production, was one of his more tantalizing exercises. Inspired by fragments of a play by Friedrich Hölderlin, the work dealt with, in Foreman's words, a professor who "through silliness and weirdness tries to introduce his students to the poetic method." Although this was not necessarily evident in the elliptical narrative, his highly stylized method captured our attention. More to the point, a demanding teacher (Thomas Jay Ryan, who was also Wellman's Dracula) confronted two unruly students in a classroom battle royal. The Ontological-Hysteric stage sizzled with Foremanesque techniques and signatures (string, clocks and the author supplying sepulchral marginal notes).

Mel Gussow Citations

Thomas Jay Ryan is pictured here in leading roles in two of the three productions cited as the season's outstanding OOB offerings: *above,* in the title role of Mac Wellman's *Dracula* ("Both literate and blood-thirsty in its view of the liveliness of the undead") at Soho Rep; and *right,* with Henry Stram and Jan Leslie Harding in Richard Foreman's *My Head Was a Sledgehammer* ("One of his more tantalizing exercises") at Ontological-Hysteric theater

Robert Wilson, who operates mostly in European opera houses, made a rare return to the Brooklyn Academy of Music with *The Black Rider*, a musical (or pop opera) written in collaboration with Tom Waits and William Burroughs. *The Black Rider* takes off from the opera *Der Freischutz*, filtering it through Wilson's perfervid imagination. In this story of a man who sells his soul for the gift of magic bullets, coffins levitated—and bullets seemed to whiz around the theater. The diverse elements coalesced into a *danse macabre* of ghoulish delight.

John Kelly was also at the Brooklyn Academy with his latest epic, *Light Shall Lift Them*, an eerie perambulation around the life of Barbette, a transvestite trapeze artist who was taken up by Jean Cocteau. In this surrealistic play, Kelly was both Barbette and Cocteau, interweaving their lives with a Copland-like score by Bill Obrecht.

Though the piece seemed disconnected, its creator remains a virtuosic talent. Fred Curchack, who astonished audiences with his one-man *The Tempest*, *Stuff as Dreams Are Made On*, returned to New York with a smaller, slighter piece, *Heddy and Teddy* (in a festival of one-man shows presented by the Watermark Theater). As intended, this was a closet drama, with Curchack offering himself a platform to rap about religion, abortion and proctology. The piece was chaotic but intriguing. Theodora Skipitares extended her scientific explorations at La Mama, with *Under the Knife*, a people and puppet show about the world of medicine.

Over the years, the York Theater Company has made a substantial reputation with a series of chamber-size revivals of Stephen Sondheim musicals. This season the company brought back Sondheim's 1981 *Merrily We Roll Along* after what amounted to a long post-Broadway reconditioning process on the road. In revised form, the show seemed sharper. But the effect was the same: fine score, problematic book about the wages of success, in a story told backwards. As directed by Susan H. Schulman, the performers Malcolm Gets, Adam Heller and, especially, Amy Ryder were exceptional in the leading roles. As its name indicates, the Second Stage generally revives shows of the recent past, but occasionally it puts on new work, this season a specialty act with a difference: *Ricky Jay & His 52 Assistants,* an evening of card tricks as performed with brilliance and charm. Jay is unparalleled at his profession, a masterly illusionist filled with arcane information about the history of sleight of hand. The show, staged by David Mamet, deservedly moved into an extended run at this tiny theater.

The CSC brought in Tony Kushner's haunting adaptation of Corneille's *The Illusion* and gave Charles Busch center stage in *The Maids*. Jean Cocteau Repertory swung from Wedekind to Pirandello to Shaw. Shakespeare was in relatively short supply, with Mark Rylance moving into the role of director with a production of *As You Like It* for Theater for a New Audience. For the same company, Julie Taymor turned her inventive mind to *Titus Andronicus*. As usual, she made magical use of tableaux. Robert Stattel was a stormy Titus, but the rest of the cast was uneven.

The multi-talented Kevin Kling was represented by his wistful dream play, *The Ice-Fishing Play*, previously staged at the Humana Festival of New American Plays at the Actors Theater of Louisville with the author in the leading role. In *Wifey*, Tom Noonan turned his playwright's camera on a slice of life—a meandering play in which the audience eavesdropped on two mismatched couples (Noonan and Julie Hagerty, Wallace Shawn and Karen Young). As director and star of the Ridiculous Theatrical Company, Everett Quinton continued to carry on the tradition of Charles Ludlam, acting in Ludlam's *How Not to Write a Play*; then, in *Movieland*, reenacting scenes in classic Hollywood films. Tisa Chang's Pan Asian Rep offered a new play, Kitty Chen's *Eating Chicken Feet*, and one from the 1930s, Cao Yu's *Wilderness*.

Every year, the Ensemble Studio Theater reinvigorates the art of the one-act play. In its annual Marathon, the company offers a festival of short works by celebrated and emerging writers. This year, theatergoers could choose from a baker's dozen of candidates. Among the worthiest entries were Herb Gardner's *I'm With Ya, Duke*, in which David Margulies was a cantankerous octogenarian and John Guare's *New York Actor*, a mischievous look at the traumas and tantrums of the title species. Promise was demonstrated in plays by Romulus Linney (*Paradise*, with Lois Smith as a survivor of domestic warfare), Edward Allan Baker and Antoine O'Flatharta. Amid these and a number of disappointments (including a comedy by Steve Martin), one play stood out: Christopher Durang's *For Whom the Southern Belle Tolls*, an uproarious spoof of *The Glass Menagerie*. Though it ran only 30 minutes, the play deserves a citation as an outstanding OOB production. There were splendid performances by Liz Mackay as the mother and Keith Reddin as her son Lawrence (Durang's delirious version of the lame Laura) who cherished his collection of glass swizzle sticks. Durang's *Belle* was a salutary tonic at the season's end.

PLAYS PRODUCED OFF OFF BROADWAY

AND ADDITIONAL PRODUCTIONS

Compiled by Camille Croce Dee

Here is a comprehensive sampling of off-off-Broadway and other experimental or peripheral 1993-94 productions in New York. There is no definitive "off-off-Broadway" area or qualification. To try to define or regiment it would be untrue to its fluid, exploratory purpose. The listing below of hundreds of works produced by more than 100 OOB groups and others is as inclusive as reliable sources will allow, however, and takes in all leading Manhattan-based, new-play producing, English-language organizations.

The more active and established producing groups are identified in **bold face type,** in alphabetical order, with artistic policies and the names of the managing directors given whenever these are a matter of record. Each group's 1993-94 schedule, with emphasis on new plays and with revivals of classics usually omitted, is listed with play titles in CAPITAL LETTERS. Often these are works-in-progress with changing scripts, casts and directors, sometimes without an engagement of record (but an opening or early performance date is included when available).

Many of these off-off-Broadway groups have long since outgrown a merely experimental status and are offering programs which are the equal in professionalism and quality (and in some cases the superior) of anything in the New York theater, with special contractual arrangements like the showcase code, letters of agreement (allowing for longer runs and higher admission prices than usual) and, closer to the edge of the commercial theater, a so-called "mini-contract." In the list below, all available data on opening dates, performance numbers and major production and acting credits (almost all for Equity members) is included in the entries of these special-arrangement offerings.

A large selection of lesser-known groups and other shows that made appearances off off Broadway during the season appears under the "Miscellaneous" heading at the end of this listing.

American Place Theater. New American plays in their world premieres. Wynn Handman artistic director, Susannah Halston executive director.

BIBLIOMANIA (one-man show) (24). By and with Roger Rosenblatt. October 3, 1993. Director, Wynn Handman; scenery, Kert Lundell; lighting, Christopher Boll.

JIMMY TINGLE'S UNCOMMON SENSE (one-man show) (46). By and with Jimmy Tingle. October 31, 1993. Director, Larry Arrick; lighting, Christopher Boll.

COME DOWN BURNING (22). By Kia Corthron. November 7, 1993. Director, Judyie Al-Bilali; scenery, Kert Lundell; lighting, Shirley Prendergast; costumes, Judy Dearing. With Kim Yancey, Serena Henry, Myra Lucretia Taylor, Tse-Mach Washington, Shona Tucker.

THE MAYOR OF BOYS TOWN (one-man show) (22). By Barnaby Spring and Elise Thoron. March 15, 1994. Director, Elise Thoron; scenery, Joel Reynolds; lighting, Brian MacDevitt and Louise C. Dizon; costumes, Emma Cairns. With Barnaby Spring.

American Theater of Actors. Dedicated to providing a creative atmosphere for new American playwrights, actors and directors. James Jennings artistic director.

ACADEMIC AFFAIRS. By John Attanas. June 9, 1993. Director, Ken Stuart. With Ellen Bradshaw, Meissa Baker, Michael Giannini, Jennifer Gibbs, Stephen Peters, Don Sheehan.

ANTIGONE. By Sophocles. June 16, 1993. Director, James Jennings. With Carolina Barcos, Tom Bruce, Michael Colombo, Kelsie Chance, Courtney Everett, Sally Graudons, Anne Jennings, Colleen Kelley, Kathleen Mancini.

THE NAVAJO CREATION STORY. By James Jennings. July 7, 1993. Director, Shep Howard. With Joseph David, Mat Sarter, Kurt Gombar, Gordon Gauntlett Jr., Vivienne Jurado, Claes Lilja, Michael Ladagana.

HOME AGAIN. By Henry Slesar. July 21, 1993. Director, David Conroy. With Michael Colombo, Ronnie Siegel, Ralph Feliciello, Mark Scherman.

CROSSFIRE. By John Walsh. July 28, 1993. Director, Dan Sturges. With Chance Kelly, Joe Reynolds, Gary Richards.

TWO GENTLEMEN OF VERONA. By William Shakespeare. Director, Diane Van Beuren. August 18, 1993. With Jerry Berk, Stephen Blackheart, Tom Bruce, Budwell, Noemi de la Puente, Anthony DiMaria, Nina Jakobsson, Amy Ketchum, Jeff Lynn, Christopher Pursil, Joe Reynolds, Larry Ratzkin, Veronika Schmidt, Gavin Smith, Jordan Torjussen.

SKEETER AN' MAYBA. By Michael Meadors. September 8, 1993. Director, Jane Culley. With William Hallmark, Lin Ciangio.

BUFFALO GRASS. Written and directed by James Jennings. September 8, 1993. With Anthony Jones, Stacey Lisk, Katie Carrico, Kevin Baskett. (Reopened September 22 and December 6, 1993.)

WHISPERS OF THE KOSHIRIS. Written and directed by James Jennings. October 6, 1993. With Don Damico, Colleen Kelley, Billy Gross.

THE SAME SQUARE OF DUST. By Mary Gage. October 13, 1993. Director, D.A.G. Burgos. With Michael Colombo, David Conroy, Sally Masakowski, Aaron Nay, Gary Richards.

ONE! TWO! THREE! SURPRISE. By Gregory Reardon. October 20, 1993. Director, James Jennings. With Ellen Bradshaw, Tom Bruce, Anne Correa, John Borras, Stewart Vigoda, Madelaine Schleyer.

WAR RABBIT. By Larry Maness. November 10, 1993. Director, Alan Osburn. With Alexander Blaise, Will Buchanan, Kelly Ann Moore, Robert Most, Robert W. Smith.

SNOW. By Stuart Edelson. November 17, 1993. Director, Michael Arzouane. With Jerry Berk, Flip Brown, John Combs, Evelyn Crawford, Ed Mahler, Bill Massof, Vickie Meyers.

BELTWAY ROULETTE. By Mark Scharf. December 1, 1993. Director, Leo Boylan. With Stephanie Barron, Robert Croft, David Erbach, D.J. Mendel, Michael Valente.

THE INTRUDER. By Bernard Myers. December 1, 1993. Director, William Gilmore. With Mark Auerbach, David Buxbaum, Chris Jennings, Patti Uhrich, William Swarts, Ray Weir, Belle Maria Wheat.

THE BOMB INSIDE. By Joseph Coyne. December 15, 1993. Director, David LeBarron. With Anthony Aziz, Julie Brimberg, Sharon Gardner, Stacey Lisk, Shawn Parr, Jeff Sass, Bryan Keith Schany.

FAMILY LINEN. Written and directed by D.A.G. Burgos. December 15, 1993. With Mark Macken, Shiek Mahmud-Bey, Sally Masakowski, French Napier, Hilda Willis.

EVENSONG. By Mary Gage. December 20, 1993. Director, Britton Payne. With Wayne Gordy, Kelly Ann Giante, Eddie Daniels, Maureen Pedala, Maria Petrone, Don Sheehan.

VOICES FROM THE HEARTLAND. Written and directed by James Jennings. February 2, 1994. With Josephine Cashman, Christopher Groenewold, Cinda Lawrence, Patrick Waggoner.

FORCES and TROT, TROT, TROT . . . (one-act plays). Written and directed by James Jennings. February 9, 1994. With John Borras, Patrick Waggoner, Mat Sarter, Courtney Everett, Jane Culley, Tom Bruce, Benjamin Quinto.

COUNTRY HOLLER. By Norman Rhodes. February 23, 1994. Director, Joe Heissan. With Judith Boxley, Flip Brown, Josephine Cashman, Jim Forsha, Christopher Groenewold, Annette Lascoe, Jonathan Peters, Madelaine Schleyer, Clark Reiner.

FLIGHT OF CHILDREN and TOGETHER AGAIN (one-act plays). Written and directed by James Jennings. March 2, 1994. With Cinda Lawrence, Frank Lewallen, Neil Potter, Catherine Corcoran, Anthony Jones, Lena Jakobsson.

HAWK DREAMING. By Frank Cossa. March 30, 1994. Director, Michael Gardner. With Cheryl Adam, Ken Coughlin, Connie Giordano, Michael Giannini, Cinda Lawrence, Stacey Lisk, Alfred Pagano, Matt Savage.

LOSERS, WEEPERS. By Frank Crow. April 20, 1994. Director, Britton Payne. With Joseph Amorando, Ellen Campbell, Katie Carrico, William Christopher, Anthony Jones, John Knox, Kathleen Erin McGuirk, Vanessa Thorpe.

STRANGERS THERE. By Eve Hammond. April 27, 1994. Director, Marc Anthony Thomas. With Vicki Acerra, Jerry Berk, Evelyn Crawford, Tim DeBaun, Orran Farmer.

GENDER WARS. By Joseph Krawczyk. May 4, 1994. Director, Vincent Apollo. With Patrick Waggoner, John Borras, Dina Comolli, Annette Lascoe, Anne Mulhall.

DANCING IN THE ELEVATOR. By R.A. Stankovic. May 4, 1994. Director, Pepe Douglas. With Judith Boxley, Cornelius J. Redmond.

MY YANKEES. Written and directed by Sean Cooney. May 11, 1994. With Mat Sarter, Tom Bruce, Eddie Daniels, Jeff Lynn, Michael Harley, Connie Jones, Jim Jensen.

THE WHITE GODDESS. By Steven Carinci. May 18, 1994. Director, Taliesin Gregory. With Jonathan Panczyk, Veronika Schmidt, Stacey Lisk, Connie Giordano, Jennifer Drake, David Gassaway, Maria Hurley, Jennifer Roberts, Maeve Webster.

THE BIRTH OF PSYCHOANALYSIS. By Dan Manassee. May 25, 1994. Director, Arthur Reel.

Atlantic Theater Company. Produces new plays or reinterpretations of classics that speak to audiences in a contemporary voice on issues reflecting today's society. Neil Pepe artistic director, Jeffrey Solis managing director.

PAYING FOR THE POOL (one-man show) (26). By and with Frank Maya. September 30, 1993. Director, John Masterson.

THE LIGHTS. By Howard Korder. November 3, 1993. Produced at the Mitzi E. Newhouse Theater; see its entry in the Plays Produced Off Broadway section of this volume.

MOTION PICTURES (dance theater work) (6). By and with Falling Angels. January 29, 1994.

SHAKER HEIGHTS (50). By Quincy Long. April 18, 1994. Director, Neil Pepe; scenery, James Wolk; lighting, Howard Werner; costumes, Laura Cunningham. With Steven Goldstein, Felicity Huffman, Jordan Lage, Mary McCann, Ray Anthony Thomas, Todd Weeks.

Circle Repertory Projects-in-Process. Developmental programs for new plays. Tanya Berezin artistic director, Abigail Evans managing director.

RED MEMORIES (2). By Seth Greenland. November 1, 1993. Director, Calvin Skaggs. With Laila Robins, Kay Walbye, Peter Bartlett, Michael Countryman, John Curless, Drew McVety.

THE TRUTH-TELLER (3). By Joyce Carol Oates. May 16, 1994. Director, Gloria Muzio. With Craig Bockhorn, Marylouise Burke, Jack Davidson, Jay Devlin, Kathy Hiler, Andrew Polk.

Classic Stage Company (CSC). Reinventing and revitalizing the classics for contemporary audiences. David Esbjornson artistic director.

FAITH HEALING (dance theater) (8). Conceived by Jane Comfort, based on Tennessee Williams's *The Glass Menagerie*. September 10, 1993. Director, David Esbjornson; scenery and costumes, Liz Prince; lighting, David Ferri. With Nancy Alfaro, David Neumann, Mark Dendy, Scott Willingham, Jane Comfort.

THE MAIDS (36). By Jean Genet, translated by Bernard Frechtman. September 21, 1993. Direction and scenery, David Esbjornson; lighting, Brian MacDevitt; costumes, Elizabeth Fried. With Charles Busch, Peter Francis James, Seth Gilliam.

THE ILLUSION (36). By Pierre Corneille, adapted by Tony Kushner. January 19, 1994. Director, David Esbjornson; scenery Karen TenEyck; lighting, Brian MacDevitt; costumes, Claudia Stevens; composer, Michael Ward. With John C. Vennema, Rocco Sisto, Rob Campbell, Cynthia Nixon, Lynn Hawley, Todd Weeks, Steve Mellor, Dan Moran.

THE TRIUMPH OF LOVE (36). By Marivaux, translated by James Magruder. March 29, 1994. Director, Michael Mayer; scenery, David Gelb; lighting, Brian MacDevitt; costumes, Michael Krass; music, Jill Jaffe. With Margaret Welsh, Thom Christopher, Randy Danson, Garret Dillahunt, Umit Celebi, Camryn Manheim, Daniel Jenkins, Christine Gummere.

En Garde Arts. Dedicated to developing the concept of "site-specific theater" in the streets, parks and buildings of the city. Anne Hamburger founder and producer.

ORESTES (20). By Charles L. Mee Jr. June 27, 1993. Director, Tina Landau; scenery, Kyle Chepulis; lighting, Brian Aldous; costumes, James Schuette; music and sound, John Gromada. With Jefferson Mays, Theresa McCarthy, Christopher Adams, William Buddendorf, Jernard Burks, Ramsey Faragallah, Gregory Gunter, Natalie Layne Kidd, Jayne Amelia Larson, Michael Malone, Sonya Martin, Phaedra Philippoussis, Frank Raiter, Sharon Scruggs, Steven Skybell, Stephen Speights, Jeffrey Sugarman, Elvin Velez, Jean-Loup Wolfman.

MARATHON DANCING (30). By Laura Harrington; musical adaptation, Christopher Drobny; conceived and directed by Anne Bogart. March 13, 1994. Choreography, Alison Shafer; scenery, Kyle Chepulis; lighting, Carol Mullins; costumes, Gabriel Berry; musical direction, Michael Rice. With P. J. Benjamin, Gabriel Barre, Steven Goldstein, Kristen Flanders, Jennifer Wiltsie, Frank Raiter, Tom Nelis, Lisa Monacelli, Andrew Weems, Maureen Silliman, Lauren Mitchell, Jonathan Fried, Myra Lucretia Taylor, Matthew Bennett, Victoria Clark.

Ensemble Studio Theater. Membership organization of playwrights, actors, directors and designers dedicated to supporting individual theater artists and developing new works for the stage. Over 250 projects each season, ranging from readings to fully-mounted productions. Curt Dempster artistic director, Jacqueline A. Siegel managing director.

OCTOBERFEST. Festival of 80 new plays by members. October 6-November 1, 1993.

ALL FOR ONE (22). By Paul Weitz. November 28, 1993. Director, Kate Baggott; scenery, David Gallo; lighting, Glen Fasman; costumes, Julie Doyle. With Calista Flockhart, Noelle Parker, Liev Schreiber, John Speredakos, Michael Louis Wells.

BLUE RARE (festival of new works). Schedule included BY THE FROG POND by Sheri Matteo, directed by Christopher A. Smith; FOURTH TIME AROUND by Michael Louis Wells, directed by Jaime Richards. February 9-21, 1994

MARATHON '94 (festival of one-act plays). EXTENSIONS by Murray Schisgal, directed by Lee Costello; THE FALLING MAN by Will Scheffer, directed by David Briggs; I'M WITH YA, DUKE by Herb Gardner, directed by Jack Gelber; PARADISE by Romulus Linney, directed by Christopher A. Smith; LUNCH WITH LYN by Marsha Norman, directed by George de la Pena; ROSEMARY WITH GINGER by Edward Allan Baker, directed by Ron Stetson; DEAR KENNETH BLAKE by Jacquelyn Reingold, directed by Brian Mertes; NEW YORK ACTOR by John Guare, directed by Jerry Zaks; MUDTRACKS by Regina Taylor, directed by Woodie King Jr.; WASP by Steve Martin, directed by Curt Dempster; THE 'FAR-FLUNG' by Julie McKee, directed by Ethan Silverman; BLOOD GUILTY by Antoine O'Flatharta, directed by Kevin Confoy; FOR WHOM THE SOUTHERN BELLE TOLLS by Christopher Durang, directed by Walter Bobbie. May 4-June 12, 1994.

INTAR. Mission is to identify, develop and present the talents of gifted Hispanic American theater artists and multicultural visual artists. Max Ferra artistic director.

INTAR—Sigfrido Aguilar and Jim Calder, authors and performers in a modern comedy adaptation of *Don Quixote*

EL GRECO (opera) (16). Libretto, Bernardo Solano; music, William Harper. September 26, 1993. Director, Tom O'Horgan; scenery, Robin Wagner; lighting, Robert M. Wierzel; costumes, Donna Zakowska. With Daryl Henricksen, Selena Cantor, Steven Goldstein, Tom Bogdan, Maggi-Meg Reed, Gabriel Barre, Don Chastain, Veronica Tyler.

SANCHO AND DON (22). By Sigfrido Aguilar and Jim Calder. May 15, 1994. Lighting, Paul Clay; music, Andy Tierstein. With Sigfrido Aguilar, Jim Calder, Andy Tierstein.

Interart Theater. Committed to producing innovative work by women theater artists and to introducing New York audiences to a bold range of theater that is non-traditional in form or theme. Margot Lewitin artistic director.

Schedule included:

ANGELS ELEGY. Written and directed by Lee Nagrin. February 18, 1994. Scenery, Jim Meares; lighting, Tony Giovanetti; costumes, Sally Ann Parsons. With Kwabena Chan Ansapilsqehsis, Cristina Bonati, Sheridan Roberts, Marta Soares, Vanessa Walters, Lee Nagrin.

Irish Arts Center. Provides a range of contemporary Irish drama, classics and new works by Irish and Irish American playwrights. Nye Heron artistic director.

LOVECHILD (30). By Gerard Stembridge. June 3, 1993. Director, Nye Heron; scenery, David Raphel; lighting, Judith Daitsman; costumes, Carla Gant. With Malcolm Adams, Mac Orange, Rosemary Fine, Michael Judd, Marian Quinn.

BROTHERS OF THE BRUSH (43). By Jimmy Murphy. March 25, 1994. Director, Nye Heron; scenery, David Raphel; lighting, Mauricio Saavedra Pefaur; costumes, Anne Reilly. With Ronan Carr, Mickey Kelly, Paul McGrane, Paul Ronan.

La Mama (a.k.a. LaMama) Experimental Theater Club (ETC). A busy workshop for experimental theater of all kinds. Ellen Stewart founder and artistic director.

Schedule included:

THE WHITE WHORE AND THE BIT PLAYER. By Tom Eyen. June 17, 1993. Director, Eric Concklin; music, Henry Krieger. With Lois Weaver, Louise Smith.

GULLIVER. By Lonnie Carter. September 30, 1993. Director, George Ferencz.

A GYPSY CARMEN. Conceived, adapted and directed from Georges Bizet's *Carmen* by Ray Evans Harrell. October 7, 1993.

AGES. Conceived and directed by PoPo. October 21, 1993. With PoPo and the GoGo Boys.

MARY. By Tom Wilson. October 21, 1993. Director, George Ferencz; music, Genji Ito.

THE BROTHERS KARAMAZOV. Adapted by Gerard McLarnon from Dostoyevsky's book. November 4,1993. Director, Mervyn Willis.

VOLODYA/RUSSIAN HERO. By Sue Harris and Walter Jones. November 4, 1993. Director, Walter Jones; music, Vladimir Vysotosky.

THE CO-OP LOFT. By Esteban Fernandez. November 18, 1993. Director, Goerge Ferencz; music, Genji Ito and Jeff Tapper.

YARA'S FOREST SONG. Written and directed by Virlana Tkacz. December 3, 1993. Music, Genji Ito. With the Yara Arts Group.

THE SEVEN BEGGARS. Adapted from Rabbi Nachman and directed by Victor Attar. December 8, 1993. Music, Ari Frenkel and David Roe. With Victor Attar.

TANCREDI AND ERMINIA. Based on Torquato Tasso's *Gerusalemme Liberatta;* music, David Sawyer, Genji Ito, Sheila Dabney and Kate Dezina; music for the lyrics and direction, Ellen Stewart. December

9, 1993. Choreography, Masahiro Kunii; scenery, Jun Maeda and Mark Tambella; lighting, David Adams. With Paul Beauvais, Erika Bilder, Sheila Dabney, Kate Dezina, Jonathan Hart Makwaia, Andrea Paciotto, Markus Scarabai.

OBJECTS LIE ON A TABLE. By Gertrude Stein. January 6, 1994. Director, David Herskovits; scenery, Sarah Edkins; lighting, Lenore Doxsee; costumes, David Zinn. With Michael Booth, Neil Bradley, Linda Donald, Rohana Kenin, Steven Rattazzi, Greig Sargeant, Noel Simmons, Yuri Skujins, Penelope Smith, Barbara Wiechmann. Co-produced by Target Margin Theater.

X TRAIN. Written and directed by Harold Dean James. January 27, 1994. Scenery, Charles Golden; lighting, Phil Sandstrom. With Paul Albe, Daniel Clymer, Robin Cornett, Shelley Crandall, Martina Degnan, Jesse N. Holmes, Anthony O'Donoghue, Harold D. James, George Patterson, Lee Pender, Tom Steinbach, Rachel Wineberg.

KARNA: A SHADOW PUPPET OPERA. Libretto and music, Barbara Benary. February 3, 1994. Puppeteer, Barbara Politt.

NO HARM/DRIVING WEST. By Jeannie Hutchins. February 17, 1994. Director, Pablo Vela. With Jeannie Hutchins, Louise Smith.

UNDER THE KNIFE. Conceived, directed and designed by Theodora Skipitares; music, Virgil Moorefield. March 3, 1994. Choreography, Marc Kotz, Shigeko Suga; lighting, Pat Dignan; costumes, H.G. Arrott; additional puppet design, Holly Laws. With George Bartenieff, Tom Costello, Preston Foerder, Mary Jo McConnell, Sarah Provost, Kate Lyn Reiter, Jack Shamblin, Jane Catherine Shaw, Shigeko Suga, Basil Twist, Daphne Vega.

FIORADES/FIZZLES. Text, Samuel Beckett; images adapted from Jasper Johns's illustrations; conceived and directed by Michael Rush. March 3, 1994. Choreography, David Maurice Sharp; scenery, Joy Wulke; lighting, Howard Thies. With Jim Donovan, Peter Lucas, Elizabeth Mozer.

BIFFING MUSSELS, CONVERSATION PIECES I AND II and A RANDOM ACT OF VIOLENCE (one-act plays). Written and directed by Michael Gorman and William Gorman. March 17, 1994. With the Fabulous Giggin' Brothers.

AMERIKA. By Maria Guevara, Michael Carley, David Letwin, Phil Pardi, Holiday Reinhorn, Rainn Wilson, based on Franz Kafka's work. April 15, 1994. Director, Maria Guevara; scenery, Chris Muller; lighting, Jennifer Tanzer; costumes, Constance Hoffman; music, Ralph Denzer. With Doug Andrews, Andrew Barr, Dan Berkey, Shaula Chambliss, Marissa Copeland, Ralph Denzer, Bruce Kennedy, David Letwin, Vernice Miller, Cornelia Mills, Ulla Neuerberg, Rebecca Ortese, Jeff Ricketts. Frank Wood.

THE STRANGE LIFE OF IVAN OSOKIN (opera). Conceived and directed by Lawrence Sacharow, from P.D. Ouspensky's novel; libretto, Constance Congdon; music, Peter Gordon. April 15, 1994. Choreography, Donald Byrd; scenery, Marjorie Bradley Kellogg; lighting, Michael Chybowski; costumes, Constance Hoffman; musical direction, "Blue" Gene Tyranny. With Jeff Reynolds, Tamara Walker, Andy Umberger, Dave Clemmons, Hugo Munday, Wilbur Pauley, April Armstrong, Patti Onorato, Jennifer Lynn Michael, Nicole Alifante, Lynnen Yakes.

SLIPPERY WHEN WET. By H. Maeoka. April 28, 1994. Director, Ching Valdes-Aran; music, Fred Carl and Yushio Torikai. With Suzen Murakoshi, Leland Gantt.

POP DREAMS. Text and choreography, David Rousseve. May 5, 1994.

FRUSTRATION (FRUSTRA-AZIONI). By and with Dario D'Ambrosi. May 5, 1994. Scenery, Jun Maeda and David Adams; lighting, Howard Thies, music, Tim Schellenbaum.

GALLATIN FESTIVAL OF ONE-ACT PLAYS: PLASTIC FLOWERS by Carmen Rivera; RESERVATIONS by Elena Megaro; ELEPHANT by Jennifer Houlton. May 19, 1994.

W. Adapted and directed by Andrea Paciotto from Georg Buchner's *Woyzeck*. May 26, 1994.

The Club:

HAUNTED TAXI RIDE. By Stan Baker and Louie Fleck. June 3, 1993.

MORTALITY WALTZ. By and with Robert Lanier. June 21, 1993. Director, Mark Greenfield.

HULAWOOD BABYLON, OR A LITTLE HULA HELL. Written and directed by Ching Valdes-Aran. September 30, 1993.

SUDDENLY SOMETHING RECKLESSLY GAY, OR CIRQUE DE CA CA. Written and directed by Assurbanipal Babilla. October 7, 1993. With Leyla Betehadj, David Cole, Assurbanipal Babilla.

WHEN WITCHES CACKLE. By and with Alien Comic. October 25, 1993.

WHEN SHE HAD BLOOD LUST. By Edgar Oliver. October 28, 1993.

WORD OF MOUTH: THE STORY OF A HUMAN SATELLITE DISH. By and with James Lecesne. November 4, 1993. Director, Eve Ensler. Reopened November 26, 1993.

SLEEPWALKER'S DINER. By Charles E. Drew. November 8, 1993. Music, Janice Lowe.

HEADS. By and with Danny Mydlack and the Mr. Big Company. November 11, 1993.

LAST FOREVER. By and with A. Leroy, Sonya Cohen, Carolyn Dutton, Bill Ruyle. November 15, 1993.

THESE SUNGLASSES BELONGED TO ROY ORBISON. By Robert I. Rubinsky and Mary Fulham. November 22, 1993. Director, Mary Fulham; musical direction, Robert Secret. With Ellen Foley.

JULIA DARES HERSELF. Written, choreographed and performed by Julia Dares. December 13, 1993.

FRIENDLY PEOPLE FROM NOWHERE: HAPPY ENDINGS by and with Kenneth Shorr, director, Cisco Heimowitz; THE STATE I'M IN: A TRAVELOGUE by and with Paula Killen (monologues). January 3, 1994.

STITCHES. By Amy Sedaris and David Sedaris. January 6, 1994. Director, David Rakoff; scenery, Hugh Hamrick; lighting, Howard Thies. With Paul Dinello, Amy Sedaris, Mitch Rouse, Becky Thyre.

STUART SHERMAN'S NINETEENTH SPECTACLE. By and with Stuart Sherman. January 10, 1994.

TWO. By Jim Cartwright. January 17, 1994. Director, Alison Summers.

LINCOLN. By Hapi Phace. February 10, 1994. Choreography, Mark Dendy. With Hapi Phace, Jennifer Miller, Hattie Hathaway, Ruby Lynn Rayner.

A VARIETY OF WOMEN (SECOND ANNUAL EDITION). Director, Mary Fulham. February 14, 1994. With Cassandra Danz, Linda Maldonado, Eva Mantell, Nicole Quinn, Amy Sue Rosen, Toni Schlesinger, Lillias White.

YOUR RACE AND MINE (one-woman show). By and with Lisa Erika James, based on Carrie B. Wiley's writings. March 10, 1994. Director, Alice Jankell.

BUCK SIMPLE. By Craig Fols. March 14, 1994. Director, David Briggs.

DARK POCKET. By Jim Neu and Bill Rice. March 17, 1994. Music, Neal Kirkwood, Harry Mann.

EDGAR OLIVER'S EASTER EXTRAVAGANZA. By Edgar Oliver. March 28, 1994. With Angela Rogers, Mary Lou Wittmer, Carine Montbertrand, Jason Bauer.

A TATTLE TALE (one-woman show). By Judith Sloan, Warren Lehrer and Deb Margolin. March 31, 1994. With Judith Sloan.

GULLIVER REDUX (staged reading). Adapted by Lonnie Carter from Jonathan Swift's book. Director, Andre De Shields. April 18, 1994.

WITHOUT APPARENT MOTIVE. Book, music and lyrics by Donald Arrington. April 28, 1994. With David Kulick.

PIE by Joan Hockey; THE LIVING ROOM PROJECT by and with Tierry Royo. May 2, 1994.

FROLICKING FROCKS. May 5, 1994. With Lavinia Co-op.

INVISIBLE EVIDENCE OF OUR ANGELIC RESIDUE. By Judith Ren-Lay. May 9, 1994.

MIXED NUTS. By and with the High-Heeled Women. May 16, 1994.

YOU'RE JUST LIKE MY FATHER (one-woman show). By and with Peggy Shaw. May 19, 1994. Director, James Neale-Kennerley; lighting, Howard Thies; music, Laka Daisical.

Lamb's Theater Company. Committed to developing and presenting new works in their most creative and delicate beginnings. Carolyn Rossi Copeland producing director.

JOHNNY PYE AND THE FOOLKILLER (49). October 31, 1993. See its entry in the Plays Produced Off Broadway section of this volume.

Mabou Mines. Theater collaborative whose work is a synthesis of motivational acting, narrative acting and mixed-media performance. Collective artistic leadership. Frederick Neumann, Terry O'Reilly, Ruth Maleczech, Lee Breuer artistic directors.

REEL TO REAL (15). Written, directed and choreographed by Frederick Neumann. April 6, 1994. Scenery, lighting and video Paul Clay; costumes, Gabriel Berry; sound, Christopher Todd; music, Al Kryszak; film director, Tony Gerber; film producer, Melissa Powell. With Ruth Maleczech, Diane Grotke, Judith Elkan, Cradeaux Alexander, Terry O'Reilly, Joyce Nielsen.

Manhattan Class Company. Dedicated to the promotion of emerging writers, actors, directors and theatrical designers. Robert LuPone and Bernard Telsey executive directors, W.D. Cantler, associate director.

THE ABLE-BODIED SEAMAN (20). By Alan Bowne. October 14, 1993. Director, Jimmy Bohr; scenery, Rob Odorisio; lighting, Howard Werner; costumes, Claudia Stephens. With Chelsea Altman, Larry Attile, Simon Brooking, Robert Floyd, Anita Gillette, Robert LuPone.

CLASS ONE-ACTS FESTIVAL (one-act plays): I CAN'T STOP THINKING TODAY by Annie Evans, directed by Max Mayer; THE AMAZON'S VOICE by Allan Heinberg, directed by Melia Bensussen; ENDLESS AIR, ENDLESS WATER by Robert Shaffron, directed by Jimmy Bohr; GOOD AS NEW written and directed by Peter Hedges. February 17, 1994-March 12, 1994. Scenery, Rob Odorisio; lighting, Stewart Wagner; costumes, Judy Jerald Sackheim. With Allison Janney, Tim Blake Nelson, Ellen Parker, Bill Christ, Scott Paetty, Bill Timoney, Penny Ejke, Jenny O'Hara, Margaret Welsh.

LIAR, LIAR (one-woman show) (12). Written and performed by Dael Orlandersmith. May 1, 1994. Director, Syd Sidner; scenery, Rob Odorisio; lighting, Howard Werner; costumes, Karen Perry.

Music-Theater Group. Pioneering in the development of new music-theater. Lyn Austin producing director, Diane Wondisford general director.

RING AROUND THE ROSIE (2). Music, Richard Peaslee; lyrics, Mark Campbell. November 15, 1993. Choreography, David Parsons; scenery, lighting and costumes, Power Boothe and Michael Chybowsky.

New Dramatists. An organization devoted to playwrights; member writers may use the facilities for anything from private cold readings of their material to public script-in-hand readings. Elana Greenfield director of artistic programming, Jana Jevnikar director of finance, Paul A. Slee director of development.

Rehearsed Readings

BROKEN LAND. By Peter Mattei. July 7, 1993.
CIGARETTES AND MOBY DICK. By Migdalia Cruz. July 29, 1993.
HADLEY'S MISTAKE. By Kate Moira Ryan. August 10, 1993.
STEVIE WANTS TO PLAY THE BLUES. By Eduardo Machado. August 30, 1993.
KATSINA. By Carol DuVal Whiteman. September 13, 1993.
SOUNDS THAT CARRY. By Heather Flock. September 22, 1993.
FORTUNE. By Hillary Bell. September 27, 1993.

MANHATTAN CLASS COMPANY—Anita Gillette and Robert LuPone in a scene from *The Able-Bodied Seaman* by Alan Bowne

TONGUE SOUP. By Erin Cressida Wilson. September 28, 1993.
THE INTERPRETER OF HORROR. By Kelly Stuart. October 4, 1993.
THE PEACOCK SCREAMS WHEN THE LIGHTS GO OUT. By Kelly Stuart. October 7, 1993.
SNOW QUEEN. By Erin Cressida Wilson. October 12, 1993.
SAN ANTONIO SUNSET, BOVVER BOYS, SABINA and THE CLOSER. By Willy Holtzman. October 26, 1993.
BROKEN EGGS, A BURNING BEACH, ACROSS A CROWDED ROOM and STEVIE WANTS TO PLAY THE BLUES. By Eduardo Machado. October 27, 1993.
BREATHING JESUS. By S. Jason Smith. November 9, 1993.
TALES FROM THE TIME OF THE PLAGUE. By Lynne Alvarez. November 10, 1993.
THE HALLS OF MENTAL SCIENCE. By Moss Kaplan. November 16, 1993.
THE SECRET WIFE. By Y York. November 22, 1993.
THE WINDOW MAN. By Matthew Maguire. December 1, 1993.

THE BEST THINGS IN LIFE. By Lenora Champagne. December 8, 1993.
CLEVELAND RAINING. By Sung Rno. December 8, 1993.
BANANA AND WATER and LOVE IN THE AFTERNOON. By Barry Jay Kaplan. December 10, 1993.
THE UNIVERSAL WOLF. By Joan M. Schenkar. January 6, 1994.
DREAM HOUSE. By Darrah Cloud. January 13, 1994.
LUSH LIFE. By Roger Arturo Durling. January 24, 1994.
LATINS IN LA LA LAND. By Migdalia Cruz. January 27, 1994.
CRAZY HORSE. By Darrah Cloud. January 28, 1994.
DANTE AND VIRGIL GO DANCING. By John C. Russell. January 31, 1994.
BLUE MOON RISING. By James Nicholson. March 17, 1994.
NEBRASKA. By Lenora Champagne. March 18, 1994.
THE DEVILS. By Elizabeth Egloff. April 18, 1994.
KNOCK OFF BALANCE. By Cherylene Lee. April 21, 1994.
DELIRIUM OF INTERPRETATIONS. By Fiona Templeton. May 9, 1994.
ISABELLA DREAMS THE NEW WORLD. By Lenora Champagne. May 16, 1994.
GIRL GONE. By Jacquelyn Reingold. May 24, 1994.
THE NEIGHBOUR. By Meredith Oakes. May 25, 1994.

New Federal Theater. Dedicated to presenting new playwrights and plays dealing with the minority and Third World experience. Woodie King Jr. producer.

16 performances each

IN BED WITH THE BLUES: THE ADVENTURES OF FISHY WATERS (one-man show). By and with Guy Davis. January 20, 1994. Director, Shauneille Perry; scenery, Kent Hoffman; lighting, Antoinette Tynes; costumes, Judy Dearing.

LOOKING BACK. Conceived and directed by Shauneille Perry; songs, Micki Grant. February 17, 1994. Choreography, Chiquita Ross-Glover; scenery, Robert Schwartz; lighting, Antoinette Tynes; costumes, Judy Dearing; musical direction, Julius Williams. With Lena Berrios, Debbie Blackwell-Cook, Anthony Gaglione, Micki Grant, Pepsi Robinson, Miki Sakaguchi, Adam Wade.

New York Shakespeare Festival/Joseph Papp Public Theater. Schedule of special projects, in addition to its regular off-Broadway productions. George C. Wolfe producer, Rosemarie Tichler, Kevin Kline associate producers, Jason Steven Cohen managing director.

Schedule included:

NEW YORK NOW (festival of staged readings). Schedule included CARTHAGE by Naomi Iizuka, directed by Robert Woodruff; A LANGUAGE OF THEIR OWN by Chay Yew; IN THE SPIRIT by Chuka Lokoli; SUNSHINE PLAYLOT by Dominic A. Taylor, directed by Donald Douglas; UNMERCIFUL GOOD FORTUNE by Edwin Sanchez, directed by Susana Tubert; TRIPPING THROUGH THE CAR HOUSE by Regina Porter, directed by Michael Meyer; STUPID KIDS by John Russell; MULTIPLE PERSONALITIES by Will Scheffer, directed by David Briggs; TALKING BONES by Shay Youngblood, directed by Robbie McCauley; BETTY AND GAUGUIN by Nilo Cruz; THE SONG OF GRENDELYN by Russell Davis, directed by John Pietrowski; works by Latino Labia and Emerging Writers' Unit. May 1-15, 1994.

New York Theater Workshop. Produces new theater by American and international artists and encourages risk and stimulates experimentation in theatrical form. James C. Nicola artistic director, Nancy Kassak Diekmann managing director.

BRAVE SMILES . . . ANOTHER LESBIAN TRAGEDY (6). By and with the Five Lesbian Brothers (Maureen Angelos, Babs Davy, Dominique Dibbell, Peg Healey, Lisa Kron). June 15, 1993. Director, Kate Stafford; scenery, Jamie Leo; lighting, Diana Arecco; costumes, Susan Young.

BLOWN SIDEWAYS THROUGH LIFE (one-woman show) by and with Claudia Shear. September 29, 1993. See its entry in the Plays Produced Off Broadway section of this volume.

THE REZ SISTERS (7). By Tomson Highway. January 4, 1994. Director, Linda S. Chapman and Muriel Miguel; scenery, Anita Stewart; lighting, Christopher Akerlind; costumes, Anne C. Patterson. With Kevin Tarrant, Louis Mofsie, Gloria Miguel, Muriel Miguel, Elvira Colorado, Sheila Tousey, Lisa Mayo, Hortensia Colorado, Murielle Borst.

UNFINISHED STORIES (24). By Sybille Pearson. February 4, 1994. Director, Gordon Davidson; scenery Peter Wexler; lighting, Ken Billington; costumes, Gabriel Berry. With Joseph Wiseman, Christopher Collet, E. Katherine Kerr, Laurence Luckinbill.

MY VIRGINIA (one-woman show) (16). By and with Darci Picoult. March 20, 1994. Director, Suzanne Shepherd.

THE MEDIUM (35). Conceived and directed by Anne Bogart, inspired by Marshall McLuhan's life and predictions. May 16, 1994. Scenery, Anita Stewart; lighting, Michitomo Shiohara; costumes, Gabriel Berry. With J. Ed Araiza, Will Bond, Ellen Lauren, Kelly Maurer, Tom Nelis. Co-produced by the Saratoga International Theater Institute.

The Open Eye. Goal is to gather a community of outstanding theater artists to collaborate on works for the stage for audiences of all ages and cultural backgrounds. Jean Erdman founding director, Amie Brockway artistic director.

BOCON! (14). By Lisa Loomer. November 11, 1993. Director, Ernest Johns; choreography, Stephanie Marshall; scenery, lighting and costumes, Adrienne J. Brockway; music, Jose Garcia. With Joey Chavez, Cynthia Firing, Marlene Forte, Kathryn Markey, Jeff Ranara, Charles Sanchez.

THE WISE MEN OF CHELM. By Sandra Fenichel Asher. December 18, 1993. Director, Amie Brockway; choreography, Alice Bergmann; scenery, lighting and costumes, Adrienne J. Brockway. With Alice Bergmann, John DiLeo, Judy Dodd, Scott Facher, Larry Hirschhorn, Michael Metzel.

FREEDOM IS MY MIDDLE NAME. By Lee Hunkins. January 20, 1994. Director, Ernest Johns; scenery, lighting and costumes, Adrienne J. Brockway. With Mary Cushman, John DiLeo, Sheryl Green Leverett, Stephanie Marshall, Ernest Toussant.

AND THE TIDE SHALL COVER THE EARTH (12). By Norma Cole, based on her novel. March 3, 1994. Director, Amie Brockway; scenery, lighting and costumes, Adrienne J. Brockway. With Mary Ellen Cravens, Catherine Dudley, Patricia Guinan, Jeremiah Jamison, Ernest Johns, Mandy Peek, Eden Riegel, Elyzabeth Gregory, Gregory Wilder.

Pan Asian Repertory Theater. Strives to provide opportunities for Asian American artists to perform under the highest professional standards and to create and promote plays by and about Asians and Asian Americans. Tisa Chang artistic/producing director.

24 performances each

EATING CHICKEN FEET. By Kitty Chen. October 26, 1993. Director, Kati Kuroda; scenery, Robert Klingelhoefer; lighting, Michael Chybowski; costumes, Hugh Hanson. With Liana Pai, Ben Lin, Wai Ching Ho, Steve Park, Mary Lee, Christine Campbell, Bobby Sacher. Co-produced by Women's Project and Productions.

WILDERNESS. By Cao Yu, translated by Christopher C. Rand and Joseph M. Lau, adapted and edited by Lili Liang and Ernest Schier. May 3, 1994. Director, Lili Liang; scenery, Robert Klingelhoefer; lighting, Richard Schaefer; costumes, Helen Q. Huang. With John Baray, Frances Calma, Noriko Kashiwakura, Kati Kuroda, Lisa Li, Jason Ma, Les J.N. Mau, Yoshifumi Nakamori, James Saito, Hua Xi.

Playwrights Horizons New Theater Wing. Full productions of new work, in addition to the regular off-Broadway productions. Don Scardino artistic director.

14 performances each

ARTS & LEISURE. By Steve Tesich. February 23, 1994. Director, JoAnne Akalaitis. With Hope Davis, Alice Drummond, Mary Beth Hurt, Angela Lanza, Harris Yulin.

CATHER COUNTY. By Ed Dixon. May 18, 1994. Director, Scott Harris; musical direction, Stan Tucker. With Brent Barrett, Brigid Brady, Glory Crampton, Herb Foster, David Hart, Judy Kaye, Alice Ripley, Anne Runolfsson, Lannyl Stephens, Mary Stout, Sal Viviano.

Primary Stages Company. Dedicated to new American plays by new American playwrights. Casey Childs artistic director, Gina Gionfriddo general manager, Janet Reed associate artistic director, Seth Gordon associate producer.

24 performances each

BREAKING UP. By Michael Cristofer. September 29, 1993. Director, Melia Bensussen; scenery, Allen Moyer; lighting, Thomas Haase; costumes, Michael Krass; with Allison Janney, Kevin O'Rourke.

ALL IN THE TIMING: SURE THING; WORDS, WORDS, WORDS; PHILIP GLASS BUYS A LOAF OF BREAD; THE PHILADELPHIA; THE UNIVERSAL LANGUAGE; VARIATIONS ON THE DEATH OF TROTSKY (one-act plays) by David Ives. November 24, 1993. A Best Play; see its entry in the Plays Produced Off Broadway section of this volume.

CRACKDANCING. Written and directed by Joseph Hindy. April 6, 1994. Scenery, George Xenos; lighting, Deborah Constantine; costumes, Amanda J. Klein; choreography, Bridgit Dengel. With Patricia McAneny, John Wojda.

THE HYACINTH MACAW. By Mac Wellman. May 14, 1994. Director, Marcus Stern; scenery and lighting, Kyle Chepulis; costumes, Robin J. Orloff; music, David Van Tieghem. With Yusef Bulos, Bob Kirsh, Steve Mellor, Melissa Smith, Francie Swift.

Puerto Rican Traveling Theater. Professional company presenting bilingual productions primarily of Puerto Rican and Hispanic playwrights, emphasizing subjects of relevance today. Miriam Colon founder and producer.

DEATH AND THE MAIDEN (18). By Ariel Dorfman. January 19, 1994. Director, Alba Oms; scenery, Michael Sharp; lighting, Spencer Brown; costumes, Carlos Marquez. With Diana Volpe, Henry Martin Leyva, Edouard De Soto.

INNOCENT ERENDIRA AND HER HEARTLESS GRANDMOTHER (26). By Jorge Ali Triana and Carlos Jose Reyes, based on Gabriel Garcia Marquez's story, translated by Felipe Gorostiza and Rene Buch. February 20, 1994. Director, Jorge Ali Triana; scenery, Liliana Villegas; lighting, Robert Weber Federico; costumes, Rosario Lozano; music, German Arrieta; English lyrics, Felipe Gorostiza; musical direction, Nicolas Uribe. With Miriam Colon, Sofia Oviedo, Alexia Murray, David Johann, Jeffrey Rodriguez, Rene Sanchez, Tatiana Vecino. Co-produced by Repertorio Espanol.

WRITTEN AND SEALED (18). By Isaac Chocron, translated by Susan J. Jones, revised and edited by Carmen L. Marin. March 9, 1994. Director, Pablo Cabrera; scenery and costumes, Randy Barcelo; lighting, Spencer Brown. With Jaime Sanchez, Ramon Albino, Rafael DeMussa, Isabel Keating, Irma-Estel LaGuerre.

Quaigh Theater. Primarily a playwrights' theater, devoted to the new playwright, the established contemporary playwright and the modern (post-1920) playwright. Will Lieberson artistic director.

THE TRAGEDY OF KING RICHARD THE SECOND. By William Shakespeare. March 2, 1994. Director, Carol Bennett Gerber; lighting and sound, Kevin Mack; costumes, Kevin Brainerd. With Charles E. Gerber, Helen Hanft, Todd Davis, Liz Amberly, Penelope Smith, Ellen O'Mara, Michael Darden.

THE BONDING (20). By Hal O. Kesler. April 8, 1994. Directors, Will Lieberson and Paul Brandt; scenery, Bob Phillips; lighting, Winifred H. Powers, With Dickson Shaw, Ken Budris, Natasha de Vegh.

ON OOB STAGES—*Right,* Miriam Colon and Sofia Oviedo in the Repertorio Espanol-Puerto Rican Traveling Theater co-production of *Innocent Erendira and Her Heartless Grandmother; below,* Ken Budris, Natasha de Vegh and Dickson Shaw in Hal O. Kesler's *The Bonding* at Quaigh Theater

Lunchtime Series. 10 performances each

1-800-HELP. By Tony Kraft. October 4, 1993. Director, Ralph Court. With Dominique Griffin, Francine Lloyd, Bill Brownlee.

A WIG FOR THE BALD HEADED SPEGAL. By Richard Froggue. October 18, 1993. Director, Henry Little. With Loring Powers, John Ford, Trisha Carney.

HOT DOGS AND COOL CANS. By Barbara Applegate. November 1, 1993. Director, Mary Powell. With Freida Lowell, Tanya Muller.

I AM MY OWN WOMAN. By Kim Meesoat. November 15, 1993. Director, Lisa Porter. With Ahn Jinah, Pablo Farji.

NO YARD TO PLAY IN. By Robert Lawson. November 29, 1993. Directors, Tona Scott and Winifred Cushing. With Rudy Cornell, John Schultz, Fred Hampton.

TOO MANY EXITS. By Harriet Jacobson. December 13, 1993. Director, Peter Kaufman. With Javier Sanchez, Paul Meridith, Edith Jane, Greta Rosenberg.

PORTRAIT OF A PORTRAIT. By Shirley Dawson. January 10, 1994. Director, Ruby Remmer. With Greta Knowland, Lydia Thomson, Joan Genet.

A SPECIAL OFFER. By Peron March. January 24, 1994. Director, Jack Spero. With David Maloy, Simone Dahlbeck, Martin Karne.

WORD IS OUT. By Frank Hamner. February 7, 1994. Director, John Farrow. With Glenda Walker, Jack Murphy, Lester Bolger.

THE WIZARD OF ODDS. By Channing. February 21, 1994. Director, Donald Smith. With Paul Gilbert, Judy Hamilton, Bessie Weiner, Burt Burke.

CHINESE PIZZA. By Bruno Frederico. March 7, 1994. Director, Andy Harris. With Lloyd Martin, Ellen Anger, Sue Riggs.

WHAT'S HAPPENING. By LeRoy Epstein. April 4, 1994. Director, Ellen Adair. With Ina Huff, Bo Jones, Tom Carson.

AGAINST THE STREAM. By Mark Gottlieb. April 18, 1994. Director, Milton Hopper. With Philip Reingess, Anna Block, Harvey Richardson.

THE HONEST POLICEMAN - A FAIRY TALE. By Jackson Calder. May 2, 1994. Director, Jules Warren. With Gene Loeb, Nicky Jonas, James Lawrence, Mark Roberts.

THE MUSKETEERS OF TIN PAN ALLEY. Book, music and lyrics, Kevin Booth. May 16, 1994. Director, Walter Weiner. With Rosa Eugene, Ben Young, Lee Paterson, Buster Miller.

THE TITANIC REVISITED. By Peter Levy. May 30, 1994. Director, Will Lieberson. With Patricia Dodd, Harry Atkinson, Frank Avoletta.

Summer Reading Series

FRIENDSHIP OF A PRINCE. By Arthur Schwartz. July 26, 1993.
LEMON GOTHIC by Dale Attias and LONDON BRIDGE IS FALLING DOWN by Hal O. Kesler. August 9, 1993.
THE HOLY TERROR. By Simon Gray. August 16, 1993.
ELLERY QUEEN'S THAT DOOR BETWEEN. Adapted by Douglas Alan Dean. August 23, 1993.

The Ridiculous Theatrical Company. The late Charles Ludlam's comedic troupe devoted to productions of his original scripts and new adaptations of the classics. Everett Quinton artistic director, Adele Bove managing director.

HOW TO WRITE A PLAY (78). By Charles Ludlam, adapted and directed by Everett Quinton. November 8, 1993. Scenery, Tom Greenfield; lights, Richard Currie; costumes, Ramona Ponce. With Everett

Quinton, Jimmy Szczepanek, Katy Dierlam, Mel Nieves, Arthur T. Acuna, Chris Tanner, Bobby Reed, Christine Weiss, Michael Lynch, Lenys Sama, Alonia King.

MOVIELAND (90). By Everett Quinton. April 5, 1994. Director, Eureka; scenery, T. Greenfield; lighting, Richard Currie; costumes, Toni Nanette Thompson. With Everett Quinton, Noelle Kalom.

Second Stage Theater. Committed to producing plays believed to deserve another look, as well as new works. Carole Rothman artistic director, Suzanne Schwartz Davidson, producing director.

LOOSE KNIT (56). By Theresa Rebeck. June 30, 1993. Director, Beth Schachter; scenery, Santo Loquasto; lighting, Frances Aronson; costumes, Elsa Ward. With Mary B. Ward, Patricia Kalember, Tamara Tunie, Kristine Nielsen, Constance Shulman, Reed Birney, Daniel Gerroll.

LIFE SENTENCES (46). By Richard Nelson. December 1, 1993. Director, John Caird; scenery, Tom Lynch; lighting, Richard Nelson; costumes, Ann Roth. With Edward Herrmann, Michelle Joyner.

RICKY JAY & HIS 52 ASSISTANTS. February 6, 1994. See its entry in the Plays Produced Off Broadway section of this volume.

Flying Solo Series. 3 performances each

INSOMNIA. By and with Dana Gould. February 7, 1994. Director, Mark W. Travis.

WAKE UP, I'M FAT! By and with Camryn Manheim. February 28, 1994. Director, Mark Brokaw.

Signature Theater Company. Dedicated to the exploration of a playwright's body of work. James Houghton artistic director, Thomas Proehl managing director.

MARRIAGE PLAY (20). Written and directed by Edward Albee. October 1, 1993. Scenery, E. David Cosier; lighting, Jeffrey S. Koger; costumes, Teresa Snider-Stein. With Kathleen Butler, Tom Klunis.

COUNTING THE WAYS written and directed by Edward Albee; LISTENING by Edward Albee, directed by Paul Weidner (20). November 5, 1993. Scenery, E. David Cosier; lighting, Jeffrey S. Koger; costumes, Teresa Snider-Stein. With Patricia Kilgariff, Baxter Harris, Jacqueline Brookes, Joe Ponazecki, Francie Swift.

SAND: BOX, THE SANDBOX and FINDING THE SUN (20). Written and directed by Edward Albee. February 4, 1994. Scenery, E. David Cosier; lighting, Jeffrey S. Koger; costumes, Teresa Snider-Stein. With Jacqueline Brookes, Aisha Benoir, Peggy Cosgrave, Jane Hoffman, Earl Nash, Edward Seamon, John Carter, Brendan Corbalis, Monique Fowler, Cheryl Gaysunas, Bethel Leslie, Neil Maffin, Mary Beth Peil, James Van Der Beek.

FRAGMENTS (A CONCERTO GROSSO) (20). By Edward Albee. April 8, 1994. Director, James Houghton; scenery, E. David Cosier; lighting, Colin D. Young; costumes, Teresa Snider-Stein. With Angela Marie Bettis, John Carter, Paddy Croft, Lou Ferguson, Cheryl Gaysunas, Edward Norton, Joyce O'Connor, Scott Sowers.

Soho Rep. Dedicated to new, non-naturalistic plays. Marlene Swartz founder and executive director, Julian Webber artistic director.

CARELESS LOVE (24). Written and directed by Len Jenkin. November 4, 1993. Scenery, John Arnone; lighting, Don Holder; costumes, Caryn Neman. With Arthur Aulisi, Garret Dillahunt, Deirdre O'Connell, Steve Mellor, Polly Noonan, Lorca Simons, Rocco Sisto, Colleen Werthmann.

DRACULA (20). By Mac Wellman. April 21, 1994. Director, Julian Webber; scenery, Kyle Chepulis; lighting, Brian Aldous; costumes, James Sauli; music, Melissa Shiflett. With Jackie Domination, Marti Domination, Patricia Dunnock, Julia Gibson, Christine Martin, Christopher McCann, Tim Blake Nelson, Brett Rickaby, Thomas Jay Ryan, Damian Young, Ray Xifo.

HOLLYWOOD HUSTLE (one-man show) (18). By and with Jeremiah Bosgang. April 22, 1994. Director, Rob Greenberg; lighting, Rick Martin.

Theater for the New City. Developmental theater and new American experimental works. George Bartenieff, Crystal Field artistic directors.

Schedule included:

BOB LOVES BONNIE. Written and directed by Bina Sharif. June 9, 1993.

DON'T WORRY: WE'RE ALL GONNA BE RICH (13). Book, lyrics and direction, Crystal Field; music, Chris Cherney. August 7, 1993. Scenery, Anthony Angel; costumes, Ilona Somogyi and Jonathan Cross. With Joe Davies, Michael David Gordon, Jerry Jaffe, Terry King, Mark Marcante, Craig Meade.

THE LOVE DEATH OF CLOWNS. Written and directed by Sarah Kornfield. August 26, 1993. Choreography, Suzanne Nece; costumes, Mary Gelezunas.

GETTING THE SONG TO JOHNNIE. By Alex McDonald. October 7, 1993. Director, Alvin Alexis; choreography, Jiggers Turner; scenery, Mark Marcante; costumes, Raymond Pizarro.

WHEN THE EAGLE SCREAMS. By Glenville Lovell. October 7, 1993. Director, Cynthia Belgrave; scenery, Paul Ferri.

THE MOON IN A RIVER THAT HAS NO REASON. By Jeff Leavell. November 4, 1993. Director, Jonathan Hamel; scenery, Mark Solan; costumes, Rhonda Roper.

URBAN RENEWAL. Written and directed by Miguel Sierra. November 11, 1993.

RED CHANNELS. By Laurence Holder. November 18, 1993. Director, Rome Neal; scenery, Chris Cumberbatch; lighting, Marshall Williams; costumes, Anita Ellis. With Dennis F. Bivings, Robert F. Cole, Ed Clarkson-Farrell, Valentino Ferriera, Elizabeth Mitchell, Nick Smith, Daniel Tuck.

TOKYO BEACH BALL. By Jed Weissberg. December 3, 1993. Director, David Grae.

LIFE'S A DRAGG. Written and directed by Terry Lee King. December 6, 1993. Choreography, Inez Guzman; scenery, Ian Gordon; costumes, Shakiesha Brooks.

ANARCHIA. Written and directed by Hanon Reznikov. December 16, 1993. Scenery, Ilion Troya; lighting, Gary Brackett; music, Patrick Grant. With Judith Malina, Joanie Fritz, Isha Manna Beck, Jerry Goralnick, Tom Walker, Rain House. Co-produced by the Living Theater.

ENOUGH SAID THE CUSTARD HEART. Written and directed by H.M. Koutoukas. December 19, 1993. Scenery, Richard Cordtz and Richard Currie; costumes, Carol Tauser.

BREAD & PUPPET THEATER: NATIVITY '93. December 20, 1993.

HOW FAR TO JAISALMEER? By Martha Worth. January 6, 1994. Director, Bina Sharif; scenery, Kevin Martin; lighting, Paul Smithyman. With Mohamed Djellouli, John Edwin Payne, Emmett McConnell, Hesh Malkar.

IRVING BERLIN: RAGTIME REVUE (musical revue). Written and directed by Robert Dahdah. February 10, 1994. Choreography, Craig Meade; scenery, Donald L. Brooks; costumes, Shana Schoepke.

IT IS IT IS NOT: TWO ROMANTIC LADIES and THE MAN WHO FORGOT. By Manuel Pereiras Garcia. February 10, 1994. Director, Maria Irene Fornes; scenery, Donald Eastman; lighting, Ellen Bone; costumes, Carol Bailey. With Angela Chale Millington, Crystal Field, Steve Hofvendahl.

LIFE IN SKETCHES. By Walter Corwin. February 10, 1994. Director, Lee Gundersheimer.

LILAC AND FLAG. Adapted and directed by Paul Zimet, from John Berger's novel. February 10, 1994. Scenery, Theodora Skipitares; lighting, Arthur Roach; costumes, Aaron Elmore and Debra Stovern. With William Badgett, Ellen Maddow, Harry Mann, Tina Shepard (The Talking Band). Co-produced by Perseverance Theater.

HE SAW HIS REFLECTION. By Miranda McDermott. March 3, 1994. Director, David Willinger.

IT'S AN EMERGENCY, DON'T HURRY (cabaret). Text and lyrics, Tom Attea and Mark Marcante; music, Arthur Abrams. March 17, 1994. Director, Mark Marcante; choreography, Craig Meade; scenery, Tony Angel; costumes, Allyson Taylor.

UBU REPERTORY THEATER—Markita Prescott and Julie Boyd in *The Orphanage* by Reine Barteve, translated by Jill MacDougall

PEN PALS. Written and directed by Barbara Kahn. March 24, 1994. Scenery, Kimberly Butts; costumes, Shana Schoepke. With Janis Astor del Valle, Janis Blair, Jennifer Gwyn, Mel Nieves.

EMIGRACION: AN AMERICAN PLAY. By Yolanda Rodriguez. March 24, 1994. Director, Crystal Field; scenery, Donald L. Brooks; lighting, Kent Hoffman; costumes, Jose Rivera. With Joe Davies, Sol Echeverria, Terry Lee King, Patrick Lee, Raul Martinez, Margie Oquendo, Jose Rabelo, Mira Rivera, Al Roffe, Michael Vasquez, Juan Villegas, Barbara Wise.

COLETTE. By Rebecca Chace. April 7, 1994. Director, Jonathan Rosenberg; scenery, Erika Belsey; lighting, Tommy Wong; costumes, Christopher Del Coro. With Sarah Buff, Rebecca Chace, Nina Hellman, Donna LaBrecque, Jane Welch.

BEYOND POSSESSED. Written and directed by Jimmy Camicia. April 8, 1994. With Hot Peaches.

GENE TIERNEY MOVED NEXT DOOR and THE SAL MINEO FAN CLUB COMES TO ORDER. By Larry Myers. April 14, 1994. Directors, Shellen Lubin and Nancy Robillard. With Chadwick Brown, Cynthia Enfield, Bobby Troika, Jennifer Vath, Rik Walter, Wonderly White.

INSTINCT. Text, Rachel Kranz; music, Ralph Denzer. April 21, 1994. Directors, Joanne Schulz and Kuang-Yu Fong; costumes, Ulla Neuerburg; masks, Stephen Kaplin. Co-produced by Ninth Street Theater and Chinese Theater Workshop as part of Theater for the New City's Eco-Festival.

HURRICANE. By and with Anne Galjour. April 23, 1994. Director, Henry Steele; scenery, John Mayne; costumes, Laura Hazlett. Produced as part of Theater for the New City's Eco-Festival.

ROOM 5. By Neville Tranter. April 27, 1994. Scenery, Ad Leijtens. With Stuffed Puppet Theater.

THE LAST SORTIE. By George Rattner. May 11, 1994. Director, Robert Landau; scenery and lighting, Fred Kolo; costumes, Helen E. Rodgers. With Fred Burrell, Anthony Grasso, Christopher Healy, Alan Levine, Kevin Martin, Frank S. Palmer, David Rosenbaum, Edward Seamon, Steven Stahl, Michael Twaine.

SUBURBAN NEWS. By Nora Glickman. May 12, 1994. Director, Iona Weissberg; scenery, Carol Bailey; costumes, Harry Nadal. With Marlene Forte, Martha Gilpin, Lidia Ramirez, Liz Sherman.

THE HEART IS A LONELY HUNTER. By Carson McCullers, adapted and directed by David Willinger. May 19, 1994. Scenery, Clark Fidelia; lighting, Lee Gundersheimer; costumes, Paula Ann Innocent; music Richard Roque. With Bruce Hlibok, Ralph Navarro, Dennis R. Jones, Terry Ballard, Laurel Holloman, Shane Blodgett.

WAITING. By Toby Armour. May 20, 1994. Director, Aileen Passloff.

Ubu Repertory Theater. Committed to acquainting American audiences with new works by contemporary French-speaking playwrights from around the world. Francoise Kourilsky artistic director.

FIRE'S DAUGHTERS (13). By Ina Cesaire, translated by Judith G. Miller. October 10, 1993. Director, Ntozake Shange; scenery, Watoku Ueno; lighting, Greg MacPherson; costumes, Carol Ann Pelletier; music, Mauro Refosco. With Darlene Bel Grayson, Alene Dawson, Harriett D. Foy, Cee-Cee Harshaw.

TALK ABOUT LOVE! (12). By Paul Emond, translated by Richard Miller. November 14, 1993. Director, Shirely Kaplan; scenery, Watoku Ueno; lighting, Greg MacPherson; costumes, Carol Ann Pelletier. With Jerry Ball, Laurie Graff, Christopher Murney.

THE ORPHAN MUSES (13). By Michel Marc Bouchard, translated by Linda Garboriau. December 5, 1993. Director, Andre Ernotte; scenery, John Brown; lighting, Greg MacPherson; costumes, Carol Ann Pelletier. With Catherine Curtin, Jacqueline Lucid, Joyce O'Connor, Keith Reddin.

THE ORPHANAGE (19). By Reine Barteve, translated by Jill MacDougall. April 10, 1994. Director, Francoise Kourilsky; scenery, Watoku Ueno; lighting, Greg MacPherson; costumes, Carol Ann Pelletier; music, Mauro Refosco. With Julie Boyd, Tanya Lopert, Chad L. Coleman, La Tonya Borsay, Markita Prescott, Eric Coleman.

Staged Readings

THE SHIP. By Michele Cesaire. October 11, 1993.
THAT OLD BLACK MAGIC. By Koffi Kwahule. October 18, 1993.
JOCASTA. By Michele Fabien. November 15, 1993.
STONE AND ASHES. By Daniel Danis. December 5, 1993.
AURELIE, MY SISTER. By Marie Laberge. December 6, 1993.

The Vineyard Theater. Multi-art chamber theater dedicated to the development of new plays and musicals, music-theater collaborations and innovative revivals. Douglas Aibel artistic director, Barbara Zinn Krieger executive director, Jon Nakagawa managing director.

PTERODACTYLS (54). By Nicky Silver. October 6, 1993. Director, David Warren; scenery, James Youmans; lighting, Donald Holder; costumes, Teresa Snider-Stein; dinosaur design, Jim Gary. With Kelly Bishop, T. Scott Cunningham, Hope Davis, Dennis Creaghan, Kent Lanier.

THREE TALL WOMEN. By Edward Albee. February 13, 1994. A Best Play; see its entry in the Plays Produced Off Broadway section of this volume.

CHRISTINA ALBERTA'S FATHER (41). Book, music and lyrics, Polly Pen, based on H.G. Wells's novel. May 4, 1994. Director, Andre Ernotte; choreography, Lynn Taylor-Corbett; scenery, William Barclay; lighting, Michael Lincoln; costumes, Gail Brassard; musical direction, Paulette Haupt. With Marla Schaffel, Henry Stram, Alma Cuervo, Don Mayo, Richard Holmes, Andy Taylor, John Lathan, Tina Johnson, Marceline Hugot, Jan Neuberger.

Lab Production

HIT THE LIGHTS (19). Book and lyrics, Michele Lowe; music, Jon Gilutin. December 7, 1993. Director, Lisa Peterson; choreography, Lynne Taylor-Corbett; scenery, Allen Moyer; lighting, Peter Kaczorowski; costumes, Michael Krass, musical director, Lon Hoyt. With Jason Danieley, Annie Golden, Ann Harada, Michael Mandell, Marti Muller, Michael O'Gorman, Joseph Palmas, John Sloman, Andrea Frierson Toney, Mona Wyatt.

YOUNG WOLFGANG (family entertainment presented in addition to its regular season). By Margaret Steele and Vineyardmusicke; music adapted from Mozart by Sarah Davol. March 5, 1994.

The Women's Project and Productions. Nurtures, develops and produces plays written and directed by women. Julia Miles founder and artistic director.

THE BROOKLYN TROJAN WOMEN (18). By Carole Braverman. June 1, 1993. Director, Margot Breier; scenery, Ted Glass; lighting, Heather Rogan; costumes, Leslie Yarmo. With Adam Barnett, Ariane Brandt, Stephanie Clayman, Joanna Merlin, Lucille Rivin.

EATING CHICKEN FEET. Co-produced by Pan Asian Repertory Theater; see its entry under Pan Asian Repertory Theater.

BLACK (24). By Joyce Carol Oates. March 8, 1994. Director, Tom Palumbo; scenery, David Mitchell; lighting, Jackie Manassee; costumes, Elsa Ward. With John Wojda, Kristin Griffith, Jonathan Earl Peck.

THE AUTOBIOGRAPHY OF AIKEN FICTION (21). By Kate Moira Ryan. April 26, 1994. Director, Adrienne Weiss; scenery, Naralle Sissons; lighting, Rick Martin; costumes, Angela Wendt. With Drew Barr, Julie Dretzin, Jennifer Dundas, Sylvia Gassell, Cristine McMurdo-Wallis. Co-produced by New Georges.

WOMEN WRITE NOW! FESTIVAL (solo performances and works-in-progress): IN NO MAN'S LAND by Susan Kander, directed by Carol M. Tanzman, with Cordis Heard, Bernadette Frankel, Carrie Preston, Angela Featherstone, Jerome Preston Bates, Eden Riegel, Susan Cella; MONKEY BONES by and with Bokara Legendre, directed by Suzanne Bennett; THIN WALLS and THE PLAY THAT KNOWS WHAT YOU WANT by and with Alice Eve Cohen, directed by Alison Summers and Juliette Carillo; KILLING TIME by Ellen MacKay, directed by Bryna Wortman, with Jennifer Daniel; 11 SHADES OF WHITE (THE STORY OF VERONICA LAKE) by Sharon Houck Ross, directed by Mary Beth Easley, with Phyllis Somerville. May 12-25, 1994.

WPA Theater. Produces new American plays and musicals in the realistic idiom. Kyle Renick artistic director, Edward T. Gianfrancesco resident designer, Lori Sherman managing director.

TEN BELOW (34). By Shem Bitterman. June 9, 1993. Director, Stephen Zuckerman; scenery, Edward T. Gianfrancesco; lighting, Richard Winkler; costumes, Mimi Maxmen. With Anthony Edwards, Kevin Conway.

SNOWING AT DELPHI (33). By Catherine Butterfield. November 19, 1993. Director, Pamela Berlin; scenery, Edward T. Gianfrancesco; lighting, Jackie Manassee; costumes, Julie Doyle. With Sam Tsoutsouvas, Ray Virta, Ellen Parker, Catherine Butterfield, John Christopher Jones, Arabella Field.

MUSIC FROM DOWN THE HILL (34). By John Ford Noonan. December 30, 1993. Director, Terence Lamude; scenery, Edward T. Gianfrancesco; lighting, Craig Evans; costumes, Mimi Maxmen. With Welker White, Alma Cuervo.

NEW YORK ROCK (42). Book, music and lyrics, Yoko Ono. March 30, 1994. Director, Phillip Oesterman; choreography, Kenneth Tosti; scenery and costumes, Terry Leong; lighting, Craig Evans; musical direction, Jason Robert Brown. With Jan Horvath, Sean Dooley, Pat McRoberts, Lynnette Perry, Pete Herber, Walter O'Neil, Aaron Blackshear, Evan Ferrante, Peter Kim.

York Theater Company. Specializing in producing new works, as well as in reviving unusual, forgotten or avant-garde musicals. Janet Hayes Walker producing director.

HOW THE OTHER HALF LOVES. By Alan Ayckbourn. October 31, 1993. Director, Alex Dmitriev; scenery, James Morgan; lighting, Jerold R. Forsyth; costumes, Holly Hynes; music, Steven D. Bowen. With Mary Kay Adams, Peter Bloch, Susanne Marley, James Murtaugh, Woody Sempliner, Tracy Thorne.

BOOTH (24). By Austin Pendleton. January 22, 1994. Director, David Schweizer; scenery, James Morgan; lighting, Mary Jo Dondlinger; costumes, Clifford Capone; music and sound, Jim van Bergen. With Frank Langella, Garret Dillahunt, Frances Conroy, Alexander Enberg, Joyce Ebert, Paul Schmidt, Jan Munroe, Molly Regan.

MERRILY WE ROLL ALONG. Book, George Furth, based on George S. Kaufman's and Moss Hart's play; music and lyrics, Stephen Sondheim. May 26, 1994. Director, Susan H. Schulman; choreography, Michael Lichtefeld; scenery, James Morgan; lighting, Mary Jo Dondlinger; costumes, Beba Shamash. With Malcolm Gets, Adam Heller, Amy Ryder, Anne Bobby, Paul Harmon, Michele Pawk, Ron Butler, Danny Burstein, Rick Crom, Jonathan Flanagan, James Hindman, Philip Hoffman, Adriane Lenox, Cass Morgan, Christine Toy, Amy Young.

Miscellaneous

In the additional listing of 1993-94 off-off-Broadway productions below, the names of the producing groups or theaters appear in CAPITAL LETTERS and the titles of the works in *italics.* This list consists largely of new or reconstituted works. It includes a few productions staged by groups which rented space from the more established organizations listed previously.

ALICE'S FOURTH FLOOR. *Portrait of My Bikini* by James Ryan. February 20, 1994. Directed by William Carden; with David Burke, Brian Tarantina, Stephen Mendillo, Christopher Shaw, W.T. Martin.

ALTERED STAGES. *Blue Collar Bay* (one-man show) by and with Steve Axelrod. October 3, 1993. Directed by Mark W. Travis. *Clown Wanted* by Matei Visniec. April 8, 1994. Directed by Moshe Yassur.

AMERICAN JEWISH THEATER. *The Workroom* by Jean-Claude Grumberg, translated by Tom Kempinski. October 26, 1993. Directed by Nicolas Kent; with Larry Block, Caroline Lagerfelt, Peter Jacobson, Deborah LaCoy, Marcia Jen Kurtz, Jennifer Gibbs, Ruby Holbrook, Jeffrey Landman, Leslie Lyles, Brett Rickaby. *The Ash Fire* by Gavin Kostick. December 19, 1993. Directed by Stanley Brechner; with Rosemary Fine, Joseph Siravo, Jenny Conroy, Michael Countryman, Andrew Polk, Terry Donnelly. *The Day the Bronx Died* by Michael Henry Brown. March 22, 1994. Directed by Gordon Edelstein. *Milk and Honey* book by Don Appell; music and lyrics by Jerry Herman. May 15, 1994. Directed by Richard Sabellico; with Ron Holgate, Jeanne Lehmann.

THE BARROW GROUP. *Lonely Planet* by Steven Dietz. February 7, 1994. Directed by Leonard Foglia; with Denis O'Hare, Mark Shannon.

BLUE HERON THEATER. *Exchange* by Yuri Trifonov, translated and adapted by Michael Frayn. March 9, 1994. Directed by Peter Westerhoff; with James Fleming, Janice Johnson, Mark Adzick, Peggy Lord Chilton, Tom Dennis, Bill DiMichele, Maureen Kenny, Ruth Kulerman, Joel Parsons, Madigan Ryan, Ennis Smith, Lynn Faljian Taylor, Anna Vitkin.

BOLD FACE THEATER. *Reproducing Georgia* by Karen Hartman. April 17, 1994. Directed by Dana Kirchman; with Jeanne Dorsey, David Haughen, Colleen Werthmann, Yuri Skujins, Malindi Fickle, David Herskovits, Lauren Howard, Anthony Rapp.

BROOKLYN ACADEMY OF MUSIC. *Next Wave Festival.* Works included *Orphee* (chamber opera) libretto based on Jean Cocteau's film; music by Philip Glass. October 27, 1993. Directed by Francesca Zambello. *Light Shall Lift Them* by and with John Kelly; music by Bill Obrecht. November 10, 1993. *The Black Rider* book by William Burroughs; music and lyrics by Tom Waits. November 20, 1993. Directed by Robert Wilson; with Heinz Vossbrink, Dominique Horwitz, Annette Paulmann, Stefan Kurt. *Njinga the Queen King* written

and directed by Ione; music by Pauline Oliveros. December 1, 1993. With M'bewe Escobar, Cynthia Oliver, Mabiba Baegne, Nego Gato. Luisah Teish, Titos Sompa.

CHARLES LUDLAM THEATER. *99% Artfree* (one-man revue) by and with Bill Dyszel. November 18, 1993. *Boys Don't Wear Lipstick* by and with Brian Belovitch. May 23, 1994. Directed by Keith Greer.

CITY CENTER. Encores: Great American Musicals in Concert. *Fiorello!* book by Jerome Weidman and George Abbott, adapted by John Weidman; music by Jerry Bock; lyrics by Sheldon Harnick. February 9, 1994. Directed by Walter Bobbie; with Jerry Zaks, Philip Bosco, Faith Prince, Adam Arkin, Liz Callaway, Marilyn Cooper, Gregg Edelman, Elizabeth Futral, Donna McKechnie. *Allegro* book and lyrics by Oscar Hammerstein II; music by Richard Rodgers. March 2, 1994. Directed by Susan H. Schulman; with Stephen Bogardus, Karen Ziemba, Christine Ebersole, Celeste Holm, Jonathan Hadary, Christopher Reeve. *Lady in the Dark* book by Moss Hart, adapted and directed by Larry Carpenter; music by Kurt Weill; lyrics by Ira Gershwin. May 4, 1994. With Christine Ebersole, Patrick Cassidy, Frank Converse, Tony Goldwyn, Edward Hibbert, Betsy Joslyn, Joe Morton, Carole Shelley, Tracy Leigh Spindler, Hank Stratton.

COURTYARD PLAYHOUSE. *My Life as a Christian* by and with Jaffe Cohen. May 18, 1994. Directed by Michael Zam.

CUCHARACHA THEATER. *The Gut Girls* by Sarah Daniels. June 5, 1993. Directed by Maria Mileaf; with Deirdre Harrison, Mollie O'Mara, Lauren Hamilton, Joseph Fuqua, Damian Young. *Bremen Freedom* by Rainer Werner Fassbinder, translated by Dennis Calandra. October 20, 1993. Directed by Paul Lazar and Annie-B Parson; with Stacy Dawson, Stephen Brantley, Joey Golden, Deirdre Harrison, Kirk Jackson, Ilyana Kadushin, Susan Maginn, Kate Malin, Brennan Murphy, Rebecca Wisocky. *The Secret Lives of the Ancient Egyptians* written and directed by Hugh Palmer; *Storm Patterns* written and directed by David Simonds (one-act plays). December 1, 1993. With Chuck Montgomery, Jan Leslie Harding, Sharon Brady, Nancy Bauer, Kirk Jackson, Hugh Palmer.

DANCE THEATER WORKSHOP. *The Family Business* written and directed by Ain and David Gordon. February 23, 1994. With Valda Setterfield, Ain Gordon, David Gordon.

DAR A LUZ. *Quotations From a Ruined City* text by Reza Abdoh and Salar Abdoh, created and directed by Reza Abdoh. February 24, 1994. With Sabrina Artel, Brenden Doyle, Anita Durst, Tom Fitzpatrick, Mario Gardner, Mel Herst, Peter Jacobs, Tom Pearl, Ken Roht, Tony Torn, Tom Walker, John Yankee.

DOWNTOWN ART COMPANY. *Promiscuous: Nightwear* by David Cale, directed by Brian Jucha; *The English Rose of Indiana* written and directed by David Cale; *Table* by Roger Babb, directed by Roger Babb and Rocky Bornstein; *Tro* by Roger Babb, directed by Brian Jucha. April 24, 1994. With David Cale, Roger Babb, Mary Schultz, Hyun Yup Lee, Lenard Petit, Vicky Shick.

EAST COAST ARTISTS. *FAUST/gastronome* written and directed by Richard Schechner. June 25, 1993. With Jeff Ricketts, Rebecca Ortese, Ulla Neuerberg, Vernice Miller, David Letwin. *Amerika* adapted from Franz Kafka's novel and directed by Maria Guevara. July 7, 1993. With Shawla Chambliss, Marissa Copeland, Adi Eventov, David Letwin, Cornelia Mills, Emmit Thrower, Rainn Wilson, Frank Wood. *Pilgrims of the Night* by Len Jenkin. July 11, 1993. Directed by Sheldon Deckelbaum; with Andrew Barr, Daniel Berkey, Peter Dobbins, Debra McArthur, Vernice Miller, Daniel Tamm, Terra Vandergaw.

HAROLD CLURMAN THEATER. *Top Girls* by Caryl Churchill. December 1, 1993. Directed by April Shawhan; with Maureen Beitler, Kelly Clark, Joanie Coyote, Irene Glezos, Susan Jon, Victoria Stern, Jeannie Zusy.

HOME FOR CONTEMPORARY THEATER AND ART. *Son of an Engineer* written and directed by David Greenspan. January 6, 1994. With Chuck Coggins, Karen Levitas, Thomas Pasley, Lisa Welti.

IMPACT THEATER. *Strange Encounters: Solitary Confinement* and *My Playground* (one-act plays) by I.C. Howe. February 27, 1994. Directed by Stephen Miller and Peter J. Triolo; with Ed Hardesty, Roger A. Syng, Jim McNicholas, Jeanene Garro, Sharon Mutter, Jill Tarah, Abraham Sparer, Ken Aronow.

INTAR THEATER. *Scaring the Fish* by Benjamin Bettenbender. October 14, 1993. Directed by Michael Warren Powell; with Jim Bracchitta, Sheridan Crist, Andrew Polk. *White Widow* book, music and lyrics by Paul Dick, based on Mario Fratti's *Mafia*. December 4, 1993. Directed by John Margulis; with William

Broderick, Carrie Wilshusen. *Theatersports, Spontaneous Broadway* and *Out of Character* (improvisation pieces). January 14, 1994. By and with Freestyle Repertory Theater.

IRISH REPERTORY THEATER. *The Au Pair Man* by Hugh Leonard. February 4, 1994. Directed by Brian Murray; with Charlotte Moore, Ciaran O'Reilly.

IRONDALE ENSEMBLE PROJECT. *Danton's Death* by Georg Buchner, translated by Howard Brenton. February 27, 1994. Directed by Jim Nielsen; with Michael-David Gordon, Carrie Owerko, Terry Greiss, Joshua Taylor, Lisa Walker, Paul Ellis.

JEAN COCTEAU REPERTORY. *The First Lulu* by Frank Wedekind, translated by Eric Bentley. August 22, 1993. Directed by Robert Hupp; with Elise Stone, Craig Smith, John Lenartz, Steve Chizmadia, Harris Berlinsky, Adrienne D. Williams, John Lynch, T. Walker Rice. *Enrico IV* by Luigi Pirandello, translated by Robert Rietty and John Wardle. October 10, 1993. Directed by Eve Adamson; with Craig Smith, Angela Vitale, Mark Waterman. *Heartbreak House* by George Bernard Shaw. November 28, 1993. Directed by Richard Corley; with Craig Smith, Elise Stone, Adrienne D. Williams, John Lenartz, Harris Berlinsky, Mark Waterman. *The Brothers Karamazov* adapted from Fyodor Dostoyevsky's novel and directed by David Fishelson. January 22, 1994. With Mark Waterman, Christopher Black, Harris Berlinsky. *Iphigenia at Aulis* by Euripides, translated by W.S. Merwin and George E. Dimock Jr. March 20, 1994. Directed by Eve Adamson; with Monique Vukovic, Craig Smith, John Lenartz.

JEWISH REPERTORY THEATER. *Show Me Where the Good Times Are* book by Leonora Thuna, based on Molière's *Imaginary Invalid*; music by Kenneth Jacobson; lyrics by Rhoda Roberts. June 13, 1993. Directed by Warren Enters; with Roslyn Kind, Robert Ari, Lauren Mitchell, Gordon Greenberg, Roy Alan Wilson. *The Cincinnati Saint* book by Norman Lessing; music by Raphael Crystal; lyrics by Richard Engquist. October 31, 1993. Directed by Ran Avni; with Robert Ari, Ellen Foley, Gordon Greenberg. *Edith Stein* by Arthur Giron. January 16, 1994. Directed by Lee Sankowich; with Laura Esterman, Jim Abele, Stacie Chaiken, Tim Lord, Susan Riskin, Terry Serpico. *Teibele and Her Demon* by Isaac Bashevis Singer and Eve Friedman. April 17, 1994. Directed by Daniel Gerroll; with Steve Mellor, Betsy Aidem, David Bishins, Liz Larsen.

JOHN HOUSEMAN THEATER. *Race* by and with Paul Mooney. June, 1993. *Buya Africa* (one-woman show) by and with Thuli Dumakude. Reopened July 16, 1993. *Gilligan's Island* book by Sherwood Schwartz and Lloyd J. Schwartz; music and lyrics by Hope Juber and Laurence Juber. October 6, 1993. *Living in Flames* by and with Todd Alcott. February 28, 1994. Directed by Lee Costello. *Shepherd!* book, music, lyrics and performed by George Fischoff. December 2, 1993.

JOHN JAY COLLEGE THEATER. *Deshima* conceived and directed by Ping Chong and Michael Matthews. December 15, 1993. With Deena Burton, Barbara Chan, Ching Gonzalez, Jennifer Kato, Michael Edo Keane, Brian Liem, Michael Matthews, Ric Oquita, Trinket Monsod.

JUDITH ANDERSON THEATER. *Whattaya Blind?* (musical revue) by and with Theater by the Blind. June 17, 1993. *The Eye of the Beholder* by Ira Wallach. October 4, 1993. Directed by John Hickok; with Kim Hunter, Bob Emmett, Ray Virta, Darby Townsend.

KATHRYN BACHE MILLER THEATER. *How to Make Love* (opera) libretto by C.C. Widdoes; music and lyrics by Lawrence Widdoes. January 13, 1994.

THE KITCHEN. *Queer and Alone* adapted from James Strah's novel and directed by Ron Vawter and Marianne Weems. October 21, 1993. With Greg Mehrten, Lola Pashalinski. *Birdbones* (one-man show) by and with Dudley Saunders. January 20, 1994. *Under the Kerosene Moon* book and lyrics by Sebastian Stuart, based on the film *The Honeymoon Killers*; music by Tony Stavick. March 3, 1994. Directed by Everett Quinton; with Grant Neale, Brenda Cummings, Mary Lou Wittmer.

LINCOLN CENTER. *Serious Fun!* Schedule included *Insekta* text and music by Diamanda Galas, directed by Valeria Vasilevski; *Unplugged* written, directed and performed by Culture Clash (Richard Montoya, Ric Salinas, Herbert Siguenza); *The Complete History of America* (abridged) and *The Complete Works of William Shakespeare* (abridged) by The Reduced Shakespeare Company; *Dark Fruit* by and with Pomo Afro Homos; *Twisted Roots: The Family Business, Act I* written and directed by Ain and David Gordon, with Ain Gordon, David Gordon, Valda Setterfield, and performance works by Instant Girl and Ken Bullock; *101 Humiliating Stories* by and with Lisa Kron; *Your Turn to Roll It #55* by and with The Kipper Kids. July 8-30, 1993.

LOOKINGGLASS THEATER. *Mind Games* by Kenneth Nowell. February 28, 1994. Directed by Tom Lile.

LOVE CREEK PRODUCTIONS. *Blackberry Frost* by Le Wilhelm. December 7, 1993. Directed by Jonathan Hart; with Ben Carney, George Cron, Morgan Forsey, Diane Hoblit, Jackie Jenkins, Nancy McDoniel, Tracy Newirth, Dusty Winniford. *A Malice in the Wood* by Le Wilhelm. February 17, 1994. Directed by Sharon Fallon; with Geoff Dawe, Jed Dickson, Carol Halstead, Michael Ray Martin. *What's My Line?* by Judy Sheehan. February 24, 1994. Directed by Philip Galbraith; with Kirsten Walsh, Diane Hoblit, Katherine Parks.

MADISON AVENUE THEATER. *A Catered Affair* by Arje Shaw and George W. George. May 9, 1994. Directed by Jay Tanzi.

MANHATTAN PERFORMING ARTS COMPANY. *The Survivor* written and directed by Susan Nanus. November 17, 1993. With Dana Chaifetz, Sean Cutler, John Fairlie, Heather Gottlieb, Sam Gray, W. Aaron Harpold, Jason Katz, Julie Lauren, Michael Oberlander, Justin Walker.

MEDICINE SHOW. *Jubilee* book by Moss Hart; music and lyrics by Cole Porter. March 10, 1994. Directed by Barbara Vann; with Marjorie Austrian, James Barbosa, Bonnie Goodman, Michael Hunold, Christine O'Rourke, Regan Vann, Barbara Vann.

MINT THEATER COMPANY. *Jeremy Rudge* by Debbie Jones. November 27, 1993. Directed by Kelly Morgan; with Austin Pendleton, Becky Ann Baker.

NAKED ANGELS. *Fat Men in Skirts* by Nicky Silver. March 9, 1994. Directed by Joe Mantello; with Marisa Tomei.

NEGRO ENSEMBLE COMPANY. *Olivia's Opus* by Nora Cole. November 17, 1993. Directed by Herman LeVern Jones; with Nora Cole, Anastacia Baron, Alan Leach.

NEW GLOBE PRODUCTIONS. *The Courtesan and the Eunuch* by Terry Bradberry. January 11, 1994. Directed by Dan McKeraghan.

NEW GROUP. *Diminished Capacity* by Tom Dulack. June 3, 1993. Directed by Scott Elliott; with Hayley Barr, Chris Delaney, James DeMarse, Neal Jones, Mitchell McGuire, Isiah Whitlock. *Halfway Home* by Diane Bank. October, 1993. Directed by Scott Elliott.

NEW THEATER COMPANY. *Eat, You'll Feel Better* by Lou Ponderoso. December 9, 1993.

NEW YORK GILBERT AND SULLIVAN PLAYERS. *Ruddigore*. December 30, 1993. Directed by Albert Bergeret; with Stephen O'Brien, Lynne Vardaman, Keith Jurosko, Katie Geissinger, Marc Heller, Del-Bouree Bach, Kathleen Larson. *The Pirates of Penzance*. January 6, 1994. Directed by Albert Bergeret; with Noel Harrison, Ray Gabbard, Kate Egan, Carson Church, Michael Collins.

NEW YORK PUBLIC LIBRARY FOR THE PERFORMING ARTS READING ROOM READINGS. *They* by Arnold Weinstein. October 18, 1993. Directed by Julian Webber; with Lillian Jenkins, Peter Maloney, Linda Hill, Robert Joy, Gary Goodrow, Eliza Foss, Ted Neustadt. *Stonewall Jackson's House* by Jonathan Reynolds. November 15, 1993. Directed by Arthur Penn; with Sharon Washington, Susan Aston, Bruce McVittie, Marian Seldes, Gerry Bamman, Stewart Gardner, Danny McNulty. *Enter the Night* written and directed by Maria Irene Fornes. December 13, 1993. With Michaela Murphy, Kelly Maurer, Steven Barkhimer, Matthew Rauch. *Why We Have a Body* by Claire Chafee. January 24, 1994. Directed by Linda Hunt; with Amy Resnick, Anne Lange, Linda Hunt, Welker White, Michelle Hurst. *Sabina* by Willy Holtzman. February 28, 1994. Directed by Michael Greif; with John Hickey, Ken Marks, Laura Linney, Jon DeVries, Michael Booth. *A Slip of the Tongue* by Marion McClinton. March 21, 1994. Directed by Liz Diamond; with Seret Scott, Adina Porter, Kim Yancey. *It Changes Every Year, Four Monologues, Coq au Vin* and *Recipe for One* (one-act plays) written and directed by Jon Robin Baitz. April 18, 1994. With Scotty Bloch, Debra Monk, Mitchell Lichtenstein, John Cameron Mitchell, Nadia Dajani, Stephen Spinella. *Young Valiant* by Oliver Mayer. May 16, 1994. Directed by Bill Hart; with Daniel von Bargen, Marissa Chibas, Victor Rojas.

NUYORICAN POETS CAFE. *The Circle Unbroken Is a Hard Bop* by Sekou Sundiata. September 9, 1993. Directed by Rome Neal; with Stephanie Alston, Craig Harris, Sekou Sundiata.

OLD THEATER. *Wordfire Festival '94* (one-person shows). Schedule included *My Virginia* by and with

Darci Picoult, directed by Suzanne Shepherd; *The Promotion, The Man in the Moon* and *Sunshine's a Glorious Bird* by and with John O'Keefe; *Heddy and Teddy, A Closet Drama* by and with Fred Curchack. February 16-27, 1994.

OLD MERCHANT HOUSE MUSEUM. *Old New York: False Dawn* adapted from Edith Wharton's novella and directed by Donald T. Sanders. January 16, 1994. With John Anson, Ed Romanoff, Nathan Smith, Andrea Weber, Karin Wolfe.

ONE DREAM THEATER. *Godot Arrives* by Nathaniel C. Hutner. November 30, 1993. Directed by Nancy Hancock; with Jacob Harran, Jim Abele, Brennan Brown, Deborah Cresswell, Fred Harlow, Jeff Knapp, Charlotta Nutley, Michael Shelle, Garrison Phillips, David Weck. *The Window Man* book and lyrics by Matthew Maguire; music by Bruce Barthol and Greg Pliska. May 5, 1994. Directed by Bill Mitchelson; with Angela Bullock, Frank Deal, John Nesci, Kaipo Schwab.

ONTOLOGICAL-HYSTERIC THEATER. *My Head Was a Sledgehammer* written and directed by Richard Foreman. January 16, 1994. With Jan Leslie Harding, Thomas Jay Ryan, Henry Stram.

OUR THEATER. *The Strange Case of Dr. Jekyll and Mr. Hyde* adapted from Robert Louis Stevenson's book and directed by Graves Kiely. January 20, 1994.

PACT. *Blinding Light* by Nancy Wallace Henderson. November 18, 1993. Directed by Mitchell Ganem.

PARADISE THEATER. *Wifey* written and directed by Tom Noonan. January 23, 1994. With Julie Hagerty, Tom Noonan, Karen Young, Wallace Shawn.

PEARL THEATER COMPANY. *Oedipus the King* by Sophocles, translated by Stephen Berg and Diskin Clay. September 21, 1993. Directed by Ted Davis; with Robert Hock, Sean Pratt, Margo Skinner, Timothy Wheeler. *The Game of Love and Chance* by Marivaux, translated by Adrianne Mandel and Oscar Mandel. November 7, 1993. Directed by Shepard Sobel; with Robert Hock, Raye Lankford, Victoria Miner, Sean Pratt, Andrew Sellon, Margo Skinner, Timothy Wheeler. *Twelfth Night* by William Shakespeare. December 26, 1993. Directed by John Rando; with Robin Leslie Brown, Robert Hock, Raye Lankford, Frank Lowe, Arnie Burton, Michael James Reed, Dominic Cuskern. *Little Eyolf* by Henrik Ibsen, translated by William Archer. February 13, 1994. Directed by Shepard Sobel; with Robin Leslie Brown, Arnie Burton, Joanne Camp, Spencer Flagg, Anna Minot, Mark Kenneth Smaltz. *The Mollusc* by Hubert Henry Davies. April 3, 1994. Directed by Anthony Cornish; with Tom Bloom, Robin Leslie Brown, Arnie Burton, Kathleen Christal.

PERFORMANCE SPACE 122. *The Opposite Sex Is Neither* by and with Kate Bornstein. August 26, 1993. Directed by Iris Landsberg. *Three Short Pieces: Sunshine's a Glorious Bird, The Man in the Moon* and *The Promotion* (one-act plays) written, directed and performed by John O'Keefe. December 2, 1993. *Holly Hughes* (one-woman show). February 17, 1994. Directed by Dan Hurlin; with Holly Hughes. *Somebody Else's House* (work-in-progress) by and with David Cale. May 5, 1994.

PERRY STREET THEATER. *Cloud 9* by Caryl Churchill. November 3, 1993. Directed by Michael Rego. *Crime and Punishment* adapted from Fyodor Dostoyevsky's novel and directed by Robert Hein. March 13, 1994. With Gregory Pekar, Rhonda Musak.

PHOENIX ENSEMBLE. *The Bathtub* adapted by Paul Schmidt from Mayakovsky's *Banya*. September 26, 1993. Directed by Ivan Popovsky; with Fred Velde, Edward Cunningham, Tony Jackson, Paul Knox, Kerry Metzler, Cecilia Arana. *Black Forest* by Jon Fraser. April 10, 1994. Directed by Karen E. Lordi; with Herman O. Arbeit, Allan Benjamin, Jeremy Brisiel, Blanche Cholet, Kim Highland, Marlene Hodgdon, Kerry Metzler.

PLANET Q THEATER. *Yabba-Dabba-Q (Still Havin' a Gay Ol' Time)* (musical revue) by and with Stephen Earley, Chrisanne Eastwood, Tony Javed, Veronica Mittenzwei, Eric Rockwell and Ann Stengel; music and lyrics by Eric Rockwell and Chrisanne Eastwood. October 7, 1993. Directed by David Mowers.

PLAYHOUSE 125. *Old Flames* written and directed by Anthony Patton. July 9, 1993. With Marion Killinger, Brian McCormack, Douglas Gibson, Mac Powell.

PLAYWRIGHTS' PREVIEW PRODUCTIONS. *The Lost Dreams and Hidden Frustrations of Every Woman in Brooklyn* by Kathleen O'Neill. February 26, 1994. Directed by Tina J. Ball.

RAINBOW AND STARS (cabaret). *The Night They Invented Champagne: The Lerner and Loewe Revue*

AT PLAYHOUSE 125—Mac Powell, Brian McCormack and Douglas Gibson in a scene from *Old Flames* written and directed by Anthony Patton

music by Frederick Loewe; lyrics by Alan Jay Lerner. July 6, 1993. Directed by Deborah R. Lapidus; with Maureen Brennan, Eddie Korbich, Juliet Lambert, Martin Vidnovic.

SAMUEL BECKETT THEATER. *What You Are About to See Is Real: Waxboy, Razorman, D.N.R.* and *Peanut* by Randy Sharp and Michael Gump. December 12, 1993. Directed by Randy Sharp; with Shari Albert, Jim Cullom, Sheryl Dold, Michael Gump, Robert Ierardi, Jon Johnson, Dee Pelltier, G.W. Rooney, Chris Swift. *Boy's Life* by Howard Korder. January 12, 1994. Directed by Vincent Bossone; with Sabrina Seidner,

Andy Bushell, Maureen Donahue, Peter Dorton, Chance Kelly, Jeanne Langston, Elissa Piszel, Christopher Prizzi, Troy Sostillio. *The Ice-Fishing Play* by Kevin Kling. May 26, 1994. Directed by Sheldon Deckelbaum; with Bob Bender, Brian David Price, Christopher A. Russell, Brian Shnipper, Suzanne von Eck, David Weynand, Raymond Munoz.

SANFORD MEISNER THEATER. *Working Out With Leona* book by Nelson Jewell and Mary Lee Miller; music by Michael Capece and Paul Radalet; lyrics and direction by Nelson Jewell. September 5, 1993. *One of the Good Guys* book, music, lyrics and performed by David Bolander and Meir Vardi. October 11, 1993.

SYMPHONY SPACE. *Don Juan in Hell* by George Bernard Shaw (concert reading). May 19, 1994. Directed by Harris Yulin; with Edward Asner, Rene Auberjonois, Dianne Wiest, Harris Yulin.

SYNCHRONICITY SPACE. *Frayed Edges: Porch & Stops Along the Way* (one-act plays) by Jeffrey Sweet. May 23, 1994. Directed by Alexander Dinelaris and Chuck Zito; with Nancy Jo Carpenter, Dennis Hearn, Jamie Morris, Rob Quadrino, Patrick Welsh, Ron Crawford, Darby Townsend.

THEATER EAST. *Sweet Daddy and Amazing Grace* book and lyrics by Clyde Wayne MacMillian; music by Clyde Wayne MacMillian and Gerald Trottman. March 18, 1994.

THEATER FOUR. *All That Glitters* by Stephan Bullard. October 13, 1993. Directed by Eleanor Reissa; with Dana Vance, Linda Cook, Barbara Gulan, Ilene Kristen.

THEATER OFF PARK. *Misconceptions* by Cherie Vogelstein. June 13, 1993. Directed by Josh Mostel; with Caroline Aaron, Anne Bobby, Michael Ingram, Trish Jenkins, Lola Pashalinski, Richard Ziman, Danny Zorn. *Marilyn Monroe, Clark Gable & Me* book, music and lyrics by Lavada June Roberts. October 15, 1993. Directed by Irving Vincent.

THEATER ROW THEATER. *Panorama* by Pieter-Dirk Uys. April 10, 1994. Directed by George Ferencz; with Bill Christ, Jacqueline Pennington, Margie Rynn, Kim Tooks.

13TH STREET THEATER. *Tin Pan Alley and the Silver Screen* written, directed and performed by Wally Peterson. February 13, 1994.

T.W.E.E.D. *The Art of Hanging Fire* by Perry Souchuk. January 28, 1994. Directed by Rebecca Holderness; with Umit Celebi, Gretchen Claggett, Gia Forakis, Peggy Gould, Raymond Lamb Jr., Jenifer Regan, Diego Reyes, Mike Villane.

28TH STREET THEATER. *The Little Prince* book and lyrics by John Scoullar, based on Antoine de Saint-Exupery's book; music by Rick Cummins. October 17, 1993. Directed by William Martin; with Daisy Eagan, Natascia Diaz, Merwin Goldsmith, Howard Kaye. *The Courtesan and the Eunuch* by Terry Bradberry. January 11, 1994. Directed by Dan McKereghan; with Paolo Seganti, Blythe Baten, Jennifer Fleming, Eleonora Kihlberg, John Marino.

UNION SQUARE UPSTAIRS THEATER. *Classified* by Fred Adler and Dan Cedeno. June 6, 1993. Directed by William Oliver; with Fred Adler.

VIA THEATER. *Loved Less (The History of Hell)* written and directed by Brian Jucha. May 12, 1994. With Jason Butler Harner, Steven Belber, Kristen Lee Kelly, Lisa Welti, E. William Keenan, Tamar Kotoske, Tina Shepard, Sheryl Dold.

VILLAGE THEATER COMPANY. *Exit Music* book by Dick Pasqual and James Merillat, based on Noel Coward's story *Me and the Girls*; music by James Merillat; lyrics by Dick Pasqual. July 9, 1993. Directed by Brian Meister. *Could I Have This Dance?* by Doug Haverty. September 9, 1993. Directed by Jules Aaron; with Alyson Reim, Isabel Keating, Toni Sawyer, Bob Horen, Randell Harris, Roger Michelson. *Madonna* by Don Nigro. April 7, 1994. Directed by Gigi Rivkin; with Pam Bennett, Jill Chamberlain, Elizabeth Daly, Marj Feenan, Mark Foley, Peter Husovsky, Craig Little, Lisa Littlewood, Christopher Marino, J.B. McLendon, Roger Michelson, Michael Pinney, Melanie Summerfield, Brenda Warren.

WAVERLY PLACE THEATER. *The Ebony Game* book, music and lyrics by Richard Wolf. September 15, 1993. Directed by Louis Johnson.

WEISSBERGER THEATER GROUP. *Down the Road* by Lee Blessing. June 10, 1993. Directed by David

Dorwart; with Eric Stoltz, Lisa Eichhorn, John Dossett. *Freefall* by Charles Smith. March 7, 1994. Directed by Donald Douglass; with K. Todd Freeman, Valarie Pettiford, Geoffrey C. Ewing, Eugene Fleming.

WEST BANK DOWNSTAIRS THEATER. *The Wonderful O* book adapted by Will Osborne from James Thurber's work; music and lyrics by Ann Sternberg and Randy Courts. September 10, 1993. *The Comings and Goings of Average People* by Nikki Harmon. February 23, 1994. With Mackenzie Phillips.

WESTBETH THEATER CENTER. *Jerker* by Robert Chesley. July 21, 1993. Directed by Stephen Stahl. *Gams on the Lam* (comedy trio). September 27, 1993. Directed by John Plummer; with Patricia Buckley, Lauren Unbekant, Leslie Noble. *Masked Men* by Anthony Cuen. October 14, 1993. Directed by Tom O'Horgan; with Rafael Alvarez, Fay Kepperson, Doug Von Nessen.

WILLOW CABIN THEATER. *S.S. Glencairn - Four Plays of the Sea: The Moon of the Caribees, Bound East for Cardiff, The Long Voyage Home* and *In the Zone* (one-act plays) by Eugene O'Neill. October 11, 1993. Directed by Edward Berkeley; with Michael Rispoli, John Bolger, Laurence Gleason, Doug Broe, Adam Oliensis, Ken Forman, Peter Killy, Angela Nevard, Linda Powell. *Who Will Carry the Word?* by Charlotte Delbo. November 8, 1993. Directed by Edward Berkeley; with Linda Powell, Dede Pochos, Fiona Davis, Maria Radman, Charmaine Lord. *As You Like It* by William Shakespeare. March 9, 1994. Directed by Edward Berkeley; with Fiona Davis, John Bolger, Laurence Gleason, Dede Pochos, Angela Nevard, Ken Forman, Adam Oliensis.

THE WOOSTER GROUP. *Frank Dell's The Temptation of St. Antony* by and with The Wooster Group. November 16, 1993. Directed by Elizabeth LeCompte. *Fish Story (An Epilogue to Brace Up)* by and with The Wooster Group. December 29, 1993. Directed by Elizabeth LeCompte. *The Emporer Jones* by Eugene O'Neill. March 24, 1994. Directed by Elizabeth LeCompte; with Willem Dafoe, Kate Valk.

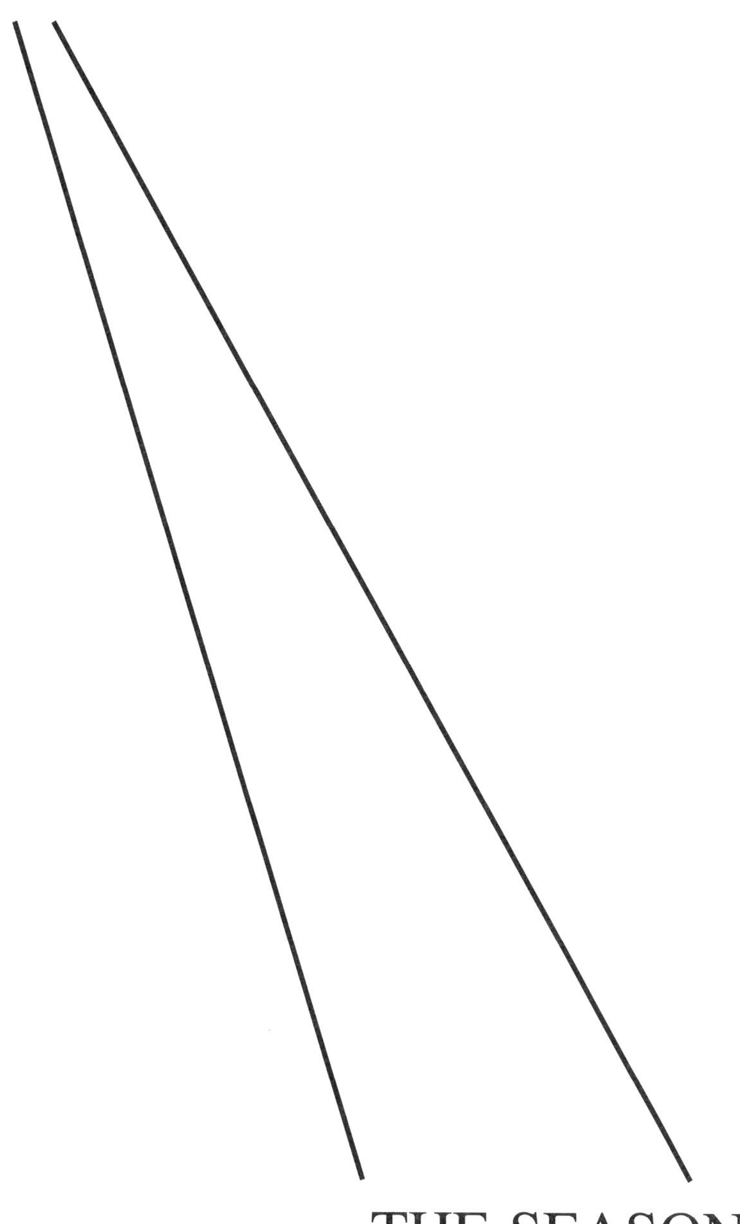

THE SEASON AROUND THE UNITED STATES

OUTSTANDING NEW PLAYS CITED BY AMERICAN THEATER CRITICS ASSOCIATION

and

A DIRECTORY OF NEW-PLAY PRODUCTIONS

THE American Theater Critics Association (ATCA) is the organization of over 250 leading drama critics in all media in all sections of the United States. One of this group's stated purposes is "To increase public awareness of the theater as a *national* resource" (italics ours). To this end, since 1974 ATCA has annually cited three outstanding new plays produced around the U.S., to be represented in our coverage of The Season Around the United States by excerpts from each of their scripts demonstrating literary style and quality. And one of these—*Keely and Du* by Jane Martin—has been designated the 1993 first-place play, receiving the 9th annual ATCA New Play Award of $1,000. Another of ATCA's citations this year is the first Elizabeth Osborn Award to an emerging playwright—Anne Galjour for her play *Hurricane*. Another 1993 citation went to Christopher Sergel's *Black Elk Speaks*.

The process of selection of these outstanding plays is as follows: any ATCA member critic may nominate a play if it has been given a production in a professional house. It must be a finished play given a full production (not a reading or an airing as a play-in-progress). Nominated scripts were studied and discussed by an ATCA playreading committee chaired by Michael Grossberg of the Columbus *Dispatch* and comprising Richard Christiansen of the Chicago *Tribune*, Lawrence DeVine of the Detroit *Free Press*, Christine Dolen of the Miami *Herald*, William A. Henry III of *Time*, Michael Sommers of the Newhouse Papers, Catherine Staddem of the Anchorage *Daily News* and alternates George Hatza of the Reading, Pa. Eagle Company, Rosalind Friedman of WMNR-FM in Trumbull, Conn. and Dennis Harvey of the San Francisco Bay *Guardian*. These committee members made their choices on the basis of script rather than production, thus placing very much the same emphasis as the editors of this volume in making the New York Best Play selections. There were no eligibility requirements except that a nominee be the first full professional production of a new work outside New York City within the 1993 calendar year. If the timing of nominations and openings prevents some works from being considered in any given year, they will be eligible for consideration the following year if they haven't since moved to New York.

We offer our sincerest thanks and admiration to the ATCA members and their committee for the valuable insights into the 1993 theater season around the United States which their selections provide for this *Best Plays* record, in the form of the following excerpts from outstanding scripts, with brief introductions provided by Michael Grossberg (*Keely and Du*), Holly Hill (*Black Elk Speaks*) and Lawrence DeVine (*Hurricane*).

Cited by American Theater Critics as Outstanding New Plays of 1993

○○○
○○○
○○○
○○○
○○○
○○○

KEELY AND DU

A Full-Length Play in One Act

BY JANE MARTIN

Cast and credits appear on page 433 of *The Best Plays of 1992-93*

KEELY AND DU: Abortion is a thorny, complex, highly personal issue that forces one to confront one's deepest assumptions about human rights, individual choice and the very meaning of what is human.

Abortion is also an intensely emotional issue. Those on both sides of this longstanding controversy have tended to demonize or caricaturize their opponents—a sad irony, since anti-abortion groups criticize abortion advocates for dehumanizing the fetus, while abortion advocates try to defend women against dehumanization via the denial of their moral autonomy.

Keely and Du, a searing drama about the abortion debate by Louisville playwright Jane Martin, plays fair with both sides of the debate.

Martin is known for her quirky comedies about feisty women (*Talking With . . .*,

Vital Signs, *Cementville*). *Keely and Du*, which also boasts strong women at its center, is her most serious and ambitious play yet.

"Martin," the pseudonym of an anonymous Louisville playwright who may be female or male, does not attempt to resolve the debate in her 95-minute, intermissionless play. Yet Martin humanizes it through sharply etched portraits of two fiercely purposeful women who form a powerful bond despite—and because of—their conflict.

As *Keely and Du* opens in an unfinished basement in a working-class home in Providence, Rhode Island, Du is making the bed in preparation for Keely's arrival. Keely, a young woman almost three months pregnant, has been kidnapped by an anti-abortion group from the street near an abortion clinic, to save her fetus.

When Keely wakes up from her anesthesia, she is shocked and angry to discover that she has been handcuffed to an old cast-iron bed, which is bolted to the floor. Soon after, she meets the man who kidnapped her.

In the darkness, we hear a buzzer. Walter, on the speaker: "I will be coming down." Lights up. Du moves to the door, pushes the speaker's button.

DU: Yes?

WALTER: I will be coming down.

DU: Yes. Good. (*She turns to Keely.*) I hope you aren't so angry that you can't listen because it would be important to listen now. Keely? He is blunt spoken sometimes, and he is a man, don't let that close your heart. Keely?

Du goes to the suitcase and puts on her mask. There is a light knock on the door. She goes to it and unlocks it. She opens the door. A man wearing a mask, dressed in a suit and tie, enters with a briefcase. He speaks to Du.

WALTER: Good morning, sister.

DU: Good morning.

WALTER: Good morning, Keely. (*No answer. He goes to the rocker and pulls it closer to Keely but still beyond her reach*) Nana is taking fine care of you, I'm sure. (*He looks at the tray on the floor.*) I see you've had your breakfast. You seem alert and well. The anesthetic we used, one hundred milligrams Ketamine, is very mild and will not harm the baby, we're very sure of that. I know you have other concerns. Funds have been arranged for your father's care. I wanted to reassure you. (*Pause.*) Will you talk to me at this point, Keely, or shall I just talk to you? I know this must be hard to take in.

KEELY: Who are you?

WALTER: I am a member, Keely, of Operation Retrieval. We are a group of like-minded Christians motivated by a belief in the sanctity of life and the rights of unborn children.

Keely puts her head in her hand.

WALTER: Now, Keely, Western man has firmly held to life-supportive principles as promoted by Hippocrates from 450 B.C. until the turn of the century. Since then, certain groups and individuals have been promoting death as a solution to social problems. I do not condone that. You are almost three months pregnant, Keely.

KEELY: I was raped.

WALTER: You were, Keely, and I find that horrifying. That a man you knew and cared for . . .

KEELY: Wait a minute; wait a minute.

WALTER: You are the injured party . . .

KEELY: Yeah, right . . .

WALTER: In God's eye, and in ours . . .

KEELY: And handcuffed, and kidnapped.

WALTER: . . . but your unborn child is separate from that issue.

KEELY: No, it isn't.

WALTER: It is a separate life which may not be taken to solve your very real problems.

KEELY: Hey, it's cells, little cells.

WALTER (*very clearly*): It is a separate life.

KEELY: And what about my life?

WALTER: I need to clarify the situation for you . . .

KEELY (*pulling on her restraint*): Oh, it's clarified.

WALTER: Keely, there are one and a half million abortion deaths on this planet each year, and that is spiritually unbearable. Now, you are one of four young women, geographically distributed, all with child, all seeking abortion, who have been taken into protective custody. Each of you sought out a clinic for different reasons and in different situations. There is, of course, a political dimension here. We chose you as a rape victim, Keely. Rape has always been understood as the extreme edge of abortion policy, and we must make clear that infant rights extend even into this catastrophic area. The rape victim must be given support on every level, but the fact of the child is critical. If medically we must lose or severely harm mother or child, we must choose. If both can survive, both must survive. We intend to document and assist these children's lives, which would otherwise have been lost.

KEELY: What do you mean, document?

WALTER: Document, Keely. We'll discuss it later.

KEELY: Who the hell are you? Screw you people. I'm not a goddamn teenager. You're not God. I want an abortion!

WALTER: Keely . . .

KEELY: What do you want from me?!

WALTER: We want you to hold your baby. We will care for you here until the seventh month of your pregnancy and then return you home for the birth in the best medical circumstances.

KEELY: Oh, man.

WALTER: We assume the following responsibilities: all expenses relating to the birth of your child will be taken care of, adoptive parents eager to raise the child and

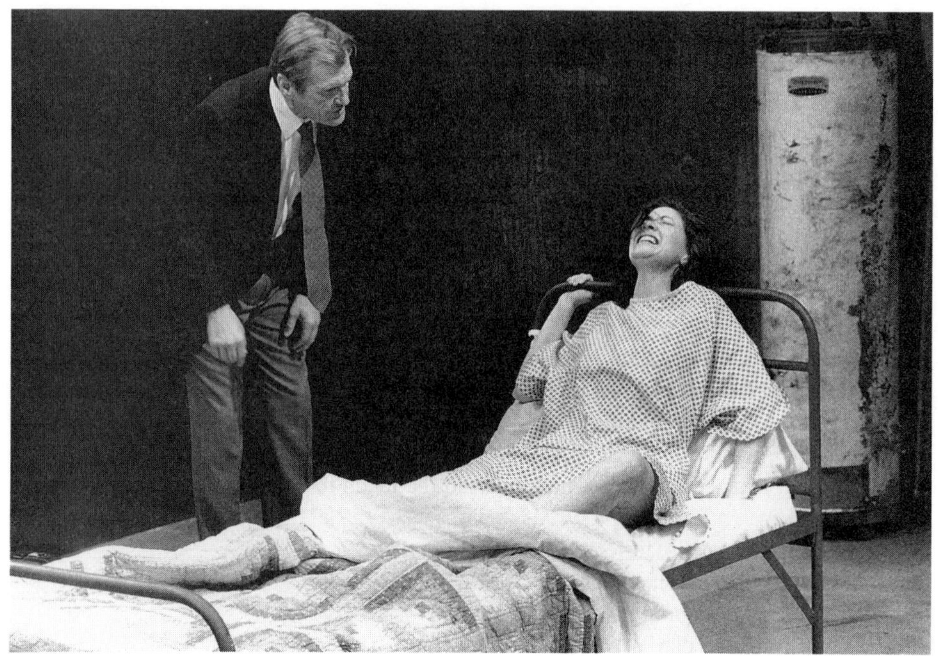

ACTORS THEATER OF LOUISVILLE—Bob Burrus (Walter) and Julie Boyd (Keely) in a scene from *Keely and Du* by Jane Martin

capable of so doing will be in touch with you, should you decide to raise your child . . .

KEELY: How the hell do you think I'm going to do that, huh? You knew I was pregnant, you knew I was raped, do you know I take care of my dad? Do you know he's paralyzed? Do you know I hold his bedpan? Is that part of what you know? Do you know I work two jobs? Do you know what they are?

WALTER: A child-care subsidy will be provided for the first two years, and there will be an education fund . . .

KEELY: What is your name? What . . . what . . . who are you?

WALTER: You're going to be famous, Keely. You're going to be a famous American. There will be many opportunities open to you and your child. This is difficult for you to understand, but your life has already changed for the better . . . (*Keely laughs.*) I know it's ironic. Are the handcuffs hurting you?

KEELY: Yes.

WALTER: I'm sure there is something we can do. Everything I know about you, Keely, and I know considerable, leads me to believe you will fall in love with your baby.

KEELY: My sister-in-law, she threw her baby on the floor. You think "in love with your baby . . . " is all that's out there?

WALTER: It's what should be out there. You are in your third month, Keely. Your baby is sensitive to the touch. If you stroke its palm, it will make a fist.

KEELY: You're going to prison, mister. I'll put you there.

WALTER: You may send me to prison . . . (*He gestures toward Du.*) . . . we are both prepared for that spiritually and practically. We have committed our lives. What can I say to you? I am a father, and caring for, learning from my children . . . well, you wouldn't understand. They resurrected my life through Our Lord Jesus Christ.

DU: She's exhausted.

WALTER: Keely, the abortion procedure you were seeking Wednesday morning is called Suction Curettage. A powerful suction tube is inserted through the cervix into the womb. The baby's body and the placenta are torn to pieces and sucked into a jar. The baby's head is crushed and then extracted.

KEELY: Screw off.

WALTER: It's sometimes hard to recognize a friend at first, Keely, we need direction sometimes, we need people to tell us what to do when we act out of panic or confusion. I have limited your options and taken control to give you the chance to step outside your runaway emotions. I will return your options to you when you are thinking clearly and ready for them.

KEELY (*indicating Du*): She took off her mask, I'll remember her.

Walter looks at Du. A pause, and then he takes off his mask.

WALTER: There, now you've seen us both. Hello.

Keely doesn't reply. Du takes off her mask. Walter looks at her again briefly. He rises and moves to the door.

I am a pastor if you wish counseling about your rape or pregnancy. One of our doctors will visit you weekly. This lady is a registered nurse. (*Pause.*) You could be my daughter, Keely, and if you were I would do this for you. I'll see about the handcuffs. Goodbye, Keely.

He exits, closing the door behind him. Du goes to the door and locks it. Turning back, she cleans up the breakfast.

DU: I'm sorry they chose you.

Keely's initial rage and despair, while always present as a bracing undercurrent, are softened by her constant contact with Du, a kindly elderly woman whose compassion for Keely belies her religious fanaticism.

Gradually, the women open up to each other about their lives and feelings, hopes and regrets.

DU: Things do change.

KEELY: Yeah, they get worse. He drank more, he got meaner, he screwed around. My dad got shot, Cole wanted to move to Arizona because he knew I'd have to take care of him. I'm waitressing, minimum wage, cashier at a car wash, seventy hours minimum, he drinks himself out of his job, real thoughtful, right? The recession came on, we just fought minute to minute any time we laid eyes on each other, I said I wanted a divorce, he hit me, and I left. I was out of there fifteen minutes after he hit me . . . I was a crazy, out-of-my-mind lunatic I lived with him all that time. Jesus! What the hell was I thinking of?

DU: It was a marriage, Keely.

KEELY: Yeah. After that, he was all over me. I'd look out the window, he'd be in the back yard. The grocery, the library, when I was hanging up laundry, walk into the same bar when I was on a date. He'd come down to the restaurant, say it was about borrowing money, but he knew I wasn't giving him money, forget that, he just liked me to be scared which is what I figured out. Then it stopped for six months, who knows why, then he came back, sent flowers, left messages, begged me to talk to him for one hour, so I invited him over, you know, I thought we could sit down and let go of it. I thought I could take his hand and say we're clear, we're two different people. You know, some dumb ass idea like that. So I fixed him something to eat, and he brought me this stuffed animal, and we were doing, well not perfect but all right, and I just touched his arm so he would know it was all right, and he locked onto my hand, and I said "let go now," and he started in . . . said he needed . . . pulled me in, you know, hard, and I got a hand in his face, and he . . . he bit down . . . bit down hard, and I . . . I don't know, went nuts . . . bunch of stuff . . . got me down on the floor . . . got me down on the floor and raped me. That's how he caught up with our marriage, that's how he changed.

They sit in silence.

DU: It's in the past, Keely.

KEELY: Well, this isn't. (*Pause.*) You believe God sees you?

DU: I do.

KEELY: He sees you now?

DU: I believe he does. (*Pause.*) Keely? . . . Keely? (*no answer.*) Almost time for your birthday.

Pause.

KEELY: How do you know that?

DU: Now, Keely, that's the least of what I know, and you know it.

KEELY: From my driver's license.

DU: The man says you can have a cake?

KEELY: The man?

DU: The man in charge.

A moment.

KEELY: If I do what, I can have a cake?

DU: Oh, a few pamphlets.

KEELY: I'm not reading that crap. I mean it. Don't you bring it anywhere near me.

DU: You're not afraid of information, are you, honey?

KEELY: You call that information?

DU: Well, there's facts to it.

KEELY: I'm not having a baby. I'm not having it and have somebody adopt it. I'm not having it and keeping it. It won't be. It won't.

Pause.

DU: What would you like for your birthday, honey? (*Keely looks at her.*) Besides that. That's not in my power.

Pause.

KEELY: I would like to get dressed. I never liked being in a nightgown. I don't like my own smell, I know that's crazy. You know how you can smell yourself off your night stuff.

DU: Oh, I can share that. That's something doesn't get a bit better with age, let me tell you.

KEELY: I want a chocolate cake. I want to stand up. I want my hands free, I don't care if it's for ten minutes, one minute. I want to walk into a bathroom. I want to stand up, not bent over on my birthday.

DU: Oh, honey. We only do this because we don't know what else to do. We can't think what else . . . I don't know, I don't . . . birthdays when they're little, the looks on those faces . . . those little hands . . .

KEELY: Little hands, little faces, you make me sick . . . Jesus, can you listen to yourself? All this crap about babies. You don't care about this baby, you just want it to be your little . . . I don't know . . . your little political something, right, God's little visual aid you can hold up at abortion clinics instead of those pickled miscarriages you usually tote around . . . hold up, Baby Tia, wasn't that the one you had downtown trying to pass it off like it was aborted? I can't believe you don't make yourself sick . . . throw up . . . you make me sick, how do you talk this garbage?

DU: (*a moment.*) I have that dress you had on . . . something the worse for wear . . . I might get it cleaned . . . cleaned for your birthday.

A moment.

KEELY: I don't hate babies, if that's what you think.

DU: I know that.

KEELY: What the hell is your name? You can . . . you can . . . you can give me that for my birthday. I would like to know what the hell to call you when I talk to you!

DU: Du.

KEELY: What?

DU: I get called Du.

KEELY: Du.

DU: Uh-huh.

KEELY: Du what? Du why? Never mind, forget it . . . I would like to be free for ten minutes on my birthday.

DU: You might have to read some pamphlets.

KEELY: What the hell happened to you, Du? Do you see where we are? Look at this where you got to. Look at me. You used to be a person sometime, right? You look like one. You sound like one. You see the movie *Alien* where they end up with snakes in their chests? What happened to you?

DU: They tear apart the babies, they poison them with chemicals, and burn them to death with salt solution, they take them out by Caesarean alive and let them die of neglect or strangulation. Over and over. Over and over. Little hands. Little feet. I've held babies. I've lost babies. I took my own baby through three heart operations and lost that baby. I need to sleep. That's what happened to me.

KEELY (*almost gently*): I can't raise this baby, Du. I'm so angry and fucked up, I just can't do it. I dream how it happened over and over all the time. I'd be angry at the baby, I think so. I'd hurt the baby sometime and might not even know it, that could happen. If I had a baby, my first one, and I gave it away, I'd just cry all the time, I would. I'm doing this on empty and, if I did that, I would be past empty and I don't know. I have such black moods, it frightens me. The baby would come out of being chained to a bed, you know what I mean. It's not my baby, it's the people's who made me have it, and I couldn't treat it as my baby, not even if I loved it, I couldn't. He'd come around, see. He wouldn't stay off if I had his baby. He would never, ever in this world leave off me, and I think sometime he'll kill me, that's all I can think. Or hurt the baby, whatever, however in his head he could get me, he would do . . . would do it. Really. And I can't have his baby . . . uh . . . it's just not something I can do . . . because I'm about this far, you know . . . right up to the edge of it . . . right there . . . right there. (*Pause.*) So I guess it's me or the baby, so I guess that's crazy, but you don't . . . I don't show you . . . just how . . . how angry I really am. I don't. I don't.

Keely and Du *was produced at the Actors Theater of Louisville March 17, 1993 during the 1993 Humana Festival of New American Plays under the direction of Jon Jory.*

BLACK ELK SPEAKS

A Play in Two Acts

ADAPTED BY CHRISTOPHER SERGEL

BASED ON THE BOOK BY JOHN G. NEIHARDT

Cast and credits appear on page 557

BLACK ELK SPEAKS: At the beginning of rehearsals for this drama about the Sioux holy man Black Elk, the Denver Center Theater Company joined in a Sioux blessing ceremony attended by Black Elk's descendants, two of whom were advisers for the production.

In the play's opening scene, the elderly Black Elk begs the Great Spirit to help him fulfill the mission he received in a boyhood vision, when he saw the sacred hoop of his people as one of many hoops sheltered by a mighty tree at the center, symbolizing world unity. He tells his rebellious grandson the tale of "the winning of the West as experienced by the Indian people," beginning with the arrival of Columbus. Black Elk ultimately realizes that the fulfillment of his mission is in telling the Indians' story as a means of re-assembling not only the sacred hoop of his own, but of all people.

A cast of nearly 30 actors and musicians enacts the events, playing Relatives (Lakota Sioux living on a reservation with Black Elk in 1931), members of diverse tribes, and Wasichus (the Lakota name for white people). The drama is enhanced by music for drums, flutes and singers, by costumes based on Lakota pictographs and by such special effects as bolas swung by warriors to signal the winds of war sweeping the plains. History never becomes a pageant because the play is laced with humor (the Indians view the Civil War as "unexpected good luck" and call Washington, D.C. "the place where everything is disputed"), and each event is personalized by highlighting one or more characters. Among these are Red Cloud and Crazy Horse.

Fort Laramie, Wyoming Territory, June 13, 1866: The Relative who will play Red Cloud enters with the magnificent staff of the Lakota nation. He wears a single eagle feather in his long hair and a bone breast-plate over his war shirt.

BLACK ELK: Chief Red Cloud is a great warrior, a skilled statesman, the most powerful chief of the Sioux Nation.

Wind whistles out. Red Cloud lifts the Lakota staff to each of the four directions.

Since he has stopped the invasion, Red Cloud hopes this may prove an unusual negotiation—one in which there is something for the Indian. The prayers of Red Cloud are for what the Indian wants most from the government; something so rare we can only pray for it.

RED CLOUD: We pray that what is spoken here be the truth.

Military and Native drums sound. The Relative who will play Commissioner Taylor enters. His top hat and long buckskin coat are painted red. He carries a star-spangled lap desk painted red, white and blue. The Commissioner is accompanied by Soldier-Aides, one carrying the Stars and Stripes, another carrying the territorial flag of Wyoming and two others who place a small campaign table and chair inside the winter-telling circle; the flags are placed behind and to each side of the chair in the classic positions. Taylor sits, takes papers from his lap desk and arranges them on the table.

At the same time, an Arapaho Chief and a Cheyenne Chief enter and cross to flank Red Cloud. Each carries the staff of his nation. Indian drums and songs match and mix with the military drums. The military and Native drums merge into a sonorous roll, rise to an honor beat and fall silent. The ceremonial arrivals have been completed. If he had not entered government service, Taylor would have become a used car salesman.

TAYLOR (*rising and speaking with great charm*): Chief Red Cloud, my name is Taylor. I am president of the Treaty Commission. The United States government is anxious to reach an agreement to open the Bozeman Road through your territory.

A murmur moves through Red Cloud's party.

We only need a little bit of land.

RED CLOUD: How little?

TAYLOR: Only as much as a wagon would take between the wheels.

RED CLOUD: There are white people all around us. They come like a river dirty with lies and greed. We have but a small spot of land left. The Great Spirit tells us to keep it.

TAYLOR (*with the demonstrated patience of one used to dealing with children*): But there's been a discovery in Montana, the yellow metal. We expect heavy travel.

RED CLOUD: Such travel would violate our treaty.

TAYLOR: Yes. The old treaty. We are here to make a new treaty.

RED CLOUD: We have signed a treaty. If your soldiers come into our country, we'll fight them.

TAYLOR: Why this talk of fighting?

As Taylor continues, two Relatives enter. One will play Colonel Henry B. Carrington; the other, a Lakota Messenger. Carrington moves to a position behind Taylor. The Messenger crosses the ridge, jumps to the floor and whispers in Red Cloud's ear.

Why not talk of our friendship for our red brothers, of the train we have loaded ready to bring presents? I have a manifest of these presents which I would like to read to you in detail. The generosity of the Great Father, his consideration for your welfare, bales of fine blankets, tins of prime tobacco . . .

RED CLOUD (*to Taylor, interrupting*): This officer was met some distance from here and asked where he and his men were going.

TAYLOR (*seeing Carrington for the first time*): Colonel Carrington! You're early, Colonel.

CARRINGTON: We made good time.

TAYLOR: Our negotiations are . . . We were not expecting you until . . .

CARRINGTON: To avoid any chance of trouble, I halted my regiment four miles east of the post.

RED CLOUD: That is very tactful. And from there, Colonel?

CARRINGTON: What?

RED CLOUD: You are now less than *two* miles east of this post. Do you intend to turn north into our territory?

CARRINGTON (*his temper flares*): You have no right to interrogate an officer of the . . .

TAYLOR (*sharply*): Colonel Carrington.

RED CLOUD (*directly to Taylor*): We have made special prayers—prayers that you tell us the truth!

TAYLOR (*a considered pause. Taylor drops his cordial mask*): The truth is that we are going to open the Bozeman Road.

RED CLOUD: Congratulations. For telling the truth.

TAYLOR: How dare you speak to me in this outrageous . . .

RED CLOUD (*interrupting with cool and controlled purpose*): Why do you treat Indians like children?

TAYLOR: I represent the government of the United States . . .

RED CLOUD: Why do you pretend to negotiate for our country while preparing to take it with your soldiers?

DENVER CENTER THEATER COMPANY—Lorne Cardinal (Red Cloud), Kenneth Martines (Commissioner Taylor), Kenneth Little Hawk (Cheyenne Chief), Peter Kelly Gaudreault (Crazy Horse) and Jack Burning (Arapaho Chief) in *Black Elk Speaks* adapted by Christopher Sergel from John G. Neihardt

TAYLOR: It is only a matter of a road, a few forts. Because of the seasonal requirements, we . . . The Great Father sends presents!

RED CLOUD: While this soldier goes to steal our land before the Indians say yes or no. This earth is my mother. For what presents should I sell my mother?

TAYLOR: You don't speak for all Indians.

Red Cloud pulls his staff from the ground.

Others would like to hear about the annuities, about the wealth of supplies . . .

RED CLOUD: Any Indian wishing to sell the home of The People stay here and negotiate.

Red Cloud turns abruptly and exits. With equal abruptness, he is followed by the other Chiefs and all of the Relatives.

TAYLOR: You haven't even heard the offer! *(But they are gone.)* Savages! Does he think we're going to leave valuable land as a camping ground for nomads! *(To*

Carrington.) In any case, I don't expect he'll give you much trouble. How many wagons are you escorting?

CARRINGTON: Two hundred—all the tools and personnel required. We'll have four new forts standing before the first snow.

TAYLOR (*as they exit*): Move them north tomorrow morning. We are authorized to use any measures to protect our citizens.

HOKSILA: They break the treaty!

BLACK ELK: Yes. We are at war. A war we must win to survive. Then we discover the most formidable weapon ever created by the Indian people . . .

HOKSILA: Weapon?

Black Elk points to the highest ledge where the Hooded Figure, enclosed by the wings of the Eagle Dancer, sits in prayer. The music of the flute and the Aleut drum speak to the other world.

BLACK ELK: He purifies himself in preparation for the battle. He seeks strength from the world of his vision.

As the Eagle Dancer releases him, smoke rises around the Hooded Figure. When he looks to the sky, his buffalo robe drops away revealing a young man clad only in a breechclout.

THE YOUNG MAN (*with soft intensity*): The world men live in is only a shadow of the real world, which is the world of the spirit. In the real world, the world beside this one, everything floats and dances because it is made of the spirit and nothing is material. (*He rises.*) In the real world, I am on my horse, and we dance through trees and rocks.

He disappears. The Eagle begins to dance slowly to the flute and drums.

BLACK ELK: He cares nothing for possessions, not even ponies. If game is scarce and The People are hungry, he will not eat. He is usually so preoccupied, he does not see or hear others. Yet within his young body there is something that spreads around him in battle like wind blowing fire through grass. When he leaves his vision quest, he brings us what we need much more than courage—a genius for military tactics.

Music out. The Eagle Dancer freezes in tableau.

His name is Crazy Horse.

The Eagle Dancer sends the scream of an eagle.

Near Fort Kearny, Wyoming Territory, July 16, 1866: The Relatives who play Red Cloud and Crazy Horse enter in animated discussion. Crazy Horse has added leggings to the breechclout; his upper body is painted with blue spots. A blue lightning bolt slashes across one side of his face.

CRAZY HORSE: Decoys! They cannot resist if they see one of us make an insulting gesture; they get hot, make mistakes. I dismounted, showed myself in front of some young cavalry officers. They left the fort, came charging after me. As soon as I had them strung out behind, my men hit them from the side.

RED CLOUD: A useful skirmish.

CRAZY HORSE (*pressing his point*): The same tactic could entice a large number of troops into a useful *battle*!

RED CLOUD: You discovered this is so. (*Considering.*) A useful battle . . . (*He decides to move on it.*) If others will join us, we will try it. This will require special organization. (*Exits.*)

December 12, 1866: The drums begin. From the center of the circle, Crazy Horse sends prayers; on the ridge, the movements of the Eagle Dancer carry his prayers to the sky.

BLACK ELK: The warriors prepare a few miles from Fort Kearny. Red Cloud assembles an unusual war party of Cheyenne, Arapaho and Sioux—at last, three nations united as one people.

Red Cloud appears on the bluff with the Lakota staff.

When Red Cloud has our main party in position, Crazy Horse and his decoys make the first move.

CRAZY HORSE (*whispers*): Hoka Hey.

The drums crescendo. In a choreographed sequence, Crazy Horse crawls to the downstage side of the hoop where he leaps to his feet, waves a red blanket and sends the cry of an eagle. He then faces "the fort." There is the heavy thump of a howitzer firing; Crazy Horse appears terrified. He runs this way and that as though confused. He stops, again faces "the fort" and lifts the front of his breechclout in an insulting gesture. This is answered with the classic bugle call for a U.S. Army cavalry charge, followed by a thundering of hooves and the confident shouts of men who know they have their enemy on the run. Crazy Horse leaps onto the ridge and turns to watch with clinical interest.

RED CLOUD (*also clinical*): They committed a major force, almost a hundred men.

CRAZY HORSE: Because an Indian is impudent! I will keep them coming.

Crazy Horse disappears; the Eagle Dancer exits.

BLACK ELK: The force from the fort is commanded by Captain Fetterman who is under explicit orders from Colonel Carrington not to pursue beyond Lodge Trail Ridge. But Crazy Horse rides along that ridge!

Crazy Horse reappears.

CRAZY HORSE: Cowards. COWARDS!

With a thunder of hooves, the cavalry charges into view with flags flying; Crazy Horse races off the ridge into the valley created by the circle. The soldiers pursue him down from the ridge. Red Cloud raises his lance and is answered by a burst of war cries topped with gunfire. The soldiers fall dead, arrows sticking from their bodies in various angles. Silence. Hoksila breaks into the circle with a shout. He leaps over the bodies as he counts coups and sings, "One little, two little, three little whities; four little, five little . . ." The musicians and the Relative who plays Red Cloud drop character to laugh at the boy.

BLACK ELK: Captain Fetterman, who foolishly got himself and all his men killed, had a fort named in his honor. Colonel Carrington, whose sensible orders were disobeyed, was recalled from command.

HOKSILA: We may win this war, yet.

Black Elk laughs—this time joined by the Relatives who are playing dead soldiers.

Near Fort Laramie, Wyoming Territory, Spring 1868: The Relatives who play Commissioner Taylor and General Sherman enter and are startled by the spectacle that greets them. Black Elk gestures for the "dead" to resume their prone positions. Taylor eyes the dead soldiers and then petulantly stamps his foot.

TAYLOR: We want to make a new treaty.

RED CLOUD: No.

TAYLOR: But why not?

RED CLOUD: I will not talk peace until your soldiers leave my country.

GENERAL SHERMAN (*calls up to the bluff where Red Cloud stands with the Lakota staff*): Chief Red Cloud . . .

BLACK ELK (*identifies the general for Hoksila*): Great Warrior General Sherman.

GENERAL SHERMAN: If, on examination, we find the road hurts you, we will give it up. Or pay for it. We sent a supply of tobacco . . .

RED CLOUD (*from above*): And I will smoke it. As soon as the soldiers leave my country.

GENERAL SHERMAN (*to Taylor*): This is an embarrassment and a humiliation, but I don't see alternatives.

TAYLOR (*under*): The only way to deal with these . . .

GENERAL SHERMAN: The only way is to end it. It's too expensive. The Indian Wars are costing us millions. And what do we have to show for it? A handful of dead Indians. The War Department wants an immediate treaty. Tell Red Cloud . . .

RED CLOUD (*calling down to them*): When we see the soldiers moving south and the forts abandoned, I will come down to talk about a treaty. (*Exits.*)

SHERMAN (*swears under his breath, then makes the decision*): Abandon the forts north of the Platte.

TAYLOR: Sir?

SHERMAN: My special competence is military reality. Red Cloud has given us a beating. Abandon the forts.

With this, Sherman exits leaving Taylor aghast. A bugle sounds "retreat"; the dead soldiers rise, form into ranks behind their flags and march in retreat.

Fort C.F. Smith, Wyoming Territory, July 30, 1868: Red Cloud, Crazy Horse and two other Chiefs appear on the ridge with the staffs of the Sioux, Cheyenne and the Arapaho nations.

RED CLOUD: Burn their forts.

Four warriors with torches rise from behind the ridge and move into the winter-telling circle. They dance the burning of the forts . . . . .

Near Fort Laramie, Wyoming Territory, November 6, 1868: As the Torch-Dancers exit, Black Elk unrolls a buffalo robe center. The four Chiefs move to the buffalo robe and plant the three staffs behind it. Crazy Horse stands beside the Sioux staff, the other Chiefs by the Arapaho and Cheyenne staffs. Red Cloud sits on the buffalo robe, waiting. Taylor enters behind a soldier carrying a white flag. When he sees the Indians, he stops, considers his options and then reluctantly sits on the buffalo robe where he removes the treaty, pen and ink from his lap desk.

What does this treaty say about the home of The People?

TAYLOR (*reads*): No white person shall be permitted to settle upon or occupy any portion of the Black Hills, or, without the consent of the Indians, to pass through the same.

Red Cloud looks to the Cheyenne Chief who nods; he looks to the Arapaho Chief who nods.

RED CLOUD: Present the pen. Our peoples desire peace, and I pledge my honor to maintain it.

Taylor passes two copies of the treaty to Red Cloud and offers the pen. Red Cloud takes the pen and signs both copies.

BLACK ELK: I am angry with our chief, Red Cloud.

HOKSILA: Why?

BLACK ELK: From the moment he touched the pen to the treaty renouncing war, he never fought again.

Red Cloud returns the treaty copies to Taylor, who signs both and returns one. Red Cloud rises with his copy and leads the procession of the four Chiefs up the ridge and off. The musicians break into a Lakota victory song. From over the ridge, dancing and singing Lakotas pour into the winter-telling circle. Hoksila lifts the buffalo robe and begins to spin in exultant celebration.

BLACK ELK (*shouts down the demonstration*): No. No.

He pulls the buffalo robe from Hoksila and throws it to the ground. The music and dancing stop. There is a stunned silence.

Why do you celebrate this treaty? Do you really believe the United States will keep this treaty? Hotheads among the Southern Cheyenne give their government an excuse to break it.

The celebrating Lakotas sit outside the hoop as Relatives.

Railroad tracks are laid toward the Smoky Hill, cutting across our land, dividing what is left of the buffalo herds. Some young fools derail a train, break in, drink whiskey, then tie ends of cloth bolts they find in the baggage to their ponies' tails and ride out across the prairie.

A Relative spins a wind-whistle, and another Relative (who will play Custer) enters on the ridge and stands looking down. His elaborate gold-fringed buckskin shirt is painted blue on top with vertical red and white stripes around the bottom. From under his hat cascades long, auburn horse hair; a blue lightning bolt slashes across a cheek of its wearer telling us that Custer is played by the same Relative who plays Crazy Horse.

The forces sent to deal with this "threat to civilization" include the glory-hunter George Armstrong Custer. At twenty-three, he became their youngest general. He led large forces in their Civil War. When he finished with the graycoats, his trail turned north into a collision with our youngest, Crazy Horse! They are almost exactly the same age; they each have a strangeness; they are both great leaders; but there is a difference—one of them is a savage!

Black Elk Speaks *was produced at the Denver Center Theater Company October 1, 1993 under the direction of Donovan Marley.*

HURRICANE

A Full-Length Play in One Act

BY ANNE GALJOUR

Cast and credits appear on page 574

HURRICANE: Reading Anne Galjour's Gulf Coast plays is like reading the affectionate lyrics of Lorenz Hart or Cole Porter: you automatically perform them in your head, but you know the musical accents are nowhere near those of the original. From Cut Off, Louisiana (population 5,325), Galjour performs the play's six characters herself—the narrator Sherelle Dantin, her sister Inez, and neighbors like Urus Arceneaux who was struck, not once, but twice by lightning, which is why his hair is all white. Galjour wrote *Hurricane* as the latest in a series of Cajun country monologues with names like *Alligator Tales* and *The Krewe of Neptune*. *Hurricane* won the 1993 American Theater Critics Association's first Elizabeth Osborn Award for emerging playwrights and is by turns natively funny, uniquely Southern and describes the faith that some good people have in the face of life-long nemeses that, in the case of Sherelle Dantin and her loved ones, begin with the baleful power of weather in the region of Grand Isle, Louisiana.

SHERELLE: Urus! What you got in that bucket?

URUS: My chickens laid some extra eggs during that thunderstorm last night. I wanted to give you some. You know, Sherelle, you and Inez might want to be careful back there. Clip Ayo was underneath his house fixing a water pipe. They had an alligator down there. Bit off a big chunk a meat from his arm below the elbow. I just got back from the hospital giving some blood. The doctor had to give his wife a shot to calm her down. When I left, she was getting hypnotized just to get her to walk out the building.

SHERELLE: We both looked around the yard. Everything seemed calm. Then the sky got dark. The air pressure fell. It made Urus's hair almost stand up on end . . . He sat at my table still staring at the TV screen. I turned around to serve him his food. I was not two feet away from him when the sky cracked and lit the windows. His hair went up. When I put his bowl in front of him, I felt a sharp prick from his electric hair as it brushed against my skin. It made all the saints' medals I have pinned to my bra rise. I watched his hair slowly fall while I sat down to eat. I asked him, "Urus, was it getting struck by lightning that made your hair turn white like that?"

URUS: My hair turned white the second time I got hit. The first time just made it kind of frizzy . . . the first time I was bending over, pouring some gas on a red ant pile. I had my watch in my back pocket. You know, Sherelle, to this day I really think that's what did it. My palms got burned where I was holding the can. When I came to, I was on top the pile soaked in gas and red ants.

SHERELLE: But the second time, Urus. How'd it happen the second time?

URUS: Direct hit. From the top of my head to the bottom of my feet. My soles were burned where the lightning came through. My whole body fell, but my boots stayed glued to the grass. And the grass was smoking.

SHERELLE: Did you see Jesus?

URUS: And Mary and Joseph and everybody in my family that died.

Later, at Rosetta and Grady Cheramie's house.

ROSETTA: Two men came from Houston to talk to Grady about drilling for oil behind our house. They said they would have to cut a road through the woods all the way to the Forty Arpent Canal to set up a land oil rig. I told Grady I thought it would be best to talk about this over supper. They said they wanted some of our wild Cajun cookin'. So I went to my freezer and pulled out this rattlesnake Grady killed at some festival in Texas because I thought, "Let's give 'em a little taste of home." I did everything Grady told me to do. I rubbed it in olive oil till I felt it get soft. Then I marinated it for three days in red wine and garlic. And when it came time to cook it, I sliced it in strips and put it in the skillet with hot peanut oil. But then the phone rang. When I got back to the kitchen, the air was already smoking. I felt bad. But while I was scouring the skillet with Comet, I thought, "Maybe I could cook something with a duck." While I was rinsing the pot I could hear him behind me sniffing the air.

GRADY: Mon Dieu, Rosetta! You didn't burn my rattlesnake maybe.

ROSETTA: It was an accident, Grady. I didn't know to turn off the fire when the meat started to curl. Don't worry. I'm going to make a French duck fricassee with some wild rice.

GRADY: Un-uhn. Go to the freezer. Get me my turtle.

ROSETTA: I stood in front of the freezer door and I put it to him, "Grady, that turtle's for you and me for our anniversary."

GRADY: I said, go to the freezer and get my turtle. I'm gonna microwave defrost it. I'm gonna make a sauce piquante out of it.

ROSETTA: When he put it in the microwave, the whole room started to smell like

CLIMATE THEATER, SAN FRANCISCO—Anne Galjour in her play *Hurricane*

the Marsh. I said, "Grady, don't give 'em that. It's too wild. It smells like the back." He looked me in the eye and pointed his finger at me.

GRADY: They want wild, Rosetta. We got to give 'em wild!

ROSETTA: Then the bell rang. His turtle was defrosted. I pulled it out the microwave all limp in my hands. "I'm gonna fix her, Grady! I'm gonna rub her down with oil and roll her in a sheet of flour till she's white like a ghost. Then I'm gonna lay her on a bed of soft yellow onions and dot her with garlic for flavor. I'm gonna make a soup out of her for your oil men to eat her. Just as soon as you get out of my kitchen!"

Later, at Sherelle and Inez Dantin's house.

INEZ: I was in the kitchen when I heard the news. Sherelle was in the bathroom scouring. I was on my knees with the bucket and the scrub brush. Then a weather bulletin came on, saying that tropical storm in the Gulf turned into a hurricane. Her winds were up to one hundred twenty miles an hour. And her name was Wanda. She was expected to hit the Gulf Coast somewhere between Gulfport, Mississippi, and Galveston, Texas, within the next five days. That's when I started noticing a lot of hair in the water and in the bristles of the brush. Sherelle was shedding again. "Sherelle, lie down on the counter. I'm gonna give you a protein conditioning shampoo treatment." I got out the Prell and two eggs from Urus's bucket. I scrambled them while Sherelle lay on her back, her neck resting at the edge of the sink. The air turned from Windex to Prell and eggshells. I could tell she was relaxing. "Your hair's gonna shine and be so bouncy with all this yoke. I bet if we did this twice a week it would get to the point where you couldn't fit it all in the rubber band. And if you put two raw eggs in the blender with a milkshake, I bet your blood would get so red you wouldn't need no rouge." Her eyelids peeled open slowly from their lull, and she smiled.

SHERELLE: Inez, I heard the Virgin Mary's been appearing in Galveston. Would you like to go?

INEZ: Sherelle, we got a hurricane coming our way. Her name is Wanda. We gotta go to the store and get some water and bread and cookies and pork 'n beans. We gotta get food we can eat if the power goes out.

Later.

INEZ: My great grandmere died in a hurricane with all of her children except for my gram. They were living on Grand Isle at the edge of the world. My great grandpere was out hunting and she was with the kids. When it hit, the water rose so high they went out on the roof. It rose higher and higher till my great grandmere took all of her five kids and tied each of them to branches of the *cheniere*, the tree by their house. My gram said they saw cows and dogs and people swimming past. They were trying to hold on to trees and chimneys. But she said she could hear them crying in the wind. But the water kept rising so high that it swallowed the littlest ones. And all my great grandmere could do was to untie the ones who were left so they could make it to safety. My gram floated for three days on the hull of a boat broken in two, all dazed and wind-blown from the shock. She woke up near a cow who let her suck with its calf. Then it bit off the blades of grass that were stuck to her face like darts from the wind. If you saw pictures of my gram, her face wore the scars from the blades like real bad acne. And if you ever wanted to hear the story of the Cheniere Caminada, you had to get her a glass of milk, sit on her lap and rub her cheek for her to begin.

Later.

SHERELLE: It was past sunset when the hurricane hit.

INEZ: It's funny how the hot summer sun could make me feel so cold. I was in my kitchen listening to the radio and hearing gunshots out my window. The weather man was talking about how hurricanes are good. They clean out the mouth of the Mississippi and push out the silt that builds up the wetlands. I look out the window at my old dog Michael's grave. I thought, "Maybe it's time for me to leave here." Then I heard a knock at my screen door. It was Urus. He was holding some kind of squeaming animal in a towel. By the way it was growling, I thought it was a puppy. But when he opened it, I saw it was a baby. It was about this long. It was sunburned and hungry. "Give me that child," I said. I undid its diaper. His little wienie and butt were scarlet red from lying in his waste. Urus touched his navel and rubbed his little head.

URUS: I found him in my cow pasture holding on to his little baby blanket. One of the cows was trying to lick him clean. Il est beau, ehn?

INEZ: Wea, il est beau. I turned on the water in the sink. I said, "Urus, go to the store. Get me three baby bottles, a box of diapers and a case of Pet Milk. And Urus, I need some more of your eggs. I was noticing this morning, they been doing wonders on Sherelle's hair."

Hurricane *was produced by Climate Theater, San Francisco, May 20, 1993 under the direction of Henry Steele. It has since been produced by Ohlone College, Fremont, Calif. September 24, 1993; Magic Theater/Solo Mio Festival, San Francisco, October 1, 1993; New City Theater, Seattle, January 20, 1994; and Diablo College, Contra Costa County, Calif. February 23, 1994.*

DIRECTORY OF NEW-PLAY PRODUCTIONS

Compiled by Sheridan Sellers

Professional 1993-94 productions of new plays by leading companies around the United States that supplied information on casts and credits at Sheridan Sellers's request, plus a few reported by other reliable sources, are listed below in alphabetical order of the locations of 75 producing organizations. Date given is opening date, included whenever a record was obtained from the producing management. All League of Resident Theaters (LORT) and other Equity groups were queried for this comprehensive Directory. Those not listed here either did not produce new or newly revised scripts in 1993-94 or had not responded by press time. Most of the productions listed—but not all—are American or world premieres. Some are new revisions, second looks or scripts produced previously but not previously reported in *Best Plays*.

Ashland: Oregon Shakespeare Festival

(Artistic director, Greg Leaming; managing director, William Chance)

THE POOL OF BETHESDA. By Allan Cubitt; music by Todd Barton. February 26, 1994. Director, Fontaine Syer; scenery, Richard L. Hay; costumes, John Paoletti; lighting, James Sale.

Dr. Daniel Pearce .... Mark Murphy
Jane .... Dawn Lisell
Kate .... Linda Alper
Ruth .... Kirsten Giroux
Hogarth; Simon .... Michael J. Hume
Maid; Sally .... Yumi Sumida
Figg; Doctor .... Tyrone Wilson
Fancy .... James Newcomb
Patient; Doctor; The Sick .... Shawn Galloway
Doctor; The Sick .... Russ Appleyard
Doctor; The Sick .... Dan Donohue
Doctor; The Sick .... Evelyn Frank
Doctor; The Sick .... Naomi Monroe
Doctor; The Sick .... Davon Russell
Doctor; The Sick .... Judith Sanford

Time: The present. Place: St. Bartholomew's Hospital, London. One intermission.

Unstaged Readings:

ASPARAGUS. By Jeanne Drennan. November 15, 1993. Directed by Cynthia White.

TROUPERS. By Syl Jones. January 24, 1994. Directed by Cynthia White.

BLOOD AND MILK. By John Lee. March 11, 1994. Directed by Mark Murphey.

EUGENE ONEGIN. By Kira Obolensky and Craig Wright. March 18, 1994. Directed by Cynthia White.

UNDER YELENA. By Buffy Sedlachek. April 14, 1994. Directed by Cynthia White.

Atlanta: Horizon Theater Company

(Co-artistic/managing director, Lisa Adler; co-artistic/technical director, Jeff Adler)

MANY THINGS HAVE HAPPENED SINCE HE DIED . . . AND HERE ARE THE HIGHLIGHTS. Adapted from the novel by Elizabeth Dewberry Vaughn by Elizabeth Dewberry Vaughn and Tom Key. January 14, 1994. Director, Tom Key; scenery, Michael S. Brewer; costumes, Joanna M. Schmink; lighting, Kevin McDermott; sound, Brian Kettler.

She .... Cathy Larson
Malone .... Jeff Portell
Her Mother; Malone's Mother .... Janet Wells
Wendy; Angie; Carolyn; Receptionist; Virginia Woolf; Nurse; Girl on Hall; Sunday School Teacher .... Shelly McCook
Doctor; Mr. Ballard; Father; Mr. Jackson;

HORIZON THEATER, ATLANTA—Janet Wells, Cathy Larson, Richard Fagan and Shelly McCook in *Many Things Have Happened Since He Died . . . and Here Are the Highlights* by Elizabeth Dewberry Vaughn and Tom Key

Preacher; Kenny; Mr. Brooks; Policeman; Organ Recipient; Librarian; High School Friend .... Richard Fagan

Time and Place: Birmingham, Ala., today. One intermission.

Baltimore: Center Stage

(Artistic director, Irene Lewis; managing director, Peter W. Culman)

THE TRIUMPH OF LOVE. By Marivaux; newly translated by James Magruder. October 8, 1993. Director, Irene Lewis; scenery, Neil Patel; costumes, Jess Goldstein; lighting, Mimi Jordan Sherin; sound and composer, John Gromada.

Léonide (a Princess, disguised as Phocion) .... Pamela Gray
Corine .... Kristine Nielsen
Harlequin .... Jefferson Mays
Dimas .... Jarlath Conroy
Agis .... Jay Goede
Léonide (sister to Hermocrate) .... Judith Marx
Hermocrate .... Mario Arrambide

Place: The garden retreat of the philosopher Hermocrate.

Buffalo, N.Y.: Studio Arena Theater

(Artistic director, Gavin Cameron-Webb; producing director, Raymond Bonnard)

THE GAME OF LOVE AND CHANCE. Translated and adapted from Marivaux by Neil Bartlett; music by Nicolas Bloomfield. March 22, 1994. Director, Gavin Cameron-Webb; scenery, Bob Cothran; costumes, Laura Crow; lighting, Frances Aronson; musical direction, Randall Kramer; choreography, Tom Ralabate.

Mr. Prowde .... Christopher Wynkoop
Silvia .... Alexandra O'Karma
Maurice .... Tim Howard
Arlecchino .... Brad Bellamy
Lisette .... Sue Brady
Mr. Dorant .... Martin Kildare

One intermission.

Burbank, Calif.: Victory Theater

(Artistic director, Tom Ormeny)

CUT FLOWERS. By Sage Allen. March 10, 1994. Director, Jules Aaron; scenery, D. Martyn Bookwalter; costumes, Tamara Summers; lighting, Jarrett S. Mager; sound, Karin Masseng.

Devon .... Joanna Miles
Skeet .... Tim Bohn
Katy .... Salome Jens
Jamie .... Chris Jordan
Carla .... Zilah

Time: The present, late September, about 6 p.m. Place: A Studio City, Calif. apartment.

Cambridge, Mass.: American Repertory Theater

(Artistic director, Robert Brustein; managing director, Robert J. Orchard)

HOT 'N' THROBBING. By Paula Vogel. April 16, 1994. Director, Anne Bogart; scenery, Christine Jones; costumes, Jenny Fulton; lighting, John Ambrosone; sound and original music, Christopher Walker.

Woman .... Diane D'Aquila
Man .... Jack Willis
Girl .... Amy Louise Lammert
Boy .... Randall Jaynes
Voice Over .... Alexandra Loria
Voice .... Royal Miller

SHLEMIEL THE FIRST. Conceived and adapted from Isaac Bashevis Singer by Robert Brustein; music by Hankus Netsky; additional music by Zalmen Mlotek; lyrics by Arnold Weinstein. May 18, 1994. Director, choreographer and editorial supervisor, David Gordon; musical direction and arrangements, Zalmen Mlotek; scenery, Robert Israel; costumes, Catherine Zuber; lighting, Peter Kaczorowski; sound, Christopher Walker; orchestrations, Hankus Netsky; co-produced with American Music Theater Festival and in association with Lincoln Center Productions.

Tryna Rytza .... Rosalie Gerut
Shlemiel .... Larry Block
Gittel; Sender Shlamazel;
Yenta Pesha .... Marilyn Sokol
Mottel; Moishe Pippik;
Chaim Rascal .... Remo Airaldi
Zeinvel Shmeckel .... Vontress Mitchell
Mendel Shmendrick;
Man in House .... Scott Cunningham
Dopey Petzel; Zalman Tippish .... Benjamin Evett
Gronam Ox .... Charles Levin

Others: Bret Bailey, Ricardo Engerman, Anne Gardiner, Wendell Goodrum, Nicholas Leary, the Kletzmer Conservatory Band.

One intermission.

Chapel Hill, N.C.: Playmakers Repertory Company

(Producing director, Milly S. Barranger; administrative director, Mary Robin Wells)

BEAUTY AND THE BEAST. By Tom Huey; music by John Gromada. December 1, 1993. Director, Michael Wilson; scenery, Jeff Cowie; costumes, Caryn Neman; lighting, Michael Lincoln; sound, John Gromada.

Belle .... Kristine Watt
Regene .... Dede Corvinus
Chloetilde .... Brett Halna du Fretay
LaPage .... Ray Dooley
Claude .... Mark Eis
Doctor .... Brent Langdon
Judas Tree .... Ed Wagenseller
At The Beast's Haunted Castle:
Droog .... Alexander Yannis Stephano
Rose .... Max Perlmutt, Karl Whittington
The Beast .... Ken Strong
Chambermaids .... Cheryl Jones, Christine Suhr, Ronda Music
Madame Vanity .... Barbara Ellingson
Mannequins .... Kim Ann Clay, Julie Padilla M.

Prince .... Michael H. King

Chorus of Magical Trees: Thomas D. Carr, Pat Cartmel, Kim Ann Clay.

Owls, Statues and Sprites: Michael Hunter, Paige Johnston, Cheryl Jones, Michael H. King, Brent Langdon, Tif Luckenbill, Julie Padilla M., Ronda Music, Jody Strimling, Christine Suhr, Ed Wagenseller.

Time and place: Once upon a time in a land not so far away . . .

Charlotte, N.C.: Charlotte Repertory

(Managing director, Keith T. Martin)

MIRACLE AT GRACELAND. By Dorothy Velasco. January 12, 1994. Director, Claudia Carter Covington; scenery, Johann Stegmeir; costumes, Stan Poole; lighting, Eric Winkenwerder; sound, Fred Story Productions.

Mama .... Deborah Rhodes
Jolene Jenkins .... Mitzi Gunter
Earl Jenkins .... Duke Ernsberger
Ruby Rayburn .... Katherine Harrison
Presley Ann .... Molly Gross

Time: A 16-year period during the 1980s and 1990s. Place: Memphis, Tenn. Act I, Scene 1: Graceland, the home of Elvis Presley; Scene 2: The following March, the Jenkins trailer in Graceland Mobile Estates. Act II: Graceland Mobile Estates.

BOCA. By Christopher Kyle. February 8, 1994. Director, Steve Umberger; lighting, Anna Sartin.

Jay .... Mike Harding
Teddy .... Rob Treveiler
Leo; Bill .... Randall Haynes
Elmer; Bowen; John .... Mark Lazar
Edna .... Claudia Carter Covington
Linda .... Andrea Powell
Ginny .... Mary Lucy Bivens
Amy .... Emily Wilson

Time: Winter 1990

SECRET INGREDIENTS. By Mary Jane Roberts. February 9, 1994. Director and lighting, Anna Sartin.

Sonja Patak .... Mary Lucy Bivens
Nada Patak .... Rebecca Cairns
Milan Patak .... Randall Haynes
Rulij Patak .... Steve Umberger
Marija Patak .... Rebecca Koon

Time: November 1991, the day before Thanksgiving. The cooking class is present time. The night of the fight is one week prior to the cooking class. Place: A cooking class in Orange County, Calif. and the kitchen at Sonja's house.

CATFISH MOON. By Laddy Sartin. February 10, 1994. Director, Mitzi Gunter Corrigan; lighting, Anna Sartin.

Curley .... Michael Mattison
Gordon .... Jim Gloster
Frog .... Buddy Osborne
Betty .... Katherine Harrison

Time: The present; late spring to early summer. Place: An old fishing pier.

MESSAGES. By Kate Hawley. February 11, 1994. Director, Terry Loughlin ; lighting, Anna Sartin.

Liz Hardy .... Pam Galle
Simon Davies .... Carl McIntyre
Jen Hardy; Jessica .... Claire Whitworth
Matthew Hardy .... Jason Loughlin
John Hardy .... Terry Loughlin
Nellie Byron .... Rebecca Koon
Maggie Cooper .... Deborah Rhodes
Mark .... Michael Corrigan
Devon .... Heather Loughlin

Time and place: The Anderson home, midnight. One intermission.

Chelsea, Mich.: Purple Rose Theater Company

(Artistic director, T. Newell Kring; executive director, Jeff Daniels)

THE VAST DIFFERENCE. By Jeff Daniels. October 15, 1993. Director, T. Newell Kring; scenery and lighting, Peter Beudert; costumes, Jeanette DeJong; sound, Steve DeDoes.

George Noonan .... John Seibert
Rita Noonan .... Jean Lyle Lepard
Earl Noonan .... Guy Sanville
Dr. Howard .... Janet Maylie

Others: Peter Bellanca, Daniel C. Jacobs Jr., Wayne David Parker, Brian Schulz.

One intermission.

Chicago: Goodman Theater

(Artistic director, Robert Falls; executive director, Roche Schulfer)

CRY THE BELOVED COUNTRY. Newly adapted from Alan Paton by Frank Galati; music by Kurt Weill; lyrics by Maxwell Anderson. June 28, 1993. Director, Frank Galati; scenery, Loy Arcenas; costumes, Susan Hilferty; lighting, James F. Ingalls; sound, Rob Milburn.

With Ernest Perry Jr., Cheryl Lynn Bruce, Brian A. Grandison, Kingsley Leggs, McKinley Johnson, Dathan B. Williams, Ora Jones, Brandon Bush, Michael Bush, Bereniece Jones, Johnny Lee Davenport, JoNell Kennedy, Aisha de Haas, Ellis Foster, Ajay K. Naidu, La Chanze, William J. Norris, John Reeger, Darius de Haas, J. Patrick McCormack, Frances Limoncelli, Michelle Elise Duffy, Raul E. Esparza, Deon Opperman, John Reeger, Tracy Hultgren, David Bonanno, Matthew Brennan.

Time: 1946. Place: South Africa—Ndotsheni, a small village in Natal, and Johannesburg.

THE NOTEBOOKS OF LEONARDO DA VINCI. Adapted by Mary Zimmerman; music by Miriam Sturm and Michael Bodeen. Director, Mary Zimmerman; scenery, Scott Bradley; costumes, Allison Reeds; lighting, T.J. Gerckens; sound, Michael Bodeen.

With Christopher Donahue, Laura Easton, Mariann Mayberry, Christopher Pieczynski, Paul Oakley Stovall, Marc Vann, Tracy Walsh, Meredith Zinner.

BRUTALITY OF FACT. By Keith Reddin; music by Rob Milburn. February 21, 1994. Director, Michael Maggio; scenery, Linda Buchanan; costumes, Birgit Rattenborg Wise; lighting, Robert Christen; sound, Rob Milburn.

Jackie .... Barbara E. Robertson
Maggie .... Leslie Lyles
Val .... Caitlin Hart
Judy; Janet; Amy .... Carmen Roman
Chris .... Philip E. Johnson
Corrinne; Kate .... Donna Jay Fulks
Harold .... Patrick Clear
Marlene .... Ann Keating

One intermission.

THE TIES THAT BIND (in two parts). By Regina Taylor. Director, Shirley Jo Finney; scenery, John Culbert; costumes, Allison Reeds; lighting, Robert Christen; sound, Michael Bodeen.

I. *Inside the Belly of the Beast*

John de Conquer .... Shanesia Davis
Walter Gaines .... Phillip Edward VanLear
Shoe Shine Man; Langley; Child .... Ernest Perry Jr.
Doctor .... Ora Jones
Ellis .... Lizan Mitchell
Sheldon; 007; Malice .... Darryl Alan Reed
Wife .... Felicia P. Fields
Marilyn .... Yolanda Androzzo

Time and place: Today, in an American city. One intermission.

II. *Watermelon Rinds*

Jes Semple .... Darryl Alan Reed
Lottie Semple .... Shanesia Davis
Willie Semple .... Phillip Edward VanLear
Liza Semple .... Felicia P. Fields
Pinkie Semple .... Ora Jones
Mama Pearl Semple .... Lizan Mitchell
Papa Tommy Semple .... Ernest Perry Jr.
Marva Semple-Weisse .... Yolanda Androzzo

Time and Place: Today, at the Semple home.

Chicago: Steppenwolf Theater Company

(Artistic director, Randall Arney)

LIBRA. Adapted by John Malkovich from Don DeLillo. May 13, 1994. Director, John Malkovich; scenery, David Gropman; costumes, Erin Quigley; lighting, Kevin Rigdon; video/media, John Boesche; sound, Richard Woodbury.

CAST: Lee Harvey Oswald—Alexis Arquette; Marina, Lynette—Ingeborga Dapkunaite; Sproul, Dupard, Raymo, Agent Bateman—K. Todd Freeman; Marguerite, Ferrie—Laurie Metcalf; Karlinsky, Banister, Frank—Ron Perkins; Everett, Tony Astorina—Ned Schmidtke; Ruby, Parmentier—Rick Snyder; Marine Guard, T-Jay Mackey—Craig Spindle; Sproul's Sister, Brenda Jean—Meredith Zinner.

One intermission.

Chicago: Victory Gardens Theater

(Artistic director, Denis Zacek; managing director, John P. Walker)

DEED OF TRUST. By Claudia Allen. December 9, 1993. Director, Sandy Shinner; scenery, Kurt Sharp; costumes, Karin Kopischke; lighting, Ellen E. Jones; sound, Galen G. Ramsey.

C'Dale .... Deanna Dunagan
Oliver .... John Judd
Hugh .... Ned Schmidtke
Millie .... Linda Kimbrough
Junia .... Seana Kofoed
Buckley .... Timothy Hendrickson

Time: The late 1930s. Place: Rural Michigan. One intermission.

MICHAEL, MARGARET, PAT AND KATE. One-man performance by Michael Smith; written by Michael Smith and Peter Glazer; songs by Michael Smith. February 3, 1994. Director, Peter Glazer; scenery, James Dardenne; costumes, Gayland Spaulding; lighting, Michael Rourke; sound, Galen G. Ramsey.

One intermission.

WIPE THAT SMILE. By Kay M. Osborne. March 6, 1994. Director, Jaye Stewart; scenery, Brian Traynor; costumes, Michael Alan Stein; lighting, David Gipson; sound, Jaye Stewart.

Putus .... Velma Austin
Phanso .... Kenn E. Head
Prettywalks .... Christian Payton
Dread .... W. Allen Taylor
Miss Scarlett .... Jacqueline Fleming

Place: Trench Town, a ghetto of Kingston, Jamaica. Two intermissions.

GET READY. By Jaye Stewart and Joe Plummer; music by Joe Plummer; lyrics by Jaye Stewart, Joe Plummer, and Debi Stewart. May 19, 1994. Director, Dennis Zacek; scenery, James Dardenne; costumes, Claudia Boddy; lighting, Todd Hensley; sound, Galen G. Ramsey; choreography, Joe Plummer.

Knobby .... W. Allen Taylor
Johnson .... Kenn E. Head
Bunch .... John Steven Crowley
J.R. .... Trent Harrison Smith
Frankie .... Allan Louis
Roscoe .... Danne E. Reese
Eva Dee .... Laura Walls
Vern .... Rick Worthy

Time: The present. Place: A large Midwestern metropolitan city. One intermission.

Staged Readings:

FAMOUS FOR 15 MINUTES. By Jamie Pachino
PALS (A FUNNY PLAY ABOUT STAYING FRIENDS). By Dan Conway. August 22, 1993.
BLINDSIDED. By Marjie Rynearson. September 12, 1993.
CASSATT. By Mary Ellen McGarry. September 26, 1993.
CAIRO. By Arthur Pearson. October 10, 1993.
SWEET COLINDA. By Stephen Serpas. October 24, 1993.
BRIDGES. By Carol Adjoran. November 28, 1993.
DON'T DISAPPOINT CAPTAIN JANUARY. By Joseph Urbinato. December 18, 1993.
LEON ESCHE! THE TRIALS OF '42. By Mark Wolghenaut. January 9, 1993.
DROWNING SORROWS. By Douglas Post. February 1, 1994.
DOLLS. By Ann McGravie. February 13, 1994.
YOUR WEB-FOOTED FRIENDS. By David Rush. March 20, 1994.
IS, WAS, ISN'T. By Richard Conlon. May 1, 1994.

Cincinnati: Ensemble Theater of Cincinnati

(Artistic director, David A. White III; managing director, John W. Vissman)

FRAGMENTS; A CONCERTO GROSSO. By Edward Albee. October 6, 1993. Director, Edward Albee; scenery, Kevin Murphy, Ruth D. Sawyer; costumes, Rebecca Senske; lighting, James H. Gage.

With Michael Blankenship, Gordon Greene, Dale Hodges, Paul Kennedy, Mack C. Miles, Regina Pugh, Lee Walsh, Julia White.

One intermission.

LITTLE RED RIDING HOOD (A BRITISH PANTOMIME). By Mark Mocahbee and Robert B. Rais. December 1, 1993. Director, David A. White III; musical direction/composer, David B. Kisor; scenery, Kevin Murphy; costumes, Rebecca Senske; lighting, James H. Gage.

Jowls .... David W. Adams
Little Red Riding Hood .... Tricia Allen
Yelper .... Gary Anaple
Links .... D. Richardson Brown
Hood; Gretel .... Erin Cowan
Crooked Old Man .... Brian Griffin
Mom .... Paul Kennedy
Weasel .... Mark Mocahbee
Hamlet .... Kristin Orr

ENSEMBLE THEATER OF CINCINNATI—Buz Davis, Keith A. Brush, Robert Browning and Joanna Olsen in Lee Blessing's *The Rights*

Little Bo Peep; Hood .... Joanna Parson
Humpty; Hood .... Stacy Jordan Pershall
Wolf .... Robert B. Rais
Grandma .... Diana Rogers
Barker .... William Schwarber
Woody .... Claire Slemmer
Hanse .... Kim Tuvin

THE RIGHTS. By Lee Blessing. March 23. 1994. Director, Jeanne Blake; scenery, Kevin Murphy; costumes, Gretchen H. Sears; lighting, James H. Gage.

Riley .... Cecelia Birt
Worth .... Robert Browning
Pryor .... Keith A. Brush
Joy .... Nicole Callender
Lyle .... Buz Davis
Dulcie .... Joanna Olsen

Place: A few hours out of New York City. One intermission.

POOR SUPERMAN. By Brad Fraser. April 27, 1994. Director, Mark Mocahbee; scenery and costumes, Ronald A. Shaw; lighting, James H. Gage.

Matt .... Damian Baldet
David .... Michael J. Blankenship
Kryla .... Annie Fitzpatrick
Violet .... Shannon Rae Lutz
Shannon .... David Schaplowsky

Time: Recently. Place: Calgary, Alberta, Canada. One intermission

The 5th Annual Production of New Works in Children's Theater:

SILAS MARNER. Newly adapted from George Eliot by Joanie Leverone. January 8, 1994. Director, Jason Minadakis; scenery, Nathan Unger; costumes, Lori Hiltenbeitel; lights, Nathan Unger, Lori Hiltenbeitel.

Godfrey .... Gary Anaple
Eppie .... Erin Cowan
Squire Cass; Bryce .... Steve Ewing
Silas .... Brian Griffin
Dunstan .... Jason McCune
Sally; Molly .... Maria A. Miller
Nancy .... Joanna Parson
Mrs. Osgood .... Stacy Jordan Pershall
Mrs. Kimble .... Kin Tuvin
Keating; Dr. Kimble .... Michael Wirick

Local Playwrights Festival:

GOING THE DISTANCE. By Norma Jenckes. May 7, 1994. Director, Julie Beckman.

Tex Larue .... Michael Conn
Roberta Barlow .... Diane Neiman
Bobby O. Barlow .... Bob Maguire
Helen Maguire.. Josephine
Brau-Jack Hanlon .... Artie Kidwell.

BLIND RAFTERY. By Sam Henry. May 7, 1994. Director, Regina Pugh.

Patrick Raftery .... Michael Burnham
Hilaria .... Kim Tuvin
Gillie; Prior .... William Schwarber
Sergeant; O'Connell; Piper .... Robert B. Rais
Dafydd Evans .... Bob Allen
Inkeeper; Chaplain; Farmer .... David Adams
Dominic; Crawford; Preacher;
Peddler; O'Rourke .... Jason McCune
Servant; Lady O'Rourke .... Stacy Jordan Pershall

THE COATS. By Yevsey Kats. May 7, 1994. Director, Lori Hiltenbeitel.

1st Woman .... Kim Tuvin
2d Man .... Susan Schuckmann
Man .... John Bruggen
Russian Woman .... Erin Cowan
Manager .... Maura Cronin
Russian Man .... Nathan Unger

THE BIG DIG. By Michael DeFrancesco. May 7, 1994. Director, Eric Weisheit.

Dee .... Laura Otis
Ickey .... Gary Anaple
Harry Snago .... Brian Griffin
Johnny Ram .... Greg Procaccino
He .... Chris Armbrister
She .... Sonya Leslie

Cincinnati: Playhouse in the Park

(Producing artistic director, Edward Stern; executive director, Buzz Ward)

THE WINGFIELD TRILOGY. By Dan Needles. January 11, 1994. Director, Douglas Beattie; scenery, John Thompson; costumes and lighting, Rod Beattie.

Walt Wingfield; 42 Other Characters .... Rod Beattie

Time and place: Present day rural Ontario. One intermission.

ALCHEMY OF DESIRE/DEAD-MAN'S BLUES. By Caridad Svich. March 31, 1994. Director, Lisa Peterson; scenery, Neil Patel; costumes, Candice Donnelly; lighting, Mimi Jordan Sherin; choreographer, Denise Gabriel.

Simone .... Sheila M. Tousey
Tirasol .... Patricia Mattick
Caroline .... Camille D'Ambrose
Selah .... Susan Barnes
Miranda .... Kate Malin
Jamie .... Scott Ripley

Time and place: A fluid space evocative of a burnt-out bayou in the present-day American South.

Cleveland: The Cleveland Play House

(Artistic director; Josephine R. Abady; managing director, Dean R. Gladden)

GRACE IN AMERICA. By Antoine O'Flatharta. October 26, 1993. Director, Josephine R. Abady; scenery, David Potts; costumes, Alyson L. Hui; lighting, Marc B. Weiss; sound, Jordan Davis.

Finbar .... Dylan Chalfy
Maggie .... Aideen O'Kelly
Sean .... Edward Tully
Con .... Jack Wallace
Understudy .... David Wilkerson

Time: The present. Place: Manhattan, Buffalo, Nashville, Graceland and places in between. One intermission.

Coconut Grove, Fla.: Coconut Grove Playhouse

(Producing artistic director, Arnold Mittelman)

THE ROOSTER AND THE EGG. By Luis Santeiro. May 1994. Director, Arthur Storch; scenery, James Tilton; costumes, Ellis Tillman; lighting, Todd Wren; sound, Steve Shapiro.

Johnny Morales .... Frank Galgano
Elsa Morales .... Loli Rainey
Juancho Morales .... Abraham Alvarez
Nati Rafferty .... Evelyn Perez
Phil Rafferty .... Bjorn Johnson
Belen Morales .... Lillian Hurst

Time and place: Present day Miami. One intermission.

Costa Mesa, Calif.: South Coast Repertory

(Producing artistic director, David Emmes)

NIGHT AND HER STARS. By Richard Greenberg. March 4, 1994. Director, David Warren; scenery and projections, Cliff Faulkner, Wendall K. Harrington; costumes, Walter Hicklin; lighting, Peter Kaczorowski; original music and sound, Michael Roth.

Daniel Enright .... Peter Frechette
Charles Van Doren .... Dylan Baker
Herb Stempel .... Patrick Breen
Jack Barry .... Ron Boussom
Albert Freedman .... John Ellington
Toby Stempel .... Mariangela Pino
Geraldine Bernstein .... Colette Kilroy

Others: Don Took, John-David Keller, David Kaufman, Tracy Yates, Robert Curtis-Brown, Becky Ann Baker, Bonnie Mikoleit, Matthew Oliva, David Reed.

One intermission.

Dallas: Dallas Theater Center

(Artistic director, Richard Hamburger; managing director, Jeff West)

The Big D Festival of the Unexpected. June 3 - 12, 1993

PORCELAIN. By Chay Yew. June 3, 1993. Director, Richard Hamburger; scenery, Beje Fort; costumes, Donna M. Kress; lighting, Ed Schmitt.

With Bruce DuBose, Steven Eng, Stephen Kalstrup, Allen McCalla, Martin Rayner.

THE AMERICA PLAY. By Suzan-Lori Parks. June 5, 1993. Director, Liz Diamond; scenery, Riccardo Hernandez; lighting, Deborah Reitman; sound, Guy Whitemore.

Woman .... Rhonda Boutte
Foundling Father .... Ben Halley Jr.
Man .... Billy Jones
Lucy .... Adina Porter
Brazil .... Michael Potts

One intermission.

SIMPATICO. By Roger Babb. June 7, 1993. Director, Roger Babb; scenery, Michael Fajans; costumes, Gabriel Berry, Angela Wendt; lighting, Pat Dignan; sound, Keith Duncan.

With Roger Babb, Rocky Bornstein, Mary Shultz, Gene Tyranny.

A CHRISTMAS CAROL. Adapted from Charles Dickens by Evan Yionoulis and Thomas Cabaniss; original music by Thomas Cabaniss. November 30, 1993. Director, Evan Yionoulis; music director, Thomas Cabaniss; scenery, E. David Cosier; costumes, Donna M. Kress; lighting, Donald Holder; sound, Lamar Livingston.

Stave One: Marley's Ghost

Ebenezer Scrooge .... Robert Dorfman
Narrator/Vendor .... Rene Moreno
Fred, Scrooge's nephew .... Billy Eugene Jones
Bob Cratchit .... Michael Waldron
Mrs. Cratchit .... Candy Buckley
Charitable Gentleman .... Ron Quade
Charitable Woman .... Liz Mikel
Marley's Ghost .... Randy Moore

Stave Two: The First of Three Spirits

Spirit of Christmas Past .... Beverly May
Youngest Scrooge .... Adrien Elizondo
Young Scrooge .... Jesse Elizondo
Fan; Scrooge's sister .... Erin Buckley
Fezziwig .... Ron Quade
Scrooge as a young man .... Mark Wilson
Dick Wilkins .... Patrick Amos
Mrs. Fezziwig .... Phyllis Cicero
Belle, Scrooge's fiancee .... Sally Nystuen

Stave Three: The Second of the Three Spirits

Spirit of Christmas Present .... Akin Babatunde
Peter Cratchit .... Cameron McElyea, Garland Hampton
Belinda Cratchit .... Marti Etheridge
Martha Cratchit .... Leslie McDonel
Tiny Tim .... Evan Figg
Fred's Wife .... Sally Nystuen

Stave Four: The Last of the Spirits

Spirit of Christmas Yet to Come .... Patrick Amos
Charwoman .... Connie Nelson
Laundress .... Phyllis Cicero
Undertaker's Man .... Randy Moore
Poor Mother .... Beverly May
Poor Son .... Mark Wilson

Stave Five: The End of It

Turkey Boy .... Huntley Russell
Londoners; Carolers; Party Guests .... Company

Time and place: 19th century London.

REAL WOMEN HAVE CURVES. By Josefina Lopez. March 22, 1994. Director, Evan Yionoulis; scenery, James Youmans; costumes, Teresa Snider-Stein; lighting, Don Holder; sound, Guy Whitmore.

Carmen .... Divina Cook
Ana .... Mariana Vasquez

Pancha .... Wilma Bonet
Rosali .... Leticia Magaña
Estela .... Francine Torres

Time: The first week of September 1987. Place: A sewing factory in East Los Angeles. One intermission.

Staged Readings:

ALKI. by Eric Overmyer. June 8, 1993. Director, Melissa Cooper.

DOSTOEVSKY GOES TO THE BEACH. By Marco Antonio de la Parra. June 4, 1993. Director and translator, Melia Bensussen.

Denver: The Changing Scene

(Executive producers, Al Brooks, Maxine Munt)

FLOWERS OUT OF SEASON. By Edward Crosby Wells. June 3, 1993. Director, Jeremy Cole; scenery, Jeremy Cole; costumes, Marianne Appel; lighting, Carol Lyn McDowell; sound, LA Bourgeois; choreography, Wilhelmina Evans.

Dawn Rose .... C. Beaner Higgins
Buck Rose .... Travis Shakespeare
Mrs. Philip Winter .... Vicki K. Febbraro

Time: Act I: 4:30 a.m. Thursday, October 1, 1992; Act II: Later that same day. Place: Hobbs, New Mexico—a small city one mile from the west Texas border. One intermission.

Summerplay: Series I—July 8 - 25, 1993

SLAVIA & HUGO. By Robert Shaver. Director, Tery Edelen.

Slavia .... Clint Heyn
Hugo .... Stephen Remund

DIMSUMZOO. By Rikki Ducornet and Rosanna Yamagiwa Alfaro. Director, Sallie Diamond.

Murasaki .... Katharyn Grant
Mimi .... Susan Ross

Place: A Chinese Restaurant

THE PARTY. By Ken Crost. Director, Tracy Oakley.

Richard .... Eric Walter
Richard .... Charles Kolar
Mildred .... Tawnya Kristen Bingham

Summerplay: Series II—August 5 - 22, 1993

THE RAINBIRD. By Katherine Dubois. Director, Mark Higdon.

With: Thom Blahnik, Robin Manuel.

THE PRISONER OF ST. PIERRE. By Pat Gabridge; music by Brenda Matson. Director, Greg Sorich-Ward.

The Prisoner .... Vincent C. Robinson
Varant; Keenan; Barker .... Joseph McDonald
Angel of Death .... Jean Sorich-Ward
Monique .... Gwen Harris

WHEN THE WOOD IS GREEN. By Sarah Fisher Lowe. Director, Stephen R. Kramer.

Ruth Vough .... Betsy Grisard
Constance Vough .... A. Lee Massaro
Ducie .... Robin Erwin
Dr. Warden .... Howard R. Ancell

THE PLAGUESONG. By David Nuss; music by Andrew Monley. Director, Jennifer Thero; scenery, Angie Lee; costumes, Jeremy Cole; lighting, Michael A. Bybee; choreography, Marta Barnard.

Meryl .... David Knudten
Farold .... Travis Shakespeare
Helmsley .... Bill Selig
Mayor .... Paul Curran
Lasha .... Robynne Lopez
Philip; Man One .... Steve Kosmicki
Man Two .... Lee Irvine
Jan; Man Three .... Bob Peterson
Woman One .... Laura Thomas
Woman Two .... Robin Ganse

Time and place: A small town in the Old West; it is late summer, the season of pending fruition. One intermission.

DESERT TIME. By Eric Walter and Doug Goodwin. Music by Eric Walter, Craig Barber, and Courtney von Drehle. November 5, 1993. Director, Doug Goodwin; lighting and sound, Dante Dunlap.

With Eric Walter, Ed Lee.

STRAWBERRY ENVY. By Kitty Johnson. ELVIS AND ELEANOR. By Mark Dunn. February 4, 1994. Director, Greg Ward.

With: Jean Sorich, Craig Cline, Kurt Soderstrom, Kathryn Gray, S.B. Neilson.

Program of Ten-Minute Plays, March 11, 1994:

(All Plays: Directed by the authors; music, Jay Shaffer; scenery, Scott Neilson; lighting, Michael A. Bybee)

CRASH. By Kathleen Hopkins.

Rick .... Jeffrey Miller
Julia .... Sherrie Scott

YELLOW-HEADED BLACKBIRDS. By Steve Hunter.

Tom .... Mark Ogle
Alice .... Rosie Goodman
Carla .... Tamara Willner
Kraft .... Joel Hudgins

ON THE FRONT LINES. By Ken Crost.

Ted .... Jeffrey Miller
Kristen .... Julie Hoffman
Molly;Girl .... Rosie Goodman

Joseph .... Brian Freeland
Father .... Larry Bailey
ESPRESSO, ANYONE? By Wesley Webb.
Gene .... Jesse Greenblatt
Nate .... Larry Bailey
FOUND OASIS. By Leroy Leonard.
Ellen .... Sherrie Scott
Bobby .... Wesley Webb
TRUDY & NATALIE. By Tami Canaday.
Trudy .... Julie Hoffman
Curtis .... Larry Bailey
Child .... Daniel Osborne
DAVID IN GOLIATH. By Pat Gabridge.
Mother .... Rosie Goodman
Father .... Doug White
David .... Brian Freeland
One intermission.

RETURN OF CRANE. By Stuart Boyce. April 22, 1994. Director, Jeffrey Pavek; scenery, Brenda Vang; costumes, Tricia Stevens; lighting and sound, Michael A. Bybee.
Tom Wiley; Sheriff .... Terry Wood
Kate Van Brunt .... Jean Black
Brom Van Brunt .... Larry Bailey
Curly .... Theodore Dawson
Big Horse Sue .... Julia Irish
Nos .... Vint Lavender
Red .... James Sharp
Sackett .... Rob O'Haire
Bea Crandall .... Peggy Miller
Ichabod Crane .... Creston McKim
Agnes Lake (Madame Virina) .... Patricia Madsen
One intermission.

THE GOLDEN GATE BRIDGE. By Ludmilla Bollow. May 13, 1994. Director, Sara Wright.

Denver: Denver Center Theater Company

(Artistic director, Donovan Marley)

BLACK ELK SPEAKS. Adapted by Christopher Sergel from the book by John G. Neihardt. October 1, 1993. Director, Donovan Marley; choreography, Jane Lind; musical direction and composition, Dennis Yerry; scenery, Bill Curley; costumes, Andrew W. Yelusich; lighting, Don Darnutzer; sound, David R. White.
Black Elk .... Ned Romero
Hoksila .... Kennetch Charlette

Relatives (names in parentheses are characters who appear in the script excerpt in the introduction to this section): John Belindo (Gen. Sherman), Jack Burning (Arapaho Chief), Lorne Cardinal (Red Cloud), Gregory Norman Cruz (Torch Dancer), Luke Dubray (Torch Dancer), Peter Kelly Gaudreault (Crazy Horse), Jane Lind (Eagle Dancer), Kenneth Little Hawk (Cheyenne Chief), Loon Hawk (Col. Carrington), Dara Marin, Kenneth Martines (Commissioner Taylor), David Medina, Jill Scott Momaday, Gracie Red Shirt-Tyon, Maria Antoinette Rogers, Tachara Maraya Salazar, Larry Swalley (Torch Dancer), Stephan Ray Swimmer (Torch Dancer), Kateri Walker.

Act I: South Dakota, 1931; The Americas, 1492-1830; New Mexico, 1861-1868; Minnesota, 1862-1863; Colorado Territory, 1864. Act II: South Dakota, 1931; Wyoming Territory, 1866-1868, The Washita River, Oklahoma Territory, 1868; Somewhere in the East, 1873; The Rosebud River and the Little Big Horn, Montana Territory, 1876; Fort Robinson, Nebraska, 1877; London, England, 1887; Wounded Knee Creek, South Dakota, 1890.

An ATCA selection; see introduction to this section.

THE SCARLET LETTER. Adapted from Nathaniel Hawthorne by Phyllis Nagy. March 21, 1994. Director, Jamie Horton; scenery and costumes, Andrew V. Yelusich; lighting, Don Darnutzer; music, Lee Stametz; sound, David R. White.
Hester Prynne .... Jacqueline Antaramian
Master Brackett .... Michael Hartman
Pearl .... Sara Fernandez-K
Mistress Hibbins .... Suzanne Bouchard
Gov. Bellingham .... Michael Santo
Arthur Dimmesdale .... Sean Hennigan
Roger Chillingsworth .... Richard Risso
One intermission.

STORIES. Adapted from Isabel Allende by Pavel Dobrusky and Per-Olav Sorensen. March 25, 1994. Direction and design, Pavel Dobrusky, Per-Olav Sorensen; music, Larry Delinger; fights, Gregory Norman Cruz; choreography, Suzanne Phillips, Sven Toorwald.
Eva Luna .... Patricia Maucieri
Rolf Carle .... John Hutton
Padre Miguel .... Michael Cullen
Gilberto .... Jim Baker
El Mulato .... Bernard K. Addison
Filomena .... Kathleen M. Brady
Belisa Crepusculario .... Feiga M. Martinez
Amadeo .... Leandro Cano
Azucena; Hortensia .... Lizette Carrion
Eloisa .... Suzanne Phillips
El Capitan .... Sven Toorwald

Others: Gabriel Cavallero, Gregory Norman Cruz, Kenneth Marines.
One intermission.

LOVE, JANIS. Adapted from Laura Joplin by Randal Myler. May 2, 1994. Director, Randal Myler; musical direction, Jerry Ragavoy; scenery and costumes, Andrew V. Yelusich; lighting, Charles R. MacLeod; sound, David R. White.

Janis, Onstage .... Laura Theodore
Janis .... Catherine Curtin
Interviewer's Voice .... Michael Santo

One intermission.

East Farmingdale, N.Y.: Arena Players Repertory Company of L.I.

(Producer/director, Frederic De Feis)

WITHIN MY ZAYDAH'S HOUSE. By Ronald Schultz. April 14, 1994. Director, Frederic De Feis; scenery, Fred Sprauer; costumes, Karen Ackley; lighting, Al Davis.

Josh .... Brian McMullan
Abe .... Leon Benedict
Maury .... Alan J. Czak
Lorraine .... Linda Bub
Shimmy .... Bill Hine

Time and place: 1969, in an old two-story home on Long Island, N.Y. One intermission.

Fort Worth: Hip Pocket Theater

(Artistic director, Johnny Simons)

HUZZYTOWN! By Johnny Simons. June 4, 1993. Director, Johnny Simons; scenery, Lake Simons, Mark Evan Walker; costumes, Diane Simons; lighting, John Leach; sound, Molemo.

Memaw .... Peggy Bott Kirby
June .... Dena Brinkley Phillips
Jane .... Dee Dee Hamilton
Odessa Faye .... Mary Hill
Dodson .... Bob Allen
David .... Chris Pelham
Dan .... Harold Lehmann
Townes .... David Yeakle
Jimmy .... Chris Lewin
Odie .... Tricia Franks
Grady .... Ric Swain
Arthur Clinton Bostick .... Perry Brown
Margaret Jane .... Kristi Ramos
Scotty .... Peggy Bott Kirby
Big Betty .... Melinda Wood
Lil' Betty .... Mary Austin-Harper
The Old Lamplighter .... Jim Hopkins
June Marshal .... Linda Boydston
Brother Swank .... Zelmer Phillips
Queen of the Vortex Huzzies .... Zoë Stein Pierce

Huzzytown Denizens: Cynthia Cranz, Barbara George, Valari Haney, Courtney Jennings, Holly Nelson Leach, Charlee Neimeyer, Melinda Wood, Kristi Ramos, Mary Austin-Harper, Elizabeth Bowie.

THE SCARFISH VIBRATO. Musical with book and lyrics by Johnny Simons; music by James Hinkle. September 3, 1993. Director, Johnny Simons; scenery, Johnny Simons, John Leach; costumes, Diane Simons; lighting, John Leach.

Scarfish .... David A. Armendariz
Catfish Charley .... Perry Brown
Minnow Mollie .... Kristi Ramos

Lake Spirits: Linda Boydston, Mary Hill, Peggy Kirby, Lisa Peterson, Dena Brinkely Phillips.

One Intermission.

THE NOSE SHOW. One-man pantomime with Johnny Simons. April 15, 1994. Scenery, John Leach, Molemo; lighting, John Leach; sound, Molemo.

FLYING SAUCERS—A MODERN MYTH OF THINGS SEEN IN THE SKIES. Adapted by Johnny Simons from C.G. Jung. May 6, 1994. Director, Johnny Simons; scenery, John Leach, Molemo; costumes, Diane Simons; lighting, John Leach; sound, Molemo.

C.G. Jung .... Richard Harris

Ensemble: Cynthia Cranz, Barbara George, Pete Gooch, Kristi Price-Jenkins, Carter Selby, Greg Turley.

Gloucester, Mass.: Gloucester Stage Company

(Artistic director, Israel Horovitz)

FIGHTING OVER BEVERLEY. By Israel Horovitz. August 27, 1993. Director, Patrick Swanson; scenery, Charles F. Morgan; costumes, Jane Alois Stein; lighting, John Ambrosone.

Beverley Shimma .... Judy Holmes
Archie Bennett .... David Jones
Zelly Shimma .... Ted Kazanoff
Cecily Shimma .... Marina Re

One intermission.

HARTFORD, CONN. STAGE—Curtis McClarin and Michael Genet in a scene from *Bailey's Cafe* by Gloria Naylor

Hartford, Conn: Hartford Stage Company

(Artistic director, Mark Lamos; managing director, Stephen J. Albert)

FALSE ADMISSIONS. Newly translated from Marivaux's *Les Fausses Confidences* by Timberlake Wertenbaker. February 18, 1994. Director, Mark Lamos; scenery, Michael Yeargan; costumes, Suzanne Palmer Dougan; lighting, Christopher Akerlind; sound, Bruce Elliot.

Arlequi .... Ben Bode
Dorante .... Jack Hannibal
Dubois .... Evan Pappas
M. Remy .... Benjamin Stewart
Marton .... Oni Faida Lampley
Araminte .... Olivia Birkelund
Mme. Argante .... Mary Louise Wilson
Le Comte .... A. Bernard Cummings

Two intermissions.

BAILEY'S CAFE. By Gloria Naylor. March 26, 1994. Director, Novella Nelson; original music, Dwight Andrews; scenery, Marina Draghici; costumes, Gabriel Berry; lighting, Jennifer Tipton; sound, David Budries.

Bailey .... Tommy Hollis
Eve .... Cheryl Lynn Bruce
Sister Carrie; Sadie .... Yolande Bavan
Sugarman; Vice President .... Curtis McClarin
Miss Maple .... Michael Genet
Esther; Miriam .... Inger Tudor
Peaches .... Renee Joshua-Porter
Daddy Jim; Jones .... Helmar Augustus Cooper
Jesse .... Phyllis Yvonne Stickney

Place: A narrow street that clings to the end of the world on a barren strip of earth. No sun. No rain. No seasons. But Bailey's Cafe is more of an experience than a place. It exists in the space where the human heart makes the ultimate decision to either die—or dream. One intermission.

Hollywood, Calif.: Theater West

(Artistic moderator, Norman Cohen; managing director, Douglas Marney)

LITTLE PRISONS, BIG ESCAPES. By Drew Katzman. June 18, 1993. Director, E.W. Swackhamer; scenery, Joel Sherry; costumes, Bernie White, Phyllis Sylvester; lighting, Eileen Cooley.

With Anne Haney, Drew Katzman.

Act I: Little Prisons—The home of Roscoe and Lillian. Act II: Big Escapes—An office in the upper stratosphere of corporate America.

ONCE A MAN, TWICE A BOY. One-man performance by Joe Lucas; written by Joe Lucas. May 6, 1994. Director, Mark W. Travis; scenery, Robert Smith; lighting, Larry Oberman; sound, Andy Parks.

Place: The porch of the O'Neil home; Muddy Creek on Shanty Ridge, Schuylkill County, Pa.

Kansas City, Mo.: Missouri Repertory Theater

(Artistic director, George Keathley; executive director, James D. Costin)

WHISPER IN THE MIND. By Jerome Lawrence and Robert E. Lee. May 4, 1994. Directed by George Keathley; scenery and costumes, Robert Fletcher; lighting, Jeff Davis; sound, Tom Mardikes; composer, Greg Mackender; choreographer, Jennifer Martin.

Franz Anton Mesmer .... Daniel Oreskes
Benjamin Franklin .... Theodore Swetz
Mme. Annette Duchland .... Cynthia Hyer
Joseph Guillotin .... James Shelby
Jean Sylvan Bailly .... Tom Troupe
Anton Laurent Lavoisier .... Gary Neal Johnson
Edouard .... Will Wiloughy
Michelle Duchland .... Milly Hands
Marie .... Brenda Mason
Marquis .... Gary Holcombe

Others: Michael Linsley Rapport, Woody Bengoa, Nicholas Gray, Chris Johnson, Michael Mastrocesare.

One intermission.

Kansas City, Mo.: Unicorn Theater

(Producing artistic director, Cynthia Levin)

THANTOS. By Ron Simonian. January 28, 1994. Director, Sidonie Garrett; scenery, Atif Rome; costumes, Gregg Benkovich; lighting, Ruth E. Cain; sound, Roger Stoddard.

Ted .... William Harper
Sam .... Phil Fiorini
Mary .... Tess Brubeck
Larry .... Daniel Barnett
Security Guard .... Walter Coppage

Time and place: 10 p.m. in a hotel room in a typical mid-Western city. One intermission.

Laguna Beach, Calif.: The Laguna Playhouse

(Artistic director, Andrew Barnicle; executive director, Richard Stein)

TEACHERS' LOUNGE. By John Twomey. January 11, 1994. Director, Andrew Barnicle; scenery, Jim Ryan; costumes, Jacqueline Dalley; lighting, R. Timothy Osborn; sound, David Edwards.

Nora O'Reilly .... Sarah Lilly
Marty Goldberg .... Eric F. James
Wallace Johnson .... Barry Wallace
Stan Cohen .... Skip Hamilton
Felix White .... Glen Vecchione
Sal Vincent .... John Ross Clark
Susan Wagner .... Alice Ensor

Time: The present. Place: The English Department's teachers' lounge of Amsterdam High School, a fictitious New York City public high school. One intermission.

Lancaster, Pa.: Fulton Opera House

(Artistic director, Kathleen Collins; managing director, Lettie Herbert)

THE NUTCRACKER. By Barry Kornhauser, based on E.T.A. Hoffman's novella. December 9, 1993. Director, Kathleen Collins; scenery, Robert Klingelhoefer; costumes, Beth Dunkelberger; lighting, Bill Simmons; sound, Michele Mercure.

Mouse King; Dame Mouserinks .... Randall Forte

Marie; Pirlipat .... Annie Meisels
Frau Stahlbaum; Queen .... Nancy Nichols
Drosselmeier .... Guy Paul
Fritz; Nutcracker .... Ward Saxton
Doctor Stahlbaum; King ... Stephen Anthony Spiese

Others: Alexa Andersen, Christina M. Anderson, Andrew P. Brubaker, Nathan Neal Fox, Rachel Howell, Brendan O'Donnell, Sara Elizabeth Pencheff.

One intermission.

Little Rock: The Arkansas Arts Center

(Artistic directory, Bradley D. Anderson)

SNOW WHITE AND THE SEVEN DWARFS. Adapted from the Grimms' fairy tale by P.J. Powers; music by Lori Loree. December 3, 1993. Director, Bradley D. Anderson; scenery, Alan Keith Smith; costumes, Mark Hughes; lighting, Chris Davis; choreography, Shirlene Gills.

Minstrels .... Jonathan P. Tatus, Matthew R. Tatus
Queen; Mother .... Michelle McFall
King .... John Christopher
Huntsman .... Shannon E. Farmer
Snow White .... Pamela Adam
Queen; Stepmother .... Misty Heather Dupree
Miss Crabbottom .... Kathleen Ferman
Hannah .... LeAnn Smoot
Johns .... Tyrell Jacob Funkhouser
Prince .... Matthew R. Tatus

Dwarfs: Emily Faulkner, Laura Morache, Jaclyn Elizabeth Napier, Rebekah Scallet, Collette Simmons, Erin West, Jennifer Wiggs. Ice Fairies: Collette Simmons, Erin West. Carolers: Laura Morache, LeAnn Smoot, Jonathan P. Tatus, Matthew R. Tatus.

AESOP'S FABLES. By Thomas W. Olson. January 28, 1994. Director, Thomas W. Olson; scenery, Alan Keith Smith; costumes, Mark Hughes; lighting, Chris Davis; choreography, Pamela Adam.

The Sibyl .... Pamela Adam
Aesop .... Curtis B. Tate
Athena .... Misty Heather Dupree
Iris .... Kathleen Ferman
Hades .... Jimi Brewi
Zeus .... Paul Gregory Nelson

Time: Mid-6th century B.C. Place: Temple of the Oracle of Apollo at Delphi, Greece.

GIANTS. By Alan Keith Smith. March 11, 1994. Director, Bradley D. Anderson; scenery, Mary Alyce Hare; costumes, Mark Hughes; lighting, Chris Davis.

Grymhild .... Misty Heather Dupree
Erik .... John Wildung
Thoskald .... Paul Gregory Nelson
Kara .... Lakeetra D. Knowles

Place: The Mountains of Jotunnheim - mythological home of the Frost Giants.

THE EMPEROR'S NEW CLOTHES. Adapted from Hans Christian Andersen by Alan Keith Smith. April 22, 1994. Director, Alan Keith Smith; scenery, Pamela Adam; costumes, Mark Hughes; lighting, Chris Davis; choreography, Brian Holman.

Boy .... Case Dillard
Aristotle .... Brian Holman
Darling .... Misty Heather Dupree
Clothiers .... Lyn Campbell, Bliss Daniel
Cobblers .... Ashley Goodspeed, Jamie Saltmarsh
Hatters .... Aaron Sanford, Jonathan P. Tatus
Wiggists .... Jimi Brewi, Paul Sheperd
Palace Guards .... Lakeetra D. Knowles, LeAnn Smoot
Minister Glove .... Kelly O'Sullivan
Imperial Page .... Bernie Baskin
Emperor .... Robb Sullivan
Minister Feather .... Kathleen Ferman

Los Angeles: Colony Studio Theater

(Producing director, Barbara Beckley)

17 DAYS. By Rick Garman; original music by Rick Garman. August 21, 1993. Director, Robert O'Reilly; scenery, Richard D. Bluhm; costumes, Ted C. Giammona; lighting, Gary Christensen; sound, Paul-Anthony Navarro.

Lucy Baker .... Erin J. Dean
Breeann Baker .... Debra Jean Rogers
MaryAnn Baker .... Laura Wernette
Edith Anderson .... Sandra Kinder
Jenny MacArthur .... Bonita Friedericy
Elizabeth MacArthur-Jennings .... Lisa Gates
Jeff MacArthur .... Nick DeGruccio

Time: Late August through early September. Place: The MacArthur family home in Cedar Rapids, Iowa. One intermission.

Los Angeles: Mark Taper Forum

(Artistic director, Gordon Davidson)

TWILIGHT: LOS ANGELES, 1992. One-woman performance by Anna Deavere Smith; written by Anna Deavere Smith. June 13, 1993. Director, Emily Mann; scenery, Robert Brill; costumes, Candice Donnelly; lighting, Allen Lee Hughes; sound, Jon Gottlieb; original music, Lucia Hwong; multimedia design, Jon Stolzberg.

No intermission.

Louisville: Actors Theater of Louisville

(Producing director, Jon Jory; literary manager, Michael Bigelow Dixon)

AIN'T WE GOT FUN? By Val Smith. September 29, 1993. Director, Julian Webber; scenery, Paul Owen; costumes, Laura Patterson; lighting, Matthew J. Reinert; sound, Peter Still, Casey L. Warren.

Hollis Bell .... Bob Burrus
Old Man; Priest; Wilmer Morty Crimp .... Ray Fry
The Operative .... William McNulty
Mrs. Cantor; Flapper; Angie; Ada; Woman; Billy Tears .... Sybil Walker
Claude Winslow; Jackson; Ledford .... Time Winters
Lindbergh; Pole-sitter .... Adam Whisner
The Staff .... Sheila Daniels, Lee Soroko

Time: The 1920s. Place: The City.

1969. Written and directed by Tina Landau. February 23, 1994. Scenery, Paul Owen; costumes, Laura Patterson; lighting, Mary Louise Geiger; sound, Darron L. West, Casey L. Warren.

Royce Martinson .... J. Ed Araiza
Stefanie Teller .... Sheila Daniels
Lester Moscowitz .... Jesse Sinclair Lenat
Howie Raskin .... Barney O'Hanlon
Roz Berringer .... Dee Pelletier
Robert Pererra .... Neil David Seibel
Curtis Callender .... Timothy D. Stickney

Time: The final weeks of Howie's senior year in high school, 1969.

MY LEFT BREAST. One-woman performance by Susan Miller; written by Susan Miller. February 27, 1994. Director, Nela Wagman; scenery, Paul Owen; costumes, Hollis Jenkins-Evans; lighting, Matthew Reinert; sound, Darron L. West.

Time: The present.

BETTY THE YETI. By Jon Klein. March 3, 1994. Director, Jeff Steitzer; scenery, Paul Owen; costumes, Laura Patterson; lighting, Kenneth Posner; sound, Casey Upton.

Claire Kutz .... Adale O'Brien
Iko .... Mary Lee
Terra Sawyer .... Mia Dillon
Trey Hugger .... V Craig Heidenreich
Russ T. Sawyer .... Stephen Yoakam
The Creature .... Carolyn Swift

Time: Maybe never, maybe tomorrow. Place: A grove of old-growth trees in the Willamette National Forrest in central Oregon, not far from the Santiam River. One intermission.

Program of Two Plays:

TRIP'S CINCH. By Phyllis Nagy. March 9, 1994. Director, Lisa Peterson; scenery, Paul Owen; costumes, Esther Marquis; lighting Mary Louise Geiger; sound, Casey L. Warren.

Benjamin Trip .... Steven Culp
Val Greco .... Barbara eda-Young
Lucy Parks .... Mary Shultz

SLAVS! (THINKING ABOUT THE LONG-STANDING PROBLEMS OF VIRTUE AND HAPPINESS). By Tony Kushner. March 9, 1994. Director, Lisa Peterson; scenery, Paul Owen; costumes, Esther Marquis; lighting, Mary Louise Geiger; sound, Casey L. Warren.

Vassily Vorovilich Smukov .... Michael Kevin
Serge Esmereldovich Upgobkin .... Gerald Hiken
Aleksii Antedilluvianovich Prelapsarianov .... Ray Fry
Ippolite Ippopolitovitch Popolitipov .... Fred Major
Yegor Tremens Rodent .... Steven Culp
Katherina Sesafima Gleb .... Kate Goehring
Bonfila Bezhukhovna Bonch-Bruevich .... Mary Shultz
Mrs. Shastlivyi Domik .... Barbara eda-Young

Time and place: Moscow, March 1985; Talmenka, Siberia, 1992; and Heaven.

THE SURVIVOR; A CAMBODIAN ODYSSEY. By Jon Lipsky. March 10, 1994. Director, Vincent Murphy; scenery, Paul Owen; costumes, Esther Marquis; lighting, Kenneth Posner; sound, Darron L. West; choreography, Eva Lee.

Haing Ngor .... Peter Kwong
Huoy My Chang .... Yunjin Kim
Pen Tip .... Mark W. Conklin
Naga Man .... Eric Steinberg
Naga Woman .... Midori Nakamura
Girl .... Nicole Scherzinger
Cambodian Dancer .... Sokhanarith Moeur

Act I: Cambodia 1975-1979. Act II: The scene shifts back and forth between Cambodia, Los Angeles, and the set of *The Killing Fields*.

JULIE JOHNSON. By Wendy Hammond. March 16, 1994. Director, Jon Jory; scenery, Paul Owen; costumes, Esther Marquis; lighting, Kenneth Posner; sound, Darron L. West.

Julie Johnson .... Lily Knight
Lisa Johnson .... Jennifer Carpenter
Frankie Johnson .... Wilder Schwartz
Claire .... Carolyn Swift
Mr. Miranda .... V Craig Heidenreich

Time: The present. Place: Hoboken, N.J., 4th and Monroe. One intermission.

SHOTGUN. By Romulus Linney. March 22, 1994. Director, Tom Bullard; scenery, Paul Owen; costumes, Laura Patterson; lighting, Kenneth Posner; sound, Casey L. Warren.

John .... Tom Stechschulte
Fred .... Michael Kevin
Beth .... Jeanee Paulsen
William .... Bob Burrus
Sarah .... Gloria Cromwell.

Time: Summer, 1993. Place: A small vacation home on a lake. One intermission.

STONES AND BONES. By Marion McClinton. March 26, 1994. Director, Marion McClinton; scenery, Paul Owen; costumes, Kevin R. McLeod; lighting, Matthew Reinert; sound, Casey L. Warren.

Mister Bones .... Timothy D. Stickney
Sistuh Stones .... Stacy Highsmith
Bone .... Terry E. Bellamy
Stony .... Fanni Green

Time: The ever-present now.

THE LAST TIME WE SAW HER. By Jane Anderson. March 26, 1994. Director, Frazier W. Marsh; scenery, Paul Owen; costumes, Hollis Jenkins-Evans; lighting, Matthew Reinert; sound, Casey L. Warren.

Hunter .... Fred Major
Fran .... Jennifer Hubbard

Time: The present. Place: An office, somewhere in Ohio.

Lowell, Mass: Merrimack Repertory Theater

(Artistic director, David G. Kent; general manager, Keith Stevens)

MAGGIE'S RIFF. By Jon Lipsky, based on Jack Kerouac's *Maggie Cassidy*. Director, David G. Kent; scenery and costumes, Gary M. English; lighting, Kendall Smith; original composition and musical direction, Steve Cummings.

Jack .... David Zoffoli
Musician .... Jeff Robinson
Mouse; Pop .... John Plumpis
Maggie; Moe Cole; Mamere .... Angela Christian

No intermission.

Metuchen, N.J.: Forum Theater Group

(Artistic director, Peter J. Loewy; managing director, Vicki Tripodo)

SPITTIN' IMAGE. Book by Karin Kasdin; music by Stephen A. Weiner; lyrics by Laura Szabo-Cohen; adapted from Jesse Stuart's *Taps for Private Tussie*. April 1, 1994. Director, Peter J. Loewy; musical direction, Larry N. Rothweiler Jr.; scenery, Perry Arthur Kroeger; costumes, Jose M. Rivera; lighting, Matthew J. Williams; sound, Nancy R. Mannon; orchestrations, Steve Cohen; additional choreography, Dan Siretta.

Sid .... Joe Giopco
Matt .... Charlie Hofheimer
Boy .... Ramzi Khalaf
Grandpa .... Leonard Drum
Mama .... Janine LaManna
Grandma .... Judi Wilfore
Mott .... R. Peter Mogens
Becca .... Eden Riegel
Lucy .... Sarah Hubbard
Matt's Father .... John Carroll

Others: Jeremy Leiner, Maria Weiner, Debbie Zeidner, Jasmine Bloch, Erika Insana, Gerald Crawford, Michael C. Gomborone, Val Disanto, Gail Montgomery.

One intermission.

Millburn, N.J.: Paper Mill Playhouse

(Artistic director, Robert Johanson; executive producer, Angelo Del Rossi)

PAPER MOON. Book by Martin Casella; lyrics by Ellen Fitzhugh and Carol Hall; music by Larry Grossman. September 8, 1993. Director, Matt Casella; musical direction and vocal arrangements, Steve Marzullo; scenery, Michael Anania; costumes, Jeffrey Kurland; lighting, Pat Collins; sound, David R. Pater-

PAPER MILL PLAYHOUSE, MILLBURN, N.J.—Christine Ebersole and Gregory Harrison *(foreground)* with Chandra Wilson and Natalie DeLucia in *Paper Moon,* a new musical by Martin Casella, Ellen Fitzhugh, Carol Hall and Larry Grossman

son; choreography, Alan Johnson.

With Keith Perry, Mary Stout, Norrice Raymaker, Roxie Lucas, Kathryn Kendall, Kathy Garrick, Ruth Gottschall, Natalie DeLucia, Raegan Kotz, Gregory Harrison, Joe Locarro, John Bolton, Rebecca Holt, Monica M. Wemitt, Roy Leake Jr., Christine Ebersole, Chandra Wilson, Linda Hart, John Dossett.

Time and place: Various locales in the south in 1935. One intermission.

A TALE OF TWO CITIES. Adapted from Charles Dickens by Robert Johanson; music by Albert Evans. February 16, 1994. Director, Robert Johanson; scenery, Michael Anania; costumes, Gregg Barnes; lighting, Ken Billington; sound, David R. Paterson.

With Timothy Altmeyer, Nancy Bell, Steve Boles, Sabrina Boudot, Kermit Brown, William Carl, Kevin Chamberlin, Matthew D'Antuono, Jeffrey Force, Larry Grey, Margaret Hall, Verl John Hite, Christopher Innvar, Mark Irish, Stephanie Jones, John Juback, Donald S. Kilcoyne, Ken Kliban, Kathleen Mahony-Bennett, Wilma Mondi, Ron Parady, James Pritchett, John Rainer, Michael James Reed, Judith Roberts, Eliza Schlesinger, Adam Slater, Elizabeth Timperman, Suzanne Toren, Patrick Tull, Kristin Kay Wiegand.

Staged Reading:

THE RED BADGE OF COURAGE. Adapted from Stephen Crane by Leland Ball. November, 22, 1993.

Milwaukee: Theater X

(Artistic director, John Schneider; managing director, Pamela Percy)

BODE'-WAD-MI: KEEPERS OF THE FIRE. By John Schneider and John Kishline. February 4, 1994. Director, John Schneider; scenery and lighting, Rick Graham; costumes, Carri Skoczek; sound, John Dereszynski.

With George Amour, Amber Ante, Deborah Clifton, Flora Coker, Marcie Hoffman, John Kishline, Ruth Pemma, Louis Shepard, John Starmer, Huston Wheelock.

Time: The present. Place: Around a council fire, a discussion between the actors and the audience. One intermission.

Minneapolis: The Cricket Theater

(Artistic director, William Partlan)

DESPERATE AFFECTION. By Bruce Graham. February 4, 1994. Director, Ann Justine D'Zmura; scenery, Thomas Barrett; lighting, Tina Charney; sound, Peter Still.

Maddie .... Barbara Kingsley
Richard .... William Francis McGuire

Place: A Manhattan apartment on the day of a Presidential visit.

SACRED JOURNEY. By Matthew Witten. March 5, 1994. Director, William Partlan; scenery, Rick Regan; costumes, Jim Alford; lighting, Tina Charney, Michael Klaers.

Indian John .... Adan Sanchez

Place: On the streets of New York City. One intermission.

UNDER YELENA. By Buffy Sedlachek. April 7, 1994. Director, William Partlan.

Ruta Zemlyan .... Barbara Kingsley
Antonas Zerbitska .... John Patrick Martin

Place: The science bunker at Chernobyll.

A DROP IN THE BUCKET. By Edward Belling. April 30, 1994. Director, William Partlan; scenery and lighting, Nayna Ramey; costumes, Kathleen Egan; sound, Ben James.

Beatrice Freeman .... Barbara June Patterson
Barry Freeman; Son; Bus Driver;
Casino Manager .... Stephen DiMenna
Doris Claffee .... Shirley Venard

Place: New York City, Atlantic City and the bus route in between. One intermission.

Minneapolis: The Guthrie Theater

(Artistic director, Garland Wright; executive director, Edward A. Martenson)

NAGA MANDALA (PLAY WITH A COBRA). By Girish Karnad; music by David Philipson. July 16, 1993. Director, Garland Wright; scenery, Douglas Stein; costumes, Susan Hilferty; lighting, Peter Maradudin.

Playwright .... Richard Ooms
The Story .... Miriam Laube
Rani .... Nirupama Nityanandan
Appanna; Naga .... Stan Egi
Kurudavva .... Isabell Monk
Kappanna .... William Francis McGuire

The Flames: Cheryl Moore Brinkley, Jennifer Jordan Campbell, June Gibbons, Rita Mustaphi, Monica E. Scott, Sally Wingert. Village Elders: John Bottoms, Bob Davis, Charles Janasz, Stephen Pelinski. Attendants, Townspeople, Additional Flames: Brian Chapman-Evans, David Fischer, Jeana Johnson, Joseph Johnson, Runa Lahiri, Lisa Oglesby, Christopher Peterson, Joseph Ramstrom, Naomi Smith.

Place: The inner sanctum of a ruined temple. One intermission.

THE TRIUMPH OF LOVE. Adapted from Marivaux by Paul Schmidt. August 6, 1993. Director, Dominique Serrand; scenery, Dominique Serrand, Ray Forton; costumes, Sonya Berlovitz; lighting, Marcus Dilliard.

Dimas .... Richard S. Iglewski
Merino .... Nathaniel Fuller
The Princess .... Jacqueline Kim
Corinne .... Julie Briskman Hall
Countertenor .... Tom Gibis
Harlequin .... Christopher Bayes
Agis .... Reg Rogers
Leontine .... Isabell Monk
Aglaia .... Miriam Laube
Hermocrates .... Stephen Yoakam
Azor .... Enrico Colantoni

Montgomery: Alabama Shakespeare Festival

(Artistic director, Kent Thompson)

FLYIN' WEST. By Pearl Cleage. January 14, 1994. Director, Edward G. Smith; scenery, Felix Cochren; costumes, Judy Dearing; lighting, William H. Grant; sound, Kris Kuipers.

With Kim Brockington, June Duell, Andrea Frye, Cee-Cee Harshaw, Robert Owens, Cedric Young.

One intermission.

GROVER. By Randy Hill. January 14, 1994. Director, Peter Hackett; scenery, Robert N. Schmidt; costumes, Elizabeth Novak; lighting, Liz Lee; sound, Kris Kuipers.

With Stuart Culpepper, Greta Lambert, Elizabeth Omilami, Sam Gordon, Barry Boys, Joan Ulmer, Tony DeBruno, Andrew Long, Kurt Kingsley, Joey Collins, Danny Gilroy, Baylen Drew Thomas.

One intermission.

Nashville: Tennessee Repertory Theater

(Artistic director, Mac Pirkle; managing director, Brian J. Laczko)

A HOUSE DIVIDED. Book and additional lyrics by Mac Pirkle; music and lyrics by Mike Reid. May 12, 1994. Director and choreographer, Bill Castellino; scenery, Michael Anania; costumes, Howard Tsvi Kaplan; lighting, Brian J. Laczko; sound, Eric Swartz; vocal arrangements and direction, Gerald Sternbach; orchestrations, Michael Morris.

Will Jr. .... Evan Broder
Priscilla's Friends .. Brooke Bryant, Angela Pridgen
Taylor .... Mark Cabus
Sergeant .... Matthew Carlton
William Montgomery .... Giles Chiasson
Virginia Montgomery .... Rhonda Coullet
Mozart .... Keith Fortner
Priscilla's friend .... Carolyn German
Mule .... Scott K. Ivey
Josh .... Gary Lowery
Ridely Stewart; Union Official .... Brian Mathis
Hollister; Preacher .... Chris McDaniel
Priscilla Stewart .... Shelean Newman
Ben Montgomery .... Christopher Rath
Silas McAllister .... Jon Rider
Moses .... Rudy Roberson
Jasper .... Ricky Russell
Buckshot .... Mark Sanders
Jeb Montgomery .... John Wilkerson

Act I: From spring to December, 1861. Act II: The winter of 1865.

New Brunswick, N.J.: George Street Playhouse

(Producing artistic director, Gregory S. Hurst; managing director, Diane Claussen)

SHEER BOREDOM. By John Viscardi. October 23, 1993. Director, Tom Bullard; scenery, John Lee Beatty; costumes, David M. Covach; lighting, Jackie Manassee.

With Matthew Arkin, Harsh Nayyar, Joel Rooks.

Time: The present. Place: The lobby of a luxury high rise. One intermission.

SUMMER FEET HEARTS. By Lynn Martin. November 27, 1993. Director, Wendy Liscow; scenery, Deborah Jasien; costumes, Barbara Forbes; lighting, Monique Millane.

With Franchelle Stewart, Dion Graham, Ariel Harris, Reggie Montgomery, Joanna Rhinehart.

Time: The present. Place: The backyard of the Golightly house. One intermission.

TANGENTS. By Elizabeth Hansen. January 8, 1994. Director, Alyson Reed; scenery, Ray Recht; costumes, David M. Covach; lighting, F. Mitchell Dana.

With Kirstin Allen, Susan Cash, Lauren Graham, Susannah Hoffmann, Valerie Leonard, Deirdre Madigan, Marge Redmond.

Time: The present. Place: A university. One intermission.

A CRITIC AND HIS WIFE. By John Ford Noonan. February 5, 1994. Director, Wendy Liscow; scenery, Atkin Pace; costumes, Barbara Forbes; lighting, Monique Millane.

With Robert LuPone, Linda Throson.

Time: The present. Place: An Upper East Side apartment, New York City. One intermission.

SWINGING ON A STAR: A MUSICAL CELEBRATION OF JOHNNY BURKE. By Michael Leeds. April 16, 1994. Director, Michael Leeds; scenery, Deborah Jasien; costumes, Judy Dearing; lighting, Richard Nelson; choreography, Kathleen Marshall.

With Lisa Akey, Claire Bathe, Terry Burrell, Lewis Cleale, Kathy Fitzgerald, Michael McGrath, Alton F. White.

Time: The 1920s through the present. Place: A 1920s speakeasy; a street corner during the Depression; a 1930s radio show; a USA show in the Pacific Islands; a Chicago hotel; the back lot of a movie studio; a New York City nightclub. One intermission.

New Haven, Conn.: Long Wharf Theater

(Artistic director, Arvin Brown; managing director, M. Edgar Rosenblum)

THE TIMES. Book and lyrics by Joe Ross; music by Brad Ross. October 5, 1993. Director, Gordon Edelstein; musical direction, Tom Fay; scenery, Hugh Landwehr; costumes, Jess Goldstein; lighting, Peter Kaczorowski.

Ted .... Philip Hoffman
Liz .... Mary Gordon Murray
Fran; Naomi; etc. .... Nora Mae Lyng
Ann; Maggie; etc. .... Jennifer Smith
Lindsay; Model; etc. .... Cheryl Stern
George; John Updike; etc. .... James Judy
Bob; Alan; etc. .... Ron Bohmer

Tom; Matt; etc. .... Bobby Daye

Time: 1975-1990. Place: Various places in New York City. One intermission.

BROKEN GLASS. By Arthur Miller; music by William Bolcom. March 1, 1994. Director, John Tillinger; scenery and costumes, Santo Loquasto; lighting, Brian Nason.

Phillip Gellburg .... Ron Rifkin
Margaret Hyman .... Frances Conroy
Dr. Harry Hyman .... Ron Silver
Sylvia Gellburg .... Amy Irving
Harriet .... Lauren Klein
Stanton Case .... George N. Martin

Time and place: Brooklyn in the last days of November 1938.

Workshop Series:

KING OF COONS. By Michael Henry Brown. January 25, 1994. Directed by Gordon Edelstein.
SUNDAY ON THE ROCKS. By Theresa Rebeck. May 3, 1994. Directed by Susann Brinkley.

Playreading Series:

THE AMEN CORNER. By James Baldwin. January 18, 1994. Directed by Donald Douglass.
MOURN IN RED. By Regina Porter. January 19, 1994. Directed by Marion Isaac McClinton.
ONE LAST LOOK. By Steve Carter. January 19, 1994. Directed by Marion Isaac McClinton.
FLYIN' WEST. By Pearl Cleage. January 20, 1994. Directed by Ricardo Khan.
CANNED GOODS. By Silas Jones. January 21, 1994. Directed by Marion Isaac McClinton.
THE LAST AMERICAN DIXIELAND BAND. By Phillip Hayes Dean. January 22, 1994. Directed by John Stix.

New Haven, Conn.: Yale Repertory Theater

(Artistic director, Stan Wojewodski Jr.; managing director, Victoria Nolan)

THE GREEN BIRD. Translated by Albert Bermel and Ted Emery from Carlo Gozzi's *L'Augellino Belverde*. December 2, 1993; collaboratively produced by Theatre de la Jeune Lune. Director, Vincent Gracieux; scenography/puppetry, Steven Epp; costumes, Felicity Jones; lighting, Frederic Desbois; composer and musical director, Eric Jensen.

Tartaglia .... Vincent Gracieux
Tartagliona .... Barbra Berlovitz Desbois
Ninetta .... Sarah Corzatt
Renzo .... John Bolding
Barbarina .... Felicity Jones
Pompea .... Angela Lewis
Calmon .... John Plummer
Brighella .... Dominique Serrand
Truffaldino .... Robert Rosen
Smeraldina .... Heather K. Wilson
Musician .... Eric Jensen
Green Bird .... Masanari Kawahara

Chorus: Kyle Ackerman, Laura Janik, Robert de los Reyes.

One intermission.

Palo Alto, Calif.: TheaterWorks

(Managing director, Randy Adams)

JOSEPHINE. By Ernest Kinoy. August 12, 1993. Director, Anthony J. Haney; orchestrations, Michael Gibson; dance and vocal arrangements and incidental music, Marvin Laird; scenery, John Bonard Wilson; costumes, Susan Archibald Grote; lighting, John G. Rathman.

Josephine .... Natalie Venetia Belcon
Virgil; Preacher .... Milton Williams
Ida .... Della Reese, Jeanne Cuffey
Le Fevre; Jonny .... Jack Davis
Declas .... John Zic
Mistinguet; Louella .... Donna Cima
Cesare .... Rudy Guerrero
Sophie .... Katie Johnston, Katy Walters
Winchell .... Nick Lymberis
Cholly .... David Garrett
Grace Kelly .... Loretta Rezos

One intermission.

HONOR SONG FOR CRAZY HORSE. By Darrah Cloud. April 28, 1994. Director, Robert Kelley; musical direction, Tom Lindblade; choreography, Henry Smith; scenery, Joe Ragey; costumes, Fumiko Bielefeldt; lighting, John G. Rathman.

Crazy Horse .... James Apaumut Fall
Iktomi .... Stuart Bird
Father .... J. Reuben Silverbird
Mother .... Cynthia Marie Davis
Black Buffalo Woman; Spirit ... Natalie Kaye Arazi
No Water; Lakota Policeman .... Joseph Donés
Black Shawl .... Leta Rector
Little Hawk; Warrior .... Adam Jacobs
Wolf; Sitting Bull .... Jose R. Andrews III
Little Thunder; Red Cloud ... Peter Anthony Acosta
White Owl; Spotted Tail;
Lakota Man .... Jim Clearwater.
Woman's Dress .... Richard S. Sanchez

Hump; Horse Man .... Jack Kohler
Dove .... June Golveo
Spoon .... Jeanne Cuffey
Rabbit; Hawk Spirit;
Little Big Man .... Conrad Cimarra
Always Star .... Diane Way
Rainbow .... Kira Leigh Dixon, Samantha Valerio Flick
Swan .... Jessica Reiko Granger, Arielle Cherise Jacobs
Three Stars; Cavalryman .... Ron Evans
Long Hair; Cavalryman .... Peter Schmuckal

Cavalrymen: Anthony Bernal, Joe Colletti, Don Paterson, Derek Wood, Adrian Wood.

Time and place: The play takes place in various locations in the Northern Plains, 1854-1877.

Philadelphia: American Music Theater Festival

(Artistic director, Ben Levit)

FLOYD COLLINS. Book by Tina Landau; music by Adam Guettel; lyrics by Adam Guettel and Tina Landau. April 13, 1994. Director, Tina Landau; musical direction, Ted Sperling; scenery, James Schuette; costumes, Melina Root; lighting, Scott Zielinski; sound, Darron L. West; orchestrations, Bruce Coughlin; choreography, John DeLuca.

Floyd Collins .... Jim Morlino
Nellie Collins .... Theresa McCarthy
Johnnie Gerald .... Stephen Lee Anderson
Homer Collins .... Jason Danieley
Skeets Miller .... Martin Moran
Miss Jane .... Mary Beth Peil
Lee Collins .... Nick Plakias

Others: Trent Bright, Scott Coulter, Kent Faulcon, Michael Malone, James Pringle, Steven Skybell, Scott Wakefield.

One intermission.

SHLEMIEL THE FIRST. Conceived and adapted from Isaac Bashevis Singer by Robert Brustein; music by Hankus Netsky; additional music by Zalmen Mlotek; lyrics by Arnold Weinstein. May 18, 1994; co-produced with American Repertory Theater; see its full entry in the Cambridge, Mass. section.

THE MYSTERY OF LOVE. Book and lyrics by Sekou Sundiata; music by Douglas Booth. May 13, 1994. Director, Talvin Wilks; choreography, Marlies Yearby; scenery, James Schuette; lighting, Jackie Manassee; sound, Darron L. West; masks, Natalie Walker.

Cissy .... Angela Lockett
Maceo .... Ramon Melindez Moses
Shine .... Robert Tyree
Eartha .... Fuschia Walker
Swamp .... Craig Harris
Poet .... Sekou Sundiata

Philadelphia: InterAct Theater Company

(Artistic director, Seth Rozin)

6221—PROPHECY AND TRAGEDY. By Thomas Gibbons. October 1, 1993. Director, Seth Rozin; scenery and lighting, Peter Whinnery; costumes, Chryss Hionis; sound, W. Scott Roberts.

Cast: Commissioner, Agent, Jim Ramp, Gregore Sambor—John Barrett; Janine Africa, Ramona Africa—Shelita Birchett; Neighbor, Orderly, Walter Jackson, Frank Africa—Amani Kuwasha Gethers; Television Broadcaster (voice over)—Larry Kane; Commissioner, Photographer, Inspector, Pilot—Phillip Lynch; Donald Glassey, Cop, Frank Powell—Jeff Morrison; Commissioner (voice over)—Neill Hartley; Birdie Africa—Shelby Hughes; Robert Africa, Wilson Goode—Bruce Robinson; Sue Africa, Reporter, Berghaier's Wife—Lillian Rozin; Commissioner, Marie Jackson, Nurse, Theresa Africa—Shirley Scott; Merle Africa, Louise James—Cathy Simpson; Neighbor, Officer, Lucien Blackwell, Conrad Africa—Mets Suber; Jim Berghaier—Bradley Thoennes; Agent, Cop, Tommy Mellor, William Richmond—Russ Widdall; Commissioner, Delbert Africa, Leo Brooks—Frank X; John Africa—Vincente Yate.

Two intermissions.

Philadelphia: Philadelphia Theater Company

(Producing artistic director, Sara Garonzik)

NIGHT SKY. By Susan Yankowitz. Music by Glen Roven. March 9, 1994. Director, Jack Hofsiss; scenery, David Jenkins; costumes, Julie Weiss; lighting, F. Mitchell Dana; sound, Scott Lehrer.

WILMA THEATER, PHILADELPHIA—Edmund C. Davys and Benjamin Lloyd in Tom Stoppard's new revision of his *Travesties,* a 1975-76 Best Play

Anna .... Laura Esterman
Daniel .... Joseph Breen
Jennifer .... Orli Cotel
Speech Therapist (and Others) .... Sandra Daley
Aphasic Patient (and Others) .... Yusef Bulos
Bill .... Kenneth L. Marks

Time: The present. Place: New York City. One intermission.

Philadelphia: Walnut Street Theater

(Executive director, Bernard Havard)

A WORM IN THE HEART. By Paul Minx. January 4, 1994. Director, Bill Roudebush; scenery, Peter C. Harvey; costumes, Kevin Ross; lighting, Wes Hacking; sound, Eileen Tague.

Serge Toussaint .... Rozwill Young
Darlene Fischer .... Tara Carnes
Donna Jane Fischer .... Donna Snow
Yvette Ganier .... Isabel Banks
Thomas Roy .... Karl Fischer

Time and place: Lawn and patio of the Fischers' home in Indianapolis, late August, 1964. One intermission.

Philadelphia: Wilma Theater

(Artistic/producing directors, Blanka and Jiri Zizka; managing director, Teresa Eyring)

TRAVESTIES. Newly revised by Tom Stoppard. April 27, 1994. Director, Blanka Zizka; scenery, Jerry Rojo; costumes, Hiroshi Iwasaki; lighting, Jerold Forsyth; sound, Adam Wernick.

Henry Carr .... Edmund C. Davys
Tristan Tzara .... Robert Christophe
James Joyce .... Tony Azito
Gwendolen Carr .... Grace Gonglewski
Lenin .... Benjamin Lloyd
Cecily Carruthers .... Kim Rhodes
Nadya Krupskaya .... Jilline Ringle
Percy Bennett .... Benjamin Lloyd

Time and place: Zurich, Switzerland, 1917. One intermission.

Portland, Me.: Portland Stage Company

(Artistic director, Greg Leaming; managing director, William Chance)

LOSING FATHER'S BODY. By Constance Congdon. April 17, 1994. Director, Greg Leaming; scenery, Rob Odorisio; costumes, Tom Broecker; lighting, Christopher Akerlind; sound, Jim van Bergen.

Kim Anderson .... Christina Rouner
Scott Anderson .... T. Scott Cunningham
Pauline Anderson .... Jeannine Moore
Dr. Ryan .... Don LaBranche
George Boyle .... Peter Boyden
Jerri .... Catherine Lloyd Burns
Dorothea Croft .... Alison Edwards
Todd .... Paul Drinan
Michelle .... Maura O'Brien
Alice Bear .... Jan Leslie Harding
Clarence Bear .... Chad Henry
Cecil Anderson .... Benjamin Steart
Felicia .... Catherine Lloyd Burns

Act I, Scene 1: The Anderson home, midnight. Scene 2: The next morning. Scene 3: Noon. Scene 4: Cocktail time. Scene 5: Later that evening. Act II, Scene 1: The woods, upstate New York, pre-dawn. Scene 2: The Anderson home, dawn. Scene 3: 7 a.m. Scene 4: The station wagon. Scene 5: The Anderson home, 8 a.m. Scene 6: The woods. Scene 7: The limo, a short time later. Scene 8: The woods, later that morning.

Staged Readings: 1994 Little Festival of the Unexpected

THIS DAY AND AGE. By Roger Rueff. May 4, 1994. Directed by John Swanbeck.

CHURCH OF THE SOLE SURVIVOR. May 5, 1994. By Keith Curran. Directed by Ray Cochran.

TALES FROM THE TIME OF THE PLAGUE. May 6, 1994. By Lynne Alvarez. Directed by Greg Leaming.

Princeton, N.J.: McCarter Theater

(Artistic director, Emily Mann; managing director, Jeffrey Woodward)

THE PERFECTIONIST. By Joyce Carol Oates; music by Lucia Hwong. September 28, 1993. Director, Emily Mann; scenery, Thomas Lynch; costumes, Jennifer Von Mayrhauser; lighting, Pat Collins.

Tobias Harte .... David Selby
Paula Harte .... Betty Buckley
Kim Harte .... Dina Spybey
Jason Harte .... Josh Hamilton
Willy Rebb .... Peter Maloney
Nedra Minsk .... Shareen Mitchell

Time: The present, over a period of approximately one week. Place: The affluent suburb of Mt. Orion, New Jersey. One intermission.

Winter's Tales '94 New Play Festival, January 12-23, 1994

THE NANJING RACE. By Reggie Cheong-Leen. January 12, 1994. Director, Loretta Greco; scenery, Philip Creech; costumes, Catherine Homa-Rocchio; lighting, Christopher Gorzelnik; sound, Stephen G. Smith.

Philip .... Thom Sesma
Yu Ahn .... B.D. Wong
Bao .... David Chung

Place: China

Winter's Tales '94 Short Plays Collection I:

MY DEAD FATHER'S BODY AT THE CARLTON FLOPHOUSE REDISCOVERED AS ANTHROPOLOGY. By Han Ong. Director, Jorge Ledesma.

Young Mr. Chang .... Stephen Lee
Flophouse Resident #1 .... Lynne Thigpen
Flophouse Resident #2 .... James Puig
Flophouse Resident #3 .... Jere Edmunds
Old Mr. Chang .... Karl Light

Voice of Slides .... James Morrison

AN ACT OF DEVOTION. By Deborah Tannen. Director, Evan Yionoulis.
Father .... Allen Swift
Daughter .... Katherine Borowitz

HE WAS A BIG BOY, STILL IS. By Leigh Bienen. With Katherine Borowitz.

MOTHERHOOD 2000. By Adrienne Kennedy. Director, Michael Kahn.
Mother; Writer .... Lynne Thigpen
Richard Fox .... Karl Light
Passion Play Actors: James Morrison, Stephen Lee, Brandan McClain.

SMART CHOICES FOR THE NEW CENTURY. By Jane Anderson. Director, Tamsen Wolff.
Arden Shingles .... Katherine Borowitz
Rudy .... Stephen Lee

Winter's Tales '94 Short Plays Collection II:

TO KNOW A MONSTER (PROLOGUE). By Emily Mann. Director, Nikki Appino.
Young Man .... Brandan McClain
Man .... James Morrison
Anonymous Man .... Karl Light

WHITE FOLKS SHO' IS CRAZY. By Russell Banks. Director, Nikki Appino.
Little Eva .... Karen Garvey
Huck Finn .... Brandan McClain
Frederick Douglas .... Terry Alexander
Shields Green .... Jere Edmunds
John Brown .... Karl Light
Owen Brown .... James Morrison

WHAT'S A HEAVEN FOR. By Nicole Burdette. Director, Laura Huntsman.
Bobby .... Richard Thompson

AND I AM NOT RESIGNED. By Gayle Pemberton. Director, Jennifer Nelson.
Annie .... Lynne Thigpen
Larry .... Terry Alexander

MINI-MALL HEROES. By Hector Tobar. Director, Laura Huntsman.
Developer .... James Morrison
Al Greenwood .... Allen Swift
Yesnia .... Lynne Thigpen
Basiliso .... James Puig

THE INTERVIEW. By Joyce Carol Oates. Director, Adam Arkin.
The Immortal .... Allen Swift
The Interviewer .... Richard Thompson
Kimberly .... Karen Garvey

C'MON & HEAR — IRVING BERLIN'S AMERICA. Conceived by George Faison and David Bishop; music and lyrics by Irving Berlin. March 22, 1994. Director, George Faison; choreography, George Faison; musical arrangements, David Bishop; scenery, Chris Barreca; costumes, Toni-Leslie James; lighting, Richard Nelson; sound, Stephen G. Smith; musical director and conductor, Linda Twine; dance arrangements, Timothy Graphenreed.
Rose Santos .... Carol Woods
Nathan Singer .... James Hindman
Sophie Stendhal .... Mary Testa
Gino da Vinci .... Ted L. Levy
Percy Ishmael .... Alton Fitzgerald White
Anna Schiller .... Karyn Quackenbush
Ida Mae Lewis .... Stephanie Pope
Eric Carlson .... John Hickok
Bruno Marcus .... Rodney Scott Hudson
Molly McGuire .... Laurie Beechman
Time: Act I: 1900-1919. Act II: 1924-35.

CHANGES OF HEART. Adapted and translated from Marivaux's *The Double Inconstancy* by Stephen Wadsworth. May 3, 1994. Director, Stephen Wadsworth; scenery, Thomas Lynch; costumes, Martin Pakledinaz; lighting, Christopher Akerlind.
Silvia .... Natch Roi
Trivelin .... Laurence O'Dwyer
Prince .... Robert Sean Leonard
Flamina .... Mary Lou Rosato
Lisette .... Sheryl Taub
Harlequin .... John Michael Higgins
Lord .... Nicholas Kepros
Valets .... Reid Armbruster, Michael Collins
Ladies-in-Waiting .... Roberta Kastelic, Jennifer Thomas
Place: In the palace of the Prince. Two intermissions.

Rockford, Ill.: New American Theater

(Producing director, J.R. Sullivan)

MURDER CENTER STAGE. By Margaret Raether. May 6, 1994. Director, Richard Raether; costumes, Jim Bacino; lighting, Laurie Oliver.
Jackie Donnelly .... Mandy Howard
Detective Jake Granite .... Greg Lackner
D. Saunders .... Kathleen Muldowney
Mabel Mackenzie .... Patricia Newman
Brian; Director Guy; Conway ....Jack Rabito
Jimmy Barstow .... Christopher Drew Vidal
Veronica LaRue .... Sue Ann Westlund
Stanley Exton .... Gary Wingert

Sacramento: Sacramento Theater Company

(Artistic director, Mark Cuddy; managing director, David M. Hagar)

GOLF WITH ALAN SHEPARD. By Carter Lewis. January 11, 1994. Director, Mark Cuddy; scenery, Rosario Provenza; costumes, Phyllis Kress; lighting Kathryn Burleson.

Griff .... Robert Kelly
Milt .... Devoy White
Larkin .... Bruce Mackey
Ned .... Robert Parnell
The Microphone .... Gary S. Martinez

Place: A public golf course in Ohio. Act I: The front nine. Act II: The back nine. One intermission.

A CAPPELLA. Book by Richard Hellesen; music and lyrics by David de Berry. March 29, 1994. Director, Tim Ocel; musical direction, David de Berry; scenery and costumes, Loren Tripp; lighting, Kathryn Burleson; choreography, Cynthia Mitterholzer.

Willie .... Mark Booher
Paul .... Christopher Gurr
Darlene .... Kathryn Morison
Brandon .... Rob Robinson

Time: The present. Place: A state office.

St. Louis: Repertory Theater of St. Louis

(Artistic director, Steven Woolf; managing director, Mark D. Bernstein)

YOUNG RUBE. Book by John Pielmeier; music and lyrics by Matthew Selman; based on the play by George W. George. September 8, 1993. Director, Susan Gregg; musical direction and vocal arrangements, Albert Ahronheim; scenery, John Ezell; costumes, Dorothy L. Marshall; lighting, Dale F. Jordan; choreography, David Holdgrive; orchestrations, Michael Gibson.

Tillie; Pearl His Girl .... Mana Allen
Boob McNutt .... Bill Bowers
Secretary; Copyboy; Eau D'Alisque; Adenoida Sourgrapes; Miner .... Amanda Butterbaugh
High School Principal; Professor Slate; Boss Ruef; Mike; Bartender ... Frank DiPasquale
Secretary; Copyboy; Galatea de Teets; Countess Lala Palooza; Miner .... Susan Ericksen
Little Rube; Mole; Mr. P.; Little Cop; Old Man Alf of the Alphabet; Black Bart ... Gregory Grant
Professor Christy; Bunker; Big Cop; Liberty Undaunted; Minister .... Steve Liebman
Max; Prof. Lucifer Gorgonzola Butts .... Michael Mulheren
Young Rube .... Marcus Neville
Secretary; Copyboy; Moany Lisa; Miss Medulla Oblongata; Miner .... Kristine Nevins
Woodward; Mayor Schmitz; Ike; Dying Miner .... Russ Thacker

Time: From the turn of the century to early 1900s.

Salt Lake City: Pioneer Theater Company

(Artistic director, Charles Morey; managing director, Christopher Lino)

THE HUNCHBACK OF NOTRE DAME. Adapted from Victor Hugo by Charles Morey; original music by James Prigmore. October 27, 1993. Director, Charles Morey; scenery, Peter Harrison; costumes, Linda Sarver; lighting, Karl E. Haas.

Dom Claude Frollo .... Craig Wroe
Quasimodo .... Michael Lewis
Esmeralda .... Kristen Wilson
Pierre Gringoire .... Christopher Mixon
Clopin Trouillefou .... Edward James Hyland
Jacques Charmolue .... Robert Peterson
Jean Frollo .... David Valenza
Phoebus de Chateaupers .... Mark Lewis
La Recluse de la Tour Roland .... Ann Cullimore Decker
Medieval Chorus of Three Deadly Sins:
Madame de la Luxure .... Anne Stewart Mark
Madame de L'Orguiel .... Darla Davis
Madame de la Cupidite .... Rebecca Hunt
Ensemble:
Mlle. Fleur de Lys Gondelaurier; Beggar .... Christy Summerhays
Lienarde; Beggar .... Angel Hayes Sabala
Gisquette; Beggar .... Britt Sady
Duenna; Mme. Falourdel; Beggar .... Jayne Luke
Actor; Bishop; Francois .... Richard Mathews
Actor; Provost; Andry .... Gene Pack
Actor; Torterue; Beggar .... Frank Gerrish
Actor; Soldier .... Trevor Black
Father; Beggar .... Thomas E. Jacobsen
Boy; Acolyte; Beggar .... Aaron Nelson
Sergeant .... Adam Middleton Watts
Beggar; Reveler .... Steven Patrick Sater
Soldier .... Christopher Ivins
Bellevigne .... Mark Larson

Time: From the Feast of the Epiphany through the Sunday after Easter in the year 1482. Place: In and about the Cathedral of Notre Dame de Paris.

San Diego: Old Globe Theater

(Artistic director, Jack O'Brien; managing director, Thomas Hall)

BURNING HOPE. By Douglas Michilinda. July 1993. Director, Andrew J. Traister; scenery, Kent Dorsey; costumes, Andrew V. Yelusich; lighting, Ashley York Kennedy; sound, Jeff Ladman.

Padraig Henry O'Donney .... James Greene
Chaser O'Donney .... Dave Florek
Micky Gates .... Wren T. Brown
Lucia Scibelli .... Rosina Widdowson-Reynolds
Sisopha Van Ngoc .... Kim Miyori
Danielle Scibelli .... Jennifer Stratman
Larry Clark .... Dan Gunther

Time: The summer of 1991. Place: Hanley, a mill town in New England. One intermission.

MR. A'S AMAZING MAZE PLAYS. By Alan Ayckbourn. January 1994. Director, Craig Noel; scenery, Greg Lucas; costumes, Clare Henkel; lighting, Michael Gilliam; sound, Jeff Ladman.

1st Narrator .... Ralph Elias
2d Narrator .... Katherine McGrath
Suzy .... Jennifer Hugus
Mother .... Lynne Griffin
Neville .... Sean Sullivan
Father .... Steve Jones
Mr. Passerby .... Richard Easton
Mr. Accousticus .... Jonathan McMurtry

Place: In and around Suzy's house in a small English village. One intermission.

Staged Reading:

BONES. By Lillian Garrett-Groag. July 26, 1993.

San Diego: San Diego Repertory Theater

(Managing director, Sam Woodhouse)

BURNING DREAMS. Libretto by Julie Herbert and Octavio Solis; music by Gina Leishman. February 16, 1994. Directors, Julie Herbert, Sam Woodhouse; choreography, Deborah Slater; scenery, Robert Brill; costumes, Mary Larson; lighting, John Phillip Martin; sound, Jeff Ladman.

Anselmo .... Alex Britton
Leone .... Cheryl Carter
Rosaura .... Anita De Simone
Segismundo .... Rinde Eckert
Midwife .... Catalina Maynard
Clown .... Deborah Slater

Time and place: The present, at Isla Mujeres, an island off the coast of the Yucatan Peninsula in Mexico. One intermission.

San Francisco: American Conservatory Theater

(Artistic director, Carey Perloff)

PECONG. By Steve Carver. October 20, 1993. Director, Benny Sato Ambush; musical direction and composition, Wayne Wallace; scenery, Kate Edmunds; costumes, Richard W. Battle; lighting, Peter Maradudin; sound, Stephen LeGrand.

Granny Root .... Barbara Montgomery
Mediyah .... Rosalyn Coleman
Cedric .... Leland Gantt
Faustina .... Margarette Robinson
Persis .... Renee Joshua-Porter
Creon Pandit .... Graham Brown
Sweet Bella .... Chanella Schaffer
Jason Allcock .... Michael Gene Sullivan

Time: Well in the past. Place: Trankey Island (Ile Tranquille), an island of the mind in the Caribbean, and Miedo Wood Island, a dark and mysterious place.

UNCLE VANYA. By Anton Chekhov, newly translated by Paul Schmidt. Music by Stephen LeGrand. January 19, 1994. Director, Carey Perloff; scenery, Kate Edmunds; costumes, Beaver Bauer; lighting, Peter Maradudin.

Prof. Alexander Serebriakov .... Ken Ruta
Yelena .... Vilma Silva
Sonya .... Sharon Omi
Maria Voinitsy .... Wanda McCaddon
Vanya .... Tony Amendola
Dr. Mikhail Lovovich Astrov .... Wendell Pierce
Ilya Ilych Telegin .... Frank Ottiwell
Marina .... Roberta Callahan
Hired Man .... Guiesseppe Jones

Time and place: A country house in Russia. Act I: The garden, late summer. Act II: The dining room, a few weeks later. Act III: The living room, an autumn afternoon. Act IV: Vanya's room, the same evening. One intermission.

San Francisco: Climate Theater

(Directors, Joegh Bullock, Marcia Crosby)

HURRICANE. One-woman performance by Anne Galjour; written by Anne Galjour. May 20, 1993. Director, Henry Steele; scenery, John Mayne; costumes, Laura Hazlett; lighting, Novella Smith.

Characters: Sherelle Dantin, Urus Arceneaux, Inez Dantin, Marlon Skinner, Rosetta Cheramie, Grady Cheramie.

No intermission. The 1993 Elizabeth Osborn Award winner; see introduction to this section.

COUSIN MARTIN. By Andrew O'Hehir. April 12, 1994. Director, Bill Talen; scenery, costumes and lighting, Kate Boyd; sound, Shelby Gaines.

Anthony Dever .... Joel Mullennix
Bridie MacMahon .... Deirdre Herbert
Martin MacMahon .... Owen Murphy
Mary Margaret Byrne .... Esther Mulligan
Seamus MacMahon .... Dennis Matthews
Fionnuala MacMahon .... Stephanie Hunt
Carla MacMahon .... Katie Meagher
Paul Donovan .... Paul Colley

One intermission.

WHAT'S WRONG WITH THIS PICTURE? One-woman performance by Grace Walcott; written by Grace Walcott. April 22, 1994. Director, Mary Forcade; scenery, Henry Gutman; lighting, Dave Gebhard, David Holcomb.

No intermission.

San Francisco: Magic Theater

(Artistic director, Mame Hunt)

GIANTS HAVE US IN THEIR BOOKS. Program of six one-act plays by Jose Rivera: *A Tiger in Central Park, Flowers, The Winged Man, Gas, The Crooked Case, Tape*. November 9, 1993. Director, Roberto Gutierrez Varea; scenery, Lauren Elder; lighting, Jeff Rowlings; costumes, Chrystene Ells; sound, J.A. Deane.

With Sean San Jose Blackman, Michael Girardin, Margo Hall, Dennis Matthews, Selena Navarro, Michelle Pelletier, Megan Blue Stermer.

San Francisco: Theater Rhinoceros

(Artistic director, Adele Prandini)

THE SECRETARIES. By the Five Lesbian Brothers. January 15, 1994. Director, Kate Stafford; scenery, Amy Shock; costumes, Susan Young; lighting, Lori E. Seid; sound, Peg Healy.

Dawn Midnight; Buzz Benikee ... Maureen Angelos
Ashley Elizabeth Fratangelo .... Babs Davy
Patty Johnson .... Dominique Dibbell
Susan Curtis .... Peg Healy
Peaches Martin .... Lisa Kron

San Jose: San Jose Repertory Theater

(Artistic director, Timothy Near)

LONELY PLANET. By Steven Dietz. January 14, 1994. Director, Steven Dietz; scenery, Scott Weldin; costumes, Carolyn Keim; lighting, Rick Paulsen; sound, Sergio Avila.

Jody .... Michael Winters
Carl .... Laurence Ballard

One intermission.

Santa Maria, Calif.: PCPA Theaterfest

(Artistic director, Greg Leaming; managing director, William Chance)

THE DALY NEWS. By Jonathan Gillard Daly; music by Larry Delinger and Gregg Coffin. December 2, 1993. Director, Paul Barnes; musical direction and arrangements, Gregg Coffin; scenery, Tim Hogan; costumes, Abby Hogan; lighting, Michael A. Peterson; sound, Dirk Mahabir; choreography, Karen Barbour.

Martin Daly; Jon .... Jonathan Gillard Daly
Claudia Schatzie Daly .... Debi Mason
Their Sons:
Bob .... Gregg Coffin
Chuck .... Brad Carroll
Gene .... Jack Greenman
Dave .... Nathan Galloway Lacey
Catherine .... Kerry Neel
Marion .... Alysa Sylvia Lobo
Ruth .... Christine Jugueta
Lou; Messenger .... Brad Heberlee

Time: 1943 to 1946, and the present. Place: Milwaukee; Santa Maria, Calif.; various locales around the world. One intermission.

Santa Monica, Calif.: Santa Monica Group Theater

(Artistic director, Evelyn Rudie; artistic and managing director, Chris DeCarlo)

KILLJOY. By Jerry Mayer; original music composed and performed by Steve Mayer. June 18, 1993. Director, Chris DeCarlo; scenery, Scott Heineman; lighting, James Cooper; sound, Linn Yamaha.

With Mickey Callan, Tracy Effinger, Sandy Faison, Deborah Harmon, Jane Harnick, Allison Holmes, Michael Horton, Peter Jason, Tim Kirkpatrick, Andy Lauer, Matthew Laurence.

Time: The present. Place: The living room of Carol's Townhouse. One intermission.

EMPRESS EUGENIE. One-woman performance by Agnes Bernelle; written by Jason Lindsey. October 1993. Director, Marianne Macnaghten; lighting, James Cooper; sound, Linn Yamaha.

Time: 1919. Place: Chateau de Compiegne. One intermission.

HERO IN THE HOUSE. By Brenda Krantz. February 10, 1994. Director, Chris DeCarlo; scenery, Scott Heineman; lighting and sound, James Cooper.

With Nicholas Cascone, Suzanne Ford, Lee Ryan, Christopher Spiro.

Time: The present. Place: The Felders' living room. One intermission.

AUTHOR! AUTHOR! AN EVENING WITH SHOLOM ALEICHEM. Newly adapted from Sholom Aleichem by Evelyn Rudie and Chris DeCarlo; music by Ben Weisman. April 1994. Directors, Chris DeCarlo, Evelyn Rudie; scenery, Tim Chadwick; costumes, Ashley Hayes, Cheryl Moffatt; lighting and sound, James Cooper.

With Laura Aaronson, Chris DeCarlo, Dani Dechter, Sophia Elias, Cheryl Moffatt, Evelyn Rudie, Aisha Waglé, John Waroff, Sharon Webster.

Time: Early 1900s. Place: New York City. One intermission.

1994 - A TELLING OF TOMORROW. Extended bilingual version of 1992 musical by Evelyn Rudie and Chris DeCarlo. May 22, 1994. Director, Chris DeCarlo; scenery, Daren Rice, Timothy Chadwick; costumes, Ashley Hayes, Timothy Chadwick; lighting, James Cooper; sound, Linn Yamaha.

Survivalists:
Jo .... Evelyn Rudie
Jad .... Ann Grennan
Genesis .... Inara George
Tampopi .... Kacy Boray
Tari .... Stacy Endman
Nobi .... Monica Schneider
Lawrence .... Martin Barron
Kharma .... Toshiko Tano
Masami .... Maki Hirabayashi
Dwan .... Laura Aaronson
Steena .... Sara Beck
Cosmo .... Dani Dechter
Heart .... Ashley Griffin-Dworman
Annie .... Karina Longworth
Mando .... Jon Martin
Rika .... Keiko Mitsunaga
Honani .... Yoshima Nakagomi
Woody .... Ronen Segal
Lisbeth .... Allison Sego
Peak .... Adam Sires
Chomi .... Nao Takahashi
Courage .... Matt Wrather
Vandalists:
Brother Rat .... John Waroff
Roache .... Elana Bell
Carter .... Noah Gershman
Nostalgities:
Fossie .... Cheryl Moffatt
Yumee .... Aisha Waglé
Pierrette .... Wendi Glodery
Nani-Nani .... Chrissy Lowe
Flip .... Samara Friedman
Flopsy .... Veronica Riglick
The Tracker .... Chris DeCarlo
Runt .... Daren Rice

Time: 35 A.D. Place: Enclave and Wasteland.

Seattle: A Contemporary Theater

(Founding director, Gregory A. Falls; artistic director, Jeff Steitzer; producing director, Phil Schermer)

AGNES SMEDLEY: OUR AMERICAN FRIEND. By Doris Baizley. September 16, 1993. Director, Steven E. Alter; choreography, Mayme Paul-Thompson; Chinese movement, Ernest Abuba; scenery, Shelley Henze Schermer; costumes, Jeanne Arnold; lighting, Michael Wellborn; sound, Steven M. Klein.

Agnes Smedley .... Susan Barnes
Chu Teh (Zhu De) .... Ernest Abuba
Lily Wu (Wu Guangwei) .... Jeanne Sakata
The Guard .... David Mong

Time: 1937. Place: Yen'an, China and Agnes's memory.

DREAMS FROM A SUMMER HOUSE. Book and lyrics by Alan Ayckbourn; music by John Pattison. October 21, 1993 (co-produced with the Arizona Theater Company). Director, Jeff Steitzer; co-director, David Ira Goldstein; musical direction, Jerry Wayne Harkey; scenery, Tom Butsch; costumes, Laura Crow; lighting, Rick Paulsen; sound, David Pascal.

Mel .... Liz McCarthy
Robert .... Greg Zerkle
Chrissie .... Darcy Pulliam
Grayson .... Burt Edwards
Amanda .... Suzanne Bouchard
Sinclair .... R. Hamilton Wright
Belle .... Rachel Coloff
Baldemar .... David Dollase
Musicians .... Jerry Wayne Harkey, Chris Kimbler

One intermission.

A CONTEMPORARY THEATER, SEATTLE—Liz McCarthy and Rachel Coloff in the musical *Dreams From a Summer House* by Alan Ayckbourn and John Pattison

Seattle: Intiman Theater Company

(Artistic director, Warner Shook; managing director, Laura Penn)

Staged Readings:

BAD AXE. By P.J. Barry. Directed by Daniel Renner.
BURNING DESIRE. By William Mastrosimone. Directed by Victor Pappas.
EXECUTION OF THE CAREGIVER. By Michael Cristofer. Directed by Scott Rosenfelt.
BE IT REMEMBERED. By Jamie Baker. Directed by Victor Pappas.
DOG OPERA. By Constance Congdon. Directed by Victor Pappas.
A LANGUAGE OF THEIR OWN. By Chay Yew. Directed by Daniel Renner.

Silver Spring, Md.: Round House Theater

(Artistic director, Jerry Whiddon)

THE MISANTHROPE. Adapted from Molière by Neil Bartlett. May 11, 1994. Director, Daniel Fish; scenery, James Kronzer; costumes, Jane Schloss Phelan; lighting, Joseph B. Musumeci Jr.; sound, Neil McFadden.

Celimene .... Carol Monda
Oronte .... Lawrence Redmond
Arsinoe .... Kimberly Schraf
Clitandre .... Craig Wallace
Eliante .... Jane Beard
Philinte .... Jason Kravits
Acaste .... Marty Lodge
Alceste .... Jerry Whiddon

Stockbridge, Mass.: Berkshire Theater Festival

(Artistic director, Julianne Boyd; managing director, Chuck Still)

CAMPING WITH HENRY & TOM. By Mark St. Germain. July 21, 1993. Director, Paul Lazarus; scenery, James Leonard Joy; costumes, Candice Donnelly; lighting, Donald Holder; sound, Timothy J. Anderson.

Thomas Alva Edison .... Robert Prosky
Henry Ford .... John Cunningham
Warren G. Harding .... Ralph Waite
Col. Edmund Starling .... John Prosky

One intermission.

Syracuse, N.Y.: Syracuse Stage

(Artistic director, Tazewell Thompson; producing director, James A. Clark)

HOLIDAY HEART. By Cheryl West. January 4, 1994. Director, Tazewell Thompson; scenery, Riccardo Hernandez; costumes, Paul Tazewell; lighting, Jack Mehler; sound, James Wildman.

Niki Dean .... LaShonda Hunt
Holiday Heart .... Keith Randolph Smith
Wanda Dean .... Harriett D. Foy
Silas Jericho .... Ron C. Jones
Mark, Ricky .... Leon Sanders

Time and place: A South Side Chicago neighborhood, in the present. One intermission.

THE INDOLENT BOYS. By N. Scott Momaday; music by Terry Tsotigh. February 8, 1994. Director, Tazewell Thompson; scenery, Amy Shock; costumes, Janice Benning; lighting, Marc B. Weiss; sound, James Wildman.

Musician .... Terry Tsotigh
Mother Goodeye .... Ching Valdes-Aran
G.P. Gregory .... Robert Hogan
Barton Wherritt .... Kelly Morgan
John Pai .... Jonathan Fisher
Carrie .... Twyla Hafermann
Emodotah .... Gordon Tootoosis

Others: Justin Alexander, Oliver Cabiles, Ryan Cabiles, Aaron John Curtis, Brandon Homer, Stewart Homer, Robert Mendoza, Weheh Myers, Atsabetsaye Schenandoah, Gabrial Tarbell, Owen White.

Time and place: The Kiowa Boarding School, Anadarko, Oklahoma Territory, January 1891.

Troy, N.Y.: The New York State Theater Institute

(Producing director, Patricia Di Benedetto Snyder)

AMERICAN ENTERPRISE. By Jeffrey Sweet; original songs by Jeffrey Sweet. March 13, 1994. Director, Patricia Birch; incidental music and vocal arrangements, Michael Vitali; additional vocal arrangements, Betsy Riley; scenery, Richard Finkelstein; costumes, Brent Griffin; lighting, John McLain; sound, Matt Elie.

George M. Pullman .... John Romero
J. Patrick Hopkins .... Erol K.C. Landis
George Jr.; Paymaster .... David Bunce
Eugene V. Debs; Beman; Businessman
McCormick; Priest .... Gerard Curran
John P. Altgeld; Jackson; Clayton;
Porter .... Bernard J. Tarver
Stephens; Harahan; Agent .... Paul Villani
Thomas Wickes; Commissioner;
Wright; Porter .... Marshäll Factora
Heathcote; Railroad Owner; Commissioner
Worthington .... Joel Aroeste
Jennie Curtis; Florence Pullman .... Erika Newell
Soloists .... Betsy Riley, Kelley Sweeney
Rev. E.C. Oggel; Businessman
Field .... John T. McGuire III
Mayor Harrison; Businessman Swift; Delegate
Crosgrove; Federal Marshal .... Michael Steese
Railroad Assistant; Porter; Servant .... Jack Seabury
Club Attendant .... Jason W. Bowman
Secretary .... Tracey E. Madison
Ensemble .... Laura Roth, Allison Sharpley

Time and place: Chicago during the latter half of the 19th century. One intermission.

Tucson: Arizona Theater Company

(Artistic director, David Ira Goldstein; managing director, Robert Alpaugh)

DREAMS FROM A SUMMER HOUSE. Book and lyrics by Alan Ayckbourn; music by John Pattison. December 4, 1993; co-produced with A Contemporary Theater; see its full entry under Seattle heading.

Staged Readings:

THE EDUCATION OF WALTER KAUFMANN. By Kevin Kling. March 2, 1994.

THE OLD MATADOR. By Milcha Sanchez-Scott. March 3, 1994. Directed by Peter Brosius.

CRIME AND PUNISHMENT. Adapted from Fyodor Dostoyevsky's novel by Andrzej Wajda. Translated by Roger Downey and Stefan Rowny. March 4, 1994. Directed by David Vining.

Washington, D.C.: Arena Stage

(Artistic director, Douglas C. Wager; executive director, Stephen Richard)

DIRTY WORK. By Larry Brown and Richard Corley. January 21, 1994. Director, Richard Corley; scenery, Andrew Wood Boughton; costumes, Mildred Brignoni; lighting, Christopher Driscoll; sound, Timothy Thompson.

Walter James .... David Marks
Braiden Chaney .... Jeffrey V. Thompson
Diva .... Linda Cavell
Beth .... Kristina Smith
Randall; Sergeant .... Ralph Cosham
Buelah .... Sarah Marshall
Willie May .... Beverly Cosham
Young Braiden; Preacher;
Orderly .... Teagle F. Bougere
Jesus; Hugh-Jean; Big King
Hobbs .... Michael W. Howell
African Boy; Angel Child .... Anthony L. Thomas

Time: The late 1980s. Place: A V.A. Hospital. One intermission.

A SMALL WORLD. By Mustapha Matura. February 11, 1994. Director, Kyle Donnelly; scenery, Loy Arcenas; costumes, Paul Tazewell; lighting, Nancy Schertler; sound, David E. Smith.

Herman .... Wendell Wright
Carol .... Franchelle Stewart Dorn

Time and place: The play takes place in a small bar in Brooklyn in the early 1980s. One intermission.

SIN. By Wendy MacLeod. February 18, 1994. Director, Laurence Maslon; scenery, Andrew Wood Boughton; costumes, Joyce Kim Lee; lighting, Michele M. McDermott; sound, Timothy Thompson.

Avery Bly .... Cynthia Hood
Man .... Michael W. Howell
Michael .... Jerry Whiddon
Date .... TJ Edwards
Fred .... Richard Bauer
Jason .... M.E. Hart

Gerard .... Teagle F. Bougere
Act I, Scene 1: Lust. Scene 2: Sloth. Scene 3: Greed. Scene 4: Gluttony. Scene 5: Envy. Scene 6: Wrath. Scene 7: Pride. Act II: The streets of San Francisco.

BABES IN BOYLAND. By Lynn Martin. March 18, 1994. Director, Kyle Donnelly; scenery, Andrew Wood Boughton; costumes, Joyce Kim Lee; lighting, Christopher Driscoll; sound, Timothy Thompson.

Elaine .... Holly Twyford
Gigi .... Kate Fleming
Charlie .... Teagle F. Bougere
Stan .... TJ Edwards
Llew .... M.E. Hart
Fi .... Kristina Smith
Woman .... Sarah Marshall
Time: The present. Place: New York City. One intermission.

Waterbury, Conn.: Seven Angels Theater

(Artistic director, Semina De Laurentis)

THE CRIMSON THREAD. By Mary Hanes. Director, Dan Lauria; scenery, Thomas Cariello; costumes, Donna Trelford Fontana; lighting, Gene Lenahan; sound, Patrick Barrett, Jack Nardi.

CAST: Eilis McDermott Connelly, Fionnuala Connelly Kennedy—Stephanie Zimbalist; Bridget McDermott Flynn, Maggie Kennedy—Kathleen Noone; Kathleen Connelly Wright, Nora Kennedy Fitzpatrick—Shanna Reed.

Act: Ireland, 1869. Act II: New Bedford, Mass., 1889. Act III: A meeting hall in New York City, a week after the Shirtwaist fire.

Waterford, Conn.: Eugene O'Neill Theater Center

(Artistic director, Lloyd Richards)

1993 National Playwrights Conference, July 4-July 31, 1993

WHITE OAK. By Hunt Scarritt. July 10, 1993. Director, Oz Scott.

Stage Directions .... John Joseph
Hart .... Eric Roemele
Tater; Rocky; Jim; Priest .... Bryan Clark
T.C. .... John Seitz
Ted .... John Braden
Weston .... Walker Jones
Queenie .... Laurie Kennedy
Grand; Amy; D.D. .... Helen Stenborg
Mabel; Betty Sue .... Marcell Rosenblatt
Place: The Childerson residence, a decaying Victorian house.

YOU SEND ME. By Rick Cleveland. July 12, 1993. Director, Jay Broad.

Marty .... Bruce MacVittie
Pete; Mark: Young Marty .... Kevin Geer
Hanna .... Susan Knight
Bonnie; Judge; Ticket Agent; #3 Dog Owner; Doctor .... Julie Boyd
Cockrum; Dr. Berger; Tourist; #2 Dog Owner; Don; Rich .... Victor Raider-Wexler
Billy Shakespeare; Louis; Trooper; #1 Dog Owner; Scott; Weber; Truck Driver; Robertson .... Count Stovall

ENTRIES. By Bernardo Solano. July 13, 1993. Director, Amy Saltz.

Jorge Garcia .... Joe Urla
Timothy Adams; Paco; Bert; Arturo; Mosquitoes; Amaru; Madremonte; Jaguar .... Susan Gibney
Celestino; Boat Driver; Ernie; Ants; Termites; Trumpeter .... Adan Sanchez
Place: A virgin rain forest in the Colombian Amazon.

THE BOOK OF LAMB. By Kirk Aanes. July 15, 1993. Director, William Partlan.

Peter .... Jon DeVries
Luke .... Richard Thomsen
Frances .... Phyllis Somerville
Nick .... Reed Diamond
Popper .... Christopher Curry
Time: The present. Place: The sunroom and patio garden of a suburban home in Richfield, Minn. One intermission.

KILLING JAZZ. By Frederic Glover. July 16, 1993. Director, Oz Scott.

Blue .... Robert Knepper
Silas .... John Seitz
Ruth .... Laurie Kennedy
Jazz .... Angie Phillips
Time: December. Place: Keene Valley, an isolated community among the high peaks of the Adirondack Mountains in Upstate New York. One intermission.

TENDERNESS. By Jonas Gardell. July 16, 1933.

THE CRADLE OF MAYBE. By Gay Walch. July

19, 1993. Director, Jay Broad.
Jamie MacPherson .... Ryan Kistner
Selena Hollander; Sally .... Sharon Schlarth
Melissa Rayburn; Claire .... Susan Gibney
Dr. John Selpha; Charlie .... Victor Raider-Wexler
Aaron Auerback; Bill .... Kevin Geer
Judge Bennett .... Bryan Clark
Caroline Reese .... Susan Knight
Clifford Backus .... Kenneth L. Marks
Alfred Feyer .... Count Stovall
Jeffrey Krebs .... Bruce MacVittie
Dorice MacPherson .... Julie Boyd
Dolly Krebs; Susan .... Marcell Rosenblatt
One intermission.

THE INTERROGATION. By Evert Eden. July 21, 1993. Director, Amy Saltz.
James Mbongeni .... Michael Rogers
Hennie Potgieter .... Joe Urla
Dladla Mzamane .... Adrian Bethea
Colonel Goosen .... Jon DeVries
Sarah Jabavu .... Rosalyn Coleman
Time: 1990—on the eve of Nelson Mandela's release from jail. Place: An interrogation room in Johannesburg, South Africa.

A NAME FOR THE MOON. By Thomas W. Stephens. July 21, 1993. Director, William Partlan.
Lurine .... Katherine Borowitz
Kirby .... Christopher Curry
Tisha .... Alice Haining
Tay .... Reed Diamond
Alice .... Helen Stenborg
Rosalia .... Martha Thompson
Paulina .... Laurie Kennedy
Phronsie .... Phyllis Somerville
Camille .... Elizabeth Keiser
Act I, Scene 1: Kirby's kitchen, a day in late summer. Scene 2: A shed at Tay's place, later that day. Scene 3: Alice's porch, the next morning. Scene 4: The kitchen, that afternoon. Scene 5: Paulina's bedroom, later that afternoon. Scene 6: The yard at Tay's place, the next morning. Act II, Scene 7: The porch, the next day. Scene 8: The shed, that night. Scene 9: The bedroom, the next midday. Scene 10: The kitchen, that night. Scene 11: The yard, the next morning.

MYSTERIOUS CONNECTIONS. By Peter Hardy. July 23, 1993. Director, Oz Scott.
Pamela .... Angie Phillips
Travis; Dream Man .... Robert Knepper
Jonesy .... Greta Lambert
Isobel .... Zoey Zimmerman
Time: The present day. Place: Southeast. One intermission.

MARINA. By Youri Volkov. July 24, 1993.

17 BLACK. By William S. Leavengood. July 26, 1993. Director, Jay Broad.
John Wheelright .... Kenneth L. Marks
Houseboat .... Victor Raider-Wexler
Joe Marucci .... Count Stovall
Nance Wheelright .... Julie Boyd
Henry Wheelright .... Bruce MacVittie
Clyde Wheelright .... Bryan Clark
Robbie Wheelright .... Ryan Kistner
One intermission.

IN THE VALLEY OF THE HUMAN SPIRIT. By Lesli-Jo Morizono. July 28, 1993. Director, Oz Scott.
Cory .... Kiya Ann Joyce
Sam .... Ernest Abuba
Cory's Mother; Cory's Grandmother .... Lori Tan Chinn
Sam's Father; Husband .... Ron Nakahara
Wife .... Ginny Yang
Real Estate Broker .... Susan Knight
Michael; Soldier; Thatcher Brother; Cop #1 .... Kevin Geer
Sanders; Soldier; Thatcher Brother; Cop #2 .... Joe Urla
Time: 1989. Place: Fresno, Calif.

LOCKED DOORS AND LIGHTNING BUGS. By Jett Parsley. July 30, 1993. Director, Oz Scott.
Robert Madison; Phil .... Reed Diamond
Shannon Anchor .... Laurie Kennedy
Philadelphia .... Theresa Jarvis
Thurman Anchor .... Christopher Curry
Philly Anchor .... Kellie Overbey
Davis Banks .... Marcus Giamatti
Jane Patterson .... Helen Stenborg
Time: A timeless place. Place: Act I: Elon, N.C., upstairs in the Anchor household. Act II: The house in Elon and Jane Patterson's house in Charleston. Act III: The house in Elon.

All National Playwrights Conference plays: Scenery, G.W. Mercier, Charles McClennahan; lighting, Tina Charney; sound, Philip Hanson, Michael Sonnenschein.

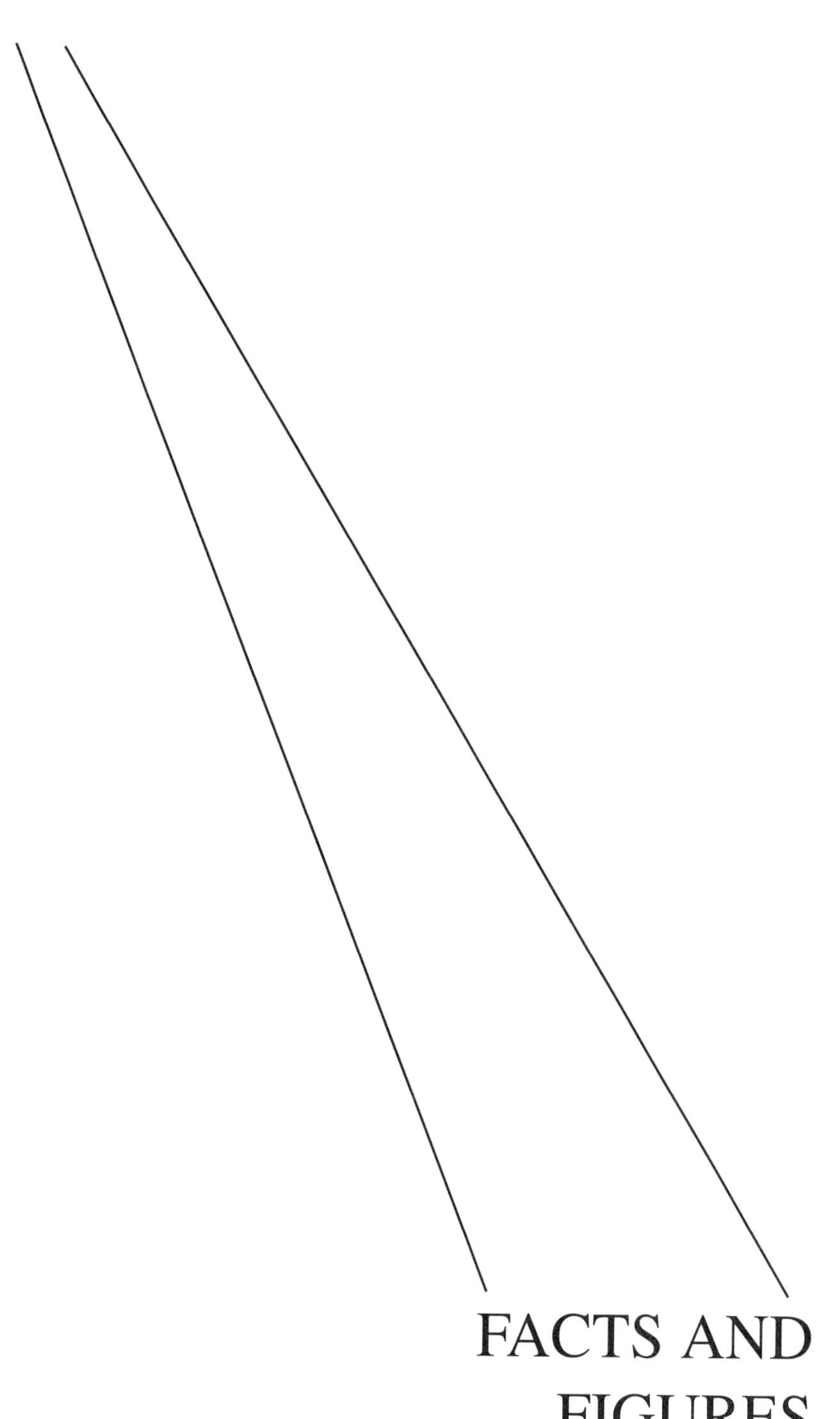

FACTS AND FIGURES

LONG RUNS ON BROADWAY

The following shows have run 500 or more continuous performances in a single production, usually the first, not including previews or extra non-profit performances, allowing for vacation layoffs and special one-booking engagements, but not including return engagements after a show has gone on tour. In all cases, the numbers were obtained directly from the show's production offices. Where there are title similarities, the production is identified as follows: (p) straight play version, (m) musical version, (r) revival, (tr) transfer.

THROUGH MAY 31, 1994

(PLAYS MARKED WITH ASTERISK WERE STILL PLAYING JUNE 1, 1994)

Plays	*Number Performances*
A Chorus Line	6,137
Oh! Calcutta! (r)	5,959
*Cats	4,862
42nd Street	3,486
Grease	3,388
Fiddler on the Roof	3,242
Life With Father	3,224
Tobacco Road	3,182
*Les Misérables	2,949
Hello, Dolly!	2,844
My Fair Lady	2,717
*The Phantom of the Opera	2,650
Annie	2,377
Man of La Mancha	2,328
Abie's Irish Rose	2,327
Oklahoma!	2,212
Pippin	1,944
South Pacific	1,925
The Magic Show	1,920
Deathtrap	1,793
Gemini	1,788
Harvey	1,775
Dancin'	1,774
La Cage aux Folles	1,761
Hair	1,750
The Wiz	1,672
Born Yesterday	1,642
The Best Little Whorehouse in Texas	1,639
Ain't Misbehavin'	1,604
Mary, Mary	1,572
Evita	1,567
The Voice of the Turtle	1,557
Barefoot in the Park	1,530
Brighton Beach Memoirs	1,530
Dreamgirls	1,522
Mame (m)	1,508
Same Time, Next Year	1,453
Arsenic and Old Lace	1,444
The Sound of Music	1,443
Me and My Girl	1,420
How to Succeed in Business Without Really Trying	1,417
Hellzapoppin	1,404
The Music Man	1,375
Funny Girl	1,348
Mummenschanz	1,326
*Miss Saigon	1,310
Angel Street	1,295
Lightnin'	1,291
Promises, Promises	1,281
The King and I	1,246
Cactus Flower	1,234
Sleuth	1,222
Torch Song Trilogy	1,222
1776	1,217
Equus	1,209
Sugar Babies	1,208
Guys and Dolls	1,200
Amadeus	1,181
Cabaret	1,165
Mister Roberts	1,157
Anni Get Your Gun	1,147
The Seven Year Itch	1,141
Butterflies Are Free	1,128
Pins and Needles	1,108

Plays	Number Performances
Plaza Suite	1,097
They're Playing Our Song	1,082
Grand Hotel (m)	1,077
Kiss Me, Kate	1,070
Don't Bother Me, I Can't Cope	1,065
The Pajama Game	1,063
Shenandoah	1,050
The Teahouse of the August Moon	1,027
Damn Yankees	1,019
Never Too Late	1,007
Big River	1,005
The Will Rogers Follies	983
Any Wednesday	982
A Funny Thing Happened on the Way to the Forum	964
The Odd Couple	964
Anna Lucasta	957
Kiss and Tell	956
*Crazy for You	952
Dracula (r)	925
Bells Are Ringing	924
The Moon Is Blue	924
Beatlemania	920
The Elephant Man	916
Luv	901
Chicago (m)	898
Applause	896
Can-Can	892
Carousel	890
I'm Not Rappaport	890
Hats Off to Ice	889
Fanny	888
*Guys and Dolls (r)	888
Children of a Lesser God	887
Follow the Girls	882
City of Angels	878
Camelot	873
I Love My Wife	872
The Bat	867
My Sister Eileen	864
No, No, Nanette (r)	861
Song of Norway	860
Chapter Two	857
A Streetcar Named Desire	855
Barnum	854
Comedy in Music	849
Raisin	847
You Can't Take It With You	837
La Plume de Ma Tante	835
Three Men on a Horse	835
The Subject Was Roses	832
Black and Blue	824
Inherit the Wind	806
Anything Goes (r)	804
No Time for Sergeants	796
Fiorello!	795
Where's Charley?	792
The Ladder	789
Forty Carats	780
Lost in Yonkers	780
The Prisoner of Second Avenue	780
M. Butterfly	777
Oliver!	774
The Pirates of Penzance (1980 r)	772
Woman of the Year	770
My One and Only	767
Sophisticated Ladies	767
Bubbling Brown Sugar	766
Into the Woods	765
State of the Union	765
Starlight Express	761
The First Year	760
Broadway Bound	756
You Know I Can't Hear You When the Water's Running	755
Two for the Seesaw	750
Joseph and the Amazing Technicolor Dreamcoat (r)	747
Death of a Salesman	742
For Colored Girls, etc.	742
Sons o' Fun	742
Candide (m, r)	740
Gentlemen Prefer Blondes	740
The Man Who Came to Dinner	739
Nine	739
Call Me Mister	734
West Side Story	732
High Button Shoes	727
Finian's Rainbow	725
Claudia	722
The Gold Diggers	720
Jesus Christ Superstar	720
Carnival	719
The Diary of Anne Frank	717
I Remember Mama	714
Tea and Sympathy	712
Junior Miss	710

Plays	*Number Performances*
Last of the Red Hot Lovers	706
The Secret Garden	706
Company	705
Seventh Heaven	704
Gypsy (m)	702
The Miracle Worker	700
That Championship Season	700
Da	697
The King and I (r)	696
Cat on a Hot Tin Roof	694
Li'l Abner	693
The Children's Hour	691
Purlie	688
Dead End	687
The Lion and the Mouse	686
White Cargo	686
Dear Ruth	683
East Is West	680
Come Blow Your Horn	677
The Most Happy Fella	676
The Doughgirls	671
The Impossible Years	670
Irene	670
Boy Meets Girl	669
The Tap Dance Kid	669
Beyond the Fringe	667
Who's Afraid of Virginia Woolf?	664
Blithe Spirit	657
A Trip to Chinatown	657
The Women	657
Bloomer Girl	654
The Fifth Season	654
Rain	648
Witness for the Prosecution	645
Call Me Madam	644
Janie	642
The Green Pastures	640
Auntie Mame (p)	639
A Man for All Seasons	637
Jerome Robbins' Broadway	634
The Fourposter	632
The Music Master	627
Two Gentlemen of Verona (m)	627
The Tenth Man	623
The Heidi Chronicles	621
Is Zat So?	618
Anniversary Waltz	615
The Happy Time (p)	614

Plays	*Number Performances*
Separate Rooms	613
Affairs of State	610
Oh! Calcutta! (tr)	610
Star and Garter	609
The Mystery of Edwin Drood	608
The Student Prince	608
Sweet Charity	608
Bye Bye Birdie	607
Irene (r)	604
Sunday in the Park With George	604
Adonis	603
Broadway	603
Peg o' My Heart	603
Street Scene (p)	601
Flower Drum Song	600
Kiki	600
A Little Night Music	600
Agnes of God	599
Don't Drink the Water	598
Wish You Were Here	598
Sarafina!	597
A Society Circus	596
Absurd Person Singular	592
A Day in Hollywood/A Night in the Ukraine	588
The Me Nobody Knows	586
The Two Mrs. Carrolls	585
Kismet (m)	583
Gypsy (m, r)	582
Brigadoon	581
Detective Story	581
No Strings	580
Brother Rat	577
Blossom Time	576
Pump Boys and Dinettes	573
Show Boat	572
The Show-Off	571
Sally	570
Jelly's Last Jam	569
Golden Boy (m)	568
One Touch of Venus	567
The Real Thing	566
Happy Birthday	564
Look Homeward, Angel	564
Morning's at Seven (r)	564
The Glass Menagerie	561
I Do! I Do!	560
Wonderful Town	559

Plays	*Number Performances*
Rose Marie	557
Strictly Dishonorable	557
Sweeney Todd, the Demon Barber of Fleet Street	557
The Great White Hope	556
A Majority of One	556
Sunrise at Campobello	556
Toys in the Attic	556
Jamaica	555
Stop the World—I Want to Get Off	555
Florodora	553
Noises Off	553
Ziegfeld Follies (1943)	553
Dial "M" for Murder	552
Good News	551
Peter Pan (r)	551
Let's Face It	547
Milk and Honey	543
Within the Law	541
Pal Joey (r)	540
What Makes Sammy Run?	540
The Sunshine Boys	538
What a Life	538
Crimes of the Heart	535
The Unsinkable Molly Brown	532
The Red Mill (r)	531
Rumors	531
A Raisin in the Sun	530
Godspell (tr)	527
Fences	526

Plays	*Number Performances*
The Solid Gold Cadillac	526
Biloxi Blues	524
Irma La Douce	524
The Boomerang	522
Folies	521
Rosalinda	521
The Best Man	520
Chauve-Souris	520
Blackbirds of 1928	518
The Gin Game	517
Sunny	517
Victoria Regina	517
Fifth of July	511
Half a Sixpence	511
The Vagabond King	511
The New Moon	509
The World of Suzie Wong	508
The Rothschilds	507
On Your Toes (r)	505
Sugar	505
Shuffle Along	504
Up in Central Park	504
Carmen Jones	503
The Member of the Wedding	501
Panama Hattie	501
Personal Appearance	501
*The Sisters Rosensweig	501
Bird in Hand	500
Room Service	500
Sailor, Beware!	500
Tomorrow the World	500

LONG RUNS OFF BROADWAY

Plays	*Number Performances*
*The Fantasticks	14,103
*Nunsense	3,513
*Perfect Crime	2,908
The Threepenny Opera	2,611
Forbidden Broadway 1982-87	2,332
Little Shop of Horrors	2,209
Godspell	2,124
*Tony 'n' Tina's Wedding	2,062
Vampire Lesbians of Sodom	2,024

Plays	*Number Performances*
Jacques Brel	1,847
*Forever Plaid	1,794
Vanities	1,785
You're a Good Man Charlie Brown	1,597
The Blacks	1,408
One Mo' Time	1,372
Let My People Come	1,327
Driving Miss Daisy	1,195
The Hot 1 Baltimore	1,166

Plays	*Number Performances*
I'm Getting My Act Together and Taking It on the Road	1,165
Little Mary Sunshine	1,143
Steel Magnolias	1,126
El Grande de Coca-Cola	1,114
The Proposition	1,109
Beau Jest	1,069
*Tubes	1,044
Tamara	1,036
One Flew Over the Cuckoo's Nest (r)	1,025
The Boys in the Band	1,000
Fool for Love	1,000
Other People's Money	990
Cloud 9	971
Sister Mary Ignatius Explains It All for You & The Actor's Nightmare	947
Your Own Thing	933
Curley McDimple	931
Leave It to Jane (r)	928
The Mad Show	871
Scrambled Feet	831
The Effect of Gamma Rays on Man-in-the-Moon Marigolds	819
A View From the Bridge (r)	780
The Boy Friend (r)	763
True West	762
Isn't It Romantic	733
Dime a Dozen	728
The Pocket Watch	725
The Connection	722
The Passion of Dracula	714
Adaptation & Next	707
Oh! Calcutta!	704
Scuba Duba	692

Plays	*Number Performances*
The Foreigner	686
The Knack	685
The Club	674
The Balcony	672
Penn & Teller	666
America Hurrah	634
Oil City Symphony	626
Hogan's Goat	607
Beehive	600
The Trojan Women	600
The Dining Room	583
Krapp's Last Tape & The Zoo Story	582
The Dumbwaiter & The Collection	578
Forbidden Broadway 1990	576
Dames at Sea	575
The Crucible (r)	571
The Iceman Cometh (r)	565
The Hostage (r)	545
What's a Nice Country Like You Doing in a State Like This?	543
Forbidden Broadway 1988	534
Frankie and Johnny in the Clair de Lune	533
Six Characters in Search of an Author (r)	529
Oleanna	513
The Dirtiest Show in Town	509
Happy Ending & Day of Absence	504
Greater Tuna	501
A Shayna Maidel	501
The Boys From Syracuse (r)	500

NEW YORK DRAMA CRITICS CIRCLE AWARDS, 1935–36 TO 1993–94

Listed below are the New York Drama Critics Circle Awards from 1935–36 through 1993–94 classified as follows: (1) Best American Play, (2) Best Foreign Play, (3) Best Musical, (4) Best, regardless of category (this category was established by new voting rules in 1962–63 and did not exist prior to that year.)

1935–36—(1) Winterset
1936–37—(1) High Tor
1937–38—(1) Of Mice and Men, (2) Shadow and Substance
1938–39—(1) No award, (2) The White Steed
1939–40—(1) The Time of Your Life
1940–41—(1) Watch on the Rhine, (2) The Corn Is Green
1941–42—(1) No award, (2) Blithe Spirit
1942–43—(1) The Patriots
1943–44—(2) Jacobowsky and the Colonel
1944–45—(1) The Glass Menagerie
1945–46—(3) Carousel
1946–47—(1) All My Sons, (2) No Exit, (3) Brigadoon
1947–48—(1) A Streetcar Named Desire, (2) The Winslow Boy
1948–49—(1) Death of a Salesman, (2) The Madwoman of Chaillot, (3) South Pacific
1949–50—(1) The Member of the Wedding, (2) The Cocktail Party, (3) The Consul
1950–51—(1) Darkness at Noon, (2) The Lady's Not for Burning, (3) Guys and Dolls
1951–52—(1) I Am a Camera, (2) Venus Observed, (3) Pal Joey (Special citation to Don Juan in Hell)
1952–53—(1) Picnic, (2) The Love of Four Colonels, (3) Wonderful Town
1953–54—(1) The Teahouse of the August Moon, (2) Ondine, (3) The Golden Apple
1954–55—(1) Cat on a Hot Tin Roof, (2) Witness for the Prosecution, (3) The Saint of Bleecker Street
1955–56—(1) The Diary of Anne Frank, (2) Tiger at the Gates, (3) My Fair Lady
1956–57—(1) Long Day's Journey Into Night, (2) The Waltz of the Toreadors, (3) The Most Happy Fella
1957–58—(1) Look Homeward, Angel, (2) Look Back in Anger, (3) The Music Man
1958–59—(1) A Raisin in the Sun, (2) The Visit, (3) La Plume de Ma Tante
1959–60—(1) Toys in the Attic, (2) Five Finger Exercise, (3) Fiorello!
1960–61—(1) All the Way Home, (2) A Taste of Honey, (3) Carnival
1961–62—(1) The Night of the Iguana, (2) A Man for All Seasons, (3) How to Succeed in Business Without Really Trying
1962–63—(4) Who's Afraid of Virginia Woolf? (Special citation to Beyond the Fringe)
1963–64—(4) Luther, (3) Hello, Dolly! (Special citation to The Trojan Women)
1964–65—(4) The Subject Was Roses, (3) Fiddler on the Roof
1965–66—(4) The Persecution and Assassination of Marat as Performed by the Inmates of the Asylum of Charenton Under the Direction of the Marquis de Sade, (3) Man of La Mancha
1966–67—(4) The Homecoming, (3) Cabaret
1967–68—(4) Rosencrantz and Guildenstern Are Dead, (3) Your Own Thing
1968–69—(4) The Great White Hope, (3) 1776
1969–70—(4) Borstal Boy, (1) The Effect of Gamma Rays on Man–in–the–Moon Marigolds, (3) Company
1970–71—(4) Home, (1) The House of Blue Leaves, (3) Follies
1971–72—(4) That Championship Season, (2) The Screens, (3) Two Gentlemen of Verona (Special citations to Sticks and Bones and Old Times)
1972–73—(4) The Changing Room, (1) The Hot 1 Baltimore, (3) A Little Night Music
1973–74—(4) The Contractor, (1) Short Eyes, (3) Candide
1974–75—(4) Equus (1) The Taking of Miss Janie, (3) A Chorus Line
1975–76—(4) Travesties, (1) Streamers, (3) Pacific Overtures
1976–77—(4) Otherwise Engaged, (1) American Buffalo, (3) Annie
1977–78—(4) Da, (3) Ain't Misbehavin'
1978–79—(4) The Elephant Man, (3) Sweeney Todd, the Demon Barber of Fleet Street
1979–80—(4) Talley's Folly, (2) Betrayal, (3) Evita (Special citation to Peter Brook's Le Centre International de Créations Theâtrales for its repertory)
1980–81—(4) A Lesson From Aloes, (1) Crimes of the Heart (Special citations to Lena Horne:

The Lady and Her Music and the New York Shakespeare Festival production of The Pirates of Penzance)
1981–82—(4) The Life & Adventures of Nicholas Nickleby, (1) A Soldier's Play
1982–83—(4) Brighton Beach Memoirs, (2) Plenty, (3) Little Shop of Horrors (Special citation to Young Playwrights Festival)
1983–84—(4) The Real Thing, (1) Glengarry Glen Ross, (3) Sunday in the Park With George (Special citation to Samuel Beckett for the body of his work)
1984–85—(4) Ma Rainey's Black Bottom
1985–86—(4) A Lie of the Mind, (2) Benefactors (Special citation to The Search for Signs of Intelligent Life in the Universe)
1986–87—(4) Fences, (2) Les Liaisons Dangereuses, (3) Les Misérables
1987–88—(4) Joe Turner's Come and Gone, (2) The Road to Mecca, (3) Into the Woods
1988–89—(4) The Heidi Chronicles, (2) Aristocrats (Special citation to Bill Irwin for Largely New York)
1989–90—(4) The Piano Lesson, (2) Privates on Parade, (3) City of Angels
1990–91—(4) Six Degrees of Separation, (2) Our Country's Good, (3) The Will Rogers Follies (Special citation to Eileen Atkins for her portrayal of Virginia Woolf in A Room of One's Own)
1991–92—(4) Dancing at Lughnasa, (1) Two Trains Running
1992–93—(4) Angels in America: Millennium Approaches, (2) Someone Who'll Watch Over Me, (3) Kiss of the Spider Woman
1993–94—(4) Three Tall Women (Special citation to Anna Deavere Smith for her unique contribution to theatrical form)

NEW YORK DRAMA CRITICS CIRCLE VOTING, 1993–94

Three Tall Women by Edward Albee was voted the best play of the season in New York Drama Critics Circle balloting, closely contested by *Angels in America, Part II: Perestroika* by Tony Kushner and with strong support for Anna Deavere Smith's *Twilight: Los Angeles, 1992,* Robert Schenkkan's *The Kentucky Cycle* and Alan Bennett's *The Madness of George III*. After no play received a majority on the first ballot (first–place votes only), with *Three Tall Women* and *Perestroika* leading, under the Critics rules the 18 members present proceeded to a second, weighted ballet naming first, second and third choices receiving 3, 2 and 1 points, respectively, for each vote (see summary of this ballot below). *Three Tall Women* won with 31 points (to win on this ballot a play must receive a point total of three times the number of members present, divided by two, plus one—28 this year), against 26 for *Perestroika*, 14 for *Twilight: Los Angeles, 1992*, 10 for *The Kentucky Cycle* and *The Madness of George III*, 7 for Arthur Miller's *Broken Glass*, 3 for Brian Friel's *Wonderful Tennessee* and Howard Korder's *The Lights* and one each for John Patrick Shanley's *Four Dogs and a Bone*, Terrence McNally's *A Perfect Ganesh* and Diane Samuels's *Kindertransport*.

Having cited an American play as the best of the season regardless of category, the Critics then decided to give no award this year for a best foreign play (though *The Madness of George III* had strong support in the previous balloting) or for a best musical. They did, however, award a special citation to Anna Deavere Smith for her "unique contribution to theatrical form."

SECOND BALLOT FOR BEST PLAY

Critic	*1st Choice (3 pts.)*	*2d Choice (2 pts.)*	*3d Choice (1 pt.)*
Clive Barnes *Post*	Three Tall Women	Wonderful Tennessee	Four Dogs and a Bone
Mary Campbell AP	Angels in America, Part II: Perestroika	Broken Glass	The Kentucky Cycle
Greg Evans *Variety*	Perestroika	Twilight: Los Angeles, 1992	Three Tall Women
Michael Feingold *Village Voice*	Twilight: L.A.	Three Tall Women	Broken Glass
Jeremy Gerard *Variety*	Perestroika	Three Tall Women	Broken Glass
William A. Henry III *Time*	The Kentucky Cycle	Three Tall Women	A Perfect Ganesh
Melanie Kirkpatrick *Wall St. Journal*	Three Tall Women	Kindertransport	The Madness of George III
Howard Kissel *Daily News*	Three Tall Women	Madness George III	Wonderful Tennessee
Michael Kuchwara AP	Perestroika	Three Tall Women	Broken Glass
Jacques le Sourd Gannett Newspapers	Three Tall Women	Madness George III	The Lights
Julius Novick *Newsday*	Madness George III	Perestroika	Broken Glass
Frank Scheck *Monitor*	The Kentucky Cycle	Perestroika	Three Tall Women
John Simon *New York*	Three Tall Women	Madness George III	Twilight: L.A.
Michael Sommers Newhouse Newspapers	Twilight: L.A.	Three Tall Women	Perestroika
David Patrick Stearns *USA Today*	Perestroika	The Kentucky Cycle	Twilight: L.A.
Jan Stuart *Newsday*	Perestroika	The Lights	Twilight: L.A.
Edwin Wilson *Wall St. Journal*	Three Tall Women	Broken Glass	The Kentucky Cycle
Linda Winer *Newsday*	Perestroika	Twilight: L.A.	Three Tall Women

CHOICES OF SOME OTHER CRITICS

	Best Play	*Best Musical*
Joy Browne WOR	Medea	Passion
Casper Citron Casper Citron Program	Angels in America	Beauty and the Beast
Stephen Dubner *New York Magazine*	Broken Glass	Passion
Alvin Klein N.Y. *Times* Suburban, WNYC	An Inspector Calls	She Loves Me
Joseph Koenenn *Newsday*	Three Tall Women	Hello Again
Pia Lindstrom WNBC, NBC	Three Tall Women	Passion
Art Martinez Newark *Star Ledger*	An Inspector Calls	Carousel
James McLaughlin CBS	Perestroika	Passion
Joel Siegel WABC-TV	Three Tall Women	Abstain
Leida Snow	Three Tall Women	Abstain
Marilyn Stasio	Three Tall Women	Passion
Roma Torre New York-1	The Kentucky Cycle	Beauty and the Beast
Allan Wallach	Perestroika	Passion
William Wolf William Wolf Features	Perestroika	Passion

PULITZER PRIZE WINNERS, 1916–17 TO 1993–94

1916–17—No award
1917–18—Why Marry?, by Jesse Lynch Williams
1918–19—No award
1919–20—Beyond the Horizon, by Eugene O'Neill
1920–21—Miss Lulu Bett, by Zona Gale
1921–22—Anna Christie, by Eugene O'Neill
1922–23—Icebound, by Owen Davis
1923–24—Hell-Bent fer Heaven, by Hatcher Hughes
1924–25—They Knew What They Wanted, by Sidney Howard
1925–26—Craig's Wife, by George Kelly
1926–27—In Abraham's Bosom, by Paul Green
1927–28—Strange Interlude, by Eugene O'Neill
1928–29—Street Scene, by Elmer Rice
1929–30—The Green Pastures, by Marc Connelly
1930–31—Alison's House, by Susan Glaspell
1931–32—Of Thee I Sing, by George S. Kaufman, Morrie Ryskind, Ira and George Gershwin
1932–33—Both Your Houses, by Maxwell Anderson
1933–34—Men in White, by Sidney Kingsley
1934–35—The Old Maid, by Zoe Akins
1935–36—Idiot's Delight, by Robert E. Sherwood
1936–37—You Can't Take It With You, by Moss Hart and George S. Kaufman
1937–38—Our Town, by Thornton Wilder
1938–39—Abe Lincoln in Illinois, by Robert E. Sherwood
1939–40—The Time of Your Life, by William Saroyan
1940–41—There Shall Be No Night, by Robert E. Sherwood
1941–42—No award
1942–43—The Skin of Our Teeth, by Thornton Wilder
1943–44—No award

1944–45—Harvey, By Mary Chase
1945–46—State of the Union, by Howard Lindsay and Russel Crouse
1946–47—No award
1947–48—A Streetcar Named Desire, by Tennessee Williams
1948–49—Death of a Salesman, by Arthur Miller
1949–50—South Pacific, by Richard Rodgers, Oscar Hammerstein II and Joshua Logan
1950–51—No award
1951–52—The Shrike, by Joseph Kramm
1952–53—Picnic, by William Inge
1953–54—The Teahouse of the August Moon, by John Patrick
1954–55—Cat on a Hot Tin Roof, by Tennessee Williams
1955–56—The Diary of Anne Frank, by Frances Goodrich and Albert Hackett
1956–57—Long Day's Journey Into Night, by Eugene O'Neill
1957–58—Look Homeward, Angel, by Ketti Frings
1958–59—J.B., by Archibald MacLeish
1959–60—Fiorello!, by Jerome Weidman, George Abbott, Sheldon Harnick and Jerry Block
1960–61—All the Way Home, by Tad Mosel
1961–62—How to Succeed in Business Without Really Trying, by Abe Burrows, Willie Gilbert, Jack Weinstock and Frank Loesser
1962–63—No award
1963–64—No award
1964–65—The Subject Was Roses, by Frank D. Gilroy
1965–66—No award
1966–67—A Delicate Balance, by Edward Albee
1967–68—No award
1968–69—The Great White Hope, by Howard Sackler
1969–70—No Place to Be Somebody, by Charles Gordone
1970–71—The Effect of Gamma Rays on Man–in–the –Moon Marigolds, by Paul Zindel
1971–72—No award
1972–73—That Championship Season, by Jason Miller
1973–74—No award
1974–75—Seascape, by Edward Albee
1975–76—A Chorus Line, by Michael Bennett, James Kirkwood, Nicholas Dante, Marvin Hamlisch and Edward Kleban
1976–77—The Shadow Box, by Michael Cristofer
1977–78—The Gin Game, by D.L. Coburn
1978–79—Buried Child, by Sam Shepard
1979–80—Talley's Folly, by Lanford Wilson
1980–81—Crimes of the Heart, by Beth Henley
1981–82—A Soldier's Play, by Charles Fuller
1982–83—'night, Mother, by Marsha Norman
1983–84—Glengarry Glen Ross, by David Mamet
1984–85—Sunday in the Park With George, by James Lapine and Stephen Sondheim
1985–86—No award
1986–87—Fences, by August Wilson
1987–88—Driving Miss Daisy, by Alfred Uhry
1988–89—The Heidi Chronicles, by Wendy Wasserstein
1989–90—The Piano Lesson, by August Wilson
1990–91—Lost in Yonkers, by Neil Simon
1991–92—The Kentucky Cycle, by Robert Schenkkan
1992–93—Angels in America: Millennium Approaches, by Tony Kushner
1993–94—Three Tall Women, by Edward Albee

THE TONY AWARDS, 1993–94

The American Theater Wing's Antoinette Perry (Tony) Awards are presented annually in recognition of distinguished artistic achievement in the Broadway theater. The League of American Theaters and Producers and the American Theater Wing present the Tony Awards, founded by the Wing in 1947. Legitimate theater productions opening in eligible Broadway theaters during the eligibility season of the current year—May 6, 1993 to May 11, 1994—were considered for Tony nominations.

The Tony Awards Administration Committee appoints the Tony Awards Nominating Committee which makes the actual nominations. The 1993–94 Nominating Committee consisted of Donald Brooks, costume designer; Marge Champion, choreographer; Betty L. Corwin, theater archivist; Gretchen Cryer, composer; Thomas

BEAUTY AND THE BEAST—Terrence Mann and Susan Egan as the Beast and Belle in the Howard Ashman-Alan Menken-Tim Rice-Linda Woolverton musical produced by Walt Disney Productions, a multiple Tony nominee and the winner of the Best Costumes Tony for the designs of Ann Hould-Ward

Dillon, administrator; Brendan Gill, historian, writer; Jay Harnick, artistic director; Eileen Heckart, actress; Arthur Kopit, playwright; Robert Lewis, director, educator; Suzanne Sato, arts executive; Sister Francesca Thompson, theater educator; and George White, administrator.

This year, for the first time, because of the large number of revivals that opened on Broadway, the category of best revival was split in two (for play and musical). Also, the 1994 rules and regulations required the Nominating Committee to select four nominees in each category. In three categories they unanimously requested a reduction in the number of nominees. In two of these categories (best musical and best score) that request was denied by the Tony Administration Sub Committee.

The Tony Awards are voted from the list of nominees by the members of the governing boards of five theater organizations: Actors' Equity Association, the Dramatists Guild, the Society of Stage Directors and Choreographers, the United Scenic Artists and the Casting Society of America, plus the members of the designated first night theater press, the board of directors of the American Theater Wing and the membership of the League of American Theaters and Producers. Because of fluctuation within these boards, the size of the Tony electorate varies from year to year. For the 1993–94 season, there were 687 qualified Tony voters.

The list of 1993–94 nominees follows, with winners in each category listed in **bold face type**.

BEST PLAY (award goes to both author and producer). ***Angels in America, Part II: Perestroika*** by **Tony Kushner**, produced by **Jujamcyn Theaters, Mark Taper Forum/Gordon Davidson, Margo Lion, Susan Quint Gallin, Jon B. Platt, The Baruch–Frankel–Viertel Group, Frederick Zollo, Herb Alpert;** *Broken Glass* by Arthur Miller, produced by Robert Whitehead, Roger L. Stevens, Lars Schmidt, Spring Sirkin, Terri & Timothy Childs, Herb Alpert; *The Kentucky Cycle* by Robert Schenkkan, produced by David Richenthal, Gene R. Korf, Roger L. Stevens, Jennifer Manocherian, Annett Niemtzow, Mark Taper Forum/Intiman Theater Company, The John F. Kennedy Center for the Performing Arts, Benjamin Mordecai; *Twilight: Los Angeles, 1992* by Anna Deavere Smith, produced by Benjamin Mordecai, Laura Rafaty, Ric Wanetik, New York Shakespeare Festival, Mark Taper Forum, Harriet Newman Leve, Jeanne Rizzo, James D. Stern, Daryl Roth, Jo–Lynne Worley, Ronald A. Pizzuti, The Booking Office, Inc., Freddy Beinstock.

BEST MUSICAL (award goes to the producer). *A Grand Night for Singing* produced by Roundabout Theater Company, Todd Haimes, Gregory Dawson, Steve Paul; *Beauty and the Beast* produced by Walt Disney Productions; *Cyrano: The Musical* produced by Joop Van Den Ende, Peter T. Kulok; ***Passion*** produced by **The Shubert Organization, Capital Cities/ABC, Roger Berlind, Scott Rudin, Lincoln Center** Theater.

BEST BOOK OF A MUSICAL. *A Grand Night for Singing* by Walter Bobbie; *Beauty and the Beast* by Linda Woolverton; *Cyrano: The Musical* by Koen Van Dijk; ***Passion*** by **James Lapine.**

BEST ORIGINAL SCORE (music & lyrics) WRITTEN FOR THE THEATER (only three nominees in this category). *Beauty and the Beast*, music by Alan Menken, lyrics by Howard Ashman and Tim Rice; *Cyrano: The Musical*, music by Ad Van Dijk, lyrics by Koen Van Dijk, Peter Reeves and Sheldon Harnick; ***Passion,*** music and lyrics by **Stephen Sondheim.**

BEST LEADING ACTOR IN A PLAY. Brian Bedford in *Timon of Athens*, Christopher Plummer in *No Man's Land*, **Stephen Spinella** in *Perestroika*, Sam Waterston in *Abe Lincoln in Illinois*.

BEST LEADING ACTRESS IN A PLAY. Nancy Marchand in *Black Comedy,* **Diana Rigg** in *Medea,* Joan Rivers in *Sally Marr . . . and Her Escorts,* Anna Deavere Smith in *Twilight: Los Angeles, 1992*.

BEST LEADING ACTOR IN A MUSICAL. **Boyd Gaines** in *She Loves Me*, Victor Garber in *Damn Yankees*, Terrence Mann in *Beauty and the Beast*, Jere Shea in *Passion*.

BEST LEADING ACTRESS IN A MUSICAL. Susan Egan in *Beauty and the Beast*, Dee Hoty in *The Best Little Whorehouse Goes Public*, Judy Kuhn in *She Loves Me*, **Donna Murphy** in *Passion*.

BEST FEATURED ACTOR IN A PLAY. Larry Bryggman in *Picnic*, David Marshall Grant in *Perestroika*, Gregory Itzin in *The Kentucky Cycle*, **Jeffrey Wright** in *Perestroika*.

BEST FEATURED ACTRESS IN A PLAY. **Jane Adams** in *An Inspector Calls*, Debra Monk in *Picnic*, Jeanne Paulsen in *The Kentucky Cycle*, Anne Pitoniak in *Picnic*.

BEST FEATURED ACTOR IN A MUSICAL. Tom Aldredge in *Passion*, Gary Beach in *Beauty and the Beast*, **Jarrod Emick** in *Damn Yankees*, Jonathan Freeman in *She Loves Me*.

BEST FEATURED ACTRESS IN A MUSICAL. Marcia Lewis in *Grease*, Sally Mayes in *She Loves Me*, Marin Mazzie in *Passion*, **Audra Ann McDonald** in *Carousel*.

BEST DIRECTION OF A PLAY. **Stephen Daldry** for *An Inspector Calls*, Gerald Gutierrez for *Abe Lincoln in Illinois*, Michael Langham for *Timon of Athens*, George C. Wolfe for *Perestroika*.

BEST DIRECTION OF A MUSICAL. Scott Ellis for *She Loves Me*, **Nicholas Hytner** for *Carousel*, James Lapine for *Passion*, Robert Jess Roth for *Beauty and the Beast*.

BEST SCENIC DESIGN. **Bob Crowley** for *Carousel*, Peter J. Davison for *Medea*, Ian MacNeil for *An Inspector Calls*, Tony Walton for *She Loves Me*.

BEST COSTUME DESIGN. David Charles and Jane Greenwood for *She Loves Me*, Jane Greenwood for *Passion*, **Ann Hould–Ward** for *Beauty and the Beast*, Yan Tax for *Cyrano: The Musical.*

BEST LIGHTING DESIGN. Beverly Emmons for *Passion*, Jules Fisher for *Perestroika*, **Rick Fisher** for *An Inspector Calls*, Natasha Katz for *Beauty and the Beast.*

BEST CHOREOGRAPHY. Jeff Calhoun for *Grease*, **Kenneth MacMillan** for *Carousel*, Rob Marshall for *Damn Yankees*, Rob Marshall for *She Loves Me.*

BEST REVIVAL OF A PLAY (award goes to the producer). *Abe Lincoln in Illinois* produced by Lincoln Center Theater, Andre Bishop, Bernard Gersten; ***An Inspector Calls*** produced by **Noel Pearson, The Shubert Organization, Capital Cities/ABC, Joseph Harris;** *Medea* produced by Bill Kenwright; *Timon of Athens* produced by National Actors Theater, Tony Randall, Michael Langham.

BEST REVIVAL OF A MUSICAL (award goes to the producer). ***Carousel*** produced by **Lincoln Center Theater, Andre Bishop, Bernard Gersten, The Royal National Theater, Cameron Mackintosh, The Rodgers & Hammerstein Organization;** *Damn Yankees* produced by Mitchell Maxwell, PolyGram Diversified Entertainment, Dan Markley, Kevin McCollum, Victoria Maxwell, Fred H. Krones, Andrea Nasher, The Frankel–Viertel–Baruch Group, Paul Heil Fisher, Julie Ross, Jon B. Platt, Alan J. Schuster, Peter Breger; *Grease* produced by Barry and Fran Weissler, Jujamcyn Theaters; *She Loves Me* produced by Roundabout Theater Company, Todd Haimes, James M. Nederlander, Elliot Martin, Herbert Wasserman, Freddy Bienstock, Roger L. Stevens.

SPECIAL TONY AWARDS. 1st Lifetime Achievement Award to **Jessica Tandy** and **Hume Cronyn**; Regional Theater Award to **McCarter Theater**, Princeton, N.J.

TONY AWARD WINNERS, 1947–1994

Listed below are the Antoinette Perry (Tony) Award winners in the categories of Best Play and Best Musical from the time these awards were established until the present.

1947—No play or musical award
1948—Mister Roberts; no musical award
1949—Death of a Salesman; Kiss Me, Kate
1950—The Cocktail Party; South Pacific
1951—The Rose Tattoo; Guys and Dolls
1952—The Fourposter; The King and I
1953—The Crucible; Wonderful Town
1954—The Teahouse of the August Moon; Kismet
1955—The Desperate Hours; The Pajama Game
1956—The Diary of Anne Frank; Damn Yankees
1957—Long Day's Journey Into Night; My Fair Lady
1958—Sunrise at Campobello; The Music Man
1959—J.B.; Redhead
1960—The Miracle Worker; Fiorello! and The Sound of Music (tie)
1961—Becket; Bye Bye Birdie
1962—A Man for All Seasons; How to Succeed in Business Without Really Trying
1963—Who's Afraid of Virginia Woolf?, A Funny Thing Happened on the Way to the Forum
1964—Luther; Hello, Dolly!
1965—The Subject Was Roses; Fiddler on the Roof
1966—The Persecution and Assassination of Marat Performed by the Inmates of the Asylum of Charenton Under the Direction of the Marquis de Sade; Man of La Mancha
1967—The Homecoming; Cabaret
1968—Rosencrantz and Guildenstern Are Dead; Hallelujah, Baby!
1969—The Great White Hope; 1776
1970—Borstal Boy; Applause
1971—Sleuth; Company
1972—Sticks and Bones; Two Gentlemen of Verona
1973—That Championship Season; A Little Night Music
1974—The River Niger; Raisin
1975—Equus; The Wiz
1976—Travesties; A Chorus Line
1977—The Shadow Box; Annie
1978—Da; Ain't Misbehavin'
1979—The Elephant Man; Sweeney Todd, the Demon Barber of Fleet Street
1980—Children of a Lesser God; Evita
1981—Amadeus; 42nd Street
1982—The Life & Adventures of Nicholas Nickleby; Nine
1983—Torch Song Trilogy; Cats
1984—The Real Thing; La Cage aux Folles
1985—Biloxi Blues; Big River
1986—I'm Not Rappaport; The Mystery of Edwin Drood
1987—Fences; Les Misérables

1988—M. Butterfly; The Phantom of the Opera
1989—The Heidi Chronicles; Jerome Robbins' Broadway
1990—The Grapes of Wrath; City of Angels
1991—Lost in Yonkers; The Will Rogers Follies
1992—Dancing at Lughnasa; Crazy for You
1993—Angels in America, Part I: Millennium Approaches; Kiss of the Spider Woman
1994—Angels in America, Part II: Perestroika; Passion

THE OBIE AWARDS

The *Village Voice* Off-Broadway (Obie) Awards are given each year for excellence in various categories of off-Broadway (and frequently off-off-Broadway) shows, with close distinctions between these two areas ignored. The 38th annual Obies for the 1993-94 season, listed below, were chosen by a panel of judges chaired by Ross Wetzsteon and comprising Michael Feingold, Alisa Solomon, and Jan Stuart.

BEST PLAY. ***Twilight: Los Angeles, 1992*** by Anna Deavere Smith.

SUSTAINED ACHIEVEMENT: **Edward Albee**.

PLAYWRITING. **Eric Bogosian** for *Pounding Nails in the Floor With My Forehead*; **Howard Korder** for *The Lights*.

DIRECTION. **Andre Ernotte** for *Christina Alberta's Father*; **David Warren** for *Pterodactyls*.

DESIGN. **Kyle Chepulis**, sets; **Brian MacDevitt**, lighting.

CITATIONS. **Ain Gordon, David Gordon, Valda Setterfield** for *The Family Business;* **Holly Hughes; Ricky Jay** for *Ricky Jay & His 52 Assistants;* **Michael John LaChiusa** for *First Lady Suite* and *Hello Again;* **John Moran** and **Bob McGrath; Tom Noonan** for *Wifey;* **Claudia Shear** for *Blown Sideways Through Life;* ***Stomp.***

PERFORMANCES. **Carolee Carmello** in *Hello Again*, **Myra Carter** in *Three Tall Women*, **Gail Grate** and **Michael Potts** in *The America Play*, **Danny Hoch** in *Some People*, **Judith Ivey** in *The Moonshot Tape*, **Peter Francis James** in *The Maids*, **Jefferson Mays** in *Orestes*, **Christopher McCann** in *The Lights*, **Alice Playten** in *First Lady Suite*, **Robert Stanton** in *All in the Timing*, **Tom Nellis** in *The Medium*.

VILLAGE VOICE GRANTS. **The Changing Scene, HERE, Anna Deavere Smith, Edward Albee.**

ADDITIONAL PRIZES AND AWARDS, 1993–94

The following is a list of major prizes and awards for achievement in the theater this season. In all cases the names and/or titles of the winners appear in **bold face type.**

9th ANNUAL ATCA AWARDS. For outstanding new plays in cross–country theater, voted by a committee of the American Theater Critics Association. New Play Award: ***Keely and Du*** by Jane Martin. 1st Elizabeth Osborn Award for emerging playwrights: ***Hurricane*** by Anne Galjour. Citation: ***Black Elk Speaks*** by Christopher Sergel.

1993 ELIZABETH HULL–KATE WARRINER AWARD. To the playwright whose work dealt with controversial subjects involving the fields of political, religious or social mores of the time, selected by the Dramatists Guild Council. **Tony Kushner** for *Angels in America, Part I: Millennium Approaches*.

13th ANNUAL WILLIAM INGE AWARD. For lifetime achievement in the American Theater. **Terrence McNally**.

MARGO JONES CITIZEN OF THE THEATER

MEDAL. For lifetime achievement in theater, in support of playwrights and playwriting. **Henry Hewes**.

16th ANNUAL KENNEDY CENTER HONORS. For distinguished achievement by individuals who have made significant contributions to American culture through the arts. **Stephen Sondheim, Johnny Carson, Arthur Mitchell, George Solti, Marion Williams**.

10th ANNUAL JUJAMCYN THEATERS AWARD. Honoring outstanding contribution to the development of creative talent for the theater. **Alliance for New American Musicals.**

2d ANNUAL ROBERT WHITEHEAD AWARD. For distinguished producing. **Dennis Grimaldi.**

1994 AMERICAN THEATER WING DESIGN AWARDS. For design originating in the U.S., voted by a committee comprising Tish Dace (chair), Michael Feingold, Alexis Greene, Henry Hewes and Michael Sommers. Scenic design, **Tony Walton** for *She Loves Me*. Costume design, **Ann Hould-Ward** for *Beauty and the Beast*. Lighting design, **Beverly Emmons** for *Passion*. Noteworthy unusual effects, **David Schulder** for the props in *Movieland*.

1994 ASTAIRE AWARDS. For achievement in dance in the Broadway theater. **Lar Lubovitch** for the choreography and **Margaret Illmann** for performance in *The Red Shoes*. **Scott Wise** for performance in *Damn Yankees*.

10th ANNUAL GEORGE AND ELISABETH MARTON AWARD. To an American playwright, selected by a committee of Young Playwrights Inc. **Jose Rivera** for *Marisol*.

JOE A. CALLAWAY AWARD. To the author of a first New York production. **Paula Vogel** for *Baltimore Waltz*.

1993 MR. ABBOTT AWARD. Presented by the Stage Directors and Choreographers Foundation for lifetime achievement. **Trevor Nunn**.

1992–93 GEORGE JEAN NATHAN AWARD. For drama criticism, administered by Cornell University's English Department. **David Cole**.

50th ANNUAL THEATER WORLD AWARDS. For outstanding new talent in Broadway and off–Broadway productions during the 1993–94 season. Selected by a committee comprising Clive Barnes, Frank Scheck, Douglas Watt and John Willis. **Marcus D'Amico** and **Aden Gillette** in *An Inspector Calls*, **Jarrod Emick** in *Damn Yankees*, **Arabella Field** in *Snowing at Delphi* and *Four Dogs and a Bone*, **Sherry Glaser** in *Family Secrets*, **Michael Hayden** and **Audra Ann McDonald** in *Carousel*, **Margaret Illmann** in *The Red Shoes*, **Burke Moses** in *Guys and Dolls* and *Beauty and the Beast*, **Jere Shea** in *Passion*, **Anna Deavere Smith** in *Twilight: Los Angeles, 1992*, **Harriet Walter** in *Three Birds Alighting on a Field*.

1993 JOSEPH KESSELRING PRIZES. For best new American plays, selected under the aegis of the National Arts Club. ***Fires in the Mirror*** by Anna Deavere Smith. ***Swoony Planet*** by Han Ong.

60th ANNUAL DRAMA LEAGUE AWARDS. For distinguished achievement in musical theater: **George Abbott**. For unique contribution to the theater: **Arthur Miller**. For distinguished performance: **Sam Waterston**.

1994 LUCILLE LORTEL AWARDS. For outstanding achievement off Broadway, selected by a committee comprising Clive Barnes, Jeremy Gerard, William A. Henry III, Howard Kissel, Alvin Klein, Michael Kuchwara, Edith Oliver, Allan Wallach, Edwin Wilson and Lucille Lortel. Play: ***Three Tall Women*** by Edward Albee. Musical: ***Wings***, book and lyrics by Arthur Perlman, music by Jeffrey Lunden, based on Arthur Kopit's play. Revival of a play: ***Owners*** and ***Traps*** by Caryl Churchill, produced by New York Theater Workshop. Performance by an actor: **Ron Rifkin** in *Three Hotels*. Performance by an actress: **Myra Carter** in *Three Tall Women*. Direction: **Lawrence Sacharow** for *Three Tall Women*. Institutional body of work: **Theater for a New Audience**. Individual body of work: **A.R. Gurney**, playwright; **Irene Worth**, actress. Unique accomplishment: **Ricky Jay** for *Ricky Jay & His 52 Assistants*. Special award: **Alliance of Resident Theaters/New York**, Virginia P. Louloudes executive director, for its Passport to Off Broadway program.

1993 MUSICAL THEATER HALL OF FAME AWARDS. **Carol Channing** and **Jule Styne**.

39th ANNUAL DRAMA DESK AWARDS. For outstanding achievement in the 1993–94 season, voted by an association of New York drama reporters, editors and critics. New Play: ***Angels in America, Part II: Perestroika*** by Tony Kushner. New musical: ***Passion***, book by James Lapine, music and lyrics by Stephen Sondheim. Actor in a Play: **Stephen Spinella** in *Perestroika*. Actress in a play: **Myra Carter** in *Three Tall Women*. Supporting actor in a play: **Jeffrey Wright** in *Perestroika*. Supporting actress in a play: **Jane Adams** in *An Inspector Calls*. Actor in a musical: **Boyd Gaines** in *She Loves Me*. Actress in a musical: **Donna Murphy** in *Passion*. Supporting actor in a musical: **Jarrod Emick** in *Damn Yankees*. Supporting actress in a musical: **Audra Ann McDonald** in *Carousel*. Director of a play: **Stephen Daldry** for *An Inspector Calls*. Director of a musical: **Nicholas Hytner** for *Carousel*. Music: **Stephen Sondheim** for *Passion*. Lyrics: **Stephen Sondheim** for *Passion*. Book: **James Lapine** for *Passion*. Play revival: ***An Inspector Calls.*** Musical revival: ***She Loves Me.*** Solo performance: **Anna Deavere Smith** in *Twilight: Los Angeles, 1992*. Orchestrations: **Jonathan Tunick** for *Passion*. Music in a play: **Stephen Warbeck** for *An Inspector Calls*. Choreography: **Kenneth MacMillan** and **Jane Elliott** for *Carousel*. Set design: **Ian MacNeil** for *An Inspector Calls*. Costume design: **Howard Crabtree** for *Howard Crabtree's Whoop–Dee–Doo*. Sound design: **John A. Leonard** for *Medea*. Lighting design: **Rick Fisher** for *An Inspector Calls*. Unique theatrical experience: ***Stomp.*** Revue: ***Howard Crabtree's Whoop–Dee–Doo.*** Special effects: **Gregory Meeh** for *An Inspector Calls*.

Special achievement: **John Willis** for his devotion to the theater and its artists, as expressed in his 50 years of meticulous documentation in *Theater World*; **Janet Hayes Walker** for 25 years of revivals and new plays at the York Theater Company.

50th ANNUAL CLARENCE DERWENT AWARDS. For the most promising male and female actors on the metropolitan scene. **Jeanne Paulsen** in *The Kentucky Cycle*. **Robert Stanton** in *All in the Timing*.

10th ANNUAL NEW YORK DANCE AND PERFORMANCE AWARDS (BESSIES). For exceptional achievement in the field of dance and related performance in the 1992–93 New York season, presented by Dance Theater Workshop. **Joan Duddy** of Dia Center for the Arts for "creating a safe haven for dance artists in an unsafe time." Sustained achievement: **Beverly Blossom** for dance theater, **Nikki Castro** for dancing, **Eileen Thomas** for performing, **Arthur Russell** for his music, **Robert Wierzel** for lighting design, **Dona Ann McAdams** for photography. Choreography/performance art: **David Cale** and **Roy Nathanson** for *Deep in a Dream of You*, **Laurie Carlos** for *White Chocolate*, **Rhodessa Jones** and **Idris Ackamoor** for *Big–Butt Girls, Hard–Headed Women*, **Merce Cunningham** for *Enter*, **Yvonne Meier** for *The Shining*, **Alyson Pou** for *To Us at Twilight*, **Sally Silvers** for *Small Room*, **Mary Ellen Strom** for *Witness*, the **Five Lesbian Brothers** for collective work. Performing: **Niles Ford, Mimi Goese, Everett Quinton, Sam Weber**. Musical scores: **Tan Dunn, Christopher Hyams–Hart, James Lo**. Visual design: **Bloolips** ensemble, **Kyle Chepulis, Bill Morrison**.

44th ANNUAL OUTER CRITICS CIRCLE AWARDS. For outstanding achievement in the 1993–94 New York theater season, voted by an organization of critics on out–of–town periodicals and media. Broadway play: ***Angels in America, Parts I and II: Millennium Approaches*** and ***Perestroika*** by Tony Kushner. Performance by an actor: **Sam Waterston** in *Abe Lincoln in Illinois*. Performance by an actress: **Myra Carter** in *Three Tall Women*. Broadway musical: ***Kiss of the Spider Woman***, book by Terrence McNally, music by John Kander, lyrics by Fred Ebb, based on the novel by Manuel Puig. Actor in a musical: **Boyd Gaines** in *She Loves Me*. Actress in a musical: (tie) **Audra Ann McDonald** in *Carousel* and **Chita Rivera** in *Kiss of the Spider Woman*. Off–Broadway play: ***Three Tall Women*** by Edward Albee. Off–Broadway musical: ***Annie Warbucks***, book by Thomas Meehan, music by Charles Strouse, lyrics by Martin Charnin, based on the comic strip *Little Orphan Annie*. Design: ***Carousel***, scenery and costumes by Bob Crowley, lighting by Paul Pyant. Director of a play: **George C. Wolfe** for *Angels in America* and *Twilight: Los Angeles, 1992*. Director of a musical: **Scott Ellis** for *She Loves Me*. Choreography: Rob Marshall for ***Damn Yankees*** and ***She Loves Me***. Revival of a play: ***An Inspector Calls.*** Revival of a musical: ***She Loves Me***. Solo performance: **Lynn Redgrave** in *Shakespeare for My Father*. Debut of an actor: **Jeffrey Wright** in *Angels in America*. Debut of an actress: **Hynden Walch** in *The Rise and Fall of Little Voice*. John Gassner Playwriting Award: **David Ives** for *All in the Timing*.

Special achievement awards: **Anna Deavere Smith** for documenting and interpreting events of our time in a unique theatrical form. **Lucille Lortel** for a lifetime of service and devotion to the American theater. **Jane Alexander**, always a distinguished voice *in* the theater and now an important voice *for* the theater, as chairman of the National Endowment for the Arts.

1994 BOSTON THEATER AWARDS (formerly Elliott Norton Awards). For distinguished contribution to the theater in Boston, voted by a panel of critics comprising Carolyn Clay, Iris Fanger, Arthur Friedman, Joyce Kulhawik, Jon Lehman and Caldwell Titcomb. **Carol Channing** for "her unflagging devotion to the stage and her pride in her Boston theatrical roots." Outstanding production by a large resident company, American Repertory Theater's ***Henry IV, Parts 1 and 2.*** Outstanding production by a small resident company, Nora Theater Company's ***Death of a Salesman***. Outstanding production by a visiting company, Royal National Theater of Great Britain's ***The Madness of George III***. Outstanding actor, **Diego Arcinegas** in *Amadeus* and *God's Country*. Outstanding actress, **Sandra Shipley** in *Medea* and *Two*. Outstanding director, **Eric Engel** for *Death of a Sales-*

man. Outstanding design, **George Tsypin** (scenery) and **Frances Aronson** (lighting) for *The Cherry Orchard.* Sustained excellence, **Thomas Derrah.**

10th ANNUAL HELEN HAYES AWARDS. In recognition of excellence in Washington, D.C. theater, presented by the Washington Theater Awards Society. Resident productions—Play: ***Dancing at Lughnasa*** by Brian Friel, produced by Arena Stage. Musical: ***The Pirates of Penzance***, produced by Interact Theater. Charles MacArthur Award for outstanding new play: ***Free Will and Wanton Lust*** by Nicky Silver, produced by Woolly Mammoth Theater Company. Director: **Michael Kahn** for *Mother Courage and Her Children.* Lead actress, play: **Pat Carroll** in *Mother Courage and Her Children.* Lead actor, play: **Hugo Medrano** in *Kiss of the Spider Woman.* Supporting actress, play: **Mary Vreeland** in *Mother Courage and Her Children.* Supporting actor, play: **Edward Gero** in *Richard II.* Actress, musical: **Lorraine Serabian** in *Show Me Where the Good Times Are.* Actor, musical: **Steve Cramer** in *The Pirates of Penzance.* Set design: **Linda Buchanan** for *Dancing at Lughnasa.* Lighting design: **Deirdre Kelly Lavrakas** and **Kim Peter Kovac** for *Kiss of the Spider Woman.* Costume design: **Reggie Ray** for *Spunk.* Sound design: **Keith Thomas** for *Julius Ceasar.* Choreography: **Mike Malone** for *Spunk.*

Non–resident productions—Play or musical: ***Three Hotels*** by Jon Robin Baitz. Director: **Joe Mantello** for *Three Hotels.* Lead actress: **Debra Monk** in *Three Hotels.* Lead actor, **Stacy Keach** in *The Kentucky Cycle.* Supporting performer: **Tuck Milligan** in *The Kentucky Cycle.*

25th ANNUAL JOSEPH JEFFERSON AWARDS. For achievement in Chicago Theater during the 1992–93 season. Production—Play: ***King Lear***, produced by Shakespeare Repertory. Musical: ***Sweeney Todd***, produced by Marriott's Lincolnshire Theater. Revue: ***Puttin' on the Ritz***, produced by National Jewish Theater. Touring: ***Miss Saigon***, produced by Cameron Mackintosh. Director—Play: **Barbara Gaines** for *King Lear*; **Michael Maggio** for *Black Snow.* Musical: **Michael Maggio** for *Wings.* Revue: **Sheldon Patinkin** for *Puttin' on the Ritz.* Actress in a principal role—Play: **Marji Bank** in *Lost in Yonkers.* Musical: **Linda Stephens** in *Wings.* Revue: **Jackie Hoffman** in *The Disgruntled Employee Picnic, or The Postman Always Shoots Twice.* Touring: **Dee Hoty** in *The Will Rogers Follies*; **Stephanie Mills** in *The Wiz.* Actor in a principal role—Play: **Richard Kneeland** in *King Lear.* Musical: **Ross Lehman** in *Hot Mikado.* Revue: **Stephen Wade** in *On the Way Home.* Touring: **Martin Short** in *The Goodbye Girl.* Actor in a supporting role—Play: **Allan Pinsker** in *The Price.* Musical; **Jim Corti** in *Grand Hotel.* Touring: **Keith Byron Kirk** in *Miss Saigon.* Actress in a supporting role—Play: **Barbara Robertson** in *Black Snow.* Musical: **Kelly Prybycien** in *Grand Hotel.* Touring: **Ebony Jo–Ann** in *The Wiz*; **Valerie Wright** in *And the World Goes 'Round.* Ensemble: ***Xenogenesis***. Design—Scenery: **Linda Buchanan** for *Black Snow.* Costumes: **Nancy Missimi** for *Hot Mikado.* Lighting: **Rita Pietraszek** for *King Lear.* Sound: **Adam Kroloff** for *Xenogenesis.* New work/adaptation: ***Wings*** by Jeffrey Lunden and Arthur Perlman. Original music: **Rob Milburn, Miriam Sturm** and **Michael Bodeen** for *Black Snow.* Choreography: **Danny Herman** for *Song and Dance.* Musical direction: **Kevin Stites** for *Sweeney Todd.*

25th ANNUAL LOS ANGELES DRAMA CRITICS CIRCLE AWARDS. For distinguished achievement in Los Angeles Theater during 1993. Production: ***Crazy for You***, produced by Roger Horchow and Elizabeth Williams; ***The Tavern***, produced by Joseph Stern. Direction: **Jules Aaron** for *Equus*; **Marilyn Fox** for *Ondine*; **Tony Giordano** for *The Tavern.* Writing: **Roger Rueff** for *So Many Words.* Lead performance: **Ron Campbell** in *Monsieur Shaherzad*, **Kandis Chappell** and **Dakin Matthews** in *Shadowlands*, **Glenn Close** in *Sunset Boulevard*, **Harold Gould** in *Incommunicado*, **Jack Noseworthy** in *Equus*, **Cotter Smith** in *The Tavern*, **Juliet Stevenson** in *Scenes From an Execution.* Featured performance: **J.D. Daniels** in *Conversations With My Father*, **Tony Maggio** in *La Bête.* Creation performance: **John Robert Hoffman** in *Northern Lights*, **Anna Deavere Smith** in *Twilight: Los Angeles, 1992.* Scenic design: **Cliff Faulkner** for *Hay Fever*, **Gerard Howland** for *Great Day in the Morning*, **John Napier** for *Sunset Boulevard.* Lighting design: **Andrew Bridge** for *Sunset Boulevard*, **Peter Maradudin** for *Great Day in the Morning.* Costume design: **Walter Hicklin** for *Great Day in the Morning*, **Anthony Powell** for *Sunset Boulevard.* Sound design: **Martin Levan** for *Sunset Boulevard.* Musical direction: **Paul Gemignani** for *Crazy for You.* Choreography: **Susan Stroman** for *Crazy for You.* Original music: **Tom Gerou** for *Ondine.* Musical orchestration: **William D. Brohn** for *Crazy for You.* Special awards: **South Coast Repertory** in recognition of its 30th year of excellence; **Artists Confronting AIDS** for creating and presenting theater pieces that memorably dramatize an urgent health care crisis. Ted Schmitt Award (for an outstanding script having its world premiere in Los Angeles): ***So Many Words*** by Roger Rueff. Margaret Harford Award (for continuous achievement in the smaller theater arena): **Pacific Resident Theater Ensemble**. Angstrom Award (for a career or body of work in stage lighting by a designer whose career was established in the small theaters of Los Angeles): **J. Kent Inasy**.

THE THEATER HALL OF FAME

The Theater Hall of Fame was created to honor those who have made outstanding contributions to the American theater. Members are elected annually by the nation's drama critics and editors (names of those so elected in 1994 appear in ***bold face italics***).

GEORGE ABBOTT
MAUDE ADAMS
VIOLA ADAMS
STELLA ADLER
EDWARD ALBEE
THEONI V. ALDREDGE
IRA ALDRIDGE
JANE ALEXANDER
WINTHROP AMES
JUDITH ANDERSON
MAXWELL ANDERSON
ROBERT ANDERSON
MARGARET ANGLIN
HAROLD ARLEN
GEORGE ARLISS
BORIS ARONSON
ADELE ASTAIRE
FRED ASTAIRE
BROOKS ATKINSON
PEARL BAILEY
GEORGE BALANCHINE
ANNE BANCROFT
TALLULAH BANKHEAD
RICHARD BARR
PHILIP BARRY
ETHEL BARRYMORE
JOHN BARRYMORE
LIONEL BARRYMORE
NORA BAYES
S.N. BEHRMAN
NORMAN BEL GEDDES
DAVID BELASCO
MICHAEL BENNETT
RICHARD BENNETT
IRVING BERLIN
SARAH BERNHARDT
LEONARD BERNSTEIN
EARL BLACKWELL
KERMIT BLOOMGARDEN
JERRY BOCK
RAY BOLGER
EDWIN BOOTH
JUNIUS BRUTUS BOOTH
SHIRLEY BOOTH
ALICE BRADY
FANNIE BRICE
PETER BROOK
JOHN MASON BROWN
BILLIE BURKE
ABE BURROWS
RICHARD BURTON
MRS. PATRICK CAMPBELL
ZOE CALDWELL
EDDIE CANTOR
MORRIS CARNOVSKY
MRS. LESLIE CARTER
GOWER CHAMPION
FRANK CHANFRAU
CAROL CHANNING
RUTH CHATTERTON
PADDY CHAYEFSKY
INA CLAIRE
BOBBY CLARK
HAROLD CLURMAN
LEE J. COBB
GEORGE M. COHAN
JACK COLE
CY COLEMAN
CONSTANCE COLLIER
BETTY COMDEN
MARC CONNELLY
BARBARA COOK
KATHARINE CORNELL
NOEL COWARD
JANE COWL
LOTTA CRABTREE
CHERYL CRAWFORD
HUME CRONYN
RUSSEL CROUSE
CHARLOTTE CUSHMAN
JEAN DALRYMPLE
AUGUSTIN DALY
E.L. DAVENPORT
RUBY DEE
ALFRED DE LIAGRE JR.
AGNES DEMILLE
COLLEEN DEWHURST
HOWARD DIETZ
DUDLEY DIGGES
MELVYN DOUGLAS
ALFRED DRAKE
MARIE DRESSLER
JOHN DREW
MRS. JOHN DREW
WILLIAM DUNLAP
MILDRED DUNNOCK
ELEANORA DUSE
JEANNE EAGELS
FRED EBB
FLORENCE ELDRIDGE
LEHMAN ENGEL
MAURICE EVANS
JOSE FERRER
DOROTHY FIELDS
HERBERT FIELDS
LEWIS FIELDS
W.C. FIELDS
MINNIE MADDERN FISKE
CLYDE FITCH
GERALDINE FITZGERALD
HENRY FONDA
LYNN FONTANNE
EDWIN FORREST
BOB FOSSE
RUDOLF FRIML
CHARLES FROHMAN
GRACE GEORGE
GEORGE GERSHWIN
IRA GERSHWIN
JOHN GIELGUD
JACK GILFORD
WILLIAM GILLETTE
CHARLES GILPIN
LILLIAN GISH
JOHN GOLDEN
MAX GORDON
RUTH GORDON
ADOLPH GREEN
PAUL GREEN
CHARLOTTE GREENWOOD
JOEL GREY
JOHN GUARE

Tyrone Guthrie
Uta Hagen
Lewis Hallam
Oscar Hammerstein II
Walter Hampden
Otto Harbach
E.Y. Harburg
Sheldon Harnick
Edward Harrigan
Jed Harris
Rosemary Harris
Sam H. Harris
Rex Harrison
Lorenz Hart
Moss Hart
Tony Hart
Helen Hayes
Leland Hayward
Ben Hecht
Theresa Helburn
Lillian Hellman
Katharine Hepburn
Victor Herbert
Jerry Herman
James A. Herne
Al Hirschfeld
Raymond Hitchcock
Celeste Holm
Hanya Holm
Arthur Hopkins
De Wolf Hopper
John Houseman
Eugene Howard
Leslie Howard
Sidney Howard
Willie Howard
Barnard Hughes
Henry Hull
Josephine Hull
Walter Huston
William Inge
Elsie Janis
Joseph Jefferson
Al Jolson
James Earl Jones
Robert Edmond Jones
John Kander
Garson Kanin
George S. Kaufman
Danny Kaye
Elia Kazan
Gene Kelly
George Kelly
Fanny Kemble
Jerome Kern
Walter Kerr
Michael Kidd
Sidney Kinglsey
Joseph Wood Krutch
Bert Lahr
Burton Lane
Lawrence Langner
Lillie Langtry
Angela Lansbury
Charles Laughton
Arthur Laurents
Gertrude Lawrence
Jerome Lawrence
Eva Le Gallienne
Robert E. Lee
Lotte Lenya
Alan Jay Lerner
Sam Levene
Robert Lewis
Beatrice Lillie
Howard Lindsay
Frank Loesser
Frederick Loewe
Joshua Logan
Pauline Lord
Lucille Lortel
Alfred Lunt
Charles MacArthur
Steele MacKaye
Rouben Mamoulian
Richard Mansfield
Robert B. Mantell
Fredric March
Julia Marlowe
Mary Martin
Raymond Massey
Siobhan McKenna
Helen Menken
Burgess Meredith
Ethel Merman
David Merrick
Jo Mielziner
Arthur Miller
Marilyn Miller
Helena Modjeska
Ferenc Molnar
Lola Montez
Victor Moore
Zero Mostel
Anna Cora Mowatt
Paul Muni
Tharon Musser
George Jean Nathan
Mildred Natwick
Nazimova
James M. Nederlander
Elliot Norton
Clifford Odets
Donald Oenslager
Laurence Olivier
Eugene O'Neill
Geraldine Page
Joseph Papp
Osgood Perkins
Molly Picon
Christopher Plummer
Cole Porter
Robert Preston
Harold Prince
Jose Quintero
John Raitt
Michael Redgrave
Ada Rehan
Elmer Rice
Lloyd Richards
Ralph Richardson
Chita Rivera
Jason Robards
Jerome Robbins
Paul Robeson
Richard Rodgers
Will Rogers
Sigmund Romberg
Harold Rome
Lillian Russell
Gene Saks
William Saroyan
Alan Schneider
Arthur Schwartz
George C. Scott
Robert E. Sherwood
J.J. Shubert
Lee Shubert
Herman Shumlin
Neil Simon
Lee Simonson
Edmund Simpson
Otis Skinner
Oliver Smith
Stephen Sondheim
E.H. Sothern

Kim Stanley
Maureen Stapleton
Roger L. Stevens
Ellen Stewart
Dorothy Stickney
Fred Stone
Lee Strasberg
Jule Styne
Margaret Sullavan
Jessica Tandy
Laurette Taylor
Ellen Terry
Tommy Tune
Gwen Verdon
Eli Wallach
James Wallack
Lester Wallack
Tony Walton
David Warfield
Ethel Waters
Clifton Webb
Joseph Weber
Margaret Webster
Kurt Weill
Orson Welles
Mae West
Robert Whitehead
Thornton Wilder
Bert Williams
Tennessee Williams
Lanford Wilson
P.G. Wodehouse
Peggy Wood
Irene Worth
Ed Wynn
Vincent Youmans
Stark Young
Florenz Ziegfeld

MUSICAL THEATER HALL OF FAME

This organization was established at New York University on November 10, 1993. Its first eight honorees are the following:

George Gershwin
Ira Gershwin
Oscar Hammerstein II
Jerome Kern
Alan Jay Lerner
Frederick Loewe
Ethel Merman
Richard Rodgers

1993–94 PUBLICATION OF RECENTLY-PRODUCED NEW PLAYS AND NEW TRANSLATIONS/ADAPTATIONS

A . . . My Name Is Still Alice. Joan Micklin Silver and Julianne Boyd (libretto). Samuel French (acting edition).
Absence of War, The. David Hare. Faber & Faber (paperback).
Angels in America, Part II: Perestroika. Tony Kushner. TCG (paperback).
Arcadia. Tom Stoppard. Faber & Faber (paperback).
Broken Glass. Arthur Miller. Penguin (paperback).
Cherry Orchard, The. Anton Chekhov, newly translated by Elisaveta Lavrona. Dramatic (acting edition).
Conversations With My Father. Herb Gardner. Random House (also paperback).
Dark Rapture. Eric Overmyer. Broadway Play (paperback).
Destiny of Me, The. Larry Kramer. New American Library (paperback).
Eating Raoul. Paul Bertel with Boyd Graham and Jed Feuer (libretto). Samuel French (acting edition).
Falsettos. William Finn and James Lapine (libretti). New American Library (paperback).
Fires in the Mirror. Anna Deavere Smith. Doubleday (paperback).
Gift of the Gorgon, The. Peter Shaffer. Viking (paperback).
Gray's Anatomy. Spalding Gray. Random House (paperback).
Heliotrope Bouquet by Scott Joplin and Louis Chauvin, The. Eric Overmyer. Broadway Play (paperback).
Here. Michael Frayn. Methuen (paperback).
Houseguests. Harry Kondoleon. Dramatists (acting edition).
Jeffrey. Paul Rudnick. New American Library (paperback).
Jelly's Last Jam. George C. Wolfe and Susan Birkenhead. TCG.
Later Life and Two Other Plays. A. R. Gurney. New American Library (paperback).
Mambo Mouth. John Leguizamo. Bantam (paperback).
Mastergate and Power Failure. Larry Gelbart. Applause (paperback).
Medea. Euripides, newly translated by Alistair Elliot. Oberon (paperback).
Month in the Country, A. Turgenev, newly adapted by Brian Friel. Dramatists (acting edition).
Moonlight. Harold Pinter. Faber & Faber (paperback).
Murmuring Judges. David Hare. Faber & Faber (paperback).
Night Larry Kramer Kissed Me, The. David Drake. Doubleday (paperback).
Odyssey, The. Derek Walcott. Farrar, Strauss (also paperback).
One Shoe Off. Tina Howe. Samuel French (acting edition).
Perfect Ganesh, A. Terrence McNally. Dramatists (acting edition).
Persians: A Modern Version by Robert Auletta. Newly adapted from Aeschylus. Sun & Moon Press (paperback).
Playland/A Place with the Pigs. Athol Fugard. TCG (paperback).
Secret Garden, The. Marsha Norman. TCG (also paperback).
Song of Jacob Zulu, The. Tug Yourgrau. Arcade/Little Brown (also paperback).
Sunset Boulevard. Christopher Hampton and Don Black (libretto). Faber & Faber (paperback).
Time of My Life. Alan Ayckbourn. Faber & Faber (paperback).
Trojan Women. Euripides, newly adapted by Brendan Kennelly. Dufour (paperback).
Twilight: Los Angeles, 1992. Anna Deavere Smith. Anchor Doubleday (paperback).
Ugly Man, The. Brad Fraser. NeWest Press (paperback).
Wonderful Tennessee. Brian Friel. Faber & Faber (paperback).
*Years, The.*Cindy Lou Johnson. Dramatists (acting edition).

A SELECTED LIST OF OTHER PLAYS PUBLISHED IN 1993–94

Bad Infinity: Eight Plays, The. Mac Wellman. John Hopkins University.

Best American Plays: Ninth Series—1983-1992. Clive Barnes, editor. Crown.

Best American Short Plays 1992-1993, The. Howard Stein and Glenn Young, editors. Applause (paperback).

Calderon de la Barca: Six Plays. Calderon de la Barca, translated by Edwin Honig. IASTA Press (paperback).

Collected Plays of Ronald Harwood. Ronald Harwood. Faber & Faber (paperback).

Crosswinds: An Anthology of Black Dramatists in the Diaspora. William B. Branch, editor. Indiana University Press (paperback).

Drama. Jeffrey D. Hoeper, James H. Pickering and Deborah K. Chappel, editors (anthology). Macmillan (paperback).

Eric Overmyer: Collected Plays. Smith & Kraus (also paperback).

Figaro Plays, The. Beaumarchais, newly translated by Graham Anderson. Absolute Classics (paperback).

Horton Foote: Four New Plays. Horton Foote. Smith and Kraus (paperback).

Four Plays Translated by Barbara Bray. Marguerite Duras. Oberon Books (paperback).

Humana Festival '93—The Complete Plays. Marisa Smith, editor. Smith & Kraus (paperback).

Landmarks of Contemporary Women's Drama. Emilie S. Kilgore, editor. Methuen (paperback).

Lanford Wilson: 21 Short Plays. Lanford Wilson. Smith & Kraus (paperback).

Mirror to the Cage: Three Contemporary Hungarian Plays, A. Clara Gyorgyey, editor and translator. University of Arkansas.

Moon Marked & Touched by Sun: Plays by African-American Women. Sydne Mahone, editor and translator. TCG (paperback).

Mother and Other Unsavory Plays, The. Stanley Ignacy Witkiewicz. Daniel Gerould and C.S. Durer, editors and translators. Applause (paperback).

Nine Plays. Eugene O'Neill. Modern Library/Random House.

Plays of the New Democratic Spain (1975-1990). Patricia W. O'Connor, editor. University Press of Amerca (paperback).

Professor Bernhardi & Other Plays. Arthur Schnitzler, translated by G. J. Weinberger. Ariadne Press (paperback).

Selected Plays 1963-83. Vaclav Havel. Faber & Faber (paperback).

Seven Gothic Dramas 1789-1825. Jeffrey N. Cox, editor. Ohio University Press (also paperback).

Sharing the Delirium: Second Generation AIDS Plays and Performances. Therese Jones, editor. Heinemann (paperback).

Six Plays. Romulus Linney. TCG (paperback).

Television Plays: 1965-1984. Tom Stoppard. Faber & Faber (paperback).

Theater of Tennessee Williams: Volume Four. Tennessee Williams. New Directions (also paperback).

Vietnam Plays: Volumes One and Two, The. David Rabe. Grove.

Waiting for Lefty and Other Plays. Clifford Odets. Grove (paperback).

William Mastrosimone: Collected Plays. William Mastrosimone. Smith & Kraus (paperback).

Women on the Verge: Seven Avant Garde Plays. Rosette C. Lamont, editor. Applause.

NECROLOGY

MAY 1993—MAY 1994

PERFORMERS

Adler, Clyde (67)—Sepember 4, 1993
Aidman, Charles (68)—November 7, 1993
Akins, Claude (67)—January 27, 1994
Aldridge, Michael (73)—January 10, 1994
Allen, Adrienne (86)—September 14, 1993
Ameche, Don (85)—December 6, 1993
Ames, Leon (91)—October 12, 1993
Auger, Arleen (53)—June 10, 1993
Baker, Bill (58)—June 8, 1993
Barclay, Steve (75)–February 2, 1994
Barrault, Jean-Louis (83)—January 23, 1994
Bellaver, Harry—August 8, 1993
Bellin, Steve (43)—April 14, 1994
Bernardi, Jack (85)—March 23, 1994
Berry, Eric (80)—September 2, 1993
Bittner, Jack (75)—June 26, 1993
Bixby, Bill (59)—November 21, 1993
Blackburn, Royce P. (69)—April 14, 1994
Blake, Marie (74)—December 5, 1993
Booke, Sorrell (64)—February 11, 1994
Borisov, Oleg (64)—April 28, 1994
Boucher, Gene (60)—January 31, 1994
Bozyk, Reizl (79)—September 30, 1993
Brafa, Tony (72)—September 30, 1993
Brian, David (82)—July 15, 1993
Brooks, Eda Helen (94)—October 15, 1993
Brox, Lorayne (94)—June 14, 1993
Bruce, Ida Parkinson (93)—February 20, 1994
Burr, Raymond (76)—September 12, 1993
Buttram, Pat (78)—January 8, 1994
Caine, Howard (67)—December 28, 1993
Callen, Michael (38)—December 27, 1993
Candy, John (43)—March 4, 1994
Carey, Macdonald (81)—March 21, 1994
Carey, Timothy (65)—May 11, 1994
Carlon, Fran (80)—October 4, 1993
Carroll, Janice (61)—September 10, 1993
Clarke, Michael (31)—February 12, 1994
Cobain, Kurt (27)—April 8, 1994
Conrad, William (73)—February 11, 1994
Copeland, Vincent (77)—May 31, 1993
Corday, Josephine (79)—September 6, 1993
Cotten, Joseph (88)—February 6, 1994
Crain, Charles (83)—July 4, 1993
Cuny, Alain (85)—May 16, 1994
Cusack, Cyril (82)—October 7, 1993
Damita, Lili (85)—March 21, 1994
Dano, Royal (71)—May 15, 1994
Dano, Royal Jr. (47)—February 25, 1994
Davies, Richard (80)—April 2, 1994
Davis, Robert (76)—July 19, 1993
De Voll, Ray (66)—August 24, 1993
DeFabees, Richard (46)—November 18, 1993
DeFore, Don (80)—December 22, 1993
DeLoache, Benjamin (88)—March 15, 1994
Donald, James (76)—August 3, 1993
Douglas, Gordon (85)—September 30, 1993
Douglas, Hugh (78)—September 1, 1993
Drylie, Patricia (69)—November 11, 1993
Duffy, John Paul (42)—March 28, 1994
Duke, Edward (40)—January 8, 1994
Edwards, Kenneth (75)—August 7, 1993
Ellison, James (83)—December 23, 1993
Farnsworth, Ralph (71)—February 2, 1994
Feld, Fritz (93)—November 18, 1993
Frederick, Lynne (39)—April 27, 1994
Fuccello, Tom (55)—August 16, 1993
Gari, Giulio (84)—April 15, 1994
Gifford, Frances (72)—January 22, 1994
Gilbert, Ruth (71)—October 12, 1993
Gillette, Ruth (89)—May 13, 1994
Gloo, Peter Alan (37)—December 3, 1993
Gordon, Timothy (71)—October 4, 1993
Goya, Carola (88)—May 8, 1994
Granger, Stewart (80)—August 16, 1993
Greene, Jan Wiley—May 27, 1993
Grey, Nan (75)—July 25, 1993
Gunn, Moses (64)—December 17, 1993
Gwynne, Fred (66)—July 2, 1993
Hackes, Peter (69)—April 17, 1994
Hall, Adelaide (82)—November 7, 1993
Hall, Don (44)—September 2, 1993
Hall, Natalie (89)—March 4, 1994
Hammer, Alvin (78)—October 31, 1993
Hart, Muriel Williams (80)—Winter 1994
Haynes, Tiger (79)—February 16, 1994
Hicks, Bill (32)—February 26, 1994
Holland, John (85)—May 21, 1993
Horen, Robert (68)—January 12, 1994
Huber, Gusti (78)—July 12, 1993
Hugo, Lawrence (76)—March 2, 1994
Ide, Letitia (84)—August 29, 1993
Innocent, Harold (60)—September 12, 1993
Jensen, Sterling (68)—December 8, 1993
Johann, Zita (89)—September 24, 1993
Johnson, Marv (54)—May 16, 1993
Jordan, Richard (56)—August 30, 1993
Karin, Rita (73)—September 10, 1993
Keats, Steven (49)—May 8, 1994
Kelly, Patrick (40)—December 20, 1993

Kibbee, Lois (71)—October 18, 1993
Killian, Phil (47)—August 14, 1993
Kosleck, Martin (89)—January 16, 1994
Kozlovsky, Ivan (93)—December 21, 1993
Langton, David (82)—April 30, 1994
Lanteau, William (70)—November 3, 1993
Lavoe, Hector (46)—June 29, 1993
Ledoux, Fernand (96)—September 21, 1993
Lewis, Edwina (42)—August 23, 1993
Liebgold, Leon (83)—September 3, 1993
Logan, Marian (73)—November 25, 1993
Loy, Myrna (88)—December 14, 1993
Lynch, Christopher (73)—April 13, 1994
Maier-Forsythe, Tracy-Kai (32)—February 13, 1994
Manoa, Gloria (69)—July 6, 1993
Margolin, Janet (50)—December 17, 1993
Marshall, Joseph (28)—April 15, 1994
Masina, Giulietta (74)—March 23, 1994
Mathis, Sherry (44)—January 23, 1994
May, Winston (57)—April 29, 1994
Mays, Joe (45)—January 27, 1994
McCall, Barbara (50)—February 4, 1994
McHugh, Burke (77)—May 15, 1994
McLiam, John (76)—April 16, 1994
McNeil, Claudia (77)—November 25, 1993
Meiser, Edith (95)—September 26, 1993
Mercouri, Melina (68)—March 6, 1994
Millhollin, James (77)—May 23, 1993
Moloney, Jim—March 23, 1994
Monti, Carlotta (86)—December 8, 1993
Moore, Garry (78)—November 28, 1993
Moreno, Rosita (85)—April 25, 1994
Morgan, Henry (79)—May 19, 1994
Morley, Robert (84)—June 3, 1993
Moro, Frank (48)—June 21, 1993
Morris, Anita (50)—March 3, 1994
Morrow, Jeff (86)—December 26, 1993
Nelli, Herva (85)—May 31, 1994
Nelson, Kenneth (60)—October 7, 1993
Nigh, Jane (68)—October 5, 1993
Niles, Wendell (89)—March 28, 1994
Novotna, Jarmila (86)—February 9, 1994
O'Connell, Helen (72)—September 9, 1993
O'Hara, Patrick J. (55)—June 11, 1993
Ormont, David (79)—February 2, 1994
Peppard, George (65)—May 8, 1994
Pepple, Sydney C. (83)—October 20, 1993
Phoenix, River (23)—October 31, 1993
Pithey, Wensley (79)—November 10, 1993
Popesco, Elvire (98)—December 11, 1993
Price, Vincent (82)—October 25, 1993
Ralston, Esther (91)—January 14, 1994
Ramsey, Gordon (63)—November 5, 1993
Reed, Peter (40)—May 1, 1994
Reiman, Elise (79)—August 26, 1993
Reinheart, Alice (83)—June 10, 1993
Revier, Dorothy (89)—November 19, 1993
Rey, Fernando (76)—March 9, 1994
Rogers, Will Jr. (81)—July 10, 1993
Roland, Gilbert (88)—May 15, 1994
Romanoff, Dimitri (86)—February 9, 1994
Romero, Cesar (86)—January 1, 1994
Sablon, Jean (87)—February 24, 1994
Sadoff, Fred (68)—May 6, 1994
Sanford, Mary Duncan (98)—May 9, 1993
Savalas, Telly (70)—January 22, 1994
Schwartz, Michael (47)—May 17, 1994
Seymour, Dan (78)—May 25, 1993
Sharkey, Ray (40)—June 11, 1993
Shirley, Anne (74)—July 4, 1993
Shore, Dinah (76)—February 24, 1994
Simek, Vasek (66)—May 16, 1994
Simms, Ginny (81)—April 4, 1994
Simms, Hilda (75)—February 6, 1994
Smaney, June (71)—June 4, 1993
Smith, Alexis (72)—June 9, 1993
Smith, Willie Mae Ford (89)—February 2, 1994
Soule, Olan (84)—February 1, 1994
Sten, Anna (80s)—November 12, 1993
Stevens, Mark (44)—March 16, 1994
Stone, Ezra (76)—March 3, 1994
Strivelli, Jerry (61)—June 21, 1993
Strong, Robert B. (87)—July 4, 1993
Sullivan, Jeremiah (58)—December 12, 1993
Swann, Donald (70)—March 23, 1994
Tazewell, Louise (93)—May 25, 1993
Thomas, Jess (66)—October 11, 1993
Thor, Jerome (69)—August 21, 1993
Tomlinson, Kate (96)—October 30, 1993
Travers, Bill (72)—March 29, 1994
Troyanos, Tatiana (54)—August 21, 1993
Trueman, Paula (96)—March 23, 1994
Turgeon, Virginia (70)—September 21, 1993
Twitty, Conway (59)—June 5, 1993
Tyeska, James (43)—September 5, 1993
Vawter, Ron (45)—April 16, 1994
Venable, Evelyn (80)—November 16, 1993
Villechaize, Herve (50)—September 4, 1993
Wanamaker, Sam (74)—December 19, 1993
Warren, Joseph (77)—October 1, 1993
Welles, Gwen (42)—October 13, 1993
Wilbern, George E, (77)—February 17, 1993
Williams, Bradford C. (42)—October 17, 1993
Zane, Bartine (96)—May 20, 1994
Zetterling, Mai (68)—March 17, 1994

PLAYWRIGHTS

Dreifus, Arthur (85)—December 31, 1993
Frankel, Doris C. (84)—February 1, 1994
Gilliat, Sidney (86)—May 31, 1994
Gow, Ronald (95)—April 26, 1994
Hansen, James Lee Jr. (36)—December 1, 1993

Herlihy, James Leo (66)—October 21, 1993
Ionesco, Eugene (81)—March 28, 1994
Kondoleon, Harry (39)—March 16, 1994
London, Roy (50)—August 8, 1993
MacDougall, Roger (82)—May 27, 1993
Peyton, Bruce (44)—December 25, 1993
Russell, John C. (31)—April 22, 1994
St. Joseph, Ellis (82)—August 21, 1993

PRODUCERS, DIRECTORS, CHOREOGRAPHERS

Bartlett, Hall (70)—September 8, 1993
Beck, John (83)—July 18, 1993
Becker, Robert (47)—May 6, 1993
Bortoluzzi, Paolo (55)—October 16, 1993
Bronston, Samuel (85)—January 12, 1994
Butler, John (74)—September 11, 1993
Caro, Jacobina (90)—September 13, 1993
Clare, Gary (32)—January 28, 1994
Cort, William (53)—September 23, 1993
Dance, William (53)—February 14, 1994
de Mille, Agnes (88)—October 6, 1993
Dewell, Michael (62)—March 4, 1994
D'Orsa, Lonnie (96)—July 24, 1993
Douglas, Jack (72)—April 13, 1994
Eolis, Miriam I. (80)—August 18, 1993
Fellini, Federico (73)—October 31, 1993
Freedland, George (83)—December 23, 1993
Gatchell, Taylor (50)—July 1, 1993
Grigas, John (71)—March 6, 1994
Hack, Monroe B. (93)—June 16, 1993
Harlib, Matthew (68)—March 26, 1994
Harvey, Michael (49)—September 23, 1993
Henderson, Spencer III (44)—November 14, 1993
Hughes, Thomas L. (62)—April 10, 1994
Jarman, Derek (52)—February 19, 1994
Kogan, Jay (67)—November 5, 1993
Kravetz, Walter J. (66)—October 17, 1993
Landau, Richard (79)—September 18, 1993
Lawrence, Peter (74)—March 21, 1994
Layton, Joe (64)—May 5, 1994
Lilo, Larry (46)—June 2, 1993
Mackendrick, Alexander (81)—December 22, 1993
Martin, William R. (59)—December 29, 1993
Matofsky, Harvey (60)—January 3, 1994
McGriff, Heywood (36)—May 8, 1994
Negulesco, Jean (93)—July 18, 1993
Nettles, Gene (65)—April 15, 1994
Nichtern, Claire (73)—March 26, 1994
Nikolais, Alwin (82)—May 8, 1993
O'Neil, Bradford (38)—August 15, 1993
Paley Irving (77)—April 28, 1993
Parham, Ernest R. Jr. (64)—January 22, 1994
Pierce, Edward (77)—August 1, 1993
Raedler, Dorothy (76)—December 11, 1993
Raitt, James (41)—April 25, 1994
Riggs, Marlon (37)—April 5, 1994
Rubenstein, Harry (69)—December 1, 1993
Ruud, Tom (50)—February 28, 1994
Salmon, Scott (51)—July 17, 1993
Schifter, Peter Mark (44)—September 10, 1993
Schneider, Harold (55)—February 4, 1994
Smith, Clinton Wilding (40)—February 10, 1994
Soelberg, Louise (90)—January 5, 1994
Subber, Saint (76)—April 26, 1994
Walker, Paul (41)—December 5, 1993
Wonder, Tommy (78)—December 11, 1993
Woodward, Charles (71)—February 23, 1994
Young, Marvin (90)—May 26, 1993
Zevin, Harry (74)—September 9, 1993

MUSICIANS

Adonaylo, Raquel (67)—March 15, 1994
Baller, Adolph (84)—January 22, 1994
Barker, Danny (85)—March 13, 1994
Benford, Tommy (88)—March 24, 1994
Bloom, Robert (85)—February 13, 1994
Cathcart, Dick (69)—November 8, 1993
Clarke, Michael (49)—December 19, 1993
Collins, Albert (61)—November 24, 1993
Cores, Alexander (93)—February 5, 1994
Creach, John (76)—February 22, 1994
Hopkins, Douglas (32)—December 5, 1993
Jackson, Oliver (61)—May 29, 1994
Jordan, Steve Philip (74)—September 13, 1993
Kaufman, Louis (88)—February 9, 1994
Lombardo, Lebert J. (88)—June 16, 1993
Lombardo, Victor (82)—January 22, 1994
Majeske, Daniel (61)—November 28, 1993
Mikhashoff, Yvar (52)—October 11, 1993
Nikolayeva, Tatyana (69)—November 22, 1993
Pass, Joe (65)—May 23, 1994
Peterson, Harold E. (93)—December 17, 1993
Pike, Craig (30)—May 23, 1993
Pratt, Bobby (67)—January 7, 1994
Sabinsky, Raymond (80)—January 9, 1994
Scholz, Janos (89)—June 3, 1993
Sharrock, Sonny (53)—May 26, 1994
Slag, Gregory (33)—March 22, 1994
Smeck, Roy (94)—April 8, 1994
Sun Ra (79)—May 30, 1993
Tucker, Luther (57)—June 17, 1993
Villa, Micaela (83)—March 27, 1994

COMPOSERS, LYRICISTS

Alexander, Arthur B. Jr. (53)—June 9, 1993

Altman, Arthur (83)—January 18, 1994
Bergsma, William (72)—March 18, 1994
Bjorlin, Ulf (60)—October 23, 1993
Cary, Dick (77)—April 1994
Couper, Monroe (40)—February 1994
Dana, Gus (60)—August 13, 1993
David, Mack (81)—December 30, 1993
Fisher, Marvin (76)—August 21, 1993
Flagello, Nicholas (66)—March 16, 1994
Flaum, Harley (48)—May 8, 1994
Getz, Donald—August 22, 1993
Glyde, Rosemary (46)—January 18, 1994
Haieff, Alexei (80)—March 1, 1994
Hartman, Dan (43)—March 22, 1994
Hiller, Lejaren (69)—January 26, 1994
Kuller, Sid Charles (43)—September 16, 1993
Lutoslawski, Witold (81)—February 7, 1994
Nilsson, Harry (52)—January 15, 1994
Poné, Gundaris (61)—March 15, 1994
Ramirez, Roger (80)—January 11, 1994
Rieti, Vittorio (96)—February 18, 1994
Rome, Harold (85)—October 26, 1993
Ronell, Ann (85)—December 26, 1993
Scott, Raymond (85)—February 8, 1994
Wilcox, Larry (58)—November 24, 1993
Zappa, Frank (52)—December 4, 1993

CONDUCTORS, BAND LEADERS

Abravanel, Maurice (90)—September 22, 1993
Bauza, Mario (82)—July 11, 1993
Black, Robert (43)—November 14, 1993
Blackton, Jay (84)—January 8, 1994
Del Mar, Norman (74)—February 6, 1994
Ferden, Bruce (44)—September 19, 1993
Hawkins, Erskine R. (79)—November 11, 1993
Hawthorne, Joseph C. (85)—March 20, 1994
Leinsdorf, Erich (81)—September 21, 1993
Levine, Joseph (83)—March 23, 1994
Rodney, Red (66)—May 27, 1994
Trace, Al (92)—August 31, 1993
Van Vactor, David (87)—March 24, 1994
Zoob, Andy (46)—March 30, 1994

CRITICS

Beiswanger, George W. (91)—October 6, 1993
Burgess, Anthony (76)—November 25, 1993
Corrigan, Robert (65)—September 1, 1993
Gallo, Clifford (31)—March 8, 1994
Gould, Jack (79)—May 24, 1993
Harwood, Jim (55)—September 4, 1993
Knight, Bob (72)—August 30, 1993
Myers, Harold (83)—March 17, 1994
Prideaux, Tom (85)—March 8, 1994
Raidy, William A. (70)—September 4, 1993
Raven, Seymour S. (75)—January 14, 1994
Tatelman, Milton (50)—June 11, 1993

DESIGNERS

Ballard, Lucinda (87)—August 19, 1993
Brainard, Joe (52)—May 25, 1994
Checchi, Robert J. (67)—June 4, 1993
Eckart, Jean (72)—September 6, 1993
Falabella, John M. (40)—July 6, 1993
Fingerhut, Arden (48)—May 13, 1994
Harp, Bill (70)—March 16, 1994
MacDonald, Richard (74)—May 29, 1993
Samaritani, Pier Luigi (51)—January 5, 1994
Scarfiotti, Ferdinando (53)—April 30, 1994
Sharaff, Irene (83)—August 16, 1993
Smith, Oliver (75)—January 23, 1994
Truscott, John (57)—September 5, 1993

OTHERS

Allen, Raymond (72)—January 26, 1994
Light Opera of Manhattan
Boulle, Pierre (81)—January 30, 1994
Author
Boyars, Albert (69)—February 18, 1994
Publicist
Brakefield, Charles Brown (73)—August 13, 1993
N.Y. *Times* Broadcasting
Bunin, Lou (89)—February 17, 1994
Puppeteer
Burdick, Elizabeth (74)—May 6, 1994
International Theater Institute
Campbell, Bruce (42)—June 18, 1993
Publicist
Chute, Marchette (84)—May 5, 1994
Biographer
Citron, Harold (79)—May 21, 1993
Theater executive
Conn, Billy (75)—May 28, 1993
Boxer
DeRita, Curley Joe (83)—July 3, 1993
Last of the Three Stooges
Dolbier, Maurice (81)—October 20, 1993
Book editor
Ellison, Ralph (80)—April 16, 1994
Author
Falk, Richard (81)—January 28, 1994
Publicist
Fernbach, John R. (73)—December 25, 1993
Lawyer

Fitelson, H. William (89)—May 19, 1994
Lawyer
Furness, Betty (78)—April 2, 1994
Actress and reporter
Golding, William (81)—June 19, 1993
Author
Hacker, George J. (81)—April 11, 1994
Advertising executive
Heinsheimer, Hans W. (93)—October 12, 1993
Music publisher
Herscher, Seymour (82)—February 12, 1994
Production manager
Hoguet, Robert (88)—October 14, 1993
Lincoln Center
Hughes, Dorothy B. (88)—May 6, 1993
Author
Jablons, Josephine (69)—October 5, 1993
Reporter, editor
Jollie, Mark (41)—September 9, 1993
N.Y. City Opera
Kataoka, Nizaemon (90)—March 26, 1994
Kabuki actor
Lazar, Irving (86)—December 30, 1993
Talent agent
Lewine, Robert (80)—December 13, 1993
Creative Management Association
Locher, Mark R. (37)—January 7, 1994
Screen Actors Guild
Lowry, W. McNeil (80)—June 6, 1993
Ford Foundation
McClelland, Maurice (53)—September 19, 1993
International Theater Institute
McFarland, Spanky (64)—June 30, 1993
Our Gang
North, Henry Ringling (83)—October 2, 1993
Ringling Brothers Circus
Otway, Howard (72)—April 18, 1994
Theater designer
Pulitzer, Joseph Jr. (80)—May 26, 1993
St. Louis *Post-Dispatch*
Rainwater, John (32)—September 3, 1993
Stage manager
Rao, Vincent P. (79)—May 4, 1993
Jurist
Reinglas, Fred (58)—March 31, 1994
Stage manager
Renoir, Claude (79)—September 5, 1993
Cinemaphotographer
Schilts, Randy (42)—February 17, 1994
Reporter
Sherman, Esther (56)—February 13, 1994
Agent
Sommers, Estelle (74)—March 23, 1994
Capezio Dance-Theater Shops
Specter, Jack E. (95)—December 20, 1993
Publicist
Tatum, Donn B. (80)—May 31, 1993
Walt Disney Company
Uttal, Larry (71)—November 25, 1993
Pop music excutive
Wagner, Lee (83)—September 7, 1993
TV Guide-New York
Washbaugh, Charles (33)—September 25, 1993
Production manager
Way, David (75)—February 4, 1994
Musicologist
Weiss, Mandell (102)—December 29, 1993
Angel
Wells, Frank (62)—April 3, 1994
Walt Disney Company
West, John Spencer (37)—July 24, 1993
Publicist
Wilson, Woody S. (71)—July 27, 1993
Daily Variety librarian
Zolotow, Sam (94)—Otober 21, 1993
Drama reporter

INDEX

Play titles appear in **bold face.** ***Bold face italic*** page numbers refer to those pages where complete cast and credit listings for New York productions may be found